FOUNDATIONS OF CANADIAN
NATIONHOOD

FOUNDATIONS OF CANADIAN NATIONHOOD

By

CHESTER MARTIN

Professor Emeritus
Department of History
University of Toronto

UNIVERSITY OF TORONTO PRESS
TORONTO   1955

FOREWORD

THE POLITICAL TRADITIONS culminating in Canadian nationhood are now the oldest in the American hemisphere—the only political traditions unbroken by revolution or civil war.

For more than half of their history these traditions were not only shared but developed with exemplary resourcefulness by the thirteen provinces which abandoned them in the American Revolution and built upon the fragments of a divided empire the structure of an independent republic. For the provinces which remained British vis-à-vis the United States the traditions of the first empire came to possesses a melancholy interest. In a very real sense that century and a half of common history before the revolution belonged—much of it vicariously—to them also. In one sense it now belongs more appropriately to them than to the United States, for the provinces which remained British perpetuated the parliamentary tradition and out of it evolved a type of nationhood which has since come to maturity in every quarter of the Commonwealth. It is a curious fact that the priority among the British provinces in the early stages of that achievement is directly traceable, as we shall see, to the relative continuity of their traditions from the first empire.

In these studies an attempt is made to trace the foundations, the containing-walls, upon which the structure of Canadian nationhood now squarely rests. There is no attempt, even in outline, to write another "history of Canada" or to propound another "interpretation." Many economic or cultural by-products of nationhood are attributable to chance or to circumstance, but the four "Parts" of this theme have all been the work of builders inspired by a common cause. In the struggle for survival, for self-government, for union, for expansion "from sea to sea," for international recognition, they followed their star, hesitantly at times, as we shall see, with much diffidence and improvisation. But they never lost sight of the parliamentary tradition. They appropriated its evolution in the parent state, and nationhood in its widest amplitude was claimed at last in 1917, 1919, 1923–26, 1930–31 as a direct corollary of that maturing tradition.

By comparison with this slow but unbroken process of evolution, the nationhood of the United States was a prodigy of rapid and spectacular achievement. In the first chapter of these studies this theme of Canadian evolution vis-à-vis the United States is explored in greater detail. The attributes of nationhood which were acquired piecemeal and at long intervals of time by Canada, Australia, and New Zealand were forced upon the American republic by an imperative and immediate necessity. Complete self-government was a corollary of their independence, and it tended, for better or for worse, to stereotype the parliamentary tradition at the colonial stage. The thirteen colonies were precipitated into full self-government before the conventions of the cabinet system of parliamentary government had been reduced to a body of doctrine in the parent state. Election of the governor was substituted for appointment by the crown and infirmities from the old colonial system are still discernible in the technique of congressional government. Union too was an immediate and imperative necessity, but it required one of the most concerted exploits of statesmanship in the modern world to transform the Articles of Confederation of 1781 into the Constitution of the United States in 1787, and it required a civil war three-quarters of a century later to preserve and confirm that union in its final form. The expansion of the republic from behind the barriers of the Alleghany Mountains to the Rio Grande in the south, the Pacific in the west, and Alaska in the north was achieved in the span of eighty years. This conquest of half a continent was one of the most rapid and dynamic feats of territorial expansion in modern history but it did not outstrip the vision of Benjamin Franklin for an undivided empire in 1774, "adding province to province, as far as the South Sea" thereby "assuring to the *British* name and nation a stability and permanency that no man acquainted with history durst have hoped for, 'till our *American* possessions opened the pleasing prospects." A fourth prerequisite of nationhood—functional recognition abroad for the new republic—began tentatively on a scale desperately meagre and hazardous, in grim contrast to the entrancing destiny which Franklin had forecast for the British nation in America on foundations "broad and strong enough to support the greatest political structure that human wisdom ever yet erected." It was Franklin himself, nevertheless, as plenipotentiary to the French court who guided the infant footsteps of the republic towards international recognition and lived to secure for the United States a sure footing among the nations of Europe.

All these attributes of nationhood, as we shall see, were acquired in due time also by the provinces which remained British at the revolution, but they were acquired piecemeal and in every instance the method as well as the function itself left its stamp upon them. It was half a century before the technique of responsible government emerged from the controversies of the second empire, though happily it was then found to possess virtues that were not to be found in the "clumsy irresponsible mechanism" of the old colonial system. For union the British provinces had to await a solution at the hands of the next generation. Here also the coercive factors were highly distinctive and the resulting federation was charged with a distinctively Canadian tradition. The expansion of the original Canadian confederation to a transcontinental destiny was less spectacular than that which carried the United States from the Alleghanies to Alaska in the span of eighty years, but it was no less deliberate and imperative. The national superstructure which came to be reared upon these foundations—the full functioning of nationhood at home and abroad—was also a highly distinctive process. In many ways it was unique. Unlike that of the United States it was not the first but the last of the major attributes of Canadian nationhood, and it is coming to maturity only in our own day.

II

The attempt to trace these traditions in causal sequence in Canada may startle the observer who is content to accept superficial resemblances or differences at their face value and to speculate upon them in terms of sheer plausibility where one guess is almost as good as another. The truth is that Canadian history is so largely the by-product of other issues, in many cases beyond our own border, that conventional plausibility is apt to be misleading as well as worthless. The achievement of each of the major attributes of nationhood cited above was the work of discerning men who have left behind them, in most instances, convincing records of their work. Their motives and methods are now traceable with considerable certainty, not infrequently in correspondence which was both secret and confidential. An effort has been made to understand the task of these men on their own terms and to trace their work where possible in their own words.

The factual record alone is not seldom found to be the most difficult to reconstruct. Plausible fictions are usually based upon faulty facts, and nothing but confusion can be expected to follow. The source materials for Canadian history are now becoming fairly convincing and no apology is offered for trying to purvey this evidence convincingly from authentic sources. While it has been necessary to dispense, as far as possible, with elaborate footnotes and bibliographies which would have increased beyond feasible bounds the length of the book in its final form,[1] the author acknowledges an added obligation to observe with scrupulous care the sanctions of accurate scholarship. The claim to have met this obligation must of course rest upon the record of previous work and like Bob Acres's courage in Sheridan's famous play it must emulate Bob's modest resolve not to disgrace his ancestors. Let us hope at least for something more than Bob's success.

III

The dominant political tradition which these studies are intended to trace has been evolved in juxtaposition with two others which have never been far removed from it.

One of these, the tradition of an independent republic, founded by revolution and inspired for more than a century by antipathies generated in that bitter conflict, can never be forgotten or ignored on this continent. Canadian nationhood has been conditioned at so many points by that of the United States that their immediate proximity vis-à-vis has long been a commonplace. The preliminary chapter on "Prospect and Retrospect" is an attempt to fix the terminal signposts of this long association and to illustrate, if only at widely separated milestones along the way, a few of the crises at the cross-roads. Antipathies as well as affinities—on occasion antipathies rather than affinities—have sometimes been dominant. But the significant fact is not the conflict or concord between the two traditions but their persistent association. For nearly a century and a half, whether in juxtaposition or in co-operation, the two have existed side by side in peace. The one has been evolved from the oldest unbroken political tradition in the American hemisphere. The other, a republic under a written constitution, now functions under the oldest fixed instrument of government in the modern world.

There was a third tradition of government in America with origins as old as those of the British colonies, and with functions in New France which came to an end only as the first British empire in America was drawing to a close. The deceptive neatness and despatch of French colonial government had a fatal fascination for hard-pressed British officialdom. From Shirley of Massachusetts, who was deceived

[1]See Bibliographical Note, pp. 519–24.

by illusions of its efficiency, to Carleton of Quebec who set his indomitable mind to the design of appropriating the French system in its
entirety ("to get rid of the Proclamation of 1763 with the Commissions
and Ordinances depending thereon and to restore the old Law and
Constitution")[1] British governors had envied the apparent simplicity
and "system" of French administration. At the risk of repetition in
greater detail in another context (chapter III) the place of this French
colonial tradition in the "design" of officialdom for America may be
anticipated here. When the new American Department was being
organized to deal specifically for the first time with America, the
permanent under-secretary was William Knox who deplored the "total
want of plan or system" in all the British colonies "except Quebec"—
"there is really no material difference between any of them, (except
Quebec) and the others":

The government of the French colonies particularly deserves our attention,
and is worthy of our imitation; they take every precaution of a wise and
prudent nation, to secure good order and government; a governor is
appointed with a proper power. . . . Without any of those pompous ideas of
popular government, which our countrymen are elated with, the people
are happy. . . . Happy would it be for this Kingdom, were such plans
adopted for the government of our colonies, instead of that disorder and
anarchy, that almost universally reigns in them. . . . The northern colonies
would have experienced a much greater degree of felicity, had their
government consisted only of a governor and council.

When the time came in 1774 for the *Quebec Act* along with the four
other "intolerable Acts" of that fatal year Knox was ready with his
"system" for Quebec and added the revealing commentary that "the
noble personages who planned this bill [the *Quebec Act*] warily considered these material points; and in giving them a government, had
the view of making a great and flourishing body of people happy;
instead of creating in them a power of destroying their peace and
tranquility."[2]

Whether this denial of an Assembly altogether was intended to be
the corner-stone of a new American "system," as Burke and Chatham
and Fox in Britain and many a perplexed observer in America
suspected, remains one of the inscrutable and neglected problems of
the revolution. Knox who regarded himself as "a principal actor in the

---

[1]Carleton's Memorandum in the Dartmouth Papers. "To render," he added, "the
Colony of that Advantage to Great Britain, it certainly is capable of, would
require the reintroducing of the French Criminal Law, and all the Powers of its
Government."
[2]*Thoughts on the Act*, 13 ff.

executive Government" during the revolution—"the most important of all the subordinate offices of the State"—afterwards boasted that he had "served as Under Secretary to every Secretary of State that has filled the American department from its institution to its suppression." He wrote no fewer than six pamphlets of prime importance and he afterwards published two whole series of papers and memoranda amplified by contemporary correspondence and other data gathered during these critical years.[1] In the *Extra Official State Papers* (1789) Knox was still defending his American policy and protesting unrepentantly against "fine spun theories, for promoting the happiness of the French Canadians, by converting them into English Republicans."

It is not surprising that the veneration of French Canada for the religious aspects of the *Quebec Act* (with which we are not here concerned) concealed the significance of that fatal measure for the struggle now opening in America. When Carleton, after an absence of five years behind the scenes with the new American Department, returned to Quebec, there were songs of rejoicing by the "petites pensionnaires" of l'Hôpital-Général:

> Peuple du Canada tu dois
> A ses soins salutaires
> La Religion, et les Lois
> Que suivirent tes Pères.

The "people of Canada" had no means of knowing that the *Quebec Act* supplanted a train of policy far more generous than this for the Roman Catholic "new subjects" of Quebec. Burke advocated the tithe without the reservations of Wedderburn that it was "subject to his Majesty's approbation": in case of recalcitrance on the part of the French clergy "all tithes are subject to be taken from them." "I want as much of law as you please," exclaimed Burke, "and as little of the King's pleasure as possible." The Board of Trade in 1765 and in its

---

[1]His *Present State of the Nation* in 1768 commanded, as Knox himself was afterwards proud to prove from George Grenville's own letter, the unqualified approbation of that "stout and resolute" man for its "temper and force," its "knowledge and precision" on American policy. A second pamphlet in 1769 interpreted the election of 1768 *ex cathedra* to America in terms calculated, as James Otis afterwards wrote, to "make the wisest mad and the weakest strong." "If you do not avail yourself of the information I have given you," wrote Knox, "perhaps the people of England may be led by it to conceive more justly of their *Rights,* and of your *Intentions,* than they have hitherto done; and may compel you to submit, if they unhappily find no argument, but force can induce you to obey." Knox's two elaborate pamphlets on the *Quebec Act—The Justice and Policy of the Late Act* and *Thoughts on the Act*—were published anonymously but it would be absurd to suppose that they did not carry the approval and encouragement of the American Department.

great Report in 1769 advocated Roman Catholic emancipation more than sixty years before it came in England. Fox challenged the House of Commons to deny the parliamentary tradition to the French because they were Roman Catholics. North's reply was that "there is something in that religion, which makes it not prudent."

On the other hand Knox stated with assurance that if attached by religion the French Canadians would be "a security against the insurgents of the other parts of America; for in a case of emergency, a force can easily be raised from thence." His authority for that fatal miscalculation, as we shall see, was on record even before Carleton left Quebec. Memoranda in the handwriting of both Carleton and Knox in the Dartmouth Papers indicate only too conclusively the real authorship of the *Quebec Act*; while Dartmouth, North's half-brother at the head of the American Department at this time, enjoyed an enviable reputation in America for philanthropy. Knox's open avowal of policy could scarcely have been made with more provocative audacity: "The old mode of treating our dependencies must be exploded and a new system formed."

The protests of Burke and Chatham and Fox against the rising portents of this "system new and strange" in 1774 have been quoted with incredulity by generations of otherwise credulous historians. The *Quebec Act*, said Chatham, would "put the whole people under arbitrary power." "It was a most cruel, oppressive, and odious measure, tearing up justice and every good principle by the roots." The measure was "tyrannical and despotic" and it "established a despotic government in that country." The bill, exclaimed Fox, contained "not a spark or semblance of liberty." It was "a perfectly despotic government, contrary to the genius and spirit of the British constitution." It had "the appearance of a love of despotism, and a settled design to enslave the people of America." "By being made perpetual," Burke protested, "it is evident that this constitution is meant to be both an instrument of tyranny to the Canadians, and an example to others of what they have to expect; at some time or other it will come home to England." "Canada will become a dangerous instrument in the hands of those who wish to destroy English liberty in every part of our possessions." In America Alexander Hamilton discerned "two great purposes" in the *Quebec Act*—"first, the subjugation of the colonies and afterwards that of Great Britain itself." "It is clear beyond a doubt," the Continental Congress resolved, "that a resolution is formed, and is now carrying into execution to extinguish the freedom of these colonies, by subjecting them to a despotic government."

Is it possible that Knox and his associates in the King's secret counsels had a "design" in 1774, as Burke surmised, to make the *Quebec Act* "an example to others of what they have to expect"? Assuredly none but a madman could have deemed it possible to tear up by the roots a century and a half of parliamentary traditions in America and to plant in their place "a governor with a proper power," as Knox openly advocated, "without any of those pompous ideas of popular government, which our countrymen are elated with" in America. But it may be recalled that there was similar incredulity about *Mein Kampf* until Hitler proceeded to put it into practice. Washington at first confessed that he was "unsuspicious of design" but by 1774 he was "convinced beyond the smallest doubt, that these measures are the result of deliberation" and that there was "a regular systematic plan formed to enforce them." "Government is pursuing a regular plan at the expense of law and justice to overthrow our constitutional rights and liberties." Embodied in the Declaration of Independence itself is the charge of establishing in Quebec "an arbitrary government, and enlarging its boundaries, so as to render it at once an example and fit instrument for introducing the same absolute rule into these colonies."

A still more hypothetical thesis has gone almost unexplored by historians obsessed with the cis-Atlantic aspects of the revolution. How far was the decision "to *coerce* America"—the decision which destroyed the hope of further evolution in the thirteen colonies—based upon the fatal delusion built up in the closely knit circle of the new American Department by Carleton from Quebec that "a force can easily be raised from thence" for use "against the insurgents of the other parts of America"?[1] It was the beginning of this insensate policy rather than its futility which proved so fatal. When Carleton's delusions with regard to Quebec resulted in fiasco and his own recall it was too late to retreat. A month after Dartmouth's decision to endow Carleton with the "full appointments of Commander-in-Chief"

---

[1]Knox, *Thoughts on the Act*, p. 28. Cf. Carleton to Shelburne, Nov. 25, 1767: "The New Subjects could send into the Field about eighteen thousand Men. . . . As the common People are greatly to be influenced by their Seigneurs, I annex a Return of the Noblesse of Canada." Hillsborough to Carleton, March 6, 1768: "His Majesty approves of every Sentiment. . . . Corresponds in almost every part with His Majesty's Opinions." Cf. Barré's "detestation" of the Quebec Bill: "From this time, all hope of peace in America will be destroyed. The Americans will look on the Canadians as their task-masters, and, in the end, their executioners. I smelt this business out from the beginning. . . . I wash my hands of this business. I here declare my solemn aversion to it. I know what you mean. *Liberavi animam meam*! I have foretold the thing. There is not a man in the government that means to deny it." Cavendish's *Debates*, 227 ff.

in America there was another mad suggestion from the American Department for 20,000 men to be supplied by Catharine the Great of Russia: "the greatest part of the Russians will be sent to Quebec." In the end the resort to Hessian and other mercenaries proved equally detestable to Chatham and all who shared his goodwill towards America.[1] Beyond a doubt Carleton's policy for Quebec had no small share in precipitating armed conflict. The Continental Congress cited "indubitable evidence that a design is formed by the British Ministry of making a cruel invasion from the province of Quebec, upon these colonies, for the purpose of destroying our lives and liberties." The *Declaration on Taking Arms*, which was drafted a few weeks later by John Dickinson, and placed in the hands of George Washington, cited, truly enough, "certain intelligence that General Carleton, the Governor of Canada, is instigating the people of that province and the Indians to fall upon us." Thus the illusory tradition of French colonial government, reinforced by designs all too palpable for "a force . . . from thence" against "the other parts of America," found its climax in the American Revolution.

IV

This illusory tradition of French colonial government was extinguished in the thirteen colonies of the first empire but it lingered on unimpaired for seventeen years in Quebec until the *Constitutional Act* of 1791 restored the conventional forms of a "royal province" to the loyalists of Upper Canada and extended them for the first time to the uninitiated "new subjects" of Lower Canada. How that tradition was to fare with such a background became one of the most difficult problems of the second empire. Meanwhile in the loyalist province of New Brunswick as in Upper Canada the exiles from the old provinces took the parliamentary tradition for granted. In Nova Scotia where it survived uninterruptedly from the first empire it throve, as we shall see, in exemplary "moderation and harmony."

In Lower Canada, however, these vicissitudes left behind a legacy of bitterness and frustration. Had the Board of Trade as they had proposed in their magnanimous report of 1769 succeeded in inducting Quebec, with unprecedented generosity to Roman Catholic "new subjects," into "those Privileges, which exist in the principles of a British Constitution," it is possible that British parliamentary traditions might have been associated from the outset with the cultural traditions from

---

[1]"If I were an American, as I am an Englishman, while a foreign troop was landed in my country, I never would lay down my arms—never—never—never."

the French régime in the first loyalties of French Canada. But the Board, as we shall see, came into fatal conflict with Carleton and Knox in the counsels of the American Department. The parliamentary tradition was proscribed completely and, as it seemed, permanently. By the terms of the *Quebec Act* every vestige of it was specifically "revoked, annulled, and made void." When it was reinstated in 1791 after the revolution it was conceded grudgingly and it was received without gratitude. After the *Quebec Act* it appeared to contravene in its very nature the gentleman's agreement with the seigneurs and the church. The vast patrimony which Carleton was ready to promise to them in 1774 was now divided with the loyalists of Upper Canada, though the seigneurial system in Lower Canada lingered on until 1854 when it disappeared at the hands of French Canadian reformers themselves under the Canadian union.

Meanwhile the cultural traditions of the French régime came to be associated with the *Quebec Act* and took priority over the parliamentary traditions which eventually supplanted the abortive project of government from the old French colonial system. The religion of French Canada, cradled and nurtured in the Counter-Reformation, survived the French revolution unscathed, to become the most consistent and ultramontane outpost of the Roman Catholic church in the modern world. The classical language of eighteenth-century France survived on the St. Lawrence to challenge the purity of the mother tongue on the banks of the Seine. The first loyalties of French Canada remained true to their origins in New France. But a miasma of misunderstanding enveloped the constitution. Derailed by statute from the normal evolution of a British province[1] Quebec could be restored only by a series of statutes, each one more controversial than the last. The parliamentary tradition, introduced in its most primitive form in 1791, was denied the attributes which Durham claimed as the "necessary consequences of representative institutions." For more than half a century the instinctive loyalties of French Canada remained on the defensive.

La Fontaine, in turning resolutely from the republican models of the Papineau era to the British parliamentary models of Hincks and Baldwin, still followed inflexibly the cause of "his people" for their religion, their language, and their laws. For the first time perhaps, and in the closest association ever experienced by the two historic races

[1]Nova Scotia, New Brunswick, and Prince Edward Island attained responsible government by "convention" or usage without a single imperial statute complicating the process.

in Canada—the political bonds of a legislative union—the special interests of French Canada were committed by La Fontaine to full association with the British parliamentary tradition. It was by the consummation of that tradition under responsible government in the united province of Canada that La Fontaine was able to win back the cherished rights of "his people," and to the end of his days he never ceased to venerate the union.

V

In Part II on "Self-Government" and in Part III on "British American Union" an attempt is made in greater detail to trace the evolution towards Canadian nationhood after "the great divide" of the American revolution. With the confluence of these two streams—self-government and union—the unmistakable set towards nationhood is measurably quickened. It is here particularly that mere plausibility becomes so unsafe in interpreting the trends of the times. Fortunately the factual background is now traceable from authentic records of the men who brought these things to pass. In many instances it is possible to follow their work in their own words in correspondence so confidential that its publication has sometimes been protested to our own day. The decent restraint which the most exacting scholarship must acknowledge in the use of materials of this sort must be observed in these cases with more than usual care. Muck-raking can be as reprehensible and as misleading too as conventional plausibility. The historian's task in Canada for another generation, it may be, will be beset with many pitfalls, and he will be well advised to tread warily if he is not to defeat the cause he has at heart. It makes all the difference, as Archbishop Whately used to say, whether we put Truth in the first place or in the second place. If there is a stronger loyalty than this the historian has no business with it. The best he can hope to do is to cite his evidence without malice, without extenuation, and without fear.

Part IV of the studies in this series—"Expansion"—has been based upon evidence now available in truly ponderous profusion. The volumes of the "Canadian Frontiers of Settlement" series and the truly voluminous material accumulated from official sources by no fewer than three Natural Resources Commissions are invaluable. The political expansion of Canada was already foreshadowed in the B.N.A. Act of 1867. The physiographical expansion across the continent in the building of the Canadian Pacific Railways was made good, as we shall see, by prodigies of statesmanship as well as enterprise. Only with the political and physiographical expansion was it possible to attempt the demographic expansion of Canada—the real task of mature nationhood —with any hope of success. With the organization of Alberta and Saskatchewan in 1905 the giant's causeway of provinces across the continent was complete and our immediate concern with the foundations of Canadian nationhood may well come to an end.

The completion of this theme—tracing the superstructure of nationhood which is already rising upon these foundations—was originally to have been written by the late J. W. Dafoe in a joint volume for the series on *The Relations of Canada and the United States* for the Carnegie Endowment for International Peace. Dafoe's own share in that development will no doubt find its way into history in due time but his preoccupation to the last with affairs and, alas, his sudden death have deprived the record of an authoritative review. As a result I have been content to expand "Foundations of Canadian Nationhood" to its present size without attempting to complete the theme except in outline in the closing chapter on "The Functioning of Nationhood." That this superstructure conforms to the pattern of foundations so deeply laid in the past is now a commonplace of Canadian history, and it would be strange indeed if a tradition so tough and infrangible were to fail now. Lord Morley records the whimsical reflection: "How curious it is to see how exactly people follow their own characters all through life." If history is to a nation what character is to an individual, and especially a history as tough and pragmatic as that of Canada and the United States, the two traditions which they represent may be expected to survive side by side in North America in mutual respect and association.

My obligations in the preparation of this book are many and few of them can be acknowledged here. To various other publishers some form of acknowledgement is due for the use of source-material already cited in other contexts: in *Empire and Commonwealth* published by the Clarendon Press, in *"Dominion Lands" Policy* published by the Macmillan Company of Canada in the "Canadian Frontiers of Settlement" series, in articles published by the *Canadian Historical Review*, in the *Transactions* of the Royal Society of Canada, in the reports of the Canadian Historical Association and in various other journals. In two such quarters my obligations call for special acknowledgment. To Mr. John Gray of the Macmillan Company of Canada and to Principal Mackintosh of Queen's University, one of the editors of the "Canadian Frontiers of Settlement" series, I am indebted for permission to use maps and plans already published in *"Dominion Lands"*

Policy, volume II of that series. To the University of Toronto Press I am indebted not only for assistance towards publication provided by their Publications Fund but for their patience in delaying publication during the author's protracted illness. To the Editorial Office of the Press and particularly to Miss Francess Halpenny and Miss Jean Houston I am grateful for exhilarating criticism and indefatigable attention to detail. They must not be held accountable for the solecisms that still survive in a difficult and complicated theme. For the Index I am gratefully indebted to Mrs. G. M. Craig.

The subject-matter of these studies has long been an absorbing preoccupation. To attempt to distinguish individuals over so long a range of university teaching would be like the hypothetical task which Aristotle once set for the plaintiff in a law case: how could a man who had plunged through a bramble hedge pick out any particular thorn that had scratched him? So much research in Canadian history remains to be done—much of it of the lilliputian variety—that it may be too soon for many a day to expect "great" history yet. But the future is in safe hands. The contours of Canadian history are steadily rising and they will never recede. What would it be to be young again in that cause?

CONTENTS

I

SURVIVAL

Chapter One

PROSPECT AND RETROSPECT

IN 1613 Captain Button, bearing letters by way of the northwest passage, as he thought, to the Emperor of Cathay, passed the winter at the mouth of the Nelson River on Hudson Bay and claimed that vast hinterland for King James I of England. This is now the oldest continuously British territory on the continent. Six years before this event and under the auspices of the same prince a much more promising venture in colonization had begun at Jamestown in Virginia. This too remained British for more than half of its history. These two regions now bear allegiance to different states but it is a fact of the first importance that they both speak the English tongue and that even in political allegiance they have been united longer than they have been divided.

Out of that first British empire in America have come the basic institutions and traditions which now distinguish Canada among the nations of the new world. It is true that Rupert's Land, Nova Scotia, and the newly acquired province of Quebec were still in swaddling clothes at a time when some of the older colonies were passing through the advanced stages of political adolescence. But though the primitive Assembly of Nova Scotia was just coming of age at the Declaration of Independence it did remain an unbroken bridge—perhaps the only unbroken bridge—between the first empire and the second. In tradition as well as association, therefore, the first empire belongs fairly to Canada as well as to the United States. For both of them half their history lies beyond "the great divide" of the American Revolution. For half their existence on this continent the two English-speaking nations of North America were undivided, and they still share uninterruptedly that range of common history.

The most careful and deliberate measures were already under way to incorporate into this colonial empire the newly won province of Quebec as a "royal government" with unprecedented privileges to the "new subjects" when the American Revolution launched thirteen of the southern colonies into political independence. The most discerning observers of the undivided empire had already been speculating upon a destiny of continental proportions. Both before and after the revolution the attempt was made to keep it united. Benjamin Franklin who dared to predict for the first empire "the greatest political structure that human wisdom ever yet erected" was still the stoutest advocate of North American union for all the provinces when the die was finally cast for revolution and independence.

More than a century and a half of history has since intervened. Two destinies instead of one have become manifest for English-speaking America. In their political institutions and in their outlook upon world problems characteristic contrasts as well as similarities have developed. But sharing an identity of colonial origin before the parting of the ways they now share an identity of international standing though not of stature at the end. Before attempting to trace the distinctive development of the northern provinces to this equality of nationhood—a process which is in many ways unique among the nations of the modern world—it may be fitting to point the contrast between the undivided empire in the middle of the eighteenth century and the accomplished facts at the middle of the twentieth.

EIGHTEENTH-CENTURY PROSPECTS

I

A realist with a sense of history and in search of the most entrancing prospect that ever lay before the English-speaking world would probably select the decade which intervened between the martial glory of the Seven Years' War and the political tragedy of the American Revolution. By 1759, "the year of victories," Chatham's dream of a British America had fairly captured the imagination of his countrymen on both sides of the Atlantic. By 1769 inscrutable designs behind the newly formed American Department were already set towards "the fatal decision to *coerce* America" which made the evolution of that first American empire into an eighteenth-century British Commonwealth forever impossible.

The generation which lived to see that decade in America had just passed through one of those periods of faith and exaltation which sometimes trouble so beneficently the waters of human enterprise. Edmund Burke was at this time agent for the Assembly of New York. "Nothing in the history of mankind," he exclaimed, "is like their progress. For my part I never cast an eye on their flourishing commerce and their cultivated and commodious life too but they seem to me rather ancient nations grown to perfection through a long series of fortuitous events, and a train of successful industry, accumulating wealth in many centuries, than the colonies of yesterday." There were at this time in America a score of British colonies stretching from the Gulf of Mexico to the Arctic Ocean. Between two and a half and three millions of the most resourceful pioneers of modern history here found themselves surrounded by opportunity on every side. Population had doubled within the span of twenty years. It was Benjamin Franklin's opinion that the prolific birth-rate in the American colonies was "doubling their numbers every twenty-five years, by natural generation only."[1] Within the twenty-year period from 1747 to 1767 their trade had more than trebled. So vast was the range of this first American empire that some of its constituent provinces were scarcely conscious of each other's existence.

In the north, Rupert's Land under the charter of the Hudson's Bay Company was lost and almost forgotten. In area it comprised more than half of what is now Canada. The newly acquired province of Quebec lay astride the St. Lawrence, gateway to the Great Lakes and the vast central hinterlands of the continent. Virginia too claimed a hinterland westward to the Mississippi. The new provinces of East and West Florida stretched from the Atlantic seaboard along the Gulf of Mexico to the Mississippi River. Pennsylvania was already torn between the older settlements on the lower reaches of the Delaware and Susquehanna rivers and the expanding frontier beyond the Blue Mountains. New York, astride another gateway to the hinterlands, had long since found within her grasp some of the factors of a commercial empire. On the Ohio was a realm upon which the acquisitive gaze of the land-jobber was already fixed. Little land booms which were later to spread like numberless ripples before the breeze from Baltimore to San Francisco were already beginning to move from one little centre to another, stirring dreams of local importance as they passed. Some of these colonial merchants and planters with vision sharpened, no doubt, by their own share of good fortune were beginning to speculate without false modesty upon the days to come.

There were two shrewd observers in a position to watch the trend of the time with peculiar insight. One, a printer and newspaper man, felt as accurately perhaps as any man of his day the pulse of new life in America. The other, for better or for worse, felt and perhaps stimulated the pulse of officialdom during these decisive years with un-

[1]Albert H. Smyth, ed., *Life and Writings of Benjamin Franklin*, IV, 54.

ceasing assiduity. In temper and in outlook few contemporaries could have been further apart. In one respect, however, their views were curiously corroborative. This British empire in America was approaching a dayspring of illimitable promise.

William Knox was one of those sedulous and indomitable men who thrive best in the throes of public administration. Burke once reflected that "men too much conversant in office are rarely minds of remarkable enlargement." Officialdom itself was personified in Knox's career. He could boast with authority of his early experience "in America, and as an American planter . . . deeply interested in the prosperity and security of that country."[1] He had gone to Georgia just after the preliminary trusteeship of twenty-one years, devised as an official experiment for the infancy of that colony, had come to an end and the province had taken its place as the newest among the "royal governments" in America. At the close of the Seven Years' War Knox found congenial employment under Grenville when that inflexible minister with "stout and resolute heart" set about the regimentation of the old colonial system in the interests of "public justice and integrity." With Grenville himself Knox could boast a closer intimacy than "that Great Minister's nearest relations," and he took Grenville's benediction as well as his uncompromising principles with him into the new American Department under Hillsborough when those fatal decisions began to take form in the inner counsels of the King to "*coerce* America."

During the critical years which followed, the seals of office passed from Hillsborough to Dartmouth, from Dartmouth to Germain, and from Germain to Shelburne, but the mordant influence of William Knox remained paramount among the permanent officials of the American Department. Whatever may have been Knox's infirmities of temper the evasion of responsibility was not one of them. He never ceased to avow his role as "a principal actor in the executive Government" throughout the revolution. He regarded his function as "the most important of all the subordinate offices of the State," and he afterwards reminded his disciples at the humble beginnings of the second empire in America that he had "served as Under Secretary to every Secretary of State that has filled the American department from its institution to its suppression."[2] With Carleton and the King behind the scenes it was Knox who added the *Quebec Act* to the four other "intolerable Acts" of 1774 for the discipline of America, and it was

[1]*Extra Official State Papers* (1789), II, 54.
[2]*Ibid.*, I, 34.

Knox[1] who hinted openly for the first time its most sinister historic purpose. By the restoration of the French seigneurial system in Quebec armed forces could "easily be raised from thence" against "the insurgents of the other parts of America." After the loss of the thirteen colonies Knox was yet to draft for North a daring project for a second empire in America. His *Extra Official State Papers*, published in 1789, are a revelation of the official mind, undaunted amidst the ruins and as resolute as ever against "fine spun theories, for promoting the happiness of the French Canadians, by converting them into English Republicans." In such a context there may have been a taint of sour grapes in Knox's reflections upon the lost potentialities of the first empire. "Had America," he wrote in 1789, "continued a part of the British Empire for half a century longer, under the same mode of Government as subsisted in the several provinces before the war, the navigation, manufactures, and a great part of the people of Great Britain and Ireland would probably have transported themselves thither."[2] As the lost colonies began to integrate their interests and move westward into the hinterlands Knox consoled himself with the reflection that "the Transallegany mountain people" would wander there like the Scythians and the Tartars for thousands of years before they should be able to found a settled state. Such were the resources of the first empire in the mind of the permanent official who had more to do perhaps than any other man in the ranks of permanent British officialdom with bringing it to an untimely end.

II

The counterpart to this bitter philosophy was to be found in the most famous of Knox's American contemporaries. From 1764 to 1775 Benjamin Franklin was in London as the agent of the Massachusetts, Pennsylvania, New Jersey, and Georgia assemblies. In the ante-rooms of the Southern Department and later on of the American Department when that branch was organized to deal specifically with the slowly emerging problems of America, Franklin's path must have crossed a thousand times the inflexible course of the permanent under-secretary. Beyond the fact that Franklin supplanted Knox as agent for Georgia there seems to be little record of direct encounter, but both must have been thoroughly aware of the widening gulf between them. It would be interesting to speculate how far the forces now moving into collision

[1]*Thoughts on the Late Act* (1774) and *Justice and Policy of the Late Act* (1774).
[2]*Extra Official State Papers*, II, 12.

were shaped by the mutual antipathies of these two men. Franklin, urbane, humorous, and wily, had the faith of an astrologer in the rising star of America. Knox had visions no doubt of an equally resplendent empire, but it was not to be built, he exclaimed, upon the *"polypus* government" of colonial assemblies "where a head sprouts out of every joint." While Franklin struggled manfully to retain his faith in Parliament, in "great men," and above all in the young King, he was far too shrewd to mistake the substance for the shadow or to ignore the permanence of the under-secretary as an abiding symptom of royal policy in the midst of faction. Confidence between these two men must have been impossible. In temper, in technique, in political philosophy, there was no common ground between them. It is curious to reflect upon the narrow orbit in which these implacable adversaries must have moved in London for so many years, measuring each other no doubt instinctively for signs of accommodation or of conflict. One trait they had in common. They were both realists. Neither was disposed to ignore the evidence of his senses. The greatest portent of their day was the illimitable prospect before the British empire in America.

For Franklin this conviction was a part of his birthright. Long before the Seven Years' War appeared upon the horizon he was discussing the theme with William Shirley, "the ablest colonial governor of his time." Both were Massachusetts men, one by birth and the other by adoption. If Franklin's removal to Philadelphia and Shirley's elevation to the governorship of his adopted province placed barriers of distance and of station between them there is little evidence of it in their confidential correspondence. The manner and temper of their intercourse was characteristic of both, for neither was disposed to look upon juristic interpretation as the norm of life for the British Empire.

From the walls of Louisbourg after its capture by New England troops in 1745 Shirley had launched his "Great Plan" for the completion of a British American empire. Nova Scotia, already a frontier of New England in its primitive economy, was to become "the Key to British interests in America"; for this bastion in the North Atlantic could safeguard both the inevitable assault upon Quebec and British maritime expansion by way of the St. Lawrence into the northern hinterlands of the continent. Shirley's "Great Plan," frustrated for a time by the vicissitudes of eighteenth-century politics, was left at last to others to achieve. Halifax at the Board of Trade, General Wolfe at Louisbourg in 1758, and Governor Lawrence, Shirley's own disciple, in Nova Scotia, brought the first phase of the project to pass within a few months of Shirley's own departure from the American scene. The enterprise on the St. Lawrence followed almost immediately. With Chatham in power in Great Britain, the capture of Quebec by Wolfe in 1759 and of Montreal by Amherst in the following year seemed like the dawn of a new day in America.

To Franklin there was a touch of destiny in these events. No American of his time had ventured more daringly into the scientific and philosophical speculation of that age. By 1760 Franklin's political speculations too appear to have settled into a deeper conviction. It is only too evident that to his European contemporaries these views were less acceptable than the scientific theories for which St. Andrews and Glasgow and Oxford were so eager to acclaim him. "I refrain," he wrote to Lord Kames at the close of one of these political forecasts, "for I see you begin to think my notions extravagant, and look upon them as the ravings of a mad prophet." Lord Kames was to live long enough to give melancholy approbation to the prophet's sanity.

As early as 1754, two years before the final struggle for America officially began, Franklin had drafted his "Albany Plan" for the union of the British American colonies. Thirty-five years later, at the close of a long life of almost incredible vicissitudes, Franklin maintained that his *Plan of Union* might have forestalled a revolution. The plan itself, based upon colonial sanctions and parliamentary enactment, still commands the respect of modern scholarship but it is less important here perhaps than the ensuing correspondence with Shirley. This was prophetic not only of the dangers which threatened the first empire in America but of the spirit which saved the second. Ten years before the *Stamp Act* and twenty years before the *Quebec Act* he wrote:

In Matters of General Concern to the People, and especially where Burthens are to be laid upon them, it is of Use to consider as well what they will be apt to think and say, as what they *ought* to think. . . .

They will say, and perhaps with Justice, that the Body of the People in the Colonies are as loyal . . . as any Subjects in the King's Dominions. . . .

That to propose taxing them by Parliament . . . shews a Suspicion of their Loyalty to the Crown, or Regard for their Country, or of their Common Sense and Understanding which they have not deserv'd. . . .

That a Power in Governors to march the Inhabitants from one End of the British and French Colonies to the other would put them on a Footing with the Subjects of France in Canada. . . .

That if the Colonies in a Body may be well governed by Governors and Councils . . . without Representatives, particular Colonies may as well or better be so governed; a Tax may be laid upon them all by Act of Parliament; for Support of Government, and their Assemblies dismiss'd, as a useless Part of their Constitution. . . .

Five years after this intercourse with Shirley, Franklin found himself in London. It was the "year of victories" and the king's ministers were wavering in their policy for the ensuing peace. In Franklin's *Autobiography* for the period of the Seven Years' War the most significant caption appears in the words of Cato: *Canada delenda est*. In a pamphlet of great power Franklin now viewed the regions of the St. Lawrence and the Great Lakes as the logical appanage of a British American empire. "With *Canada* in our possession," he wrote from London, "our people in *America* will increase amazingly." The colonies, doubling their numbers "by natural generation only" every twenty-five years, "would probably, in a century more, make the number of *British* subjects on that side the water more numerous than they now are on this," thereby "assuring to the *British* name and nation a stability and permanency that no man acquainted with history durst have hoped for, 'till our *American* possessions opened the pleasing prospects."

To Chatham, the revered architect of victory in the Seven Years' War, Franklin could speak the language of a common faith. In 1774, upon the brink of irremediable decisions in British policy, Franklin was invited to the secret interview in Chatham's own house at Hayes which has survived in one of the most poignant passages of the *Autobiography*. "In former cases," said Franklin, "great empires had crumbled first at their extremities," through distance, misgovernment, and misunderstanding. "This Empire had happily found and long been in the practice of a method whereby every province was well governed, being trusted in a great measure with the government of itself." From these trends had arisen "such satisfaction in the subjects, and such encouragement to new settlements, that had it not been for the late wrong policies . . . we might have gone on extending our western empire, adding province to province, as far as the South Sea." Deploring the "ruin which seemed impending over so fine a plan, so well adapted to make all the subjects of the greatest empire happy," Franklin appealed, not in vain, for one supreme effort of statesmanship to rescue it "out of the mangling hands of the present set of blundering ministers" in order to restore "the Union and harmony between Britain and her colonies so necessary to both."

Even after the die was cast for revolution and independence, the acquisition of Canada remained for Franklin an obsession. Scarcely had he taken his seat in the Continental Congress after his return from England before he hurried off, at seventy years of age, to Montreal, to forestall the design which Carleton's indomitable mind had formed for the subjugation of New England. Franklin had commanded too accurate information in London to be mistaken about the ulterior purposes of the *Quebec Act*. It may well have been from him that the Continental Congress received its "indubitable evidence that a design is formed by the British Ministry of making a cruel invasion from the province of Quebec, upon these colonies."[1] The mission of Franklin and Carroll in Montreal, with the ensuing enterprise of Fleury Mesplet in the founding of the Montreal *Gazette*, forms one of the strangest passages in the early history of Canada. When Franklin again crossed the Atlantic—this time not as colonial agent in London but American plenipotentiary to France—he still retained Canada and Nova Scotia within the orbit of the revolutionary cause in North America. He still held his grants of land in Nova Scotia and he still pressed, though in vain, for the inclusion of the northern provinces in the United States of America at the treaty of Versailles in 1783.

It is doubtful if Franklin ever surrendered his early vision of an undivided empire. Questioned in 1766 as to the prevailing temper in America towards the mother country before 1763, Franklin replied that it was "the best in the world. . . . They had not only a respect but an affection for Great Britain, for its laws, its customs and manners and even a fondness for its fashions that greatly increased the commerce." "Of all Americans," writes Van Doren, Franklin "had the largest vision of the Empire that might be shaped by political wisdom, and perhaps the strongest affection for the idea." There can scarcely be a doubt that this vision attended Franklin to England on his early mission during the Seven Years' War and remained with him until his faith in the statesmanship requisite for such a destiny was utterly extinguished.

No one [he wrote to Lord Kames[2] after the fall of Quebec] can more sincerely rejoice than I do, on the reduction of Canada; and this not merely as I am a colonist, but as I am a Briton. I have long been of opinion, that the *foundations of the future grandeur and stability of the British empire lie in America*; and though, like other foundations, they are low and little now, they are, nevertheless, broad and strong enough to support the greatest political structure that human wisdom ever yet erected. . . . All the country from the St. Lawrence to the Mississippi will in another century be filled with British people. Britain herself will become vastly more populous, by the immense increase of its commerce, the Atlantic sea will be covered with your trading ships; and your naval power, thence continually increasing, will extend your influence round the whole globe, and awe the world!

[1] *Journals*, ed. Ford, II, 56.
[2] Jan. 3, 1760; John Bigelow, ed., *The Life of Benjamin Franklin Written by Himself*, I, 399.

TWENTIETH-CENTURY RETROSPECT

I

In comparison with this resplendent prospect from the middle of the eighteenth century, the retrospect from the middle of the twentieth is at first sight a bewildering vista. Over much of the distance hangs the pall of conflict and political frustration on both sides of the boundary. Many signs of a common origin and of common enterprise in a North American environment are still discernible, but the prospect which still lay unbroken before Franklin and Chatham in the year of destiny 1774 is no longer there. In its place is a series of landmarks stretching backwards over the century and a half from the Imperial Conference of 1926 to the Declaration of Independence like the traps and pitfalls which Bunyan's pilgrim surveyed in the clear light of morning after his fearsome journey through the Valley of the Shadow of Death. Many of the terrors of darkness and of lost direction—"the hobgoblins, and satyrs and dragons of the pit"—have been dissipated by the light of day. On the other hand many real dangers, many hair-breadth escapes from more serious pitfalls and conflicts, are discernible from this distance of time with great clearness.

For many years after the revolution, nostalgic memories of the first empire survived on both sides of the boundary. To the Simcoes, the Winslows, the Putnams, the Chipmans, the Beverley Robinsons of the second empire, the attempt to transplant three or four generations of American traditions to a new soil in the north was an experience too grim to be forgotten. Many of the maritime loyalists still wrote of "home" in the old colonies and not a few of them returned thither after the dust of conflict had settled. In Upper Canada the loyalists were followed in increasing numbers by post-loyalist migrations from the United States which settled the southwestern reaches of the peninsula. On the other side of the boundary the former advocates of conciliation and reunion quickly fell into step in obedience to the marching orders of the young republic. Even Franklin seems to have abandoned the hope of a united America, and Jay's treaty sealed the separation of the north with a restoration at least of goodwill and common interests. But the generations that followed, fired by the phenomenal westward expansion of the republic, recaptured Franklin's vision and sanctified it into "manifest destiny." Then as a second destiny became slowly manifest in the north a clearer and perhaps profounder conception of North Americanism became possible. The late Lord Bryce once remarked that if there had been no Dominion of Canada it would have been in the interests of the United States to create one.

There are now two English-speaking nations in North America instead of one. They are unequal in resources and in power, dissimilar and in some respects perhaps divergent in association, and separated, it may be, by deeper cleavages of political technique and temper than may appear upon the surface. But they are now equal at least in the sovereign attributes of nationhood, and for more than a century they have given the most effective demonstration of friendly intercourse to be found among contiguous peoples in the modern world. Parting company midway through their North American career in their approach to the gravest problem of pioneer communities—their relations to the sanctions of the parent state—they have now circumvented or surmounted that problem by methods characteristically different. In the process they have developed for more than a century and a half traditions that are never likely to be obliterated. But from the sovereign vantage-ground of nationhood they may now reflect with mutual respect that historic antipathies have been known to yield to dominant national interests. If these interests can be brought into conformity for the future, the two nations may now move forward again in many respects not only in parallel lines but *pari passu* towards the second greatest problem of their destiny on this continent, their relations to basic issues of peace and international order in the modern world. Upon their agreement here may well depend their relations to each other for many years to come.

For both countries much of the way from the Declaration of Independence to the Imperial Conference of 1926 was beset with unpredictable vicissitudes, and the tendency in retrospect to read back into it a uniform pattern of friendly intercourse can play strange pranks with history. National traditions crystallizing over so long a period of time may be expected to condition the method of co-operation and in some respects to dictate the terms of association. To the two generations that lived through the revolution and the War of 1812 it seemed that the patterns of national life were already set in indelible colours. Mutual antipathies were translated deliberately into divergencies of political technique and temper, ensuring, as they thought, permanent differences in the forms and functions of government. In the long contest for reform in the second empire these antipathies still complicated the issue and probably impeded the outcome. When self-government was finally achieved it was deliberately devised to follow British parliamentary rather than American congressional models. The antipathies too of the Civil War period had a profound effect upon the process of Canadian federation. Many of these immediate historic motives have long since passed away. To all but the superficial observer, nevertheless, the trends remain. Even instinctive traits may not be without significance. Lord Morley's whimsical reflection, "how curious it is to see how exactly people follow their own characters all through life," applies to nations as well as to individuals. To divorce either the United States or Canada from a history like theirs is no more feasible than divorcing an individual from his character. For many reasons which will emerge in the course of these studies the Canadian legacy from these formative years may be expected to remain characteristically Canadian. The epic of America too may be expected to remain, even in a world setting, as characteristically American as the Declaration of Independence. Many of the prejudices and anti-pathies that have gone into the compound of national life in both countries have been sublimated in due time by wise statesmanship— by recognizing rather than by perverting or ignoring history. With goodwill now in the ascendant, the present generation may hope to survey antipathies as well as affinities with what Burke once called "the freedom of history."

Many of these divergencies were rooted during the formative years of both countries, in the conditions of their being. The United States emerged from the first empire in America by revolution—a republic with profound convictions against monarchical forms of government, with a written constitution involving a presidential execu-tive and a congressional system of legislation, and with an ineradicable bias against British officialdom and statecraft. Canada has emerged by evolution from the second empire, after historic passages of political conflict but with parliamentary government fortified by British pre-cedents and so charged by common traditions and practice that she remains in association with kindred nations of the British Common-wealth in every quarter of the world. It can scarcely be denied that the method itself determined function as well as form; for if the high road of revolution led to isolation, the low road of evolution led to association. Canada assuredly did not reach nationhood first but the record would seem to show that she reached it in the end by a process which kept her more closely in association with world forces of peace and freedom, and left her for nearly a generation before the outbreak of war in 1939 much nearer to an international world order.

The rise to nationhood in both the thirteen colonies and those that remained British in the north was conditioned, moreover, by factors in many respects peculiar to each. It would be easy to cite controls of geography, of demography, of economic resources, which have functioned so distinctively in each case that even contiguity in a North American environment has left them almost untouched by mutual association. The St. Lawrence and the Great Lakes have not always meant the same thing to both nor canalized to the same extent the sense of national direction. Had the region of Hudson Bay and the Hudson Bay watershed proved, as its location on the map would seem to imply, to be the counterpart in the north to the Gulf of Mexico and the Mississippi prairies in the south, the distinctive problem of the "Canadian Shield" in the expanding Canadian frontier would never have arisen. This problem has forced some of the most imperative innovations in Canadian policy. The fur trade and the Indian had a vast influence upon the early development of Canada, but these are not the counterpart of cotton and the Negro in the economic or demographic development of the United States. In issues such as public ownership the contrasts between Canada and the United States are so marked that superficial observers have assumed organic differences in social structure. Many of these contrasts originated in very commonplace ways and warrant no such implications. The vast resources of water power in Canada, for example, were largely unalienated, or were still largely recoverable, at a time when modern techniques of power development were coming into vogue, and there was a very natural tendency to look to the province or the city for rapid development of public utilities. It is apt to come as a surprise to an American observer that publicly owned enterprises like the Ontario Hydro-Electric Power Commission, the Manitoba telephone system, the Winnipeg Electric Company, the Ontario Northland Railway, the Toronto Transportation Commission, the Canadian National Railways, have all reflected not socialistic or "new deal" trends towards "the left" like the Bonneville dam or the Tennessee Valley Authority but empirical experiments of a relatively frontier economy, inaugurated, as it happens in most of the instances just cited, by Conservative governments.

Certain cultural cleavages, too, are deeply set in history and will remain permanent. Nearly one-third of the present population of Canada is of French origin—perhaps the most self-conscious and tenacious cultural group in North America. Representing a tradition as distinctively North American as that of the thirteen British colonies to the south, they parted company from the parent state at approximately the same time, though for vastly different reasons. By the middle of the eighteenth century both groups had developed a sturdy brand of frontier localism which was beginning to give concern to colonial officials. When a famous line regiment once arrived in New France, the Intendant Bigot marched them up to Montreal instead of sending them by water in order to impress unruly *habitants* with the resources of royal power in America. Beginning with fewer than 100,000 inhabitants at the close of the American Revolution, French-speaking Canada has followed the horoscope cast by church and seigneurs in the throes of that conflict. After a century and a half of history as a British province which one of their historians has truly called an epic in itself, this section of Canada has developed a philosophy of "survival" against "assimilation" by the prevailing spirit of English-speaking America, whether from Canada or from the United States, which is probably the most distinctive achievement of the French race on this continent. On the other hand the problem of the Negroes in the United States—a group which outnumbers the whole population of Canada—has no counterpart in Canada. The tragic story of the North American Indian too is divided at the international boundary. The incomparable success of the Hudson's Bay Company in dealing with the aborigine in the north was reinforced in the east by French traditions appropriated by the British Indian department after the fall of New France.

These and many other less obvious contrasts are apt to escape the Canadian observer who does not know the United States or the American observer who does not know Canada, or the European observer who does not happen to know either. Even superficial resemblances are sometimes deceptive. One of the most prominent Japanese visitors in Great Britain once remarked that during the first six months of his stay in London all Britons looked alike to him, and he could scarcely tell them apart.

II

These differences and contrasts between Canada and the United States could be multiplied by any competent observer who was searching for them, but it is equally true that they are quite as easily ignored by those who have no occasion to distinguish them. The truth appears to be, as one of the shrewdest French observers once remarked, that the problem of international relations in Europe has no counterpart in America. In Europe the nations resemble each other in little things and differ in big things. In America they differ in little things and resemble each other most in the biggest things of all. In Europe the

cultural and other resemblances may be many in little things, while
the political differences are profound and implacable. In North
America the cultural and physical differences may be many but as a
rule they are relatively unimportant, while the basic resemblances—resemblances which are shared in varying degree by the whole English-
speaking world—are the most important attributes which can concern
the modern state.

Many of the basic factors in the development of two English-
speaking nations in North America are of this order. The method of
their development from their common origin in colonial America to a
common nationhood has been in many respects fundamentally different. At almost every stage there have been differences of sequence, of
tempo, and of association. But to a complex world torn by conflicting
ideologies the net results at the end are apt to appear remarkably
similar; and their association in the comity of nations has come at a
time when both countries have completed cycles of remarkable
similarity.

In the United States several of the stages through which the British
provinces have since passed were attempted by a single generation
within less than a single decade. Self-government was a corollary of
revolution and political independence. In that respect the United
States followed the pattern of the United Netherlands almost exactly
two centuries before, in vindicating self-government by successful
revolt against constituted authority. Union, too, was the product of
revolution, confirmed by one of the great constructive achievements
of modern statesmanship, the constitution of 1787—though it required
a civil war three-quarters of a century later to safeguard and preserve
that union. National status in international relations—the last phase of
nationhood for the British nations overseas—came almost automatically
for the United States in defiance of one European power and with the
aid of two others. In this respect the American achievement was much
happier than its European prototype, for nearly half a century separated
the beginning of successful revolt in the Netherlands in 1572 from the
recognition accorded the northern provinces by England and France
in 1609, and another generation was yet to pass before the independence of the Netherlands was formally recognized by Spain in 1648. A
fourth factor in the United States was perhaps the greatest single
ingredient in the unity and expansion of the republic. With independence from European entanglements the union turned deliberately to
attack a much more lucrative and immediate task, the conquest and
settlement of half a continent. Almost every major aspect of policy in

the United States was affected by this process. The public domain of the republic, created when the original states of the union dedicated to the national government their conflicting claims to the hinterlands, was enlarged by purchase, by conquest, and by diplomacy from the Alleghany Mountains to Alaska in the span of eighty years. This expanding frontier was the background for the great transcontinentals, for the conflict between north and south in the deadly rivalry of "slave" and "free" for new territory, and for the widest range of land settlement ever administered by one government. With the completion of this task early in the twentieth century, the gates were barred to immigration, and a new set of problems began to emerge in the United States—the establishment of a stable society and a stable economy on this continent, and another equally prodigious experiment, whether the greatest aggregation of population, wealth, and resources under one government in the world could remain isolated and insulated from a world in which air transport promises to make oceans and mountain ranges almost meaningless for the intercourse of nations.

In Canada also these same four factors have attended the development of nationhood, but they have appeared in a different order, one at a time, and with long intervals between. The associations that attended the development have resulted in a distinctive tradition, and there is a distinctive outlook at the end.

The prime factor, self-government, though implanted in the primitive legislation of colonial assemblies, began to function over the executive only with the achievement of responsible government in 1848—the beginning of a long process which has come to include many of the attributes of nationhood only in our own day. Union of the British provinces was the work of the next generation, and after seventy-five years—the stage marked by civil war in the United States—the growing-pains of federalism were still with us. Expansion to the Pacific, though less spectacular than that of the republic, was undertaken long before the young dominion was ready for it. Here too the settlement of the new frontier under federal auspices has formed a cycle of Canadian development—a cycle like that of the United States now rounding into completion in our own day. The final functioning of Canada, in international affairs, has come last of all, and perhaps most rapidly of all, but this outcome is now seen in retrospect to have been foreshadowed by trends in Canadian self-government for nearly a century.

All four of these major factors and many others that have emerged in the evolution of Canadian nationhood have been profoundly influenced by relations with the United States in a North American environment. These relations have been mutual but for obvious reasons their reciprocal effects have been far from equal. The United States, obsessed as a rule with its own domestic problems, has responded only incidentally to conditions upon its northern frontier, while Canada has found the preponderance of her neighbour in wealth, in population, and in state policy, in one aspect or another inescapable. Antipathies as well as affinities have played their part, and it would be a strangely perverted view of history that ignored the causes and consequences of both. For the development of Canadian nationhood, however, their importance lies not in the balance between them but in their unbroken continuity. In each of the major factors of a common nationhood that continuity has been inescapable, and this preliminary survey may be an appropriate place to illustrate at the outset so dominant a characteristic of the Canadian scene.

III

The early stages of self-government in the second empire were almost indistinguishable from those of the first. During the century and a half of their common history practical self-government had developed much farther than British officialdom was willing to concede. It was the awakening of men like Knox and Grenville and Hillsborough to these trends and to the uncanny speed of colonial development that aroused their worst suspicions of colonial "intentions." Many of the colonial governors also, after a bitter round or two with exuberant colonial assemblies, added to the reaction which followed Chatham's fine gesture of co-operation during the Seven Years' War. A few prophets of the Commonwealth like Chatham himself and Franklin and Burke were concerned less with imperial organization than with those empirical adjustments of "day to day opportunism" which have since been found so efficacious in the modern Commonwealth. The colonists too were adepts at this sort of improvisation. By a score of devices they contrived to circumvent official regimentation. In New York the Assembly contrived to supervise the expenditure of their own appropriations by agents under their own appointment. In Rhode Island and Connecticut the governors themselves were elective, and Stephen Hopkins, the last of them, stated roundly that "the Parliament of Great Britain had no more right to make laws for them than they had for the Mohawks." Already these two provinces were regarded by a neighbouring governor as "two Republics . . . the Allies of Great Britain and not the Subjects." It is true that the technique of self-government in the first empire was not that finally evolved so successfully in the second. The conventions which came to be called responsible government in the Canadian provinces would have been repudiated in Georgian England of the eighteenth century where the monarchy still shuffled and re-shuffled its ministers in defiance of the House of Commons, and where the House itself, as an American observer once said of the fateful election of 1768, could be "sold for about two millions, and might be bought . . . by the very devil himself." In practice, however, self-government was a familiar theme in eighteenth-century America. The Stamp Act Congress claimed for each of the colonies "all the inherent rights and liberties of . . . natural-born subjects within the Kingdom of Great Britain"—a principle which Dickinson in his *Farmers' Letters* called "the American Declaration of Rights." Knox still scouted this "idea of a *polypus* government, where a head sprouts out of every joint," but Franklin's boast was already warranted: the British Empire "had happily found and long been in the practice of a method whereby every province was well governed, being trusted in a great measure with the government of itself."

The reaction which attended the beginnings of the second empire was sanctioned by the short-sighted lessons drawn from the disastrous ending of the first. For generations the revolution remained almost incomprehensible. When the representative institutions which the Board of Trade had advocated in vain for French Roman Catholics in Quebec in 1769 were finally conceded in 1791, William Knox, as we have seen, still deplored these "fine spun theories, for promoting the happiness of the French Canadians, by converting them into English Republicans." For the new republic Knox predicted an age of chaos in the illimitable hinterlands of America. This diffusion, it was thought, made disintegration safe for the neighbouring colonies. The old province of Nova Scotia was broken into four fragments, three of them never to be reunited. The old province of Quebec was broken into Upper and Lower Canada. There were local reasons as plenty as blackberries for this separation, but the policy behind it was too uniform and too subtle to be the result of local preferences; and it is traceable long before the "spring fleet" of New Brunswick loyalists left New York in 1783. The second empire in America, as we shall see, began in a new environment, with a picked personnel, and with mutual confidence in the ascendant, but it is a commonplace of Canadian history that it went the way of the first empire until at last it invited the same dissolution. How far was American neighbourhood responsible for the policy which transformed it into the Commonwealth?

The association of the Papineau and Mackenzie risings in the Canadas with the tide of Jacksonian democracy in the United States has survived that day to conceal many of the more distinctive features of the Canadian scene. Even Murdock of the Colonial Office attributed the "moderation and harmony" in Nova Scotia to its "remoteness from American institutions and habits." The intercourse of the Upper Canadian frontier with up-state New York and the new frontier state of Ohio is traceable in countless aspects of frontier life from building-bees and camp-meetings to spelling-books, farm implements, and stoves. But agricultural frontiers in America have had a way of generating distinctive patterns of their own not through contagious contacts with other similar frontiers but by the play of their own primitive and spontaneous vitality. Nova Scotia, in many respects, was still a frontier of New England. As late as 1817 Dalhousie found that "the connection between the respectable inhabitants of this Province, and the States, is yet very intimate; scarcely is there a family that has not Fathers, Brothers, and near relations settled there." This, however, had never implied "the most distant doubt of the loyalty of this Province." In Upper Canada also the temper which finally prevailed was neither tory nor republican. In a very real sense it was in conflict with both, and the American neighbourhood was exploited by both to embitter every issue. In the loyalist migrations at the close of the revolution the United States had sown the neighbouring provinces with dragon's teeth, and every reformer from Gourlay to Baldwin reaped a harvest of ineradicable prejudice and suspicion. Whatever Mackenzie may have owed in his political ideas to the neighbouring republic he was credited in tory annals with little else. Robert Baldwin, whose profound convictions, as Elgin afterwards wrote, were worth more than so many regiments to the British connection, was associated by Metcalfe with "treason and republicanism": his professions were "utterly worthless." Howe in Nova Scotia challenged his adversaries to point that "antiquated old blunderbuss" at him, but the elections of 1836 and 1844 in Canada are scarcely to be explained apart from this devastating tradition. Egerton Ryerson finally surrendered to it and contributed in no small measure to its ravages.

The counterpart to this is the progress, and in the end the solid achievement, which was made by another approach. As early as 1836 New Brunswick secured not only the control of its crown lands revenues but a change in the personnel of the Executive Council which commanded the confidence of the representative branch. Durham reported, all too confidently, that "the constitutional practice" which he advocated had been "fully carried into effect in this Province; the

Government had been taken out of the hands of those who could not obtain the assent of the majority of the Assembly, and placed in the hands of those who possessed its confidence." Here was responsible government in embryo, if not in practice; but the Assembly obligingly disavowed any intention of holding the Executive Council responsible "at all times" in accordance with the "claims set up by another colony." Glenelg in reply at the Colonial Office commended the "just delicacy" of the New Brunswick delegates in waiving any "peremptory rule" during the turmoil in the Canadas. For Nova Scotia the Colonial Office stated the difficulty more ingenuously: responsible government "if conceded in any one colony . . . must be granted in all." What would happen in Lower Canada, asked Lord John Russell, with a "ministry headed by M. Papineau"? Joseph Howe, with the ball at his feet in the masterly resolution of no confidence in February, 1840—carried in a reform assembly by a disciplined party of thirty to twelve—responded to Sydenham's appeal not to complicate his problem in the Canadas. Nova Scotia which was the first to secure responsible government was the remotest from the frontier influences of Jacksonian democracy, while in all the provinces alike the technique itself as expounded by Baldwin and Hincks, by Howe and Huntington, by Buller and Grey and Elgin, represented a deliberate departure from republican models —in Elgin's phrase a "departure from the American model not an approximation to it." The crucial vote in the caucus of the Canadian Reform party after the election of 1848 followed a duel in the French language between La Fontaine and Papineau who continued to impugn responsible government as the product of a "narrow and malevolent genius," designedly "ominous and disastrous" to the province. Self-government in Canada was modelled so closely upon British parliamentary practice in distinction to the congressional system of her neighbours that the sequel is scarcely more than a commentary upon Elgin's robust faith in that practice.

It is not necessary to disparage Mackenzie and Papineau for what Howe was pleased to call "the maddest rebellions on record." At any rate they forced the issues of colonial government into major British politics for the first time since the American Revolution: a fact attested by the deluge of print and the succession of able men—Durham, Buller, Sydenham, Bagot, Metcalfe, Elgin, and Sir Edmund Head— who gave their best services, and four of them their lives, to Canada. The net effect of American neighbourhood, however, is not so easily estimated. As Franklin observed of the earlier crisis, where the ravages of prejudice are involved it is of use to consider as well what men are "apt to think and say, as what they *ought* to think." Mackenzie plunged

into rebellion after being bludgeoned into defeat in the elections of
1836 by indiscriminate charges of treason and republicanism. Beyond
a doubt his method and his own temper lent colour to those charges.
His genius for "grievances" ranging far beyond the voluminous
Seventh Report on Grievances—"grievances here and grievances there"
as the lieutenant-governor jeered "which the Committee, he said, had
not ventured to enumerate"—had one fatal defect as a medium for
reform. Every new "grievance" added to the list merely complicated
the problem and multiplied the difficulties. In both the Canadas sheer
obstructiveness, often in the most offensive terms, was the order of
the day. Papineau's ninety-two resolutions multiplying and magnifying
these accumulated "grievances" invited nothing but conflict. Was
there no solution but revolution and independence?

To Baldwin and to Howe and eventually to the whole school of
British American reformers who won responsible government, "grievance-mongering" as such was worse than useless. In that sense "the
great divide" in reform—the watershed between revolution and responsible government, between the old colonial system and the
Commonwealth—was to be found within the ranks of the reformers
themselves. The Mackenzie–Papineau school with their meticulous
accumulation of "grievances" invited futile conflict and frustration.
The Baldwin–Howe school concentrated inflexibly upon redressing
their own grievances through the sovereign device of responsible
government. That device was "perfectly *simple* and eminently *British*."
It was based upon confidence rather than conflict. It invited association
rather than separation. In seeking first responsible government they
were persuaded that all other things should be added unto them:

It is vain [Baldwin wrote desperately to Lord Durham in 1838] to direct
their attention to this or that grievance—Many that have been harped upon
in the political heat of the day as evils of appalling magnitude are no
grievances at all and many others would cease to be such under the system
proposed. . . . You must give those in whom the people have confidence
an interest in preserving the *system* of your Government, and maintaining
the connection with the Mother Country, and then you will hear no grievances because real ones will be redressed, imaginery ones will be forgotten.[1]

"Give us this truly British privilege," wrote Howe to Lord John
Russell, "and colonial grievances will become a scarce article in the
English market."

[1]"These are the views which I laid before Sir Francis Head when he sent for
me on my first arrival in the Province—These views I again pressed upon the
consideration of Lord Glenelg and Lord John Russell when in England in 1836,
and I now again and for the last time would most earnestly urge them upon the
consideration of Your Lordship."

Had the British provinces at the close of the American Revolution been towed out into the Pacific, out of the orbit of the United States, what is known as "the fight for responsible government" must still have arisen in every legislature almost as a necessity of its nature. But beyond question it would have been less complicated by false analogies, and it might have been settled without bloodshed. It was Howe's conviction, confirmed by a confidential interview with Glenelg himself in 1838 and by lifelong antipathies to the upper provinces, that responsible government was feasible in Nova Scotia without the ten years of turmoil—"the siege of Troy"—which followed the Canadian rebellions; and it was won at last, as Howe was wont to boast, without a blow, without the breaking of a pane of glass.

IV

For confederation, the second prerequisite for Canadian nationhood, American neighbourhood appears in a vastly different light. If self-government *plus* union equals nationhood—a very rough and ready formula—it might almost be claimed that the Civil War which saved the American union created the Canadian. Had the British provinces, in this instance, been towed out into the Pacific, out of the orbit of the United States, Canadian federation might have been as protracted and infirm as that of Australia. Without the influence of American relations during the Civil War, and without in turn the coercive influence of the Colonial Office upon New Brunswick and Nova Scotia, it would be impossible to reconstruct a federation of the British provinces in 1867, or indeed a federation at any time endowed with the preponderant federal powers which came to function in 1867.

After the annexation of Texas and of Oregon, the danger of the piecemeal disintegration of the British provinces into the United States was never lost to sight in British policy. The fur-trading technique of the Hudson's Bay Company had been powerless to cope with American pioneers in Oregon, confirmed in their enterprise by grants of free land (a whole section to a family) nearly a decade and a half before the great *Homestead Act* of 1862. The grant of Vancouver Island to the Hudson's Bay Company in 1849 for purposes of settlement was an attempt to forestall this technique north of the forty-ninth parallel of latitude; and nothing perhaps but the existence of the Red River Settlement and the awakening interest of Canada and the Colonial Office falsified the prophecy of Consul Taylor in 1865 that "the Americanization of the fertile belt is inevitable." "I doubt not," wrote Governor McTavish of the Hudson's Bay Company as late as 1869, "this will be its ultimate destiny. . . . Indeed it is for the interests of settlers here that annexation should take place at once."

After the *Report from the Select Committee on the Hudson's Bay Company* in 1857, British policy, guided by the penetrating sagacity of Sir Edmund Head in Canada, moved rapidly towards a series of preliminary regional unions across the continent. The remotest and perhaps the most urgent was the union of Vancouver Island and the mainland area of British Columbia. Nelson defended the shores of England from Napoleon's flotillas at Boulogne by blockading Toulon in the Mediterranean where Villeneuve and the remotest squadron of the French fleet had to move first in order to secure, even for a fortnight, the necessary command of the channel. In a sense British Columbia was the Toulon of British policy, the remotest and therefore the first instead of the last, or almost the last, phase of Canadian confederation. Had Polk's objective of "fifty-four forty or fight" during the Oregon trouble been combined with the Alaska purchase two decades later, the Canadian provinces would have been cut off forever from the Pacific. This problem of the West was clearly in Lytton's mind in opposing the highly partisan project of Sir Edmund Head and Alexander Tilloch Galt for federation in 1858 without enlisting in that great enterprise the support of George Brown and the Clear Grits, "the party of westward expansion." The union of Vancouver Island and British Columbia was the only one of the projected regional unions of that time that was ever consummated in its original form.

The second, the transfer of the Red and Saskatchewan river areas to "Canada," was not to be effected until 1870, after federation and an insurrection at Red River; but to Macdonald and his colleagues it was this central area, "the keystone of the arch," which caused the gravest concern for the future of a transcontinental British dominion. The third regional union, that of the Maritime Provinces, was supported by the widest range of opinion on record at that time: by Sir Edmund Head and by Lord Mulgrave, by Lieutenant-Governors Manners-Sutton, Gordon, and Macdonnell, by Howe and Tupper, George Young, Dickey, Archibald, McCulley, Tilley, Fisher, and many others on this side of the Atlantic; and by Newcastle, Lytton and Merivale, Carnarvon, Fortescue, Blackwood, Elliot, and Cardwell, at the Colonial Office. But athwart the Charlottetown Conference, convened in September, 1864, to implement maritime union, there appeared, with dramatic impact and suddenness, the Canadian project of federal union for all the provinces, advocated by the most impressive array of talent that had ever left "Canada" on such a mission. The success of these

dauntless Argonauts, first at Charlottetown and Quebec, then behind
the scenes at Downing Street, and finally behind the scenes also in the
shrewd tactics of 1866 with New Brunswick and Nova Scotia, was
more than a miracle of advocacy. "Stronger than advocacy," as Thomas
D'Arcy McGee once said, was the pressure of events; and the strongest
pressure, it is safe to say, came from the United States.

While the breakdown of the Canadian union—"deadlock," as
Goldwin Smith was so fond of insisting—may have been in one sense
"the real author of confederation," the coalition which met the crisis
in 1864 is scarcely to be explained apart from the imperative trends
of American politics. When George Brown in 1859 carried the Clear
Grit convention in favour of a dual federation of Canada East and
Canada West, his opponent was George Sheppard behind whose project of "simple dissolution" for the Canadian union is now known to
have lurked the subtler design of annexation to the United States. In
1862, when the Militia Bill was thrown out in the Canadian legislature,
George Brown resented the scathing comment of the British press and
still relied upon the solid good sense of both peoples to keep the peace.
By 1864 however Brown was prepared to vote a million dollars for the
militia and to fortify Montreal. The cumulative effect of these years it
is impossible for this generation to estimate: the Trent affair, the long
series of border incidents culminating in the St. Albans crisis at the
time of the Quebec Conference, the abrogation of the Reciprocity
Treaty and the threatened abrogation of the Rush-Bagot convention,
the Union Pacific charter and *Homestead Act* of 1862, the Northern
Pacific project in 1864, the moral effect of Gettysburg and Vicksburg
in 1863, the march of "manifest destiny" quickened by the impending
triumph of the North. No better emissary for the defence of the British
provinces, for a general federation as distinct from maritime union, and
for a national effort to safeguard the West could have been sent to
London in November, 1864, than George Brown himself, the only
Canadian behind the scenes when the epochal decision of the Colonial
Office was announced in December, 1864. During these critical months,
defence overshadowed every other aspect of Canadian policy on both
sides of the Atlantic. The unremitting pressure from the Colonial
Office which carried New Brunswick and finally Nova Scotia into confederation is set to the same major key, and without this intervention
it could be demonstrated with almost mathematical precision that
confederation, for that generation at least, could never have been
brought to pass. There were other forces without number, but the
abnormal pressure and temperature, so to speak, under which federations are almost invariably consummated, are almost measurably

traceable in this instance to the American neighbourhood. Many of the most characteristic features of the Canadian federal system are traceable to the same quarter. The preponderance of federal powers in the *British North America Act of 1867* was the work of Canadian statesmen at a time when the issues of state sovereignty were being decided by two millions of armed men across the border.

V

A third stage in Canadian nationhood—expansion to the Pacific—was forced upon the British provinces from the outset by the gigantic strides of the republic across the continent. Nothing like the speed and momentum of that movement had ever been seen. After Texas and Oregon and the failure of the Hudson's Bay Company in Vancouver Island, it was obvious to the select committee of the British House of Commons in 1857 that the Company was a broken reed. Nothing but an expanding Canada could hope to hold the West. By 1860 nearly seven and a half millions of people had poured into the north-central states, sped and directed like a torrent by the Illinois Central, the first of the great land-grant railways of the republic. The transfer of Rupert's Land to a Canadian federation was foreordained as early as the mission of Macdonald, Galt, Cartier, and Brown to London in April, 1865; and it was the first task of the new dominion—a premature function which taxed its resources to the breaking point—to complete the design by the political annexation of Rupert's Land, the North-Western Territory, and British Columbia to the original federation, and to make good that political expansion by a transcontinental railway on Canadian soil.

The Illinois Central in 1850, the Hannibal and St. Jo, the Union Pacific, and the great *Homestead Act* of 1862 were all wonders of their day; but it was the Northern Pacific two years later—in 1864, "the year of destiny" for Canada—which filled Canadian statesmen with concern. It is now possible to discount much of "manifest destiny" and "annexation" in the United States as political propaganda for home consumption, but it is not so safe to discount the contemporary effect upon Canadian policy. In the midst of the Riel insurrection, Brydges of the Grand Trunk reported to Macdonald a conversation with Governor Smith of Vermont, then president of the Northern Pacific. "There is some political action," he wrote, "at the bottom of this . . . to prevent your getting the control for Canada of the Hudson's Bay Territory." "It is quite evident to me," Macdonald replied, "not only from this conversation, but from advices from Washington, that the United States Government are resolved to do all they can, short of war, to get possession of the western territory, and we must take immediate and vigorous steps to counteract them." The first governor-elect for the new territory had to reach his province by way of the United States, and the McDougall fiasco, the Riel insurrection, the endless toil of the Wolseley expedition through the Canadian wilderness, were not forgotten. When British Columbia entered confederation in 1871 the resources of the dominion were pledged anew to a transcontinental railway. The national endowment for the C.P.R. was beyond all precedent for those days—a cash subsidy of $25,000,000, completed lines and surveys to the value of $38,500,000, government loans of nearly $35,000,000, and a princely land grant of 25,000,000 acres, more than half the area of New England. Such was the measure of the national emergency.

With the achievement of these major attributes of nationhood—self-government within, a national federation which reached the Pacific in 1871, and a transcontinental railway on Canadian soil—relations with the United States underwent a characteristic change. The Treaty of Washington in 1872, which liquidated a decade of the worst relations since the War of 1812, has been regarded in Canadian tradition as a double achievement: a place in British policy for the newly federated dominion which supplied one of the plenipotentiaries and ratified the treaty, and a recognition (it was hoped) on the part of the United States of another "manifest destiny" in North America. Apocryphal as much of this tradition must now be regarded there was never to be a return of the antipathies which dominated the formative stages of Canadian nationhood. The range of American experience in the development of the public domain of the United States was appropriated with abounding admiration and goodwill in the development of this new empire of "Dominion lands" in the West. The sectional survey, thirty-six sections to the township, railway land grants, school lands and swamp lands, pre-emptions and free homesteads, and above all the insistence upon federal control "for the purposes of the Dominion" instead of the provincial control conceded to the original provinces of confederation, all attest the influence of American practice, though the analogies are almost lost sometimes in the differences of adaptation. For a decade and a half at the turn of the century, the physiographical and economic factors which have almost invariably determined sustained movements of migration to the agricultural frontiers of the continent were at last propitious. The tide which had been flowing in succession over the east north-central and west north-central states reached at last the Prairie Provinces of

Canada. Even the personnel of settlement in such enterprises as the Saskatchewan Valley Land Company was a response to this era of goodwill and friendly intercourse. No more resourceful settlers have ever come to western Canada than these well-to-do pioneers with experience in dry farming and with capital to buy two or three additional quarter-sections of land for hard cash from the railway or the enterprising land company. The very soil has drifted to and fro across the boundary in the dust storms of recent years. Nowhere are institutions more characteristically Canadian, and nowhere is good neighbourhood more cordially appreciated and reciprocated.

VI

External developments in Canadian nationhood culminating in international recognition in the League of Nations and confirmation by the *Statute of Westminster* within the Commonwealth have owed little to the neighbourhood of the United States. In the main, international recognition has been but the corollary of a much longer and less spectacular process. Responsible government began in 1848 with purely local and internal issues, and Durham conceived it fairly possible to reserve foreign policy and trade, crown lands, and even the form of the constitution for imperial control. The piecemeal expansion of these primitive local powers to include all the attributes of nationhood has been one of the commonplaces of Canadian national development. The technique of self-government has remained the same. What has changed has been the range of its application; and that range from beginning to end has been determined, as we shall see, by the legitimate interests of the Canadian people. It would be possible to illustrate this process during the past century by scores of instances—one for every other year—including at last Sir Arthur Currie's command in World War I, the participation of Sir Robert Borden and his colleagues in the peace treaty, the control of foreign policy, the accession to the throne, and the declaration of war in 1939. This evolution to full nationhood by incubation, so to speak, has followed a characteristic technique of the British Commonwealth, and other nations have had very little to do with it.

But in another sense these attributes of nationhood have been but outward signs of inward growth. To that inward growth a multitude of factors have contributed, and none perhaps more pervasively for Canada than her destiny of sharing this continent with the United States. For four thousand miles a nation of fourteen millions of people faces the greatest aggregation of material resources to be found in the modern world. The pace set by the United States has been a perpetual stimulus to Canadian development—in some respects a stimulus towards impossible standards. With the retreat of historic antipathies into the past, "the time of good neighbours," as Benedick calls it in *Much Ado about Nothing*, has drawn nearer in international relations. It would be idle to assume that antipathies have altogether disappeared, or that they are to be exorcised by platitudes about the century of peace and the undefended frontier. Nobody knows better than the historian how much courage it still takes to tell the truth about American-Canadian relations, and how near the surface some of these antiquated but latent prejudices are still to be found. The combined scholarship of both countries has been clearing the ground for a more discerning understanding based upon history rather than hagiology. "In the time of good neighbours" such scholarship may truly hope to function without the lurking suspicion of devious motives and ulterior purposes.

In this understanding may lie a happy function not only for sound scholarship but for Canadian nationhood. By Great Britain and by the United States alike the national development of Canada has been at times profoundly misunderstood. So long as Canada remained a sort of no-man's land for the traditional feud between them, there have been those in both countries who persisted in regarding the development of Canadian nationhood as a movement to or fro from one to the other. Those who inspired and directed that development in its later stages have known very well that it was nothing of the sort. There have been times, for example the Alaska boundary award, when Canadian statesmen have been inclined to invoke "a plague o' both your houses." In pursuit of a self-conscious and indigenous nationhood Canadian opinion has never turned back. But among those who have brought it to pass there has not been wanting a less assertive purpose. The traditional function of Canada as an interpreter between Great Britain and the United States has been honoured in the breach rather than in the observance so long as the traditional antipathies between them were allowed to play upon the domestic issues of British North America: so long too, it may be added, as Canada found it necessary to run the gauntlet between them in the pursuit of a sentient nationhood of its own. It is only by transcending these traditional antipathies of both, in a national destiny conceded and sanctioned by both, that Canadian nationhood can hope to make a modest contribution of its own to mutual co-operation and goodwill.

Measured by results this newly won nationhood began to function barely in time to cope with the gravest emergencies in Canadian history. Peace may be expected to bring no less exacting responsibilities than war. The new age of air transportation has brought a third world neighbour—the prodigious apparition of the U.S.S.R.—within the sphere of Canadian national interests in the northern hemisphere. These conditions of contiguity and of mutual concern have now become inescapable. Moreover, in a sense never hitherto true in world history, they would seem to be final and irrevocable. The oar of the Mediterranean long-ship and the sail of the oceanic round-ship were both alike transient. The wooden clipper-ship too had its day. The iron steamship, the railway, and the motor-car have still to pass no doubt through many new phases of propulsion. But the era of the air, with stratosphere and outer space beyond, is here to stay. Man has now embarked upon his last medium of transportation on this planet. Oceans and mountain ranges and polar solitudes have lost their terrors and are fast losing their accustomed meaning for the modern world. In this new age Canada now stands astride the crossroads of the world—"the dead centre of the new heartland of air geography"—the nearest neighbour of all three paramount powers of the modern world, nearer to each of them than any two of them are to each other. For better or for worse Canada is the Belgium of the world to come, and the prospect is calculated to challenge every re source of Canadian statesmanship.

If Canadian nationhood has had a modest function to play—barely in time—between the two great English-speaking neighbours in the northern hemisphere, what will be its function in the unpredictable contingencies of the future? The role of understanding and of conciliation, all too lightly esteemed in the past, is now complicated immeasurably by differences in language and ideology and economic structure between each of our kindred neighbours and the U.S.S.R. Permanent accord between these three would leave Canada cradled in a shield of national security. Conflict between them might possibly be fought out in Canadian skies and on Canadian soil. It must be apparent that the historic associations of Canada with the Commonwealth alone would not be enough, and Canadian accord with the United States alone would not be enough, and accord with the U.S.S.R. would not be enough even if "cold war" and "iron curtain" were to yield to the amenities of civilized and rational intercourse. Canadian traditions of goodwill and association can scarcely hope to prevail over these stubborn eventualities. There must be not only accord with each of the great powers on the part of Canada but accord

among themselves—all three of them and with each other—if Canada
is not to become the battleground between them. Neither the United
States nor the U.S.S.R. could afford to tolerate Canadian neutrality even
if Canada could afford to claim it; and all the resources of the Commonwealth would be unequal to the task of vindicating it. Meanwhile
the atomic age is already upon us and the elimination of time and
space, to the attendant drum-beat of radio and television, has reached
the point where every impact is accentuated with unpredictable
speed and contiguity. To problems such as these a belated and im-
mature Canadian nationhood must now address itself willy-nilly, and
let us hope without too much false modesty. These studies are an
attempt to discern something of the historic method and temper which
may be expected to emerge from the past to govern this experiment.

Chapter Two

FRAGMENTS OF AN EMPIRE: GEOGRAPHY

FOR nearly two generations the gloom which attended the loss of the first empire in America was unrelieved by any abiding faith. Carleton himself, redoubtable still in the ruins of all his plans, faced the future with foreboding. As the last British regiment "wheeled off the key-wharf and embarked" at New York, Ward Chipman remarked that Sir Guy "looked unusually dejected"—probably the only occasion on record when Sir Guy Carleton was visibly daunted. Thirteen years later, as Lord Dorchester, he was leaving America forever with rueful reflections upon the "ruinous consequences" of the "old Colonial System."

The military and especially the naval history of the American Revolution filled the darkest pages of defeat and humiliation in the records of the English nation. In Professor Coupland's moving chapter on "England in Defeat"[1] the evidence closes in like nightfall. In 1779 a Spanish fleet anchored with impunity in Falmouth Bay. Darker than the surrender of Yorktown was the naval disaster which made it inevitable. Sea power, as Washington had seen, was to have the casting vote. The Caribbean was lost. By 1783 nearly 3,000 British merchantmen had been taken by French, Spanish, and American frigates and privateers. The revolution had been "an incongruous, illogical, detestable interlude" in the championship of freedom against Louis XIV and Napoleon. The nation learned to hurry on in its history from Quiberon Bay and the Plains of Abraham to Trafalgar and Waterloo. The truth was that a quarter of the white population of the empire had been lost to the British Crown. "The sun of Great Britain is set," said Shelburne. Horace Walpole lamented that "England totters to its foundations. Disgraced it is forever." The time came when the King himself could write of "the downfall of this once respectable Empire."

For the remnants in America too the prospects were so profoundly

[1] *The American Revolution and the British Empire* (Longmans, Green and Co., 1930), chap. i.

changed that generation after generation refused to retrace their traditions through this Valley of Humiliation to their legitimate origins in the first empire. But it was not so easy in America to pass from Quiberon Bay and the Plains of Abraham to Trafalgar and Waterloo. Basic elements of their history are to be found there. For French Canada the *Quebec Act* became a "sacred Charter" as remote in contemporary tradition from the American Revolution as it was from the generous policy of the Board of Trade which the *Quebec Act* so ignominiously supplanted. The loyalist migrations in the north were separated from their "cultivated and commodious life" in the first empire by deeper revulsions of feeling than any their ancestors had suffered in exchanging the old world for the new. Even for the fur trader and the lumberman the new prospects which opened up for them in the north carried them away from the continental destiny in which Franklin had seen "the true foundations of the British Empire."

In two respects in particular—in geography and in personnel—the British Empire in America could never again be the same. In both there were permanent elements of destiny for Canadian nationhood, for if the life of a people dominates the land in which they live, it is equally true that the land is apt to have an abiding influence upon the people. The twin problems of race and geography are visible like mountain ranges throughout the length and breadth of Canadian history. It is not always possible to chart their contours or to record precisely the watersheds into which these mountain ranges have divided the terrain of Canadian nationhood. But though obscured at times by the foothills, the peaks are seldom lost to sight on the horizon. In this and the following chapter on "Demography and Traditions" it may be as well to attempt a few bearings for future reference.

I

In Shirley's "Great Plan" which had inspired a whole generation of soldiers and prophets in America, expansion was to follow the sea and the Great River, as well as the Hudson and the Mohawk, to the hinterlands of the continent. The Great Plan was truncated at its base by the revolution. Now for both sections of English-speaking America geography was to prove a hard and tyrannical taskmaster. In some respects the provinces which remained British followed the easier route and encountered fewer international complications. The hinterland was still a wilderness but at least the title from Cape Breton to Vancouver Island was to be found in the British Crown.

"The key of all the Eastern Colonies upon the Northern Continent," in Shirley's Great Plan, was to be at the apex of the triangle, in Nova Scotia. To develop the "Cod fishery" and the "King's woods whence the Royal Navy is almost wholly supply'd," 6,000 families were to be entrenched in that province. The reduction of Louisbourg and Quebec would then open to British enterprise the vast reaches of the St. Lawrence system for the fisheries, the fur trade, and the expanding settlement of the British provinces. From the walls of Louisbourg soon after its capture by New England troops in 1745 Shirley had launched his Great Plan, only to witness the return of that dearly won prize to France at the treaty of Aix-la-Chapelle, and reluctantly to pass on his mantle to others at the opening of the Seven Years' War. By 1760, under Halifax and Chatham in Britain, vindicated by Lawrence, Wolfe, and Amherst in America, the Great Plan was an accomplished fact, sanctified by imperishable exploits on land and sea. Franklin, who must have warmed to Shirley's memory after the years of intimate association with his compatriot in Massachusetts, predicted twice as many English-speaking settlers as there were already French on the St. Lawrence. "All the country from the St. Lawrence to the Mississippi will . . . be filled with British people. Britain herself will become vastly more populous, by the immense increase of its commerce; the Atlantic sea will be covered with your trading ships; and your naval power, thence continually increasing, will extend your influence round the whole globe, and awe the world!" When this vision of an undivided empire was finally lost in 1776, Franklin still clung, as we have seen, to the hope of an undivided republic. His unavailing mission to Montreal, his lost land grants in Nova Scotia, the final failure to include Nova Scotia and Quebec north of the lakes in the Treaty of Versailles marked the end of the Great Plan. Thenceforth the regional trends of geography were doomed to frustration by arbitrary political controls on both sides of the boundary.

Compared with the easy and early approach of Champlain, Frontenac, and La Salle to the hinterlands of New France by way of the St. Lawrence and the Great Lakes, the westward movement of Daniel Boone and his fellow frontiersmen through the Cumberland Gap of the Alleghany ranges was a slow and precarious enterprise. William Knox's sour forecast as late as 1789 seemed warranted by the prospects at that time: the "Transallegany mountain people" would wander in the wilderness like the Scythians and the Tartars before they should be able to found a settled state. The chaos of "land rights" claimed by the constituent states could be resolved only by vesting in the public domain of the federal government the conflicting claims to the hinterland. Not only the vindication of the old claims but the establishment of new ones by purchase, by conquest, and by diplomacy taxed the most resourceful and acquisitive statesmanship of the republic. From the widest range of neighbouring powers, friendly and otherwise—France, Spain, Mexico, Great Britain again in the Oregon country, and Russia in Alaska—the widest range of territory to be acquired by a single state in the nineteenth century was accumulated by the United States in the span of eighty years. This conquest of transcontinental geography by frontal assault stands in striking contrast to the programme of Shirley and his disciples for an easier approach by the waterways. Spectacular as that conquest must have seemed to those who inherited Franklin's vision of an undivided America, there were limits both north and south to their success. In the end the "manifest destiny" they pursued in its widest amplitude eluded them, and thus geography has had its vicissitudes on both sides of the boundary.

II

For the second empire too, and particularly for its economy, geography proved to be a variable and unpredictable factor. Of the four or five distinctive regions across the continent the Pacific slope and the Hudson Bay watershed were as yet too remote for the vision of the most discerning seer. Of the two major economies left in the east the one was determined by the sea and the other by the Great River. These were to have been integrated in the designs of an undivided empire by a vision of continental proportions. Resources of personnel and of economic enterprise were already at work there when the revolution appeared upon the horizon. The population of Nova Scotia at the time of the revolution was already more than half "American" from the old colonies. The settlement which moved into Upper Canada after the loyalist migrations came from the frontier states of the union in spite of the revolution. In the opinion of the late Professor Hansen the range of the original loyalist migrations, had there been no revolution, would have been dwarfed by a voluntary migration of American frontiersmen already beginning to flood the new channels to the north and west. The sources of that flow were now dried up for the British provinces, and the teeming expansion from the south was deflected to other channels. Even the Ponds and the Henrys and their successors from the old colonies, who had been quick to exploit the success of the Great Plan in 1760 for the Montreal fur trade, found themselves expelled by Jay's Treaty of 1794 from the

Indian posts south of the lakes, and barred altogether by Congress in 1816 from the fur trade of the republic.

No less inexorable perhaps than the decrees of a divided allegiance were some of the decrees of nature itself which neither Shirley nor Franklin could have foreseen in the northern twilight of the first empire. Between the remote regions of Hudson Bay and the Pacific in the west and the divergent economies of the Maritimes and the St. Lawrence in the east, lay the Precambrian "shield" against which all the tides of agricultural settlement from the old colonies at their flood would have beaten in vain. For any enterprise but that of the fur trade the southwestern peninsula of Upper Canada was almost as completely separated from the alluvial prairies of Rupert's Land as though the granite wilderness between them were still in the grip of the ice age. The mineral wealth buried in these rocky fastnesses was as yet beyond the reach of the puny technique of those days for its discovery and reclamation. Meanwhile the agricultural settlement of Upper Canada was barred towards the north by the "shield," and open towards the south to one of the most rapid movements of population in modern history. In a single decade more than two millions of people swarmed about the southern borders of the Great Lakes. By the early sixties it was suspected that even the Grand Trunk was canalizing settlement by way of the St. Lawrence towards the richest agricultural frontier on the continent, the Mississippi prairies of the United States. Such were some of the hazards of geography for the second empire.

In Nova Scotia the new boundaries set by the revolution were as unnatural as the issues of the revolution itself. Governor Shirley had planned a frontier community under his own governorship from Massachusetts. Nova Scotia remained a frontier of New England but it was cut off from its base and broken into four fragments, three of which have never been reunited. For a time the maritime economy of the separate provinces was directed with scarcely warranted optimism to the task of freeing themselves from the trammels of the old colonies and supplanting them in the lucrative West Indian trade. Lord Sheffield was the patron saint of this new mercantilism, and his portrait hangs with that of Glenelg in the Legislative Assembly chamber of New Brunswick. By 1794, however, it was obvious that the West Indies needed the old colonies as much as the old colonies had ever needed the West Indies. The remote and sparsely populated fragments from the first empire in the north could not hope to supplant two million resourceful settlers of tide water America. Oak staves for West Indian rum and molasses, fish and provisions for their supply, were not to be found in sufficient quantities in the primitive economy of the Maritimes. The *Enabling Act* of 1794 which restored New England to much of its natural priority in the West Indian trade marked the end of self-sufficiency for the second empire.

Trade with the independent states soon outdistanced the old trade with the dependent colonies. Mercantilism, as we shall see, was to pass through some strange phases in British North America before it was finally abrogated by the formal repeal of the Navigation Acts in 1849. The economy of the Maritimes tended to remain static and individualistic and decentralized. Fish, timber, and ships, in their frontier life as in their coats of arms, were staples which required a wider setting for successful enterprise. While their trade continued to be complementary rather than competitive—the fish of Nova Scotia went chiefly to the West Indies, the masts and timber of New Brunswick chiefly to Great Britain, and the products of Prince Edward Island chiefly to the United States—it was far from covering the "Atlantic sea" as Franklin had predicted. Geography was little better than a step-mother to the Maritime Provinces during the formative stages of the second empire. It was cruellest of all perhaps just before Confederation, and it remained a baffling factor in the fortunes of the provinces as part of Canada.

III

In the old province of Quebec—or what was left of it after the revolution—the second empire confirmed for a time the trends that were already discernible at Montreal and Quebec for the exploitation of the North American fur trade. To a maritime and trading power the east-west direction of the St. Lawrence may well have been the most coveted geographical feature of the Atlantic seaboard. For more than a century it had been a challenge to the boldest spirits of adventure in New France.

The lure of the wilderness was one of the most seductive features of a frontier community through which the waters of the world's greatest lakes and the greatest of North American waterfalls passed to the ocean. The success of the French *voyageur* and *coureur-de-bois* with the Indian was all too often the result of compromise between the civilization of ordered settlement and the wild licence of the wilderness. At his worst the Indianized Frenchman was scarcely distinguishable from the Frenchified Indian. But his adventurous spirit ranged over the widest network of waterways on the continent; and at his best his success in discovery and adventure passed into a tradition in America. Before such a tradition the hard acquisitive technique of the fur trade often fell into second place, not only for the Radissons, the La Vérendryes, and La Salles of the French régime but for the Kelseys, the Mackenzies and the Thompsons of the British fur trade. There remained indeed a world of difference between French and English in their relations with the Indian. At Albany Sir William Johnson as Indian Commissioner had to cope incessantly with the ruthless brutality of the frontiersman in subordinating and eventually supplanting the Indian. In New France, bishop, governor, and intendant alike were concerned with the deteriorating standards of French civilization among the Indians in the *pays d'en haut*.

The combination of these two traditions of adventure and ruthlessness was perhaps the most distinctive feature of the Canadian fur trade. In a single generation it carried the North West Company to the Arctic and Pacific oceans. It is curious how completely the political issues of the revolution were left behind in this first great expansive and cohesive enterprise of the second empire. Peter Pond, the first intrepid trader to cross the Methy Portage into the Athabaska, was a resourceful Connecticut Yankee who had enlisted twice during the Seven Years' War, was at Ticonderoga with Abercrombie, and served with the victorious British forces in the final descent from Niagara upon Montreal in 1760. He killed his man in the Detroit fur trade, and his characteristic shrewdness, truculence, and resourcefulness did much to set the pace of the North West Company in the first lucrative enterprise of staple production in Canada. Alexander Henry too had come to Montreal in the wake of the Great Plan, as a merchant in General Amherst's commissariat. The Ellices who came into the Canadian fur trade from a wide range of commercial enterprise in New York, and a host of other adventurers both American and Scottish, early discovered the advantages of the Great River over the Albany route for the fur trade. Reinforced by Scottish thrift and brawn the North West Company was soon the hardest and most ruthless enterprise of its sort in the second empire, "surpassing," Sir Alexander Mackenzie wrote in 1801, "anything known in America."

The Canadian ingredients in this enterprise were perhaps the most distinctive and certainly the most lucrative. The light *canot du nord* of birch-bark west of Fort William, and even the commodious *canot du maître* from Montreal, could be made and repaired almost anywhere with a saw, a knife, and an axe. Launched upon the Saskatchewan at Fort Cumberland near the centre of a fur trader's paradise, the birch canoe could reach the Arctic Ocean, the Pacific, the Atlantic, or the Gulf of Mexico with no delays longer than a single day's portage. The woodcraft and hardihood of the French-Canadian *voyageurs* matched the intricacy and range of the waterways. From Ste Anne on the Ottawa to the Athabaska no fewer than 60 large lakes, 130 portages where canoes as well as goods were carried, and 200 smaller *décharges* where goods alone were taken from the water, were known to the geographer of the fur trade. Neither the winter-partners west of Fort William nor the Montreal partners at head-quarters could have functioned without the *voyageurs*. Colin Robertson pronounced them the best in the world, "spirited, enterprising, and extremely fond of the Country." "However dismal the prospect they follow their Master." They "sing while surrounded with misery; the toil of the day is entirely forgot in the encampment; they think themselves the happiest people in existence; and I do believe they are not far mistaken. It is from these active Subordinate Men, that the North West Co. derive their greatest profit." Exploited without scruple at every stage of the enterprise, the *voyageur* often escaped his debts to the Company by taking his discharge, at the end of his indenture, in the up-country where these "freemen" and their Indian progeny, the Métis, soon began to refer to themselves as the "New Nation."

For nearly half a century the "commercial empire of the St. Lawrence," marked out for disillusionment and frustration at almost every other stage of its development, came nearest to success in the technique of the fur trade. Thus while geography was buffeting the old colonies against the Alleghanies and forcing them through the Cumberland Gap and the Mohawk Valley towards the central plains of the continent, the central British provinces were enjoying the most expansive period in their history. Geography for a time was a friend of the second empire.

IV

This auspicious beginning which might have subserved almost indefinitely an undivided empire was not to last. The first rift in the commercial empire of the St. Lawrence came with Jay's Treaty when the Indian posts south of the lakes—retained since 1783 as surety for reparations to the loyalists—were finally surrendered. For practical purposes the St. Lawrence and the Mississippi waterways were never again to meet in a single national economy. After the War of 1812 the fur trade south of the boundary was barred by Congress to all but citizens of the United States. The Canadian fur trade was thrust farther and farther afield until the lengthening chain fairly brought the North West Company to their knees. There were many other factors of prime importance in the triumph of the Hudson's Bay Company over the Nor'Westers at the coalition of 1821, but geography alone would probably have been decisive in the long run. The Hudson's Bay Company "brought their goods to the Indian Country," wrote the most redoubtable of the Nor'Westers in 1821, "at less than one half the Expence that ours cost us." Colin Robertson's estimate was more favourable to Hudson Bay than William McGillivray's: "one-third of the expense which it costs the North West Company." With such odds in its favour geography could scarcely fail to win.

The other factors in the historic conflict between the North West and Hudson's Bay companies may be traced elsewhere. About the outcome in 1821 there could be no manner of doubt. The Bay had beaten the River. Beneath the specious appearances of accommodation in the indenture of 1821 the triumph of the Hudson's Bay Company was complete. The control of the Company, the manipulation of its capital, its direction from London by way of Hudson Bay, were all utilized in the shrewd strategy of Colvile and Simpson to establish a commercial empire by way of Hudson Bay that far excelled and out-lasted the dreams of the Frobishers, the McTavishes, and the Mc-Gillivrays for the St. Lawrence.[1] To the claims of the Company under the Charter of 1670 the British government added in 1821 a twenty-one year licence, under statutory sanctions, over the whole of British North America "not being part of any of our provinces in North America." From 1821 to 1838, when the licence was renewed for twenty-one years, and up to 1870, when most of the original chartered rights of the Company were surrendered to the Crown as the prelude to the transfer of Rupert's Land and the North-Western Territory to the new Dominion of Canada, the Hudson's Bay Company wielded an empire over the widest range of territory ever administered by one government in British North America. But it was no longer tributary to the St. Lawrence. "The Fur Trade," William McGillivray reflected bitterly in 1821, "is forever lost to Canada. . . . I was the first English Clerk engaged in the service of the N.W. Co. on its first Establishment in 1784, and I have put my Hand and Seal to the Instrument which closes its *career*—and *name* in 1821." In 1836 the sixth Earl of Selkirk found only a few wigwams at Fort William, "that once famous establishment which has now shared the fate of ancient Rome, and truly it once reigned over a territory little less extensive." For half a century in the technique of the fur trade after the coalition of 1821 the commercial empire of Hudson Bay was an unqualified success. Geography had broken the second empire in two.

With the passing of the fur trade the St. Lawrence inspired a more

[1]See Chester Martin, Introduction to *Simpson's Athabasca Journal* (Champlain Society and Hudson's Bay Record Society, 1938), 50 f.

elusive dream of commercial empire in wheat and timber and potash
and other staples of an agricultural hinterland. Above Quebec the
laws of oceanic trade and navigation yielded to local adjustments
across the international boundary. Why should not the agricultural
staples from the boundless hinterlands of a continent yet find their
outlet to world markets by way of the St. Lawrence? Much could still
be done to exploit the promise of the Great River. Duties on Riga
timber and preferences for Canadian flour in the British market lent
an ephemeral prosperity to the Canadian lumberman, miller, and
merchant. But the republic to the south was no less astute than the
Canadian merchant on the St. Lawrence in terms of national advantage. The Erie Canal, completed in 1825, short-circuited the
boasted monopoly of the St. Lawrence in the bid for the trade of the
hinterlands. By 1861 the imports into the United States by way of the
St. Lawrence amounted to $21,500 while the imports by way of the
Erie Canal to Upper Canada amounted to $7,690,000. The Welland
Canal, designed by William Hamilton Merritt to cope with its pro-
gressive rival south of the lakes, despite improvements was usually
obsolete before it could restore the balance of water transportation to
Canadian channels. By 1849 the dream of the St. Lawrence, like
colonial mercantilism and the old colonial system itself, threatened to
go up in smoke with the burning Parliament Buildings of Montreal.
The tory annexation manifesto of that year added the last touch of
petulance to an obsolete and discredited cause. The boasted patriotism
of privilege in government and preference in trade had stultified itself
beyond the power of any tradition to revive.

The new liberal-conservatism of the fifties, as we shall see, was a
hardy indigenous growth of another stock. A touch of realism—a
Peelite characteristic of both Hincks and Macdonald, of both Elgin
and Sir Edmund Head—was brought to bear upon the vestigial problems of the old order. The clergy reserves disappeared from Canada
West and seigneurial tenure from Canada East. Secure, as Elgin
believed, in the superiority of the new parliamentary system of responsible government over the congressional system with which tory
tradition had invariably confused it, Canadian policy began to respond to the hard realism of the new age. In Elgin's robust philosophy
reciprocity in trade with the United States would be the antidote to
annexation not its antecedent. For a time the Reciprocity Treaty of
1854 reopened for the St. Lawrence the old prospect of a continental
instead of a narrowly national economy. Despite the barriers of divided
allegiance geography exerted for ten years a beneficent influence

across the common boundary. The Grand Trunk from Sarnia to Rivière du Loup capitulated to a tide water terminus at Portland in the United States. Under the Reciprocity Treaty the trade of the Maritimes with the United States was doubled, and that of the Canadas began to dominate their economy. Edward Watkin once presented to Thomas Baring a plan for the projection of the Grand Trunk across the continent south of Lake Michigan, leaving the impenetrable "shield" north of the lakes as a hostage to international co-operation. For one brief decade it seemed possible that Shirley's Great Plan and Franklin's vision of a continental empire might be recaptured in the realm of commerce, at any rate, for the St. Lawrence economy.

V

The tensions of Civil War in the United States culminating not only in the abrogation of the Reciprocity Treaty altogether but in the threatened abrogation of the Rush-Bagot convention for an unguarded waterway, brought home to the British provinces the disintegration to which they had surrendered in following the lines of least resistance. Never perhaps was geography less propitious to the dream of a transcontinental British dominion than during the critical years before the Canadian confederation; and indeed the challenge of geography itself supplied for George Brown and Macdonald and Taché and many another anxious patriot no small part of the incentive to that achievement. The troops that embarked for Canada during the Trent affair, had they followed the normal channels of commerce, would have reached their destination over the Grand Trunk by way of Portland, Maine. At the transfer of Rupert's Land to the new dominion, the Lieutenant-Governor-elect, William McDougall, reached his prospective bailiwick through the United States by way of St. Paul. Of the four or five disintegrated segments of British territory across the continent, the Pacific area had already lost the Oregon territory north of the Columbia during the forties; Red River, in Macdonald's opinion, would have followed Oregon into the American union during the sixties had the deluge of migration (two millions in a single decade) south of the lakes not been checked by the Civil War; even the two central sections were in jeopardy, and Sir E. P. Taché, prime minister of the Canadian coalition, warned his countrymen in 1865 that without federation, Canada would be "forced into the American Union by violence, and if not by violence, would be placed upon an inclined plane which would carry us there insensibly." Between the Maritimes and Canada East, commercial intercourse had scarcely improved since the War of 1812 when the 104th New Brunswick Regiment had marched overland to Canada (February, 1813) on snowshoes. Had the Charlottetown Conference of 1864 met in February instead of September, the Canadian delegates must have travelled by way of the Grand Trunk through Portland, Maine.

Confederation alone could scarcely have coped with all these problems. South of the boundary as well as north, the broad economic advantages of geography for both countries, had they remained in association, were lost by conflict with the narrower interests of the national state. The inshore fisheries of the Maritime Provinces which Webster had undertaken to obtain—"hook and line, bob and sinker"— before the Reciprocity Treaty of 1854, remained a tantalizing bait to the Marblehead and Gloucester fishermen of New England after the abrogation of the treaty in 1866. Overtures were begun from Congress for a renewal of reciprocity with the Maritimes alone. Central Canada meanwhile sought a renewal in vain. When Macdonald went to Washington as a British plenipotentiary in 1871 to liquidate the antipathies of the Civil War, he took as his chart for the Treaty of Washington a memorandum drafted by Sir Francis Hincks with reciprocity as its prime objective. The inshore fisheries of the Maritime Provinces were to be dangled a second time, "hook and line, bob and sinker," before Hamilton Fish and the acquisitive interests of New England. Meanwhile some of the barriers of physical geography within Canada itself were as baffling as the political frustration across the international boundary. The task of westward expansion was undertaken a whole generation before the new dominion was able to make it good by systematic settlement; and the building of the C.P.R. meant a national enterprise of heroic proportions with the resources then available to safeguard a transcontinental dominion against the earlier approach of the Union Pacific, the Northern Pacific, and the Great Northern south of the boundary.

The development of a national economy and the functioning of national life in Canada may well be conditioned, both favourably and otherwise, by many other geographical controls, some of which are reminiscent of the early dreams of an undivided empire. The St. Lawrence waterways project and the unpredictable future of transportation by air may bring to pass not only the Great Plan of commercial expansion by way of the St. Lawrence, but the earliest project of British commercial expansion in the new world, the discovery of a northwest passage to the commercial highways of the world.

Chapter Three

THE SECOND EMPIRE:

DEMOGRAPHY AND TRADITIONS

THE bearing of race and tradition on the second empire, like that of geography, was transformed by the revolution. Several promising movements of population towards the northern frontiers were already discernible when the new American Department with its fatal policy of coercion put an end to many of the old trends and created others that were altogether unforeseen.

Shirley's "Great Plan" in its demographic aspect had already begun to function so successfully for the old province of Nova Scotia that by the time of the revolution more than half the population was classified as "American." Among the four new provinces added to the first empire at the close of the Seven Years' War, Quebec was put first among the "Places where Planting, and perpetual Settlement and Cultivation ought to be encouraged and consequently where regular Forms of Government must immediately be established." The Board of Trade, with "the Overflowing of . . . ancient Colonies" in mind, instructed Governor Murray to invite settlers to Quebec by "Proclamation in all the Colonies in North America." These swarming pioneers who had doubled their numbers in twenty years could be relied upon, Franklin predicted, to double them again in twenty-five years "by natural generation only." No fewer than sixteen sections in Murray's Instructions related to the "advantageous and effectual Settlement" of the St. Lawrence valley. Franklin recorded the prediction that "double the number of *English*, that it now has of French inhabitants" would find their way thither; and it may be added that the settlers who followed the loyalists into Upper Canada, outnumbering them four or five to one within a decade and a half, came from up-state New York, Pennsylvania, and the Ohio country in spite of the revolution. The post-loyalist migration into the western reaches of Upper Canada was in truth one of the first of those onward movements of population which swept across the continent like the rolling and receding waves of a rising tide. The same irresistible tide was to flow about the south-western borders of the Precambrian Shield towards the distant prairies of Rupert's Land during the middle of the nineteenth century, and again in tidal proportions it was to reach the prairie provinces of Canada in the early years of the twentieth century.

For the Great Plan of an undivided empire, however, the revolution substituted a divided allegiance, embittered by ineradicable traditions of civil war and exile. The loyalists of the revolution were settled like disbanded legions on the marches of a hostile frontier. In Quebec itself, as we shall see, both Murray and Carleton had already begun to conceive a vastly different function for that province in the manage-ment of the first empire, long before the conflict with the thirteen colonies had become irremediable. The French Canadians, wrote Murray to Amherst in 1762, "may become very useful to us if properly managed." Two years later he believed they could become "the most useful set of Men in this American Empire." Carleton too had a role for the new province which reversed the policy of Shirley and Halifax and the Board of Trade at almost every point. "Barring Catastrophe shocking to think of," he wrote to Shelburne, "this Country must to the end of Time be peopled by the Canadian Race." It will be observed how instinctively Carleton assumed that the teeming colonies to the south would share the northern provinces in the event of such a "Catastrophe." "It is one object of this measure," said Wedderburn as sponsor of the *Quebec Act* in the House of Commons, that British settlers from the old colonies "should not settle in Canada." Dartmouth, who was then secretary of the American Department, added that "nothing can more effectually tend to discourage such attempts." The reasons became clear in the developing details of the *Quebec Act*. The boundaries of the province were to be carried down the Ohio to the Mississippi and the whole watershed of the St. Lawrence and the Great Lakes was to revert to seigneurial tenure, "with the avowed purpose of excluding all further settlement therein."

Under such auspices the "Catastrophe shocking to think of" came to pass, and the whole area of Quebec south of the Great Lakes was lost to the first empire. But the revolution was stayed at the Sault-au-Matelot and the Près-de-Ville barricade—in Carleton's valiant defence of Quebec. The St. Lawrence valley was still to be peopled "to the end of Time . . . by the Canadian Race." There were consequences how-ever which could not have been foreseen in the "design" of Knox and Carleton. They had sought to keep Quebec French in order to keep

it British. By remaining British Quebec could no longer remain exclusively French, for it became (with the old province of Nova Scotia)
the only refuge in North America for the expatriated loyalists of the
old empire which it had been one of the purposes of the *Quebec Act*
to circumscribe.

Thus was the perversion of the Great Plan by the revolution perverted in turn by the outcome of the revolution. Both of these facts
were to prove stubborn and ineluctable elements in the future of
Canada. In its demographic as well as in its geographical and economic
aspects the Great Plan for the expansion of the first empire was now
truncated at its base. That teeming reservoir of two and a half or three
millions of the most resourceful pioneers of modern history turned
westward rather than northward, burst the barriers of the Alleghanies
like a mill-race, overran the Ohio country and the Mississippi valley in
half the time it had taken the original settlers on Massachusetts Bay
to reach the Hudson, and occupied the Pacific territory of Oregon on
the distant reaches of the Columbia in half the time it had taken to
reach the Ohio.

Meanwhile for the provinces which remained British the whole
balance of population was destroyed by the unforeseen results of the
revolution. The French population of Quebec numbered perhaps one-
fortieth of the first American empire. In the second empire in America
the French population of Quebec outnumbered that of all the other
provinces combined. The migration from the undivided empire which
Franklin expected almost immediately to flood the regions north of the
Great Lakes was either deflected altogether by the barriers of the
Quebec Act or reached Upper Canada in such attenuated volume that
the normal rapid settlement of the province was postponed for half a
century. The loyalist migrations, however, left an abiding influence
upon the second empire. Three or four generations of American history
were rooted out of the old empire and transplanted to the new. Thus
two distinctive traditions, both of them the aftermath of desperate
counsels during the American Revolution, were added to the old traditions of an undivided empire. The distinctive traditions of the loyalist
migrations and the equally distinctive preponderance of French Canada
were destined to modify profoundly the normal course of colonial
development. In many respects the Canadian scene was dominated
for many years by these two exotic traditions. Demography like
geography was to prove a variable and baffling factor in the development of Canadian nationhood.

THE PROBLEMS OF RACE
I

There is little evidence that the Board of Trade at first regarded the French population on the St. Lawrence—scarcely one-fortieth of the teeming population of the old colonies—as a problem of serious or unusual proportions. After all, the Dutch of New York, the Germans of Pennsylvania and Nova Scotia, had already taken their place in the thriving economy of the first empire. In 1763 Quebec, like the new province of Grenada in the French West Indies, was proclaimed a "royal province" and endowed with the conventional institutions of governor, council, and assembly which royal provinces like Virginia, New Hampshire, and Nova Scotia had regarded for generations as the staple of a British constitution. The assembly of Quebec was never convened, for reasons which became clearer with the approach of revolution from the south; but Lord Mansfield stated with authority[1] that an assembly had been "irrevocably granted," and it was only by the highest instrument known to the British constitution—an Act of Parliament—that this concession was finally "revoked, annulled, and made void" by the *Quebec Act*. By one of the most generous and tolerant gestures of that day, the Board of Trade in 1765 and 1769 proposed to extend to the French Roman Catholic "new subjects" of Quebec the enjoyment of the franchise and other inalienable rights of British subjects. The same policy was projected and implemented with conspicuous success by the same Board of Trade in the newly acquired French province of Grenada in the West Indies. Within twenty years a deluge of more than 25,000 settlers poured into the Spanish provinces of East and West Florida, ceded to Britain by the same treaty as Quebec and Grenada in 1763. The subsequent expansion of the old colonies in Louisiana, in Texas, and in California, goes far to vindicate Franklin's forecast in 1760 for the regions of the St. Lawrence, and his prophecy to Chatham in 1774 that "we might have gone on extending our western empire, adding province to province, as far as the South Sea." Such was the spirit in which the most prophetic minds of that day approached the prospects of 1763.

A curiously perverted tradition has found its way backward from the later record of racial strife in Lower Canada to these early years between the cession of 1763 and the "catastrophe" of civil war and revolution in 1783. Never, in all probability, were racial associations more kindly or religious antipathies less bitter than immediately after the capture of Quebec in 1759. Sir Arthur Doughty, the best of authori-

[1]In the leading case of *Campbell* v. *Hall*.

ties on such a problem, has left a lifetime of research to illustrate the chivalry and goodwill of these promising years. The first Protestant service was held by invitation in the chapel of the Jesuits. On the evening of the Battle of the Plains Townshend himself went to L'Hôpital Général to reassure the Mother Superior of safety and protection. During the winter Murray reported that "the troops have lived with the inhabitants in a harmony unexampled even at home"—a record attested by French-Canadian knitting circles for the bare-kneed Highlanders and by the Scottish names which still survive in the French countryside of Murray Bay. In the background signs of prejudice, so characteristic of that age, may be found by those who search diligently for them. Murray in his feud with the British traders once maligned them as "Licentious Fanaticks," made up of "Quakers—Puritants, Anabaptists, Presbeterians, Atheists, Infidels, and even the Jews." Egremont shared the distrust of religious orders in Great Britain at a time when the Jesuit Order itself was confronting expulsion from France and dissolution by the Papacy. It is on record, nevertheless, that these "Licentious Fanaticks" were the first to propose the franchise for the Roman Catholic "new subjects" of Quebec, a whole generation before the younger Pitt dared to authorize the same measure of toleration in Ireland and more than half a century before Roman Catholic emancipation was won in Great Britain. In this the British traders merely anticipated the Board of Trade in their official policy of 1765 and 1769.

It is clear that the Board's policy, so curiously ignored in the traditions of Quebec and the American Revolution, was exacted by no terms of capitulation in 1760 or "treaty rights" in 1763. French civil law, afterwards established by the *Quebec Act,* had been demanded at the capitulation of Montreal; but Article XLII that "the French and Canadians shall continue to be governed according to the custom of Paris, and the Laws and usages established for this country" had been categorically refused by the reply that "they become Subjects of the King." At the Treaty of Paris the status of the Roman Catholic Church was conceded only "as far as the laws of Great Britain permit"; and when the French plenipotentiaries "proposed to insert the Words *comme ci-devant,* in order that the Romish Religion should continue to be exercised in the same manner as under their Government," they were "plainly told that it would be deceiving them to admit those words." The special rights of French Canada today are no less sacrosanct than "treaty rights" but they are not to be found at the cession of New France to Great Britain in 1763.

It is equally clear that the Board of Trade's policy for Quebec was but a phase of the struggle against the slowly maturing designs in the inner counsels of the king for the control of the American colonies. Until 1769 the functions of the Board in devising general policies and in drafting the usual instruments of colonial government under the Secretary of State for the Southern Department remained unimpaired. In that year, however, the evidence begins to accumulate for "a scheme of government new in many things," geared to reaction in America. The design was entrusted to a new department—the American Department—of which William Knox, after careful consultation with Grenville, was selected as permanent under-secretary. It was Knox's conviction that "the old mode of treating our dependencies must be exploded and a new system formed." Under instructions from this new American Department duplicates of the governor's despatches in Quebec were no longer to be sent to the Board of Trade. A few months later Carleton himself at his own urgent request returned to England.

With this train of policy in view the mounting interest of the Board in the French Roman Catholic "new subjects" of Quebec takes on a deeper meaning. In June, 1765, they referred their status to the law officers of the crown. It was found, in point of law, that they were "not subject . . . to the Incapacities, disabilities, and Penalties, to which Roman Catholics in this Kingdom are subject by the Laws thereof." The Board lost no time, therefore, in recommending the franchise for them since there was "no Law by which Roman Catholicks, as such, are disqualified from being Electors." From that point the Board's plan to "extend to His Majesty's new Subjects those Provisions which exist in the principles of a British Constitution" grew in force and emphasis until it was violently reversed by the *Quebec Act*. As an instrument of toleration and political freedom the great Report of the Board of Trade in 1769, in almost every detail, stands athwart the fatal decision to "*coerce* America." For an assembly, they maintained, "the Faith of the Crown stands fully pledged," and the "new subjects" were to be admitted not only "into the Council and House of Representatives, but also into the Courts of Judicature and other Offices of Government." "Above eighty thousand brave and loyal Subjects, do . . . Stand prescribed from every privilege, and denied every right the possession of which can alone ensure their affection, and fix their attachment to the British Government." The Report of 1769, the Board repeated, was "founded on the fullest Information." It was supported "in those parts that include great constitutional Questions, by the opinions of the ablest Lawyers in this Kingdom." "No information necessary in this important consideration is wanting."

"The subject matter has undergone the most mature examination." The issue in Quebec was "a case of so great Importance, as to affect not only the security of this Colony, but with it, that of all His Majesty's other Dominions in America."

In transmitting a copy of the Report of 1769 to Carleton in Quebec the Secretary of State for the new American Department instructed him, under the most carefully guarded secrecy, to "bring back the Copy of the Report . . . without suffering it to fall into any other hands whatever," and assured him that no action was to be taken without his presence and advice. Carleton returned immediately to London and was there behind the scenes with William Knox and "the King's friends" until the new policy of coercion was put into effect five years later in 1774. It is scarcely too much to say that the Board of Trade went down fighting for the civil liberties of Quebec against the arbitrary provisions of the *Quebec Act*.[1]

II

By North the *Quebec Act* was associated with the four "intolerable acts" of 1774 designed to put "an immediate stop to the present disorders in North America" and to make "permanent provisions" for the "just dependance of the colonies." Even had this desperate policy succeeded it would have destroyed, almost as completely as the revolution itself, the dream of Shirley, Franklin, and the Board of Trade for the expansion of British settlement into the regions of the St. Lawrence and the Great Lakes beyond. It was one of the chief purposes of the *Quebec Act* to interpose the barriers of French feudalism in Quebec to the northern expansion of the old colonies. This design, as we have seen,[2] is avowed by Wedderburn who had charge of the *Quebec Bill* in the House of Commons, by Dartmouth the secretary of state for the American Department who introduced it in the House of Lords, and by William Knox himself, the permanent under-secretary, whose sponsorship for the policy at this time is unmistakable. It was "one object of this measure," that British settlers "should not settle in Canada." "Nothing can more effectually tend to discourage such attempts." The whole hinterland north of the Ohio and westward to the Mississippi, in Knox's own assertion, was to be "put under the jurisdiction of the governor of Quebec, with the avowed purpose of ex-

---

[1]Cf. Greville to Dartmouth, July 18, 1774: "I must tell you that the dissatisfaction among the Lords of Trade is general & it has been often said that if no other business but signing was expected that [*sic*] it would be unnecessary to attend as the Papers might be sent." P.A.C., Dartmouth Papers, VII, 2368.

[2]See above, p. 46.

cluding all further settlement therein." "This is the border," exclaimed
Wedderburn on the second reading of the *Quebec Bill*, "beyond which
. . . you shall not extend yourselves." The resentment of the old
colonies at this deliberate policy of "circumvallation" remained one
of the major factors of the revolution.

In the contest for civil liberties for the "new subjects" in Quebec,
there was a still more violent reversal of British policy. By the *Quebec
Act* every promise of representative institutions for which "the Faith
of the Crown stands fully pledged" was "revoked, annulled, and made
void."[1] The Board of Trade's plan for the franchise and its attendant
civil rights to French Roman Catholic "new subjects" of Quebec was
of course unknown to the House, for the government refused to produce the Report of 1769; but Burke and Fox argued, in vain, for an
assembly with toleration—"that healing shower from heaven"—in the
ascendant. "Is it safe," North retorted, "to put the principal power into
the hands of an assembly of Roman Catholic new subjects? . . . There
is something in that religion, which makes it not prudent."

But the uprooting of an assembly went deeper than mere intolerance,
and the first minds of that age on both sides of the Atlantic registered
their detestation of the new "design." Here was a "constitution such as
the world never saw before"—a constitution, said Fox, with "not a
spark or semblance of liberty." For the first time in British colonial
history it was established by statute, since there was no other procedure known to the realm by which the "principles of a British constitution," once "irrevocably granted" as Lord Mansfield maintained,
could be "revoked, annulled, and made void." It was a "perfectly
despotic government," said Burke, with "the appearance of a love of
despotism, and a settled design to enslave the people of America."
"This constitution is meant to be both an instrument of tyranny to the
Canadians, and an example to others of what they have to expect; at
some time or other it will come home to England." Even the restoration of tithe to the Roman Catholic Church, Chatham observed, was
"a child of inordinate power." How could the bishops in the House of
Lords, he asked there dramatically, "hold it out for baptism"? Wedderburn pointed out suggestively that "all this indulgence" was "subject to
his Majesty's approbation. . . . So that all tithes are subject to be taken
from them." To Chatham the Bill was a "most cruel, oppressive, and
odious measure, tearing up justice and every good principle by the
roots." It would "finally lose the hearts of all his Majesty's American
subjects." Alexander Hamilton and a host of his contemporaries in

[1] 14 Geo. III, c. 83.

America suspected "first the subjection of the colonies and afterward that of Great Britain itself." "It is clear beyond a doubt," resolved the first Continental Congress at Philadelphia after the passing of the *Quebec Act*, "that a resolution is formed, and is now carrying into execution, to extinguish the freedom of these colonies, by subjecting them to a despotic government."

How near this was to the truth is now apparent from Knox's own exposition of the *Quebec Act*. A governor and council could dispense with "those pompous ideas of popular governments, which our country-men are elated with. . . . Happy would it be for this Kingdom, were such plans adopted for the government of our colonies, instead of that disorder and anarchy, that almost universally reigns in them." "The northern colonies," he added, "would have experienced a much greater degree of felicity, had their government consisted only of a governor and council." The Canadians if attached by "lenity and indulgence" might prove a "security against the insurgents of the other parts of America; for in case of exigency a force can easily be raised from thence." Thus the new plan for America, as the greatest of Americans was slowly driven to conclude, was "the systematic assertion of an arbitrary power." Though long "unsuspicious of design," Washington was now "convinced beyond the smallest doubt, that these measures are the result of deliberation," and that there was "a regular systematic plan formed to enforce them."

It was this aspect of coercion in the *Quebec Act*—the fatuous plan of using French feudalism in Quebec to raise an army for the subjuga-tion of New England—which gave the measure so devastating an effect upon any further hope of conciliation in America. Despite the secrecy with which the *Quebec Act* was surrounded, the plans of Carleton and of Knox for the restoration of seigneurial tenure in Quebec and the use to which it could be put in raising a feudal French army against the southern colonies could scarcely have escaped the shrewd insight of Benjamin Franklin. Barré reserved his deepest "detestation of this bill" for this insensate policy: "From this time, all hope of peace in America will be destroyed. The Americans will look on the Canadians as their task-masters, and in the end, their executioners. I smelt this business out from the beginning. . . . I wash my hands of this business. I here declare my solemn aversion to it. I know what you mean. *Liberari animam meam!* I have foretold the thing. There is not a man in the government that means to deny it."

As early as 1767 Carleton had propounded his plan for the fortifica-tion of Quebec and New York with a chain of forts on the Lake

Champlain and Lake George route in order to "separate the Northern
from the Southern Colonies" and "facilitate the Transport of ten or
fifteen thousand Men in the Beginning of a War." The seigneurial
system in New France, as Carleton explained, had "established
Subordination, from the first to the lowest." By restoring French civil
law to Quebec—Carleton favoured the restoration of French criminal
law also—the seigneur, holding his land directly from the king, could
be called upon "to pay Faith and Homage to him in his Castle of
St. Lewis; The Oath, which the Vassals take upon the Occasion, is
very Solemn," and bound them "to appear in Arms for his Defence."
The automatic mustering of the *censitaires* for military service under
their seigneurs had not been so simple a process in New France as
Carleton was led to believe, but the "New Subjects could send into
the Field about eighteen thousand Men."

The day following Carleton's return to Quebec after the passing
of the *Quebec Act* (September 18, 1774) General Gage in Boston
called for "a Body of Canadians and Indians . . . to form a Junction
with the King's Forces in this Province." Carleton replied that "two,
three or more Battalions" would be available for this plan, which had
been "long since Recommended" by himself. In the following spring
Lord North was prepared "to arm the Roman Catholics of Canada and
to employ them in that service." In July, 1775, Dartmouth directed
Carleton to "raise a Body of 3000 Canadians." Meanwhile the Continental Congress was weighing "indubitable evidence that a design is
formed by the British Ministry of making a cruel invasion from the
province of Quebec, upon these colonies, for the purpose of destroying
our lives and liberties." A few weeks later the momentous *Declaration
on Taking Arms* was drawn up, based upon "certain intelligence that
General Carleton, the Governor of Canada, is instigating the people
of that province and the Indians to fall upon us." The *Declaration on
Taking Arms* was placed in the hands of George Washington as commander-in-chief. Three weeks after Dartmouth's first instructions for
"a Body of 3000 Canadians" the news from Boston was more serious,
and Carleton was instructed to raise "double what was first proposed."
A week later Carleton was given full command "in Quebec and upon
its Frontiers," while Howe was to command the forces "in the Colonies
upon the Atlantic" until the two forces should effect a junction.
Carleton, moving south by way of Lake Champlain, was then to take
over the "full appointments of Commander-in-Chief." While Dartmouth was thus disposing of a hypothetical 6,000 men from Quebec,
Carleton found himself "equally unprepared for Attack or Defence:

Not six hundred Rank & File fit for Duty upon the whole Extent of
this great River." Six months later, in the ruins of the *Quebec Act*, he
was defending the Sault-au-Matelot in the last stronghold of British
territory in the province.

There were few more egregious miscalculations, even in 1774, than
the immediate purposes of the *Quebec Act*. Carleton's own delusions
were swiftly dispelled. The direct beneficiaries of the Act—the church
and the seigneurs, restored to their status of privilege under the old
Coutume de Paris—discharged loyally their obligations of "gratitude
and zeal in support of the interests of the British Crown." Bishop
Briand in a special *Mandement* cited "the recent favours with which
he has loaded us" in an appeal to support the Crown against those "in
revolt against their lawful Sovereign." The seigneurs too, Carleton reported, "testified great Zeal." But "neither their Entreaties or their
Example could prevail upon the People." The reason was not far to
seek. The *censitaires* whose "Duty and Submission" had been taken for
granted developed ideas of their own about "Subordination, from the
first to the lowest." The seigneurs themselves, in the opinion of Chief
Justice Hey, were not without blame. "Elated with the advantages
they supposed they should derive from the restoration of their old
Privileges and customs," they "indulged themselves in a way of thinking and talking that gave very just offence." The *habitants*, added Hey
in reporting the state of the province to the Lord Chancellor, showed
their resentment by "every shape of contempt and detestation." The
Quebec Act itself had "become the first object of their discontent and
dislike." Carleton found that "the Canadian peasantry . . . not only
deserted their duty but numbers of them have taken arms against the
Crown." The American forces that captured Montreal were "two thirds
Canadian." South of the lakes in the Ohio country several regiments of
French-Canadian militia served in the armies of the revolution and
found themselves expatriated at the end of the war. The site of
Columbus, now capital of the state of Ohio, was granted to these
French "patriots," counterpart to the land grants in Nova Scotia and
Quebec to the expatriated loyalists from the old provinces.

In the ruins of all his plans Carleton charged his misfortunes upon
the "Base Desertion of the Canadian Peasantry." Absolving the authors
and direct beneficiaries of the *Quebec Act*, his resentment was reserved
for the *habitants*. They were a people of "stupid baseness," and of
"blind Perverseness." They were "a wretched People . . . blind to
Honor, Duty and their own Interest"—"the most ungrateful Race under
the Sun." The author of the *Quebec Act* might have found more valid

reasons for their "unprecedented Defection" nearer home. Meanwhile French feudalism remained rooted upon the banks of the St. Lawrence. It was eighty years before the plans of the Board of Trade for French Canada in 1769 were to catch up with the *Quebec Act,* and seigneurial tenures were abolished by the legislature of the united province of Canada in 1854.

III

The place of the *Quebec Act* in the veneration of French Canada would be hard to account for had the magnanimous policy of the Board of Trade been known in 1765 and 1769, or had the *Quebec Act* which supplanted it been known for what it was in the dissolution of the first empire. For the chief beneficiaries of the Act certain by-products of it came to overshadow its immediate purposes. The egregious failure of those purposes was buried in the catastrophe which the *Quebec Act* helped to precipitate, but the by-products have grown into an unhistorical tradition with all the force of fixed ideas in the cherished cause of French race and culture on this continent.

The truth is that the alternative of 1769 to the *Quebec Act* was far more tolerant in its temper, broader in its outlook, and beyond all comparison more magnanimous in its concern for the "new subjects" in Quebec than the measure of 1774 which, as Chatham protested, "put the whole people under arbitrary power." Nor would the honoured role of the Roman Catholic Church in the cultural survival of French Canada have varied appreciably from its traditional function under the *Quebec Act.* Burke advocated the tithe more ingenuously than Wedderburn, who made no secret of the price at which it was to be conceded: "all this indulgence [was] given subject to his Majesty's approbation . . . So that all tithes are subject to be taken from them." Burke argued that tithe ought to be a fixed "legal provision not an arbitrary provision" which was "dispossessable at the King's pleasure." "I want as much of the law as you please," he added, "and as little of the King's pleasure as possible." Fox who found "not a spark or semblance of liberty" in the Bill challenged the government to cite "the circumstance of the people of Canada being Roman Catholics as an objection to an assembly." It was North himself who questioned the safety and prudence of putting "the principal power into the hands of an assembly of Roman Catholic new subjects." There were no provisions, of course, for the French language in the *Quebec Act,* and it is hard to believe that in either language or religion the prevailing cultural trends of French Canada were profoundly altered by it.

While the chief beneficiaries of the Act—the seigneurs and the church—discharged loyally their obligations of "Duty and Submission," both the immediate results and the ultimate consequences of the Act were curiously unforeseen. Towards the seigneurs the immediate response of "the Canadian Peasantry," as we have seen, ranged from stolid indifference to "every shape of contempt and detestation"; and it was reserved for the legislature of a reunited province of Canada in 1854, under French Canadian parliamentary leaders, to abolish the vestigial anomalies of French feudalism received as the price of "Loyalty and Fidelity" in 1774. The church, on the other hand, under Bishop Briand's *Mandement*, repaid "His Very Gracious Majesty" with no small effect for the "recent favours with which he has loaded us." Aided by the blunders of the American invaders they won back the *habitants* to their own cause, and repaid with compound interest at more than one crisis of Canadian history their obligations to "loyal and stable government." To their guardianship of religion and language and culture a devoted race has accorded in turn a measure of veneration to be found perhaps in no other community in the modern world. And thus the *Quebec Act*, absolved of its ignoble purposes in the eclipse of British freedom during the revolution, has survived in French Canadian tradition as a measure of "lenity and indulgence"— "the charter of the special privileges which the French-Canadians have enjoyed ever since."

The "new subjects" were finally inducted into British institutions in 1791 but there was scarcely one major prerequisite for this great experiment in which the conditions had not changed for the worse since the Board of Trade had championed "the principles of a British constitution" in 1769. Knox and Carleton and Haldimand assumed instinctively that an assembly for the "new subjects" in Quebec would have been "in their hands a sword, that like the Bostonians they in turn may brandish [it] and put us at defiance." But the weight of evidence stands to the contrary. In Nova Scotia—a frontier province of New England already more than half "American" in population—an assembly convened by the same Board of Trade drafted, a few weeks after Lexington, an address to the Crown, Lords, and Commons of Great Britain, deploring separation as "the greatest political evil which can befall us or our posterity"; and if there were "loaves and fishes" in Nova Scotia, was there any other commercial prospect of that time to match the lucrative fur trade of the St. Lawrence? The preliminaries of the North West Company are traceable to the year before the *Quebec Act*, and the names of many of the partners appear alike in petitions for an assembly and in addresses attesting Carleton's "unshaken Constancy" in the defence of Quebec. Franklin himself failed to establish a permanent revolutionary interest in Montreal. Had self-government rather than arbitrary governance and coercion been the order of the day it would be hard to find a more opportune setting for the induction of "80,000 brave and loyal subjects" into the practice of British parliamentary institutions than the receding traditions of the conquest.

It was Carleton's obsession that "the better Sort of Canadians fear nothing more than popular Assemblies, which, they conceive, tend only to render the People refractory and insolent"; but even Lotbinière who accompanied Carleton to London conceded that "the natural inclinations of the Canadians" would have favoured an assembly had they not been "informed, that, in that Assembly, they would not be allowed as Roman Catholics, to sit." It is clear that Carleton had obeyed only too well his instructions to bring back the great Report of 1769 "without suffering it to fall into any hands whatever."

By 1791 the whole outlook in America had deteriorated irremediably, and there had been introduced into Quebec so many unforeseen by-products of the revolution that the problem of race in the second empire could never remain the same. To church and seigneurs alike the Assembly of 1791 appeared to be a violation of the gentleman's agreement of 1774. "You do not know my Countrymen," wrote Bishop Denaut in 1791, "they are not at all prepared for the Constitution you wish to give them; once let the rein loose and be assured they will never know when to stop." The *Quebec Act* had envisaged an exclusively French province stretching to the Ohio and the Mississippi, and including the whole watershed of the St. Lawrence and Great Lakes as far as the territory of the Hudson's Bay Company. The area south of the Great Lakes was now lost to the revolution, and even what was left could not "to the end of Time, be peopled by the Canadian Race." By remaining British it could no longer remain exclusively French. Loyalists at the end of the revolution and a still larger post-loyalist migration from the same source divided the patrimony and disputed the very title deeds of the old régime. And if assemblies were calculated to "render the People refractory and insolent" during the American Revolution, what was likely to be their effect during the French Revolution? It is easy to sense the derision of William Knox for "fine spun theories" as his coadjutor in the *Quebec Act*, now Lord Dorchester, returned to Quebec to promote "the happiness of French Canadians, by converting them into English Republicans."

It is a poignant reflection that the nobler conception of a common freedom at the outset for both races never had a chance. What was left of the old province of Quebec was divided in 1791. An assembly was granted to Lower Canada grudgingly and at a price because it could not in decency be withheld from French Canadians when the loyalists of the two neighbouring provinces demanded one as a matter of course. By that time there were already implanted in Lower Canada vested interests which made the "château clique" a byword of privilege and racial discord for every province of the second empire. Within a generation British institutions were being used on both sides, by Assembly and Council, only to be abused. Under Papineau the French Assembly with its proclivity for logical direct action and its impatience of subtler accommodations and compromises, brought the province to such a pass that Lord John Russell at last did to Lower Canada in 1838 what George III had done to Massachusetts in 1774—virtually suspended its constitution. Durham added fuel to the conflagration by attacking the whole basic concept of survival and advocating the ruthless assimilation of French racialism to a North American English-speaking environment. Lord John Russell's policy towards responsible government in "Canada" was haunted throughout by this unanswerable conundrum: how could there be "a ministry headed by M. Papineau"? To the end of the chapter Papineau impugned responsible government for "Canada" as a system "false, tyrannical and calculated to demoralize its people." It was "conceived by statesmen of a narrow and malevolent genius" and it would be "ruinous and disastrous" to the province. A nobler conception of collaboration at the outset might not have fared better in establishing at once the golden rule of toleration and of compromise, but it could scarcely have fared worse.

It is a remarkable fact that the noblest chapter in the relations of the two historic races in Canada was to open with the enforced reunion of Lower and Upper Canada in 1841. No auspices at that time could have been more forbidding. Compared with the halcyon traditions of mutual chivalry after the conquest, the aftermath of the Papineau rising was a grim setting for Elgin's "great experiment." Not only the immemorial bitterness of French Canada but the prejudices of uninformed opinion in Great Britain cast a sinister shadow over the Canadian scene. Here at the nadir of racial defeat and humiliation in the second empire the healing therapy of association under La Fontaine and Baldwin, inspired by the political sagacity of Francis Hincks, restored the broken tissues and set a pattern for racial co-operation in Canada for all time to come. French-Canadian assemblymen who in Durham's opinion would "never again . . . yield a loyal submission to a British Government" were the shock-troops, as we shall see, who helped to win the most cherished of Durham's own recommendations, the concession of responsible government in 1848. Under this sovereign alchemy of co-operation and compromise the rights won for French Canada under the union were underwritten in the Canadian confederation.

It is a curious commentary upon racial segregation in Canada that the recovery of those special rights and privileges which distinguish French Canada above every other element in the nation took place under the closest association, the only complete integration, the two historic races of Canada have ever experienced—the legislative union of Lower and Upper Canada. And it is a fair corollary of that reflection that those rights and privileges were retrieved by political action after British models of parliamentary government. In that sense the most distinctive achievement of the French race on this continent would seem to be found not before the cession of 1763 but after it: not before 1800, nor before 1840, but in that teeming laboratory of constructive statesmanship, the troubled years of the Canadian union.

THE LOYALIST TRADITION

I

Less intractable than the problem of race, but scarcely less dominant for many years, was the temper of the loyalist migrations at the close of the revolution. It was for this that Upper Canada and New Brunswick were detached from the old provinces of Quebec and Nova Scotia, and this distinctive survival from the first empire long continued to colour their outlook. The traditions that were planted there sprang up, like the dragon's teeth, during the War of 1812 and survived to dominate many issues of the second empire for half a century.

Spontaneous migrations propelled, as Shirley and Franklin had foretold, by the expansive resources of an undivided empire were already under way when British policy during the revolution sought to interpose barriers of French feudalism and arbitrary governance to this normal expansion into the Ohio and St. Lawrence watersheds. But the revolution, in its own despite, destroyed this design and directed to the British provinces the most highly concentrated strain of population ever to settle there. Many of the loyalists had been rooted for three or four generations in American soil. In that sense their enforced migration was in many respects a reversal of the normal pattern of pioneer settlement. The Niagara frontier and the reaches of the Saint John River were settled not from the overflow of contiguous frontiers but by the selective transplanting, root and branch, of some of the most conservative elements of the first empire. The loyalist tradition may not always have been founded on fact but it remained in itself one of the basic facts of the second empire.

The numbers of those who might have been called loyalist during the revolution will never, in all probability, be accurately known. Of the three main groups, one only—the exiles to the northern provinces—has been followed and enumerated with any degree of accuracy. The numbers of those who migrated from the south to the West Indies or succeeded in returning "home" to Great Britain can only be guessed, though their influence is traceable in many curious ways in the history of the second empire. Sir Edmund Head, grandson of a loyalist who returned to England, came back to America as governor of the loyalist province of New Brunswick and governor-general in the united province of Canada. He became one of the architects, as we shall see, of federation for the provinces of British North America. The third group, for obvious reasons, is probably the most difficult to estimate—those who found it possible to remain in the old colonies until the dust of conflict had settled, and who contrived to fall into step, with the best grace they could, with the new republic. The relations between the first and last of these groups continued to affect the outlook of settlement in the British provinces for many years.

The first group—those who shared the enforced emigration to the north—exerted an influence out of all proportion to their numbers. In Nova Scotia, where the names on the muster-rolls and other registers have been traced through to permanent settlement, the final estimate stands at a little less than 20,000. Many thousands in addition had reached the province only to leave it eventually in their pilgrimage to remoter destinations. Not a few found their way back to friends and neighbours in the old colonies. Shelburne was said to be at one time the most populous town in British America, surpassing Montreal, Quebec, and Three Rivers combined and excelled in English-speaking America only by New York, Philadelphia, and Boston. An accurate estimate of loyalists in New Brunswick would probably be less than 14,000, with less than a thousand for Prince Edward Island and Cape Breton. In the old province of Quebec, divided into Upper and Lower Canada in 1791, the total number of those entitled to the suffix U.E. by virtue of their enforced migration, was less than 7,000, though many who followed from the old colonies and quickly outnumbered

them were distinguished from their predecessors by few characteristics except their freedom of choice. In all it is doubtful if more than
50,000 settlers participated in the enforced loyalist migrations at their
peak; 40,000 would probably be a fair estimate of the numbers that
settled permanently in the British provinces.

Between the migration into the Maritimes and the Upper Canadian
movement, however, there was another difference which still further
distinguished the range of their influence. The sea route to the Maritimes was by far the easiest and the shortest from the seaboard
colonies. For most of the "military loyalists"—the disbanded troops of
the loyalist regiments of the revolution—there could of course be no
return to their old homes. For others, however, as the conflict receded
or was supplanted by local contests between radicals and whigs in
the new republic, intercourse with their old neighbours was easily
resumed, and many thousands must have returned to the old soil in
which their families had been rooted for generations in America.
Loyalist and "patriot" newspapers reflected this fluctuating temper.
In many respects cultural and educational contacts remained, particularly in the official and professional circles to be found in dispropor-
tionate numbers in the maritime migration. The son of Ward Chipman
himself returned to Harvard and became valedictorian of his class. No
fewer than six members of the first Assembly of New Brunswick returned to their old homes before the end of the first session. From
Nova Scotia the re-migration to the old colonies must have reached
imposing proportions and it is doubtful if it has ever substantially
ceased. In 1817 Dalhousie found "the connection between the respectable inhabitants of this Province and the States . . . yet very
intimate; scarcely is there a family that has not Fathers, Brothers, and
near relations there," though this association implied not "the most
distant doubt of the Loyalty of this Province."

In Upper Canada, on the other hand, the original loyalist migration
was followed, not by a recession to the old colonies but by a second
migration of "late loyalists" and by subsequent migrations from the
same region until the War of 1812 interrupted for the second time
the normal movement towards the western and northern frontiers. It
was estimated in 1812 that four-fifths of the population of Upper
Canada were definitely "American" by birth or descent or both. Of
100,000 inhabitants at that time probably one-fifth were the original
U.E.L.'s or their descendants, and three-fifths were either "late
loyalists" or resourceful frontiersmen from up-state New York and
Pennsylvania. This later migration was one of the earliest of those

tides of westward settlement which flowed and ebbed in periodical cycles for more than a century across the agricultural frontiers of the republic.

The third group of loyalists—those who made terms with destiny and remained in the republic—would have been of prime importance for the British provinces had it been possible to estimate and invoke their numbers, for from these reserves of loyalism it was Lieutenant-Governor Simcoe's deliberate policy to recruit the settlement of Upper Canada. For obvious reasons the loyalist tradition south of the boundary died out after independence, just as the much more attenuated "patriot" tradition passed away in French Canada and in Nova Scotia. Meanwhile the loyalism of the "late loyalists" in Canada was often more assertive than that of the U.E.L.'s themselves—and it is altogether probable that the patriotism of many of the late "patriots" in the revolution was equally vociferous in the new republic.

Much of the loyalism during the revolution must have been instinctive. At the close of the Seven Years' War the normal temper of the old colonies was still unmistakably loyalist—it was the "patriot" movement which was "created" and mobilized into an inveterate cause. As late as 1774 Washington himself, writing from the first Continental Congress at Philadelphia to his friend Captain Robert Mackenzie, avowed on his honour that "it is not the wish or interest of that government [Massachusetts], or any other upon this continent, separately or collectively, to set up for independence. This I advance with a degree of confidence and boldness, which may claim your belief, having better opportunities of knowing the real sentiments of the people you are among, from the leaders of them, in opposition to the measures of the administration, than you have." This remained Washington's opinion after having "spent the afternoon with the Boston gentlemen." The cumulative measures of that fatal year, however, soon convinced Washington "beyond the smallest doubt," that they were "the result of deliberation" and that there was "a regular systematic plan to enforce them." No doubt this revulsion was shared by great numbers of customary loyalists. By 1776 there could have been little difference of opinion between them and the "patriots" with regard to the folly of official policy. It was the line of retreat—the terms of reconciliation—that baffled them both. Many like the Otises and the Curwens and the Galloways were still ready to settle "without guarantees" in the hope of wiser and more salutary counsels to follow. Like the official group in Nova Scotia, who approved the "doctrines and principles" of the old colonies and were prepared to concede "the justice of their cause," they still regarded separation as "the greatest evil which can befall us or our posterity." But the radicals had gone too far to retreat. "Returning were as tedious as go o'er" and much more dangerous. For many of the loyalists, too, Paine's *Common Sense*—more than 120,000 copies of which were sold in three months—must have focused inarticulate convictions about policy and destroyed any lingering hope of reconciliation. With the Declaration of Independence the lines were drawn on the basis not of principle but of procedure. The reluctant parting of Joseph Galloway and Franklin, of Jonathan Sewell and John Adams must have been symptomatic of many thousands: "the die is now cast . . . swim or sink, live or die, survive or perish."

For loyalists therefore who contrived to escape the committee men without losing their property and their livestock it was easy to acquiesce in the new order and old debates took a new form. Whigs and derelict tories were soon coalescing against "upstart lawless committee men." Numbers alone must have been decisive. General Robertson estimated the "patriots" as only one-third of the population, although both he and Cornwallis conceded that they were "inveterates" and "typical Americans." John Adams, on the other hand, claimed that one-third of the population had been "seduced and deluded" by loyalist interests. Even on the basis of this estimate more than 750,000 loyalist sympathizers might have welcomed reconciliation, and had it succeeded would have carried on a loyalist tradition into the new era. As the war of independence developed it became obvious that the whole navy and mercantile marine of Great Britain could scarcely have transported that number of hypothetical or latent loyalists and their property to other scenes. Those who escaped to Canada must have left behind them many times that meagre number who would have acquiesced with equal readiness in a parliamentary reconciliation under the auspices of the British Whigs. It was from these reserves of loyalism that Simcoe and his disciples must have drawn much of their support in the post-loyalist settlement of Upper Canada.

II

New Brunswick which became *par excellence* the province of the loyalists proved in many respects a unique experiment. Never perhaps in the second empire, nor indeed in the first, did the old colonial system come nearer to success. By comparison with the stormy history of the Canadas that of New Brunswick was placid and harmonious. In temper the province remained the Martha rather than the Mary of the Canadian family, and the key to this practical phlegmatic outlook in politics was undoubtedly to be found in the survival there of an official tradition which remained dominant long after Confederation. "It is impossible," wrote Sydenham in 1840, fresh from his pacification of Joseph Howe in Nova Scotia, "not to be struck with the difference between the political state of New Brunswick and that of the other provinces of British North America. While elsewhere Society is distracted . . . there reigns in New Brunswick the most perfect tranquillity and an entire harmony between the Executive and the Legislature. . . . No doubt much is due to the good sense of the Inhabitants." To many of the New Brunswick reformers this phlegmatic temper was not altogether praiseworthy. After the "great election" of 1847 which established responsible government in Nova Scotia, Charles Fisher, son of a New Brunswick loyalist, reported to his Nova Scotian ally that New Brunswick was still *too loyal* and given over to their idol of £.s.d."

At the mouth of the Saint John River a city was born in a day (May 18, 1783), and it was the first to be incorporated (1785) in British North America. Within a year there were nearly two thousand houses, three-quarters of them built of sawn lumber issued under the unimaginative supervision of Major Studholme at Fort Howe. It was originally planned to settle the disbanded loyalist regiments of the revolution— the Maryland Loyalists, the Royal Guides, the Queen's Rangers, the Pennsylvania Loyalists, De Lancey's of New York, Prince of Wales and Loyal American Regiments, 1st, 2nd, and 3rd New Jersey Volunteers, King's Regiment of Foot, the Royal Fencibles, and Arnold's American Legion—in blocks of twelve miles on the upper reaches of the river, but this plan was eventually abandoned, and it is doubtful if they settled there at all at more than quarter strength. Though a bitter tradition of flight and privation attended the less fortunate "refugees" during the early years of the revolution, even to the first generation of "military loyalists" the well-organized routine of the muster-rolls, half-pay, and army rations must have assured a modest competence. A few years later Edward Winslow found many of his compatriots with well-stocked farms "of more value than their ancestors in New Jersey or New England possessed for three generations before they were born." A fair share of the £3,300,000 eventually granted by the British government as indemnities to the loyalists was awarded to New Brunswick claimants. Even the New Brunswick assemblymen, as a Nova Scotian tory remarked a generation later, were "men of considerable, and some of them of large property." The truth was that loyalism in New Brunswick was a distinction so generally shared that it ceased to be distinctive. On occasion it tended, as in Nova Scotia, to become assertive and self-conscious as a tradition; as an issue it scarcely emerged into politics. The reason is probably to be found in the philosophy of the Duke of Plaza Toro in *The Gondoliers*:

> When everybody's somebody
> Then no one's anybody.

The predominance of the professional type from the old colonies accounted for much of this official harmony. In both the Winslow and the Ward Chipman Papers there is an official *camaraderie* which could be urbane and magnanimous within the charmed circle although it could be hard and uncharitable and truculent to their old enemies "without the gates." Jonathan Sewell, brother-in-law of John Hancock, James Putnam, leader of the Massachusetts bar, with whom John Adams once lived as a law student, Justice Upham, Jonathan Bliss, Ward Chipman, Edward Winslow Sr., great-grandson of Governor Edward Winslow of the Plymouth Colony, and his son Edward Winslow whose sprightly correspondence illuminates one of the gloomiest pages of Canadian history, were all Harvard men. The first governor, Thomas Carleton, brother of Sir Guy, Lord Dorchester, held office for thirty-three years, and was absent from the province for fourteen. "We are really a self-governing people," wrote Ward Chipman, "and get on just as well without a governor as with one."

The organization of New Brunswick as a separate province, long attributed to loyalist influence, is now known to have been approved by the King as early as 1778 and it was christened in advance (New Ireland) by William Knox as early as 1780.[1] The new province, in Knox's opinion, could be relied upon to "cherish monarchial principles and to repress republican ideas," to be "abhorrers of Republicanism" and of the "American spirit of innovation." It became the policy of the second empire, as we shall see, to disintegrate representative institutions and to concentrate the executive, as Knox advocated, under the "direction and control of a Governor-General." Nova Scotia was broken up into four fragments, three of which have never been reunited. Cape Breton was left, like Quebec, without even an assembly. When this fatal policy of disintegration was reversed by the Colonial Office three-quarters of a century later, it was already too late to effect a reunited province in time for it to function in the larger federation.

Meanwhile the relations of the province of New Brunswick with the Colonial Office were exemplary. The full-length portrait of Lord

---

[1] As late as June, 1784, Ward Chipman was still in London advocating his scheme for a separate province but in complete ignorance of the fact that the province of Nova Scotia had already been divided.

Sheffield in the New Brunswick Assembly chamber attests the popularity of his rejuvenated mercantilism in the eighteenth century, and that of Lord Glenelg commemorates the control which New Brunswick was the first to secure over crown lands policy and revenue in the nineteenth century. Although it was the first among the British provinces (1836) to force a change in the Executive Council to command the "confidence" of the Assembly, New Brunswick was the last, as we shall see, to adopt responsible government "at all times" in its final form. The relations with old enemies in the United States remained equally paradoxical. The intercourse with New England during the War of 1812 was so friendly that the buoyant customs revenues collected at the improvised clearing-house at Castine were afterwards used to found Dalhousie University. Meanwhile the 104th Regiment, including names that might almost have been taken from Winslow's muster-rolls of the revolution, marched overland on snowshoes, three hundred miles in thirteen days, to the defence of Canada. It was from New Brunswick, too, that Sir Edmund Head, grandson of a loyalist, drafted the first project of a federal union of the British provinces, based squarely upon self-government in a "powerful and independent State" dedicated to a "national destiny" under the British Crown. It is perhaps characteristic of the loyalist temper that Head's report of 1851 remained undiscovered for nearly eighty years.

In Nova Scotia and Upper Canada the results of the loyalist migrations were less uniform. The early "refugees" after the evacuation of Boston and a large proportion of those who shared in the mushroom growth of Shelburne became a serious problem to the old government of Nova Scotia. Many quickly disappeared from the scene. By 1789 two-thirds of the population of Shelburne had migrated elsewhere or returned to the United States. Some crossed the Bay of Fundy in order to be "among their own people" in New Brunswick. During the revolution Nova Scotia had remained technically loyalist only by a miracle, for no more truculent martinet was to be found at that "alarming crisis" than Governor Legge. His recall at the entreaty of the whole province had restored to influence a group of pre-revolutionary New Englanders whose conciliatory policy seemed little better than neutrality to some of the militant loyalists of 1783. A few of the newcomers staged a brief and not very creditable intrigue to have the Council and Assembly "thoroughly purged and the outcasts succeeded by honest loyalists." The creation of New Brunswick in 1784, however, appeased the malcontents and left the old pre-revolutionary New England tradition dominant in Nova Scotia for many years. Though outnumbered by the loyalist newcomers, the Uniackes and Haliburtons and other pre-revolutionary whigs became the official tories of the second empire. By the close of the War of 1812 the fusion of the dominant elements of Nova Scotian settlement into a provincial tradition was already far advanced. The loyalist migrations, coming mid-way between the basic pre-revolutionary New England settlement of the eighteenth century and the Scottish migrations of the nineteenth, acted as a catalyst for the local patriotism of all the rest.

The fisheries and shipbuilding, reinforced by lucrative privateering during the War of 1812—twenty-three ships were once put up for sale by the Admiralty in a single day—soon created an economy in which the West Indian trade from Halifax became the staple of provincial prosperity. Nova Scotia was perhaps the first among the provinces of the second empire to evolve a distinctive patriotism of its own. Free from those racial asperities which began to dominate the politics of Lower Canada, the various elements of the population could sink their heterogeneous origins in a sense of common interest. By 1835 the pre-revolutionary Yankees, the English group in Halifax, the stolid Germans of Lunenburg County, the continental loyalists from half a dozen of the old colonies, the enterprising Scots of Pictou and Inverness, were all Nova Scotians. In such a community the loyalist tradition though less dominant than in New Brunswick and Upper Canada was even more characteristic perhaps of the maturing temper of the first empire from which it had come. Thus Joseph Howe, son of a Massachusetts loyalist, could avow the cause of reform in Nova Scotia without inviting those charges of sedition and republicanism which bedevilled so much of the contest against privilege in the other provinces. Allied with the son of a pre-revolutionary "Cumberland rebel" who became in 1848 the first prime minister overseas under responsible government, Howe once challenged his adversaries to point the "antiquated old blunderbuss" of the loyalty cry at their common cause of reform. It was Howe's unerring instinct that this cause was to be won only by an alliance between reformers on both sides of the Atlantic, and it may be that the loyalist tradition of Nova Scotia had something to do with that beneficent approach.

In the old province of Quebec the loyalist migration was a reversal of Carleton's original policy in the *Quebec Act* at almost every point. One of the prime purposes of the Act had been to keep the regions of the St. Lawrence and the Great Lakes exclusively French. Now the rising tide of United Empire Loyalists, the "late loyalists," and immigration from the new republic threatened their hegemony. The new province of Upper Canada was lopped off at the Ottawa. From old

Fort Frontenac to Detroit tithe and seigneurial tenure and French civil law were replaced by clergy reserves for a protestant clergy and by fee simple and British common law for an expanding frontier. Representative institutions, introduced into Lower Canada in 1791 almost as a matter of course, had the appearance of an alien political system, while church and seigneur alike, daunted by the distant thunders of the French Revolution, awaited the changing times with fear and foreboding.

In Upper Canada Simcoe's policy of recruiting settlers from the reserves of loyalism still latent in the old colonies was a partial return to the normal trends of frontier settlement. Simcoe's proclamation of 1792 is charged with all the enthusiasm of Lawrence's from Nova Scotia after the reduction of Louisbourg, and copies of it were ingeniously circulated in many areas where friendly intercourse with loyalist communities was again possible. The staple of Simcoe's land policy—the free grant of 200 acres to actual settlers instead of the old unwieldy grants to sanguine but ineffectual promoters—was in many respects a forecast of the free homestead system of the United States, adopted in 1862 by the North in order to forestall the South in the settlement of the West. Simcoe's new policy was already beginning to function when conflict with Carleton, now reinstated as Lord Dorchester to supervise the salvaging of the *Quebec Act* in Lower Canada, led to Simcoe's resignation. "All my reasonable Hopes and Views," he wrote bitterly to Dorchester, "are blighted and destroyed." His whole policy had been "checked, counteracted and annihilated, in consequence of Your Lordship's opinion." Immigration into Upper Canada from the republic continued however under its own momentum, those who came outnumbering the original loyalists four to one, until it seemed to Jefferson at the outbreak of the War of 1812 that "the acquisition of Canada this year, as far as the neighborhood of Quebec, will be a mere matter of marching." Among the most recent arrivals there were a few conspicuous examples of treason—Willcocks, once a member of the Upper Canadian Assembly, was killed at Fort Erie as a colonel in the United States army—but the American frontiersman was no longer fighting the battles of the revolution. After the war Bathurst, secretary for the colonies, attempted a second time to dam back the tide of continental migration by refusing land grants to settlers from the United States. In contrast to the Maritime Provinces and to most of Lower Canada, the upper province thus continued to nourish the antipathies from the revolutionary war. Here alone along the international boundary the military operations of the War of 1812 took on the form of conquest. In loyalist tradition the War of 1812 was the last phase of the revolution, the defence of the second empire in America, "the national war of Canada."

For many years the officials of the province, most of whom had no personal connection with the loyalist migration, appropriated the loyalist tradition and labelled every movement of reform which assailed their privileges as "treason and republicanism." In the motto of the province "fidelis" was interpreted as fidelity to the old colonial system. In 1818 Robert Gourlay, a brilliant young Scot, fellow-student of Chalmers and associate of Wilberforce, was prosecuted under the *Alien Act* while on a visit to relatives in Upper Canada, and expelled from the province. William Lyon Mackenzie was defeated in the crucial election of 1836 by appeals to the loyalist traditions of the province. Even Robert Baldwin was associated by Lord Metcalfe with "treason and republicanism." The British parliamentary technique which finally prevailed was in conflict, it will be seen, with both toryism and republicanism, but the loyalist tradition lingered on to permeate responsible government when it was finally won and to influence many another issue of British American politics. The fact that loyalism coalesced in the end almost everywhere with the prevailing temper of the British provinces was proof not only of its own vitality but of a congenial environment.

The second empire and the republic thus began with traditions mutually diverging from the norm of the century and a half which they had shared in common. The one, in perpetuating that tradition unbroken, was reinforced by the most conservative elements from the first empire. The other, in breaking with that tradition altogether, renounced the Crown for a written constitution and stereotyped at the colonial stage the evolution of the parliamentary system. On both sides the loss was incalculable. The northern provinces lost their unique advantage, in the St. Lawrence waterways system, for the exploitation of the hinterlands of the continent—an advantage which might have attracted untold resources of personnel and capital to that great enterprise. The loss to the republic was equally serious. "Manifest destiny" was stayed at the Great Lakes and the forty-ninth parallel, and even the immediate loss in the loyalist migrations was not without its bearing upon the politics of the republic. In *The Epic of America*, James Truslow Adams has attributed in no small measure what he calls the "Virginia Dynasty" of presidents and statesmen to the exodus from the northern provinces of "several thousands of families who had been most prominent in the public affairs of their colonies."

Chapter Four

PROMISE AND REACTION

IN some respects the independence of the thirteen colonies forced a new beginning for the British provinces that remained. There were still imposing resources to be explored and there were signs too of a new spirit as well as a new chance. As the younger Pitt surveyed the ruins of the empire which had been his father's crowning glory in the Seven Years' War he addressed himself to the task with the noble resolve which Professor Coupland has taken as the theme of a new era. "Let us examine what is left with a manly and determined courage. Let us strengthen ourselves against inveterate enemies and reconcile our ancient friends. The misfortunes of individuals and of kingdoms that are laid open and examined with true wisdom are more than half redressed."

None could have foreseen in 1783 the expansion to their present proportions of either nation emerging from the Atlantic provinces of the first empire. For the republic the pace of that expansion outdistanced the most sanguine expectations. By comparison the British provinces remained hopelessly disintegrated. There were solid advantages nevertheless to be explored. When Dorchester resigned in 1796 with nothing but despair for "the ruinous consequences of the old colonial system" the elements of vast and distinctive enterprises were already gathering at Montreal. In 1797 a Massachusetts Yankee, Philemon Wright, had already selected a site on the Ottawa River for the beginnings of a lumber industry that revolutionized the timber trade. From what is now Parliament Hill in the capital of Canada his rafts of logs were soon to be seen like regiments moving towards mills and markets all over the world. The North West Company was already functioning in the fur trade with ferocious energy. Alexander Mackenzie had already reached the Arctic over one of the most intricate networks of water communications on the continent, all of it through British territory. There was more promise in the range and personnel of the second empire than in its administration.

PROMISE

I. The Range of a New Empire

For both territory and settlement, as we have seen, Shirley's Great Plan was truncated by the revolution. The immediate problems of the second empire were distorted by the change although in one respect at least the barriers to their expansion were less formidable than those which confronted the new republic. The vast area now federated in Canada was administered piecemeal by every variety of government known to the old empire, and by one at least—the "statutory" province of Quebec—that was altogether new, but the title to every yard of it was already vested in the British Crown. While these primitive provinces, almost lost to each other in the northern wilderness, were groping for mutual contacts across the continent, the republic to the south was driving through the Alleghanies, clearing Spain out of the Floridas, bargaining with France for Louisiana at a time when Napoleon was quite powerless to defend it, and exploiting the claims thus acquired until the "Louisiana purchase" reached the boundaries of the Hudson's Bay Company. In the south and west a ouitlanders' war against Mexico carried the republic to the Rio Grande and to the Pacific. Oregon in the forties and Alaska in the sixties rounded out a transcontinental destiny. In the presence of this unremitting pressure the frontiers of the second empire were precarious and insecure.

The chief concern of the British provinces was to hold what they could claim already. In this they were only partially successful. Had a convention of 1803 with the United States been ratified, the sources of the Mississippi might have remained in British territory. Nearly half the area of Selkirk's Red River Settlement, held and subsequently vindicated by title from the Charter of 1670, found its way into the frontier territories of the United States. The Ashburton Treaty in the east and the settlement of the Oregon boundary at the forty-ninth parallel were signs too of conflict avoided at the cost of much prestige, and in the case of Oregon no small loss of territory. The retreat from the Columbia in the Oregon Treaty and the march of the frontiers of the United States into Mexico overshadowed the equanimity of the British provinces for more than a generation. Grey at the Colonial Office granted Vancouver Island in fee simple to the Hudson's Bay Company in order to establish there a vested interest of agricultural settlement so fatally wanting in the contest for Oregon. The failure of the Company to implement this policy moved not only the Colonial Office but the restive province of Canada to focus attention upon the West.

The reverberations of "manifest destiny" in the United States, it is now known, were in many instances sounds of domestic politics rather than of militant imperialism. Nevertheless, from the War of 1812 to the Treaty of Washington there was scarcely a decade when the designs of militant expansionists—from Old Hickory himself to Polk and Sumner and Banks and Seward and President Grant—were not known and pondered with grave concern in the British provinces. Many contemporaries in the United States—and historians since—may have dismissed the play on "manifest destiny" as a boisterous symptom of the growing-pains of the republic. The disintegrated communities across the boundary, however, could affect no such equanimity. This tension which may safely be ignored in the dynamic expansion of the United States can scarcely be omitted from the record of Canadian survival and expansion without distorting one of the most critical periods in the development of the nation. The first names in Canadian politics on both sides were the most deeply moved by it. Irrevocable decisions in both self-government and association were made in this atmosphere. In the throes of the Civil War Alexander T. Galt reported an interview with Abraham Lincoln at which that great man's "straight-forward strong common sense" left a profound impression. "He pledged himself as a man of honor," wrote Galt, "that neither he nor his cabinet entertained the slightest aggressive design upon Canada." But Galt was constrained to add that "the policy of the American government is so subject to popular impulses that no assurances can or ought to be relied on under present circumstances." It was not until much of this miasma was lifted by the Treaty of Washington that this traditional uneasiness could be supplanted by a sense of security for the range and safety of the second empire.

II. Personnel

The first empire in America had astonished its closest observers by its variety and exuberance. To officialdom in London this diversity may have been attributable to a "total want of plan or system." But from the very nature of its origin and early growth the first empire was baffling in its complexity. America had become a refuge for almost every variety of religious dissent in western Europe, and every dominant race in the expansion of Europe was represented there. Puritans had escaped to Massachusetts, Rhode Island, and Connecticut; Roman Catholics to Maryland; Quakers and German Mennonites to Pennsylvania. There were French in Quebec and Nova Scotia, Dutch in New York, Spaniards in the Floridas, Germans in Pennsylvania and

Nova Scotia, Scots of the Stuart period in the Carolinas, Highlanders after "the forty-five" among the Frasers in Quebec and in Nova Scotia, and English under the Hanoverians in Georgia. The Indian presented almost as many problems as the white man—the fierce Tuscaroras of the Carolinas, the versatile Iroquois of the Six Nations, the restless Algonquins of the Pontiac War, the unnumbered tribes of Rupert's Land. Even at Albany Sir William Johnson had been almost too late to bring order out of chaos. By comparison with this diversity of race and religion the second empire, despite the basic cleavages between French and English on the St. Lawrence, may well have seemed relatively homogeneous in its allegiance and temper.

In Nova Scotia the peninsular area to which the province was reduced after 1784 was in itself a harmonizing factor in the development of a provincial patriotism. Like the insularity of Britain itself, it bound its inhabitants, English, pre-revolutionary American, German, Scottish, Acadian, loyalist American alike, to a sense of common interest. For purposes of government the prevailing temper of the province, reinforced by the loyalist tradition, left little to be desired. By the turn of the century the royal flag of Nova Scotia under provincial registry was known upon the seven seas. A few years later an ingenuous governor like Dalhousie could move about the province like a laird on his native heath, exchanging anonymous letters in the public press with "Agricola" on the problems of provincial agriculture and sharing his enthusiasm with half a dozen cultural agencies of permanent value in the life of the province. Across the Bay of Fundy the new loyalist province of New Brunswick—New Ireland was the name originally chosen by William Knox for the new experiment—was endowed by traditions rooted in America since the Plymouth colony. By virtue of its history in colonial America sublimated by its loyalist temper during the revolution the province remained for two generations the most harmonious experiment, perhaps, in the old colonial system in either empire. From its foundation in 1784 to the brink of Confederation not a single major conflict ruffled the surface of relations with the mother country. At least one governor resigned in high dudgeon because the Colonial Office took sides against him in his feud with the local Assembly. Even Prince Edward Island, though bedevilled from beginning to end by "the eternal land question," carried on its implacable contest with absentee proprietors without questioning the sanctions of the parent state.

In Lower Canada the success of the church in retrieving and consolidating its ancient sway during the critical interlude between the

Quebec Act and the *Constitutional Act* proved to be one of the basic factors of Canadian history. The expatriated *habitants* of the French Canadian regiments that sided with the revolution in the attack upon Montreal and the conquest of the Old North West, never returned. Many no doubt were lost not only to the British Crown but to the church. In Quebec the restiveness under the seigneurial system continued, but it was counteracted by the mollifying and ingratiating guidance of the clergy under Haldimand's adroit administration which came to be identified with the *Quebec Act,* while the seamy side of that desperate measure was lost in the disaster to which it had so prevocatively contributed. The same steadying influence which had survived the American Revolution prevailed over the more subversive doctrines of the French. The church which had been the last to disappear beneath the deluge in old France stood firmly in Quebec, sustained by a growing tradition of its own and by recruits from the émigrés and clergy of old France. The empire of Napoleon was as powerless as that of Louis XVI to shake the attachment of church and people during the War of 1812. In the upper province where the tides of frontier settlement had already met and mingled across the boundary, that inglorious war, unredeemed as between Britain and the United States by any enobling elements of national policy, became in Canadian tradition "the national war of Canada."

Indigenous issues of privilege and authority soon forced both provinces into a conflict of their own. By the time of the Mackenzie and Papineau risings these issues had settled into a series of bitter and immoderate feuds not unlike the ubiquitous conflicts in the old colonies. But there was this difference. The "evidence of design" in the American Department soon fused these local feuds into a conflict with the parent state in which "the systematic assertion of an arbitrary power" threatened to undermine the whole fabric of representative government. It was now easy for the whig pamphleteers to sweep all before them until every local contest of privilege was swallowed up in the more sinister threat of coercion. The Canadian risings never assumed the aspect of resistance against the repressive designs of an imperial policy. More than one of the British provinces had the best of evidence—the experience of their own delegations to the Colonial Office—that there was a new spirit abroad. The policy of Glenelg in particular was benevolent and co-operative. The attempt of Joseph Hume in Great Britain to attribute the woes of William Lyon Mackenzie to "the baneful domination of the mother country" cost Mackenzie's party half his majority in the election of 1834 and placed in the hands of his opponents the weapons with which he was bludgeoned into insurrection in 1836. The insurrection itself was not a concerted rebellion but a sporadic rising inspired by a dozen local feuds against privilege and authority. Papineau was more successful in Lower Canada by directing discontent into racial channels, but the foundations of authority in both church and state remained stolidly unmoved. For a time it seemed that Lord John Russell's ten resolutions against responsible government, reinforced by the Russell–Sydenham régime, were designed to set up a system of governance as autocratic as the "design" by which William Knox had hoped to repair the "total want of plan or system" in the first empire. But the spirit was vastly different. The truth was that the political temper of the second empire in relation to the sanctions of the parent state was never seriously in doubt. The happy solution of 1848, as Lord John Russell himself maintained, "carried into effect the theory of responsible government with so much moderation and good sense as to reconcile in the happiest manner the interest of the colony and the mother country." During the world revolutions of 1848 Charles Buller reflected upon the new spirit of "confidence and kindliness" in colonial policy. "Amid all these convulsions," he wrote to Joseph Howe "may *we* not think with pride and satisfaction on the establishment, and working of Responsible Government?"

III. The New Mercantilism

The first and second empires present few contrasts more curiously paradoxical than that between the old mercantile system which economic historians long associated with the revolution, and the mercantilism which lingered on into the middle of the nineteenth century in the form of imperial preferences for staple products of the colonies in America. The mercantile system in the first empire culminated in the *Stamp Act* riots and the "Boston tea party." The Montreal mob which pelted the governor-general and burnt down the parliament buildings in 1849 was protesting, among other things, against the passing of mercantilism in the repeal of the timber duties and the preferences on Canadian flour.

The association of the revolution with the *Stamp Act*, the Port Duties, and other aspects of "taxation without representation," long suffused the struggle with unhistorical traditions. The merchants of the old colonies, accustomed to fish in troubled waters, exploited the opposition to these measures only to find themselves swept away by the revolution from their deep and long-range moorings in British commerce and naval protection all over the world. Until 1774 every colonial patriot from Daniel Dulany and John Adams to the authors of the fourth article in the Declaration of the first Continental Congress upheld the *bona fide* "regulation of our external commerce." "This," wrote John Adams, "the Colonies ever have been, and will be, ready and willing to concede." To this, added James Otis, "every honest man will subscribe." In the end it was not the mercantile system itself but the abuse of this glittering imperial machinery for ulterior purposes that precipitated the revolution. The *Stamp Act* to support a standing army was to be enforced by Admiralty courts without juries. The Port Duties advanced boldly to the task of raising a revenue "for defraying the charge of the administration of justice and the support of civil government." Governors were thus to become "Independent of the Assemblies for their Subsistence." Instead of approaching "*by sap* as the stamp duties would have done," wrote William Knox, this was "attacking them by storm in open day; every man therefore saw into the design." The use of the mercantile system for the legitimate control of trade was "unquestionable," but the abuse of the system for the control of government struck at "constitutional rights and liberties," British as well as American, "in the establishment of which [added Washington] some of the best blood in the Kingdom has been spilt."

In the second empire the *Declaratory Act* of 1778 disavowed at the outset the use of imperial taxation in the colonies for imperial purposes. The mercantile system resumed its normal functions. Its general purpose was still roundly avowed by William Knox in 1789: "it was better to have no colonies at all, than not to have them subservient to the maritime strength and commercial interest of Great Britain." In practice, however, the regulations were intended to be not only beneficent but mutually advantageous. For a decade or two there was a prospect of the maritime provinces supplanting the old colonies in the West Indian trade. Timber and fish, flour and fur and potash, the most lucrative staples of the second empire, fitted admirably into the system. Lord Sheffield, the patron saint of the new mercantilism, redeemed it from its evil associations during the revolution and opened up the most lucrative channels of imperial trade to colonial enterprise.

When it was discovered that British trade with the independent republic far outdistanced the old trade with the dependent colonies, the old theories of mercantilism began to undergo a sea change. *The Wealth of Nations* appeared in the same year as the Declaration of Independence. Pitt's commercial regulations with Ireland, strangled though they still were by the selfish mercantilist temper of the House of Commons, marked a brave beginning for the new empire. His abortive trade regulations with France, the "traditional enemy" of Great Britain, might have been a forecast of economic emancipation, had the French Revolution not cast its shadow over peaceful commerce and drawn the nation's enterprise once again to the "cadaverous haut goût of lucrative war." In America it was clear by this time that the maritime provinces of the second empire could not hope to supplant the abounding commerce of the old colonies with the West Indies. By the *Enabling Act* of 1794 the West Indian trade was thrown open to their ancient customers. A vision of international trade was beginning to supplant the narrow conceptions of the old mercantile system. Even within the orbit of mercantilism itself broad principles of reciprocity were replacing the hard acquisitive temper of monopoly. The Huskisson reforms after the Napoleonic Wars marked a great advance over the postulate of William Knox that it was "better to have no colonies at all, than not to have them subservient to the maritime strength and commercial interest of Great Britain."

The colonies of British North America, nevertheless, did continue to subserve the maritime strength and commercial interest of Great Britain. The commercial interests of Nova Scotia, New Brunswick, and the Canadas throve also in the process. Many of the masts and spars of Nelson's fleet at Trafalgar must have grown along the reaches of the Saint John River. The masting industry of New Brunswick, the wheat and timber and potash of Canada, the furs of the North West and Hudson's Bay Companies, were staples of solid weight and value. When preferences on Canadian flour were added in the British market not only the Canadian farmer but the Canadian miller and merchant and banker reaped a rich harvest which was still further augmented by the wheat from the American hinterland pouring across the lakes in order to enjoy the British preference. The duties on Baltic timber in the British market operated like hydraulic pressure on the banks of the Ottawa and the St. Lawrence. The simultaneous attack on the corn laws and timber duties in Great Britain brought a chorus of self-interested protest from British North America. The exponents of privilege in government and of mercantile preferences in trade joined forces to pelt the governor-general with missiles which (Elgin ruefully observed) must obviously have been brought for the purpose: to burn the parliament buildings in Montreal to the ground and to flaunt in reprisal a peevish threat of annexation to the United States. From both the first empire and the second the mercantile system disappeared in riot and frustration. It was defended by the rioters of Montreal because it subserved the acquisitive vested interests of the old colonial system. Perhaps it was execrated in Boston as an "instrument of tyranny" only because it was being exploited for ulterior purposes by those whose baleful "design," in the opinion of many a patriot in America, came to include a "regular plan at the expense of law and justice to overthrow our constitutional rights and liberties." Mercantilism in reverting to its normal function redeemed itself and became again, for half a century, a cohesive force in the second empire.

IV. British Parliamentary Supremacy

An equally paradoxical contrast between the close of the first empire and the course of the second is to be found in the place of the British Parliament in their traditions of self-government.

The first Continental Congress could "cheerfully consent to the operation of such Acts of the British parliament as are bona fide restrained to the regulation of our external commerce," but the storm aroused by the *Stamp Act* and the Port Duties soon spread to the foundations of imperial legislation. British parliamentary supremacy became a symbol of "arbitrary power" in America. No barriers of chartered rights or long-established precedents could withstand its authority. By the "intolerable Acts" of 1774 Parliament destroyed the chartered government of Massachusetts and closed the port of Boston. It tore out—"by the roots" as Chatham said—the constitution of a royal province in Quebec for which the faith of the Crown had stood "fully pledged" by proclamation, commissions, and instructions, for ten years. In its place the *Quebec Act* created a "government such as the world never saw before" without a "spark or semblance of liberty"; and the *Quebec Revenue Act* proceeded to tax that province for its civil government not only "without representation" but without representative institutions. If this was the sovereignty of Parliament what was to be expected from further parliamentary enactment? "If that sovereignty," exclaimed Burke, "and their freedom cannot be reconciled, which will they take? They will cast your sovereignty in your face. Nobody will be argued into slavery." In the end the fatal design to coerce America was so closely associated with parliamentary sanctions that the House of Commons shared with the Crown itself the odious implications of the revolution. William Knox at last conceded that the colonies had "lost all confidence in the integrity of Parliament," and that confidence was to be restored only "by putting it out of its own power to deceive."

The first colonial experiment after the revolution reflected this moral bankruptcy. The course of the "independent parliament of Ireland" from 1782 to the union in 1800 is probably the most convincing demonstration to be found in the second empire that the solution for colonial government was not to be found in the repeal of British parliamentary supremacy. In 1782, in the throes of disaster and humiliation in America, legislative independence was conceded to the Irish parliament at St. Stephen's. Grattan saluted the first session with the sententious greeting, "I am now to address a free people." The difference between freedom and mere legislative independence without control of the executive became apparent from the sequel. It is fair to reflect that the experiment was perverted by the French Revolution as well as by the American. For Ireland in 1794 as for Lower Canada in 1791 the franchise was thrown open to the Roman Catholic in the hope that this might prove a conservative and moderating influence in the midst of revolution. When Pitt's programme of emancipation came to a halt at the Fitzwilliam episode without admitting Irish Roman Catholics either to office or to parliament, Burke prophesied truly that half-citizens would soon become whole Jacobins. The rebellion of 1798 was more barbarous on both sides than anything in the Canadas in 1837. In both cases a quick and ready-made solution was sought in political union—the Irish union in 1800, the Canadian in 1841. In Ireland the "independent parliament" was extinguished by methods which turned the period from the rebellion of 1798 to the union into a chamber of political horrors. Lord John Russell's method for Canada was less truculent but it was no less effective. The constitution of Lower Canada, like that of Massachusetts in 1774, was suspended in 1838 because there seemed no other method of rendering the province governable. One thing at least was obvious from both experiments. The secret of successful colonial government was neither legislative independence nor legislative subordination.

For the second empire in America the supremacy of the British Parliament survived the odious traditions of the American Revolution and the equally odious era of the Irish union. There were many uses for it in practice which not only dispelled its terrors but transformed it into an asset of the first importance. The *Declaratory Act* of 1778 renouncing imperial taxation for imperial purposes was in itself a salutary gesture; and there were positive as well as negative uses for parliamentary supremacy. How could the free institutions of a royal province be restored to Quebec? The *Quebec Act* had created a new type of province by a new procedure, and the process would perhaps have warranted a new name. Unlike the chartered or proprietary or royal provinces of the first empire Quebec was a statutory province, and the only method known to the law by which a statute could be amended was by another statute. Thus while the "royal" provinces of Nova Scotia and New Brunswick, like Britain herself, were developing by "convention" or usage to full responsible government without legislative intervention by the British Parliament, the old province of Quebec, derailed by the *Quebec Act,* was being salvaged by one constitution after another, all of them established and in turn supplanted by Act of Parliament. When the *Quebec Act* which was already obsolete by more than a century in British America was repealed in 1791 there was a partial return to normal usage in the *Constitutional Act.* When this proved impracticable after the Papineau rising the constitution of Lower Canada was suspended by statute in 1838. The *Act of Union* reunited the two provinces in 1841, and when reunion became unworkable by reason of deadlock and external danger in 1864 the British Parliament enacted a federation with two other provinces by the *British North America Act, 1867.* Amendments to this Act, from those in 1871, 1875, 1886, 1907, 1915, to the *B.N.A. Act, 1949* (13 Geo. VI, c. 81) and beyond, have all been effected by British statutes. This record of usefulness could be expanded to imposing dimensions. The *Statute of Westminster* itself, establishing at last legislative autonomy for the British dominions in 1931, provided, at the express stipulation of the Canadian government, that the "repeal, amendment or alternation of the British North America Acts, 1867 to 1930" must still be effected by Act of the British Parliament. The reason for this stipulation is perhaps the best commentary upon the function of British parliamentary supremacy throughout most of the second empire: no more expeditious or convenient method of amending a federal constitution has yet been devised than the perfunctory enactment by British statute of a joint resolution of the Canadian Houses of Parliament. The empirical usefulness of this procedure in normal cases has been deemed to outweight the grotesque anomaly of colonial subordination. It was in this pragmatic spirit that British parliamentary supremacy survived so usefully into the second empire.

There were salutary uses for it, too, which were much more discerning and constructive than the blind escape from the train of policy introduced by the *Quebec Act.* It is safe to say that the federation of 1867 could never have been achieved in that decade had it been necessary to rely upon constituent conventions after the American model with subsequent ratification by the constituent provinces. The Quebec Resolutions of 1864 were never formally ratified in the Maritime Provinces.

It was the undisputed parliamentary supremacy of Great Britain at that time that enabled a group of far-seeing Canadian and British statesmen to carry the B.N.A. Act, 1867 "per saltum," as Macdonald advocated, thus cutting at one stroke the Gordian knot of state sovereignty which had dragged the United States through the horrors of civil war. The fact that the instrument of federation was a statute and not in any sense a comprehensive written constitution has permitted practices of incalculable value in the functioning of the Canadian federation. The use of the parliamentary as distinct from the congressional system remains one of the "unwritten" conventions of the Canadian constitution.

Not only the union of the British provinces but their successful expansion to the Pacific was aided incalculably by British parliamentary supremacy. It was the Rupert's Land Act of 1868—next to the B.N.A. Act, 1867 probably the most important statute relating to Canada— that provided for the "surrender" by the Hudson's Bay Company to the Crown and the transfer to the new dominion of an area four or five times the size of the original federation. Without this ready expedient the accession of Rupert's Land and the North-Western Territory might have been so complicated and protracted a process that a transcontinental British dominion might have become forever impossible.

To John Adams or James Otis the action of the Montreal rioters in 1849 or of the prime minister of Canada in 1931 must have appeared fantastic and incomprehensible. The truth is that neither the mercantile system nor British parliamentary supremacy was abused in the second empire for the sinister purposes which John Adams and James Otis discerned in the British policy of their day. From the Stamp Act of 1765 to the "intolerable Acts" of 1774 almost every encroachment upon "constitutional rights and liberties" in America had come in the guise of an Act of Parliament. Had the "mangling hands . . . of blundering ministers" been withheld, as Franklin reminded Chatham in the secret interview at Hayes in 1774, parliamentary supremacy might still have played the beneficent role in the first empire which in fact it did play in the second. Franklin's own "Albany Plan" for colonial union, though drafted in America, was to have been sanctioned, like the Canadian confederation in 1867, by Act of Parliament. Revolution put an end to these "pleasing prospects" and to the continental destiny which Franklin had predicted so confidently in 1760: with "foundations . . . low and little" then but "broad and strong enough to support the greatest political structure that human wisdom ever yet erected."

Thenceforth British parliamentary supremacy, however benevolent, was destined to play a less heroic role in America.

REACTION IN GOVERNMENT

I

The elements of promise in territory, personnel, and temper in the second empire were accompanied by such vestiges of reaction in government that it is not easy to fix the starting-point of departure in terms of reference to the first empire. Knox and Franklin though in substantial agreement with regard to actual trends in America must have sensed with deadly accuracy their mutual repugnance with regard to the new American Department's "plan or system" for America. For the place of Quebec in that system it is unnecessary to go far beyond the evidence of Knox himself. In Quebec alone the new American Department was able to discard "the absurdity of . . . a *polypus* government, where a head sprouts out of every joint." "Without any of those pompous ideas of popular governments, which our countrymen are elated with, the people are happy." The authors of the *Quebec Act,* added Knox, "warily considered these material points," instead of "creating in them a power of destroying their peace and tranquility." The British colonies too "would have experienced a much greater degree of felicity, had their government consisted only of a governor and council." "The old mode of treating our dependencies must be exploded and a new system formed."

With this background the second empire could scarcely hope to begin where the first empire left off. In Quebec, Governor Haldimand bluntly dismissed the plea that the loyalist migrations were "an Argument in favor of the Repeal of the Quebec Act and for Granting a House of Assembly." "These unfortunate People," he reflected, "have Suffered too much by Committees and Houses of Assembly, to have retained any prepossessions in favor of that Mode of Government." When it became apparent that even the New Brunswick loyalists, "abhorrers of Republicanism," took an assembly for granted, and their compatriots in Upper Canada did the same, every precaution was taken to circumscribe its powers, to disintegrate the representative institutions of the second empire, to concentrate the civil and particularly the military powers of the executive, and to create in all the provinces vested interests both religious and secular, in order to "render them useful, and retain them in subordination to Great Britain."

These precautions were easily taken. The power of the purse in the "sole framing of money bills" which the burgesses of Virginia or the assemblymen of New York had fairly won in the first empire was grudgingly conceded. It "ought not to be resisted," Dundas wrote to Dorchester, but it was not to be "extended by overstrained refinements." In effect the buoyant "casual and territorial revenues" of the crown in the northern provinces transferred the power of the purse bodily to the executive. By 1836 in New Brunswick a tidy surplus of £150,000 from the administration of crown lands was in the hands of the commissioner. In Nova Scotia the transfer of these revenues to the Assembly in return for a fixed civil list was not made until after the achievement of responsible government.

Meanwhile the disintegration of the remaining provinces went on apace. Long before the "spring fleet" of loyalists left New York in 1783 the decision had been reached to break the old province of Nova Scotia into four fragments. In 1783 William Knox was busy with a plan for a fifth colony on the St. Croix as a buffer against the old colonies. Cape Breton Island, like Quebec, was denied an assembly altogether. That of Prince Edward Island narrowly escaped suppression at the hands of Lord Sydney. The old province of Quebec, as we have seen, was divided into Upper and Lower Canada. This disintegration was deemed not only salutary but safe, in view of the disintegration of the new republic. The policy of the government, Durham shrewdly surmised in 1839, was "to govern its Colonies by means of division, and to break them down as much as possible into petty isolated communities, incapable of combination, and possessing no sufficient strength for individual resistance." Dorchester himself before he left Canada came to deplore "our present policy . . . to divide and subdivide, and of this Remnant to form many independent Governments with as little communication and as little connexion as possible; while that of our Neighbours is to consolidate, and of many independent States to form one Government."[1]

The counterpart of this policy "to divide and subdivide" the remaining provinces was the attempt to concentrate the military and civil powers of the executive. After the *Quebec Act* Carleton was to receive the "full appointments of Commander-in-Chief" in America for the reduction of the refractory colonies in order to supervise North's fatuous plan "to arm the Roman Catholics of Canada and to employ them in that service."[2] Carleton's recall in disgrace by Germain after

[1]To Portland, Feb. 20, 1795, P.A.C., Q Series, 71, part 2, p. 313.
[2]Q Series, 11, 198; *Parliamentary History*, XVIII, 681.

the failure of this insensate policy left the design of centralized authority frustrated but not foresworn. In the plan drafted for Lord North in 1783 on the *Establishments for the American Loyalists* William Knox stipulated the "direction and control of a Governor-General." Carleton returned to the American scene as Commander-in-Chief in time to supervise the loyalist concentrations at New York and to evacuate the last British regiment from the new republic. In 1786 he returned as Lord Dorchester, "Captain General and Governor in Chief." Over Upper Canada his authority remained paramount. Evidence already cited in another context will suffice for illustration. Simcoe resigned in protest because his project of loyalist expansion from the reserves of loyalism in the old colonies were "blighted and destroyed." "All my measures," he added bitterly, "were checked, counteracted and annihilated, in consequence of Your Lordship's opinion." Over Nova Scotia, on the other hand, and over New Brunswick where Dorchester's younger brother Thomas Carleton was lieutenant-governor for thirty-three years, the control of the Governor in Chief must have been remote indeed. Fourteen of Lieutenant-Governor Carleton's years of office were spent in England, and a member of his own executive council observed that the province could "get on just as well without a governor as with one."

Within the provinces themselves the reinforcement of executive authority was more successful. In Nova Scotia the executive and legislative councils were identical in personnel—an expedient which multiplied their powers not by two but by three or four. Both executive and legislative functions were discharged behind closed doors. The result, there and elsewhere, was a circle of influence which the governor himself was frequently unable to dominate and which developed chronic tendencies towards "family compacts," "château cliques," and other forms of irresponsible privilege. As late as 1837 in Nova Scotia the executive councillors, twelve in number, were still the same as the legislative councillors. They included five members of two family connections, and five partners of the Halifax Banking Company. For thirty years every councillor but one had lived in Halifax. Sustained by "casual and territorial revenues" over which the Assembly had no control, "the twelve" wielded the power of the purse over their own emoluments and could defy the Assembly to cut off the supplies. As legislative councillor the Chief Justice helped to make the laws; as executive councillor he helped to administer them, and on the bench he interpreted them. Nine of the twelve were members of a religious denomination which numbered less than a quarter of the population of the province.

II

These precautions against the nascent powers of assemblies were augmented by two expedients which proved singularly futile for their purpose. One was so incongruous that even Dorchester's robust sagacity rejected it as a solution for "the American question." The other sowed seeds of strife, envy, and all uncharitableness in Upper Canadian politics for three generations and left scars which are still visible in the religious life of Canada.

The plan of establishing an hereditary aristocracy as a stabilizing vested interest in colonial government was not new in 1791. In the Carolinas the original proprietary grants of 1669 had been made under a fantastic constitution graced by the approbation of John Locke. Like palatinates on the frontiers of colonization the new provinces with their landgraves and caciques were to safeguard by this vicarious authority the distant functions of the Crown. When the proprietors surrendered the government back to the Crown in 1729, the titles lapsed, despite vested interests of the Carterets and others in the soil, and the Carolinas took their place with all but two of the old proprietary governments in America as royal provinces under the Crown.

In the royal provinces the expectation that the councils with their vested interests of place and privilege would prove "bulwarks of royal prerogative" in chronic conflict with the assembly was not always warranted. In Pennsylvania where there was no legislative council the proprietary governor and the popular assembly stood face to face, and it was Franklin's chief mission in London for six years to elevate the proprietorship to the dignity of a royal province. In the chartered provinces the council itself was elective. In the royal provinces during the revolution many a tory councillor paid for his prerogatives by the confiscation of his estates. It is probable that the property of the loyalist attracted more patriots than it daunted. The futility of landed councillors during the American Revolution was matched by the fate of the *noblesse* during the French Revolution.

To Pitt and to Grenville it was obvious that the British peerage and the established church were the bulwarks of stable government. The British constitution, said Pitt in 1791, was "the model and envy of the world," and aristocracy was "the true poise" of the constitution. The *Constitutional Act* was to provide for "an hereditary Council, an imitation of our House of Lords." "There was something," added Pitt, "in the habits, customs, and manners of Canada, that peculiarly fitted it for the reception of hereditary honours. . . . Some of the Seignors

. . . should be among others named to those honours. . . . The aristocracy flowing from the Imperial Crown of Great Britain, would tend materially to strengthen the system of connexion between the colony and the mother Country. The want of those honours had tended to accelerate the separation of the former Colonies."

The provisions for "hereditary titles of honour" to be associated with the "Hereditary Right of being summoned to the Legislative Council," were duly embodied in the Act. Fortunately for Canada they were never implemented in practice. In the House of Commons Fox observed dryly that "the sort of titles meant to be given were not named in the bill; he presumed the reason was that they could not be named without creating laughter." Dorchester with all his zeal for the royal prerogative hinted that "the fluctuating state of property in these Provinces would expose all hereditary honours to fall into disregard." In the end legislative councillors were appointed for life only; and "family compacts" and "château cliques" alike came to rely for their influence not upon hereditary honours in the service of the Crown but upon the self-interested control which they were able to exert by a score of subtle devices over the administration of the transient governor.

One result at least emerged from these tendencies towards privilege and vested interests. Instead of a conflict between the colonies and the mother country over the sanctions of imperial authority, colonial government generated a contest between two rival sets of interest within each province. The most discerning of these interests came to see that the pearl of great price—the prize which could be relied upon to add all other things unto itself—was the control not of legislation after the pattern of "Grattan's parliament" in Ireland but of the executive. If the councils could claim this control by virtue of appointment under colonial practice in America for two hundred years, the assemblies could claim it by virtue of representation and historic trends in Great Britain since the Grand Remonstrance. By 1836 these trends were settling into a body of doctrine intelligible to Britons everywhere; and the contest for responsible government was finally won by allies on both sides of the Atlantic.

A second expedient for reinforcing vested interests favourable to the sanctions of the parent state went much farther in practice and jeopardized the political as well as the religious peace of the colonies.

Plans for an established church, like those for a colonial aristocracy, were not new in 1791. It is clear that when "the accustomed Dues and Rights" of the French régime were restored to the Roman Catholic

Church by the *Quebec Act* these were intended to depend upon the favour of the Crown. "All this indulgence," said Wedderburn, was "subject to his Majesty's approbation," in default of which "All tithes are subject to be taken from them." The clergy, including the bishop himself, were to function under "Licence and permission . . . for and during Our Will and Pleasure"; and the parochial clergy were subject to suspension by the council "upon due proof of seditious Attempts to disturb the Peace and Tranquillity of Our Government." The shadow of impending revolution already lay upon the province, and the Act (in the words of Chatham) was "a child of inordinate power." By the *Quebec Act* the Protestant clergy also were to share in "the accustomed Dues and Rights" from the French régime. When the crisis had passed, however, these dues and rights were left by the *Constitutional Act* in the possession of the Roman Catholic Church under French civil law, and support for a Protestant clergy was sought by another expedient which played havoc with the religious and political peace of Upper Canada.

The "clergy reserves" of Upper Canada became the storm centre of privilege until the issue was finally settled in 1854. Sydenham in 1842 referred to it as "the root of all the troubles of the province, the cause of the rebellion—the never-failing watchword at the hustings—the perpetual source of discord, strife, and hatred." Many misconceptions, then and since, attended the inception of the plan and its function. By the *Constitutional Act* (s. xxxvi) reserves of land "equal in Value to the Seventh Part" of all lands granted were to be set aside for the "Support and Maintenance of a Protestant Clergy." The unseemly wrangle to share in this patrimony or to secularize it brought one Protestant denomination after another into the field against the original beneficiaries of the system.

The Church of Scotland as one of the two legally established churches in Great Britain early made good its claim to participate in the endowment. Sydenham succeeded for a time in settling the issue, as he thought, by admitting the Methodists under the responsive leadership of Egerton Ryerson to a share in the Protestant patrimony. Sydenham's settlement, however, was blocked in Great Britain by vested interests of the old order. The obstructionists went farther and fared worse, for when the issue was finally settled in 1854 the major part of the endowment was diverted to secular purposes. As an expedient for reinforcing the paramount authority of the Crown and the British connection the clergy reserves were no more efficacious in the second empire than other religious devices of special privilege had been in the first.

In New Brunswick the claim of the Church of England to function as an "established" church encountered less opposition. Through the Executive Council it long enjoyed undisputed pre-eminence in the religious and educational life of the province. Yet even here the assumption was open to question long before the Judicial Committee of the Privy Council in the leading cases from South Africa (1865) determined once for all that the functions of church establishment in Great Britain did not extend to the colonies. In Nova Scotia where scarcely one-fifth of the population belonged to the Church of England, Brenton Halliburton, afterwards Chief Justice, once expressed the convictions of Anglicans themselves when he reported that "every attempt on the part of the Government to give pre-eminence to the Church creates ten enemies for one friend. . . . People on this side of the water are even more tenacious of religious equality than of political. . . . The generality of Churchmen themselves participate in it." The Assembly rejected "without a dissenting vote" a proposal to commute quit rents for a permanent endowment for the Church of England. The resolutions were "brought in by a Churchman." The bishop himself deprecated as "worse than useless" the use of crown lands in the special interest of his diocese. This freedom from religious strife was not to last in Nova Scotia, but the province escaped at least the short-sighted attempt to use vested interests in religion as an expedient in colonial policy. Dalhousie once forwarded to Bathurst at the Colonial Office a joint address of council and assembly in refreshing contrast to the prevailing temper of religious controversy in the second empire: "The mild and tolerating spirit of the majority" in the Church of England itself could be relied upon to "command the attachment of its Members and the respect even of those who dissent from it. And it can only be injured in the Province of Nova Scotia, by the misguided zeal of its intemperate friends."

TRIAL AND ERROR: ANOTHER CHANCE

The elements of promise and reaction at the narrow beginnings of the second empire in America are curiously reminiscent of the first. In the Canadas as in the Carolinas the enterprise of the frontiersman, the planter and farmer, the fur trader, the lumberman, the merchant, was the best promise for the future. Official policy, as a rule, was short-sighted and applied at short range; and the immediate objective was frequently a short cut which proved to be the longest way home. A few enthusiasts of the second empire like Simcoe and Edward Winslow and R. J. Uniacke developed a sense of direction frustrated though it came to be by the vicissitudes of their day. The outlook called for more courage than enthusiasm. The chronic "American question" had just been settled irremediably wrong with the thirteen colonies. The solution which the remaining provinces came to regard as demonstrably right was still far off, and not a sign of it appeared as yet above the northern horizon. Meanwhile the best that could be hoped for was a third sort of solution which may be credited with showing more empirical wisdom than contemporaries are apt to accord to it—to forgo any solution for the present; *solvere ambulando*; to avoid at all costs a solution irremediably wrong; to lower sights and aim only at the commonplace survival of primitive frontier communities.

In that sense the Peter Ponds, the Alexander Henrys, the Philemon Wrights, the Simon McTavishes, and the Samuel Cunards were the best builders of their day. One looks in vain in their record for the sort of maturity or discernment which illuminated for a moment the generation of Shirley, Halifax, and Franklin. Of all the thirty decades of British colonization in America, before the revolution or after it, this at the beginning of the second empire must have been the most despondent. The revolution was still incomprehensible, and the lessons that were drawn from it were sterile and negative. The most promising elements in the first empire, the vitality and resourcefulness of a maturing society, bursting with youthful vigour and charged (as Franklin said) with the government of itself, had overflowed the normal channels of colonial subordination like the Mississippi in floodtime. The whole empire in America had been submerged. It was too soon to expect the survivors in the northern provinces to reflect upon the illimitable resources of water-power in such a deluge if only it could be harnessed to the mill-wheels of industry or the beneficent uses of commerce. They were concerned rather with its recent ravages in colonial government. They were content to build higher the levees and dam back the flood into safer channels. In the debate on the Canada Bill Fox alone seems to have kept his faith in the trends toward freedom in the old colonies. The lifelong estrangement between Fox and Burke on this occasion was a sign that Britain herself was passing from one eclipse to another—from the gloom of the American Revolution to the alarming portents of the French.

The first experiment in colonial policy after the American Revolution, as we have seen, was the attempt to apply one of the most short-sighted of its lessons to Ireland. No more appropriate prelude could be found to the struggle for self-government in the second empire than the sequel to that ill-fated experiment. The miasma of revolution was still in the air. Many of the Irish Volunteers who had extorted Grattan's "independent parliament" in 1782 had brothers or cousins marching with Washington. Young Robert Stewart—afterwards as Lord Castlereagh the arch-tory of the Irish union and the long struggle with Napoleon—was at this time a whig in the Volunteers and led a company of infantry in a regiment of which his father was colonel. The Parliament which had enacted the "intolerable Acts" of 1774 now renounced altogether its right to legislate for Ireland: endeavouring, as Knox advised for America, to "beget confidence by putting it out of its own power to deceive." It is probable that many a "patriot" in the Continental Congress shared Grattan's delusion after 1782 when he arose, as he thought, to "address a free people."

But the cardinal defect in Ireland as in Canada was not legislative subordination. It would be hard to find a more convincing display of representative but not "responsible" government than the eighteen years of the independent parliament of Ireland. With reagents which had been tried again and again in colonial America, the experiment now went forward in a European laboratory for all men to see. The time had long since passed when Gibbon could boast his ignorance of a "remote and petty province." Irish legislation could no longer be reviewed at Westminster, but the executive was still appointed and directed by the British government. No governor in America ever received more detailed instructions under the sign manual than the Lord-Lieutenant and the Irish Secretary now received in rescripts from Downing Street. It was necessary for this executive, irresponsible to the Irish parliament, to carry out a British policy by means of a sectional legislature of different origin and temper, of which less than half could be said to owe their seats to popular support. Seats, rated at their market value, were quoted on the stock exchange, and government measures had to be carried by systematic political jobbery. "It is anarchy," said Grattan, "and must become slavery." The rebellion of 1798, fomented by the French Revolution, completed the breach between the Irish parliament and the British executive. When Pitt, distracted by the opening struggle with Napoleon, turned to union as "the great necessity," it became necessary to "buy up," as Castlereagh himself put it, "the fee simple of Irish corruption." With the country under martial law and garrisoned by 40,000 troops, a parliament elected three years before with no reference to such an issue was "bought and bullied out of existence." The price included every species of bribery from peerages and legal advancement to less refined promises of places, pensions, and hard cash. It was obvious that the independence of the legislature was no panacea for the woes of Ireland. It was not so obvious, in the midst of the political horrors of 1798 and 1800, how the relations between a colonial legislature and the executive were to be harmonized. At the union the grim problems of Ireland were buried alive or distorted by other issues. It remained for the second empire in America to find a happier solution for the problem of colonial government.

In British North America the second empire began more auspiciously, though it was destined to pass through stage after stage of frustration to the brink of the same disaster. In Lower Canada the French Revolution, instead of turning half-citizens into whole Jacobins, confirmed the historic role of the Roman Catholic Church as a bulwark against revolution whether American or French. British Americans began at least as more than "half-citizens." This was true not only for the pre-revolutionary Nova Scotian and Prince Edward Islander but for the French of Lower Canada and the newcomers in New Brunswick and Upper Canada. The struggle for reform in all the provinces was not uniform in pattern, and the underlying conditions, social and economic, were as varied as the provinces themselves. In Prince Edward Island "the eternal land question" was never far from the surface. In Lower Canada the political conflict was soon charged with racial antipathies. In Upper Canada frontier conditions were complicated by distance and by religious strife of exceptional virulence. In Nova Scotia and New Brunswick a more settled economy was reflected in more "harmony and moderation." But it is surely significant that however diversified the background, all the provinces began the movement for political reform about the same time and found the solution for their varied economic and social ills through the agency of the same political technique. For all of them, it would seem, there was an element of original sin in the old colonial system. The concession of responsible government enabled them all to work out their varied problems in their own way.

Before that solution was reached, however, the reformers of the second empire were almost as desperate as Franklin and James Otis and John Adams in the first. The most impetuous of them yielded to despair and committed their cause to futile rebellions. Francis Hincks was about to organize a group of Upper Canadian reformers for migration to Iowa in the United States when the news of Lord Durham's mission revived their hopes of reform. Robert Baldwin who had failed in London in 1836 to forestall the Mackenzie rising, waited upon Lord Durham with the same plea in Toronto in 1838 and added the solemn note that without responsible government Britain would "continue to retain these Colonies by means of her troops alone." Joseph Howe, who had dissociated his party almost savagely from the Canadian *débâcles* of 1837 as "the maddest rebellions on record," wrote desperately to Charles Buller in 1846 that "if this Whig Government disappoints us, you will have the questions I have touched discussed in a different spirit, ten years hence, by the Enemies of England, not by her friends."

But these desperate men encountered no sinister "design" such as Franklin and Washington discerned in the counsels of the new American Department after 1769. It is doubtful if there was ever a time in the second empire when a measure of mutual confidence was altogether wanting. Matthew Arnold once remarked that "what attaches people to us is the spirit we are of, not the machinery we employ." The dissolution of the first empire, in the opinion of the profoundest statesmen of that day, had become irremediable in the last analysis from the poisoning of all official intercourse by suspicion on the one side and coercion on the other. In the end Knox himself had declared the bankruptcy of official policy: "State chicane or lawyers craft will not do with the Colonies, they have lost all confidence in the integrity of Parliament, and until confidence is restored, treaty is impossible. Parliament must therefore endeavour to beget confidence by putting it out of its own power to deceive."

Official relations in the second empire never reached this sorry pass. Several of the provinces began with mutual confidence already in the ascendant. In Nova Scotia Governor Legge, nephew of Dartmouth himself, had been recalled during the American Revolution at the entreaty of every articulate agency in the province. It was during the stormy months of the Mackenzie and Papineau risings that a delegation from New Brunswick, the third since 1832, was completing with exemplary skill the greatest measure of reform in the British provinces since the American Revolution, the control of crown lands and land revenues by the Assembly. Glenelg added a curiously spontaneous tribute to their candour and "just delicacy." A long series of memoranda and special missions from Nova Scotia—the names of R. J. Uniacke, Charles Fairbanks, George Young, Herbert Huntington, Joseph Howe and many others come to mind—attested the easy access of provincial visitors to the confidence of the Colonial Office.

Other provinces were less fortunate. Cooper's mission on "the eternal land question" of Prince Edward Island found the vested interests of the absentee proprietors too firmly entrenched. Relations with the Canadas, too, tended to follow the pattern of the first empire. The choice of Hume and Roebuck as agents of the two provinces was unfortunate. Their Ishmaelitish temper left the impression in the House of Commons of equally immoderate counsels in the colonies. William Lyon Mackenzie was cordially received by Lord Goderich in 1832, but the torrents of abuse that deluged "Goosie Goderich" from Upper Canada were not calculated to prompt a repetition of the experiment. When Baldwin went to London in 1836 at his own expense in order to forestall if possible the impending insurrection, Glenelg usually the most accessible and kindly of men, hesitated to countenance the Upper Canadian "ultra." Baldwin was constrained to register his protest in the famous memorandum on responsible government which found its way, after a more successful interview with Lord Durham in Upper Canada two years later, into the majestic diction of Durham's *Report.*

For the happier results of the second empire little credit can be given to the "system" which Knox had hoped to devise from the lessons of the revolution. But while the new system was both more primitive and more reactionary than the prevailing trends in the first empire, there was a new season in a new soil, and the harvest was attended by better husbandry on both sides of the Atlantic. Instead of Grenville and Hillsborough and Germain served by the mordant temper of William Knox there was the dour empiricism of the third Earl Grey attended by the gracious spirit of Charles Buller. Instead of Sir Guy Carleton with "a war of this sort constantly in view"[1] there was Sir John Harvey's benign candour in Nova Scotia and Elgin's prophetic sagacity in Canada. The second empire was happy in the ministration not only of better measures but of better men.

[1]"In all my political letters, I had a war of this sort constantly in view . . . and have not the least reason to change my opinion of these matters." Carleton to Germain, Sept. 28, 1776, Q Series, 12, 188.

II

SELF-GOVERNMENT

Chapter Five

BRITISH AND AMERICAN TRADITIONS

PARLIAMENTARY self-government by a process of evolution was the crowning achievement of the second empire. The original thirteen colonies, resisting what they conceived to be a "design," "a regular systematic plan," to overthrow "constitutional rights and liberties," resorted to revolution, broke a train of evolution already a century and a half old in America, and established a congressional system embodied in a written constitution. The hazards of war and of adventitious foreign alliances with traditional enemies were almost as formidable as those which had confronted the Netherlands in their first successful revolt against constituted authority in the sixteenth century. The remaining colonies were content to explore again the traditional method. This protracted the contest for half a century but the method proved in the end not only safer and more peaceful but easier and more successful in appropriating the accruing advantages of parliamentary practice in the parent state.

As this process developed it was found in each particular province that success was conditioned in no small measure by relations with the first empire. Much of the baffling diversity of the second empire is a commentary upon this fact. In Nova Scotia where tradition and association were alike unbroken the transition from governance to self-government was made without a single major conflict between the province and the parent state. The Canadas on the other hand began with a constitution which had already been obsolete for more than a century in America. Constrained to pass through stage after stage of reversal and frustration they survived these vestigial defects from the first empire only to undergo two abortive rebellions which in some respects forced, and in other respects distorted, the solution. Between these extremes the loyalist "royal" province of New Brunswick and the proprietary provinces of Prince Edward Island and Rupert's Land followed, more narrowly, the pattern of their own peculiar interests. It was one of the penalties of this technique that the pace was often set by the most complicated and troublesome of the provinces. Even when the goal was fairly in sight for Nova Scotia, responsible government, as a Colonial Office annotation on one of the Nova Scotia despatches attests, could not be granted piecemeal: "if conceded in any one Colony it must be granted in all." Thus it was more than half a century before the practices were conceded which saved the second empire from the fate of the first.

There were two supreme advantages nevertheless which attended this method. The remaining British provinces, claiming as their birth-right the accruing advantages of British parliamentary procedure in the parent state, were spared not only the bloodshed of revolution but the century of inveterate antipathies which the republics of both American continents have come to associate with their independence. "The fight for responsible government," as it was called, came also at times to smack of the field rather than the forum; but the "fight" was parliamentary. It went on concurrently in half a dozen correlated experiments, each one disposed to appropriate the gains of all the others in the contest. In this process a second advantage appeared scarcely less fortunate than the first. Individual provinces could make contributions out of all proportion to their size or wealth or population. Precedents were claimed where they could be found. In that sense each of the British American provinces had a contribution to make. The supreme advantage of the evolutionary technique was that a single eminently successful experiment in self-government could do more to achieve success for all of them than all their potential re-sources for a military revolution put together. The end was intended to be peaceful and it was sought most effectually by methods truly pacific. As a technique of acquiring political freedom in association with others that were politically free this method of the British Com-monwealth was not without a wider significance. After more than a score of successful experiments all over the world, it may be that in our own day it holds a livelier hope for world peace and freedom than counsels of indiscriminate revolution.

On both sides of the Atlantic this process of evolution towards political freedom was already far advanced when the American Department determined to challenge the prevailing trends of the first empire. On both sides of the Atlantic, too, this promise of success was lost to sight in the bitter traditions of the revolution. On both sides there has been a tendency, as instinctive as it is unhistorical, to regard the American Revolution as inevitable. For British statesmen as well as historians it has become, as we have seen, a "detestable interlude" in their history, sinister and forbidding in every aspect. The prospects of an undivided empire, like the sour grapes in the fable, were placed forever beyond their reach by the bitterest chapter of defeat in their long history. For the United States, on the other hand, the elements of fatalism were suffused by the exultant traditions of the republic. Evidence that the revolution was inevitable has been sought in a wide variety of causes. Economic historians have attributed the revolution to an obsolescent mercantilism, constitutional historians to irreconcilable sovereignties, social historians to inevitable divergencies between a cosmopolitan society and the frontier. Yet far wider divergencies of economic interest, of constitutional antinomy, of social complexity, have obtained all over the world in the second empire without destroying their peaceful evolution into the mutually stimulating associations of the Commonwealth. To a British American the inevitableness of revolution is belied by the results of evolution which have been as nearly inevitable as any process in the long range of British constitutional history can be said to be. No province of the first empire presented divergencies comparable to those of South Africa or of India. With the concession of responsible government a century ago the trends toward national destinies for regional groups of self-governing provinces have become self-evident in every quarter of the world.

To a Canadian, therefore, viewing the loss of the first empire at closer range, the elements of failure are apt to be found in less ponderable factors, not unrelated to prevailing human infirmities of temper and character and insight. With goodwill on both sides—and on both sides goodwill was indispensable—few problems in the second empire proved "inevitably" insoluble. That axiom may stand confirmed not only by the long history of the Canadian, the Australian, the South African, the New Zealand provinces, but by the elements of frustration for so many years in India or Jamaica or Newfoundland. The deterioration in the first empire from the *Stamp Act* to "the intolerable Acts" of 1774 was inevitable only as the Black Death was inevitable—because the knowledge and skill were not forthcoming to forestall it. It was Franklin's opinion that relations at the close of the Seven Years' War were still "the best in the world." The colonies "had not only a respect but an affection for Great Britain, for its laws, its customs and manners and even a fondness for its fashions that greatly increased the commerce." In this estimate, as in the traditional estimate to the contrary, there may have been a measure of wishful thinking, but recent scholarship in the United States would seem to concede unheralded elements of promise in the first empire had mutual confidence not been recklessly poisoned by foolhardy "design" on the one side and in-eradicable suspicion on the other.

It is true that the empirical methods devised by Virginia or Massachusetts for the control of the executive in 1748 were not those of Nova Scotia after responsible government in 1848. Nor had the practices of party government in Great Britain in 1770 settled into the body of political doctrine recognized by the party which conceded responsible government in the despatch of November 3, 1846. The fact remains that in long-range perspective—from the Grand Remonstrance of 1641 to Peel's resignation in 1846, or from the primitive House of Burgesses in Virginia in 1624 to the first responsible government overseas in Nova Scotia in 1848—the parliamentary sanctions of 1763 on both sides of the Atlantic were worthy of a better use. The American colonies rebelled, Fox afterwards maintained, "because they did not think themselves sufficiently free"; it is equally true that there were sounder elements in British politics than those so infamously misinterpreted by William Knox in 1768.[1] In that sense the American Revolution was almost as epochal for Britain as for America. Had the American Department succeeded in America the King might have succeeded in Britain. "Sooner or later," said Burke, "it will come home to England." In America, however, no governor could hope for long to "play the despot among the ruins of parliamentary parties." By the close of the first empire the representative elements in the provinces had got their tentacles so effectively about the executive functions of the government that more than one harassed governor began to "suspect they will not mend much." William Knox could deride "the absurdity of their idea of a *polypus* government, where a head sprouts out of every joint," but every province ("except Quebec," he added) shared in these trends, and "a real and pure democracy must soon be the true description of their Constitutions."

II

By virtue of the tactics employed in the winning of responsible government, all the remaining provinces of the second empire were enabled to play a part. Two of them, however, made distinctive and conclusive contributions. Nova Scotia was the first to win the concession from the Colonial Office, and it had been advocated there, as Murdock pointed out to Sydenham in 1840, not only "before the question was mooted in Upper or Lower Canada" but in a spirit of "exemplary forbearance and moderation." The Reform party of Nova

[1]See above, p. 53.

Scotia was the most disciplined and responsive, their parliamentary tactics were the most skilful, their leaders the most sagacious and discerning, and the relations of those leaders with their allies in Great Britain the most intimate and harmonious. Nowhere was this confidential intercourse more fruitful. The Howe-Buller correspondence reveals this intercourse at its best. If Howe was the only Canadian behind the scenes when the vital decision to concede responsible government was finally reached, he owed this distinction to his friend Charles Buller, the most gracious spirit surely to be found on either side of the Atlantic for such a role. Making broad his phylacteries, Howe was wont to boast that the day was won in Nova Scotia without bloodshed, without a blow, without the breaking of a pane of glass. Not without self-righteousness he aspired to make his native province "a 'Normal School' for the rest of the Colonies" in the attainment of self-government after British parliamentary models.

In the united province of Canada, on the other hand, the issue was by far the most critical and the most decisive. Had it failed there the failure might have been fatal. In both the constituent provinces of Upper and Lower Canada before the union desperate reformers had resorted to violence and bloodshed. In both, a gloomy sense of frustration, the gravest perhaps since the American Revolution, had settled upon the cause of political reform. The turmoil in the Canadas left little room for self-righteousness. But whatever the Mackenzie and Papineau risings did or did not do, they forced the issues of colonial government upon the best attention of government on both sides of the Atlantic. The colonial secretaries during these eventful years were among the best minds in Great Britain. Three of them— Lord John Russell, Lord Stanley (afterwards Earl of Derby), and Gladstone—eventually became prime ministers. A long succession of the ablest governors who ever left Great Britain on such a mission came to Canada during the decade and a half after the Canadian rebellions. For four of them—Durham, Sydenham, Bagot, and Sir Charles Metcalfe—that mission may be said to have cost their lives. The bitter price paid also by the "turbulent agitators" was equally distinctive of the Canadian scene. These too perhaps could forgiveness give and take at the hands of those in the other provinces who entered so complacently into their patrimony.

Although the goal was reached first by Nova Scotia and the united province of Canada, the earlier stages of the conflict owed much to the other provinces and to Upper and Lower Canada before the union. In all the provinces the parliamentary practices of the parent state supplied the readiest precedents for their own evolution. In some cases there were local inhibitions which impeded them in the race for reform and effectually barred them from the laurels. Their progress in almost every case reflected very curiously the nature of their relations with the first empire. This was particularly true of Nova Scotia where British parliamentary traditions remained unbroken and of Lower Canada where they had yet to begin.

To the pre-revolutionary New Englander of Nova Scotia some of the precedents of Virginia and New York and New Hampshire were as familiar as his own. He had invoked them with effect at the first session of the first Assembly, and his Yankee skill in parliamentary procedure continued without interruption. The loyalist migrations into New Brunswick and Upper Canada on the other hand had brought still older traditions from the first empire. The two provinces were the newest in British America but their inhabitants, in many cases, represented four or five generations of settled American life. Embittered by exile and "abhorrers of Republicanism," they resumed nevertheless in their new environment, as a matter of course, the familiar functions of assemblies and grand juries after a century and a half of representative government in America. To expect these veterans of American life to eschew assemblies, as Governor Haldimand expected, simply because they had suffered at the hands of assemblymen in the old colonies, was characteristic of the wishful thinking in high places. In both the new loyalist provinces they took an assembly as their birthright. To those of Upper Canada the *Quebec Act* was as intolerable an anachronism as to any "patriot" of the revolution. In New Brunswick they managed, even in the Governor's absence for fourteen years, to govern themselves with exemplary tranquillity and to "get on just as well without a governor as with one."

In Nova Scotia and Upper Canada, however, there was a distinction between the loyalist tradition and that of their "American" compatriots both before and after the revolution. In Nova Scotia the venerable pre-revolutionary American tradition was the older. It survived the revolution and continued unbroken in many curious ways until "the American question" was fairly settled by responsible government. Though the Yankee officials of Nova Scotia during the revolution, as Edward Winslow afterwards reported from Halifax, had approved in general "the doctrines and principles" of the old colonies, and were "finally persuaded of the justice of their cause," they had dreaded a separation from Great Britain as "the greatest political evil which can befall us or our posterity." In that spirit an accommodation with their loyalist compatriots within the peninsula of Nova Scotia, at any rate, was easily effected, though their militant loyalist neighbours in New Brunswick were less conciliatory. Loyalist regiments of the revolution were in no mood for compromise. "Irritable [as Edward Winslow described them] from a series of mortifications—scarcely cooled from the ardor of resentment—jealous to an extreme, some of 'em illiberally so," a few of them hoped to see the Nova Scotian Council and Assembly "thoroughly purged and the outcasts . . . succeeded by honest loyalists." These antipathies survived the division of the old province in 1784. As late as 1836 the New Brunswick Assembly, having secured an executive council to command their "entire confidence" for the administration of crown lands, went out of its way to "repudiate the claims set up by another Colony" for a responsible government "at all times." Ten years later the foremost of the New Brunswick re-formers—Charles Fisher, himself the son of a loyalist—still deplored to Howe that his native province was "*too loyal* and given over to their idol of £.s.d." Meanwhile many of the old pre-revolutionary reformers of Nova Scotia like the Haliburtons and the Uniackes had become the tories of the second empire, while the leadership in "the fight for re-sponsible government" passed to the son of a Massachusetts loyalist. The fusion of the two traditions was aptly consummated in the first responsible government overseas in 1848. The first prime minister was James Boyle Uniacke, son of the old "Cumberland rebel" of the revolution, and the provincial secretary was Joseph Howe.

III

In the evolution of self-government, normal relations with the first empire may be said to provide the surest index to success or frustration in the second. Nowhere were these relations more tragically compli-cated than in the tangled story of the Canadas. Two violent reversals of policy, in 1774 and 1791, attended in both cases by unhistorical traditions based upon vested interests, left a legacy of frustration which has never to this day been liquidated. It was William Knox's creed, cherished to the bitter end, that "the old mode of treating our dependencies must be exploded and a new system formed." With the triumph of the revolution destiny itself took a hand in the affairs of the old province of Quebec. Of that vast feudal province stretching to the Ohio, the Mississippi, and the territories of the Hudson's Bay Company, more than a third, comprising the present states of Ohio, Iowa, Indiana, Illinois, and Michigan, was lost to the new republic. The rest was divided at the Ottawa River, and for both provinces the attempt was made to restore the familiar pattern of a royal province. Unfortunately this familiar pattern had now been permanently impaired, since the only method known to the constitution for the reversal of a British statute was another statute. But the reversal, for the second time, of the policy with regard to settlement in Quebec destroyed the *Quebec Act* in its most vulnerable feature—its "avowed purpose of excluding all further settlement therein." To the chagrin of seigneur and churchman alike this policy was now reversed not only by the division of what was left of the old province in order to provide for the loyalist migrations, but by the much larger movement of population into the western reaches of the new province from the United States after the revolution.

Many of the newcomers, in all probability, had come, as Simcoe believed, from reserves of loyalism still unassimilated in the early growth of the republic; but the discrimination between loyalist and "late loyalist" in Upper Canada soon developed deadly antipathies in the charged atmosphere of the War of 1812. In Bathurst's land regulations after the war an attempt was made for the second time to dam back the teeming population from the south. Succeeding generations of loyalists tended to look backward with repugnance to the pit whence they were digged, and forward with foreboding to the rise of familiar trends from the old empire in the new soil. By the time of the first reform Assembly of 1828 the familiar contest against privilege and vested interests in the first empire was already countered by indiscriminate charges of "treason and republicanism," frequently laid by those who had the least claim to the loyalist tradition. The play upon this tradition in the elections of 1836 and 1844 (to cite only two examples) generated the bitterest antipathies perhaps to be found in the turbulent politics of that province. Hincks's scathing comment upon the election returns of 1844 was the savage jibe that the province deserved a tory government. Only with the achievement of responsible government four years later did these traditional antipathies yield at last to other tensions of the new order.

In Lower Canada where every normal association with the healthy traditions of the first empire had been deliberately "revoked, annulled, and made void" by the *Quebec Act*, the perversities of that fatal policy are to be seen at their worst. It will be unnecessary to review again the vain attempt of the Board of Trade to establish for French Canada the "privileges which exist in the principles of a British Constitution": to "ensure their affection, and fix their attachment to the British Government," and to safeguard "not only the security of this Colony, but with it, that of all His Majesty's Dominions in America." Quebec, in the policy of the American Department, was finally cast for a different role: "Without any of those pompous ideas of popular government, which our countrymen are elated with." "The old mode of treating our dependencies [as Knox insisted] must be exploded and a new system formed." For twenty-eight years after the "cession" in 1763 the "new subjects" in Quebec remained in ignorance of the "privileges which exist in the principles of a British Constitution."

For Lower Canada therefore representative institutions appeared in 1791 almost as a new creation, without those vital traditions which British subjects had venerated for centuries in both Britain and America. The interval between 1769 and 1791 had been filled with bewildering vicissitudes most of which complicated the concession at every point. The American Revolution was now succeeded by the French. The concession which had been conceived in a spirit of unprecedented magnanimity and toleration in 1765 and 1769 was made ungraciously in 1791 and was received without gratitude. The seigneurs and the church, clinging legitimately to the implications of the *Quebec Act*, added their protests, as we have seen, to those of William Knox. "You do not know my Countrymen," wrote Bishop Denaut. "They are not at all prepared for the Constitution you wish to give them; once let the rein loose and be assured they will never know when to stop."

With this background, or lack of background, the smooth functioning of representative institutions in Lower Canada would have been a miracle. As representation in the Assembly passed to the notary and the doctor rather than to the seigneur, the concentration of privilege in the Executive Council combined all the qualities likely to antagonize a primitive and sensitive people. Exploring for the first time the novel technique entrusted to them in 1791, the rapidly predominant French element in the Assembly quickly discovered the use to which it could be put in thwarting the acquisitive and arrogant temper of the *château clique*. Among more than a score of provinces in the old colonial system in both the first empire and the second, Lower Canada was distinguished by intractable controversies. The contest over supply was more primitive in Lower Canada in 1820 than it had been in New Jersey in 1720. Half the provincial revenues were still raised from the *Quebec Revenue Act* of 1774—the financial counterpart of the *Quebec Act*—and the casual and territorial revenues of the crown. The defalcation of the receiver-general to the amount of £96,000 added fuel to the flames. The best of intentions were often distorted by these perversities. Dalhousie, whose administration in Nova Scotia was as beneficent and unassuming as that of a kindly laird on his native heath, found himself submerged in Lower Canada in insoluble problems of race. He is remembered in Nova Scotia as the patron of agriculture and of letters, the correspondent of Agricola, the real founder of a distinguished university. In Lower Canada he lavished no less ingenuous an interest upon the economic and cultural life of the province but he is associated with Craig and other *bêtes noires* in the nationalistic traditions of French Canada.

In such an atmosphere the Assembly sought not to control but to impeach the executive councillors. With "the power of the purse" virtually in the hands of the Crown, the Assembly cut off their own supplies in order to demonstrate their implacable opposition. Without the long traditions of shrewd practice in the first empire towards the control of the executive, the French mind, logical and impatient of indirection, had little incentive until the day of La Fontaine and Morin and Cartier to trust the more devious accommodations of the parliamentary technique which resulted at last in responsible government. Papineau led his assault upon the *château clique* from the Speaker's chair. When Mondelet in the Assembly accepted a seat in the Executive Council—a procedure fraught with the greatest promise in the shrewd tactics of Fairbanks, Uniacke, and Howe in Nova Scotia—he was driven altogether from the Assembly by a single word of devastating effect in the reform movement of Lower Canada: "vendu." He had sold out to the enemy.

As Papineau moved farther and farther towards republican models, an elective legislative council and an elective governor, the possibilities of accommodation or compromise with his enemies became increasingly remote. He inspired with his zeal half a dozen young French Canadians who afterwards left their mark upon the province and upon Canada, but the method of their achievement was not that of Joseph Papineau. After the rebellion when Papineau returned from his exile with ideas confirmed by association with French republicanism, he began the old routine of uncompromising obstruction, and threw all the weight of his invective against the technique which La Fontaine and his faithful followers had perfected in the meantime with Hincks and Baldwin and the other English-speaking reformers of the united province of Canada. Responsible government, Papineau still maintained, was *tromperie*, "conceived by statesmen of a narrow and malevolent genius." The debt of French Canada, at this nadir of its fortunes, to British parliamentary procedure was subsequently to be vindicated by an unbroken line of French-Canadian statesmen of all

parties from La Fontaine and Cartier to Laurier and Lapointe and
St. Laurent. But theirs was the method which the early years of uncompromising conflict had taught Papineau to distrust. The seed had
fallen upon stony ground and among thorns. The mastery of the older
parliamentary tradition was thus a belated and bitter experience for
French Canada. It is possible that a happier blend of co-operation and
of compromise might have attended the attempt of the old Board of
Trade in 1765 and 1769 to induct Quebec generously and graciously
into British institutions during the closing years of the first empire. The
vicissitudes of reversal and frustration from the *Quebec Act* to the
suspension of the constitution in 1838 are without a parallel in British
America. The old province of Quebec was scarcely equipped to lead
the way towards the solution of self-government in the second empire.

IV

In Prince Edward Island the beginnings of self-government were
equally remote from the main currents of British parliamentary practice. Like Maryland during the first empire, the province had never
escaped from the blight of proprietary ownership. The thirty-one "lots"
of the Island had been drawn, literally, from a hat in a single hour by
absentee proprietors. "The trail of absentee landlordism" is to be
found at every turn. Between the proprietors and the "escheaters" every
government official had to run the gauntlet until Governor Smith
(1813–24) could boast he was ready to take on "the whole round of
devils" in the interests of "the sanctity of property."

The first Assembly of Prince Edward Island was elected from the
province at large; and the first impulse of Lord Sydney at the close of
the American Revolution was to reduce the Island to the status of
Quebec and Cape Breton by dispensing with an assembly altogether.
For Prince Edward Island as for Quebec, other counsels prevailed
in the spirit of the loyalist experiments of New Brunswick and Upper
Canada. Between "the eternal land question" and the meagre resources
of the province—the whole revenue appropriated by the Assembly in
1828 was less than £2,500—the local feuds of Prince Edward Island
were notoriously bitter in British North America. The Governor of
Nova Scotia feared their contagious influence "both in this province
and in New Brunswick." In local experience as well as in association
the province remained isolated from healthier traditions in the second
empire. A few promising ventures like that of Lord Selkirk—who had
bought out some of the absentee proprietors and supervised in person
the most distinctive colonizing enterprise in the province—helped to

redeem even "the eternal land question" from charges of selfishness and neglect; but as late as 1839 Durham could charge "a handful of distant proprietors" with stifling the colony "in the very cradle of its existence." While Simonds and Crane and Chandler from the adjoining province of New Brunswick were moving the Colonial Office with ingratiating tact and success to concede the greatest measure of reform up to that time in the second empire—the control of the land revenues and administration by the Assembly—the feud between proprietors and "escheaters" in Prince Edward Island poisoned the relations with the Colonial Office at their source. Cooper, the Speaker of the Assembly, sought audience in vain from Lord John Russell in 1839. From 1852 to 1875 the land question monopolized 360 days of discussion in the Legislature "to the exclusion of all sound politics." An imperial commission including Joseph Howe of Nova Scotia pointed the way to the final solution of 1875, but they reported in 1862 that "the amount of money and time wasted in public controversy no man can estimate." It was "Ireland on a small scale"; and the controversy was "unexampled, perhaps, for length and virulence, in the history of colonization." The land question complicated every move towards both maritime union and confederation until 1873 when Prince Edward Island at last joined the Canadian federation. The land clauses in the terms of union functioned on into the twentieth century before the problem was finally disposed of by enforced purchase and sale to resident settlers.

While the whole struggle for self-government was vitiated by these chronic asperities, it was stimulated by them too. This smallest of the British North American provinces narrowly missed the distinction of evolving for the first time the technique which the second empire in America came to venerate under the name of responsible government. The feud between Lieutenant-Governor Huntley and a few of his councillors in 1846 soon followed the pattern of "the fight for responsible government" in Nova Scotia and in Canada, and Huntley deserves the distinction of pledging his "best support" to a resolution of the Assembly (March 18, 1847) that the Executive Council "ought to resign" when it ceased to "retain confidence of the majority." The fearless leadership of Coles and Warburton and Whelan in the Assembly was so ably seconded by Huntley in his despatches to the Colonial Office that responsible government seemed fairly within their grasp nearly a year before its final achievement in Canada.

The chronic infirmities of Prince Edward Island, however, impaired the cause and deferred the victory. Grey, whose career in the

Colonial Office was marked by more than one gesture of concern for vested interests, was unwilling to throw the feud between the "escheaters" and the proprietors into the orbit of responsible government. He referred the issue to Elgin in Canada who began to suspect that Huntley was more anxious to dispose of Pope and Haviland, two of his troublesome executive councillors, than he was to remedy an obsolete colonial system. It was not until 1851 that Coles, acting squarely, in Grey's historic phrase, "on the faith of the Crown," was called upon as prime minister to form the first responsible government in Prince Edward Island.

V

New Brunswick, too, despite the most successful and harmonious demonstration of the old colonial system to be found in the second empire, played a subordinate and belated part in the achievement of responsible government. The "perfect tranquillity" which Sydenham found there in 1840 was in keeping with a long and unbroken tradition. The pre-revolutionary New Englanders on the Saint John River and in the Cumberland district were so completely submerged by the loyalists under whose auspices the province was founded in 1784 that the control of the administration was never seriously in dispute between them. Above all other provinces of British America, New Brunswick reflected the conservative elements of the first empire. The personnel of the executive and legislative councils might almost have been transplanted from New Jersey or Massachusetts. The selection of Fredericton as the capital of the province removed this official circle from the commercial turmoil of Saint John or the Miramichi. Sir Howard Douglas tried in vain to include "the commercial interests" of the province in the Executive Council: there was "no precedent for such a procedure." In an atmosphere of affluence and staid respectability official life moved placidly forward in a constituency that could be relied upon to be "abhorrers of Republicanism." For more than a generation, as we have seen, Lieutenant-Governor Thomas Carleton, younger brother of Lord Dorchester, floated serenely upon the current of provincial administration. His absence for fourteen years made little difference to the closely knit circle which dominated policy, managed appointments, and contrived to build up in Fredericton a cultural circle of considerable promise. When an arch-tory like Ward Chipman, as we have seen, could boast complacently that "we are really a self-governing people" it would seem that self-government in New Brunswick had not far to go.

The oldest, with one exception, of British American universities—King's College, afterwards the University of New Brunswick—reflected here the provincial pretensions of its namesake in more than one of the royal provinces of the first empire. Cultural conservatism ran to seed until Sir Edmund Head appointed a commission, including Egerton Ryerson from Canada and William Dawson from Nova Scotia, to modernize the college in 1851. Official life was equally complacent. The Provincial Secretary, Jonathan Odell, had been secretary to Sir Guy Carleton. He and his son William after him held office for nearly sixty years. Saint John, incorporated in 1785 with functions modelled upon those of London, had but two mayors in the span of thirty years. The first three attorneys-general of the province held office for sixty-three years, the first lieutenant-governor for thirty-two, the first solicitor-general for twenty-five. The members of the Council, wrote Dr. Raymond, "grew old together."

This serenity in official circles was not always reflected in the ward politics of Saint John or for that matter in the deliberations of the Assembly. Commercial enterprise was much more widely diversified than in the rest of British North America, and the interests of the lumberman, the ship-builder, the affluent farmer, and the merchant were all represented, as an envious tory once reflected in the adjoining province of Nova Scotia, by "men of considerable and some of them of large property." In this setting the political issues that arose in New Brunswick were so closely geared to local self-interest that they seldom impinged upon colonial policy. It was Charles Fisher[1] whose constituency was the hotbed of loyalist officialdom in York County, who once deplored to his fellow-reformer Joseph Howe in Nova Scotia that his associates in New Brunswick were much "*too loyal* and given over to their idol of £.s.d." Fisher himself on at least one occasion was known to bow down to the same idol.

This was the temper and these were the dominant motives behind the first considerable measure of reform in the British provinces. The lucrative masting and timber trade yielded "casual and territorial revenue" so buoyant that an accrued surplus of £150,000 was soon in the hands of the Crown. The Assembly's claim to control this windfall drew a wide measure of support from the fact that Baillie, the Commissioner of Crown Lands, had been one of Bathurst's appointees, and was therefore a "stranger, i.e. not the descendant of a loyalist." This, added the Governor, was "sufficient *of itself* to create ill-will." Stumpage dues and timber limits were also at stake. It was found that

[1]See above, p. 103.

the Commissioner's salary and fees of £2,600 per year were nearly half the cost of administration, and the cost of administration was nearly half the net revenue. By 1833 both the Governor and the Commissioner were charging "self-interest and mischievous demagogues" with a "love of innovation which . . . would speedily lay the respectability and prosperity of the Province prostrate at its feet."

The tactics adopted by the Assembly in their approach to the Colonial Office were so successful that the New Brunswick technique became a model for the Maritime Provinces. After months of committee work behind closed doors two assemblymen, Simonds and Chandler, were entrusted with a brief for the Colonial Secretary. Lieutenant-Governor Sir Archibald Campbell, referring them to Lord Goderich's "well known accessibility"—the tories of Upper Canada had just deluged "Goosie Goderich" with abuse for granting an interview to William Lyon Mackenzie in 1832—refused them letters of introduction, and they found their antagonist, Commissioner Baillie himself, already upon the scene armed with Sir Archibald's "unreserved confidence." The contrast between the studied courtesy and moderation of the assemblymen and the stubborn obstructiveness of Sir Archibald himself was not lost upon the Colonial Office. When Stanley agreed to the Assembly's terms for a fixed civil list in return for the control of land revenues, Sir Archibald, almost inarticulate with vexation, asked to be transferred to another government, while the Commissioner clung grimly to his post and succeeded at last in riding out the storm. A second delegation, in 1836, won from Glenelg a tribute to their "most liberal and handsome manner" and to their "just delicacy" in waiving their demand for a "peremptory rule" that the Assembly should control the administration of the crown lands as well as the revenues from them. Here was responsible government itself at stake in characteristic New Brunswick fashion, with the emphasis not upon abstract theory but upon empirical practice. With an eye upon this goodly mess of pottage they were content to leave to others the winning of their birthright.

When Sir Archibald Campbell resigned in high dudgeon, his successor, Sir John Harvey, changed the personnel of the Executive Council to command the "entire confidence" of the Assembly. This historic phrase with the gesture behind it seemed on the surface to carry the concession of responsible government. And so, for that particular occasion, it did. When delegates from New Brunswick, elated by their sudden opulence and prospects, described to Durham in Quebec in 1838 the success of the New Brunswick reforms, Durham

himself seems to have accepted the reorganization of the Executive
Council as the vindication of the principle which his *Report* was soon
to advocate for all the provinces: "the constitutional principle had
been, in fact, fully carried into effect in this province; the Government
had been taken out of the hands of those who could not attain the
assent of a majority in the Assembly, and placed in the hands of those
who possessed its confidence." But this exuberant opinion of 1839 was
scarcely warranted by the facts of 1836 in New Brunswick. With
rebellions brewing in the Canadas and with growing criticism of his
policy behind him not only in both Houses of Parliament but in the
cabinet itself, Glenelg had still maintained an "unfettered" prerogative for the Crown. In response the Assembly of New Brunswick had
obligingly dissociated itself from "the claims set up by another Colony"
(Nova Scotia) for an executive council subject "at all times" to the
confidence of the House. Having won a responsible government in
practice for their immediate purposes—including the expenditure of
that accrued surplus of £150,000 from the land revenues—they proceeded to disavow responsible government "at all times" as a basic
principle of colonial government. It was left to other provinces, with
less lucrative reasons for renunciation, to continue the fight for those
vital principles "until they should prevail."

Though the first in harmony and in freedom from costly controversy,
New Brunswick was the last of the British American provinces to put
responsible government into normal practice in the form of a homogeneous executive council responsible to a dominant "party" in the
Assembly. In 1843 Wilmot the reform leader took office in the Council
single-handed in a coalition with seven tories, and the Executive
Council passed a gratuitous address of loyalty in support of Metcalfe's
"noble stand" in resisting the "extravagant demands" of his Executive
Council for the control of patronage in the united province of Canada.
When Lieutenant-Governor Colebrooke proceeded to appoint his own
son-in-law as provincial secretary in New Brunswick the shoe was on
the other foot. Wilmot and four of his tory colleagues resigned and
carried a vote of protest, 24 to 4, in the Assembly. Stanley himself at
the Colonial Office cancelled the appointment. Loyalty and patronage
in New Brunswick, it would seem, were not unrelated to loaves and
fishes. As late as 1850 Wilmot deplored to Howe the amorphous state
of New Brunswick politics: "You say you do not understand our
political parties. I am not surprised at this when I cannot understand
them myself—Our People are running wild." Two years later Sir
Edmund Head, himself the grandson of a loyalist, avowed the same

system as "that pursued in Nova Scotia or Canada" but was still presiding over a coalition in the Executive Council. The individual members of the Assembly ("given over to their idol of £.s.d.") were still unwilling to forego the old colonial practice of introducing money bills in their own interest from any quarter of the House. It required more discipline than this to work the conventions of parliamentary government and surrender the introduction of money bills to a depart-mentalized and responsible executive council. It was not until 1854 that the reformers of New Brunswick, reaping where they had not strawed, closed their ranks and exacted an approach to the "party government" which the reformers of the other provinces were by this time taking for granted.

Chapter Six

BACKGROUNDS IN NOVA SCOTIA
AND "CANADA"

THE theme of parliamentary self-government in the British provinces may be simplified by citing at the outset two axioms which became self-evident only after the contest was over—axioms which confirmed the priority already enjoyed by Nova Scotia and "Canada" in the contest by virtue of their traditions from the first empire.

The first is to be found in the conviction, subsequently vindicated by the event, that by seeking first the control of the Executive Council—holding it "responsible" to the Assembly and responsive to their "confidence"—all other things could be added unto them. In that sense, as we have seen,[1] the watershed between revolution and responsible government, between the independence of a republic and the associations of the Commonwealth, was to be found within the ranks of the reformers themselves. The indiscriminate accumulation of "grievances" in Papineau's ninety-two resolutions and even in Mackenzie's *Seventh Report* invited collision and conflict at every point. With "grievances here and grievances there," as Sir Francis Head jeered, the policy of sheer obstruction, increasingly offensive and defiant, carried both movements towards insurrection and bloodshed. It was the resolute purpose of the Howe-Baldwin school to discard "grievance-mongering" as worse than useless and to concentrate upon the one sovereign device, the more devious but dynamic little "trick" of responsible government. This procedure called for mutual confidence and accommodation rather than defiance and frontal assault. Instead of separation in mortal enmity it sought association, with goodwill in the ascendant. The dynamic little trick itself, as Howe exclaimed, was "perfectly *simple* and eminently *British*." It would enable every prov-

[1]See above, p. 23.

ince to redress its own grievances, each province in its own way, each grievance in the order of its importance. With this "truly British privilege" grievances would soon "become a scarce article in the English market." It would be hard to find a more appropriate signpost to the modern Commonwealth than the desperate appeal which Robert Baldwin made to Lord Durham:

It is in vain to direct . . . attention to this or that grievance. . . . Many that have been harped upon in the political heat of the day as evils of appalling magnitude are no grievances at all and many others would cease to be such under the system proposed. . . . You must give those in whom the people have confidence an interest in preserving the *system* of your Government, and maintaining the connection with the Mother Country, and then you will hear no grievances because real ones will be redressed, imaginery ones will be forgotten.

The second axiom too became self-evident only after the fact, and it was mastered only by painstaking and sometimes costly discipline: responsible government was won at last by disciplined political parties. Without disparaging the advocacy of Baldwin and Fairbanks, Durham and Howe and Buller and many others, the fact emerges that one coercive factor carried conviction at last to every critic. There was no peaceful alternative. A disciplined majority in the Assembly, by the exercise of the same attributes by which the parliamentary system functions best at all times, could bring to naught every peaceful device that could be brought to bear against them. It was this lesson— learnt largely from the Falkland experiment in Nova Scotia and the Metcalfe crisis in Canada—which enabled Lord Grey to concede responsible government at last with the acquiescence of Lord John Russell himself in 1848.

As early as 1830 both these axioms had been mastered by two or three discerning men in the British provinces, and at least one of them had penetrated to the Colonial Office with the prophetic claim that the House of Representatives in Nova Scotia ought to possess powers over the executive "similar to those exercised by the House of Commons. They have repeatedly claimed these as their rights and *will* exercise them." By 1840 the parliamentary leaders in both provinces—Huntington, Howe, and Uniacke, Baldwin, Hincks, and La Fontaine—had seized upon this conviction with unshakable tenacity. Baldwin assured Lord Durham that the only alternative was to hold the province "by troops alone"; Grey conceded that no sane British statesman could contemplate such an alternative "in the present state" of political thought in Great Britain. By 1852 Stanley himself had acquiesced in responsible government, and the most stubborn tories of two provinces had begun to practise it. Even Sydenham in 1842 must have succumbed to it had he lived. Bagot and Sir John Harvey who capitulated to it with goodwill, Sir Edmund Head, with shrewd hard Peelite empiricism, Sir Allan MacNab and J. W. Johnston, with calculated advantage to their own parties, all reached the same conviction with varying degrees of insight or resignation. Elgin stated frankly that responsible government was simply "party government" in its most familiar form: by parties it was won and by parties would it continue to function. "The system now established in Canada," added Grey, "is that of Party Government, that is to say government by means of parties." It will suffice here to repeat Howe's claim, advanced all too confidently as early as 1839, that this British practice was the birthright of the British provinces, and that the old colonial system was "now become contemptible in the eyes of every man of common understanding, who has no interest in keeping it up." Within a decade and a half this doctrine had become so firmly established that no administrator in the face of a disciplined parliamentary majority ventured to dispute it.

With these axioms by way of preface the mutual relations between "Canadian" and Nova Scotian reformers are seen to have an importance far beyond the range of official intercourse. The antipathies between the two provinces at various stages of the conflict only sanctioned the ground which they shared in common—the functioning of disciplined political parties in order to control the executive. Mutual co-operation, often in spite of themselves, is traceable in curious counterpoint between the reformers in both provinces even when the two movements appeared hopelessly at cross purposes. Here as in the first empire the springs of human conduct are seldom far removed from the infirmities as well as the virtues of human nature. Without elaborating this theme at this stage the cross currents of "Canadian" and Nova Scotian politics may be explored in advance for evidence of their mutual influence.

The only defender of Papineau in the Nova Scotian press was Jotham Blanchard in the Pictou *Colonial Patriot*. Howe rejected the overtures of Henry S. Chapman, the Lower Canadian delegate to London in 1835, to make common cause with Papineau's "uncompromising and offensive" temper, and his refusal was published broadcast in the *Novascotian* two years later in order to salvage the cause of reform in Nova Scotia from the *débâcle* of the Papineau rising. It was Howe's conviction, based largely upon the confidential interview with Glenelg himself in 1838, that responsible government was feasible in Nova Scotia as early as 1840 had it not been for the *impasse* in the Canadas, and it was Sydenham's adroit appeal to strengthen his hands there which lured Howe into the ill-fated coalition of 1840. At the Metcalfe crisis in "Canada" in 1843 Howe in a moment of exasperation at the rash tactics of the reformers dropped the word "bungled," and not even his letter of explanation to Hincks in the Montreal *Pilot* could make amends to the Canadian "ultras." "I have not more confidence in him," wrote La Fontaine, "for all that."

Many of these instinctive antipathies between the Canadian and Nova Scotian reformers grew rather than diminished as time went on. Howe's correspondence with Adam Fergusson is abruptly suspended at the Metcalfe crisis. A visit to Kingston in 1841 must have brought a meeting with Canadian reformers, but Howe was then deep in Sydenham's confidence and the absence of comment on either side is easily understood. Isaac Buchanan once tried to induce Howe to launch into Canadian journalism by moving to Montreal. He replied truly that he "would not be sufficiently ultra" for Canadian politics. With Egerton Ryerson Howe's relations were more cordial at this time. He once referred to Ryerson as "a man after my own heart," but Ryerson's pointed reference to Howe during the Metcalfe crisis as "the father of Responsible Government in British North America" was not calculated to soothe Canadian sensibilities. Later on in 1849 Howe emptied the vials of his wrath in the other direction upon Moffatt and the tories of the Montreal riots. There can be no doubt that these early antipathies coloured his whole outlook towards Confederation. His correspondence with John Kent of Newfoundland who had caught the "Promethean fire . . . from Nova Scotia" was full of frank and mutual counsels. From Charles Fisher and L. A. Wilmot of New Brunswick came many a neat turn of political finesse. But in the Baldwin Papers and the La Fontaine Papers on the one side and the voluminous Howe Papers on the other not half a dozen letters are to be found in exchange between them. Even the private letters between Howe and Hincks were strained and unresponsive. In the newspapers, comment on both sides is sometimes very unreserved, but as a rule sympathetic and constructive. Indirectly, friends common to both in Great Britain—Charles Buller in particular—left an abiding influence upon the discipline of political parties in both provinces.

II

It is curious, nevertheless, how close a parallel is to be found in temper and political principles between Baldwin, La Fontaine, and Hincks in Canada and the Nova Scotian triumvirate Huntington, Uniacke, and Howe.

Baldwin in the one case and Huntington in the other were the men whose unwavering consistency will stand the closest scrutiny. From the Hume resolution and Glenelg memorandum of 1836 to the last interview with Elgin, Baldwin was the Robespierre of responsible government, the "sea-green incorruptible" whose every political act was oriented to one inflexible principle. Huntington, too, from the Glenelg reforms to the final achievement of responsible government held inflexibly, as he wrote, "to the good old cause." He saw from the first the futility of coalitions. The first of the reformers to enter the Executive Council, he seized the first opportunity of resigning; and he rejected, no fewer than six times, the adroitest inducements of Howe and Sydenham and Falkland and Sir John Harvey to take office, unless the principles of responsible government were unreservedly conceded. It would be easy to prove that Baldwin and Huntington both lacked the genius for those practical compromises and accommodations upon which the successful practice of responsible government so largely depends. Huntington would have stood to his arms in 1840 even though his success might perhaps have wrecked not only the Canadian union but his own cause. Reforms of the Bagot and Metcalfe crises were jeopardized by the same uncompromising temper on the part of Baldwin. Measured by what General Smuts has called the movement of the benign stars, however, the course of each was fundamentally sound. There is the same sombre and austere piety, kept as a rule for the sanctity of the secret chamber. Baldwin arose from his knees before making one of the most fateful decisions of his life. Huntington, who traced his lineage through New England to the Cromwells, brought the inflexible integrity "of the Hampden school," as Bourinot says, to the cause in Nova Scotia. His political principles were necessities of his nature. Puritan though he was in temper, he stood as Howe's second in the duel with Halliburton; and even after Howe, yielding to Sydenham's blandishments, had entered the futile coalition of 1840, thus leading his party, as it proved, for seven years into the wilderness, it is not on record that Huntington ever said "I told you so." With the death of Huntington in 1851, and the retirement of Baldwin in the same year, their work was done, and the day passed to the practical politician.

Between La Fontaine and Uniacke the parallel is perhaps more fanciful. Both were won over to responsible government during the same critical months of 1839–40; La Fontaine, convinced by the adroit and insinuating advocacy of Hincks and anchored at last to the incorruptible character of Robert Baldwin; Uniacke, convinced by Howe almost against his will, against his private interests, and certainly against the instinctive tastes of the set which he adorned in Halifax. Grey, the most exacting of critics, once exclaimed that La Fontaine was a gentleman. Howe has more than one tribute to Uniacke's "noble form, easy deportment, graceful manners . . . a mind ever fruitful, a tongue ever eloquent, humour inexhaustible." Uniacke became the first prime minister and La Fontaine the second in the British provinces overseas.

The parallel between Hincks and Howe is more startling: less perhaps a parallel than a series of contacts and intersections which developed at last into open rivalry. Both were newspaper men, of prodigious energy, of unrivalled insight, of incomparable resourcefulness in practical politics. It would be safe to say that Hincks in the *Examiner* and the *Pilot,* and Howe in the *Novascotian,* trained and educated and disciplined the dominant political parties by which responsible government was eventually won. Howe has much of the gorgeous imagery, the philosophical insight of Burke. His letters and many of his speeches are political literature. Within the narrow columns of a newspaper, however, one is inclined to credit Hincks with the sharper pen. Incisive and ruthless in every conflict, shrewd and discreet in every emergency, versatile, almost mercurial, in a hundred shifts of policy, Hincks was recognized by Sydenham, by Bagot, and by Elgin, as the ablest man in Canadian politics. He had "more energy," Elgin wrote, "than all the Canadian Statesmen I have yet had to do with put together." There is scarcely one of Hincks's innumerable changes of front which cannot somehow be justified from the standpoint of public policy; there are few indeed which did not subserve the interests of Francis Hincks. He had a profound distrust of Sydenham. "*We think it policy,*" he wrote to La Fontaine, "*to assume that Mr. T. is sincere.*" No one had laboured more assiduously than Hincks for the *coup* of June, 1841; to the end he insisted upon fighting through the session in the hope of better fortune with the return of "the tyrant" (Sydenham) to England. Two weeks before Sydenham's death Hincks was ready to take office under him for the expenditure of the imperial loan of £1,500,000. It was Hincks who organized the ranks of Irish repealers in Montreal, and used without scruple the bludgeon-men from the canal for the by-election of April, 1844. The contrast here with Howe's integrity is never impaired. During the Metcalfe crisis Hincks once stated bluntly that patronage was "the essence of Responsible Government," and that without it "all the advantages of Responsible Government are lost." In Nova Scotia, Howe not only set his face against the "spoils system" in opposition, but distributed patronage with unequalled magnanimity after 1848 in defiance of many of his patronage-mongering supporters. Imputations of dishonesty Howe would have resented with might and main. Hincks once printed in his own newspaper, as we shall see, the casual charges of the tory press that he was a "Villainous Liar," a "Penniless Vagabond," a "Cowardly Blackguard," and a master of "cool and steady villainy."

The fight for responsible government was followed by the war of the railways in which Howe, the rugged exponent of public ownership and an intercolonial railway to be built by imperial guarantees, proved no match for his nimbler rival in the race for imperial favours and the subtler accommodations of British bankers and contractors. The story of the Grand Trunk, however, belongs to another chapter.

Without these two groups of men responsible government might have been long and perhaps fatally deferred. Their monument is the British Commonwealth. Their names are more closely linked in tradition than in history, for the play of personal idiosyncrasies often obscured the essential unity of their cause. That cause required the contribution of both provinces. If the Nova Scotian achievement was the first and perhaps the most skilfully executed, it was also the easiest. If the Canadian achievement was the most turbulent, it was also the most critical, the most complicated, and the most epochal for the whole empire. A third group, the little band of Durhamites in Great Britain, was the counterpart of the other two. Without the mutual counsels of these discerning allies on both sides of the Atlantic, the day of reckoning might have been sought in another spirit, as Howe truly said, "by the Enemies of England, not by her friends."

III

The exploits and idiosyncrasies of individuals, however, will not go far to explain the contrast in temper between Nova Scotia and the united province of "Canada" in the "fight for responsible government." If the key to that achievement is the functioning of disciplined political parties it would be hard to find a background for that purpose more congenial than the Nova Scotia of the forties, or more forbidding than

the welter of complications in the province of Canada after the
union. In the old Province Building at Halifax tory and reformer
had long met on a level of moderation almost quixotic in its de-
corum. In the Canadas the habitual political turmoil was so forbidding that Francis Hincks himself, the real architect of the reform
party after the union, and the least squeamish of men, sometimes
despaired of the consequences.

Geography itself accounts for much. A small self-contained and
self-conscious community was a more promising constituency for a
disciplined political party than a vast sprawling province in the hinterlands of the continent. Nova Scotia was a peninsula; its trade was
maritime, chiefly with the West Indies and Great Britain. A sense of
association with British naval and commercial traditions was never
wanting. To a merchant in Halifax, Liverpool and London lay just
over the horizon, while the remoteness of York or the Huron tract in
Upper Canada frequently overwhelmed the British immigrant with
a sense of distance from any community but his fellow-frontiersmen
in up-state New York or Ohio. Differences of language and religion
cut him off from his French compatriots of Lower Canada and complicated unceasingly his political associations with them after the union.
Communications were vital for both provinces. In Nova Scotia the
roads were the best in British America. There were 250 miles of car-
riage roads in 1827, and the coasting trade by sea was easier and
cheaper still. In Upper Canada Sydenham once abandoned his
itinerary into the western reaches of the province in despair and rode
the rest of the way on horseback.

Other geographical and economic factors in Nova Scotia helped to
impart a truly provincial outlook. The shipping interests were predominant. In 1830 nearly 1,400 ships were under provincial registry.
The Cunard shipping interests flourished in Halifax, and Bagot in
1842 could write of "Cunarding it" across the Atlantic. Howe and
Haliburton ("Sam Slick") crossed the Atlantic together on a Cunarder
in 1838 and speculated upon the glowing prospects of oceanic trade.
The flag of Nova Scotia—the St. Andrew's cross charged with the
royal arms of Scotland under King James I—was to be found on the
seven seas. The banking and mercantile interests which gathered about
this lucrative trade appealed to provincial pride, and every Nova
Scotian shared in it. The very insularity of the province, like that of
Britain itself, gave a sense of compactness and common interest to its
inhabitants. The population of Nova Scotia was heterogeneous in its
origin—a few Acadian French after the exile, English in Halifax,

Germans in Lunenburg County, Highland Scottish in Pictou and Inverness, northern Irish in Cumberland, pre-revolutionary New England in dominating proportions in the Annapolis valley and on the south shore, and loyalists from the old colonies merging with the rest after the revolution. But by 1830 they were "all Nova Scotians" with a remarkably homogeneous outlook upon the North American scene.

This provincial patriotism became almost an obsession in the columns of the *Novascotian,* and Howe must have shared it with thousands of his readers who followed him in his rambles to the remotest villages of the province, extolling the busy life of the fishing-fleets and the ship-yards, the orchards of the Annapolis valley, the consoling solitudes of woodland roads and the sea, the lure of trout and salmon, the autumn camp-fires of hunters "calling moose." The British press reinforced this solidarity. British newspapers reached the province with every packet. Howe was astonished at the range of their circulation. British politics and history were familiar themes in the provincial press. The issues of the Reform Bill and the Whig ascendancy under Melbourne were probably as closely followed in Halifax, Nova Scotia, as in its Yorkshire namesake.

The contrasts between this tight and somewhat complacent little community and the sprawling expanses of the Canadas must have impressed every observer. Even before the union of 1841 complicated their politics the upper province was hopelessly attenuated by distance and diversity. The contest against privilege and vested interests degenerated into scores of local conflicts each with its own train of rivalry and bitterness. On both sides the land itself was the focus of controversy in a province so predominantly agrarian. Even when the poor frontiersman and the land-poor official never saw each other the basic patterns of Upper Canadian life brought them into conflict. Wheat, lumber, and potash, barley, potatoes, and whiskey, brought solid wealth and neighbourliness at last to Upper Canada, but it lacked the robust stimulus of ships, fish, and rum which Sam Slick observed so indulgently in the spontaneous politics of Nova Scotia.

The population of Upper Canada, almost as heterogeneous as that of Nova Scotia in its origin, became more so with every expansion of the frontier. By 1820 the loyalist pioneers and their descendants were outnumbered, four or five to one, but the loyalist tradition grew in intensity and exclusiveness with every relative decline in their numbers. The Dutch from Pennsylvania, unlike their counterpart in Lunenburg County, Nova Scotia, brought a North American strain to their new settlements in Upper Canada. Scots in both provinces demonstrated their proclivities for office, but radical Scottish reformers like Gourlay and Mackenzie found in Upper Canada every accessory to irritate their infirmities of temper. Had Mackenzie gone to Pictou instead of York his stormy career might have blended with the congenial radicalism of the Blanchards and the McCulloughs in that rugged Scottish community. Conversely Howe's self-righteousness and boasted moderation might have yielded to a different spirit had he encountered the truculent "family compact" of Upper Canada: he might have proved "sufficiently ultra" for the "ultras" themselves. The curious fact that so many of the reformers—Wyatt and Thorpe and Willcocks of the early period as well as the Baldwins, Francis Collins, Hincks, and Sullivan during the last phase of the contest—were Irish, brought that growing element of the population instinctively into contact with Canadian politics. The Irishman's politics at home however were calculated to start him off on the wrong foot in Canada. Party and cabinet government at Westminster he took for granted. His *bête noire* was the Irish union. It required more than usual discernment to support the Canadian union as the most promising basis for a dominant reform party and to subordinate every other aspect of reform to the paramount necessity for responsible government. The fierce passions of Irish politics, at any rate, were easily transplanted to Canadian soil. Tens of thousands of plague-stricken immigrants, with Fenian compatriots of Hunters' Lodges and the Irish Republican Union just across the border, invited political exploitation. In a famous by-election of April, 1844, the presence at the polls of Irish labourers from the Lachine Canal armed with shillelaghs for the occasion was attributed by Metcalfe to the machinations of Francis Hincks. La Fontaine, he was ready to believe, was "out of his Element in haranguing an Irish mob," and Morin was probably guiltless of the "grossly false" reports of *Minerve* and the *Pilot,* but Hincks's "ruffianlike proceedings" must be met with firmness. The gregarious technique and discipline of French-Canadian politics under La Fontaine, Morin, Perreault, and Viger added characteristic ingredients to the Canadian compound.

A friend of Elgin's once assured him that any man who could govern Canada would be equal to anything. For the edification of those "whose vocation it is to invent wrongs for Ireland," Elgin sent to Grey, at the concession of responsible government, the list of five Irishmen, four Frenchmen, one Englishman, and two Scots in his new Executive Council. Responsible government itself was the only issue that could fuse these fissiparous elements into a political party. Beyond this discipline, wrote Elgin, lay all sorts of "affections and antipathies, national, sectional, and personal," all "making political capital out of whatever turns up," and most of them "so occupied with squabbles that the bent of men's opinions on graver subjects can hardly be conjectured." Controversy was "rabid and unreasonable." "With a thousand other mutual suspicions and repulsions, it is hardly possible to touch any part of this rickety machine without bringing the whole about one's ears."

IV

The chief advantage of Nova Scotia in the achievement of reform was an instrument of unique power and maturity among the provinces of British North America. The press was truly provincial. The periodicals of the day, from the *Nova Scotia Magazine* of 1789 to the *Halifax Monthly* of 1830, frequently strained at impossible standards, but the coterie which gathered about Thomas Chandler Haliburton set the pace for a literary movement of great originality and considerable distinction. Sam Slick not only founded a school of American humour but peddled his racy and whimsical wares in lucrative editions to a British public. The newspaper press, robust and ingenuous, carried some of the best writing to be found in the record of Canadian journalism. The Holland family in the *Acadian Recorder,* Jotham Blanchard in the *Colonial Patriot,* Joseph Howe in the *Novascotian* and later on in the *Chronicle,* made the whole province their constituency. For several years Howe's rambles through the countryside, his articles and editorials on their needs and commodious life too, made him a familiar figure in a thousand households. His legislative reviews, both Canadian and British, made his readers familiar with kindred issues in other communities. It was no idle boast to Lord John Russell that the great names of British politics were "familiar in their mouths as household words." Conversely Howe's own "Legislative Reviews" of Nova Scotia, reported by his own hand in the *Novascotian,* left him with an unrivalled mastery of parliamentary procedure and tactics. At the same time his tory background and judicious impartiality were well known in a truly provincial constituency. Thus when "Joe Howe" doffed his coat and plunged into the fray as a reformer his readers assumed instinctively that there was something wrong with the old colonial system. The famous libel case was much more than a personal triumph for the young editor of the *Novascotian.* Howe bade his supporters teach their children the names of the twelve jurors who had established the freedom of the press in Nova Scotia.

The press of "Canada"—and particularly of Upper Canada before the union—reflected the paralysing effect of remoteness and distance in a frontier community. Isolated pockets of settlement with corduroy roads for communication doomed for many years any hope of a truly provincial press. Journals like Egerton Ryerson's *Christian Guardian* for the Methodists or the *Freeman* of Francis Collins for Irish Catholics found their way to special constituencies over a wide area of the province, but many a valiant journalist gave up the fight with the wilderness and sold his press and type to newcomers with more enthusiasm than experience. Much of the type of the primitive press of Upper Canada must have done service to a variety of names and causes. The early numbers of Mackenzie's *Colonial Advocate* had to be printed in Syracuse, and when his stormy career approached a climax in 1836 the press of the *Constitution* had to be sold to his enemies to found the *Paladium*. The *Cobourg Star's* long and consistent record in that interesting constituency is perhaps the nearest approach to the *Acadian Recorder* of the Holland family in Nova Scotia. Before the time of the Durham mission the *Freeman* with its appeal to its Irish constituency on the basis of reform for Ireland was perhaps the most radical of Upper Canadian journals, but too narrow in its appeal for the cause of Upper Canadian reform. The necessity for a truly provincial press was recognized when the *Examiner* was launched by private subscription among the leading reformers themselves under the editorship of Francis Hincks. The first number was presented to Lord Durham. It flew from its mast-head the motto "Responsible Government" and it never struck its flag. When the capital was moved to Montreal the *Examiner* gave way to the *Pilot,* still under Hincks's redoubtable editorship. By this time the *Minerve* was attempting the same coverage of French Canada for the reform cause. The vituperation to be found on both sides in the Canadian press became a by-word. Hincks once assured a Toronto audience in 1877 after the Pacific Scandal that federal politics could not match the fierce rancour of the early days.

V

The purely political problems of the two provinces, similar though they were in fundamentals, were sharpened by these contrasts. Political unrest in Upper Canada often broke down into innumerable local feuds revolving as a rule about land grants and petty offices rather than general principles. "Grievances" against the "family compact" and their henchmen were more effective as political ammunition than abstractions about responsible government. The vast majority in the province could have known little and must have cared less about either, until cant phrases about clergy reserves and vested interests and monopoly in high places began to reach their ears to the accompaniment of countercharges against "treason" and "republicanism." Since the real protagonists seldom saw each other, much of the turmoil must have taken on the impersonal aspect of a plague. Attorney-General Hagerman habitually referred to William Lyon Mackenzie as "that reptile," and Mackenzie charged the family compact with "the iron rule of the czar of Muscovy." Robert Baldwin with the doctrine of responsible government locked in his indomitable mind must have passed Mackenzie on the street a dozen times a month for several years. It is not on record that they ever met in confidential talk upon the greatest issue that ever concerned them both.

In Nova Scotia the concentration of power and privilege in Halifax brought many of the antagonists face to face, sometimes in familiar and confidential association. Until 1839 Halifax was the only free port in the province. The shipping and banking interests were so closely knit that "family compact" was no empty phrase. Five of the twelve members of the Executive Council were partners in the Halifax Banking Company. The officers of the garrison and of the navy—Halifax was the north Atlantic base of the British fleet—and all but one of the legislative and executive councillors were to be found there. James Stephen, of the Colonial Office, in a confidential minute for Lord John Russell, once deprecated the straining after impossible standards—"the extinction of Public Spirit in the effeminate passion for mere social and fashionable distinction." But the homespun virtues of assemblymen like Herbert Huntington from Yarmouth moved in these official circles without embarrassment. In Great Britain too the Nova Scotian abroad usually found himself at home. A long succession of visitors to London—R. J. Uniacke in 1826, Charles R. Fairbanks in 1830, Howe and Haliburton in 1838, Huntington and George Young in 1839—found their way without difficulty to the Colonial Office. Howe, disdaining a letter of introduction from Sir Colin Campbell, sent in his card and was received by Clinton Murdock, the under-secretary, and by Glenelg himself with ingratiating confidence. "What passed," Howe records in his diary, "not fit to put into Note Book which might fall into other hands."

For Canada such salutary official contacts were either wanting altogether, or added to the virulence of local faction. The news of Mackenzie's interview with Goderich in 1832 was greeted in Upper Canada with such execration that neither "Goosie Goderich" nor

Glenelg—the most kindly and approachable of men—dared to repeat the experiment. The assemblies of both the Canadas, resorting to the old colonial device of appointing agents at Westminster, selected of all the members of the House of Commons the two men whose Ishmaelitish temper was least likely to advance their cause with the Colonial Office—Roebuck for Lower Canada and Hume for the upper province. In Nova Scotia Roebuck's "talent and judgment" were profoundly distrusted; Hume's gratuitous reference to the "baneful domination of the mother country" in 1834 cost Mackenzie a large section of his majority in the election of that year.[1] When Baldwin sought to forestall the rising of 1837 by an appeal in person in London, Glenelg was afraid to grant him an interview, and Baldwin had to content himself with the memorandum which proved so significant two years later for the Durham *Report.* When the austere Robert Baldwin was brought to such a pass in order to "free his soul," unofficial relations must have been strained indeed. Francis Hincks had better luck with Charles Buller. Between them the foundations of the Reform party under the union were well and truly laid.

Two other complications added to the bitterness of Canadian politics. The clergy reserves, wrote Sydenham, were "the root of all the troubles of the province, the cause of the rebellion—the never-failing watchword at the hustings—the perpetual source of discord, strife, and hatred." Long after the final settlement of 1854 they continued to poison Canadian politics. The uncompromising temper of Bishop Strachan may have been inspired in some measure by the failure of Bishop Inglis to attempt a similar programme in Nova Scotia. When a Scottish Presbyterian becomes the champion of colonial Anglicanism the temper of ecclesiastical polity is apt to harden. Bishop Inglis regarded a policy of endowments for the church from the public lands of the province as "worse than useless." The threadbare device of commuting quitrents for church endowments was rejected by the Nova Scotia Assembly, as their resolution records, "without a dissenting vote," and the resolutions were "brought in by a Churchman." Brenton Halliburton, afterwards Chief Justice and himself a staunch Anglican, was once chairman of a committee to report upon the status of the Church of England in Nova Scotia. They reported that "every attempt on the part of Government to give pre-eminence to the Church creates ten enemies for one friend. . . . People on this side of the water

[1]Broughton records in his diary that he once found the members of the House of Commons streaming out into the lobbies. He inquired of Stanley: "Is the House up?" "No," Stanley replied, "Hume is."

are even more tenacious of religious equality than of political. . . . The generality of Churchmen themselves participate in it." In a joint address of Council and Assembly Anglicans themselves subscribed to the view that the church "can only be injured in the Province of Nova Scotia by the misguided zeal of its intemperate friends."

Scarcely less endemic than religious strife in Upper Canada were the traditions of the revolution and the War of 1812. In Nova Scotia the relations with New England improved after the dust of conflict had settled in the old provinces. The trend of migration upon the whole was "back home" to New England. Thousands of the over-optimistic inhabitants of Shelburne must have found their way thither, and no fewer than six members, as we have seen, of the first New Brunswick Assembly. The opposition of New England to the War of 1812 and the clandestine trade at Castine maintained a tradition of almost un-interrupted intercourse. A joint address of the Nova Scotia Council and Assembly commended the "proud and just spirit of their British ancestors" in the temper of "our nearest neighbours in the United States." Dalhousie, as we have seen, found that "the connection between the respectable inhabitants of this Province, and the States, is yet very intimate; scarcely is there a family that has not Fathers, Brothers, and near relations settled there." Yet there was scarcely a trace of political influence and not "the most distant doubt of the Loyalty of this Province." The fact that piecemeal migration back to New England remained for many generations one of the prevailing trends of population softened the asperities of a divided allegiance and robbed it of any serious influence upon the contest that was about to open for responsible government.

In Upper Canada where the tide of migration flowed so strongly in the other direction the political views of the newcomers were exploited and often misrepresented by vested interests intent upon safeguarding their waning influence in a rapidly expanding economy. The contacts here were not with conservative New England but with up-state New York and the new frontier states of the old Northwest. New ideas on every variety of frontier life, from school-books and stoves to taverns and camp-meetings, came over the border. The elective principle in politics and government found a ready reception in the rough soil of another frontier, but as an alternative to the tech-nique which finally solved "the old colonial question" in both Upper Canada and Nova Scotia—the control of the executive through the conventions of the parliamentary system—the elective principle alone was to prove a delusion and a snare. It was not by electing a governor,

or a president, or a judge, or a legislative council, that the solution
was found at last to the abuses of privilege. Even the stimulus to
politics traceable to Jacksonian democracy across the border was
counteracted by so much prejudice in Upper Canada against republicanism in any form that the reform movement was frequently compromised rather than helped by the association. Every reformer from
Gourlay to Baldwin was charged at some time or other with republicanism and credited with little else. Where prejudice and exploitation
were so prevalent the net result of republican influences would be
hard to estimate.

In its final form the basic pattern of Canadian reform, as Elgin
discovered, was a departure from republican models, not an approximation to them. The ground swell and cross currents from the south,
however, left the surface of provincial politics littered with prejudice
and false analogies. Thousands of his countrymen recently arrived
from Britain must have shared the perplexities of "Tiger" William
Dunlop of the Canada Company who brought a sharp tongue and a
varied experience in Scotland and in India to bear upon the Canadian
scene. Before Mackenzie's committee which produced the *Seventh
Report on Grievances* Dunlop had gone on record in favour of responsible government. He afterwards conceded with characteristically
whimsical humour that neither he himself nor anybody else appeared
to know exactly what the term implied or how it was to function.
Against republicanism, however, his conviction never wavered. When
the storm broke in 1837 he feared so deeply for the British connection
that he raised a company of militia on his own responsibility, com-
mandeered blankets and supplies for them from the Canada Company
in defiance of official protests from Longsworth, their egregious agent,
and marched his men down towards the London district to head off
an imaginary American invasion. The Governor's own conduct was
scarcely less quixotic. Broughton describes in his diary the mingled
astonishment and amusement of his colleagues in the government at
some of Sir Francis Head's hysterical despatches; and when Head
afterwards demanded his reward for saving the province Melbourne
is said to have burst into laughter with the exclamation, "My dear
chap, you are such a damn'd odd fellow!"

Chapter Seven

POLITICAL PARTIES IN THE MAKING

W ITH these contrasts in background, reform in "Canada" and in Nova Scotia varied in pace and temper with the conditions out of which it grew. In both provinces reformers had the sagacity, as Durham pointed out, to concentrate upon the control of the executive council, with the conviction, vindicated by the event, that in seeking first this kingdom all other things should be added unto them. The discipline which they attained and the effectiveness of their strategy depended in no small measure upon their discernment of this historic principle. That discernment, however, came slowly and haltingly in both provinces. Even when it came it was frequently obscured by local grievances and personal animosities. Without official sanction, moreover, from governor and Colonial Office alike, the most impeccable doctrine must have remained inoperative. Extorted though that sanction might be by hard experience, it could function at its best only with goodwill and mutual confidence. Every issue which brought assembly and executive council into direct juxtaposition added a lesson to the experiment, but it was not by chance that the historic formula reached its most convincing demonstration in circumstances where it was least complicated by the play of fierce and irrelevant animosities.

I

In Nova Scotia the executive and legislative councils were composed of the same twelve men, and the doubling of their functions must have trebled or quadrupled their power. It was in their legislative function that "the twelve" first challenged the firmness of the Assembly. The Legislative Council sat behind closed doors and in the "brandy dispute" of 1830 had the assurance to throw out a money bill because the Assembly, in sending it forward only two days before the expiration of the old law, had "outraged the rules which regulate the intercourse of gentlemen." The ensuing election returned a determined majority for reform, and the revenue bill passed without comment. In this the Council sensed the rising "domination of a Democratic faction," while the Speaker of the Assembly asserted roundly that the rejection of a revenue bill would "form a new era" in the traditions of Nova Scotia:

This is my native land, and my home . . . but if its freedom is lost . . . I will travel from it as far as the City of Destruction. . . .
They have distracted the peace of a Colony, the most quiet and orderly within His Majesty's realms. . . . God knows I come with reluctance to this discussion and bring to it a melancholy mind.

Perhaps the most discerning comment on the "brandy dispute" is to be found in a memorandum which an assemblyman, Charles R. Fairbanks, left at the Colonial Office in 1830. Fairbanks, whose lucrative practice in vice-admiralty cases assured him access not only to British legal circles in London but to the confidence of Under-Secretary Hay at the Colonial Office, singled out the executive rather than the legislative function of "the twelve" as the chief defect in the colonial constitution. The Executive Council was "defective, inasmuch as the popular branch and People of the Colony are not represented in it." Urging the separation of the two councils, Fairbanks continued:

The remedy is to be found in applying to the colonies the same principles on which the Government is conducted at home—and by seeking in the House *some at least* of the Advisers of the Executive. . . . The freedom of the Colonial Institutions has conferred much of the real power on the popular Branch. . . . Seats in the Executive Council . . . can consequently be held only during pleasure. . . . It can hardly be questioned that the House of Representatives ought to possess powers similar to those exercised by the House of Commons. They have repeatedly claimed these as their rights and *will* exercise them. . . . The restoration of harmony is not to be expected until after very material changes of Men and measures.

In the debates of 1834 the Assembly joined issue with "the twelve" in terms which admitted of no retreat. In 1832 Goderich at the Colonial Office had authorized the separation of the executive and legislative councils. The directions were withheld from the Assembly until 1834 on the cool assumption that it would have a "tendency to disturb the peaceful state of the Colony." The temper of the House nevertheless remained unruffled by this imputation of "improper motives." Resolutions for the separation of the councils and the opening of the debates of the Legislative Council to the public passed without a division. On the position of the Executive Council—the core of the whole contest for responsible government—opinion was still divided. Stewart and Fairbanks, Blanchard, Huntington, and Uniacke all advocated an Executive Council "selected from both Branches of the Legislature." Fairbanks, now solicitor-general, added a note, however, which Joseph Howe reported with suggestive discernment in the columns of the *Novascotian*:

In England the people operate upon the King through the Ministers, and these have seats in the Legislature. So far from this being the case in (Lower) Canada, there the Assembly deprived Mr. Mondelet of his seat because he accepted the situation of an Executive Councillor. . . .

Let the Executive Council be chosen . . . from both branches of the Legislature and from others unconnected with either. Let a part of them come here, Sir, to seek support to the measures of the administration; and when they cannot procure the sanction of the people's representatives to the measure they propose, let them either abandon them or resign. . . . The principles of the British Constitution ought to be in operation here as far as they can be introduced. . . . The present system cannot continue.

Here in embryo was the dynamic principle which was to transform the second empire into the Commonwealth. Howe's ominous report of this debate in the *Novascotian* found its way into many quarters. A tory correspondent in Halifax sent a copy to the Colonial Secretary as a timely warning of "political troubles" ahead.

II

The sedate temper of reform in Nova Scotia until the election of 1836 is easily traceable to a policy of long-standing and conspicuous success on the part of the Executive Council and the Colonial Office. The veteran Speaker of the House, S. W. G. Archibald, who could boast a long record of no mean distinction in pouring oil on troubled waters, remarked that "Assemblies require to be moulded by men of understanding." "God knows," he once exclaimed, "I seek peace. I am the last person to revolutionize the Country, or excite confusion." "No man in this Assembly has exerted himself more than I have done to preserve the peace and order of the Colony, and no man has been more successful . . . indeed I have not escaped censure for my unwearied efforts in this cause." But Archibald too ended his days as an executive councillor, and like many another assemblyman was not without "honourable ambition" for such promotion. His appointment as Solicitor-General and Master of the Rolls was an earnest of favours to come. Stewart, long the ranking whig leader in the Assembly, passed in due time to a seat in the Executive Council—the meed, in this case, not only of "honourable ambition" but of jealousy for the rising star of Joseph Howe. No fewer than three of "the twelve" had served their apprenticeship for "order and moderation" in the Speaker's chair, and one of them once observed sardonically that without great care "a Supply of Patriots will be produced greater than the demand, and they will thwart and embarrass the Executive Government because it cannot employ and reward them." Charles R. Fairbanks, probably the most discerning of them all, once indicated that the translation of his own father-in-law from the Assembly to the Council would "allay all unpleasant feeling in the two Branches of the Legislature." His own appointment as Solicitor-General was followed by a more lucrative promotion as Master of the Rolls and Judge of Vice-Admiralty; the Assembly, sensing his defection from their cause, barred him in both capacities from a seat in the House. A couplet in Howe's common-place-book must have depicted a practice so notorious that the Governor himself was beginning to find it less than "proper and laudable":

> As Bees, on Flowers alighting, cease their hum
> So, settling upon Places, Whigs grow dumb.

In the Colonial Office itself this method of dealing with reform by decapitation and translation of its leaders became approved tactics for Nova Scotia. Four years later, as we shall see, when Sydenham was confronting the sharpest test of the new Russell-Sydenham régime at Howe's resolutions of no confidence in February, 1840, Clinton Murdock, Sydenham's secretary, who had met Howe in London in 1838, drew upon a long tradition at the Colonial Office in drafting a memorandum for the guidance of his chief at Halifax. The "demand for a responsible Executive Council," he noted, had arisen there "before the question was mooted in Upper or Lower Canada," but such was the "exemplary forbearance and moderation" of the province that "if a more turbulent and energetic individual at times arose, it was easy by well-timed concession, to disarm his opposition, if not to secure his support." For Howe too, as we shall see, the honeyed trap was spread, and Sydenham's "magic wand" never waved more magically for a time. But the old mimic battles of "honourable ambition" were over in Nova Scotia. The rise there for the first time of a disciplined political party with a clear sense of direction on this greatest of issues for the future of British North America was largely the work of Joseph Howe.

III

Howe's definition of party on the eve of his greatest victory in 1847 may stand as his immediate objective for ten years: "a healthy tone of public feeling, based on sound political knowledge, pervading not a class or a coterie, but the great body of the people; and an organized party in the Lower House, acting on general principles which the constituencies understood and feeling in honour bound to advance those principles until they should prevail." In a moment of elation he once exclaimed that "a more manly, public-spirited, united, and disinterested body of men were never exhibited by the legislative conflicts of any country."

Much of this public spirit and discipline Howe himself created. His father, a Massachusetts loyalist, had been king's printer, postmaster-general, and founder of the *Weekly Chronicle*. Howe's own paper, the *Novascotian,* quickly became a familiar feature in every constituency of the province before its young editor threw off his tory traditions and plunged into politics in the cause of reform. Since 1830 the *Novascotian's* "Legislative Reviews," written by Howe himself, had been perhaps the best medium of political education in Nova Scotia not only for provincial but for Canadian and British politics. The well-known libel case had brought him into direct conflict with the Executive Council, since the magistrates of Halifax who brought the action had the official sanction of "the twelve" who appointed them in the attempt to silence their critics. Howe's speech in his own defence revealed for the first time, to himself perhaps as well as to his enemies, his matchless gifts in moving and inspiring his countrymen. For the first time "the twelve" executive councillors had met their match in the "twelve good men and true" of the jury, whose names Howe bade his followers teach to their children as the founders of the freedom of the press in Nova Scotia.

The Reform party in 1835, however, was far from "public-spirited, united, and disinterested." "They have the numbers," Howe wrote to Jotham Blanchard of the Pictou *Colonial Patriot*, "but in knowledge, discipline, able leaders, everything in fact which ensures success in any struggle, they have been and are miserably deficient." The election of 1836 resulted in a "majority pledged to the people and kept in salutary awe of them," but the process of welding them into the disciplined political party which carried the resolution of no confidence, 30 to 12, in February, 1840, was probably the most brilliant and constructive feat of reform in the British provinces.

Howe's first election to the Assembly in 1836 was won upon the issue of responsible government. Laying impious hands again upon the shewbread he singled out the Executive Council as the cardinal defect of the constitution. "In England [he said upon the hustings] one vote of the people's representatives turns out a ministry and a new one comes in. . . . In this country, the government is like an ancient Egyptian mummy, wrapped up in narrow and antique prejudices—dead and inanimate, but likely to last forever." A few "Bees on Flowers alighting" ceased their hum but Howe's first foray in the House, The Twelve Resolutions, proved to be a turning-point in his career. One of these resolutions, charging "the twelve" with protecting "their own interests and emoluments at the expense of the public," was so hotly resented that they demanded its rescinding under the thinly veiled threat of stopping the supplies. More than one candidate for "honourable promotion" with polished sarcasm passed the word in the lobbies that "young Mr. Howe" had shot his bolt. With a characteristic gesture of magnanimity Howe rescinded all twelve of his resolutions and substituted an address to the throne which carried the issue of responsible government irretraccably into imperial politics. It was the first of those "flashes" of insight which established among his followers the tradition of Howe's uncanny mastery of parliamentary tactics, his magnanimity in success, his profound conviction that "upon a right understanding of these principles, a fair adjustment of these institutions, depends the security and peace" of every quarter of the empire, "embracing many, many millions of people, more than the islands to which they belong." With deep veneration for Glenelg himself and rare understanding of his problems, Howe evolved a course of parliamentary tactics from the rescinding of the Twelve Resolutions to the resolution of no confidence in 1840 that remained a classic demonstration of reform by parliamentary action.

The spirit of Glenelg's response to the Address to the Throne, confirmed by Howe's own interview with him in 1838, left a conviction that responsible government was within reach had it not been overshadowed by the Canadian rebellions and the "incomprehensible disgrace" of Glenelg himself. "No man gave the old system a fairer trial," Howe afterwards wrote to Lord John Russell; "no man less deserved the fate to which it almost inevitably consigned its victims." Responsible government, James Stephen recorded in the Colonial Office, was "not yet in a state for decision, nor even for discussion." "If conceded in any one Colony it must be granted in all." It required the Durham mission and ten years of "wandering in the wilderness" to bring the issue in the Canadas to this pass of acceptability.

Meanwhile two far-reaching principles of the contest in Nova Scotia are directly traceable to Howe's insight and temper. Against the cause of reform in that province the "loyalty cry" which bedevilled politics in the Canadas for a whole generation never raised its head: responsible government was "perfectly *simple* and eminently *British.*" "All suspicion of disloyalty we cast aside, as the product of ignorance or cupidity; we seek for nothing more than British subjects are entitled to; but we will be contented with nothing less." The second principle was another of Howe's "flashes," developed with prophetic insight and catholicity. Howe was prepared to believe that "when sufficiently advanced in knowledge, resources, and population, North American Provinces with the concurrence even of the British Government shall assume the rank of free and independent States." But a contest for immediate independence by revolution based upon Papineau's republican models would be one of "the maddest rebellions on record." Instead of a conflict between the province and Great Britain "to be sought in a spirit the most uncompromising and offensive," Howe never ceased to represent his cause as an alliance between reformers on both sides of the Atlantic "struggling against the same enemies." In practice this alliance in the end took him happily behind the scenes and contributed not a little to a happy ending. The intimate correspondence between Howe and Charles Buller is perhaps the pleasantest chapter in the long contest for responsible government.

IV

The Canadian union of 1841 brought together many factions. Sydenham sorted them out complacently into no fewer than six groups so incompatible that he anticipated little trouble in neutralizing their opposition. "I will take the moderate from both sides—reject the extremes—and govern as I think right, and not as they fancy." These kaleidoscopic factions yielded at last, as we shall see, not to the "magic wand" of the Governor but to the discerning strategy of Francis Hincks, inspired, it may be, by Charles Buller, and personified by the historic alliance of Baldwin and La Fontaine. This training of a disciplined party in the Canadas was a truly herculean task, by far the most formidable of its sort in the British provinces. In truth the contrasts between the Canadas themselves before the union appeared to be irreconcilable.

In Lower Canada the Assembly had passed almost immediately after its creation in 1791 into the control of a dominant French-

Canadian majority, antagonized by the arrogance of the "château clique" and incited by a chapter of almost incredible official blunders to dedicate their powers to the defence of their racial interests. The blunt declaration of the *Mercury* that Lower Canada was "too French for a British province" found an immediate response in *Le Canadien* with its motto "notre langue, nos institutions, et nos lois." After the abortive attempt to reunite the provinces in 1822 the suspicion became ineradicable in the minds of Papineau and his compatriots that the subordination of the French-Canadian majority was the deliberate purpose of official policy. This legacy survived to embitter the union of 1841 and to complicate confederation, but the immediate effect for Lower Canada was to stultify from the outset the play of political parties. From the second election in 1796 to the Papineau rising of 1837 every major contest increased the popular majority in the Assembly, and every punitive dissolution of the Assembly added to the bitterness of the contest. The tory Assembly of Upper Canada was scarcely more truculent in expelling William Lyon Mackenzie than the French-Canadian nationalist Assembly of Lower Canada in expelling Robert Christie. From the division of the province in 1791 to the suspension of the constitution of Lower Canada in 1838 the French never lost their majority in the Assembly and the system which the Assembly was attacking never lost its domination in the Executive Council. Not a single election registered a change in this implacable conflict.

In Upper Canada, the contrast was complete: from the first reform Assembly in 1828 to the union and beyond it to the achievement of responsible government in 1848 not a single election failed to register a change in the political temper of the majority. The Assembly went "reform" in 1828, "constitutionalist" in 1830, overwhelmingly reform in 1834, overwhelmingly constitutionalist in 1836, reform in the first election after the union in 1841, constitutionalist again in the Metcalfe election of 1844, and reform for the final concession of responsible government in 1848. While the dominant majority in Lower Canada, with brief periods of fitful accommodation, used its powers with almost unvarying hostility to obstruct the government and finally to cut off supply and to challenge the whole function of government, the majority in the upper province swung left and right with the regularity of a pendulum.

But though the pendulum swings to and fro, with unvarying regularity, the force of gravity which controls this oscillation is one of the most constant and pervasive forces in the universe. It would be little to the purpose to speculate here upon this extraordinary political phenomenon in Upper Canada. Calculated with mathematical accuracy there is but one chance in more than a thousand that the ten alternations which took place from 1824 to 1854 could have "just happened" in the normal play of chance and probability. It is reasonable to suppose that some relatively constant factor must have dictated this unbroken series of change. With the possible exception of one election, one factor at least is not far to seek. Two illustrations may suffice. The first reform Assembly of 1828 passed no fewer than fifty-seven bills that were thrown out by the Legislative Council. The futility of this torrent of abortive legislation without the slightest control of practical administration to enforce even the bills which successfully ran the gauntlet of rejection or veto must have strengthened immeasurably the plea of the constitutionalists in 1830 to give the new governor, Sir John Colborne, and a new king, William IV, "a fair chance" to demonstrate their goodwill. Conversely, the short-sighted expulsion of Mackenzie no less than five times by the rampant tory Assembly of 1830, with the additional assertion—flagrantly unconstitutional—that he was ineligible for re-election, must have accounted in no small measure for the revulsion of 1834 in his favour. Had Hume's supporting letter with its gratuitous reference to the "baneful domination of the mother country" not found its way to the hustings Mackenzie's majority would probably have been overwhelming. A few constituencies, like Sir Allan MacNab's in Hamilton for the constitutionalists or Mackenzie's in North York for the reformers, stood staunchly and consistently for the same cause throughout, but the majority demonstrated consistency of another sort. There were but two ways of voting, either to uphold the record of the existing Assembly or to condemn it in the hope of electing a better one, and the invariable verdict in favour of the second course is scarcely to be interpreted as a demonstration that the electors did not know their own minds. The truth would seem to be that they knew their own minds well enough to register consistently their disapproval of extreme counsels on both sides. It may be that while the extremists on both sides were notoriously open to this criticism, the constituencies themselves might have responded to more moderate leadership.

These violent revulsions were reflected in the unpredictable temper of the Assembly itself. Even Mackenzie's *Seventh Report on Grievances* —an impressive programme of reform which probably represents Mackenzie's stormy career at its best, ballasted and dignified by responsibility—produced in practice no discerning and disciplined party "acting [in Howe's classic phrase] on general principles which the constituencies understood and feeling in honour bound to advance those principles until they should prevail." The profusion of petty "grievances" on every side must have daunted many an instinctive reformer in search of "principles." Sir Francis Head once described his adversary with characteristic vituperation: "Afraid to look me in the face, he sat, with his feet not reaching the ground, and with his countenance averted from me, at an angle of about seventy degrees . . . while with the eccentricity, the volubility, and indeed the appearance of a madman, the tiny creature raved about grievances here and grievances there which the Committee, he said, had not ventured to enumerate." The spectacle of Sir Francis (the "damn'd odd fellow" of Melbourne's badinage) berating William Lyon Mackenzie for eccentricity and volubility must have appealed to Broughton's sense of humour.

The Upper Canadian scene was littered with grotesque and fantastic incidents, many of them tragic to the participants but scarcely calculated to call forth statesmanship. Robert Courlay was bludgeoned into sheer lunacy and exile by a truculent system employing the most barbarous of laws with impeccable legal procedure. One of Captain Matthew's crimes was said to have been doffing his hat on New Year's eve when a visiting band from the United States played "Yankee Doodle" on request as the counterpart to "God Save the King." William Lyon Mackenzie was on the brink of bankruptcy when the young tories of Toronto demolished his printing-press, scattered type along the street and dumped the rest of it into the lake. With £625 from the ensuing action for damages Mackenzie was able to equip one of the best printing-presses in Upper Canada. The abuse of "Goosie Goderich" after the interview with Mackenzie in 1832 came from the outraged "family compact" of Upper Canada. The expulsions of Mackenzie—the fifth time resisting violently—confirmed his standing in one of the oldest and most prosperous constituencies of the province. His name to this day is calculated to evoke mingled cheers and jeers in the neighbourhood of Queen's Park. Scarcely less turbulent were the excesses of the lower province. *Le Canadien* could be as vituperative as the *Freeman* or the *Colonial Advocate*. Governor Sir James Craig not only seized Bédard's printing-press but jailed the printer. The union of Upper and Lower Canada in 1841 merely fused traditions of turbulent politics in both provinces.

The austere and aristocratic temper of Robert Baldwin recoiled from this turmoil, but his inflexible and uncompromising policy was not altogether out of place among the Upper Canadian "ultras." It required, as we shall see, the resourcefulness of Francis Hincks, the shrewdest coldest intellect of them all, without squeamishness and without scruple, to bring a semblance of order out of this political chaos. The contingency which gave this architect of the Canadian Reform party his chance must be examined in another context—the Russell-Sydenham régime under the Canadian union. Meanwhile the historic "principle" which was to bind these warring factions into a party had received its most convincing definition. It was in Upper Canada, in the midst of this incessant turmoil, that the Baldwins, father and son, developed the doctrine of responsible government in terms which found their way into Durham's *Report* and remain the classic formulation of parliamentary government in the British provinces.

V

Broken lights of the Baldwin doctrine are to be found at many earlier stages of colonial government. As early as 1809 Craig in Lower Canada reported to Castlereagh: "They either believe, or affect to believe that there exists a Ministry here, and that in imitation of the constitution of Britain that Ministry is responsible to them for the conduct of Government." Craig added a warning of "the steps to which such an Idea may lead them."

It may be that Pierre Bédard, with an approach to representative institutions through books and British newspapers rather than the empirical traditions of the first empire, understood the "constitution of Britain" as well as the old soldier who jailed him and seized the press of *Le Canadien*. It is deeply significant, however, that responsible government finds a place neither in the voluminous material placed before the select committee of the British House of Commons in 1828 nor in Papineau's Ninety-two Resolutions of 1834. Concentrating his attention upon "the elective principle," not only for the Legislative Council but for the governor himself,[1] upon the impeachment of executive councillors and their expulsion from the Assembly if appointed (as in Mondelet's case) from that body, upon the stopping of supply (no supplies were voted after 1832) and obstruction *à l'outrance* of government in every form, Papineau moved uncompromisingly towards republican models. To the end of the chapter responsible government with its indirect technique and accommodating temper was "false, tyrannical, and calculated to demoralize its

[1] Section 28 in the Ninety-two Resolutions of 1834.

people." It was "ruinous and destructive" of popular rights, the product of a "narrow and malevolent genius."

Perhaps the nearest approach to the doctrine of responsible government in Lower Canada was a phrase in the resolutions of the last Assembly before the Papineau rising, the last Assembly, as it proved, of the province of Lower Canada—an appeal to "the principles and practice of the British Constitution." By this time, however, it was obvious that the "practice of the British Constitution" if applied to Lower Canada would have been used to commit the province in the most immoderate and offensive terms to revolution and independence. The effect of this insoluble problem upon the cause of responsible government in the other provinces was far-reaching. Sir George Gipps of the Gosford select committee of 1828 was ready to concede independence itself if "demanded by an equal majority of an homogeneous people." In Nova Scotia Howe salvaged his cause by dissociating it altogether from Papineau's "uncompromising and offensive" tactics. The memoranda and minutes on the New Brunswick and Nova Scotia correspondence, as we have seen, attest the same baffling frustration at the Colonial Office: responsible government "if conceded in any one Colony . . . . must be granted in all." The issue was "not yet in a state for decision nor even for discussion." In the midst of the New Brunswick reforms of 1836 Glenelg commended the "just delicacy" of the Assembly in waiving any "peremptory rule" about their change in the Executive Council; and the Assembly obligingly disclaimed any intention of exacting such a practice "at all times." For Lord John Russell the spectre of "a ministry headed by M. Papineau" never ceased to haunt his colonial policy. Beyond a doubt it precipitated the fatal resolutions of 1837 which seemed to block for nearly a decade the concession of responsible government to all the provinces.

In Upper Canada the doctrine advocated by the Baldwins must have been current in reform circles many years before it found its way into the record. The Upper Canada *Herald* in October 1829 quoted a pamphlet said to have appeared during the Thorpe controversy before 1810 that "resignation of office must follow the loss of a parliamentary majority."[1] Robert Baldwin in 1838 assured Lord Durham that "as early as 1820 . . . some of the leading Members . . . adopted the principles now contended for as a part of their political creed, and assumed it as necessarily pertaining as much to the provincial Constitution as to that of the Mother Country." Robert Baldwin himself was but sixteen years of age in 1820, and he never ceased to

[1]Aileen Dunham, *Political Unrest in Upper Canada* (London, 1927), p. 168.

attribute his own dedication to the "great principle" to the doctrine learnt at his father's knee. It was Dr. W. W. Baldwin who forwarded to the Duke of Wellington in 1828 a petition against the dismissal of Judge Willis with the additional suggestion "that a legislative act be made in the provincial parliament to facilitate the mode in which the present constitutional responsibility of the advisers of the local government may be carried into effect: not only by the removal of these advisers from office when they lose the confidence of the people but also by impeachment for the heavier offences." Stanley replied truly that the views of the petitioners were not "very clearly expressed" for in point of fact "the remedy is not one of enactment but of practice." Dr. Baldwin's own covering letter, however, was unexceptionable in suggesting "a provincial ministry . . . responsible to the provincial parliament and removable from office by His Majesty's representative at his pleasure and especially when they lose the confidence of the people as expressed by the voice of their representatives in the Assembly; and that all the acts of the King's representative should have the character of local responsibility by the signature of some member of this ministry."

It is worthy of note that Mackenzie's *Seventh Report on Grievances* advocated "some heads of departments well paid, to direct the government, to prepare bills and most of the business of the session, and to hold office or lose it according as they may happen to be in the minority or majority in the House of Assembly." After the election of 1836, however, Mackenzie left the moorings of constitutional reform and sailed for the open sea. In truth the gulf between Mackenzie and the Baldwins had deepened with every issue. The avalanche of Mackenzie's grievances merely complicated the main issue and obscured the simplicity of the remedy. "Many that have been harped upon in the political heat of the day as evils of appalling magnitude," wrote Robert Baldwin to Durham in 1838, "are no grievances at all and many others would cease to be so under the system proposed." With responsible government the colonies could redress their own grievances.

Accepting Sir Francis Head's invitation to join the Executive Council in 1836, Baldwin and Rolph not only avowed their "principle" but when Head failed to take their advice resigned in order to vindicate their responsibility to the Assembly. "It is the duty of the council," said the lieutenant-governor, "to serve *him*, not *them*." The ensuing technique of voting no confidence and stopping the supplies came to grief in the *débâcle* of the election of 1836, and Baldwin left for London at his own expense to forestall if there was yet time the impending rebellion. His failure to see Glenelg and his interview with Lord John Russell alike sealed the immediate failure of his mission. His famous memorandum, drafted at Glenelg's own request, was published nevertheless in *The Times* and in the *Parliamentary Papers* of 1839. It was enclosed, as we have seen, in a still more urgent appeal to Lord Durham after the interview with him in Toronto in 1838. By this time the doctrine had acquired in Baldwin's indomitable mind the precision and consistency of natural law. Upon its acceptance would depend "the ultimate destiny of Upper Canada." The governor would continue to be responsible to the Crown, but he would act "with the Advice and Assistance of the Executive Council, acting as a Provincial Cabinet." Its "formation, continuance in office and removal" would conform to British practice. This procedure would "place the Provincial Government at the head of public opinion, instead of occupying its present invidious position of being in direct opposition to it." The principle could be applied by simple instructions from the Colonial Office: it "consists in fact merely in the ordinary exercise of the Royal Prerogative." "The Concession of the principle therefore calls for no legislative interference;—It involves no sacrifice of any branch of the Royal Prerogative . . . from being an English Principle, it would strengthen the Attachment of the People to the connexion with the Mother Country."

To the memorandum of 1836 for Glenelg Baldwin now added for Durham "the solemn assurance of my belief that sooner or later it must be adopted, and those fatal Resolutions [of Lord John Russell in 1837] abandoned, or . . . England will continue to retain the Colonies by means of her troops alone." "Give those in whom the people have confidence an interest in preserving the *system* of your Government, and maintaining the connection with the Mother Country, and then you will hear no more of grievances because real ones will be redressed, imaginery ones will be forgotten."

In the majestic diction of Durham's *Report* this precise and legalistic doctrine became the epitome of responsible government for all the British provinces:

We are not now to consider the policy of establishing representative government in the North American Colonies. That has been irrevocably done. . . . To conduct their Government harmoniously, in accordance with its established principles, is now the business of its rulers; and I know not how it is possible to secure that harmony in any other way, than by administering the Government on those principles which have been found perfectly efficacious in Great Britain. I would not impair a single prerogative of the

Crown. . . . But the Crown must, on the other hand, submit to the necessary consequences of representative institutions; and if it has to carry on the Government in unison with a representative body, it must consent to carry it on by means of those in whom that representative body has confidence. . . .

Every purpose of popular control might be combined with every advantage of vesting the immediate choice of advisers in the Crown, were the Colonial Governor to be instructed to secure the co-operation of the Assembly in his policy, by entrusting its administration to such men as could command a majority. . . . This change might be effected by a single despatch containing such instructions.[1]

If courage is the hallmark of consummate statesmanship, Durham's avowal of responsible government in defiance of Lord John Russell's Resolutions and of Lord Melbourne's official repudiation may well stand at the summit of the pass to parliamentary government and the evolution of the Commonwealth. For the first time a British official dared openly to avow this dynamic principle. No other British official had ever wielded such rank and power in America. Durham staked them both, and in the end his life, upon the outcome. He did not live to see the achievement of responsible government. It is doubtful if he ever foresaw the manner of that achievement or how it was to function in the united province of Canada. In the House of Lords he once spoke of responsible government as "an isolated topic in the report," and indeed he observed that he "had never made use of the phrase." It is possible that he gave ground when discussing the prospects with Poulett Thomson who afterwards, as Lord Sydenham, claimed that his own plans for Canada had had the acquiescence of Lord Durham. If there is one fact beyond dispute, as we shall see, it is that responsible government, to Lord Sydenham, was an "inadmissible principle." The closing months of Durham's life may have been clouded with uncertainty. One looks in vain for Buller's serene faith in the outcome, or his mastery of the mode by which responsible government was to be won and by which it was afterwards to function. Buller's last letter to Durham was the comfort of a physician for a stricken man—a man stricken unto death—and it is doubtful if Buller's sagacious counsels to the men who were to vindicate Durham's memory, La Fontaine and his followers among them, could have had his approval even had he lived.

But the real heroes of triumphant causes are those who do not live to hear the victor's song. Durham's sublime courage, his spectacular advocacy, and the manner of his death at the darkest hour of the

[1]Durham's *Report*, ed. Lucas, II, 278 ff.

contest, left his name, like the Durham flag, a rallying point for the warring factions of Upper Canada. Hincks published the *Report* in the *Examiner* with "Responsible Government" at the masthead and with a dedication to Robert Baldwin, "the zealous, eloquent, and able advocate of those constitutional principles which have been at last recognized by a Governor General of Canada." The most regal British pro-consul in America had cast his imperial mantle over responsible government. The *Report* enfiladed the old tory tradition that reform was synonymous with treason and republicanism. The solution, as Howe had exclaimed in Nova Scotia, was found to be "perfectly *simple* and eminently *British.*" It is true that advocacy, even imperial advocacy, was not enough. It is now clear that empirical statesmanship on both sides of the Atlantic was to win the day over official policy. "It does not matter very much," wrote Buller at Durham's untimely death, "what the Government repudiates and what it recognizes, for certain it is that in the Parliament of United Canada it has created a power from which no Government in this country will be able to withhold that voice in the selection of its rulers, which Lord Durham showed to be a necessary consequence of representative institutions." For seven years British colonial secretaries, three of whom lived to become prime ministers, were deaf alike to Durham's *Report,* to Howe's *Letters,* and to Charles Buller's *Responsible Government for Colonies.* Seven days, it is written, they compassed the walls of the city, and the seventh day they compassed the city seven times; and the walls of the city fell when the trumpets sounded and the people shouted with a great shout. It was the shout, as we shall see, that brought down the walls of Jericho so that the people went up into the city, every man straight before him; but among all who blew with the trumpets first place has gone to Lord Durham for the courage, the dignity, the noble diction of his *Report.* It has long been possible to claim the fulfilment of the faith in which he died that Canada would one day do justice to his memory.

Chapter Eight

THE RUSSELL-SYDENHAM RÉGIME

THE last phase of the second empire—the old colonial system in the hands of Russell, Stanley, and Gladstone at the Colonial Office—was an appropriate prelude to the Commonwealth. Never was there a nobler attempt to make the old colonial system work. Many of the ablest administrators of their day gave the best years of their lives, and four of them life itself, to the experiment. But the system which Sydenham boasted he had running "in grooves" was as fatally doomed as any which the ill-starred American Department had ever hoped to establish in the first empire. It took ten years of statesmanship on both sides of the Atlantic to demonstrate this, but the solution has since been appropriated by more than a score of parliamentary communities all over the world, with consequences that may yet have a vast field of usefulness in the service of mankind.

I

The immediate effect of Durham's *Report* and of Howe's four *Letters to Lord John Russell* a few months later was to confirm the doctrine and harden the temper of the Melbourne whigs against responsible government. "There is nothing in this report," said Lord John Russell in the House of Commons, "which has at all, in my mind, shaken the argument by which at the time I supported that resolution [of 1837 disavowing responsible government]. . . . It is in my opinion one of the most important points contained in Lord Durham's *Report* and one on which I differ with him." More emphatic than the repudiation of "Finality John" was that of Melbourne himself: "The opinion of this country and this government was entirely opposed to independent responsible government."[1] In truth Durham's *Report* merely confirmed the obsession of both with the *impasse* in Lower Canada and "the measures which a ministry, headed by M. Papineau would

[1] *Hansard,* 3rd Series, LV, 657.

have imposed upon the Governor."[1] In demonstrating that Lower Canada by itself was ungovernable even by responsible government, Durham had postponed its adoption elsewhere, since the Colonial Office had been quick to see that "if conceded in any one Colony it must be granted in all." "To recall the power conceded would be impossible," and who could "take upon himself to say that such cases will not again occur?" In this dilemma there was much to be said for a temporizing policy of delay until responsible government could be conceded safely: until the Canadas could be reunited: until efficient departments of government could be set up in the Executive Council itself, and until some sort of reconciliation could heal the deadly rivalry of races.

But while Howe and Hincks were not unmindful of these empirical problems there was a note of infallibility in "Finality John's" Olympian logic which struck dismay into their counsels. A governor, said Lord John Russell, could not emulate the "high and unassailable position" of the Crown because he received "instructions from the Crown on the responsibility of a Secretary of State." "I am not prepared to lay down a principle, a new principle, for the future government of the colonies." "Can the colonial council be the advisers of the Crown of England? Evidently not, for the Crown has other advisers, for the same functions, and with superior authority."

It may happen, therefore, that the Governor receives at one and the same time instructions from the Queen, and advice from his executive council, totally at variance with each other. If he is to obey his instructions from England, the parallel of constitutional responsibility entirely fails; if on the other hand, he is to follow the advice of his council, he is no longer a subordinate officer, but an independent sovereign.

To a Nova Scotian like Howe, intent upon "nothing more than British subjects are entitled to but . . . contented with nothing less," there was a complacency about this barren logic which seemed little short of "sophistry": as though men could be argued into subordination or as though it were necessary before contemplating matrimony to exploit all the possibilities of divorce.

It was left to Sydenham, Lord John Russell's ablest colleague and disciple, to formulate their concerted doctrine in its last phase of

[1]Cp. Howe's *Letters*: "Admitting that in Lower Canada . . . such a policy may have been necessary; surely there is no reason why the people of Upper Canada, Nova Scotia, New Brunswick, Prince Edward Island, and Newfoundland, should, on that account, be deprived of the application of a principle which is the corner-stone of the British Constitution."

assurance and infallibility, and to demonstrate for a brief year or two its plausible success:

I am not a bit afraid of the responsible government cry. I have already done much to put it down in its inadmissible sense; namely the demand that the council shall be responsible to the assembly, and that the governor shall take their advice and be bound by it. . . . I have told the people plainly that, as I cannot get rid of my responsibility to the home government, I will place no responsibility on the council; that they are a *council* for the governor to consult, but no more. . . . There is no other theory which has common sense. Either the governor is the sovereign or the minister. If the first, he may have ministers, but he cannot be responsible to the government at home, and all colonial government becomes impossible. He must therefore be the minister, in which case he cannot be under the control of men in the colony.

It was Sydenham's versatility and resourcefulness which saved this barren logic for a year or two from disaster.

II

It is now possible in retrospect to appraise the chief features of the Russell-Sydenham régime which Sydenham boasted to be "in grooves running of itself, and only requiring general directions."

The old colonial system which the Russell-Sydenham régime was to galvanize into its last febrile spasm of plausibility had changed little in essential features in more than two centuries. The function of the Colonial Office was to direct policy, and in the last analysis to "decide" on the multifarious issues of colonial administration. While there had been varying methods of direction or supervision over the centuries of British colonization, the differences between Grenville of the Southern Department, Hillsborough and Knox in the new American Department, Castlereagh as Secretary for War and the Colonies, and Lord John Russell in the Colonial Office, had been differences of degree rather than kind. The nineteenth century had brought complications in this technique, but Lord John Russell insisted as confidently as William Knox or Grenville himself upon his own authority to "decide." In dealing with a disciplined political party in Nova Scotia in 1840 this authority, as we shall see, functioned in a manner truly curious to contemplate.

The governor, whether appointed like Sir William Berkeley in Virginia by Charles I, or like Cornwallis of Nova Scotia by the Southern Department, or like Haldimand in Quebec by the American Department, or like Craig in Lower Canada by the Department of War and the Colonies, or like Sir John Colborne by the Colonial

Office, was directly charged with "the administration of the government." His function was to "govern." This was as true in Connecticut and Rhode Island where the governor was elected as it was in the "royal" provinces where he was appointed by the Crown. After the revolution the state governors continued to "govern"—to function as in colonial days except that all governors were now elected instead of being appointed by the Crown.

The legislative and executive councils, whether identical in personnel, as in many of the old colonies and in Nova Scotia until 1838, or separate in both personnel and function, as in the Canadas, continued to follow the primitive patterns of the first empire. The legislative functions of the legislative council as a second chamber had encountered the strictures of colonial assemblymen from time immemorial, chiefly in the field of taxation. The right to amend money bills was as vigorously disputed in New Jersey before the revolution as in Nova Scotia during the "brandy dispute" of 1830.[1] As a second chamber appointed almost invariably for life, the legislative council usually discharged only too well its traditional function as a check upon the popular assembly. In the first reform Assembly of Upper Canada from 1828 to 1830 no fewer than fifty-seven bills were thrown out by the tory Council. In some of the old colonies where the legislative council was elective the same latent jealousies obtained, but from the outset of the second empire it was assumed that the elective principle would improve the prospects for popular legislation. Even for the first empire Governor Pownall in 1764 had advised the general separation of legislative and executive councils. It was reserved for Elgin, with characteristic Peelite sagacity, to point out that an elective council on a higher franchise might serve a conservative function in offsetting the excesses of a popular assembly. Reformers inspired by republican models almost uniformly advocated the "elective principle" for the councils of the second empire. Those, on the other hand, who advocated British parliamentary models were quick to see, as Baldwin pointed out to Lord Durham in 1838, that the basic problems of colonial government could never be solved merely by making the legislative council elective. Responsible government was essentially—and in its immediate objective exclusively—a technique for controlling the executive. If this solid objective could be won, all other issues of privilege, legislation included, could be added unto it.[2] Under Bald-

[1]In Pennsylvania the Council had no legislative functions as a second chamber, and thus the governor and Assembly were brought into direct juxtaposition.
[2]In that sense the famous *Rebellion Losses Bill*, traditionally associated with the

win's sagacious doctrine the Canadian "ultras" could afford to by-pass the innumerable "grievances" of Mackenzie's *Seventh Report* or of Papineau's Ninety-two Resolutions. The election of the legislative council, wrote Baldwin to Glenelg, "could never supersede the necessity" of controlling the executive. An executive council responsible to the assembly became the target for the day.

The historic function of the executive council had been to "advise and assist" the governor. In Sydenham's words they were "a *council* for the governor to consult, but no more." Appointed nominally "during pleasure," they normally held office for life. "I cannot learn," wrote Lord John Russell, "that during the present or last two reigns, a single instance has occurred of a change . . . except in cases of death or resignation, incapacity, or misconduct." Jacks of all trades and masters of none, few executive councillors except the law officers, the surveyor-general, and the inspector-general could claim any expert qualifications but successful self-interest for the "advice" they gave to the governor. In the pages of Howe's four *Letters to Lord John Russell* this "small knot of public functionaries" who "fill the offices and wield the powers of the Government" receive their classic delineation. The temporary governor himself usually surrendered to their insidious influence which was fortified by lifelong self-interest and assiduity. "While the Governor is amenable to his Sovereign, and the members of the Assembly are controlled by their constituents, these men are not responsible at all." From time immemorial counterparts to the "château clique" and the "family compact" of the Canadas had flourished in the royal provinces of the first empire, and it was assumed that their own obvious interests could be relied upon to support the "connexion" with the mother country and the system which fostered their privileges.

Between the executive council and the assembly there was a great gulf fixed. This hiatus, so rigidly stereotyped in the congressional system, was the result not of design but of retarded development. The same hiatus had obtained between the king's ministers and the House

---

concession of responsible government, had nothing directly to do with it. Elgin's decision to sign the bill established no precedent against either reservation or veto, both of which were provided for in the *B.N.A. Act of 1867*, s. 55. Had Elgin reserved the bill, however, he might have been thrown into the arms of the tory opposition and the smooth functioning of responsible government might have been jeopardized. The great lesson of the *Rebellion Losses Bill* was the faculty of responsible government to force control of everything else. An equally convincing demonstration was Galt's success in carrying through the Canadian tariff bill in 1859. The only alternative was for the Colonial Office "to assume the administration of the affairs of the Colony, irrespective of the views of its inhabitants."

of Commons under the Stuarts until as a result of two revolutions and a series of lucky accidents the conventions of parliamentary government had become established. To Bacon and to Wentworth for a time parliaments could be excellent "instruments for managing a people," but nothing in the end could reconcile parliaments to such management without such ministers as "Parliament may have cause to confide in." Could provincial assemblies numbering such men as Hincks, Baldwin, and La Fontaine, Howe, Huntington, and Uniacke, remain merely useful "instruments for managing a people"—"a useful and powerful engine in the hands of the Governor"? Sydenham professed to think so, and the "system" which he and his chief devised for the British provinces was one of the most valiant attempts in more than two centuries to make the old colonial system really work.

III

By 1830 certain defects in the old colonial system had become glaringly self-evident. Two were remedied by Lord John Russell himself and two or three other expedients were devised with incomparable skill by his lieutenant in British North America.

The first link in the chain of colonial governance was the Colonial Office itself. From the Durham mission to the concession of responsible government no fewer than six colonial secretaries held the seals—Glenelg, Normanby, Lord John Russell, Stanley, Gladstone, and Grey. Mediocrity could be charged against none of these men. But how could six men in ten years presume to "decide" the administration of a dozen maturing communities from three to ten thousand miles away, each with problems that must have taxed the resourcefulness of the ablest of administrators on the spot? Charles Buller in his *Responsible Government for Colonies* overwhelmed this solemn fiction with genial derision. "Mr. Mother Country" was found to be a few permanent clerks in the attics of Downing Street.

The strengthening of this weak link in the chain was undertaken by Lord John Russell himself. The rising hope of the Whig party, "beyond all comparison the ablest man," thought Sydney Smith, "in the whole administration," Lord John took over the Colonial Office in 1839. Whatever his faults he was never accused of not knowing his own mind. The Colonial Office could now "decide." The manner of that decision in Nova Scotia after Howe's resolutions of no confidence in February, 1840, must have appealed to Buller's sense of humour.

A second link, hitherto perhaps the weakest in the chain, was the function of the average governor in the hands of his self-interested advisers. Amid the growing complexity of modern conditions the governor could not govern. In the familiar passages of Howe's four *Letters* the antiquated fiction that a newly arrived governor was carrying out the views of the Colonial Office—or indeed his own—was examined at close quarters with convincing badinage:

He may flutter and struggle in the net, as some well-meaning Governors have done, but he must at last resign himself to his fate; and like a snared bird be content with the narrow limits assigned him by his keepers. I have known a Governor bullied, sneered at, and almost shut out of society, while his obstinate resistance to the system created a suspicion that he might not become its victim; but I never knew one who, even with the best intentions . . . was able to contend, on anything like fair terms, with the small knot of functionaries who form the Councils, fill the offices, and wield the powers of the Government. The plain reason is, because, while the Governor is amenable to his Sovereign, and the members of the Assembly are controlled by their constituents, these men are not responsible at all. . . . It is indispensable, then, to the dignity, the independence, the usefulness of the Governor himself, that he should have the power to shake off this thraldom . . . and by an appeal to the people, adjust the balance of power. Give us this truly British privilege, and colonial grievances will soon become a scarce article in the English market.

Measured by sheer resourcefulness and executive ability, the governor-general selected to repair this weak link in the chain was probably the ablest administrator who ever came to Canada. Entering the House of Commons at twenty-four years of age, Charles Poulett Thomson represented Manchester for ten years. For five years he had been a member of the Board of Trade, and finally its president. He was already marked out for the chancellorship of the exchequer when Lord John Russell induced him, at thirty-nine years of age, to undertake the task of demonstrating their new régime of colonial governance in British North America. A prodigious programme of reorganization and reform, rewarded by a peerage as Lord Sydenham and by the Order of the Bath, was compassed there in less than two years. At his death he was barely forty-one. His political sagacity found avowed disciples in Francis Hincks, John A. Macdonald, and Wilfrid Laurier, the first names in Canadian politics. If Sydenham's exuberant opportunism, his almost incredible exploits of tact and versatility in winning critics to his service, his assurance and demonic energy could not "govern" the British colonies, then, as Melbourne himself sardonically observed, "all will be up with him and with those who sent him too." Like Durham before him, and Bagot and Metcalfe after him, he may be said to have paid for his mission with his life—

"literally worried to death," Gibbon Wakefield asserted, in the toils of Canadian politics. "I have been done," he confessed to his brother at the end, "by the work and the climate united, and God knows whether I shall see the other side of the Atlantic again!" In a sense he died just in time for his great reputation, for nothing can be more certain than the failure of his system had he lived and remained at his post in Canada. "When I read Lord Sydenham's despatches," wrote Elgin in 1847, "I never cease to marvel what study of human nature or of history led him to the conclusion that it would be possible to concede to a pushing enterprising people . . . such constitutional privileges . . . and yet to limit in practice their power of self Government as he proposed."

The third link in the Russell-Sydenham régime, though undoubtedly concerted between them for the Canadian scene, was perhaps Lord John Russell's most distinctive contribution. The "thraldom" to which the governor had normally been subjected by the sedulous and irresponsible executive council must be broken before the current of imperial governance could flow uninterruptedly throughout the colony. Tenure "during pleasure" had become in practice appointment for life. Howe's plea in September, 1839, that the governor should "shake off this thraldom" was designed to enable the governor to employ councillors possessing the confidence of the assembly: a "British constitution" could then be "withheld from them by no plea but one unworthy of a British statesman—the tyrant's plea of power." Lord John Russell's purpose in "shaking off this thraldom" was vastly different. Following a recommendation of the Gosford commission of 1837, the despatch of October 16, 1839, imparted for the first time flexibility and mobility to the governor's control of the executive council:

Hereafter the tenure of colonial offices held during Her Majesty's pleasure, will not be regarded as equivalent to a tenure during good behaviour. . . . Not only will such officers be called upon to retire from the public service as often as any sufficient motives of public policy may suggest the expediency of that measure, but . . . a change in the person of the governor will be considered as a sufficient reason for any alterations which his successor may deem it expedient to make.

The governor could now adjust his administration to "the well-understood wishes and interests of the people."

To the reformers this famous despatch "bestowed all that was required" for responsible government. This was literally true—if the Colonial Office and the governor were both prepared to concede responsible government and to put it into effect with mutual goodwill. But this was not the purpose of the despatch of October 16, 1839. The evidence on this point is conclusive. Perplexed by the difference between the circular despatches attuned to "the well-understood wishes of the people" and the private instructions from Lord John Russell for dealing with Howe and his party in Nova Scotia, Sir Colin Campbell interpreted the terms of October 16 for further confirmation from the Colonial Office: it was "not intended to sanction any fundamental change of the Constitution, but merely to strengthen the hands of the Governor by enabling him more effectually to control refractory Public functionaries." On the margin of Sir Colin's inquiry Vernon Smith of the Colonial Office added the convincing comment that Sir Colin was "right in his interpretation of Lord John's letter." Melbourne stated in the House of Lords that Lord John Russell's despatch was intended "directly to counteract the principle . . . and was properly understood by Sir Colin Campbell." "The opinion of this country and this government was entirely opposed to independent responsible government." The despatch of October 16 was intended to short-circuit responsible government not to concede it. "The well-understood wishes of the people" were to be interpreted not by their representatives in the assembly but by the governor under the direction of the Colonial Office. The governor was to be "free to choose his Counsellors" in order to manage the assembly not to consult their "confidence"; to enforce the responsibility of his executive council not to the assembly but to himself; to coerce his councillors into administering not their policy but his own; and to provide himself with subservient "placemen" (Sydenham's own phrase) carefully selected to sponsor the governor's policy and to supply "that aid in the management of public affairs which is absolutely indispensable."

The fourth link in the chain of governance was Sydenham's characteristic contribution to the new régime. Glenelg had tried to integrate the executive and the Assembly by appointing two or three assemblymen to the Executive Council. Under Sydenham this historic hiatus in the old colonial system was effectually to be bridged over by the stipulation that councillors "whom it may be desirable to make use of in that way, should be required, when necessary, to become members of the Assembly . . . in order to afford their assistance there." In the first instance "the most influential members of either House— but especially those of the House of Assembly" were to be utilized for that purpose. The governor was thus to "acquire the necessary strength in the Legislature; and if the proper direction be given to their labours, and due firmness evinced in controlling them, the Council will prove a very useful and powerful engine in the hands of the Governor." This was "the extent to which Her Majesty's Government wish to go in administering affairs here according to the wishes of the People, and thro' persons having their confidence, at the same time that they reject a principle incompatible with Colonial Government." Above all, no alignments of parties other than his own were to be recognized in the pattern of this "useful and powerful engine in the hands of the Governor." It was assumed that political parties—the dynamic which had forced almost every phase of parliamentary government in Great Britain from the Grand Remonstrance to the Reform Bill—could be disposed of in British America by decapitation, by enticing their leaders in neutralizing proportions into coalitions in the Executive Council, disarming them for self-defence by the executive oath of secrecy, and appropriating their influence in the Assembly for the advancement of the governor's own policy. If "family compacts" had been the normal products of the old colonial system, "coalitions" were to become indispensable prerequisites, as we shall see, for the Russell-Sydenham-Stanley régime.

IV

Two other links in the chain—the fifth and sixth in the series—bore the hallmarks of Sydenham's versatile genius. The four links already welded, as we have seen, were the strongest available. Lord John Russell was in charge of the Colonial Office. Sydenham was at the throttle as Governor in Chief in North America. The despatch of October, 1839, was designed to break the thraldom of the governor to his councillors. Sydenham with mercurial ingenuity could then transform these "placemen" into a "useful and powerful engine in the hands of the governor." The Russell-Sydenham régime now required only speed and lubrication to by-pass "abstract principles" and to establish a record for efficient administration that has probably never been surpassed in Canada.

No such exploits in political administration had ever been projected in British America to "divert men's minds from the agitation of abstract points of government." Lower Canada for the moment presented no difficulties. The constitution had been suspended and the Governor's Special Council enabled him to dictate a series of arbitrary measures there that "would have taken ten years of an Assembly." The union itself, thought Sydenham, could be "settled" for Lower Canada by these summary methods. But for Upper Canada and the united

province after the union the problem was not so simple. A deficit of
£75,000 to be turned into a buoyant surplus, public works suspended,
"emigration going on fast *from* the province," public credit unequal to
the construction of indispensable canals, roads, and bridges, finances
"more deranged than we believed even in England"—all these conditions could be reversed only by a forthright policy of "practical
measures." Above all, a loan of £1,500,000 from the British treasury
could be relied upon to lubricate this machinery. The magic of
Sydenham's "wand," the ascendancy of his "star" in the political firma-
ment, became a legend in Canadian politics. Hincks himself surrendered to the prospect, as inspector-general, of spending that
£1,500,000.[1] In Nova Scotia Howe, too, was won by Sydenham's
ingratiating confidence in an "attempt to occupy the attention of the
Country upon real improvements." Against his own better judgment
and that of his best friends in the party, Howe agreed to enter one
of those hermaphrodite coalitions which formed the last and most
essential ingredient in the Russell-Sydenham régime. The necessary
impetus for speed and efficiency was to come from the Governor himself. "He is," said Sydenham, "in fact the minister. . . . There is I feel
satisfied so much good sense amongst the People—so much respect and
reverence for the Royal Authority, and so strong a desire for improve-
ment, that he may Govern with ease to himself, and contentment to the
people." Sydenham's exuberance at this stage is easily understood, for
by enticing Howe, Uniacke, and McNab into a coalition he had just
staved off the most dangerous and skilful of tactics against the whole
Russell-Sydenham régime—a formal resolution of no confidence in the
Executive Council, passed by a disciplined political party in the Nova
Scotian Assembly by a vote of 30 to 12.

It was in Canada, however, that the technique of coalition was most
dexterously exploited. "I am more than ever satisfied," wrote Sydenham, "that the Union affords . . . the only means by which the present
abominable system of government can be broken up, and a strong
and powerful administration, both departmental and executive, be
formed." Without the union "the province is lost. . . . From all I can
hear or see, I would not give a year's purchase of it, if some great
stroke is not given which shall turn men's thoughts from the channel
in which they now run. . . . I am sure it is the last and only chance."
To Melbourne he wrote with desperate urgency: "The whole system

[1]Hincks's appointment was suggested by Sydenham a week before his death.
Bagot who confirmed it conceded that Hincks was "at heart radicalissimus but he
supported Sydenham's Government, and says he will support mine." Bagot
Papers, IV, 54.

. . . must then be broken up and remodelled; and if for no other purpose than that the Union would be most desirable. . . . I am satisfied that if we fail in carrying it you may as well give up the Canadas at once, for I know no other means of governing either." Even Upper Canada, it would seem, was ungovernable except by decapitating parties and factions, turning their leaders into complacent "placemen," and avoiding at all costs "the great mistake" of his predecessors who fell "into the hands of one party or the other, and became their slave." "I will yield to neither of them," Sydenham added confidently. "I will take the moderate from both sides—reject the extremes—and govern as I think right, and not as they fancy." The era of "family compacts" was now to end. The sovereign specific for the future was to be coalition "including all parties." The preoccupation of Lord John Russell and Melbourne, of Stanley and Peel in Great Britain, of Sydenham himself and Metcalfe and Falkland and even of Bagot and Sir John Harvey, for a time, in Canada and Nova Scotia, with this business of disparaging political parties, of disarming their dynamic faculties by specious coalitions, became for seven years the commonplace of official policy. In the end Falkland concluded that nothing short of an Act of Parliament could prevent "a party Government" in Nova Scotia: how even this *brutum fulmen* was to function Falkland did not elaborate. Grey who cut at last this ineluctable Gordian knot wrote bluntly that "the system now established is that of Party Government, that is to say government by means of parties."

V

Thus reinforced and refurbished the old colonial system entered upon its final test. Many of the links, new as well as old, were to prove singularly ineffectual. At least four of them, as appraised by British, Canadian, and Nova Scotian reformers, were calculated in the end to destroy the very system they were designed to reinforce.

Sydenham's term of incomparable finesse as governor seemed for the moment irresistible, but what was likely to happen then? "Our dictator will be gone before another session," a confidential adviser once counselled La Fontaine, "and public opinion will bring renegade Reformers back to their faith." The "great measure" of Sir Charles Bagot was to fulfil this prophecy. Lord John Russell's despatch of October 16, devised to enable the governor to "control refractory Public functionaries," had a catalytic effect, altogether unforeseen, upon the whole system. It enabled a disciplined majority in the Assembly to determine beyond question whether the Governor in the first instance and the Colonial Secretary who instructed him were disposed to employ as councillors "those who *enjoy the confidence of the people* and can *command a majority in the popular branch.*" Sydenham's policy of bridging the age-old hiatus between the executive council and the assembly in order to enable his "placemen" to manage the House for the governor's own purposes could be used still more effectively by ministers responsible to the assembly to manage the policy of the governor. The favourite device too of the Russell-Sydenham régime for keeping reformers out of mischief—a forthright programme of "practical measures" calculated to "direct men's minds from the agitation of abstract points of government"—proved invaluable to the cause of responsible government itself, for it taught the reformers what good government was and provided indispensable departmental machinery and training for some of the ablest ministers in Canadian history. Even Lord John Russell's Olympian function to "decide" was to be called in question. "Whatever decision he might come to," said Charles Buller in the House of Commons, "he did not care a pin about it (a laugh). . . . Responsible Government would inevitably be established by the people themselves."

Finally the "great stroke" of policy without which "the province is lost" and Sydenham "would not give a year's purchase of it"—the Canadian union—had consequences so ironically contrary to those forecast by Sydenham and Durham that they have left their mark upon Canadian politics to this day. Parties and factions were to be "broken up and remodelled" in order to enable the Governor to "reject the extremes—and govern as I think right and not as they fancy." It was the Canadian union which enabled Francis Hincks, the architect of the party which won responsible government in Canada, to bring Baldwin and La Fontaine together for one of the historic alliances of Canadian politics. "Never again," Durham had written, "will the present generation of French Canadians yield a loyal submission to a British Government. Never again will the English population tolerate the authority of a House of Assembly, in which the French shall possess or even approximate to a majority." Yet it was under the Canadian union that La Fontaine and his followers helped to win the most cherished of Durham's recommendations. And conversely it was under the Canadian union, in the closest association ever attempted by the two historic races of Canada, that those special rights and privileges were won back which were finally underwritten by the Canadian federation.

This train of policy was already in process before the Act of Union passed the British Parliament. The foundations of the new Canadian Reform party were already laid before Sydenham left England. For

more than two years before the first session of the united Assembly
Hincks and Baldwin, La Fontaine and Morin, with the *Examiner* and
the *Minerve* to expound their cause, had been toiling at their task.
In Nova Scotia, meanwhile, a disciplined Reform party was already
in control of the House. The *dénouement* in both provinces is largely
traceable to the success of these two parties in extricating themselves
like Samson from the green withs of specious coalitions, in reforming
their shattered ranks after defeat in 1843–4, and in resisting the
blandishments and in the end the open attempts of their adversaries
to compromise their integrity. Sanctioned by the conjunction of three
epochal elections—the return of the Whigs to power in Great Britain
in 1846, the reform victory in Nova Scotia in August, 1847, and the
overwhelming reform majority in the Canadian elections of 1848—
responsible government passed quickly into practice in both provinces.
   This development may now be traced without irrelevant details.

Chapter Nine

"THE TUG OF WAR"

THE Canadian union had been decided upon in Great Britain before Durham's *Report* was received and it is altogether probable that the prospects of a reform party for the united province were discussed with Buller before the Durham mission left Canada. Charles Buller's unfailing insight into the mode of responsible government is in evidence at every turn. At Durham's death he wrote to Lady Mary Lambton, afterwards Lady Elgin, with confidence undaunted by the official repudiation of Lord John Russell: "If there is anything certain in the course of events, it is that the great principles, with which he has linked his name, will henceforth amid all the chances of party politics, & passing events, make good their sure and steady way." "It does not matter very much," he added a few weeks later, "what the Government repudiates and what it recognizes, for certain it is that in the Parliament of United Canada it has created a power from which no Government in this country will be able to withhold" responsible government. Buller's letters to Hincks, now lost, were cited to La Fontaine as early as October, 1839,[1] and there is every indication that Hincks like Howe in Nova Scotia profited more than once from Buller's sagacious counsels.

Hincks's first letter to La Fontaine, dated April 12, 1839, was written without previous acquaintance. Between that date and the first session of the Canadian Assembly in June, 1841, no fewer than thirty-four of these confidential letters are to be found in the La Fontaine Papers. So discreet and secret was this intercourse that it could not be entrusted to the post office of those days. The good offices of trusted friends and a visit of La Fontaine to Toronto during the summer of 1840 enlarged the confidential circle to include Morin, Cherrier, Viger, Woodruff, and a few others. With the meeting of La Fontaine and Baldwin the alliance took on a deeper and more

[1]Sir Francis Hincks died of smallpox in 1885 and it is possible that the Buller correspondence was destroyed at that time.

intimate relationship. Domestic bereavement for both charged this friendship as time went on with mutual sympathy and affection. Baldwin's incorruptible character, his uncompromising rectitude, his inflexible "principle," remained the sheet-anchor of the Canadian reform party until responsible government was won. But the strategy was the strategy of Francis Hincks, and the political alliance which he advocated became a landmark in Canadian politics.

The induction of a group of young French Canadians, trained in the Papineau school of uncompromising obstruction, into the Eleusinian mysteries of responsible government was no easy task. La Fontaine's long association with Papineau, his ineradicable bitterness intensified by Durham's proscription of "his people," the brutal terms of the union and the manner of its passing in Lower Canada, must have given many a rankling reflection to a young patriot of La Fontaine's sensibilities. How he responded to the crisis, how he mastered his old prepossessions and turned with his new friends to face the unpredictable prospects of the union, with smouldering faith but with a grim sense of destiny for his country, is traceable in the La Fontaine Papers. How he succeeded in purveying that faith to others, in training them to discipline and forbearance and acquiescence if not confidence in the mysteries of a new technique, remains a more baffling problem, one to which Canadian history has not yet found the answer.

The burden of Hincks's argument was threefold: that the union which outraged La Fontaine's instincts and many of his dearest interests in detail could yet, through the co-operation of trusted allies, restore French Canada to an honourable and honoured place in Canadian politics; that responsible government, with all its indirection and conventions would be more effective for this purpose than uncompromising obstruction; and finally that the British connexion, exploited though it had been by the *château clique,* could be a better guarantee for the rights of "his people" at the darkest hour of their fortunes than the most logical application of the "elective principle" under a hypothetical republic. All three of these arguments were fairly won: sometimes by ingratiating candour, sometimes by the adroit indoctrination of events, and not infrequently by invoking the serene faith, the incorruptible character, of Robert Baldwin.

The first of Hincks's theses was perhaps the most debatable, for the details of the union—the equality of representation for the two sections of the province at a time when the population of Canada East outnumbered that of Canada West 600,000 to 450,000, the assumption of

the Upper Canadian debt by the united province, the proscription
of the French language, the despotic measures of the Special Council
after the suspension of the constitution in 1838—were "monstrously
oppressive and unjust." "Lord Durham" wrote Hincks, nevertheless, in
his first letter, "ascribes to you national objects; if he is right union
would be ruin to you, if he is wrong . . . the union would in my
opinion give you all you could desire." "On the Union question,"
he wrote a fortnight later, "you should not mind Lord D.'s motives,
but the effect of the scheme." "If we can act as Canadians for
the good of Canada," he repeated, "then a Union would I am convinced be beneficial to the French Canadians. It would remove the
pretext of national hatred and secure the common objects of all." As
a result of Hincks's shrewd tactics the Upper Canadian tories were
left to fight the Governor-General in advocating "the breaking of the
union at any cost." "Pray do try not to quarrel with Mr. Thomson."
"Be assured the Union is the only chance for us Reformers. . . . Let
the Tories fall into the pit of their own digging." After an interview
with the Governor-General Hincks's confidence in the union was "un-
bounded." "*We can not be beat.* Our Tories particularly Orangemen
are savage at the Union. They openly talk of preferring a Junction with
the Yankees to one with you French Canadians. . . . You may depend
upon it that we shall never consent to a Union unless it is founded
upon *Justice to all classes.*" "Depend upon it *all our liberties* must be
attained by that means." Under Sydenham's necromancy with men
and measures during the early days of the union La Fontaine's chronic
scepticism took on a deeper gloom, but the invincible resolve of Robert
Baldwin to "stand by the Reformers of Lower Canada" and the healing reconciliation of Bagot's "great measure" established an accord
between the two races which has never been irreparably imperilled.

The second of Hincks's theses was by far the most important for
upon it depended the validity of the other two. "I wish we could convince you," he wrote, "that a really responsible Executive Council
would accomplish all we want." "If we once had responsible government . . . we should in a very short time *obtain everything* we have
ever asked." "All that is right *must be conceded* afterwards." The pre-
dilection of La Fontaine's associates for cutting off the supplies, for
an elective legislative council, for placing Baldwin himself in the
Speaker's chair in order to lead the attack after the Papineau manner,
gave way slowly before the patient application of Baldwin's "principles." This interchange of opinion as the reformers from both provinces struggled with a concerted policy for the Legislature would make

a curious anthology of self-government in practice. It is easy in all this to trace the mastery of Robert Baldwin. More than once Hincks himself was receiving instruction in the doctrine which he was expounding to his colleagues. "Mr. Baldwin often urges on me," he wrote, "the propriety of not attacking the Governor *personally* but his Council for the acts of the Government. I know it is hard to do this as I have told him, but on our own principle we ought to consider the Governor as acting under the advice of his Council and not to make a personal quarrel with him." When La Fontaine declined office under Sydenham and a bitter conflict seemed imminent, Hincks reminded him that if he "had only taken office the Governor would have done everything he could." Obstruction would only deliver him "into the hands of the Tories." "I believe," Hincks added frankly, "His Excellency thinks you an *impracticable* man who will not work with any Government." There was a "conviction that the Reformers of Lower Canada will yield nothing to produce harmony." "I know you think we shall never get Responsible Government, that the ministry are deceiving us—granted—But *we will make them give it whether they like it or not.*" When Hincks himself charged the government with "fraud and dissimulation" Baldwin conveyed his "disapprobation of the tone and temper assumed by the *Examiner*" in terms which deserve quotation if only for the ponderous exactitude of his doctrine:

While . . . resolved, as I am fully convinced the Reformers of Upper Canada are, to unite with their Lower Canada brethren cordially as friends, and to afford them every assistance in *obtaining Justice . . . they ought . . .* fully to understand that it is not . . . to collision . . . to stop inevitably the whole machinery of the Constitution that we look for the accomplishment of this Just and necessary object, but on the contrary to the harmonious working of the Constitution *by means of the new principle to be applied to its practical administration,* coupled with that forbearance, moderation and firmness on our parts which is ever the best evidence of fitness for the exercise of political power.

This gospel according to Robert Baldwin was duly passed on to La Fontaine and his associates, reinforcing sagacious counsels from Charles Buller which Hincks had already purveyed to the same critical audience:

I feel sure [wrote Buller] that the Union with all its defects will give the people of Canada so much power that I am content. . . . Your fate is now in your own hands. Be energetic and firm but also be moderate and whatever you do do not needlessly embroil yourselves with the autocrats at home. Your public conduct has been all I could wish but I think in your private expressions to me you Judge Mr. P. Thomson too harshly. . . . The business of the Reformers of Upper Canada is to strengthen Mr. Baldwin's hands as much as possible in the United Parliament. The great principle of Responsible Government is not to be carried by any Legislative measure or any Executive coup de main. Silently, gradually and quietly must it work its way and become the real principle of colonial administration. . . . Avoid collision with the Government. . . . Lead it on but do not confront it. Attach no importance to enforcing from it a distinct recognition of an implicit conformity with the principles of Responsible Government which both its own foolish point of honour and the state of opinion here prevent it openly adopting.

"Return a Reforming majority," Buller added confidently, "and depend upon it that from that hour Mr. B. will direct the Executive Government."

It was not easy to maintain this serenity. The time was soon to come, in September, 1842, when Baldwin rather than his friend was to prove "impracticable" and uncompromising in taking office together under the benign statesmanship of Sir Charles Bagot. Hincks who had preceded them both in office was already deep in Bagot's counsels. In the Metcalfe crisis, as we shall see, all three of them staked their case on a trivial point of patronage, lost the ensuing election, and jeopardized their cause for four years. But La Fontaine lived to see the rights of "his people" vindicated at last by the "principles" which he had adopted with so many misgivings. "Je n'hésite pas à dire," he said as early as 1841, "que je suis en faveur de ce principe anglais du gouvernement réponsable. . . . Les Réformists dans les deux provinces forment une majorité immense. . . . Notre cause est commune." Less than ten years after Durham's prophecy the cause of French Canada which had reached its lowest ebb on this continent after the Papineau rising and the suspension of the constitution in 1838 was restored to the honoured position which it still occupies in the Canadian federation. It is a remarkable fact that this feat was achieved under the closest *rapprochement* which has ever subsisted between French and English in the second empire—the bonds of a legislative union.

The third of Hincks's theses required no small amount of courage in 1839. For Robert Baldwin the British connexion like the British technique of parliamentary government remained an obsession, and Hincks's task was the easier for this unflinching example. To reconcile French Canada after a whole generation of bitter recrimination from the "English" within their gates—and not only to reconcile but to attract and attach—must have required a prodigy of faith. "I can fully enter into your feelings," Hincks wrote in one of his earliest letters, "towards that infamous (*miscalled Believe me*) British party in Lower

Canada which I hate as cordially as you can do and you may perceive that the love they bear me is about the same as if I were a French Canadian." At the same time he wrote frankly that the rank and file of Upper Canadian reformers "do not like *your countrymen* whom they look on as determined republicans or rather anti-British. . . . My impression is that a large majority of the [Upper Canadian] people desire British connexion provided it is consistent with the entire management of their own local affairs. . . . I am myself for British connexion." How a disciple of Louis Joseph Papineau could come to see salvation in *perfide Albion*—how a disciple of Durham could champion the cause of French Canada—how the legacy of bitterness from Craig and Aylmer could be turned to "oil and gladness" at the hands of Bagot and Elgin, remains the miracle of these eventful years.

Beyond a doubt the answer is to be found very largely in the imponderable realm of character. Between La Fontaine and Baldwin there were depths of understanding and of sympathy which have never been convincingly fathomed. Both toiled with disgust through the "tracasseries of Political life." Usually suspicious and uncharitable in his estimates of measures and of men, La Fontaine responded to Baldwin's incorruptible integrity, his transparent sincerity, his intractable loyalties, and even the melancholy despondency of domestic bereavement, with kindred feelings deepening into profound respect and affection. In 1846, at the temporary eclipse of their political fortunes, La Fontaine still wrote of Baldwin's "patriotism," his "noble character, public and private, and above all, my sincere friendship for the man whom I always considered one of my happiest days to have become acquainted with." Others too contributed to La Fontaine's final attachment to the British connexion. He once left Bagot's presence with tears in his eyes. "Come what may," he exclaimed during the Metcalfe crisis, "I desire above every thing to remain at peace with my own convictions." At a time when Metcalfe was accusing his former ministers of treason and republicanism, La Fontaine in private was bitterly denouncing "such imputations": "Far from thinking of separation," he wrote to Baldwin, "I quite agree with you, and I do not hesitate in stating that I sincerely believe it to be the material interest both of England and Canada that the connection should subsist as long as possible." Responsible government itself would "secure the connection." The contribution of Elgin and Grey to this growing accord was of course incalculable. In the end, Sir Louis La Fontaine (the baronetcy was suggested by Lord John Russell himself), first prime minister of the united province of Canada, came to value the union for its own sake. It was La Fontaine, speaking in French in the caucus of the reform party in 1848, who withstood the bitterest attack of his old chief upon the technique and temper of responsible government. In the Assembly Papineau was unable to find a seconder to his amendment against Baldwin's address of "Loyalty and attachment to the British connexion."

II

The first test and perhaps the narrowest escape of the Russell-Sydenham régime came in Nova Scotia. The disciplined party which had carried Howe's Address to the Crown in 1836 had received the news of Lord John Russell's resolutions of 1837 with consternation. Durham's *Report* and Howe's four *Letters* did much to restore the confidence of the party in the ultimate success of their cause. Through the columns of the *Novascotian* both these classics found their way into the familiar language of political discussion in every constituency of the province. The party which Howe afterwards extolled in the hour of success—"a more manly, public-spirited, united, and disinterested body of men were never exhibited by the legislative conflicts of any country"—had now reached its prime. Its morale was probably never higher. Its solidarity was as yet unbroken by the distractions of Howe's own capitulation to Sydenham or the *gaucheries* of his quarrel with Falkland. The confidential interview with Glenelg in 1838 had left a profound impression of goodwill, of "goodness of heart and habitual suavity of temper." "No man," Howe afterwards wrote, "gave the old system a fairer trial; no man less deserved the fate to which it almost invariably consigned its victims." The delegation of Young and Huntington at their own expense to the Colonial Office in 1839 had reached London just in time to witness Lord John Russell's second repudiation of responsible government.

But two incidents of the local scene in Nova Scotia in 1839 had established the goodwill of the province beyond dispute. During the Aroostook "war of pork and beans" over the Maine boundary the Nova Scotia Assembly had voted £100,000 and called out the militia, to the accompaniment of cheers that spread from the old Province Building to the streets of Halifax. In Howe's four *Letters* (September, 1839) this prevailing temper of the province was unanswerable. Why should the British constitution be "completely reversed on this side of the Atlantic"? Admitting that in Lower Canada Lord John Russell's policy "may have been necessary," could this justify the denial to five British provinces of "a principle which is the corner-stone of the British Constitution"? "The population of British North America are sincerely attached to the parent State." They want no "other form of government here than that which you enjoy at home. . . . Why should we desire a severance of old ties that are more honourable than any new ones we can form? . . . This suspicion is a libel upon the colonist and upon the Constitution he claims as his inheritance."

Am I not justified, my Lord, in claiming for my countrymen that constitution, which can be withheld from them by no plea but one unworthy of a British statesman—the tyrant's plea of power? I know that I am; and I feel also, that this is not the race that can be hoodwinked with sophistry, or made to submit to injustice without complaint. All suspicion of disloyalty we cast aside . . . We seek for nothing more than British subjects are entitled to; but we will be contented with nothing less.

To this robust assertion Howe added a shrewd comment which became a classic before the contest was over. The solemn fiction that the governor governs by "instructions from the Crown on the responsibility of a Secretary of State" was one of those "nostrums by which the science of politics, like the science of medicine, is often disfigured for a time." In practice the governor who was "amenable to his Sovereign" was usually in thrall to executive councillors who were "not responsible at all." "It is indispensable, then, to the dignity, the independence, the usefulness of the Governor himself, that he should have the power to shake off this thraldom . . . by an appeal to the people. Give us this truly British privilege, and colonial grievances will soon become a scarce article in the English market."

The *dénouement* followed swiftly. Howe's four *Letters* were dated September 8, 1839. Lord John Russell's circular despatch of October 16 for the first time shook off this thraldom of the Executive Council by authorizing their dismissal "from the public service as often as any sufficient motives of public policy may suggest the expediency of that measure." To Lord John Russell and to Melbourne, to Sydenham and to Sir Colin Campbell, this despatch was intended, as we have seen, to "strengthen the hands of the Governor by enabling him more effectually to control refractory Public functionaries." But to Howe and Huntington it could serve a vastly different purpose. In Canada the Governor-General had just announced the Queen's commands to govern "in accordance with the well-understood wishes and interests of the people." The despatch of October 16 therefore "bestowed all that was required" for responsible government. The Governor was now free to adapt the Executive Council to "the well-understood wishes" of the people. On February 3, 1840, Howe moved four resolutions in the Assembly culminating in the historic formula that "the

Executive Council, as at present constituted, does not enjoy the confidence of the Commons." In a speech of great moderation and power he forecast a "form of government, which will, like the atmosphere, yield to every necessary pressure, preserve the balance of liberty, and yet expand with the growth of our posterity to remote generations." "Proud and happy that the commencement of these great changes should be laid here," he foretold their extension "into all the British dependencies." "The other colonies would follow her example." Two days later, on February 5, the resolution of no confidence passed by a vote of 30 to 12, and J. B. Uniacke, son of the old "Cumberland rebel" and afterwards first prime minister overseas, tendered his resignation as executive councillor and crossed the floor of the House to join the Reform party. "From that hour," Howe declared all too confidently in the Assembly, "they might date . . . a constitution of which no power on earth could now deprive them."

The sorry device by which this flawless prelude to responsible government was frustrated taxed the resourcefulness of the Russell-Sydenham régime. Sir Colin Campbell, still in thrall to his Executive Council, replied loyally that he was still "satisfied with the advice and assistance which they have at all times afforded me." Moreover he was categorically instructed by Lord John Russell himself "not to assent to the Address of the House of Assembly, for the change of the Members of the Executive Council of Nova Scotia collectively, without the previous sanction of Her Majesty." Thus had the Colonial Secretary "decided." Sydenham from Montreal added his warning to Lord John Russell that "to change the Executive Council would be to give up the principle for which we contend" and establish the "objectionable principle" of responsible government. This "could only be met when thus urged by a refusal." Meanwhile the resolute party in the Assembly, baffled by the irrefutable fact that Sir Colin had either violated his instructions or had been instructed to withhold responsible government, resolved to give Lord John Russell the benefit of the doubt. "Five-and-twenty stern men," like soldiers "called out on a firing party," voted for gallant old Sir Colin's recall. Howe once referred to this vote as "the severest trial of my life. . . . If ever I performed a task with a heavy heart it was that." There seemed no other way of "testing this Constitution," as Sir Colin himself came to see before the crisis was over. His parting handshake with Joseph Howe, "in the midst of a dozen of the Tories," must have concealed some poignant qualms about the old colonial system. "You did what you thought was right," he said to Howe in the hearing of his councillors, "you did

it fairly and honorably, and I have no unkind feeling towards you."
The old soldier was being sacrificed for carrying out his instructions.

Lord John Russell's first instincts were to regard the address for Sir
Colin's recall as "a very unusual, irregular, and inconvenient pro-
ceeding" which he declined peremptorily (so he assured Sir Colin)
to "submit to Her Majesty" for approval. To Sydenham he wrote on
the same day that "the Queen has remarked with pain" the demand
for Sir Colin's recall. Sydenham himself was not so squeamish. From
Montreal he wrote that he was "not disposed to consider the Address
of the House of Assembly for the removal of the Governor as a step
so objectionable as the other." This was the "legitimate mode for the
Legislature when it is unsatisfied with the Executive Council." And
thus it came to pass that Lord John Russell who had assumed "the
responsibility of deciding" with regard to "the total change" in the
Executive Council demanded by the Assembly, decided to recall Sir
Colin Campbell "in the present circumstances of the Canadas." To
Sydenham with his magic wand, already deep in the turmoil of
Canadian politics, was entrusted the task of arranging the details
upon the spot, and Her Majesty's Government (Lord John Russell
explained to Sir Colin Campbell) "are relieved from the necessity of
entering into many explanations."

For Howe and his cause the Colonial Secretary's function of "deciding" proved for the time equally fatal. Something of Lord John
Russell's perplexity on this score is decipherable in his own handwriting upon the margins of the Nova Scotia despatches. With a sense
of justice seldom wanting in that remarkable man he noted that there
was obviously "something untold." Reformers, in a majority of 30 to
12 in the Assembly, were put into the Executive Council "in a
Minority—They were out-voted in the Cabinet." More than two-thirds
of the Assembly had been termed "a few factious demagogues." It
was obvious that the House sought nothing "dangerous to the connection." It was equally obvious that "a considerable change in the
composition of the Executive Council is desirable." Howe himself was
an obvious choice "were it not that such an appointment at this
moment might appear a sanction to the opinions of his recent publication." Here again the exigencies of the Governor-General who was
supposed to govern took right of way over the prerogatives of the
Colonial Secretary who was supposed to "decide." Sydenham, then in
the throes of Canadian politics at Montreal, was to post down to
Halifax with his star and his magic wand in order to compose the
issue on the spot.

III

Sydenham's success in inducing Howe to forego the interests of his party and to enter the coalition of 1840—the approved specific of the Russell-Sydenham régime—was perhaps the most spectacular pass of legerdemain in the Governor-General's repertoire. Howe's motives have been examined elsewhere[1] and there can scarcely be a doubt that the key is to be found in Lord John Russell's own phrase—"the present circumstances of the Canadas." Sydenham's mercurial finesse, his exuberant infallibility, were never more in evidence. At the famous interview *in camera* every instinct of Howe's public life—his prejudices as well as his exemplary moderation and his magnanimity—left him defenceless before the Governor-General's ingratiating appeal not to complicate the herculean task that lay before them in the Canadas. Howe afterwards wrote confidentially to Sydenham of his duty "to bring out the new policy discreetly." "Your Lordship has a difficult task before you in Canada." "We will do our duty to you." To Falkland he stated the aims of the coalition without reserve: "to aid the introduction of the new system, and to lessen, if possible, the difficulties with which, at that time, the Governor General was beset." Howe's appeal to his followers was equally ingenuous: to support the Governor-General by "throwing the influence of Nova Scotia into the scale of Canadian politics, strengthening his hands, and giving the principles we value a wide circulation," in the hope of making "Nova Scotia, by her loyalty, intelligence and spirit, as it were, a normal school for British North America."

The descent from these lofty regions of political altruism was swift and disconcerting. Howe's enemies accused him of selling his principles for office. His best friends charged him with wrecking the party. Huntington, who had stood as his second in the duel with young Halliburton, resolutely refused to enter the coalition and held to "the good old cause." The effect upon the party was in truth devastating. Howe's followers never forgot and some of them never forgave his defection. He agreed to serve in the Executive Council for two years "without fee or reward," and to combine that office with the speakership of the Assembly. More than once he left the Speaker's chair to rally the wavering support for the new coalition, and to defend what he believed to be the new system of "responsible government by degrees."

When Peel and Stanley returned to office in Great Britain a few weeks before Sydenham's death in Canada, it soon became obvious

[1]*Empire and Commonwealth,* 200 ff.

that there was to be a return "by degrees" to the old régime. Shrewder than Metcalfe in Canada, Falkland took the precaution of dissolving the Assembly and securing a narrow majority for the coalition while it was still intact upon the hustings. More fortunate too than Metcalfe, he could rely upon the serene temper and incisive counsels of J. W. Johnston, his new attorney-general, who had succeeded Archibald in that office in April, 1841. Johnston like Howe was the founder of a political party in Nova Scotia. Combining the most pertinacious religious traditions in the province, the Baptist traditions of New England, with the instincts and associations of the aristocrat—the "polish of manners" which Durham and Buller had remarked during his visit to Quebec in 1838—Johnston joined mortal combat with Howe at every point. Goaded to fury by his rival's skilful tactics and rising power within the Executive Council, deprived of his own old rostrum in the *Novascotian,* baffled after the return of the tories to power in Great Britain by the open jibes of his tory colleagues that responsible government was "responsible nonsense," Howe soon found the rising discipline of the Conservative party more than a match for his own. Uniacke informed him loyally of a cabal from within the coalition "to embark in the same boat . . . and throw Howe overboard." Howe wrote bitterly to Falkland that more was needed to make an adminis-tration than "nine men treating each other courteously at a round table. There is the assurance of good faith—towards each other—of common sentiments, and kindly feelings . . . in Society, in the Legis-lature and in the Press, until a great Party is formed . . . which secures a steady working majority to sustain their policy and carry their measures." The House could not be expected to have confidence in a coalition "who were supposed to feel none for each other."

The resignation of Howe, Uniacke, and McNab from the coalition took place a month after the Metcalfe crisis in Canada, but the Canadian issue, as we shall see, was less imperative.[1] A reference in Howe's diary as late as 1850 still shows the scars of the Sydenham régime as he recalled his desperate plight at the time of his resig-nation in 1843. "Weary and sick at heart," with "debts to pay—seven children to maintain—no fortune, and . . . a four years' fight against an infernal faction before me," Howe reflected ruefully upon the "ceaseless strife, the heartless insincerity," "the appearance of trick

[1] A charge by Falkland that the issue was the same stirred the reformers to unprecedented vehemence: "In the name of the ex-Councillors, on the house-tops, before Lord Falkland's face; aye, in the presence of the Queen herself . . . we will pronounce it a base, black falsehood, without a shadow of foundation."

and humbug" that followed Sydenham's departure from Nova Scotia. If he ever suspected the real views of that wily autocrat he never admitted it. In truth the Russell-Sydenham régime never had a chance. This was the end of coalitions in Nova Scotia. Falkland tried in vain to fill the vacant chairs at the council table from the Reform party, but "the Liberals," said Howe, "will have party government . . . and the Tories can form no other." From the interminable prolixity of Falkland's despatches one fact emerged which even Stanley could not gainsay: the reformers could "force . . . a party Government." In the end, wrote Falkland, they "must triumph absolutely." That "crisis," he added, could only be met by an Act of Parliament. How an Act of Parliament could prevent reform councillors resigning from a coalition, or coerce them into joining one, Falkland did not elaborate. Grey's conclusion from this dilemma, reinforced as we shall see by the Metcalfe crisis in Canada, supplied another escape from the Russell-Sydenham régime. The governor and the home government must "belong to neither party and have nothing to do with their contests. . . . This principle must be completely established in order long to preserve our connection with the Colony."

The final stages of the Falkland régime in Nova Scotia brought the politics of that province to the lowest ebb. In the vendetta between Falkland and Howe their mutual vulnerability derived much of its deadliness from their previous intimacy. The infirmities of both came seething to the top. In Howe's case this "war to the knife" (Falkland's phrase) stultified the very principles of responsible government, as Baldwin could have told him. Concluding that "moderation and magnanimity are thrown away," Howe plunged into a "more barbarous style of warfare" which coarsened his temper, debased his name, and lost him, in all probability, the distinction which in all his life he coveted most, the first premiership overseas in 1838. He lived to become, like Falkland himself, lieutenant-governor of his native province, and he died in Government House,[1] but he never ceased to deplore "this disgraceful page from our Provincial history."

On the other side Howe's Rabelaisian humour was matched by the *gaucherie* of a lieutenant-governor defending his administration over his own name in the newspapers, and printing in the *Gazette* a letter of support from Stanley against "the pretensions of the retired Councillors." Johnston with his courtly skill and solemn resolutions against "breaches of decency and good manners" moved steadily forward to

[1]A truly ironical fulfilment of Falkland's prophecy to Stanley, August 2, 1844, that Howe's appointment to the Executive Council would "degrade the office I hold . . . and make Mr. Joseph Howe *de facto* Governor of Nova Scotia."

consolidate his party and his reputation. Here was an executive council, homogeneous in spite of itself, led by one of the most adroit parliamentarians of his day, commanding a majority, albeit a narrow one, in the Assembly; and a governor who assuredly took their advice and was bound by it. Sydenham himself could scarcely have defined more accurately responsible government "in its inadmissible sense." Years afterwards Thomas Chandler Haliburton ("Sam Slick") once claimed in a lecture in Glasgow that responsible government had been introduced in 1844 by the Conservative party of Nova Scotia. For Stanley himself as for Metcalfe in Canada and for Falkland in Nova Scotia responsible government willy-nilly had become inescapable in the presence of disciplined political parties. But what would follow a Reform victory at the polls? In Stanley's opinion "the Canadas are gone." In Falkland's the only resource would be the *brutum fulmen* of an Act of Parliament. Such seemed to be the outcome of the Russell-Sydenham-Stanley régime.

IV

The developments in Canada, though complicated in endless detail by the union, followed the same pattern. The party which Hincks and Baldwin and Dunn had built up so sedulously with La Fontaine and his associates for the first session of the union Legislature slipped through their fingers like sand before the wizardry of Sydenham's management. Baldwin in taking office as attorney-general had avowed a "reasonably well-grounded confidence that the government of my country is to be carried on in accordance with the principles of Responsible Government which I have ever held." This was reinforced by a memorandum to the Governor-General himself—one of the dozens of votive offerings, usually in the third person, made by that uncompromising conscience upon the altars of political integrity. "Come what will," Hincks wrote reassuringly to La Fontaine, "Baldwin is *incorruptible. He has taken office solely from a sense of public duty.*" The day before the House was to meet for the first session after the union, Baldwin waited upon the Governor-General to announce his "entire want of political confidence" in four of his tory colleagues in the coalition, and "coolly proposed to me," wrote Sydenham, to "replace them by men whom I believe he had not known for 24 hours." Charging Baldwin with "some principle of conduct which I can reconcile neither with honor nor common sense," Sydenham "at once treated [the proposal] . . . as a resignation" and informed Baldwin that he "accepted it without the least regret."

Had Sydenham known how long this historic alliance had already been building—not twenty-four hours but more than twenty-four months—he might have spared his concern for Robert Baldwin's honour. For the time, however, the Governor-General's incomparable *élan* carried the field. Harrison, Dunn, Daly, and many of the "moderate Reformers" joined the "Government members"—"my candidates" as Sydenham called them—on the hustings. La Fontaine and the Lower Canadian reformers resolutely held their ranks, and Baldwin resolved to stand by them even if he were "sure of being deserted by the whole of Upper Canada." "I can hardly be surprised," Hincks wrote to La Fontaine "that the Lower Canadian members are disgusted at the conduct of our Reformers—I am so myself." Before long Hincks himself began to respond to the spell of Sydenham's demonic energy and enterprise. Rated the ablest financier of his generation in Canada though "at one time [Bagot afterwards wrote] Lord Sydenham's most uncompromising and ablest opponent," Hincks was selected as inspector-general by Sydenham himself a week before his death at Alwington House. The appointment was made by Bagot who added: "He is at heart radicalissimus, but he supported Sydenham's Government, and says he will support mine, and he has quarrelled with his friend Baldwin." Hincks's acceptance was "prompt, straightforward and unconditional." With both Howe and Hincks safely entangled in the toils of coalitions it seemed that the bogie of political parties in both Nova Scotia and Canada was safely laid.

In the Governor-General's despatches, however, there was a new note of desperation after the encounter with Baldwin. He urged the "absolute necessity" of sending out as his successor "*not* a soldier, but a statesman"—"some one with House of Commons and Ministerial habits,—a person who will not shrink from work, and who will govern, as I do, himself." The truth was that Sydenham's febrile resources were fast running out, and his own mind at the end was already clouded by premonitions that his "system" like his failing health might not survive the ordeal. Baldwin's resolutions of September, 1841, formulating the "principles" of responsible government with his usual ponderous exactitude, were perhaps the last major concern of Sydenham's administration. He met them by entrusting to Harrison a series of counter-resolutions so nearly resembling Baldwin's that historians ever since have been mystified by the subtleties of the difference. One sentence, carried by 56 votes to 7, was interpreted by Harrison to Sydenham's successor in terms that proved imperative: "the chief advisers of the representative of the Sovereign, constituting a Provincial administration under him, ought to be men possessed of the confidence of the representatives of the people." Less than a year after Sydenham's death both Harrison and Draper informed Sir Charles Bagot that a resolution of no confidence would probably be carried in the Assembly and that the Executive Council, in that event, would find it necessary to resign.

V

The familiar story of Bagot's "Great Measure" and the reaction under Metcalfe completed the collapse of the Russell-Sydenham régime in Canada. Stanley's instructions to both contained all the approved specifics: "seek to withdraw the Legislature, and the People generally, from the discussion of abstract and theoretical questions"; construct the Executive Council "without reference to distinction of local party, which, upon every occasion, you will do your utmost to discourage." In addition there were two or three considerations peculiar to the Canadian scene. "Without running counter to public opinion in England" how was it possible for the governor to take into his confidence "men tainted with violent suspicion of treasonable practices"? Colonel MacNab dined with Stanley on the Queen's birthday and was promised (as it afterwards appeared) the adjutant-generalship of the militia in order to safeguard the British connexion. "If you come into difficulties," Stanley added to Bagot, "that is the class of men to fall back upon."

Against this sombre background the sprightly spirit of Sir Charles Bagot wrought for a time one of those miracles in human relations that were to play so large a part in the normal functioning as well as in the achievement of responsible government. Nephew of the Iron Duke and an intimate friend of both Stanley and Peel, Bagot brought fewer inhibitions to fetter his goodwill than any governor who had ever come to Canada. He was not trained, as Sydenham had enjoined, in "House of Commons and Ministerial habits," but he was assuredly a "statesman." Diplomacy, as Hincks afterwards remarked, was "the very best school" for Canadian politics. Bagot's record included diplomatic feats of lasting value with Russia, with the Netherlands, and in the Rush-Bagot conventions with the United States, but his greatest diplomatic exploit was yet to come: not only with La Fontaine and Baldwin whom he manœuvred into acquiescence and at last into profound attachment, but with his chief and with Peel whom he disarmed with the lightning stroke of a fencing-master. "There never was a man acted a nobler part," added Hincks, "or with more consummate statesmanship. . . . Sir Charles Bagot was a much more profound Statesman than is generally imagined." "The secret of . . . success was his *strict impartiality*."

It is clear from the blithesome pages of the Bagot Papers that his mind was not only unprejudiced but predisposed towards the French in their bitter plight under the union. His own views were corroborated from many quarters. French Canada could yet be "recovered" and Bagot might yet become their "Protector"—this from Colborne, now Lord Seaton. "*Au fond,*" Sir George Murray had written, "They are the most anti-Yankee, as well as the most Monarchical" element in British America. A colleague of Bagot's in Washington, deploring the unaccountable estrangement of a chivalrous people, attached the "deepest political and Diplomatic importance" to the recovery of their affections. Draper, whom Bagot regarded as "the most Conservative" of his councillors, urged the "overwhelming importance of gaining the confidence—and removing the distrust" of French Canada. Like Elgin and long before him, Bagot sensed their essential conservatism and anticipated the association which became under Macdonald and Cartier a commonplace of Canadian politics for more than a generation. As early as February, 1842, in "confidential" despatches to Stanley, Bagot was imploring him to "wean them from what I feel to be a false and unsafe position." "The peculiarity of their position on this continent and their habits and feelings, would, I should think, lead them to ally themselves with the Government. . . . By such an alliance alone, can they hope to maintain their peculiar laws and privileges."

The hollowness of the Sydenham régime was quickly apparent. "It was only by dint of the greatest energy," Bagot wrote confidentially to Stanley, "and I must add the unscrupulous personal interference of Lord Sydenham, combined with practices which I would not use, and your Lordship would not recommend, in addition to the promise of the Loan and the bribe of public Works, that Lord Sydenham managed to get through the Session." With studied conciliation Bagot spent a month in Montreal—"altogether the hardest I ever passed in my life," he reported, "showing my bienveillance towards them . . . thus smoothing my path hereafter." The old game of detaching individuals from the solid French bloc was frankly abandoned: it could never win the party and it invariably ruined the man, who became "immediately in their eyes "Le Vendu'—and "Le Vendu' he remains." Meanwhile the other groups in the Canadian compound were hopelessly heterogeneous and disintegrated, and such was "the narrowness of the foundations" that the government could rely upon no stable majority in the Assembly. If Sydenham's technique was no longer feasible it would be necessary, wrote Bagot, to regroup these factions in order to "merge minor differences" in pursuit of "cardinal principles." In truth this trend towards a reform coalition, coalescing still further into the semblance of a political party, was to be the greatest result, as we shall see, of Bagot's "Great Measure," and it was the work not of the autocrat but of the diplomat:

The political parties which exist in this country [he wrote to Stanley] resemble but in a very small degree those two great parties which during the last century and a half have governed the destinies of Great Britain. . . . There is here no party comprising a majority of the Representative body. . . . There are no leaders who can reckon on the support of more than a few followers . . . and there is no appreciation of the necessity of concert and cooperation among those whose opinions coincide in general matters. Hence an attempt to govern by a single party and so confer on them the whole patronage and power of the Government has invariably united all other parties in opposition.

In July, 1842, a letter from Harrison confirmed Bagot's own convictions in terms that admitted of no delay: "The Government does not now command a majority. . . . A vote of want of confidence will be brought forward and carried. . . . I who introduced and all who voted for the resolution of last session would be bound to bow to the decision of the House. . . . I do not for one moment suppose it possible to resort to the old system of Government irrespective of the views of the House of Assembly, because the consequences of such a course would be fearful in the last degree." With regard to responsible government Harrison concluded that "the Government will be held to that doctrine whoever may form the administration."

Somewhat daunted by these coercive factors but facing them unblinkingly with the true diplomat's concern for the facts, Bagot approached his first session with three or four of the most dynamic ideas in colonial government taking shape in his mind. The governor could no longer "govern" through subservient "placemen," manipulating piecemeal a heterogeneous Assembly. His chief function must be "strict impartiality." His best reagent was goodwill. His best policy was detachment and scrupulous fair play, particularly to the French. If they could be persuaded to accept the union as a *fait accompli*, to accept office as a pledge of their co-operation, and to rely for their vindication upon "the sober spirit of a constitutional Country," it might be possible for the governor, as Grey afterwards prescribed, to "belong to neither party and have nothing to do with their contests." These are familiar principles of responsible government under the Grey-Elgin régime, but they are to be found for the first time in Canadian history in the urbane and serene temper of Sir Charles

Bagot. To vindicate these convictions it might be necessary, as Bagot wrote to Stanley, to act "in the very teeth of an almost universal feeling at home—possibly . . . in opposition to a fixed and determined policy of your own—certainly (with regard to the French) in opposition to Lord Durham's recorded sentiments—and as certainly to Lord Sydenham's avowed practice." This task nevertheless was now to fill Bagot's remaining span of life with the most intractable diplomatic hazards of his career. His success with Stanley and Peel was ephemeral for it was to be followed by the reaction of the Metcalfe régime. But his success in Canada was a landmark. In circumstances far more forbidding than Elgin's, and far more complicated than Durham's, his lonely and prophetic spirit struck the key-note of a new era.

VI

Bagot's most dynamic letter to Stanley (July 28, 1842) will remain a classic of British statesmanship at its best—urbane, insinuating, inviting "a simple Yea or Nay" and disclaiming the "political courage" to decide against his instructions, yet charged with a desperate plea for magnanimity in "making friends and supporters of the French population." Clinton Murdock, who had been secretary to both Sydenham and Bagot, returned to the Colonial Office in August bearing a letter for Peel himself and another urgent plea to Stanley for a free hand "unfettered as to the course to be adopted towards the French." Here again, as in Nova Scotia, it was the function of the Colonial Secretary to "decide," and the joint decision of Peel and Stanley, had it reached Bagot in time, might have precipitated a political tragedy. Let Bagot not despair, they wrote, in the face of a hostile Assembly. Louis Philippe in France and the President of the United States were both contending successfully against hostile majorities, and "we know [this from Peel] what George the Third did in 1783–4." Let Bagot continue "the game of multiplying these 'Vendus'." The example might prove contagious. There was still "a fine opportunity of playing the game of Divide et impera." If in the end, wrote Stanley to Peel, "the combined forces of the Radical and French Party" were to acquire a majority in the Assembly, "I fear the Union is a failure and the Canadas are gone."

The timing of Bagot's "Great Measure," had it been premeditated, could scarcely have been more fortunate, for Stanley's reply enclosing "in strictest confidence" his own correspondence with Peel, arrived (September 21) less than a week after the crisis had been met and "after the power of acting upon it had passed away." In the dramatic developments of that week, and during the brief months "de joie et d'espérance" (as Bagot wrote) that were to follow, Bagot's own part, despite his self-effacing modesty to Stanley, gained in conviction and in mastery at every stage. On September 9, the day after the Assembly met, Bagot sent for La Fontaine. The negotiations reached a deadlock on the 13th when La Fontaine informed him "almost with tears in his eyes" that Baldwin "could not on principle" concede pensions for two of the retiring councillors whose appointment had been "non-political" and of long standing. That afternoon in the Assembly Baldwin moved his long-anticipated resolution of no confidence.

The famous *coup* by which Bagot carried his "Great Measure" in the Assembly and checkmated his chief's stolid obstruction at the Colonial Office bears every mark of statesmanship. Bagot's final terms to La Fontaine, unlike the earlier memoranda, were not marked "confidential": three seats in the Executive Council, including Baldwin if "brought in by the French Canadian party," and pensions for the two retiring councillors. These terms Bagot now authorized Draper to read for the first time to the French members of the House. That evening, while the debate on Baldwin's resolution of no confidence was still raging and while the last post for the packet was waiting in the courtyard of Alwington House, Bagot sent off to Stanley a note charged, even in defeat, with a new assurance of mastery. There was a savage thrust for MacNab who was at that moment intriguing with the French in his own interests—"I shall keep faith. . . . Trust him I never will." There is a shrewd thrust too for Stanley himself in the copy of a "Royal Speech" from the Canadian press which MacNab had just "delivered before mine," replete with "vaunts of loyalty and the extravagant and absurd demonstrations made to him in England." For the French there was still a note of confidence "when they learn, as they are at this moment doing in the Assembly, how abundantly large an offer their leaders have rejected, and the honest spirit in which that offer was made. The offer itself, accepted or not, will raise a prodigious outcry. . . . I care not. . . . I bespeak, till you hear from me again by the next mail, your confidence in the wisdom, and the necessity of the course that I have taken—I have no reason, even under present failure, to repent it."

In the House Bagot's disclosures to the French had an "effect . . . almost electrical." The following morning a memorandum signed by La Fontaine and Baldwin on the one side and by Harrison on the other provided for the substitution of four reformers for Draper,[1] Ogden,

---

[1] Draper's discerning advice in July involving his own magnanimous resignation received perhaps the highest tribute from Bagot in appraising the "Great Measure."

Sherwood, and Davidson in the Executive Council. Baldwin's resolution of no confidence was withdrawn, and another of "unmixed satisfaction" with the new Council passed the House by a vote of 55 to 5. From this point, through anxieties that must have clouded every surviving association with friends in England and through illness which claimed at last his life in Canada, Bagot's new faith carried him serenely. "Such had been my fixed perswasion founded upon the calmest and most careful observation of the State of Parties, and of the Colony since I arrived in it. . . . Upon my own responsibility I have decided." His last letter to Peel reaffirmed his "Great Measure" as the last will and testament of his life. "Looking back upon my Short administration of affairs here, and looking back upon it as my last act in this world . . . I do assure you that . . . I have found no reason to regret my course."

But Bagot was not accustomed to blink unpleasant facts, and his "Great Measure" was still riddled with paradoxes. Though Stanley and Peel in full cabinet council found themselves inextricably committed to Bagot's "Great Measure," they were far from convinced, and it is impossible to suppose that Metcalfe's pessimistic outlook from the beginning did not reflect their own. Bagot, they pointed out, had been "driven to take on your own responsibility, and contrary to the wishes of the Home Government . . . a step which must have . . . immense effects upon the future government and destinies of Canada." The chorus of faint praise from other intimate friends in the cabinet was equally pessimistic. The Duke of Wellington (Bagot's own uncle) was less reserved: "What a fool the man must have been . . . and what stuff and nonsense he has written! and what a bother he makes about his policy and his measures, when there are no measures but rolling himself and his country in the mire."

In Canada too the results were paradoxical. Baldwin made the most of the "Great Measure" to declare his "great principle . . . formally and solemnly recognized by the representative of the crown." Bagot himself wrote bluntly to his chief that Baldwin was now "the actual and deservedly acknowledged leader of the strongest party in the House, *and in the Country.*" "Whether the doctrine of responsible Government," he added, "is openly acknowledged, or is only tacitly acquiesced in, virtually it exists." But the fact remained, as Hincks pointed out many years afterwards, that the government was still a coalition: La Fontaine, Baldwin, Aylwin, and Small "became members of the old Government, six members of which retained their offices, and their precedence, without concessions of any kind." Bagot himself, in obedience to his instructions, sought to "admit the French as a part of, or an addition to, my own Council, and not reconstruct my Council with Mr. Baldwin and the French as the staple of it." There had been no vote of want of confidence, no general resignation of the old Council, no appointment of a new cabinet in its place. These technical defects, however, soon were lost to sight in the harmonious functioning of the Council under Bagot's ingratiating "bienveillance." The truth was that the new coalition was rapidly coalescing into a party. By the time of the Metcalfe crisis it was acting as such and with one exception it then resigned as such. The danger lay in the chronic infirmity of Canadian politics—the fierce contest between the "ins" and the "outs" for a "share of power and place." It might have taxed even Bagot's diplomacy to liquidate the promises of patronage already made by Sydenham and Stanley. A post in the West Indies, an appointment in Canada for "services . . . in the way of elections in Lower Canada," and a debate in the House of Lords as late as Elgin's day, attest the play of patronage under the union. Baldwin could defend it on "principle." Hincks and Morin, as we shall see, had more practical uses for "loaves and fishes."It is curious to find La Fontaine and Cherrier, as early as February, 1843, pouring oil on the waters troubled by the Canadian "ultras," and it was the exaction of patronage which wrecked the government under Metcalfe and jeopardized responsible government in Canada for four years.

The one feature of the "Great Measure" which threw the kindliest light upon the Canadian scene and still illuminates like a beacon the best traditions of Canadian politics was the benign spirit of Bagot. He received confidence because he gave it. In that sense his greatest work was done after the "Great Measure," not before it. "His uniform frankness and cordiality," wrote Hincks, "had so won upon his Ministers that there was not one of them that would not have gone the utmost length in his power to meet and forward his views." "Sir Charles Bagot was I hesitate not to assert the most successful Governor, that ever administered the affairs of any British Colony enjoying representative Institutions." For French Canada his name passed into a legend. Many years afterwards Hincks reflected that no governor, not even Elgin, was held in more "grateful remembrance by the French Canadian population." During his last illness masses were said in their churches for his recovery, and at his death Cherrier wrote to La Fontaine with unaffected sorrow: "Tous nos vœux ont été impuissants pour l'arracher au Tombeau qui va s'ouvrir pour lui." Well might they revere his name for it was "only in Canada [as Hincks observed] that Sir Charles Bagot's sterling qualities are properly appreciated." "In his last sad interview with his Ministers he more than once appealed to them 'to defend his memory.'" His last official letter was a tribute to their "unreserved confidence" and his own: "My reputation is in your hands. I know that you will all protect it."

VII

The pestilential atmosphere of the Metcalfe crisis like that of the Falkland administration in Nova Scotia was the *reductio ad absurdum* of the Russell-Sydenham régime. It is hard to believe that Sydenham, Bagot, and Metcalfe were all dealing with the same Assembly under substantially the same instructions reinforced by the closest liaison between Stanley and Lord John Russell. If Bagot's apocalyptic vision was a search for the highest attributes of Canadian politics, it was reserved for Metcalfe to explore the lowest. The descent took place within a period of eight months, and for a few who had the insight to see its meaning it was to prove a convincing object-lesson in those elemental human qualities which have had so much, for weal or for woe, to do with the evolution of the Commonwealth.

If Sydenham was a governor of "House of Commons and Ministerial habits," and Bagot of the "diplomatic School" at its best, Metcalfe may personify the gubernatorial school *par excellence,* at its best and worst. Stanley could rely implicitly upon his stolid and insatiable industry, his scrupulous obedience to instructions, his invincible prejudices. Buller in England suggested to him certain "stipulations" and "certain powers to act" for "essential steps" to be taken in Canada, but Metcalfe replied stolidly that his first duty was to the Colonial Office and it was "impossible to stipulate that they shall not control the Government of a colony." In due time Kaye rounded out Metcalfe's career with the most fulsome of official biographies. A peerage and laurels from Gladstone and Macaulay crowned his fidelity. Metcalfe brought to Canada a record already so distinguished that Gibbon Wakefield regarded him as "unicus homo" for the post. Returning from India with both the purse and "the pride of the Nabob," he had just presided in Jamaica over the adjustments following the emancipation of the slaves. He spent the first ten days in Canada without stirring from the house for rest or relaxation. He closed his career in Canada in a darkened room, half-blind with cancer, ready to die at his post if necessary to save the empire as he understood it.

The tragedy of this devotion was its futility. For the Canadian crisis of 1843 Metcalfe's official virtues and many of his private idiosyncrasies were worse than other men's vices. From his first awkward interview with Peel to his last council meeting with the Canadian reformers his manner was reserved and ungracious. Even Kaye pronounced it "a little intractable." Suspecting his Council of "revolutionary opinions" he came to regard their "professions of a desire to perpetuate their connexion of this Colony with the Mother Country, as utterly worthless." Those who would concede to such men the control of patronage "must be reckless as to the consequences." Inspired by the vociferous loyalty of the Canadian tories it was not long before Metcalfe was lecturing Stanley himself upon the best class of men to fall back upon in Canada. How could he submit to the "utter exclusion of those on whom the Mother Country might confidently rely in the hour of need" —of those who had defended the province "in the hour of need against foreign invasion and internal rebellion"—"without setting at defiance the operation of responsible administration which has been introduced into this Colony"? "Such a system of Government appears to me to be utterly inadmissible in a Colony," and to forego the patronage of the Crown would be to "surrender the Queen's Government into the hands of rebels, and to become myself their ignominious tool." "Whether my contest be with a malignant Minority, or with a Majority of the House of Assembly, or with the whole Colony run mad, my duty must be the same. I cannot surrender Her Majesty's Authority, or the supremacy of the Mother Country."

Metcalfe's official biographer, with less regard for "Her Majesty's Authority," stated his dilemma more bluntly: "At the nominal head of this Government-by-a-party in England was the wearer of a crown, who might be a child, a woman, or an imbecile old man . . . whilst at the head of this Responsible Government-by-a-party, in Canada, was . . . the chief ruler of our North American possessions." In the words of Metcalfe himself "the sole question is, to describe it without disguise, whether the Governor shall be solely and completely a tool in the hands of the Council." This quandary is repeated with tiresome iteration in the Metcalfe correspondence both public and private. "The truth is," Grey afterwards wrote to Elgin, "he did not comprehend responsible Government at all, nor from his Indian experience is this wonderful." Elgin's own verdict may be cited without discount: Metcalfe "profoundly distrusted the whole Liberal party" and "believed its designs to be revolutionary"; and he "imagined that when circumstances forced the party upon him, he could check these revolutionary tendencies by manifesting his distrust of them, more especially in the matter of the distribution of patronage."

With these invincible prepossessions ministered to by the egregious

Captain Higginson—"the everlasting Secretary"—the Governor-General's reserve with his official advisers became a byword. Adam Fergusson wrote to Howe of the painful contrast between Bagot's ingratiating practice of responsible government and Metcalfe's "sneering emphasis upon the term." From their correspondence a whole anthology of contrasts could be compiled. If Bagot in dealing with his advisers gave and received "unreserved confidence," Metcalfe admitted that from the outset "their manifest inclinations and conduct . . . always prevented my sympathizing with them," though he tried to suppress his "feelings of disapprobation." The deluge of addresses to Bagot after the "Great Measure," the masses in the French churches for his recovery, the more intimate tributes of "l'appui entier" (Morin), of "l'attachement" (La Fontaine), of "affection, esteem and respect" (Aylwin) were "oil and gladness" to his closing hours. It was not long before the epithets applied to Metcalfe by some of the more irresponsible among the reformers ranged from "Old Squaretoes" and "Charles the Simple" to "stupid," "hypocritical," "the old Squaw," and worse: with repercussions, as we shall see, fatal to their cause. Thus while Bagot, as his "last act in this world," saw "peace and Union" triumphant, Metcalfe foresaw from the outset nothing but a "tug of war" with disaster ahead. Hope there was none, "not even of escape." "I fear that the whole concern is rotten at the core."

VIII

The "tug of war" came in November, 1843. The immediate occasion—petty appointments to the justiceship of the peace in the Dalhousie and Bathurst districts—was merely the last of a long series of smouldering conflicts upon that issue. Even Hincks had been under fire from a few uncompromising "ultras" for his failure to make a "clean sweep" of his enemies. A bitter discussion in council with Metcalfe was followed by the resignation of all but one of the executive councillors and the dissolution of the first Assembly after the union.

It cannot be necessary to retrace here the labyrinth of charges and counter-charges through which Canadian politics descended to the lowest ebb of turbulence and vituperation in all its history. The conflict over patronage turned largely upon the ubiquitous activities of "the everlasting Secretary," Captain Higginson, through whose hands as joint private and "civil" secretary Metcalfe was determined to dispense the patronage of the Crown in order to safeguard "the British connexion." In this there can be no doubt that Metcalfe was supported by Stanley, and Stanley by both Peel and Lord John Russell in the

House of Commons. Parallel to this and upon a still lower plane of politics was the use to which patronage could be put in the interests of the Reform party. Hincks subscribed bluntly to the view that "a government that should neglect to avail itself of this power *could not long exist*"; that "all the advantages of Responsible Government are lost" if appointments were to be made by the governor "either without or against the advice of his responsible ministers"; that Metcalfe was "plotting to destroy the political influence of his ministry," and that it was necessary to "come to an understanding with His Excellency."

The understanding which was sought with His Excellency was formulated by Baldwin in punctilious conformity with his "principles": that appointments were of course to be made by the governor, but not "without previously taking the advice of the Council" and not in a manner "prejudicial to their influence." On both sides the issue degenerated into a *mêlée* in which motives and veracity itself were called in question. A casual conversation in May between La Fontaine and Captain Higginson on the subject of patronage was relayed by Higginson to Metcalfe, by Metcalfe to Stanley, and by Stanley to the House of Commons in terms which Sullivan pronounced "simply and manifestly untrue." The bitterest comment on this was added in private by La Fontaine to Baldwin, in the very shadow of Metcalfe's death in 1845: "I may forgive anything but a lie." Metcalfe on the other hand accused La Fontaine of exploiting "differences on the Theory of 'Responsible Government' . . . which had been expressed in the freedom of conversation . . . and were therefore very unfairly used." Baldwin, whose whole political life was a sleepless vigil with an uncompromising conscience, was "not scrupulous," and his professions of attachment to the British connexion were "utterly worthless," while MacNab's "gallant energy . . . in putting down Rebellion" merited "any reward that can be bestowed." In this light the promise to MacNab of the adjutant-generalship took on a new meaning.[1] Viger and Gibbon Wakefield and Egerton Ryerson for the Governor-General, Hincks and Sullivan[2] for the reformers, brought the savage war of pamphlets to a pitch of fury, while the press on both sides fairly exhausted the range of scurrilous invective in two languages. Wakefield's *Letter* was "mensonge," "déception," "duperie," "moquerie." Hincks was a "Pennyless Vagabond," a "Cowardly Blackguard," a

[1]Stanley had written to Bagot: "The great object of his [MacNab's] ambition . . . is a *Baronetcy*. . . . This is *the* object, which dangled before him will be more likely than anything to keep him quiet." Bagot Papers, IX, 110 ff.

[2]"A very able man, the readiest with his pen . . . that I ever encountered." Elgin to Grey, August 16, 1848.

"Villainous Liar," a master of "cool and steady villainy." Metcalfe himself added that Hincks was a "designing villain."

The election of 1844 added yet another oscillation—the sixth in sixteen years—to the invariable swing of the Upper Canadian pendulum since 1828. But there were conditions which accentuated the change. Beyond a doubt the British connexion was believed to be in jeopardy. In 1844 as in 1836 the appearance of Egerton Ryerson in the arena was symptomatic of that conviction. "What took place in 1837 [he wrote] was but a preface of what may be witnessed in 1847." Metcalfe attributed the results of the election to "loyalty and British feeling," and beyond a doubt the demonstration may have had its effect in reassuring public opinion in Great Britain. Stanley's relief may be measured by the peerage and other marks of official favour showered upon the victor. Many grotesque anomalies remained unknown or unnoticed— the patient work of Hincks and Baldwin in reconciling French Canada to British parliamentary institutions and the vociferous "loyalty" of some of Metcalfe's supporters who demonstrated it four years later in Montreal by pelting the Queen's representative with rotten eggs, burning the parliament buildings, and signing a manifesto for annexation to the United States. In truth Metcalfe's own choice of councillors must have astonished Stanley. Viger had been barred by Stanley himself because he had been "imprisoned on a charge of treason." D. B. Papineau was a brother of Louis Joseph.

Another note struck in the election of 1844, however, must have reverberated through many a constituency in Canada West: "Canada owes all its evils," said Egerton Ryerson, "to immoderate counsels and extreme men." There can be no doubt that the issue was forced by the reformers with a rashness which outraged the prevailing temper of the province and brought retribution at the polls. Dunn predicted a majority against the Governor "like a clap of Thunder." "Depend upon it," wrote Hincks, "Upper Canada is perfectly safe." Hincks was beaten in his own constituency and the "party completely routed." Metcalfe's obvious unpreparedness, his serene sense of duty in the midst of almost incredible vituperation, his incessant toil in defiance of a mortal disease, all reinforced his "hard-earned and hitherto unsullied reputation." Egerton Ryerson with apostolic fervor pronounced him a "misrepresented and an injured man. . . . While God gives me a heart to feel, a head to think, and a pen to write, I will not passively see honorable integrity murdered by grasping faction." Metcalfe's own avowals of responsible government drafted with his own hand in reply to addresses during the crisis—no fewer than 93 were published in 1844—would supply an anthology of that doctrine more compendious than the memoranda of Robert Baldwin. "Never," he wrote to Stanley, "did men act more wantonly to do mischief. Responsible Government was in full play. Politicians who came from the other Colonies were astonished at the extent to which it was carried." "With moderate Men," he added, "I see no impossibility in carrying on the Government . . . on the principle of Responsible Government." Howe in Nova Scotia sought in vain to reconcile Isaac Buchanan and Baldwin: "if Sir Charles Metcalfe is the man I take him for, a little tact and good temper would bring you all into line." In a letter to Hincks in the *Pilot* Howe added that there had been "no instance in three years" of a conflict over patronage in Nova Scotia. The alienation of Harrison and Gibbon Wakefield (the "arch-traitor" of reform invective), of Isaac Buchanan and Egerton Ryerson and Charles Buller, was a high price to pay for "an inconveniently strict definition." Measured by results the cost was exorbitant. The reformers sacrificed an overwhelming majority in the Assembly, lost the bitterest election in Canadian politics, and jeopardized their cause for four years. Hincks's comment was that "the people richly deserve a Tory Government," and he was absent from the province when the landslide of 1848, in the wake of the Nova Scotian election of the previous year, restored the reform majority for responsible government.

For British officialdom the Metcalfe crisis was paradoxical. The stolid British temper of the province may well have eased many an anxious fear. Gladstone in the Colonial Office cited Metcalfe's administration as a "model" for his successors. Had the election of 1844 been lost, however, Metcalfe himself was prepared to resign in order to reinstate Baldwin and La Fontaine, and in Stanley's opinion "the Canadas are gone." In charging one party with treason and republicanism Metcalfe identified himself with the other, and both himself and it with the British connexion; and he made the triumph of the first party sooner or later inevitable. There was no escape in the end from "the certainty of check-mate." His gubernatorial conception of the empire was to be safeguarded by patronage and geared to subordination. "Speaking as an Englishman I should have no hesitation in saying that I would rather offer independence and separation to a Colony than continue to hold it on terms so preposterous, and so degrading to my Country." In a private letter which reached Metcalfe only a few hours after the crisis, Stanley too had enjoined the same firmness "in the disposal of Patronage. . . . If you let your Council take it out of your hands, they will at once strengthen a party already too compact and powerful, and tend to reduce your authority, as I doubt not they would desire, to a nullity. . . . You may rely upon my support."

To this sorry pass, without faith and without hope, the old colonial system had been brought by the last attempt to implement it in Canada. In the opinion of a few statesmen in Britain and a resolute band of reformers in the British provinces there was a higher conception of the empire and a better way. Grey almost alone at this time in British public life "never approved" of Metcalfe's policy, and it was less than a year after Metcalfe's death that he took over the seals of the Colonial Office.

Chapter Ten

"THE GREAT EXPERIMENT"

RESPONSIBLE government in both Nova Scotia and the united province of Canada was the work of political parties in learning the hard lessons of the Russell-Sydenham régime, reforming their shattered ranks after the *débâcles* of 1844, and resolutely declining office until they could accept with a homogeneous cabinet. The decision of Lord Grey at the Colonial Office in 1846 to accept these inescapable eventualities as "principles of general application to all colonies, having a similar form of government," came at last with the suddenness and almost the simplicity of daylight.

In both provinces Sydenham's technique of neutralizing parties by subservient coalitions had vanished by spontaneous combustion. In Canada the reformers after Bagot's "Great Measure" had so far coalesced into a homogeneous party that Metcalfe himself conceded responsible government to be "in full play": had the reformers been discerning enough to forestall the "loyalty cry" and to await with patience and moderation the return of the Whigs to power in Great Britain, responsible government might fairly have been dated from 1842 in Canada. In Nova Scotia Falkland's struggle with "party" had been for a time more successful. He had secured his election before the collapse of the coalition, but he escaped from one party only by identifying himself with another. Under Johnston's smooth and sagacious counsels the Conservative party exploited the infirmities of both Howe and Falkland to the top of their bent. With almost incredible *gaucherie* the Lieutenant-Governor permitted the publication of a despatch to Stanley in which his overtures to five of the reformers to take office at the price of throwing Howe overboard appeared in glaring violation not only of confidence but of fact. It was an attempt, wrote Howe, to "fasten treachery on one Member—disloyalty on another—and poltroonery on all." The truth was that the consequences of the Russell-Sydenham-Stanley régime were so forbidding in both provinces that no colonial secretary was likely to repeat the experiment.

189

For Howe in Nova Scotia, degraded by the quarrel with Falkland and appalled by its consequences, it was necessary first of all to pull his party—and himself—together. The initial price was paid with his usual magnanimity: he acclaimed J. B. Uniacke "the acknowledged leader" of the Liberal party. "That gentleman and I," he said, "started from different points in life, with different friends and adverse opinions; we contended in this arena till we understood each other and until the true principles of Colonial government were developed by our collisions." "On the other side," he wrote ruefully to one of his friends, "the organization is perfect—the leadership uncompromising, the morale of the service active and elevated. We are a body of very honest and well meaning people going to capture the Sepulchre with 'good intentions'—and we have to deal with pagans, who while they trust in the Prophet, know the value of close ranks, discipline and chain mail."

Falkland's promotion to the governorship of Bombay closed a chapter "rude and intemperate" in the politics of the province. At first sight the appointment of Sir John Harvey by Gladstone a few weeks before the return of the Whigs to power in Great Britain was not reassuring. "These Military statesmen," Buller wrote, were addicted to the "notion of a Composite Ministry . . . not knowing that Coalitions always damage all engaged to them and fail all who lean on them." Howe required no warning against coalitions. The second series of *Letters to Lord John Russell*, written *de profundis* at this time, was concerned with action rather than argument. The lessons since the ten resolutions of 1837 were now plain for all men to read. "The evils . . . from such a system North America has endured; but in her name, my Lord, I think I may be pardoned for desiring that it shall have an end." Buller, whose correspondence during these grim months of frustration was perhaps the steadiest portent for the North American scene, assured Howe in September, 1846, that with Earl Grey at the Colonial Office they had at last a "Colonial Secretary who has sound views of Colonial Policy." Howe was "devilish glad . . . to see the Whigs back," but with every desire to be "deferential and respectful towards Lord John," the time was now past for subservience. "If this Whig Government disappoints us," he added frankly, "you will have the questions I have touched discussed in a different spirit, ten years hence, by the Enemies of England, not by her friends."

Sir John Harvey, who was the last of the military governors, proved to be the first of a new line. After military service in the War of 1812, in Ireland, and in Egypt, he had governed three of the four maritime provinces with conspicuous success. His term in Prince Edward Island was too brief for lasting results on "the everlasting land question," for he was transferred to New Brunswick to inaugurate the reforms of 1836–9. Here he encountered the fatal displeasure of Sydenham and Lord John Russell in the "Aroostook War" over the Maine boundary— an incident as regrettably at cross purposes with official policy as that of his brother-officer Sir Colin Campbell in Nova Scotia, and like that also leading to his recall. After a term in Newfoundland Harvey's prestige was again unimpaired, and Howe's friend Kent in Newfoundland was deeply concerned lest Harvey's success in three provinces should "meet a grave in Nova Scotia." Howe replied resolutely that "the time for seduction, intrigue and splitting parties has gone by in Nova Scotia. Johnston can give Sir John no Coalition, for not a Liberal will act with him. . . . I fear [he] may not understand my countrymen, and may fail by relying on expedients which . . . are not suited to our meridian." Harvey's first kindly note (September 14, 1846) still bears in the Howe Papers a marginal comment in Howe's meticulous handwriting: "This was my first communication . . . from Government House, after my 'proscription' and banishment therefrom for several years. During all that period I was a disaffected and dangerous man. Now I am my Sovereign's Representative's most excellent and talented friend [Harvey's term of address]. I thank God, and the steadiness and intelligence of my countrymen for the change."

Buller's confidential letter of November 16, 1846, to Howe was probably the first authentic news of responsible government to cross the Atlantic. It is clear that the prospects in Nova Scotia had been canvassed in great detail in the light of Howe's correspondence, and that Grey's epochal despatch of November 3, 1846, conveying for the first time "the fullest adoption of the principle of Responsible Government," had passed through Buller's hands. Sir John Harvey was to "entrust his Government to those who have the confidence of a majority of the Assembly." With impeccable precision worthy of Robert Baldwin himself Buller's counsels covered every contingency likely to complicate the impending change. To Howe's casual suggestion for a forced dissolution of the Assembly[1] Buller replied that so long as the Executive Council could command a majority, however narrow, in the Assembly it was of "paramount importance that the ordinary practice of Responsible Government should be rigidly respected." In the end "one hostile vote of the House would settle the matter." At the worst

[1]"Dissolve our House, and you will have no more trouble in Nova Scotia for the next four years."

"you will wait a year longer, but it will be a recognition of the Principle of Responsible Government. . . . Lord Grey's good intentions you may rely on. I do not think that even Ld. Stanley in his place could thwart you."

With this authoritative benediction from the Colonial Office (Buller was judge-advocate-general in the Whig government of Lord John Russell) the establishment of responsible government now turned upon the next election in Nova Scotia.

II

After a century of commonplace practice in more than a score of provinces and dominions in the Commonwealth it is not easy to recapture the exaltation which attended the "great election" of August, 1847, in Nova Scotia.

Lost causes are seldom venerated by posterity. The masterly retreat of the old order in Nova Scotia has received less than justice at the hands of their opponents. Nowhere in British America were honourable traditions held with deeper conviction. And indeed many of the early attributes of self-government were forbidding enough. The "spoils system" of Jacksonian democracy became a by-word in the British provinces. In Canada La Fontaine recoiled before "the universal thirst for place." "Le patronage," wrote Cherrier, "sera souvent un écueuil . . . il y a de gens trop exigeants." At times Uniacke himself shared the misgivings about "exclusive party government . . . in a small Colony like Nova Scotia." Howe too denounced the "spoils system" and the exploitation of patronage for party advantage. The unalterable opposition of Howe and three of his colleagues to a coalition, however, was announced in December, 1846. Johnston's rejoinder was a memorandum for the *Journals* of the House and another for the Colonial Office which may stand as the most formidable brief ever prepared in defence of the old order. In a small colony like Nova Scotia, wrote Johnston, with a population of scarcely a quarter of a million, a revenue of £80,000, with no efficient departmental organization and "no class born to fortune and leisure" for the exacting duties of public life, the "extravagant comparisons" and "unrestrained and unsound analogies" with British practice could only "give an air of burlesque and caricature" to the contest. Johnston begged a further "authoritative declaration" from the Colonial Office, and it was in reply to this final appeal of the old colonial system that Grey's second despatch was written on March 31, 1847. From that point "further controversy was a waste of time," and the issue, as Grey and Buller both maintained, now lay with "the people themselves."

The "great election" of August, 1847, filled the press of Nova Scotia and reverberated throughout the British provinces. In Bermuda, in Newfoundland, in Prince Edward Island, the issue was awaited with tense anticipation. "If Nova Scotia strikes the first blow," wrote Charles Fisher from New Brunswick, "I do believe that the next election in Canada will follow suit and it must have some effect here." In the technique of elections Johnston had no equal at that time in British America. Unlike the Canadian tories who later on committed hara-kiri in Montreal in 1849 and forced the organization of a new Liberal-Conservative party in 1854, the Conservatives of Nova Scotia kept their "close ranks, discipline and chain mail," and came back to office in due course to carry the province into confederation in 1866. In the "great election" of 1847 the handbills, the posters, the picnics, the political dinners, the sailing excursions, and the more devious devices of the day, exhausted the resources of both parties at the hustings. It was Howe's familiar boast that the day was won without a blow, without bloodshed, "without the breaking of a pane of glass." The election was the first in British America to be held in one day—one of Johnston's reforms bearing the label of "sound conservatism." Twelve of the seventeen counties gave the reformers a resolute majority of seven in a House of fifty-one. At Howe's homecoming after the election the cheers were "heard for miles down the valley," to be followed by weeks of less boisterous dedication with Herbert Huntington, the most unflinchingly consistent spirit of the contest in Nova Scotia. They "went into the woods and called moose with the old hunters . . . forgetting the bitterness of conflict." Thus were the "highest privileges of British subjects" won at last "by a single act, in a single day." It is doubtful if the emotional exaltation of that day has ever been equalled in Canadian politics.

The new House met on January 22, 1848. A vote of want of confidence was carried 29 to 22 and the Executive Council resigned in a body—"the coup de grace constitutionally given" not only to the old government but to the old order. Nearly eight years had passed since a similar resolution of no confidence in February, 1840, had been frustrated by the fatuities of the Russell-Sydenham régime. "Conscious of having achieved a Revolution, without bloodshed," the new government turned to the commonplace tasks of departmental organization to deal with the civil list and transportation, schools and trade and the most "important public Bills" since the days of Sydenham. The ghosts of pensions and patronage which had haunted the Canadian scene were laid with exemplary forbearance. Howe's predecessor as provincial secretary, Sir Rupert George, was "voted an adequate pension, and gazetted removed." Problems of patronage, Howe wrote to Fisher, were "very simple . . . where a Governor is acting in good faith with his Council. If *he* or *they* desire a ground of quarrel, this will answer as well as any other. . . . Do not quarrel about abstract principles if in practice all goes well." Patronage was not always to wait upon these sagacious counsels in Nova Scotia.

In truth the harmony which attended the transition of 1848 was phenomenal, and the key as usual was to be found in the realm of the imponderables. Sir John Harvey's goodwill, his "imperturbable bon-homie," quickly deepened into reliance, and his Council responded to their "venerable chief" with respect and attachment. For a time even the despatches to the Colonial Office were drafted by the provincial secretary. To Grey's own "spirit of generous confidence in our dis-cretion and right feeling" Howe replied that "he shall not be dis-appointed. It will be our pride to make Nova Scotia a 'Normal School' for the rest of the Colonies." This serenity was not always to obtain between Joseph Howe and the third Earl Grey. The "railway fiasco" of 1852 involving Grey himself, the bitter controversy with Elgin over the Reciprocity Treaty, the conflict with Cardwell over confederation, all attest the empirical adjustments inseparable from self-government. The death of Herbert Huntington in 1851 removed one of the stal-warts "of the Hampden school" whose sagacity and inflexible principles had won for him the highest record for consistency among the Nova Scotian reformers. But the death of Charles Buller, in the hour of assured success in 1848, removed the serenest influence on either side of the Atlantic for the cause of responsible government. In the *Nova-scotian* of December 25, 1848, Howe paid this tribute to the memory of his friend:

If the question had been asked a month ago, of the North American colonies, what English statesman they could least afford to spare, the almost unanimous answer of the best informed men in the five Provinces would have been—Charles Buller.

Lord Durham, Lord Sydenham, Sir Charles Bagot, Charles Buller! With these men alive and holding high stations in England, North America would have had her advocates and friends, familiar with her wants and hopeful of her destinies. . . . The grave has closed over them all. . . .

There was something safe, practical, and conciliatory in Buller's advocacy of North American interests. Unlike Hume, he never frightened or misled by counselling extreme measures; and instead of traversing boundless fields and generalizing like Molesworth, he stuck to the matter in hand and raised no difficulties, the facile removal of which was not proved to be as compatible with the parent state as with the security of the distant provinces of the empire.

It was for this quality of his mind that we chiefly admired Buller. He never did violence to the antique prejudices of Parliament or feared to give honest counsel, when they seemed to require it, to the colonists themselves. There may be rising men in both Houses, of whom we know little; but of those we do know, there is not one, in the peculiar walks he chose, who can fill Charles Buller's place.

III

If Nova Scotia aspired to be the "Normal School" for responsible government, Canada could qualify, a correspondent once assured Elgin, as *experimentum crucis*. Not only the size and population of the united province but its complexity and incalculable antipathies now dominated colonial policy. By 1850 there were nearly as many British subjects in Canada as there had been in the thirteen colonies at the beginning of the revolution. After the Papineau and Mackenzie risings the obsession of British opinion on both sides of the House with "race" and "the British connexion" was almost inevitable. Durham's *Report* magnified these impressions to alarming proportions. Lord John Russell himself was daunted by them. The paradox of his obstructive policy in 1837, his goodwill but obvious frustration at Howe's resolutions of no confidence in February, 1840, his support of Stanley at the Metcalfe crisis, and his final acquiescence in responsible government as prime minister in 1848, is perhaps to be explained only by his own obsession with this ineluctable problem: what was to be done with a "ministry headed by M. Papineau"? Responsible government was conceded at last when it could be conceded safely. In that sense the election of 1844 in Canada as interpreted by Metcalfe and Egerton Ryerson may have served its purpose in Great Britain better than a victory for phantom "rebels and republicans." By 1846 the truth about some of this vociferous loyalism was beginning to filter through. Even Sir Allan MacNab soon conceded that the reformers of 1842 were "far superior to this——Ministry," and sought a *rapprochement* with La Fontaine for his own party. Metcalfe lived to sponsor a resolution for a general amnesty[1] and the reinstatement of the French language in the Legislature. Draper at one stage opened negotiations with Caron to take Morin into the government and appoint La Fontaine to the bench. La Fontaine contemptuously declined but he added a prophecy of singular insight: "The same scene [as Bagot's 'Great Measure'] is on the eve of being re-enacted, or I am much mistaken. . . . Lord Metcalfe is the Lord Sydenham and his successor will be the Sir

[1] Though he could not forbear the comment that "one of thanks for Her Majesty's clemency would in my opinion have been more appropriate."

Charles Bagot. Come what may, I desire above everything to remain at peace with my own convictions."

The mantle of Sir Charles Bagot was indeed to fall upon Lord Metcalfe's successor, but Lord Elgin's fame in Canada rests upon foundations too sure to require unwarranted and unhistorical traditions for support. He had nothing to do with the origins of responsible government, either in doctrine or in official acceptance by the Colonial Office. He was not even a Whig. A Peelite of the first order in both practice and precept, he had seconded the resolution of no confidence which led to the fall of the Melbourne government in 1842. His marriage to the daughter of Lord Durham took place long after Grey's decision on responsible government had been made and several months after the despatch of November 3, 1846, to Sir John Harvey had put it into effect. When Elgin left England two months later he carried a copy of that despatch as the chart for his mission to Canada. "In conformity with the principles there laid down," reads Grey's official statement of 1854, revised by Elgin himself, "it was his object . . . to withdraw from the position into which Lord Metcalfe had, by unfortunate circumstances, been brought . . . and to make it generally understood that, if public opinion required it, he was equally ready to accept their opponents as his advisers, uninfluenced by any personal preferences or objections."[1]

To first appearances in British North America, in fact, Elgin was not only a Peelite but a tory. When he arrived in Halifax in 1847 the Johnston administration was still in control and Elgin lectured the House, in Johnston's best manner, on the evils of the "spoils system." His renewed overtures in Canada to Caron and Morin were interpreted as the old game of coalitions, though he contrived to convey the information to La Fontaine that "the invitation to the *French Canadians* to take office *contained no exception.*" Even Papineau, as Elgin afterwards wrote, would have been accepted "if his being included . . . should be insisted upon by the leaders of a party which can command a majority." Meanwhile Elgin gave his best advice to his conservative Council, and undoubtedly anticipated a tory victory at the polls. After the landslide for the reformers he wrote regretfully that "this change of Government occurs at an inconvenient moment."

From that moment, however, the scene was changed, and the policy already concerted with Grey in London was carried into effect with flawless sagacity and goodwill. The election of 1848 was almost as

[1]*Colonial Policy of the Administration of Lord John Russell* (London, 1853), p. 214.

great a surprise to the reformers as to Elgin himself. Hincks was elected in his absence in the constituency which had repudiated him in 1844. The new House met on February 25, 1848. Baldwin's resolution of want of confidence was carried on March 3 by a vote of 54 to 20. On March 4 the old Executive Council resigned in a body. On March 7 Elgin sent for La Fontaine and Baldwin, "spoke to them [he reported to Grey] in a candid and friendly tone, told them . . . that they might count on all proper support and assistance from us. La Fontaine's manner, (to whom Baldwin seemed desirous to yield the first place) is naturally somewhat stiff, but he soon thawed, and our intercourse has been entirely frank and satisfactory." On March 11 the La Fontaine-Baldwin ministry was sworn in and responsible government in Canada, as avowed by Colonial Office, governor, prime minister, cabinet, and an overwhelming majority in the House, became an accomplished fact.

Thus simply and without ostentation the "great experiment" which both Grey and Elgin believed to be epochal for the whole empire was begun, under conditions scarcely more tractable than those which challenged the same procedure in India exactly a century later or in South Africa in 1909. In the confidential Grey-Elgin correspondence their forebodings are still traceable in convincing detail. Long before the election of 1848 Elgin foreshadowed his official functions with true Peelite realism: to "give to my Ministers all constitutional support frankly and without reserve, and the benefit of my best advice." "I have never concealed from them that I intend to do nothing which may prevent from working cordially with their Opponents." This interchange of ministries and oppositions was not only "the very essence of our Constitutional system," but it was "probably the most conservative element which it contains"—a characteristic Peelite touch discernible in a dozen details of Elgin's political philosophy. "By subjecting all sections of politicians in turn to official responsibilities it obliges heated partizans to place some restraint on passion." This doctrine was confirmed by Grey in terms which admitted of no retreat. "You and the Home Government," he wrote, "belong to neither party and have nothing to do with their contests. . . . This principle must be completely established in order long to preserve our connection with the Colony." The governor's function was to crown the victors—a duty much more congenial than contending for the laurels in the dust and heat of the market-place, and much safer. "Even if it were necessary to include Papineau," Elgin wrote after Papineau's return by acclamation to the new House, "in spite of his manifesto I should not object if . . . insisted upon by the leaders of a party which can command a majority." That this was no idle boast became apparent as the crisis of 1848 moved to its *dénouement*. At the conclusion of that "year of trial" it was Grey's conviction that "by acting on the very different policy of Lord Metcalfe (which you know I never approved) you would have got into inextricable difficulties." Elgin, viewing the "great experiment" at closer range, descried more serious disasters had he failed in "perfect sincerity and fairness" in allowing "constitutional principles to have full scope and play": "we should by this hour either have been ignominiously expelled from Canada, or our relations with the United States would have been in a most precarious condition."

IV

Upon many aspects of the second empire in America the effect of responsible government was catalytic. Elgin, as we have seen, could not claim to have originated it, and he was not the first to implement it, but above every other name on either side of the Atlantic his was truly prophetic among those who made it work.

In many respects his conclusions were at variance with the prevailing impressions not only of that day but of our own. No man was ever less bound by shibboleths. With fearless Peelite sagacity his first concern was "to see things exactly as they are." Like the "Nelson touch" in the navy, the Elgin touch became proverbial in Canadian politics. That responsible government was not an approach to republicanism but a departure from it and more unlike it than the old colonial system; that the congressional system, though substituting election for appointment to the office of president or governor, still stereotyped the "clumsy irresponsible mechanism" of the old colonial system at its worst; that an elective second chamber could be conservative in its effect since it permitted an appeal from one popular tribunal to another with a higher franchise; that reciprocity in trade with the United States was not the antecedent but the antidote to annexation; that French Canada was generically a conservative force in the Canadian compound, disposed to act with governments rather than against them; that reliance for the "connection" upon colonial subordination or the mechanical structure of the old empire was a delusion and a snare, and that even an elective governor would not impair what Burke had called "the spirit of the communion"; that good government could not be a satisfactory substitute for self-government; these and many other aphorisms emerged from Elgin's study of Canada and left their mark upon Canadian politics.

Elgin's convictions on the prevailing conception of "loyalty" and

the "connection" have become the basic philosophy of the Commonwealth. The rampant tory monopoly of "romantic loyalty" he found
"fast waning in Canada." The tory attempt to have "the Metcalfe
game . . . played over again" at the Rebellion Losses Bill—"the Tory
rebellion of 1849" Elgin once called it—went up in smoke in the
burning parliament buildings of Montreal. Their "loyalty" appeared
in the annexation manifesto. Elgin lived to see a new brand of loyalty
that was mutual, an association that was constructive rather than repressive, beginning to manifest itself between the British provinces
and the mother country. In Baldwin and Hincks, La Fontaine and
Morin, he discovered allies in this philosophy beyond the vision of
the old order to comprehend. "The most serious cause of apprehension for the future" Grey believed to be the apathy of British
opinion even among his own colleagues. Lord John Russell's speech
"with the sting in the tail" brought consternation to a man whose
British convictions had been rated by Metcalfe as "utterly worthless"
and were now regarded by Elgin as "of more importance to the connexion than three regiments":

Baldwin [wrote Elgin] had Lord John's speech in his hand. He is a man
of singularly placid demeanor, but . . . I never saw him so much moved.
"Have you read the latter part of Lord J. Russell's speech?" he said to me.
I nodded assent. "For myself", he added, "if the anticipations therein
expressed prove to be well founded, my interest in public affairs is gone
for ever. But is it not hard upon us while we are labouring through good
and evil report, to thwart the designs of those who would dismember the
Empire, that our adversaries should be informed that the difference
between them and the Prime Minister of England is only one of time?"

In place of the barren logic of Lord John Russell's doctrine Elgin
developed a philosophy which was as profound as Burke's or Balfour's.
In this he was less a jurist than a statesman; and Lord John Russell
himself came to applaud the skill with which Elgin "carried into effect
the theory of responsible government with so much moderation and
good sense as to reconcile in the happiest manner the interest of the
colony and the mother country." The old "Colonial Empire for the
purpose of exercising dominion or dispensing patronage," wrote Elgin,
was passing away. So too was its usefulness as a "hot-bed for forcing
commerce and manufactures." The connexion was now to function
"neither by the golden links of protection, nor by the meshes of old-
fashioned colonial office jobbing and chicane." Freedom was to be
defined by those who aspired to it, and its range was no longer to be
determined by "rescripts from the Colonial Office."

In this respect Elgin's forecast for the empire was perhaps the most prophetic approach of his day to the conventions of the Common-wealth. Unlike Durham he believed it impossible to reserve vast regions of common interests for imperial control. "I see nothing for it," he wrote resignedly to Grey, "but that the Governors should be re-sponsible for the share which the Imperial Government may have . . . with the liability to be recalled and disavowed." Conflicts of interest there were likely to be, but each must be dealt with on its merits, and the expanding range of colonial interests could be recognized only by applying to them the same stringent principles of responsibility.[1] Thus while even Baldwin and La Fontaine recoiled at times from the future—"il faut jeter l'ancre" Baldwin once exclaimed—Elgin's realistic and homely philosophy faced up to it without a pang. The "great lubberly boy," as he humorously described the Canada of 1850, was coming of age, and despite the proclivities of fond parents at that critical juncture of domestic adjustment permanent estrangement was likely to result only from egregious mismanagement. In all this the "principles" of responsible government could remain the same. What was destined to change, as we shall see, was the range of their application, and that range from beginning to end, it is now seen, was to be dictated by one consideration—the legitimate interests of the Canadian people. To such "social and political development," wrote Elgin, "organized communities of freemen have a right to aspire." With this sanguine and empirical approach Elgin was the Isaiah among the major prophets of Canadian nationhood and of the Commonwealth.

In Canada itself Elgin's benign example, like Bagot's before him, wrought miracles in the amelioration of public life. Without delusions and without squeamishness he took men at their best, and raised the level of public life higher than he found it. This was no mean achieve-ment in the Canada of the early fifties. Responsible government has seldom improved immediately the standards of political conduct. It is human nature to explore the worst first and to resort to short-cuts and half-measures for partisan advantage. The French with "no notion of fair play," wrote Elgin, were prone to exploit political doctrines learnt at second hand in their own interests, and to "revive the ancient cry of nationality" unless responsible government operated uniformly in their favour. The English-speaking radicals, less docile than the French, were "rabid and unreasonable," and liable to "plunge at once into the most reckless opposition." Intent upon "making political capital out of whatever turns up," both sides were ready to exploit "a thousand other mutual suspicions and repulsions," and it was "hardly

[1]See below, chapter XXIV.

possible," added Elgin, "to touch any part of this rickety machine without bringing the whole about one's ears."

Both Baldwin and La Fontaine recoiled from the "tracasseries" of public life and escaped from it with relief. As control passed to other men of "the railway age," to Hincks and Morin, to Macdonald, Galt, and Cartier, the exigencies of Canadian politics were such that no device in the devious practices of the day could safely be ignored. On both sides of the international boundary "the railway age" played havoc with the infirmities of human nature. The exploits of Stephen Douglas with the Illinois Central were scarcely more devastating to political morals than those of Hincks and the Galts with the Grand Trunk. Elgin had left Canada before the day of the gerrymander and the "double shuffle," but the growing pains of that prodigious decade were already discernible. By example as well as precept he pointed the way to "national and manly morals." By standing resolutely alone— "literally alone," as he reported ruefully, on at least one occasion—he taught others how to stand. He once dined in Toronto with Morin, MacNab, and Papineau among his guests, and before he left Canada he could observe "symptoms of a blush rising on the cheek" of the Montreal tories. It is on record that Sir Allan MacNab in June, 1851, entertained Joseph Howe and a delegation on the proposed inter-colonial railway at dinner, and himself proposed the health of Elgin and La Fontaine. Without superciliousness and without condescension Elgin could afford to forget the folly of his enemies and to explore the promise of a nobler role for Canadian politics. The prospects for the united province of Canada warranted that magnanimity. It was "a glorious country." From Gaspé to Thunder Bay there were materials for "the future of Nations." "The main object of our policy," he wrote to Grey, "ought to be to support the hopes and courage of the Canadians until their natural advantages begin to tell."

V

In this he was near the centre not only of the most discerning British policy of that day but of the whole central theme of Canadian history. The fundamental faith which underlies a Canadian nation on this continent—a faith which required the co-operation of both French- and English-speaking for its success and which could be wrecked only by their conflict—becomes almost incandescent in the pages of the Grey-Elgin correspondence. This was "the pole star of my policy" which gleamed again and again through "obloquy and misrepresentation" as Elgin picked his way across the pitfalls of that prodigious era. The kindliest of political relations with the United States, trade relations of unprecedented accommodation under the Reciprocity Treaty, an undefended frontier and healthy rivalry in the standards and amenities of life, were woven together into a political philosophy of profound significance for British North America. This central conviction he purveyed to Grey, to Sir Edmund Head in New Brunswick, and to many a convert among his old political associates in Great Britain: "I have been possessed (I use the word advisedly, for I fear that most persons in England still consider it a case of *possession*) with the idea that it is possible to maintain on this soil of North America, and in the face of Republican America, British connexion and British institutions, if you give the latter freely and trustingly."

The crisis of the early fifties, though compounded of many ingredients now long since forgotten, was grim enough to daunt even Elgin at his best. The repeal of British preferences on flour and timber destroyed much of the lucrative trade through Canadian flour-mills, ship-yards, and warehouses which had buttressed the specious prosperity of the Metcalfe régime. Tens of thousands of plague-stricken immigrants from Ireland, many of them from Palmerston's own estates, made a combination with the Irish Republican Union and the Hunters' Lodges across the border which lent verisimilitude to every rumour. It was said that "50,000 Irish were ready to march into Canada from the United States at a moment's notice." For the benefit of those "whose vocation it is to invent wrongs for Ireland," Elgin cited the list of five Irishmen, four Frenchmen, one Englishman, and two Scots in the La Fontaine-Baldwin ministry. The petulance of the Montreal tories protesting "pay for traitors" in the Rebellion Losses Bill, and intent upon remaining "English even at the expense of not being British," was to be matched only by the bravado which almost invariably attends political and economic irresponsibility. "Whether merchants be bankrupt," wrote Elgin, "stocks depreciated, roads bad, or seasons unfavourable—annexation is invoked for the remedy for all ills imaginary or real." The Montreal newspapers—"six out of seven were anti-ministerialist"—exploited the annexation manifesto with calculated malice. To add to the turmoil, Papineau, charged with French republican ideas on the eve of "the '48," was again at large in Canada and stirred Elgin's temper, for once, from its customary composure. "Actuated by the most malignant passions, irritated vanity, disappointed ambition, and national hatred," he had appeared upon the scene with a manifesto "waving a lighted torch among these combustibles": "Lord John Russell was a deceiver and Responsible Government a delusion and a snare."

There can be no doubt that responsible government—the superiority of the parliamentary over the congressional system—was regarded by Elgin, and by posterity after him, as the corner-stone of Canadian national development on this continent. To the accompaniment of cheers from the Tory party in the House of Commons Stanley charged Grey and his governor-general in Canada with having "already established a Republic in Canada." "Now I believe, on the contrary," Elgin wrote, "that . . . the concession of Constitutional Government has a tendency to draw the Colonists the other way. . . . It habituates the Colonists to the working of a political mechanism which is both intrinsically superior to that of the Yankees, and more unlike it than our old colonial system." Critics less shrewd than Elgin were already beginning to speculate upon the inflexibility of written constitutions stereotyped into rigidity by fixed elections.

That responsible government was "a departure from the American model, not an approximation to it" Elgin had little difficulty in demonstrating to any observer of the old colonial system and its adaptation in the United States. "Of the soundness of this view of our case," he added, "I entertain no doubt whatsoever. . . . The fact is that the Yankee system is our old Colonial system with, in certain cases, the principle of popular election substituted for that of nomination by the Crown." The fatal hiatus still remained between the elective legislature and the new elective governor. In the concern of Congress or of the state legislatures exclusively with the making of laws, and of the president or the state governors exclusively with their administration, the infirmities of the old colonial system were all too faithfully perpetuated, with no possibility of breaking the deadlock between them in case of conflict. The record in Canada under the old colonial system was too recent to be forgotten. The arts of the demagogue, with no responsiblity for administration, could flood the statute-books with laws under the naïve delusion that a community could be reformed by sheer legislation. In the 1828 Assembly of Upper Canada no fewer than 57 bills were passed with the virtual certainty that they were either doomed in the Legislative Council or were to be administered by a governor who was utterly out of sympathy with their purpose. The Assembly could be as irresponsible as the Executive Council. The "confusion and riot" which Sydenham found in the last Assembly of Upper Canada must have been characteristic: "Every man proposes a vote for his own job; and bills are introduced without notice, and carried through *all* their stages in a quarter of an hour!"

With responsible government the Assembly could no longer blame a governor for not administering the laws and the Executive Council could no longer blame the Assembly for ill-conceived laws that could not be administered. Under Elgin's ingratiating tutelage the Canadian Legislature began to master those unwritten but invaluable conventions which were soon to become the commonplaces of the parliamentary system. The integration of legislation and administration in the cabinet system of parliamentary government deprived both branches of the government of valid excuses or alibis. Those who made the laws were charged, through the responsible cabinet system, with their administration. Those who were to administer the laws were usually—in the case of money bills invariably—charged with drafting and sponsoring them in the first place. The chronic conflict over supply between governor and Assembly—stereotyped in the congressional system—could now be forestalled at its source. If the responsiblity of ministers in the House, on the one hand, could be relied upon to moderate the temptations of the demagogue, the exigencies of party government, on the other hand, could be relied upon to produce cabinet ministers conversant with the subtle compromises and accommodations of parliamentary temper and procedure. In any event the government of the day could be held responsible for the consequences. The smooth transmission of public opinion into policy, of policy into party, and of party into power, could be spared the violent checks and conflicts of interest that disfigured the old colonial system. "When a people have once been thoroughly accustomed to the working of such a Parliamentary system as ours," Elgin once affirmed, "they will never consent to revert to this clumsy irresponsible mechanism." The list of converts to this robust thesis included not only Bagot's friend Wharncliffe in the Peel administration but Elgin's old colleague at Oxford (now lieutenant-governor of New Brunswick) Sir Edmund Head, and Sir Henry Bulwer in the British embassy in Washington. The subsequent development of self-government in more than a score of provinces and dominions in the Commonwealth is a fair commentary upon this shrewd diagnosis as early as 1850.

With this sheet-anchor to windward the most favourable trade relations it was possible to get with the United States lost their terrors in Elgin's philosophy. Convinced that artificial commercial restrictions were more likely than normal commercial intercourse to induce annexation, he discovered before long that the shrewdest annexationists on both sides of the boundary—the New York *Tribune*, the Montreal *Herald*, the *Courier*, and the *Witness*—shared his sagacity by opposing reciprocity, while the Southern senators, fearful of the annexation of "free" territory to the union, proved to be his best allies in the negotiations for the Reciprocity Treaty of 1854. Without malice and without chicane he sought to assuage the traces of truculence on both sides of the boundary after the tensions of the Oregon fiasco and the Mexican War. His popularity in Washington, Portland, Buffalo, and Boston, and with visiting Americans in Canada, was fairly won. With his own chief in the Colonial Office his abounding humour was mingled on occasion with a touch of impatience. "Only one absurdity," he wrote, "can be greater, pardon me for saying so, than the absurdity of supposing that the British Parliament will pay £200,000 for Canadian Fortifications. It is the absurdity of supposing that the Canadians will pay it themselves. . . . £200,000 on Defences! and against whom? Against the Yankees. Your own kindred a flourishing swaggering people who are ready to make room for you at their own table." Here was a nation "which never makes a bargain without getting at least twice as much as it gives." On Thanksgiving Day they were to be seen "pouring into their multifarious places of worship to thank God that they are exempt from the ills which afflict other men." This robust philosophy for British institutions and the British connexion "in the face of Republican America" was to encounter unforeseen stresses and strains during the next phase of Canadian nationhood. The problems of Confederation and the Civil War would have taxed even Elgin's equanimity. The sheet-anchor, however, held fast, and "the pole-star" of Elgin's policy never shone with clearer effulgence in the northern sky. With the solid achievement of self-government after British parliamentary models, the British provinces set their feet irretraceably upon the road to nationhood.

III

BRITISH NORTH AMERICAN UNION

Chapter Eleven

NATIONHOOD IN PROSPECT

THE closing years of Elgin's administration, like an effulgent sunset, suffused the Canadian scene with a deceptive glow of achievement and of destiny. The problem of self-government, after nearly two centuries and a half of unbroken tradition in America, was now at last set at rest by the adoption of British parliamentary practice, advancing *pari passu* with the conventions of parliamentary government in the parent state. Charged with a robust faith in the superiority of that system over "the clumsy irresponsible mechanism" inherited by republican models from the old colonial system, a new spirit was soon stirring in the British North American provinces. The largest of them, in wealth and population, was already advancing so rapidly in its own right that "something like a national existence," in the words of Lord Durham, was already in prospect. In the united province of Canada the ominous structural defects in the solidarity of British North America as a whole were for the moment almost forgotten.

Here was a province which stretched from the Gulf of St. Lawrence to the headwaters of the Great Lakes. Enthusiasts were prepared to assert Canadian claims to a still vaster territory. When Chief Justice Draper attended the sessions of the Select Committee of the British House of Commons on the Hudson's Bay Company in 1857 a Canadian minute of council authorized him to "recognize no western limit of Canada in that direction excepting the Pacific Ocean." "I hope to see the time," said Draper before the committee, "or that my children may live to see the time when there is a railway going all across that country and ending at the Pacific. . . . I entertain no doubt that the time will arrive when that will be accomplished."[1] The St. Lawrence system, the greatest artery of water communication from the Atlantic seaboard, traversed the province from end to end. Reinforcing the waterways, the Grand Trunk Railway from Rivière du Loup to Sarnia

[1]*Report*, p. 218.

was already at this time the longest railway in the world under one management. The Reciprocity Treaty of 1854 reopened for the first time since Franklin's early vision of an undivided empire the prospect of reaching the hinterlands of the continent by way of the St. Lawrence and of making their development tributary to it. The record of the fifties was already imposing. The population of the united province of Canada increased from a little over one million in 1841 to two millions and a half in 1861—nearly 250 per cent in the span of twenty years. Thomas Chandler Haliburton once demonstrated before a British audience that there was nothing in the neighbouring states of the American union to compare with this solid achievement.

The prospect, however, was deceptive, and it was further belied by a melancholy record of British American disunion and disintegration. The contrast between the vast united province of Canada under a legislative union and the rest of British America was only too obvious —the four maritime provinces in the east riddled by separatism and across the continent the distant colony of Vancouver Island, the vast regions of New Caledonia and Rupert's Land and the North-Western Territories. The lag between Elgin's vision of Canadian nationhood at the middle of the nineteenth century and the solid achievements of the twentieth appears at first sight to be the result of forgoing the rapid march of the unitary province of Canada in order to incorporate the remoter fragments of British North America into the more complicated pattern of a federal system. But the truth is that Canada itself was already stricken by an infirmity which perverted and complicated the functioning of Canadian nationhood. The equal representation of Canada East and Canada West in the legislature of the province had implanted in the union an element of federalism which doomed the province within two decades to the ravages of intolerable sectional strife. The necessity for federalism was endemic in the politics of Canada, and the mainspring not only of federalism but of Confederation, as we shall see, is to be found in that circumstance.

Critical as the issue of British American union became during the early sixties it was attended nevertheless by evidences of benevolent policy which contrasted at every point with the record of folly and ineptitude at the beginning of the second empire. The best efforts of the Colonial Office were exerted in vain during the fifties to repair the ravages of those early days. The futile policy of governing by division inherited from the first empire brought the provinces of the second empire to the brink of disaster before wiser counsels could be brought to bear upon their destiny.

II

A melancholy interest attaches to those abortive plans of Franklin, Shirley, and Halifax for British colonial union during the closing decades of the first empire which were supplanted by fatal designs for a "system new and strange" in the administration of the American Department. Franklin maintained to the end that his Albany plan of 1754, had it been implemented in good faith, might have forestalled the revolution:

By my plan, the General Government was to be administered by a President-General, appointed and supported by the Crown, and a General Council, to be chosen by the representatives of the people of the several colonies, met in the respective assemblies. The plan was agreed to in Congress, but the assemblies . . . thought there was too much prerogative in it, and in England it was judged to have too much of the democratic. The different and contrary reasons of dislike to my plan made me suspect that it was really the true medium. . . . The colonies so united would have been strong enough to have defended themselves; there would then have been no need of troops from England; of course the subsequent pretext for taxing America, and also the bloody contest it occasioned would have been avoided.

Franklin's *Plan of Union* for the first empire not only inspired the first plan—that of Chief Justice Smith—for the union of the second empire in America but it had one basic feature in common with the final federation of the British provinces. It was to be ratified by an Act of Parliament. Parliamentary supremacy, as yet unsullied by the fatal abuses of that sanction which precipitated the revolution, was still viewed in its beneficent aspect as an invaluable practical expedient for composing conflicting interests. The initial agreement, to be reached by the colonies themselves in their own interest, was to be confirmed also by all the sanctions of sovereign authority. But in the preliminary tensions of the Seven Years' War it was already too late to legislate an equitable plan for colonial union.

Meanwhile a second plan, more promising perhaps than Franklin's, was being developed by the Board of Trade under the sagacious counsels of Lord Halifax. Halifax's plan, like Franklin's, would have left both the total amount required for defence and the quotas to be raised by the various provinces to be determined by commissioners selected by the colonies themselves. The various provinces in turn were to raise their quotas in their own way, thus forestalling the devious suspicions which attended the *Stamp Act* and the port duties and other aspects of direct parliamentary taxation. As in the Albany plan the final ratification was to come from the sovereign authority of an Act of Parliament. In both cases the careful regard for "colonial conditions and government" was calculated to allay those suspicions of ulterior "design" which became inescapable with the short-sighted preference of officialdom for imperial taxation of the colonies as a "security for their dependence." Impressed by the spontaneity of the Albany plan Halifax deferred to the deceptive prospects of agreement there, and both plans were soon lost to sight in the Seven Years' War.

The glaring inequalities of colonial co-operation in the war merely confirmed the view of British officialdom that colonial separatism was chronic and hopelessly intractable. This was the stock-in-trade of many a perplexed governor, and many shrewd observers shared that opinion. "They never can be united into one compact empire," wrote Josiah Tucker, Dean of Gloucester, "under any species of government whatever." They would remain a "disunited people to the end of time, suspicious and distrustful of each other." Even Shirley who had sent to the Albany Congress commissioners from Massachusetts with plenipotentiary powers to conclude "articles of Union and Confederation . . . for the General Defence of his Majesty's Subjects and Interests in North America as well in time of Peace as of War," was intent upon an "Imperium over all the Colonies," leaving to the several provinces only the right to "raise the Sum assessed upon them according to their own discretion." Against these imperialistic tendencies Franklin argued with prophetic insight:

If the Colonies in a Body may be well governed by Governors and Councils, appointed by the Crown, without Representatives, particular Colonies may as well or better be so governed; a Tax may be laid on them all by Act of Parliament for Support of Government and their Assemblies dismiss'd, as a useless Part of their Constitution. . . .

The Administration . . . will probably become suspected and odious. Animosities and dangerous Feuds will arise between the Governors and the Governed, and every Thing go into Confusion.

When these sagacious counsels were vindicated by the fatal train of policy from the port duties to the "intolerable Acts" of 1774, the union of the provinces remained one of Franklin's obsessions until it became an accomplished fact. "Unite or perish." Though long "unsuspicious of design," Washington was at last "convinced beyond the smallest doubt, that these measures are the result of deliberation," with a "regular systematic plan to enforce them." The provinces that could "never be united into one compact empire under any species of government whatever" in the interests of the mother country, were united at last in self-defence against those interests into an independent republic with ineradicable traditions against the integrity of

British statesmanship. That was one way of uniting the American provinces.

III

The second empire began with this ugly lesson only partially learnt and with short-sighted precautions against its repetition. The revolution had sprung from these "polypus governments" combining into a continental congress. The second empire began with no representative institutions whatever in Quebec and Rupert's Land, and with signs of a deliberate policy of disintegrating such institutions wherever they were yet to be found. Nova Scotia was broken into four fragments, three of them still separate provinces with a combined area scarcely more than one-seventh the present area of British Columbia. Cape Breton was committed to conciliar government without an assembly and Prince Edward Island narrowly escaped the same fate. When an assembly became necessary for the Canadian loyalists Quebec also was divided and Lower Canada also endowed with an assembly. Since the "Transallegany mountain people" of the new republic, in Knox's wry opinion, were likely to wander about in the hinterlands like the Scythians and the Tartars for thousands of years before founding a settled state, it was deemed safe as well as expedient to keep the remaining provinces of the empire weak and disintegrated. The causes and consequences of this policy, as we have seen, were fatal to every plan of British American union for many years. Durham deplored this early "policy of the British Government to govern its Colonies by means of division, and to break them down as much as possible into petty isolated communities, incapable of combination, and possessing no sufficient strength for individual resistance to the Empire." Even Dorchester had protested in vain "our present policy . . . to divide and subdivide, and of this Remnant to form many independent Governments with as little communication as possible; while that of our Neighbours is to consolidate, and of many independent States to form one Government." In the end the contrast between the disintegrated provinces of the second empire and the flourishing national policy of the neighbouring republic became a matter of astonishment to every observer. Disintegration, instead of ensuring the security of the second empire, was becoming its greatest peril. The remaining colonies might disintegrate piecemeal into the United States.

While disintegration was the order of the day for the provinces in their representative institutions, deliberate attempts were made to centralize the executive and particularly the military authority of the empire. For the first time there was a Captain General and Governor in Chief in the person of Lord Dorchester.[1] Chief Justice Smith, with insight sharpened by experience in the old province of New York, drafted an abortive plea (1783) for a "General Government for the Colonies," and a few years later (1786) a more elaborate plan for a Governor-General, a strong "Board of Council" to be appointed by the Crown, and a legislature representing the assemblies (not the electors) of the several provinces, like that of Franklin's Albany plan or the senate of the United States before the seventeenth amendment. About this central theme of centralization for the executive ("uniting their general strength and interest") and disintegration for representative elements in the colonies a whole school of tory speculation seems to have grown up in opposition to the march of republican trends across the border. Chief Justice Sewell, Smith's son-in-law, and a dozen others tried their hands at similar projects, all of them geared to the old colonial system and designed to assemble while there was yet time a reserve of power in America to safeguard the remnants of the second empire. When the abortive plan for the reunion of the Canadas came up for decision in 1822 the Colonial Office was able to pass in review a variety of commentators ranging from Colonel Morse in Nova Scotia to John Beverley Robinson and Bishop Strachan in Upper Canada, and a few more detached and disinterested observers in official circles from Great Britain.

The plan for the reunion of the Canadas in 1822 under the advocacy of James Stuart and his friends in Montreal was an issue in domestic politics, a by-product of the problem of race rather than of British American union in its continental aspect. The motives behind the measure were such as to inspire the French of Lower Canada with ineradicable suspicion. The antipathies which Durham dragged into the open a few years later in his *Report* were already seething beneath the surface of Canadian politics. Had it been known at the time how near the *Union Bill* was to success, even its withdrawal might not have allayed the conflict.[2] On the other hand had the *Union Bill*, however

[1] The title governor-general, though technically inaccurate until Confederation, is used in these chapters in conformity with general practice.

[2] Wilmot Horton, then under-secretary at the Colonial Office, stated in 1838 that the government would have implemented the measure "but for the unfortunate state of the leader of the House of Commons"—Castlereagh whose breakdown culminated in suicide in August, 1822. *Exposition and Defence of Earl Bathurst's Administration of the Affairs of Canada*, by Right Hon. Sir Robert Wilmot Horton (London, 1838), p. 103.

reprehensible its motives, passed at that time it is possible that the twin movements for reform in the two Canadas might have been tempered by a measure of mutual accommodation without culminating in the *impasse* of 1836. Had some of the salutary results which La Fontaine, Hincks, and Baldwin succeeded in extracting from the Union of 1841 been feasible without the ugly preliminaries of insurrection and bloodshed, an easier approach might have been possible not only to responsible government but to confederation. Upon so narrow a margin sometimes turn the destinies of measures and of men. At Castlereagh's death, wrote Wilmot Horton, "the favourable moment was lost," and the Union of 1841, after the suspension of the constitution of Lower Canada altogether in 1838, was so riddled with antipathies that the unforeseen results of the measure at the hands of Hincks, La Fontaine, and Baldwin seemed almost a miracle of conciliation and of statesmanship.

One other project for British American union, untrammelled as yet by the impending issues of race in the Canadas, was inspired by nostalgic reflections upon the prospects of the first empire. In 1826 J. B. Uniacke, the old "Cumberland rebel" whose long career in the public life of Nova Scotia as speaker of the Assembly and attorney-general had established for him at the Colonial Office a reputation as "quite a veteran in the King's service," drafted for Bathurst his "Observations on the British Colonies in North America with a Proposal for the Confederation of the whole under one Government."[1] Dissociating himself at the outset from the narrow views of the Canadian unionists—the French, he wrote, had merely shown a "natural preference to elect their own people to be members of the House of Assembly, which, a few who are desirous to grasp at power, consider as little short of a rebellion"—Uniacke in 1826 ranged with patriarchal sanctions over the loss of the first empire. The "power, dignity and pre-eminence" of Great Britain and her North American provinces had been his "study through life, and shall continue to be the object of my most anxious solicitude during the remainder of my days":

Had the administrators of His late Majesty met the wishes of the North American Colonies fifty years ago with the same liberality and enlightened wisdom that influenced His present Majesty's Government[2] there cannot be

---

[1]One of Uniacke's sons had been solicitor-general of Lower Canada, another enjoyed a lucrative practice at Lincoln's Inn in London, and a third, as we have seen, was to be the first prime minister overseas under responsible government.

[2]The Huskisson reforms in the mercantile system.

a doubt that the separation of that Country from the British Crown would not have taken place but . . . ties of union . . . would have nearly doubled the strength of Great Britain by sea and land. Instead of this the false information of interested Individuals and a contracted policy, suddenly gave rise to a new nation. . . .

No man has had a better opportunity of forming an opinion on this subject than I have had. In the year 1774 I travelled through a large part of these Colonies. I saw their first Congress assemble at Philadelphia the same year, and I continued in America from the very commencement of the revolution to its conclusion.[1] It is impossible for me when I contemplate what nature has done for British America, to banish from my thoughts that Providence has destined such a Country for some great and mighty purpose, and that the time is come for laying its foundations.

Uniacke proposed the confederation of Upper and Lower Canada, New Brunswick and Nova Scotia (the last to include Prince Edward Island and Cape Breton) under the name United Provinces of North America in order to "shew to the world, that good government can be formed without violent revolutions." With Quebec as the capital, the central government was to be charged with the national attributes of the confederation, while the provinces were to retain their special laws and institutions and "the power of legislation for all local purposes the same as heretofore except where the power is delegated to the General Confederacy." Uniacke's plan, however, was born out of due season, for after the abortive project of reunion for the Canadas in 1822 Bathurst was not disposed to "agitate the question or bring it before the Cabinet." In the division of powers and particularly the residuary powers of the federation, and above all in the functioning of responsible government in both the federal and provincial fields, vast changes were in store for British North America before confederation was to come within the range of practical politics. A copy of Uniacke's plan was presented by his son, R. J. Uniacke, to Lord Durham in 1838, but a more critical issue than union was already at stake in British policy. In British North America as elsewhere the first prerequisite for nationhood was self-government. After responsible government the cause of British American union was found to involve a new destiny.

[1]Uniacke does not add that he took part in the attack on Fort Cumberland and was among those who accepted amnesty and threw down their muskets on that occasion. A newly elected assemblyman once recognized Uniacke as the man who had come out from behind the bushes at Fort Cumberland, but Uniacke retorted ruefully that the change had come not in his own views but in British policy.

IV

Durham's views of British North American union were quickly submerged by more imperative issues of colonial government. He had brought with him a quixotic plan of federation drafted by Roebuck, and there is no doubt that his own preferences ran strongly in favour of a union, either federal or legislative, of all the provinces.

On my arrival in Canada [he wrote] I was strongly inclined to the project of a federal union, and it was with such a plan in view that I discussed a general measure for the government of the Colonies, with the deputations from the Lower Provinces, and with various leading individuals and public bodies in both the Canadas. . . . I was gratified by finding the leading minds of the various Colonies strongly and generally inclined to a scheme that would elevate their countries into something like a national existence.

These "sentiments of national pride" Durham commended as "marks of Nationality," calculated to distinguish the British provinces from their republican neighbours "by raising up for the North American colonist some nationality of his own; by elevating these small and unimportant communities into a society having some objects of national importance." The fact that Durham reserved, as is well known, the chief attributes "of national importance" for the imperial government —the form of government, foreign relations, external trade and public lands—betrayed the limitations of his vision for both responsible government and nationhood.

In the end union itself was jeopardized by expediency, for the short-range device of Canadian reunion devoured the larger project as the lean kine devoured the fat kine in Pharaoh's vision. Durham approached the reunion of the Canadas with grave misgivings. As late as October 2, 1838, he still regarded it as "a pet Montreal project, beginning and ending in Montreal selfishness." Buller informed McGill at last that his chief with great reluctance had "abandoned his plan of a Federal Union of the Provinces, in favor of that to which he had hitherto been so strenuously opposed." Tranquillity was to be restored only by "subjecting the Province to the vigorous rule of an English majority; and the only efficacious government would be that formed by a legislative union" of Upper and Lower Canada. Durham's forecast was falsified, as we have seen, by the results. It was under the union that responsible government itself, the most important of his recommendations, was won by the closest association the two historic races of Canada have ever known. And conversely it was under the union that "French-Canadian rights" were fairly retrieved and under-written by the Canadian confederation.

For the cause of British American union, however, the Canadian "union" was to prove a curious misnomer. Despite Durham's plea to the contrary, the two sections of the Canadas were given equal representation in the united assembly, and thus a federal element was introduced into what was supposed to be a legislative union: with results which were scarcely less than devastating. For ten years, so long as Canada East outnumbered Canada West in population, the equality of representation was a valid grievance for the French-Canadian majority. By 1857 the balance of population had so far shifted to Canada West that the unanswerable case for representation by population, now forced by the Clear Grits, threatened to destroy the union. By 1864, as we shall see, the shrewdest observers in Canadian politics, John A. Macdonald among them, conceded that the days of "equal representation" were numbered, and that "representation by population must eventually have been carried." Escape was to be found only in the formula of "the great coalition"—in substituting a federal for a legislative union of the Canadas on terms that would "permit the Maritime Provinces and the North-West Territory to be incorporated into the same system of government." By that time the whole meaning of British North American union had undergone a "sea change." After responsible government it could never again be the same. Self-government was now in sight, and union endowed with self-government meant nationhood.

During the two stormy decades at the middle of the century this rough-and-ready formula that self-government plus union equals nationhood found recognition with far-reaching effect. By the turn of the half-century the watershed for both was being haltingly crossed. The theme of union as an imperial outwork, a redoubt of British power in North America, built and garrisoned by British officials and British troops, could no longer hold the field. A few realists were already struggling with a new sense of direction, a new sense of destiny built upon foundations in North America deep and strong enough to with-stand in the evil day and having done all to stand. Elgin caught something of this vision. This was the "pole star of . . . policy." There was nothing in the British connection to "check the development of healthy national life in these young communities." There were materials here for "the future of Nations." But Elgin was too obsessed with the basic problem of self-government and perhaps too elated with its success in the exuberant province of Canada to gauge the obstacles in the path of nationhood for the British provinces as a whole. Union became the concern of the next generation, and it was not by chance that the first clear-cut project fully geared to self-government came from Elgin's old colleague at Merton, Sir Edmund Head, now governor of the loyalist province of New Brunswick and soon to succeed Elgin himself in Canada.

V

Head's confidential *Memorandum on the Government of the North American Colonies* was "sent privately to Lord Grey" at Grey's own request, probably in January, 1851, and it was offered with self-effacing modesty.[1] A list of memoranda, confidential opinions, and reports drafted by Sir Edmund Head from that date to his death as governor of the Hudson's Bay Company in 1868 would make a curious anthology. At least a dozen of first-rate importance are still traceable in contexts so significant that the growing reliance of the Colonial Office upon "Sir E. Head's opinion" is easily understood. The fact that so many of the originals were lost may indicate not only the confidential nature and range of their circulation, but the esteem in which they were held in the inner circles of official policy.

The memorandum of 1851 was the first to associate fearlessly the newly acquired technique of responsible government for the British provinces with their federation into a "powerful and independent State" capable of maintaining British institutions and a national existence side by side in North America with the exuberant republicanism of the United States. With the true Peelite's fidelity to hard facts Head assumed from the outset that it was "inexpedient, if not impossible, to allow the North American Colonies to continue permanently on their present footing," while to prolong uncertainty would be "mischievous in every way." With shrewd hard empiricism he accepted the two historic foci of Canadian nationhood as fixed and inescapable. The first of these was the thesis that "the great Provinces of British North America" with "powers of self-government . . . . matured" must be fitted "gradually for an independent existence" as

[1]"The views set forth in this memorandum are professedly crude and undigested. They may appear to more experienced statesmen to be utterly impracticable and visionary. I have put them on paper with the utmost distrust of my own competency to discuss such a question and with no pretention to do more than suggest them for the consideration of others." The original has never been found, despite a careful search at Howick House. A rough draft in Head's forthright handwriting turned up in 1928 among the fragmentary Head Papers acquired by the Public Archives of Canada. See Canadian Historical Association *Report*, 1928, pp. 14–26, ed. Chester Martin.

a "powerful and independent State." In a later memorandum this doctrine is developed with a still surer touch and a deeper insight: "Let the forms and the substance of our Constitution come to maturity in this part of America. . . . They should stand in conscious strength and in the full equipment of self-Government as a free people bound by ties of gratitude and affection." The second was a thesis equally inescapable. Contiguity to the United States had implications to which it was "useless to shut our eyes." That the British provinces "should maintain their independence singly is hardly conceivable; that they should do so if formed into one compact and United body does not seem absurd especially when the natural and internal sources of division between the north and the south of the United States are taken into account." Meanwhile the danger of piecemeal disintegration into the United States could be seen without disguise, and it was "a great misfortune that in Parliament and elsewhere Englishmen talked of this contingency as a result which was predestined." "I for one," he added, "by no means consider it impossible that the connection should be maintained for an indefinite period" by raising up in North America "a power so united as never to be absorbed piecemeal and so important in itself as to take an independent position."

This basic philosophy of British North American union becomes a commonplace in Head's doctrine for more than a decade. "The duty and the interest of England in this matter seem to coincide," for since both self-government and union were indispensable it was a matter of duty "so to govern these Colonies as to fit them gradually for an independent existence," and it was equally a matter of interest to weld them into a federal system capable of "raising up on this side of the Atlantic a balance to the United States." Thus seven years before Galt's famous resolutions and upon long-range principles far more cogent and fundamental, Sir Edmund Head in the placid province of New Brunswick was exploring foundations for Canadian nationhood. For ten years, as we shall see, Head's hard, cold, analytical intellect played unceasingly upon this theme of British American union: first in the form of tentative regional unions while the larger union seemed as yet remote and unattainable, and finally in a desperate attempt to launch the larger union into practical politics with Galt and Cartier in 1858.

Head was under no delusion in 1851 that "duty" and "interest" were always to be reconciled without serious complications. With sardonic humour he recognized some of the morbid infirmities of the old colonial system. It had "fostered the notion that the government is to do everything." "Convinced that the Government in England are neither inclined nor able to thwart them" the colonies were ever prone to "extort something more by importunity." "A cry against the Colonial Office is the stock in trade" of agitators. "They possess already in troubled times many of the elements of power for evil but in ordinary circumstances they are powerless for good." The wish "to restrain their Colonies by force has long ceased to exist" in Great Britain, and it was imperative "to offer in time such terms as will place on a more solid footing their connection with Great Britain and relieve themselves and the Empire from the constant agitation in favour of organic changes." "If trouble breaks out in Canada," he wrote, "the lower Provinces will, I fear, now be always ready to swell the cry and profit by it if they can." There were no riots in Saint John to mark the passing of the preferences on colonial timber, but Head might have added that the language of the press and of the hustings was all too reminiscent of Montreal where they had just pelted the governor-general, burnt down the parliament buildings, and circulated a manifesto for annexation to the United States. Even a loyalist colony was "by no means scrupulous" in exploiting the "discontent or disturbance of its neighbours." "They have not yet learnt that their own ultimate prosperity must depend on their own exertions."

On the other hand the alternatives to the dictates of sound "interest" and "duty" were too forbidding to contemplate. In a later draft on the "Union of the Colonies" Head explores with cool and deliberate calculation the "impossibility of getting rid of them prematurely even if desired." To permit designedly "such dissatisfaction as would induce their populations to seek or demand a separation" would be "weak and wicked. It would imply bad faith." Britain would be recreant alike to honour and to her own interest if she did not foster "the feeling that a national destiny of their own is before them. The tie of allegiance to the British Crown may, it seems to me, last for an indefinite time. . . . It is one in which they feel a pride: it suggests no humiliation and it inspires no bitterness." "We are yet smarting from the results of a course of action which created [other] sentiments in the last century."

The "tolerant moderation" which Head now invoked for a British American federation carried him far beyond the limitations of his own day to a vision of attributes which even a federated Canada was long reluctant to assume. All expedients calculated to "foster a sentiment of union should be studiously attended to." Their currency "should be one and the same in all the Provinces and they should have a mint

of their own." "Their flag should be a modification of that of England
—the Union Jack with a difference of some sort." The Judicial Committee of the Privy Council was unsatisfactory as a "living interpreter"
of a federal constitution because "it sits in England." "The decisions of
such a court might embarrass the Government without satisfying the
public." A "High Court" of the most august character sitting in Canada,
on the other hand, would command the best legal talent in British
America, and it would be "free from all appearance of arbitrary or
capricious interference of an external character." The service of the
new federation would open to the whole of British North America a
"wide field for ambition and distinction." It should always be spoken
of officially as "British North America." "Might it not be hoped that
a body of Provinces acting thus in union would gradually develop
and cherish a feeling of united interest and feel a joint pride in the
name of 'British North America' as their common Country?"

VI

Sir Edmund Head's reputation at Oxford may well have added
weight to his professional opinions among his contemporaries in the
Colonial Office, but his numerous memoranda on British American
union carried exceptional authority from the study he was able to make
at close range of the federal system of the United States.

Grandson of a loyalist and now governor of the border loyalist
province of New Brunswick, he was the first Briton and perhaps the
first British American to master some of the intricacies of the federal
system, to recognize its advantages, and to distinguish some of its
inescapable defects. Above all he was perhaps the first to discern in
practice the sovereign advantage of a British Act of Parliament as an
instrument for effecting a federal union without the tensions and
a priori implications of "state sovereignty" which were at that moment
dragging the United States towards civil war. While he contemplated
in 1851 a federation of but five provinces—Upper and Lower Canada,
New Brunswick, Nova Scotia and Prince Edward Island—he was
among the first of British governors and perhaps also of British Americans to catch a glimpse of the Pacific in his vision of a transcontinental
British dominion. At one time or another he presided over the widest
range of territory in North America ever administered by a British
official before confederation—New Brunswick from 1848 to 1854, the
united province of Canada from 1854 to 1861, and the vast empire of
the Hudson's Bay Company from 1862 to his death in 1868, in the
midst of negotiations for the final transfer of that empire to the Cana-

dian federation. For ten years he was perhaps the most consistent and persistent exponent of British American union to be found on either side of the Atlantic, exploring and on one or two occasions exploiting the exigencies of the times, and enlisting with self-effacing modesty the services of others in that cause when his own were barred by the sanctions of official restraint.

He did not live to see the full consummation of his plans, and he has never been numbered among the fathers of confederation. One or two of the "fathers" might have disputed his right to sit in the circle of that august company. Assuredly Head himself would never have disputed with them the accolade of popular credit for this or any other of the unobtrusive measures of insight which marked his administration. The record of his concern, in season and out of season, for the contingencies which he foresaw in 1851, is more impressive to posterity than it was ever allowed to be to his contemporaries. Behind the scenes with the Colonial Office, in a dozen unrecorded passages with men who were moulding the shape of things to come in North America—with Elgin and Labouchere, with Blackwood and Stanley and Watkin, with Newcastle and Sir George Simpson and Galt and Cartier and John A. Macdonald—Head must have exchanged confidences during one of the most prodigiously creative decades of the century. If he was not one of the "fathers" he may fairly be regarded as the grandfather of confederation, in the priority of his views, in the range of his experience, in the scope of his imagination, in his grasp of the coercive factors for federation and for nationhood. He touched the problem of British American union at more dynamic points of contact than any other official of his day, and he was among the first, as we shall see, to forecast the crisis in Canadian politics which became at last the mainspring of federalism and drove it forward (and many of the fathers of confederation with it) until it became at last an accomplished fact. It is a curious coincidence too that he purveyed to Queen Victoria the advice which led to her selection of Ottawa as "the seat of government" for the province and eventually for the dominion of Canada.

The technical details of federalism as Head expounded them in 1851 were considerably modified in his voluminous memoranda of 1858, and both projects were profoundly modified by the exigencies of 1864. In the division of powers all three plans assigned the post office, currency, railways and canals, and commerce to the federal government, and public lands to the provinces. The lieutenant-governors of the provinces, Head thought, could safely be "elected by the Colony" or "appointed by themselves" in some other way. Residuary powers he assigned (at this stage, 1851) to the provinces after the practice of the United States—a tendency which the fathers of confederation deliberately set themselves to reverse. As a "living interpreter" of the federal constitution, as we have seen, Head advocated a "High Court" in Canada endowed, like the Supreme Court of the United States, with all the prestige and legal sanctions that could be bestowed upon it. "Physical obstacles no doubt exist which perhaps would only be removed by the construction of such a work as the Halifax and Quebec railway, though I doubt if these difficulties would be even now insurmountable." Second chambers he thought unnecessary for the provinces—a conclusion shared by Ontario alone in 1867, by Manitoba only in 1876, by New Brunswick in 1892, by Alberta and Saskatchewan in 1905, by Nova Scotia in 1928, and now by every province of Canada except Quebec.

The detailed technique of federalism, however, was less important in 1851 than Head's grasp of coercive factors abroad in North America at the turn of the mid-century, and his shrewd method of escape, if applied in time, from the Gordian knot of "state sovereignty" which was already beginning to threaten the integrity of the American union. As "events stronger than advocacy, events stronger than men" began to dominate the scene, Head's empirical temper is to be found at work again and again, revising his estimates, retreating from too advanced an optimism, reinforcing his basic convictions, exploring new avenues of approach for the West and the Maritimes, recasting the division of powers to correspond to the play of practical politics, and moving forward on occasion with almost reckless daring in the face of official opposition from the Colonial Office.

In one respect at least his foresight in 1851 was scarcely less than prophetic. A federal union of British North America if formed while the provinces were still pliable and before they could harden into the rigidities of "independent states" could avoid the fatal conflict already discernible between national functions and state rights in the constitution of the United States:

Indeed the doubt whether the constitution of the United States is or is not strictly speaking in the nature of a "Federal" league or compact is yet a grave practical question and one at this moment especially pregnant with important consequences. It has been argued that if the Union be in its essence a league of Independent States, Alabama or S. Carolina may or will withdraw from the compact and release the other parties. Accordingly Story [Justice of the Supreme Court] lays great stress on the enacting words of the Constitution "We the people of the United States do ordain and establish this Constitution" (not "We the people of each state concurring in a league or treaty") as if the Union was "de facto" existing before the Constitution and the power of the people as exerted in its establishment was exercised in this collective capacity.

"Now it is remarkable," Head concluded, "that the relative position of the Governments of these Colonies and of the British Crown would lend itself readily to a plan which would at least avoid these theoretical difficulties." A British federation "formed on a draft approved by the Colonies" could be carried into effect by simple Act of Parliament without raising ugly problems of constituent sovereignties. "In this respect therefore we have in our hand an 'a priori' mode of solving theoretical difficulties which yet exist in the Constitution of the United States of America."[1] This procedure, confirmed by Newcastle in the Colonial Office, and carried into effect with shrewd and deliberate calculation by John A. Macdonald after Head had left the Canadian scene, was the mode by which confederation was eventually won. "The measure," wrote Macdonald in 1866, "must be carried per saltum —with a rush and no echo of it must reverberate through the British provinces until it becomes law."[2] Had the procedure necessary for the constitution of the United States after their independence been followed in the British provinces—a constituent convention with terms to be ratified by the several provinces—confederation would have been impossible in 1867,[3] and any subsequent measure must have been a far weaker instrument for Canadian nationhood. It is a curious commentary upon Head's sagacity in 1851 that as late as 1931 the *Statute of Westminster* still stipulated the amendment of the *British North America Acts* by Act of Parliament as an "'a priori' mode of solving theoretical difficulties."

[1]"I do not mean by this that the assent of the several Colonies to any such Constitution would be unnecessary, but within a given time I believe they would receive with satisfaction any plan which left them a proper share of local self-government and defined that share by a written Constitution interpreted by the decisions of an impartial court."

[2]"There will be few important clauses in the measure that will not offend some interest or individual. . . . The Act once passed . . . the people will soon learn to be reconciled to it." Macdonald Papers, Macdonald to Tilley, Oct. 8, 1866.

[3]It is well known that the Quebec Resolutions were never ratified by Nova Scotia and New Brunswick.

Chapter Twelve

DISINTEGRATION AND REGIONAL UNIONS

G EOGRAPHY has had a curiously varied influence upon the destinies of British North America.[1] Its bearing was probably never more baffling than during the period of tension with the United States which attended the attainment of confederation. There were no fewer than five disintegrated areas of British territory stretching across the continent, and two or three of these were in precarious isolation.

The maritime provinces were grouped together as the "Lower Provinces" for purposes of reference, but they were far from united in outlook or economic interest. In many respects the disintegration which marked the beginnings of the second empire had degenerated into separatism if not sheer parochialism. Cape Breton Island had been reunited to Nova Scotia in 1820, but beyond this the old division of the province was never to be repaired. The trade of all three provinces was maritime, and their orientation was eastward or southward rather than westward. They were fortunate in one aspect at least of their commerce, that their trade was supplementary rather than competitive. Before the Reciprocity Treaty of 1854 the exports from Nova Scotia to the West Indies were more than three times those to Great Britain and the United States combined. Those of New Brunswick to Great Britain, chiefly spruce deals, were seven times those to the United States, while the chief exports of Prince Edward Island even before 1854 were to the United States. Under reciprocity maritime trade with the United States more than doubled in ten years but there was little trade with Canada. For two years the *Royal William*—the first ship to cross the Atlantic altogether under steam—was employed on the St. Lawrence route by the Quebec and Halifax Navigation Company but the enterprise failed and the *Royal William* was sold for debt. Until 1854 when the inshore fisheries were opened to the United States these invaluable resources were guarded by the provinces with

[1]See above, chapter II.

a jealous eye. Beyond a doubt the belated enforcement of maritime rights by the British navy reinforced by the provinces themselves was one of the factors which extorted the Reciprocity Treaty in 1854, though the concession of the inshore fisheries "hook and line, bob and sinker" to the Marblehead and Gloucester fishermen was a price which the Maritimes never ceased to begrudge. Shipbuilding, the most spectacular industry of the Maritimes, though thriving had already reached its zenith. Within a single decade a single town in Nova Scotia (Yarmouth from 1860 to 1869) built more than one hundred and forty ocean-sailing ships. Saint John at one time was the fifth largest ship-owning port in the world and her famous *Marco Polo* held the record for the China trade.

Canada East was separated from the Maritimes by an almost impenetrable wilderness of forest by land and by the ice-bound river in winter; and by more formidable barriers of race and language. When the Charlottetown conference met in September, 1864, the Canadian delegates came down the St. Lawrence from Quebec in the *Queen Victoria.* Had the conference met in February they must have come by the Grand Trunk to Portland and the rest of the way by coastal waters or over the old military Temiscouata road by sleigh. Latent antipathies stirred up by the Papineau rising were slow in dying in the Maritimes, and these antipathies were stirred to wrath when the Quebec agreement of 1862 for the joint building of the Intercolonial Railway was jettisoned by the Canadian delegates in the "railway fiasco" in London a few months later. The deliberate efforts of the Canadian exponents of confederation to ease these tensions in 1864 by underwriting the Intercolonial accounted for much of the success of their mission; but enough remained, as we shall see, to jeopardize confederation and to complicate it for many years.

Though bound to Canada East by the legislative union of 1841, Canada West was reaching by 1859 the conviction that the equal representation of the two sections of the province provided by the *Act of Union* was becoming an indefensible anachronism, and that the westward expansion of the province must be recognized either by the Clear Grit expedient of "rep. by pop." or by destroying the "intolerable bonds of Lower Canadian domination" altogether by a "simple dissolution" of the union. It was the exploration of the federal principle —a dual federation of the Canadas—by Dorion in 1856 and by George Brown at the Clear Grit convention of 1859 which eased some of these antipathies and averted a conflict which already threatened their survival as a united province. With the Reciprocity Treaty of 1854 it had seemed possible for a time that the old dream of the St. Lawrence might yet be brought to pass and that the illimitable resources of the hinterlands of the continent might find their way to world markets through Canadian channels. Realistic observers, however, soon discovered flaws in this deceptive pattern. By 1861 the Erie Canal and the railways were so effectively short-circuiting the St. Lawrence route from the sea that the bulk of imports even to the Canadian hinterland was flowing through the United States. While imports to the United States through Canadian channels were scarcely $22,000 those for Canada West by way of the United States amounted to $7,000,000. Canada West, said Taché, was "on an inclined plane towards the United States," and George Brown was quick to suspect that George Sheppard and a few other exponents of "simple dissolution" for the Canadian union were working in reality for annexation to the United States. At the crisis of 1864, after Gettysburg and Vicksburg in the Civil War presaged the triumph of an angry North, Colonel Jervois of the British War Office reported that Canada West was indefensible and advised the withdrawal of British troops to tidewater at Quebec.

Half-way across the continent lay an even more remote and isolated little community, separated from Canada West by a thousand miles of wilderness on British soil, and exposed by way of the United States to one of the most rapid and concerted movements of migration in the expansion of the republic. The Red River Settlement had owed its existence to the exotic enterprise of one man during a single decade. At Selkirk's death in 1820 his own brother-in-law Andrew Colvile wished the Red River Settlement "had been in the Red Sea twenty years ago." After 1834 when the Settlement passed from the Selkirk family back to the Hudson's Bay Company the Company was accused of locking the door upon the Settlement and putting the key into its pocket. Contacts with Canada had virtually ceased after the coalition between the Hudson's Bay and the North West companies in 1821. For nearly a generation the traditional access by way of Hudson Bay doomed "Assiniboia" (as Selkirk had named it) to perennial isolation in the heart of the continent. American traders from the south had appeared as early as 1822, but they had been held at bay by the adroit tactics of the old Company, "fighting fire with fire" (which meant on occasion fighting fire-water with fire-water) and "smoothing" unruly trouble-makers at Red River by a judicious mixture of authority and conciliation. Upper Fort Garry at the junction of the Assiniboine and

Lower Fort Garry on the lower reaches of the Red River were built to guard the southern approaches from the United States.

During the early forties the Company contrived to safeguard its monopoly against the "free traders," as Governor Christie once observed, by a "variety of indirect but powerful means." At the "Oregon trouble" in 1846 British troops under Colonel Crofton were sent to Red River "under secret instructions," and a handful of them continued at Fort Garry until 1848, giving an appearance of imperial protection to one of the most curious pockets of settlement on the continent. After 1850 the Illinois Central, the first of the "land-grant" railways in the United States, and the Hannibal and St. Jo to the Missouri began to canalize a westward movement of population around the Great Lakes which daunted even the Hudson's Bay Company and stirred the sluggish interest of the Canadas to feverish apprehension. Would Red River follow Oregon into the American union? In many ways, as we shall see, this problem was more immediately urgent than the plight of the Canadas. For a transcontinental federation on British soil the Red River district, as Lord Dufferin afterwards observed, was "the keystone of the arch." The abutments of that arch remained as yet a wilderness on either side, and the fate of the Red River and Saskatchewan region was one of the most urgent problems that awaited Sir Edmund Head on his transfer from New Brunswick to the united province of Canada in 1854.

A fifth area of British territory was still more remote. Vancouver Island and the mainland area of New Caledonia could be reached only through the passes of the Rocky Mountains or by half-circumnavigating the globe. The loss of Oregon in 1846 had stirred the Colonial Office to a belated effort to fortify British tenure north of the 49th parallel by establishing there some sort of vested interests of permanent settlement. The Puget Sound Agricultural Company had been too little and too late to make good those interests by actual possession on the Columbia. Vancouver Island was granted in fee simple to the Hudson's Bay Company for this purpose in 1849. But settlement had been so meagre and infirm that the discovery of gold on the Fraser and the Cariboo threatened the whole region with a repetition of "the forty-niners" in California. With the fate of Texas and of Oregon fresh in mind more than one British official was daunted by the mounting responsibilities of the Hudson's Bay Company and by their dwindling resources for the conflict. In point of time this was perhaps the most imperative problem of British North American survival, and the priority it received in Head's counsels met a very ready response, as we shall see, from the Colonial Office.

II

This hopeless disintegration of the British provinces was attended during the early sixties by two crises which were both traceable, in no small measure, directly to it, and which doubled in turn the element of danger and vulnerability. The attempt of the united province of Canada to cope with these impenetrable distances by means of the Grand Trunk Railway was approaching a crisis which could be met (so Watkin believed) only by heroic measures of reorganization and still more daring expansion. A second crisis was equally crucial. With the outbreak of the Civil War in the United States prospects of trade under the Reciprocity Treaty of 1854 were clouded almost from the outset by threats of abrogation. Fears proved only too well founded. The combination of these two crises—railways and reciprocity, transportation and trade—added elements of pressure which accentuated the problem of British American union and reinforced other still more coercive factors in driving it forward unremittingly towards confederation.

The era of railway projection, when editors as well as legislators took "glimpses of the moon" and could "see nothing but railroads," filled the British provinces with cruelly divided counsels. Joseph Howe in Nova Scotia became the apostle of public ownership: the railways like the highways ought to be "the Queen's," and Howe expounded his plan—an intercolonial railway to be built at half the normal cost by means of imperial guarantees for provincial debentures—as "the noblest scheme of colonial policy ever devised." Grey's initial refusal on "Black Saturday," December 28, 1850, to underwrite such a guarantee was reversed a few weeks later after Howe's spectacular exploit of advocacy at Southampton. Howe returned to Canada, to New Brunswick, and to his native province with the pledge of an imperial guarantee up to £7,000,000 for the railway, and in his exuberant mind a "great scheme of intercolonial policy . . . in our time reaching the Pacific."

The inscrutable withdrawal of this guarantee by Grey in 1852, confirmed by Pakington's formal reply from the Colonial Office to Hincks's "tart letter" of May 1, 1852, delivered the whole project of an intercolonial railway, Howe protested, "into the arms of the great contractors." The meteoric course of the Grand Trunk Railway in which Canadian interests represented by Galt and Holton and Gzowski and

Macpherson were finally reconciled with those of Jackson and Peto and Brassey and other British contractors, with the Barings and Glyn Mills and Company representing the senior bondholders in Great Britain, lodged in Canadian politics the most intractable combination of vested interests in British North America. By 1856 the railway extended from Rivière du Loup to Sarnia and from Montreal to tidewater in Portland, Maine—more than a thousand miles—the longest railway mileage in the world under one administration.

No such accumulation of capital investment could function in "Canada" at that time without destroying the equilibrium of Canadian politics. Issues much more devious than mail contracts and government guarantees were soon in conflict. To the Clear Grits of Canada West led by the uncompromising ardour of George Brown in the Toronto *Globe*, the Grand Trunk came to represent all the sinister influences of that railway age—"the arch-corruptionists"—in the exploitation of the frontier. A quarrel between Brown and Galt in the autumn of 1857 confirmed these antagonisms and launched a whole series of unpremeditated influences, as we shall see, in the direction of federation. By 1861, on the evidence of Edward Watkin acting as superintending commissioner on behalf of the London bondholders, the Grand Trunk was "an organized mess—I will not say a sink of iniquity." On one occasion the senior bondholders of the company contemplated running the rolling-stock across the boundary and foreclosing on the assets, until the general manager inquired pointedly what they proposed to do with the elephant. Meanwhile it would be hard to say whether the Grand Trunk corrupted Canadian politics or Canadian politics corrupted the Grand Trunk. In the Baring Papers is a letter from Ward, Baring's nephew in Boston, transmitting a request which had reached him through Blackwell, general manager of the Grand Trunk, for £4000 "to Messrs G. to the election Expenses" of 1861. Ward added the comment that in his opinion it was "labor thrown away to try to correct a public impression and prejudice which in all that concerned the management of the road, and the character of the friends of the road in the Government was but too well founded." Before the story of confederation was completed the Grand Trunk Railway, as we shall see, was supplying more than this for election expenses, in "Canada" and elsewhere.

By 1862 Watkin in Canada, after a chapter in political necromancy which rivals the record of Sydenham, had reached the conclusion that "returning were as tedious as go o'er," and that the Grand Trunk could be saved from bankruptcy only by expanding both east and west its already over-extended mileage. The warrant for this philosophy, as Watkin did not hesitate to avow, was to be found in the precarious balance of Canadian politics. The Reformers under Sandfield Macdonald came into power in May, 1862, and secured another narrow lease of life in the general elections of 1863. Under the growing tension of the *Trent* affair during the Civil War in the United States Newcastle in the Colonial Office renewed the imperial guarantee for the building of the Intercolonial. An interprovincial conference at Quebec in 1862 agreed to share the cost in the ratio of 10 to Canada and 7 each to Nova Scotia and New Brunswick. In London a few months later, however, Howland and Sicotte on behalf of the Sandfield Macdonald Government refused to implement the agreement and sailed for home under conditions which invited rankling charges of irresponsibility and bad faith from the Maritimes. Since the Intercolonial (as Watkin never tired of expounding) was "absolutely essential to Grand Trunk," it seemed obvious that some gesture of westward expansion would be necessary in order to placate the Clear Grit expansionists of Canada West in the Sandfield Macdonald Government.

Such was the background against which Watkin and his associates in London organized the International Financial Society in order to acquire a controlling interest in the Hudson's Bay Company and to present to George Brown and the Clear Grit wing of the Government a prospect of telegraph and railway expansion westward to match the indispensable eastward expansion of the Intercolonial. "Watkin is very strong in his opinion," wrote George Glyn to Baring, "that this scheme is essential to Grand Trunk." "Intercolonial," Watkin reiterated to Baring, "is . . . absolutely essential to Grand Trunk: and Intercolonial is, under present circumstances in Canada dependant [*sic*] upon the other movement." "To secure the vote of Upper Canada in favor of the Intercolonial," he added bluntly, "it was essential that some effort westward should be made."

The "effort westward" in the first instance was not an impressive programme. Watkin explained that it "asks for no money from Parliament" and no more than a token initial outlay for telegraph communications from the reorganized Hudson's Bay Company: "all the rest is optional & to be done or not as may be prudent some years hence and when, let us hope, G.T. difficulties may be over." The gesture, however, was too shallow for Baring's Roman probity. Drawing his spotless financial toga about him he stood aside from the speculation and left the enterprise to less squeamish enthusiasts. The foray of the

International Financial Society into Hudson's Bay stock belongs to another story but it is unnecessary to discount Newcastle's genuine interest in the West or the fact, according to Watkin, that Sir Edmund Head was appointed governor of the reorganized company "at the suggestion—almost the personal request—of the Duke of Newcastle." Meanwhile the sop to Cerberus was not without its effect. Even George Brown was impressed by Watkin's coup with the Hudson's Bay Company. During his visit to Great Britain in 1862 Brown reported also a "most satisfactory interview with the Duke of Newcastle at his request" and his conviction that "the members of the government . . . are set upon the Intercolonial Railway and a grand transit route across the continent." The British North American Association, organized in London to expound "Canada and Canadian affairs" to the British public, began to "force the Intercolonial Railway on public attention." In Canada the Grand Trunk could be relied upon to exploit the cause of British American union in their own interests. If a coalition of both parties could be induced to underwrite the Intercolonial, with a general federation of all the provinces in prospect at the end, Grand Trunk might be expected to play a role of truly national significance.

Under Watkin's dynamic initiative this entrancing prospect had begun to unfold in all directions. An excursion of delegates from the Maritimes under Grand Trunk auspices found its way to Portland, Montreal, Toronto, and as far west as Detroit and Chicago. Wined and dined by Watkin himself at Montreal they had joined forces with the Canadian Executive Council at Quebec in support of the renewal of the imperial guarantee for the Intercolonial. A smaller delegation had followed Watkin to London and was introduced with an appropriate gesture to Newcastle and Palmerston. Later on a delegation of more than a hundred from Canada including sixty-five members of the Assembly and Legislative Council brought Thomas D'Arcy McGee's classic oratory to bear upon the Maritimes in the cause of the Intercolonial and British American union. With the appointment of C. J. Brydges as general manager of the Grand Trunk a whole train of more devious practices—"means" as the governor-general once euphemistically termed them—was added to the legitimate enterprises of official policy. At one of the most critical stages of confederation Brydges and Galt themselves went to Portland with "the needful" (as Tilley called it) for the fateful election of 1866 in New Brunswick. The versatility and resourcefulness of Brydges, his confidential relations with John A. Macdonald attested by the voluminous correspondence in the Macdonald Papers, the knighthood bestowed upon Watkin at the achievement of confederation, and Watkin's own apocryphal account in his later volume of reminiscences *Canada and the United States* were calculated to leave an impression of ubiquitous activity on the part of the Grand Trunk during these eventful years. Beyond a doubt these influences, legitimate and otherwise, are traceable in a dozen contexts throughout the movement for confederation. Critics like A. A. Dorion declared roundly in 1865 that Grand Trunk was "the origin of this Confederation scheme"; that "the Grand Trunk people are at the bottom of it"; and that the object of the movement was to get "another haul at the public purse for the Grand Trunk."[1]

But these superficial appearances, like so many other exploits avowed by such redoubtable *entrepreneurs*, are sometimes subject to grave discount when the truly coercive factors of confederation are examined in their historical context. The Grand Trunk did not inherit the Intercolonial nor did it build the Canadian Pacific Railway. Watkin failed to carry even the Barings with him in his desperate project of transcontinental expansion, and by February, 1865, by his own admission to Macdonald, he was being "snubbed for interfering in Canadian affairs." After "the great coalition" of 1864 the Hudson's Bay Company quickly settled back into its traditional role from which it required all the resources of Sir Edmund Head, the new Dominion of Canada, and the Colonial Office combined to dislodge it. It would be safe to say that neither George Brown nor John A. Macdonald entered "the great coalition" of 1864—the mainspring of confederation—at the instance of the Grand Trunk Railway. It is equally true that the reversal of British policy in December, 1864, away from a series of regional

---

[1]Tantalizing bits of evidence, some of them as late as the seventies, illustrate this Grand Trunk–Hudson's Bay complex. Watkin once cited to Baring certain letters from Canada "read to you at the Board on the 31st," October, 1862, which "showed, clearly, that to secure the vote of Upper Canada, in favor of the Intercolonial, it was essential that some effort westward should be made, and the message sent to us & the Govt was clearly an appeal to us to proceed." "I know how annoyed you must be at all the Provincial difficulties—but the Pacific affair is part of our *Policy*—the success of wh[ich] will make—believe me—a vast dif[feren]ce in the value of your Grand Trunk property." In February, 1864, as we shall see, Brydges offered still more directly a sop to Cerberus by trying to induce George Brown to accept "the chair of the Canada Board of Hudson's Bay [whatever that was] at which I think he was a great deal impressed. . . . I shewed him that nothing could be done about Northwest without the Intercolonial—On the latter point he is *much* mollified. . . . He does not object I think to the marrying of Northwest & Intercolonial." Macdonald Papers, 191, 34 ff.

Brydges, after collision with the redoubtable Tupper over Intercolonial, was transferred to the Hudson's Bay Company where he ended his days as land commissioner.

unions, as we shall see, in favour of the Canadian project of a general federation—a forthright change of policy which eventually carried the Maritimes into confederation—was due to far more coercive factors than the officious lubrication proffered by Grand Trunk interests to the Colonial Office. Hincks, the real builder of the Grand Trunk, had long since disappeared from the Canadian scene. He had been appointed governor of Barbados in 1855, just as the railway was nearing completion and after Sir Edmund Head had arrived in Canada from New Brunswick to deal with the consequences. Thenceforth *"Head-quarters,"* as the general manager of the Grand Trunk used to term the play of that keen and imperturbable intellect, was to deal with far graver issues than mail contracts and government guarantees for the Grand Trunk Railway. The truly coercive factors of confederation belong to another category.

III

The other problem associated with the disintegration of the British provinces and accentuated by it beyond all precedent during the preliminaries of confederation was the issue of intercolonial trade and reciprocity with the United States. Like the twin-problem of transportation and railways it had a curiously direct and pervasive bearing upon the achievement of confederation.

It was not by chance that the annexation manifesto of 1849 came exactly half-way between the repeal of the Corn Laws with their preferences for Canadian flour and the Reciprocity Treaty of 1854 with the United States. The annexation manifesto, as Elgin shrewdly analysed it, was compounded of many elements, some of them so perverse and petulant that many of the signatories of 1849 never quite lived down the record of their shame. No Canadian who signed that manifesto, said Sir John Abbott in 1889, "had any more serious idea of seeking annexation than a petulant child who strikes his nurse has of deliberately murdering her." But beyond a doubt the economic interests involved were more serious than this. Up to 1846 the preferences in the British market to Canadian timber and flour were on the whole a cohesive force in the second empire. The *Canada Corn Act* of 1843 by reducing the duty on Canadian flour had promoted not only the enterprise of the Canadian frontiersman, the miller, the merchant, and the shipping agencies of the St. Lawrence waterways, but the lucrative trade in American wheat through Canadian mills and warehouses in order to take advantage of the British preference.

The repeal of the Corn Laws in 1846 and the final liquidation of the old mercantile system in 1849 thus synchronized with the passing of the old colonial system in government and drove the beneficiaries of privilege together into one camp. In the economic doldrums of the early fifties, added to the political doldrums of disgruntled toryism, the tradition of colonial dependency reached its lowest ebb.

To supplant this irresponsible temper by what he called "national and manly morals" Elgin sought to apply, as we have seen, three remedies. The first was a system of responsible parliamentary government "intrinsically superior to that of the Yankees, and more unlike it than our old colonial system." The second was a decision to move the capital from Montreal which had been the hotbed of the annexation movement. The third was a fearless determination to secure the best possible commercial relations with the United States, in the conviction that reciprocity in trade was the antidote not the antecedent to annexation. Economic recovery had already begun before the Reciprocity Treaty of 1854 began to function. For a time it seemed that the old dream of making the hinterlands of the continent tributary to the St. Lawrence might yet come true despite the short-circuit of the Erie Canal and the railways to tidewater on the Atlantic.

This prospect was destroyed by the Civil War which perverted for half a century, as it proved, the normal commercial function of the Great Lakes and the St. Lawrence waterway. In the throes of civil war the abrogation of the Reciprocity Treaty became a foregone conclusion. By 1863 the South, which Elgin had found so co-operative in negotiating the treaty in the interests of low tariffs and escape from the annexation of "free" territory, was not only lost to the cause of reciprocity but doomed to defeat and subjugation by the militant industrial North. The high-tariff interests there were already antagonized by the Galt differential tariff of 1859 which contravened, they claimed, the spirit if not the letter of the Reciprocity Treaty. These economic factors might have been composed in normal times of peace, but in the atmosphere of the *Trent* affair, the *Alabama* case, the St. Albans raid, and border incidents with the Fenian brotherhood, it was easy to suffuse the purely economic interests of a group with the belligerent political interests of the republic. Even when the major political issues of the day were in train for solution by arbitration and finally by the Treaty of Washington in 1871, the industrial lobby in Congress had little difficulty in holding its ground and wrecking the cause of reciprocity beyond recovery.

Abrogation, already canvassed as a measure of retaliation, was formally set in motion at the earliest date permitted by the terms of the Reciprocity Treaty. Though Adams, the American ambassador in London, regarded this abrogation as "the result rather of a strong political feeling rather than any commercial considerations," the effect upon the economic life of the British provinces was too serious to be associated with the provocative border incidents of the day. Lord John Russell and the British ambassador in Washington explored in vain the prospects of renewal by a sort of British North American *zollverein* without the political framework of organic federation. A trade delegation was despatched in desperation to South America and the West Indies under the great seal of Canada[1] in search of new markets and friendlier trade relations in America. Even the Maritimes, which had acceded to reciprocity with great reluctance at the cost of their own inshore fisheries, were so favourably impressed by the trade returns during this decade of reciprocity that Joseph Howe appeared at a trade convention at Detroit to urge renewal. His speech succeeded spectacularly at Detroit but failed to arrest "the descent to Avernus."[2]

How far purely commercial interests were merged with ulterior political purposes in the North at the close of the Civil War it would not be easy to estimate. By the time of President Grant and Hamilton Fish the lesson of Elgin's adroit diplomacy may have been only too well learnt: if reciprocity was indeed the antidote to annexation rather than its antecedent, then the abrogation of reciprocity in favour of prohibitive tariffs might be the shorter cut to "manifest destiny." As one of the plenipotentiaries for the Treaty of Washington in 1871 Macdonald was equipped with a memorandum drafted by Sir Francis Hincks, stipulating reciprocity once more as the goal of commercial relations with the United States; but Macdonald failed to lodge the issue even in the preliminary agenda of negotiations. For more than a decade reciprocity thus proved to be a unifying though provocative element in the affairs of the British provinces. The abrogation of reciprocity and the possible withdrawal of bonding privileges through Portland and New York loomed so ominously over the trade of British

[1]By the administrator General Michel during the absence of the governor-general. Michel was duly admonished for this lack of protocol.

[2]C. J. Brydges reported to Macdonald that Howe's speech "completely took the Americans off their legs. . . . At one point . . . the whole of the Americans rose and cheered as if they were mad, and it was some minutes before they were calm enough to allow him to continue. Many of them told me afterwards they had never listened to such a speech."

North America that intercolonial trade became for the first time a concern of prime importance. The speeches of Galt and George Brown and Tilley, and the columns of the Canadian press, rang the changes upon this familiar theme. Beyond a doubt it played a pervasive and constant part in the approaches to British American union.

Though both Canada and the Maritimes shared this concern for reciprocity there were diverging interests and prospects in regard to it which complicated their approach to confederation. These were less marked perhaps for trade than for transportation; the "railway fiasco" of 1862–3, as we have seen, served to embitter relations and incite diverging policies with regard to union. The prospects for a renewal of reciprocity though desperate for Canada were far from hopeless for the Maritimes. It is true that their accession to the Reciprocity Treaty in 1854 had been given grudgingly and at no small cost to their interests. In New Brunswick there had been a growing demand for the protection of their inshore fisheries with "no deviation . . . from that policy." Joint measures to that end were taken for the first time in 1852–3 by the province and the British navy, with no small effect upon the negotiations for reciprocity. Webster's well-known pledge to secure the interests of the Marblehead and Gloucester fishermen "hook and line, bob and sinker" confirmed the impression that the inshore fisheries of the Maritimes were to be the price of American concessions. As late as 1853 the Nova Scotia Assembly protested any "surrender to foreigners" of the inshore fisheries: it would have "a most disastrous effect" and could be "purchased by no equivalent." The treaty was finally signed without consultation with Nova Scotia, and both sides of the House protested "the right of Lord Elgin to concoct, or of the Imperial Government to ratify" the sacrifice of provincial rights. The terms had stultified "a century of loyal attachment and devotion."

The results of the treaty nevertheless for all the Maritimes were unexpectedly favourable. Trade with the United States doubled in ten years, and maritime opinion was overwhelmingly in favour of renewal. But while renewal was doomed for the province of Canada, a maritime union as distinct from a general federation possessed in the inshore fisheries the most alluring bait for reciprocity. As late as 1868 two advocates from Congress appeared in Prince Edward Island and Nova Scotia to explore the prospects of renewal until their activities were bluntly counteracted by the Colonial Office in the interests of confederation. Unfortunately this was not the only respect in which the Maritimes and Canadian interests were found to be at cross purposes.

IV

Head's first memorandum on federation had been written in 1851 in the serene atmosphere of New Brunswick. In 1854 he succeeded Elgin in Canada and it was not long before the alarming disintegration of the British provinces and the attendant crises which threatened their transportation and trade began to colour his views on British North American union. In 1856 he wrote confidentially to Labouchere: "I do not now believe in the practicability of the federal or legislative union of Canada with the three 'Lower Colonies'—I once thought differently but further knowledge and experience have changed my views." For nearly two years he laboured, under private encouragement from the Colonial Office, at a less ambitious but more feasible project—a series of three regional unions to forestall immediate disaster and to prepare the way for a general union under more promising auspices. Such a contingency, as we shall see, was to arise with startling suddenness in 1858; and Head's courage in projecting federation into practical politics at that time proved to be one of the most daring preliminaries to confederation.

The isolation of Canada West and the distant prairies of Rupert's Land had become by 1856 a precarious hazard for the British provinces. Two imminent factors added to their peril. The first was the westward movement of settlement south of the Great Lakes during the fifties—the most pronounced demographic trend on the continent at this time. The population of the border frontier states and territories of Ohio, Indiana, Illinois, Michigan, and Wisconsin increased by 2,400,000—more than 53 per cent—in a single decade. Quickened, as we have seen, by the Illinois Central, the first of the "land-grant railways" of the United States to be endowed (1850) from the public domain, this migration had reached a volume and momentum by 1856 which threatened to draw Canada West into its orbit and to engulf the prairies of Rupert's Land in its course. The Hannibal and St. Jo railway reached the Missouri in 1858. Minnesota, organized as a territory in 1849 and as a state in 1858, passed a resolution at the first session of its legislature advocating the annexation of the Red River district. The gesture was interpreted at Red River as the "highest tribute yet paid to this country." An observer from Chicago estimated that 500 Red River carts were already plying to St. Paul in 1856. The *Anson Northrup* was taken overland piecemeal from the Missouri and reassembled on the Red River in 1861. Thereafter a long succession of Hudson's Bay river boats began to supply not only the Red River Settlement but many of the Company's own posts in the Southern Department through American channels.

The effect of this migration upon Canada West was already visible in 1856. A lavish system of free land grants during the early years of the province had left, by the time of the Durham mission, less than 1,150,000 acres at the disposal of the crown out of a surveyed area of 13,600,000 acres. Of this vast wilderness of alienated land nine-tenths remained still unoccupied in the hands of privileged grantees or "land-poor" speculators. The inaccessibility of this squandered patrimony destroyed any hope of systematic land settlement by the government. The prospective settler could scarcely fail to contrast this chaotic confusion with the orderly administration of the "public domain" south of the border—simple, prompt, uniform, and efficient in its operation, with expanding frontiers in all directions under national control by the federal government. By 1856 this "prairie fever," as the Canadian press used to deplore, was already taking its toll from the immigration thronging the St. Lawrence. As early as 1851 the Canadian commissioner of crown lands stated that "the supply of Crown Lands for settlement is now exhausted." To George Brown and the *Globe* it seemed that the tide of immigration ebbing towards the Mississippi and Missouri prairies could be stemmed only by cheap land in Canada and by the prospect of Canadian prairies and "prairie fever" of their own beyond the Great Lakes in Rupert's Land. Two young Canadians who founded the *Nor'-Wester* at Red River in 1859 never ceased to urge annexation to Canada, and the *Globe* never ceased to commend their enterprise.

A second coincidence brought this issue into sharp focus in 1856. The old charter of the Hudson's Bay Company still held for Rupert's Land but the twenty-one year licence of 1838 for the regions beyond was to expire in 1859, and a select committee of the British House of Commons was consequently appointed in 1857 to "consider the state" of the whole vast territory "under the administration of the Hudson's Bay Company." Divergent policies quickly emerged in Canada with regard to the West. Even at this early date there is evidence of an understanding between Grand Trunk interests represented by John Ross, president of the company in Canada, and Sir George Simpson, governor of the Hudson's Bay Company. Later on when Watkin appeared upon the scene this alliance took on a deeper significance. The purchase of a controlling interest in the Hudson's Bay Company by the International Financial Society, as we have seen, was to have been a gambit in Watkin's policy for an accommodation with Canadian politics. Sir Edmund Head at Newcastle's own suggestion became governor of the reorganized Hudson's Bay Company in London. In

1856, however, the problem of saving Rupert's Land from the fate of Oregon sprang for the first time into public notice in Canada. The President of the Executive Council stated roundly that the western boundary of Canada ought to be the Pacific. The claim was "echoed throughout the province by the press and by public men of all degrees." A general federation was not yet feasible but half a loaf was better than no bread. A series of regional unions might safeguard for a time the survival of British interests across the continent.

On March 2, 1856, Head sent to Henry Labouchere in the Colonial Office a confidential memorandum on the Hudson's Bay territories, suggesting the preliminary organization of the whole region from Lake Nipigon to the Rockies and from the north branch of the Saskatchewan to the United States boundary as a territory under the name of Saskatchewan, with a lieutenant-governor and partially elective council. The province of Canada was then to "take charge of the whole territory of Saskatchewan and to provide for the fair representation in Parliament." When the Select Committee of which Labouchere was chairman presented its monumental *Report*—Head was in London at the time and the *Report* was based upon a draft by Labouchere himself—it was found that the chief recommendations were in agreement with Head's known views in 1856. The Select Committee recommended that the fertile districts on the Red and Saskatchewan rivers should be "ceded to Canada on equitable principles"; that unless Canada were "willing at a very early period to undertake the government of the Red River District . . . some temporary provision for its administration" might be advisable; and that Vancouver Island should revert to the crown to form the nucleus of a crown colony west of the Rocky Mountains.

The second of these projected regional unions had a stormier background which must have been ominously familiar to that generation in British America. By 1856 Texas and Oregon had become names of sinister import in the British provinces. "Manifest destiny" was on the march. From 1821 when the American migration under Stephen Austin began to move into Mexico, to the annexation of Texas in 1845, the conclusion of the Mexican War in 1848, the "Oregon Treaty" of Washington with Great Britain in 1846, and the Gadsden purchase of 1853 from Mexico, an area of more than 900,000 square miles— more than the whole area of the original Dominion of Canada—had been added to the republic. The loss of Oregon north of the Columbia to the United States in 1846 had been followed by the grant of Vancouver Island in fee simple to the Hudson's Bay Company in the hope of establishing there a permanent vested interest of settlement so fatally lacking in the contest for Oregon. By 1856 it was obvious that settlement under the Company could never cope with the deluge of migration already moving from the south. The gold of the Fraser and the Cariboo was as yet unknown for a year or two to this turbulent frontier, but another crisis like that of Oregon might have had irreparable consequences for British interests on the Pacific. The *Report* of the Select Committee in 1857 advised the resumption of Vancouver Island by the crown and the extension of colonial government to the mainland. This was in some respects the most urgent of their recommendations, and the subsequent regional union of British Columbia proved to be the only one of the three to be effected substantially in its original form.

A third regional union was advocated by Head with much ampler knowledge and authority than his Canadian experience could command for the remote regions of the West. Of the four maritime provinces into which the old province of Nova Scotia had been divided at the close of the American Revolution, one only—Cape Breton Island—had been reunited to the parent province in 1820. By 1856 the others had developed local traditions so strong that every attempt to repair the ravages of disintegration had come to grief upon these stubborn loyalties. Head's project for a general federation in 1851 would have recognized Nova Scotia, New Brunswick and Prince Edward Island as separate provinces but "further knowledge and experience" in the Canadas had dispelled any hope of an immediate general federation, and six months after the memorandum on the Hudson's Bay territories Head drafted (September 3, 1856) another "private and confidential" despatch to Labouchere on the feasibility of a regional reunion of the maritime provinces. Despairing still of any "federal or legislative Union of Canada with the three 'Lower Colonies'" on grounds of practicability, he believed it "possible, with great advantage to all parties concerned to unite under one Government, Nova Scotia, Prince Edward's Island, and New Brunswick." The process of such a union, he added, "would be a long one. . . . I can have no personal interest in the matter," though both eastern and western regional unions "had long occupied my thoughts."

During the summer of 1857—June 20 to November—Head returned to London in order to "communicate the results of my consideration either by word of mouth or on paper as circumstances permit." From the Athenaeum Club on July 29 he put on record again for Labouchere his fear that a general federation was still "impracticable." "It may be on the other hand," he added, "that a Legislative union of the three Lower Colonies, i.e. Nova Scotia, New Brunswick and Prince Edward Island, would be more practicable in itself, and would be desired by those Colonies. Such a step would not in any way prejudice the future consideration of a more extensive union."

Head was in London when the *Report* of the Select Committee on the Hudson's Bay Company was presented (July 31, 1857). He returned to Canada in November to find that the very foundations of the Canadian union were beginning to crumble, and that "rivalry of race, language and worship," without compromise and without quarter, threatened to make shipwreck of Canadian politics unless the Canadian union could be merged into a general British North American federation. For this last desperate foray into federation Head now found one ally in Canada after his own heart. Despite its immediate failure the Head-Galt project of 1858 brought into play coercive factors towards federal union which were never altogether relaxed until confederation became an accomplished fact.

Chapter Thirteen

CRISIS IN THE CANADAS

EDERALISM as distinct from legislative union—either regional or general—for the British provinces arose from the exigencies of politics in the old province of Canada. This truth came home in 1858 to two men who must have been singularly akin to each other. Both were supposed to be untrammelled by active partisanship—Sir Edmund Head, *ex officio*, and Alexander Tilloch Galt by choice. Both, nevertheless, discerned at this moment a political crisis which aligned their convictions with the most rancorous partisanship of their day.

Every instinct and economic interest of these two men must have led them to forestall if possible the impending "rivalry of race, language and worship" which now threatened the Canadian union. Galt had the mercurial subjective temperament of the financier, the inveterate *entrepreneur* whose enterprises were acquisitive in their immediate interest but national withal as a rule in their scope and too empirical for the conventions of party politics. Head also was an empiricist, a Peelite whose cold analytical intellect played unceasingly upon the two gravest problems of administration in British North America, the practical working of parliamentary government and an independent destiny for the British provinces in association with Great Britain. The collaboration of these two men in 1858 must have been instinctive. The relative lack of official correspondence between them during this critical period may be taken as *prima facie* evidence not of estrangement but of intimacy—the sort of intimacy which finds its most appropriate medium in talk over walnuts and port rather than in the formal interchanges of official intercourse. Much that took place behind the scenes from Head's return to Canada in November, 1857, to the Galt-Cartier-Ross mission to the Colonial Office in October, 1858, must be left for the present to conjecture. What took place between Head and Galt at the fall of the two-day Brown-Dorion Government in August, 1858? Why did Head call upon Galt, an untried independent member of the House who had never held office in his life, to form a government as prime minister of Canada? Galt's immediate declination is easily understood but what devious counsels must have attended the formation of the Cartier-Macdonald-Galt ad-ministration on August 6 with a "federal union of the British North American provinces" as the price of Galt's accession. These and many other speculations will require a brief retrospect of political parties during one of the most dynamic decades of Canadian history.

It would be hard to find a more concise and prophetic forecast of the peril which threatened the Canadian union than the undated memorandum in Head's unmistakable handwriting shortly after his appointment as governor-general. Using a famous passage in Durham's *Report* as his text he noted Durham's "foresight and wisdom" in opposing "every plan that has been proposed for giving an equal number of members to the two Provinces, in order to attain the temporary end of outnumbering the French. . . . Any such electoral arrangement . . . would tend to defeat the purposes of union and perpetuate the idea of disunion." These sagacious counsels had been ignored in the *Act of Union* and Canada West with a population of 450,000 was granted representation equal to that of Canada East with a population of 600,000. "To make the representation equal at the outset," wrote Head, "was to admit a federal principle as existing after the Union." By 1851 the population of Canada West outnumbered that of Canada East, and the shoe was on the other foot. By 1861 the numbers stood at 1,400,000 to 1,100,000, and the trends were unmistakable. In these two decades Canada East increased by 183 per cent and Canada West by 311 per cent. The population of Toronto grew from 13,000 in 1842 to 42,000 in 1856. London trebled its population in six years (1850 to 1856). Canada East had waived representation by population with what resignation she could command in the day of her adversity. Would Canada West be content to waive it perpetually in the day of her unquestioned ascendancy? Here was the "unsound spot in the Union" and the time was approaching when "the poison of disunion" could no longer be "passed by or overlooked: the difficulty must be faced." "No immediate occasion for action of any kind presents itself at the present moment," Head added reflectively, "but it is on that account more desirable to cast our eyes forward and look steadily at the questions which seem likely to arise hereafter." By 1858 this shrewd and characteristic forecast was upon the point of fulfilment. Led by the uncompromising ardour of George Brown and the *Globe*, the Clear Grit party of Canada West had adopted representation by population as their official policy in 1857. Head returned to Canada in November to find that the elections of that year had made serious inroads upon the Government's majority and that the ascendancy of the Clear Grits in Canada West (33 to 28) seemed assured.

The Clear Grit party of Canada West, however, was but one of the heterogeneous groups of reformers into which the great Reform party of 1848 had degenerated once the issue of responsible government which held it together had been irrevocably conceded. The old colonial Tory party, too, was undergoing a "sea change." In truth the turbulent fifties and early sixties, so chaotic to contemporaries, were a challenge to the enterprise and resourcefulness of the Canadian people, and that challenge was met by some of the most creative and original exploits in their history. This was particularly true of political parties.

THE LIBERAL-CONSERVATIVE PARTY

I

The old school of colonial toryism committed *hara-kiri* in the Montreal riots of 1849. "The party of the connection" which claimed a monopoly of loyalty to the Crown had pelted the Queen's representative with brickbats and worse, had impugned the undoubted will of both sections of the province in the *Rebellion Losses Bill*, had stultified themselves by repudiating responsible government, had burnt down the parliament buildings to the ground, and in large numbers had signed a manifesto for annexation to the United States. None could reflect upon this record without shame and without profit. Young Conservatives turned their backs upon the past and faced the future with foreboding. John A. Macdonald himself more than once threatened to retire from public life: the party was "damned everlastingly."

A new era now forced a realignment. That in itself was a political advantage. Old toryism had been a vicious spiral. With every loss of popular support it tended to rely upon the "connection" with the mother country, and with every effort to exploit the "connection" it tended to forfeit popular support. The acceptance of responsible government even by Sir Allan MacNab now forced the party to rely upon themselves. New enterprises too of unpredictable range and resources now dominated the scene. MacNab's blunt avowal that "railroads are my politics" became true also of Hincks and Galt and Ross and Cartier. Never since the turbulent days of the fur trade had such resources existed for the exploitation of the infirmities of human nature. In Canada as in the United States human nature proved only too frail before the exigencies of "railway politics." The Grand Trunk was indissolubly wedded to politics. Like its contemporary, the Illinois Central, it confronted the government of the day with an unprecedented range of vested interests. Though Watkin, as we have seen, found the Grand Trunk on the brink of bankruptcy in 1861—"an organized mess—I will not say a sink of iniquity"—the most rabid Clear Grit was prepared to admit that the Canada of that day could not function without it.

Other vested interests, too, found themselves associated in varying degrees with the government of the day and with each other. By 1855 the Bank of Montreal had a capital of $6,000,000, the Bank of Upper Canada and the Commercial Bank of $4,000,000 each. Three new banks were chartered in 1854–5, two in 1856, four in 1858. By 1859 industrial enterprises of no mean size had begun to group themselves behind Galt's differential tariff for their protection. The land companies, too, sharing in the buoyant prosperity from the expenditure of £15,000,000 on railway construction in four years, found their chief critics on the frontier. When the prices of cattle, flour, pork, and oats doubled from 1852 to 1854, merchants and speculators of every degree shared in the boom. With the close of the Crimean War the price of Canadian wheat fell from 10s. 11d. to 4s. a bushel. The financial crisis of 1857 in Great Britain developed into a panic in the United States, and though Canadian banks met the immediate crisis without suspending payments, the ebb tide of poor harvests in 1857 and 1858 brought widespread bankruptcy and distress. The gregarious interests of "big business," which readily lent themselves in prosperity to the devices of managerial politics, were now on the defensive and tended to look for relief to a managerial party. Against sectionalism and parochialism, moreover, there was a valid plea for cohesive national policies. Without false modesty John A. Macdonald and Cartier could claim for the new liberal-conservatism the sanctions of a national party.

There were other factors in this rejuvenated conservatism which were the result of deliberate policy. For a whole decade after the union the cause of doctrinaire constitutional reform had derived its most unwavering support from La Fontaine and his French bloc. They alone had forced Bagot's "great measure" in 1842. They alone had held their ranks in the disastrous election of 1844. *Que diable va-t-il dans cette galère?* A few British statesmen had been pondering that anomaly for many years. "Au fond," said Sir George Murray, "they are the most anti-Yankee as also the most Monarchical portion of the population." A colleague of Bagot's in Washington once begged him to rescue a chivalrous race from charges of radicalism and treason. Elgin, with his Peelite background and flair for realistic solutions, was quick to see the same anomalies. With the concession of responsible government the French would be "rescued from the false position into which they have been driven," and would become "essentially a conservative element in the Canadian compound." Elgin rated Baldwin at his retirement "the most Conservative public man in Canada," and La Fontaine's last great speech before his retirement in 1851 carried him too almost into the ranks of the conservatives. The transition from the radical French bloc in 1844 to Cartier's bloc of Bleus in 1854 was reinforced, as we shall see, by the defensive interests of French Canada after 1851 in safeguarding "equal representation" for Canada East in the Canadian union. The alliance of this generic conservatism with the acquisitive commercial interests of Montreal was less strange than it appeared upon the surface. Both lent themselves to a managerial technique in politics, and Cartier's blunt retort on one occasion to the perennial demand for representation by population—"call in de membr'"—was an unanswerable voting asset for the party. The time came when for confederation as for responsible government this voting strength was to prove invaluable, and for a whole generation French conservatism continued to play the same role.

II

The new conservatism had the best of reasons, moreover, for claiming a measure of national confidence in addressing itself to the solution of the gravest national issues of the day.

The clergy reserves had been the bane of Canadian politics. Sydenham called them "the root of all the troubles of the province . . . the perpetual source of discord, strife and hatred." The solution which that wily opportunist devised as a prelude to his régime of "practical measures" to follow was rejected by the officials of the church who went farther and fared worse. Every reformer from Mackenzie to Brown had put the settlement of the clergy reserves in the forefront of policy. The failure to dispose of them in 1854 led to the downfall of the Hincks-Morin administration. The issue was settled at last by the new Liberal-Conservative party (1854–5) as the first fruits of conservative administration.

Seigneurial tenure, a heritage of seventeenth-century feudalism perpetuated by the *Quebec Act*, had long been a target for French radicals. This too was now settled in true conservative fashion by indemnifying the seigneurs for the *droit de banalité*, the *lods et ventes*, and other dues, and by enabling the habitants to redeem at trifling cost the trivial rental charge that remained. With true managerial sagacity an equivalent grant was made to the municipalities of Canada West.

For a whole generation elective councils had been advocated by radical reformers and rejected by tories as futile and republican. King William IV in person had warned the Gosford mission against this "elective principle." Both Baldwin and Durham shared the opposition to it. An elective legislative council was now authorized (1856) as an adjunct of conservatism, reinforced no doubt by Elgin's traditional sagacity on that issue: would not a legislative council elected on a higher franchise have a conservative rather than a radical function in providing a legitimate appeal from the impulsiveness of a popular assembly? The same session (1856) provided a codification of the laws of Canada East under the pragmatic auspices of Cartier and his compliant Bleus. Instinctive tories with traditional loyalism might have been expected to impugn too close a reciprocity in trade with the United States. The new Conservative Government ratified the Reciprocity Treaty of 1854 of Elgin and Hincks with unquestioning enthusiasm under the realistic conviction that reciprocity was the antidote rather than the antecedent of annexation. Ten years later they spared no effort in the vain attempt to secure a renewal. The establishment of a militia system, 1854–5, marked a new sense of duty in the responsibilities of self-government.

Beneath these empirical experiments of the new conservatism there was discernible a resourceful and realistic temper which Elgin, for one, had done his best to promote, and which seems to have eluded, in some measure, the traditional apologists of the party in the heyday of its power. Untrammelled by abstractions and doctrinaire "principles" the new party was prepared to appeal unblushingly to liberalism and conservatism alike in addressing themselves to the practical problems of their day. The appropriation of both historic names in the nomenclature of the party was no idle gesture. And the pragmatic approach of men like Macdonald and Cayley, Cartier and Isaac Buchanan found an instinctive response in the realistic Peelite temper of both Elgin and Sir Edmund Head. In truth the real genealogy of this cast of political thought in Canada would be hard to trace in orthodox fashion. It was compounded of political experiences and vicissitudes that defied rationalization at once into a body of political doctrine. Improvisation was its life-blood and the prince of improvisers can scarcely be denied an honoured place in the evolution of Canadian conservatism. Whatever Sydenham's record may have been in British politics he was recognized in Canada as the first and perhaps the greatest master of managerial politics. Both Hincks and Macdonald avowed themselves his disciples. Practical politicians, open-minded and intent upon constructive material progress, adepts at improvisation, without false modesty and without squeamishness, they saw what somehow had to be done and they were sometimes ready to do it with a convenient absence of scruple. "Small thanks," Carlyle once exclaimed, "to the man who will keep his hands clean but with gloves on."

By 1854 the transition from the old "compact toryism" to the new liberal-conservatism was almost complete. Hincks who had been prepared to help spend that imperial loan of £1,500,000 for Sydenham and Bagot, was now prime minister, with John Ross, A. N. Morin, and other men of congenial temper as his colleagues. After the prodigious achievement of the Grand Trunk, the Canadian banking system (including the change to decimal currency), the post office taken over from imperial control and reorganized at cheaper rates, and a host of other practical measures to his credit, his retirement to a governorship in the West Indies was an opportune gesture both for himself and for his successors. The new Conservative party found it convenient to lay upon his unprotesting head—a convenient scapegoat into the wilderness—the devious sins of the Grand Trunk era, and to appropriate its political resources for a managerial party. Despite the most violent denunciation of Hincks ("steeped to the lips in corruption") by John A. Macdonald at this time, some observers, George Brown among them, shrewdly detected more of collusion than collision between them. Probably no man in Canadian politics stood higher for sheer ability in Macdonald's esteem than Sir Francis Hincks. His course had he remained in Canada during the era of confederation would be hard to conjecture, but when he returned at last from his imperial pilgrimage Macdonald did not rest until Hincks was included as minister of finance in the federal cabinet of the new Dominion. When Macdonald went to Washington as the first of British plenipotentiaries from Canada for the impending treaty of 1871 his chart was a memorandum from Hincks listing a new reciprocity treaty as the first need of the hour. Hincks had come to Canada before the stormy days of the Mackenzie rising and he lived through three eras of Canadian politics —the era of "compact colonialism," the inauguration of responsible government under the union, and the functioning of federalism "from sea to sea." He was equally at home in all of them, and he could be all things to all men. To Baldwin he was both a devoted disciple and a ruthless critic. To Bagot he was "radicalissimus" but "undisputably, and without any comparison, the best public accountant in the Country." To Metcalfe he was the author of the "ruffianlike proceedings" of 1844. In Elgin's opinion he had "more energy than all the Canadian Statesmen I have yet had to do with put together." The approbation of Elgin and the veneration of Macdonald may entitle Sir Francis Hincks to a place among the ancestors of the Liberal-Conservative party.

The final transition to the party which sponsored the first attempt at federation in 1858 took place when Sir Allan MacNab was supplanted by Taché and finally by John A. Macdonald in November, 1857. The formation of the MacNab-Morin administration in 1854 had been one of the last and most gratifying of Elgin's official duties before leaving Canada: responsible government was now safe as the avowed doctrine of both political parties. Several of the old Hincks-Morin administration—Morin himself, E. P. Taché, and John Ross of the Grand Trunk among them—readily accommodated themselves to the times and took office under the new standard. But John A. Macdonald of Canada West was the rising star of the new order. By 1856 it was obvious that Sir Allan MacNab with his "infernal lot of hangers on" was an anachronism. He was supplanted at first by Taché as president of the newly elective Legislative Council, leaving Macdonald, Attorney-General West, the recognized leader of the Government in the Assembly.[1] The appearance in the same cabinet of Cartier as Attorney-General for Canada East was a portent of a political alliance which was to rival that of Baldwin and La Fontaine in Canadian politics. With Taché's retirement in 1857 Macdonald donned the mantle of prime minister with an assurance of mastery which was curiously to be repeated upon the eve of confederation in 1865. Thenceforth for more than a generation conservatism in Canada was to be associated with his name.

THE "REFORM" PARTY

I

The heterogeneous groups in opposition to these integrated interests suffered from the sectional nature of their appeal and from the very

---

[1]"The object of some members of the Government was, no doubt, to throw over Sir Allan McNab. I could not save him inasmuch as it was clear to me he could not carry on the Government without those gentlemen who had persisted in resigning." Head to Labouchere, private and confidential, May 26, 1856.

nature of their political philosophy. Macdonald and his Liberal-Conservatives found it convenient to refer to them indiscriminately as Grits or Rouges, but no two groups among them could co-operate without compromise, and compromise was precisely the rarest of their political virtues. Scottish covenanters like George Brown, French-Canadian anti-clericals and republicans like the Dorion brothers and Laberge, separatists and annexationists like Charles Clarke and George Sheppard, frontier radicals like William McDougall, disgruntled *entre-preneurs* like Luther Holton, Christopher Dunkin, and (until 1857) A. T. Galt, stolid apostolic liberals like Oliver Mowat whose political sagacity was to dominate Ontario for nearly half a century—how could men and interests like these be expected to function as an integrated political party? One man alone perhaps believed it possible and bent every resource of shrewd pawky Scottish ingenuity to the task of reconciling east and west, Protestant and Roman Catholic, merchant, industrialist, and frontiersman in opposition to "jobbers and corruptionists" in high places. Sandfield Macdonald, a Roman Catholic highlander representing the middle interests along the St. Lawrence between Montreal and Belleville—the "mugwumps" of Canadian politics—became prime minister in 1862 and still believed it possible in 1865 to ride out the storm. Had no coercive factors from outside complicated the issue it is conceivable that a Reform ascendancy under Sandfield Macdonald might have dominated the united province of Canada for many years. In the provincial field Sandfield Macdonald, Edward Blake, and Oliver Mowat between them made good this ascendancy from the beginning of confederation to the turn of the century. Even in the federal field the remnants of the Clear Grit party which survived "the great coalition" of 1864 carried 50 out of 88 Ontario seats in the election of 1872 and 66 out of 88 in the election of 1874. In 1858, however, many of the elements in opposition to the Government seemed so disruptive that they threatened the very foundations of the Canadian union, and many of the shrewdest observers of that day—Sir Edmund Head, A. T. Galt, and George Cartier among them—turned to federation less perhaps in the expectation of achieving something better than in the hope of escaping something worse.

The Reform party which won responsible government in 1848 had the largest majority in the history of the Canadian union, and it disintegrated within eighteen months. Many reasons for this have already been noted. In Nova Scotia where party alignments were more natural and instinctive, liberals and conservatives without breaking their ranks continued with undiminished vigor to contest and to enjoy the laurels ot office. In Canada the victors of 1848 were a political party if ever there was one, in Burke's formula, for that most important of all issues "in the interests of the nation." But it was a highly factitious party, and when that sole issue which united them was irrefutably won it broke into fragments on half a dozen practical issues of the day. Less than two years after taking office, as we have seen, Baldwin himself thought it "time to throw out the anchor." La Fontaine escaped to the bench. Hincks plunged into railways and banking, currency reforms and commerce, with ferocious energy, and carried to the West Indies more maledictions from the Reformers than from kindred spirits in the new Liberal-Conservative party. Not from the "old boys" and not from the "Hincksite Reformers" was to come the dynamic element in Canadian politics which was to call the tune of reform for many a year in Canada West.

II

As early as 1850 a group of western radicals many of whose names have slipped quietly out of Canadian history—Peter Perry, Caleb Hopkins, David Christie, Malcolm Cameron, William McDougall, Dr. John Rolph—were so critical of the "old boys" in the party that a convention was called at Markham to speed up the cause of radical reform. The *North American* founded by William McDougall, a Toronto lawyer, in 1850, soon reached a circulation of 2400. Advocating radical principles, "all sand and no dirt—clear grit all the way through," the *North American* was at first a curious compound of Jacksonian democracy from the United States, radical thought from British Chartism, and Protestant resentment of "civil, political and religious degradation" at the hands of clerical interests in Canada East. The extension of the franchise and abolition of property qualifications for members, retrenchment in government expenditures, and vote by ballot were familiar features of radical reform. But "fixed biennial parliaments" and the "elective principle" for council and governor alike marked a clear departure from British parliamentary models in favour of frontier republican democracy. George Brown and the Toronto *Globe* attacked the Clear Grits at this stage as "Calebites" (after Caleb Hopkins) whose principles "would simply be a revolution." Clear Grit as a name was "too good for them": they were a "little miserable clique of office-seeking, bunkum-talking cormorants, who met in a certain lawyer's office [McDougall's] in King Street, and announced their intention to form a new party on 'Clear Grit' principles."

For a decade or more inconsistencies and heresies such as a written constitution and covert annexationism were to be found among the Clear Grits. There were indigenous practical issues in Canada, however, which soon transformed this imitative and exotic doctrinaire outlook into one of the most dynamic movements in Canadian politics. The secularization of clergy reserves, non-sectarian schools, cheap land as against the big land companies, thrift and economy as against "jobbery and corruption," westward expansion as against the Hudson's Bay monopoly, a tight hand on the public purse for the Grand Trunk ("we want no railroad government," wrote McDougall in the *North American*), and above all representation by population as Canada West rapidly outdistanced Canada East in wealth and population— these were native issues as indigenous to the agrarian frontier of Canada West as potash and corduroy roads. It was not long before George Brown himself sought allies among the Clear Grits against what the *Globe* used to call "state-churchism" in both sections of the province. As early as March, 1853, he moved a resolution in the House for representation by population. By June, 1855, "rep. by pop." was nailed to the masthead of the *Globe* and it flew there until "the great coalition" fairly accomplished it by the expedient of a federation of the British provinces. George Brown in turn committed the Clear Grits to two or three of the most fateful decisions of Canadian politics —the continued integration of Canada West in the St. Lawrence system for the commercial development of the frontier, the British connection with its attendant practices of parliamentary government, and the cause of westward expansion into Rupert's Land to keep pace with the prodigious westward expansion of the United States. Again a federation of the British provinces was found to be the only way of safeguarding all three objectives in the intolerable tensions of the Civil War.

It was Brown's attack upon the Hincks-Morin administration for their failure to deal with the clergy reserves in 1854 which carried him into this strange company. The British Parliament in 1853 had left the issue to the Canadian legislature then approaching dissolution for a new election. Since the franchise had just been extended and the representation in the House raised from 84 to 130, Hincks, supported unanimously by his cabinet and by Elgin,[1] decided to leave to this enlarged and more representative House the final settlement of so controversial an issue. In his covenanting wrath against Hincks, Brown

[1]"In these views of the Executive Council I entirely concurred." Elgin to Newcastle, June 22, 1854.

not only underwrote the zeal of the Clear Grit *North American* but found himself actually abetting John A. Macdonald in opposition to the Government. Hincks in return charged upon Brown the "absurd policy" of alienating Canada East and "forcing them into the Conservative Camp." As the pattern of the Liberal-Conservative party began to emerge with the benediction of Elgin, Brown suspected Hincks of unholy collusion in the new trends, and Hincks warned Brown and his impetuous allies that "if the union is not preserved by them . . . other combinations must be formed by which the union may be preserved. I am ready to give my cordial support to any combination of parties by which the union shall be maintained."

III

The *Globe* became a daily newspaper in 1853 and the *North American* withdrew from the field with the issue of February 14, 1855. Thenceforth Brown's ascendancy over a highly sectional but responsive constituency in Canada West carried him and them into irreparable conflict with vested interests both economic and ecclesiastical in Canada East. The new Government was the residuary legatee of Grand Trunk "jobbers and corruptionists." The *Globe*, which had supplanted not only the *North American* but the Presbyterian *Banner*, plunged with headlong recklessness into the religious controversies of the day. Legitimate issues such as separate schools and religious corporations were embittered by rankling "incidents" in the public press. During the Gavazzi riots in Quebec where the House happened to be in session at that time, a resentful mob which wrecked the Chalmers Free Church and drove Father Gavazzi from the pulpit marched off to the parliament buildings in search of George Brown. Early in 1856 the notorious Corrigan murder trial threatened to drag even the courts into the religious controversy. The *Globe* took up the cudgels and a narrow majority in the House directed a review of the judge's charge to the jury. To Taché and his colleagues these men were "Pharisaical brawlers." Even Luther Holton on one occasion found his prospects as a Rouge reformer so compromised by George Brown and the Clear Grits that he was moved to question the right of the *Globe* to "vex the Liberal party with its intolerable bigotry."

To regard this Clear Grit constituency as an agrarian frontier democracy, however, would be to over-simplify and conceal many elements of its strength and also of its weakness. George Brown's opposition to "big business" did not preclude a very lively concern for many big businesses in Toronto. In its crusade for western expansion the *Globe* associated itself more than once with the McMasters and the Howlands, with John Macdonald and John McMurrich and Allen Macdonnell whose "unconquerable *penchant* for magnificent schemes" ran counter to established vested interests in Montreal. Copper mines on Lake Superior, locks at the Soo, the organization of a North West Transit Company, the expedition of Captain Kennedy for "commerce and exploration" in Rupert's Land in 1856, and a project for a new North West Company to dispute the ancient monopoly of the Hudson's Bay Company, were not the earmarks of an egalitarian frontier democracy. The truth was that the *Globe*, which by 1862 claimed three times the circulation of its nearest rival in the Canadian press, was purveying "urban British Liberalism to a fundamentally agricultural North American society,"[1] an agrarian society which was fast becoming the most prosperous and the most populous community in British North America. As early as 1856 a defensive alliance between Ross of the Grand Trunk and Sir George Simpson of the Hudson's Bay Company was already traceable in the columns of the Toronto *Leader*.

But the Clear Grit movement was vitalized by one issue which grew steadily in momentum until it became fairly irresistible. How could the representation of Canada East and Canada West remain the same while the upper province contributed two-thirds of the revenue and seemed destined by 1861 to outdistance the lower province in wealth and population? The wasteful duplication of expenditures, the "intolerable domination" of Canada East in forcing separate schools upon the upper province in defiance of the *Globe*'s crusade against "state-churchism" in all its forms, the economic domination of Grand Trunk as against the Northern and the Great Western, and of Montreal banking and industrial enterprise sheltered behind protective tariffs —these evidences of "subordination" in Canada West could be expected to grow increasingly irksome with every census. If Canada East had submitted to equal representation from the union to 1851, the submission of Canada West until 1861 would even the score. Sooner or later just representation would become imperative. The perennial votes of the House and election after election in Canada West reflected this rising tempo for "rep. by pop." The Clear Grits adopted it in 1857 as their official policy and carried Canada West by a majority of five. In 1861 Canada West voted 40 to 9 to break the equality of representation in the Canadian union. In 1864 on the brink of "the great coalition" a

[1]See J. M. S. Careless, "The Toronto Globe and Agrarian Radicalism, 1850–67," *Canadian Historical Review*, March, 1948.

resolution to maintain that equality "inviolate" was lost in the House by a vote of 82 to 24. By that time the shrewdest observers on both sides of the House were prepared to concede the outcome. In "rep. by pop." George Brown and the Clear Grits had appropriated the most deadly weapon in the arsenal of Canadian politics.

This sectional conflict was embittered rather than neutralized by the natural failure of the Clear Grits to find effective allies in Canada East. The vicissitudes of the Rouges under the union remained almost a closed book to the self-centred sectionalists of Canada West. Skelton has followed Sir Wilfrid Laurier in a tribute to the young men, the Dorion brothers, Papin, D'Aoust, Laberge, and others—all of them under twenty-two years of age at the time—who founded the young Rouge party. "Never before nor since," adds Skelton, "has the power of the Roman Catholic Church in Canada been subjected to such strong assaults from within."[1] But the covenanting zeal of the *Banner,* the *North American,* and the *Globe* was scarcely calculated to advance the cause of anti-clericalism in Canada East. Even the courage of Eric Dorion in *L'Avenir* must have quailed before some of the diatribes cited by the Bleus from the columns of the *Globe.* The Rouges who had risen from five members in the House in 1851 to nineteen in 1854 came back with a mere handful from the elections of 1857. A. A. Dorion and Holton were both defeated. By this time Brown's uncompromising sectionalism, armed with "rep. by pop." and reckless of the consequences, had become a prime concern not only of the Macdonald-Cartier Government but of Sir Edmund Head as governor-general. "Our present business," he had written in an early memorandum on the union, "is to do the best we can from day to day and delay this crisis." Conflict could be forestalled "only by the greatest tact on the part of all."

[1]*Life and Times of Sir A. T. Galt* (Toronto, 1920), p. 169.

Chapter Fourteen

FIRST "DRIVE FOR FEDERATION," 1858

HEAD'S early memorandum on the union had begun with the observation that "no immediate occasion for action of any kind presents itself at the present moment but it is on that account more desirable to cast our eyes forward and look steadily at the questions which seem likely to arise hereafter. . . . The crisis may come sooner or later but the dualistic relation, if I may so call it, of U. and L.C. will be in constant peril." By 1858 the crisis had come and with it an "occasion for action" which Head did not hesitate to seize with all his might. In Cartier as prime minister and Galt the mover of the famous resolutions on federation, July 5, 1858, he found allies after his own heart.

Although Head's correspondence with Labouchere and his conferences in London during the summer of 1857 were immediately concerned with a series of regional unions across the continent, "such a step," he was careful to add, "would not in any way prejudice the future consideration of a more extensive union." There can be no doubt that from Labouchere and from Lord Stanley who succeeded him for a few months in the Colonial Office Head received encouragement to explore the cause of British North American union with every resource of tact and initiative.[1] In May, 1858, however, Stanley was succeeded by Lytton in the Conservative administration of Lord Derby, and

[1]Cf. Merivale's minute as under-secretary on Head's subsequent despatch of August 18, 1858, to Lytton: "Mr. Labouchere particularly requested him to take it in hand, when he was last in England. . . . Mr. Labouchere's view was not that it was a thing to be urged from this side, but that we ought to be prepared for its proposal and rather encourage it than otherwise." Cf. also a minute of Lord Carnarvon, then under-secretary, on Head's confidential despatch to Lytton of October 22, 1858, defending his initiative in launching the project of 1858: "One of the reasons . . . wh. I doubt not weighed much with Sir E. Head but to which he does not allude was the support wh. he conceived he had from Lord Stanley's private letters. Those letters undoubtedly do support his view." See W. M. Whitelaw, *The Maritimes and Canada before Confederation* (Toronto, 1934), 121 f.

Labouchere's friendly relations with the Hudson's Bay Company and with Head as the dean of British officials in America were replaced by a coolness which quickly developed into petulant hostility.

To Lytton the Hudson's Bay Company was a broken reed for the safeguarding of British interests across the continent. Obsessed with the immediate problem of British Columbia, where the *Report* of the Select Committee of 1857 was just being implemented for a regional union west of the Rockies, and with the equally critical problem of Rupert's Land, the transfer of which "on equitable principles" to "Canada" had been recommended by the same *Report*, Lytton was less concerned than Head with the perils of the Canadian union. To Lytton, as to Head and Labouchere and Stanley, the expansion of "Canada" may well have offered the best prospect of safeguarding British interests between the Great Lakes and the Rocky Mountains. But the chief advocates of westward expansion in Canada were the Clear Grits, hostile to the Hudson's Bay Company, openly contemptuous of their chartered rights, and already active in supplanting their monopoly by Canadian enterprise. If Canada was to underwrite British interests across the continent would it be wise to alienate the unpredictable enterprise of George Brown and the Canadian frontier? This, as we shall see, was a consideration which Lytton commended confidentially to the British cabinet in 1858—a consideration which Cartier, Galt, and Ross in 1858 and many historians since would have regarded with some astonishment. In truth it would be safe to say that the authentic origins as well as the results of the first "drive for federation" in 1858 are almost unrecognizable in the conventional story of the Canadian confederation.

The aims of both Head and Galt in 1858 were complicated, in spite of them both, by elements of intractable partisanship. Until 1857 Galt had passed as a Rouge, more fortunate than Holton in making friends with the mammon of the Grand Trunk but still associated with A. A. Dorion and Holton in thankless co-operation with George Brown and the Clear Grits of the upper province. By 1856 Dorion had found Rouge prospects so compromised by Brown's truculent zeal in the *Globe* that he had proposed in the House the substitution of a federal union for the existing legislative union of the Canadas in order to relegate religious and racial issues to local legislatures and permit co-operation between Rouge and Clear Grit in those national interests which they had in common. If it is true that federalism in British North America arose from the exigencies of Canadian politics, the first phase of this historic aphorism may be traced to the exigencies of co-operation between the Rouges and the Clear Grits in the turbulent politics of the Canadian union, and A. A. Dorion may be credited with launching it for the first time into practical politics. Skelton's tribute to Dorion's fearless and brilliant intellect—"singularly moderate and just-minded, of unstained integrity and sincerity . . . one of the most attractive figures of Canadian politics"—would have been corroborated in Dorion's own day by a small band of followers whose ability and eloquence, adds Skelton, were unsurpassed "by any other equal number in the House." It may be added that anti-clericalism required more courage in Quebec than in Toronto. On April 25, 1856, Dorion with the support of both Galt and Holton proposed in the House "a general legislature with control of commercial interests, railway interests, public works and navigation, while at the same time education and matters of local character might be left to local legislatures." If this dual federation was not feasible Dorion conceded that representation by population with all its unpredictable consequences was inevitable, and "I . . . cannot complain. It would not be fair or just for Upper Canada to have only equal representation when it had half to three-quarters of a million more population."

By 1857, however, Galt's moorings had shifted, not for the first time or for the last, to a safer anchorage for the business interests he represented than the uncharted rock-bound coasts of Clear Grit ascendancy. At Galt's first election to the House in 1849 his sponsors in the British American Land Company had feared his surrender to the fierce partisanship of Canadian politics. It would be hard to find a more appropriate motto for Galt's mercurial career than his reassuring statement to the Governor of that company (April, 1849): "I am not the least likely to become a political partisan; my views are all for objects of material advantage." Galt fairly "boxed the compass" in the course of the next forty years—he advocated in turn annexation to the United States, a dual federation of the two Canadas, a general federation of the British provinces, political independence, and preferential trade for the British Empire—but his "objects of material advantage" were such that he had little difficulty in identifying them with the material advantage of Canada.[1] By 1857 the fiscal credit of the province, the solvency of the Grand Trunk, the future of the land companies and the banks, the industrial development of the province, were all jeopardized by the impending crisis to the union.

But here as elsewhere in the course of confederation the immediate stimulus for action came from the fierce play of personalities in the

[1]"I consider the interests of the company and of the country to be identical."

charged atmosphere of Canadian politics. While Galt and Holton and Gzowski made terms, not without "material advantage," with the Grand Trunk, George Brown's uncompromising suspicions of "corruption and jobbery" were sharpened by every subvention between the government and the company. Goodwill contributions "to the election Expenses," as we have seen, no doubt warranted many of these devious suspicions. In May, 1857, Brown as chairman of a special committee of the House on the "condition, management and prospects of the Grand Trunk Railway Company" turned the full torrent of his "muckraking zeal" (the phrase of Galt's biographer) upon the profits made by Galt's firm from contracts for the Sarnia division of the Grand Trunk, upon the terms made by the Grand Trunk with Galt's old company, the St. Lawrence and Atlantic Railway, and upon various other aspects of Grand Trunk administration which had long been the target of the *Globe's* invective. Galt's defence satisfied the House at the time and Galt's biographer sixty years later, but in 1857 it was now obvious that "objects of material advantage" cherished by Galt were not likely to thrive in a Clear Grit ascendancy dominated by George Brown and the Toronto *Globe.* Galt lost no time in repudiating both, and on December 11, 1857, Brown retorted "we are very happy to find from the government organs that Mr. Galt has repudiated the Opposition, since it will save the Opposition the trouble of repudiating him."

It was in the midst of this bitter passage at arms that Galt found himself fairly transfixed by one of John A. Macdonald's shafts of political necromancy—one of many from the great bow of that "much-contriving Ulysses" of Canadian politics. Macdonald's letter to Galt is dated November 2, 1857:

MY DEAR GALT,

. . . You call yourself a Rouge. There may have been at one time a reddish tinge about you, but I could observe it becoming by degrees fainter. In fact you are like Byron's Dying Dolphin, exhibiting a series of colours—"the last still loveliest"—and that last is "true blue," being the colour I affect.

Seriously, you would make a decent Conservative, if you gave your own judgment a fair chance and cut loose from Holton and Dorion and those other beggars. So pray do become true blue at once: it is a good standing colour and bears washing.

Yours always,
JOHN A. MACDONALD

II

Galt's famous resolutions of July, 1858, which have been more admired perhaps than read in the traditions of the Canadian federation, were moved from the cross-benches of the House. He had not yet become "true blue," and it is obvious from the resolutions themselves that there was still a "reddish tinge" about them from the project which Dorion had concerted with him and with Holton in 1856. The preamble, too, makes it clear that Galt's first obsession, like Head's and Dorion's, was the chronic peril to the Canadian union which was fast becoming the *causa causans* of Canadian federalism: "in view of the rapid development of the population and resources of Western Canada, irreconcilable difficulties present themselves to the maintenance of that equality which formed the basis of the Union of Upper and Lower Canada." A few months later Head in explaining the project of 1858 to Lytton added the convincing commentary that Galt was "deeply impressed with the idea that in some such union alone could be found the ultimate solution of the great question which has been made a ground of agitation by Mr. Brown and his friends at the general election [of 1857], viz.—the existing equality of representation of Upper and Lower Canada."

Galt's immediate proposal in the resolutions of July, 1858, like Dorion's in 1856, was a dual federation of the two Canadas: "that the Union of Upper and Lower Canada should be changed from a Legislative to a Federative Union by the subdivision of the province into two or more divisions, each governing itself in local and sectional matters, with a general legislative government for subjects of national and common interests." To that end a commission of nine members was to be named to "report on the best means and mode of effecting such constitutional changes."

The second resolution related to "the claims possessed by this province on the Northwestern and Hudson's Bay territories and the necessity of making provision for the government of the said districts."[1] "In the adoption of a federative constitution for Canada [still a dual federation of the Canadas] means should be provided for the local government of the said territories under the general government until population and settlement may from time to time enable them to be admitted into the Canadian Confederation."

It was the third of Galt's resolutions which for the first time in "Canada" broke new ground for a general federation and entitled Galt

[1]The Select Committee of the British House of Commons, as we have seen, had just recommended in 1857 that "the districts on the Red River and the Saskatchewan" should be "ceded to Canada on equitable principles, and within the districts thus annexed to her the authority of the Hudson's Bay Company would of course entirely cease." The licence for the area outside the chartered territory of Rupert's Land was due to expire in 1859.

to a distinction which he never forfeited until confederation was won: "That a general Confederation of the provinces of New Brunswick, Nova Scotia, Newfoundland and Prince Edward Island with Canada and the Western territories is most desirable and calculated to promote their several and united interests . . . while it will increase that identity of feeling which pervades the possessions of the British Crown in North America; and by the adoption of a uniform policy for the development of the vast and varied resources of these immense territories will greatly add to their national power and consideration." A committee of nine—presumably the same already "named to report on the best means and mode of effecting" the dual federation of the Canadas—was to "report on the steps to be taken for ascertaining without delay the sentiments of the inhabitants of the Lower Provinces and of the Imperial Government on this most important subject." In a speech of great power and imagination Galt cited the prospect of trade without restriction over the vast regions of British North America; of adding to their "national strength and national prestige"; of acquiring a "great empire . . . ten times as large as the settled heart of Canada." "Such a thing had never yet occurred to any people as to have the offer of half a continent." Intent still upon "objects of material advantage" he deplored the menace of sectional hostility and discord. "Half a continent is ours if we do not keep on quarrelling about petty matters and lose sight of what interests us most."

At what stage Galt joined forces with Head and resolutely moved from the Rouge plan of a dual federation for the Canadas to a full-fledged multiple federation of all the British provinces it would not be easy to determine. Galt's notice of motion had been given on March 2 but his resolutions found no place on the order paper of the House until July 5. Meanwhile Alexander Morris's well-known lecture on *Nova Britannia*—a prophetic forecast of "a great Britannic Confederation"—had been given in Montreal on March 18, and a large edition was sold out within ten days of publication. Galt's resolutions in the House (July 5 and 7) commanded little support. No member of the Government spoke to them. Dorion continued to support the sections for a dual federation of the Canadas, but a general federation, he thought, could wait for a century. The only unqualified support came from Playfair of the old British American League of 1849 whose nebulous enthusiasm for federation had subsided with the crisis on the annexation manifesto which had called it into being. Galt's resolutions never went to the vote. In Skelton's opinion had they gone they "would undoubtedly have been overwhelmingly defeated." They were left upon the table when the Government resigned on the "seat of government question" after an adverse vote upon the Queen's choice of Ottawa. It is a remarkable fact that this was to be the only proposal for a general federation ever submitted to the Canadian legislature until George Brown's select committee on the eve of "the great coalition" in 1864 reported "in favor of changes in the direction of a Federative system, applied either to *Canada* alone, or to the whole British North American provinces." Confederation, as we shall see, was to be the achievement not of parliamentary resolutions but of concerted action in the inner circles of administration; and the first endorsation by the Canadian legislature followed the famous "Confederation Debates" of February and March, 1865, on the Quebec Resolutions.

Head's forthright approach to the plan of 1858 is more easily traceable. The first session of the new Parliament was full of action. On July 29, 1858, the Macdonald-Cartier ministry, though successful in withstanding a resolution of no confidence, chose to resign when the House registered its disapproval of the Queen's choice of Ottawa as the capital of the united province. Head, upon whose advice the choice of Ottawa had been made—one reason for his visit to London in 1857 was to discuss "the proposed reference to the Queen of the seat of Government question"[1]—then called upon Brown as "the most prominent member of the opposition" to form a government; and Brown, with a rashness and also with a measure of success which astonished his contemporaries, accepted on July 31.[2] Brown's implied acceptance of responsibility for "the affront to the Queen" must have delighted his wily adversaries, but it is probable that his acceptance of office, with far less than a majority of the House pledged to his support, was the last eventuality Head expected; while a formal declination would have eliminated one complication at least in Head's plans for a general federation.

It is hard to believe that these plans were not already far advanced. Head lost no time, both orally on July 31 and by formal memorandum bearing the same date, in withholding any "pledge or promise, express or implied, with reference to dissolving parliament." Two days later, on Monday, August 2, the Brown–Dorion–Sandfield Macdonald Government was sworn in and immediately resigned their seats in the House in order to contest their bye-elections. That evening during

---

[1] Head to Labouchere, secret and confidential, March 23, 1857.
[2] The cabinet included A. A. Dorion, John Sandfield Macdonald, Oliver Mowat, L. T. Drummond, and L. H. Holton.

their absence from the House and without notice, a motion of no confidence was put and carried by an overwhelming majority of 40 in the Assembly and of 16 to 8 in the Council. There is little doubt that Brown's chances of carrying on the government were hopeless from the outset and that his plan was a dual federation of the Canadas to be announced to the House as a "fixed determination" and an immediate dissolution on that issue or simple "rep. by pop." with safe-guards for the religion, language, and laws of Canada East. Two days later, Head formally declined to dissolve the House for a second election within a year[1] and the Brown-Dorion Government immediately resigned, opening flood-gates of vituperation which deluged Canadian politics for many years.

III

With an initiative almost as rash as Brown's and with purpose easy to surmise Head now called upon Galt to form a government. Galt who had never held office in his life and was still on the cross-benches of the House[2] wisely declined but, as Head put it, "placed himself under the guidance of Mr. Cartier," and accepted office as inspector-general under Cartier as prime minister. By means of the notorious "double-shuffle" the old members of the Macdonald-Cartier ministry evaded the necessity for awkward bye-elections, and the Cartier-Macdonald Government resumed office with Galt's stipulation of a "federal union of the British North American provinces" as an avowed policy. In view of Cartier's growing intimacy with both Head and Galt it is not hard to account for his sudden conversion to a general federation under Conservative auspices as an escape from the dual federation of the Canadas advocated by Rouges and Clear Grits under Dorion and Brown. The House was prorogued a few days later on August 16. The dual federation of the Rouges was now in full retreat before a multiple federation of all the provinces under the auspices of a Conservative administration.

Meanwhile Head had drafted for the legislature a series of seven resolutions on federal union far stronger than Galt's and with dual federation of the Canadas left completely out of the picture:

(1) That the Queen's dominions in Brit. N.A. united as they are by their allegiance to the British Crown would derive great & signal advantages from a closer union among themselves.

---

[1]Particularly in view of the fact that the Macdonald-Cartier Government had successfully defeated a vote of no confidence before resigning in protest against "the affront to the Queen" on the "seat of government question."
[2]His "position was neutral." Head to Lytton, October 22, 1858.

(2) That such union might be secured by the establishment of a Central Govt. for B.N.A., leaving in the hands of a local Govt. in each Province such powers as may be necessary for managing its own affairs & transferring to the Central Govt. such powers as would provide for control and regulation of their common interests.

Since (section 3) it would be "premature to discuss the limits or precise character" of such a system "until the principles of its expediency shall have been recognized by H.M. Govt, & by the several Provincial legislatures," an address (section 4) was to be presented to himself ("H.E. the G.G.") "praying him to transmit without delay a copy of these resolutions" for their approval. In the event of the Hudson's Bay Company relinquishing any part of their territory "it would be expedient" (section 5) for the Red River area to "form a part of H.M. Dominion in B.N.A. to be united on the principles herein before recited."[1] In the event of acquiescence by the Colonial Office and the several provinces (section 6) "in the principle of an Union," two delegates from each province were to "meet in Toronto in the month of October next in order to digest & prepare the outline of a scheme for consideration of the several Legislatures on their reassembling in the ensuing year." For this purpose Messrs (blank) and (blank) were to be "delegated on behalf of U.C." and Messrs (blank) and (blank) on behalf of Lower Canada as the "representatives of this Legislature." With this draft in the Head Papers are voluminous memoranda on the division of federal and provincial powers, the revenues and expenditures chargeable to each, the judiciary, and other technical details of a federal system. Though Head's resolutions are undated it now seems probable that they were drafted before Galt's, since Galt's resolutions of July 5 (as Head afterwards explained to Lytton) were still "before them" on the table and "not yet disposed of" when the House was prorogued on August 16, and Head's resolutions could scarcely have been drafted for the purpose of supplanting them. In any event there would hardly have been time at that late date to secure acquiescence "by H.M. Govt. & by the several Provincial legislatures" in time for two delegates from each province to "meet at Toronto in the month of October next." It was October, in fact, before Cartier, Galt, and Ross were able to leave for London to seek the preliminary acquiescence of the Colonial Office.

Fortunately for Head's relations with Lytton this *prima facie* evidence of his initiative behind the scenes was to remain unknown for

---

[1]This would seem to be the first use of "Dominion" in this sense. Red River was of course already part of Her Majesty's "dominions."

seventy years.[1] Head's draft resolutions were never presented to the House where they would almost certainly have been lost, and the announcement of government policy was confined to a sentence or two by Cartier on resuming office on August 7 and two sentences in Head's Speech from the Throne when proroguing the House on August 16:

I propose in the course of the recess to communicate with Her Majesty's Government and with the Governments of the sister Colonies, on another matter of very great importance. I am desirous of inviting them to discuss with us the principles on which a bond of a federal character, uniting the Provinces of British North America may perhaps hereafter be practicable.

On September 9 a Minute of Council, which Head afterwards admitted was "suggested by myself," urged upon the Colonial Secretary "the propriety of authorizing a meeting of delegates on behalf of each colony, and of Upper and Lower Canada respectively, for the purpose of considering the subject of such federative union." The conference was to "meet with as little delay as possible" (section 4), and the report was to be placed "before the Provincial Parliaments with as little delay as possible" (section 5). It is noteworthy that the procedure here follows Head's draft resolutions for an early meeting of "delegates from each province" rather than Galt's for a committee of nine to "report on the steps to be taken"; both stipulate action "without delay." On the same day as the Minute of Council, despatches, obviously ready for the occasion, were sent off by Head to the Colonial Secretary and to the lieutenant-governors of Nova Scotia, New Brunswick, Prince Edward Island, and Newfoundland, with copies of the Canadian Minute of Council for their approval. Though the despatch to Lytton, as we shall see, brought down upon Head a petulant censure which Lytton was careful to transmit also to the provinces, Cartier (now prime minister), Galt, and Ross left for London in October. British American federation was now fairly launched into practical politics. There were cynics who detected a device to postpone the awkward "seat of government question" pending the discussion of a new federation involving the possibility of a new "seat of government." But whatever may be said for the Government as a whole, the purpose of Head and of Galt can admit of no discount. They had gauged some of the basic causal factors of confederation and whatever the immediate result this first "drive for federation" in 1858 was not to return unto them void.

[1]See Chester Martin, "Sir Edmund Head and Confederation, 1851–1858," Canadian Historical Association, *Report*, 1929.

IV

Lytton's first reaction to Head's Speech from the Throne was a note of querulous surprise. Federation was an imperial issue involving other colonies in North America "equally bound with Canada by the common tie which unites all the Members of that Empire." It therefore "properly belongs to the executive authority of the Empire, and not that of any separate province to initiate." But there was more to follow. When Head's Minute of Council of September 9 ("suggested by myself") and his subsequent despatches launching the Galt-Cartier-Ross mission to London disclosed the concerted speed and seriousness and scope of the design, Lytton's scathing resentment knew no bounds. It was "absolutely necessary [so reads his minute on the despatch of October 22] to administer a reproof to Sir E. Head. . . . It has caused the gravest displeasure and I have been urged to recall him. . . . I think Sir E. Head has perpetrated a great indiscretion."[1] Fortunately for Head his name and fame were better known to British America and to the Colonial Office itself than to the new Colonial Secretary. Merivale and Carnarvon and Blackwood, the under-secretaries, came loyally to his support: Head had been authorized by both Labouchere and Stanley (son of the prime minister) in their private correspondence to explore the cause of British North American union. Fortunately, too, as we shall see, Lytton's brief but stormy career at the Colonial Office left Newcastle's confidence in Head still unimpaired. Most fortunately of all perhaps for Head himself, he was never called upon to explain his draft resolutions for the Canadian legislature which had probably been intended to set this whole train in motion by calling upon "H.E. the G.G." to prepare "without delay" for a meeting of delegates "in Toronto in the month of October next in order to digest & prepare the outline of a scheme" of British North American federation.

Galt, Cartier, and Ross in London also quickly vindicated the importance and urgency of their mission. Their joint letter to Lytton cited historic causes for confederation in terms that were to supply the preamble six years later to George Brown's resolutions for the epochal select committee, which proved in turn to be the prelude to "the great coalition." The rapid development of Canada West had already led to "claims . . . on behalf of its inhabitants for giving them representation in the Legislature in proportion to their numbers"; the result was "an agitation fraught with great danger to the peaceful and

---

[1]See Whitelaw, *The Maritimes and Canada before Confederation*, p. 131.

harmonious working of our Constitutional system"; and the "necessity of providing a remedy for a state of things that is yearly becoming worse, and of allaying feelings that are daily being aggravated by the contention of political parties" had impressed "the advisers of Her Majesty's Representative in *Canada* with the importance of seeking for such a mode of dealing with these difficulties as may forever remove them."

But whatever Lytton's initial impatience with the novel contingencies of his office, he must be absolved from charges of indifference and obstruction as the details of the plan began to emerge under Galt's ingratiating exposition. In compliance with Lytton's own request the functions of the proposed federation were outlined in a confidential letter signed by all three delegates but now known to have been entirely of Galt's own composition. In half a dozen brief paragraphs which proved in some respects a prophetic forecast of confederation Galt undertook to outline the forms and functions of the proposed federal government, the division of powers, and above all the method by which it was to be set up. In this as in Head's forecast of 1851 and the more voluminous memoranda in the Head Papers intended no doubt for the projected conference "in Toronto in the month of October next," there were many details which the intervening years and particularly the stresses and strains of the Civil War were to modify.[1] For both, however, there was one basic principle of far-reaching significance, no doubt the result of their common counsels behind the scenes:[2]

It will be observed [wrote Galt] that the basis of Confederation now proposed differs from that of the United States in several important particulars. It does not profess to be derived from the people but would be the constitution provided by the imperial parliament, thus affording the means of remedying any defect, which is now practically impossible under the

[1]Galt's plan of 1858 called for the control of public lands by the federal government with the distribution of the net revenue to the several provinces; the federal administration of "unincorporated and Indian territories"; "the constitution of a Federal Court of Appeal" (cf. Head's insistence in 1851 upon "an effective Court of Appeal" to supplant the Judicial Committee of the Privy Council); a "Senate elected upon a territorial basis" and a "House of Assembly, elected on the basis of population, the Executive to be composed of ministers responsible to the legislature." The distribution of residuary powers was left to "form a subject for mature deliberation." Perhaps the most striking variation from the *B.N.A. Act of 1867* was the suggestion for the "general revenue," that "having first been charged with the expense of collection and civil government" and the interest on the funded public debt, the surplus should "be divided each year according to population."

[2]Cf. Head's Memorandum of 1851, above, p. 225.

American constitution. The local legislature would not be in a position to claim the exercise of the same sovereign powers which have frequently been the cause of difference between the American states and their general government. . . . It is conceived that the proposed Confederation would possess greater inherent strength than that of the United States.

There can be no doubt that Lytton responded to these overtures with genuine interest. Within a week Galt reported days of congenial hospitality and "much conversation" with Lytton at Knebworth: "Mr. Ross and Mr. Cartier have gone to Paris for a few days and I remain here to attend to our matters with the Government." A renewed invitation came from the same quarter for the following week. After the return of Cartier and Ross from Paris there was a round of official courtesies in London and at Windsor (a private interview with Queen Victoria and the Prince of Wales), a "grand dinner" at the Canadian Club, and interviews with Lord Derby and Disraeli. It became obvious, however, that no *tour de force* such as "the great coalition" afterwards wrought at Charlottetown and Quebec within the span of six weeks was yet possible in the Victorian England of 1858. "Everybody is very courteous," wrote Galt, "but very slow." Galt was invited in confidence to draft the official reply to Sir Edmund Head (November 26, 1858): "It appears to Her Majesty's Government," reads Galt's draft of November 22, "that it would be premature to invite the proposed meeting of Delegates without communications from the Governments of the other Colonies." Lytton added that with one exception he had received "no expression whatever" of their views. Manners-Sutton of New Brunswick alone had forwarded a Minute of Council (including both Tilley and Fisher) indicating "that it deems the question of a Legislative union of some or all of the Colonies as equally deserving of consideration."[1]

In Canada the *Globe* detected in Galt's report of their mission a scheme "half-smoke, half-air," from which the *Leader* as the organ of the Conservative party expected no tangible results for ten years. In the House Cartier succeeded in carrying the Queen's choice of Ottawa as the capital of the province; in that respect at least the cause of federation was no longer practical politics. The issue of federalism in Canada was kept alive, as we shall see, by the concerted action of Clear Grits and Rouges for a dual federation of the Canadas as their method of escape from what Galt had called the "irreconcilable difficulties" of the Canadian union.

[1]Newfoundland subsequently agreed to send delegates to a conference.

V

Perhaps the most tangible results of the "drive for federation" in 1858 were to be found at the Colonial Office and in the long train of correspondence with provincial governors on every aspect of British North American union. Between Head's Speech from the Throne and Lytton's formal despatch of November 26 there were passages behind the scenes in London which neither Galt nor Galt's biographer could have surmised, and which belie the tradition that Lytton knew little and cared less about the "problems of the American colonies."[1]

The truth seems to have been that Lytton knew too much. The British cabinet was already struggling with a variety of problems on the British North American provinces. In addition to the project of federation, Cartier, Galt, and Ross were charged with negotiations on an intercolonial railway and the Hudson's Bay territories. It required no wizard to surmise a Grand Trunk interest in all three aspects of their mission when the Canadian president, the solicitor, and one of the most enterprising early magnates of the railway appeared together in London. Before the Select Committee of 1857 on the Hudson's Bay territories John Ross, fresh from an accord with Sir George Simpson, had been the first witness. His evidence as Speaker of the Legislative Council and "head of the trunk railway of Canada" ran to twelve folio pages and no fewer than 157 questions and answers.[2]

By October, 1858, Lytton was already implementing this *Report* for a regional union west of the Rocky Mountains—the resumption of Vancouver Island by the crown and "the ultimate extension of the colony" to the mainland under the name (chosen by Queen Victoria) of British Columbia. The central regions, which were to be "ceded to Canada on equitable principles," presented a more complicated problem, probably the most urgent single problem in British North America at this time. A confidential memorandum of Head's to Lytton (September 9, 1858) reaffirming his previous recommendation to Labouchere for a regional union with Canada added significantly that a federal union "at the present moment . . . will thus admit of extending west-

---

[1]"The plain fact was that neither the permanent officials nor the government nor the general public had any interest. . . . There is not the faintest sign of concern. . . . In the circles of the governing classes Canada was as much in mind as Kamschatka." Skelton, *Galt*, p. 249.

[2]Sir George's evidence ran to 63 pages and over 1400 questions and answers. The monumental *Report* with its 547 folio pages of evidence, index, maps, and appendices, preceded by the terse two-page recommendations of the Select Committee, was to prove a milestone in British policy in America.

ward the body of our North American colonies." More than a month
before the Canadian mission reached London Lytton had opened
negotiations with the Hudson's Bay Company. By November, 1858,
both Lytton and Carnarvon had come to despair of any "equitable
and conciliatory arrangement" in that quarter. It was to take twelve
years, until 1870 as it proved, to untie this particular Gordian knot and
Lytton was now proposing to cut it by a "writ of *Scire facias* brought
to repeal the Charter."[1] Preoccupied by the problem of British
Columbia and obsessed with the insoluble problem of Rupert's Land
in a setting which was fast becoming transcontinental, Lytton may
well have preferred the truculent expansionism of George Brown and
the *Globe* to any accommodation between John Ross and Sir George
Simpson in the interests of Grand Trunk and the Hudson's Bay Company.

When the British cabinet met to discuss the project of federation
they had before them not only the printed documents[2] but a confidential memorandum of Elliot, acting under-secretary in Merivale's
absence, and a "Most Confidential" recommendation from Lytton himself which may have been nearer the truth than either Head or Galt
could have surmised:

> At this moment Federation is really a question raised for the convenience
> of the present Canadian Administration, and upon which the formidable
> Opposition, headed by Mr. Brown, have not decidedly committed their
> policy. An Imperial interest of the utmost magnitude is, in short, in the
> crude state of a party question, embittered and obscured by fierce party
> passions.[3]

Elliot, with more restraint but with almost uncanny shrewdness in
the circumstances, doubted whether the Canadian ministers, "eminent

[1]Cf. Carnarvon to Berens, Nov. 3, 1858: "Unsatisfactory as this result would
be Sir E. Lytton will not feel at liberty to decline it. He desires that the Hudson's
Bay Company should distinctly understand that in his opinion the time for
arriving at some authoritative definition of conflicting claims can no longer be
postponed with safety or in justice to public interests; and that both Canada and
the British Parliament might justly complain of further and unnecessary delay."

The deadlock arose from the stolid but intelligible refusal of the Hudson's Bay
Company to refer to the Privy Council the validity of their Charter and the rights
under it which had been "exercised by the Company for a period of nearly 200
years" (Berens to Lytton, Nov. 10, 1858). Canada subsequently completed the
deadlock by declining the litigation by writ of *scire facias* in the well-founded
hope of acquiring the West by parliamentary action for nothing.

[2]*Question of Federation of the British Provinces in America, Confidential,*
Colonial Office, Nov., 1858.

[3]Public Record Office, G.D. 6, vol. 69; ed. R. G. Trotter, *Canadian Historical
Review*, 1933, 285 ff.

as is their position," could be regarded as "envoys entitled to speak the voice of the whole province. They announce the views of one great political party, but there is another party also, and we have no evidence that, if this proposal were submitted to the Legislature of the province, it would command a majority of votes. Those who desire the immediate revision of the representation in Canada might oppose this project as an evasion."

How near this too was to the truth became apparent at the Clear Grit convention a few months later in Toronto. Brown referred derisively to Galt's "speculative loyalty and businesslike patriotism," and a member of the short-lived Brown-Dorion Government (Dr. Connor) demonstrated the "fierce party passions" already playing upon the project of federation: "Nothing could be more audacious and insulting to the people of Canada than that on a great question like that Mr. Galt and his colleagues should proceed to England in order to patch up their fortunes in this country and hold on to office a few months longer."

The next "drive for federation" from Canada, as we shall see, was to prove more successful. No doubt a review of the tactics of 1858 played its part in the strategy of "the great coalition" as it moved resolutely upon Charlottetown and Quebec and London in 1864. Confederation was to be "carried per saltum," as Macdonald wrote to Tilley on the eve of the final conference in London. The procedure outlined by Head in 1858 for "Toronto in the month of October next in order to digest & prepare the outline of a scheme for consideration of the several Legislatures on their reassembling in the ensuing year" was precisely that which succeeded so fabulously at Quebec in October, 1864. Elliot in the Colonial Office, who was to have a hand in the second "drive for federation" as well as the first, was shrewd enough to see this "weighty" argument for Head's plan in 1858: an early meeting of delegates[1] "might prevent or postpone general excitement," since the "best men would be selected from each Government, and would go unfettered to the preliminary examination of the subject, whereas after eager debates in the Legislatures, the judgments of any delegates might possibly be less cool, and certainly their action more embarrassed by popular feelings." None saw this more clearly than the master-strategist of them all, John A. Macdonald, in 1864. Prodigious events, to be sure, were to intervene between 1858 and 1864—

---

[1]"For conferring with the other delegates & preparing the draft of a definite scheme or plan." Head's draft resolutions, Canadian Historical Association, *Report*, 1929, p. 14.

"events stronger than advocacy, events stronger than men"—events strong enough, as it proved, to still for a time even the "fierce party passions" in Canada and to daunt all British Americans, and many Britons too, with the imperative need for union. For "the great coalition" George Brown himself, not without real magnanimity, was to lead the way against "sectional hostility and discord."

Meanwhile at any rate federation had been launched irretraceably into imperial politics. Elliot, who shared Lytton's early fears for the consequences,[1] was not disposed to dispute the facts. There may have been grave doubts, he thought, "whether the question should be propounded at all. . . . But, then, it has been propounded by the Governor-General. . . . Whether or not a formal appointment of delegates be now provided for, enough has been done to open the topic to every newspaper editor and to every orator at public meetings, so that the danger, whether it be large or small, has been incurred already, and has passed beyond the control of the government."

The next "drive for federation" was more fortunate in the support it was to receive from the Colonial Office. In the last analysis it was the Colonial Office itself, as we shall see, that drove the Canadian confederation resolutely through to completion. The good offices there of Carnarvon—Colonial Secretary in 1866—were to prove a circumstance of the first importance, and it is safe to say that his experience as under-secretary in 1858 was not forgotten as he " 'sat at the cradle' of the new Dominion."[2]

[1]It is fair to add that Lytton afterwards thought Elliot's memorandum inadequate for "the arguments in favour of Federation, both as regards the safety of British North America and the interests of the mother-country."
[2]Macdonald Papers, Macdonald to Carnarvon, March 5, 1867.

Chapter Fifteen

REGIONAL UNIONS AGAIN

THE failure of the first "drive for federation" in 1858 had two unforeseen results which complicated the problem of British North American union until both were swept away by the rising tensions of the American Civil War.

At the Colonial Office Newcastle and his subordinates, inspired by Head, reverted to the plan of regional unions as the only feasible approach to a general federation. For five years the movement for a legislative union of the maritime provinces received the widest range of support and encouragement since Knox's ill-fated policy had broken the old province of Nova Scotia into fragments at the close of the American Revolution. Meanwhile the Rouges of Canada East and the Clear Grits of Canada West, confronted by the dire prospects of conflict on the rising issue of "rep. by pop.," turned to a dual federation of the Canadas as the only feasible method of allaying sectional strife without sacrificing the advantages of the St. Lawrence system. One group of provinces thus found themselves approaching a legislative union at the very moment that the two Canadas were finding their legislative union intolerable. It was this rip-tide between "Canada" and the Maritimes which complicated their approach to federation and many of their traditions with regard to it to this day.

Meanwhile the rest of British North America remained in jeopardy. For the regions west of the Rocky Mountains Lytton had lost no time in implementing the *Report* of the Select Committee for Vancouver Island and British Columbia. For the central regions from the Great Lakes to the Rocky Mountains the best that could be hoped was to reorganize the Hudson's Bay Company and await a more favourable opportunity for the transfer of Rupert's Land to Canada "on equitable principles." The purchase of a controlling interest in the old Company by the International Financial Society in 1862, as we have seen, was a gambit in Watkin's desperate game for the rescue of the Grand

Trunk.[1] Head with his New Brunswick and Canadian experience behind him was induced by Newcastle to take the governorship of the
Company in London. A prospectus was issued for "colonization under
a liberal and systematic scheme of land settlement," in accord with
"the industrial spirit of the age."

The Colonial Office, however, proved to be as chary as Canada in
conceding the "equitable principles" involved in the organization of
a crown colony in Rupert's Land. The new régime like the old ended
in frustration. Watkin's grandiose schemes in that quarter had very
quickly come to grief. The licensed area beyond Rupert's Land reverted
to the crown in 1859, but the problem of Rupert's Land itself was left
in abeyance. Three years after Confederation the "transfer" was to
confront the new Dominion with the first major crisis of its existence.

In British Columbia and the Maritimes alone the cause of regional
union made substantial progress. In "Canada" the exigencies of provincial politics forced both political parties back upon the federal
solution. In the end it was this federal solution—a general federation
of all the provinces under the unpredictable tensions of the American
Civil War—which finally fixed the pattern of British North American
union from sea to sea.

I

The collapse of the two-day Brown-Dorion Government of 1858
had left the Reformers saddled with the opprobrium of flouting the
Queen's choice of Ottawa as the provincial capital, and completely
out-manœuvred in parliamentary tactics. Macdonald, whose uncanny
flair for attaching friends to his own party and detaching the most
tractable of his opponents from theirs was by this time notorious,
never plied his art with greater versatility and success. Galt was now
"true blue" beyond retreat. When Sidney Smith too joined the Conservative cabinet in 1858 his colleagues in reform greeted his defection
with execration while one of the editorial stalwarts of the Conservative
press responded to Macdonald's appeal to support the new minister
with a famous telegram: "It's a damned sharp corner but I guess I can
make it." Overtures to John Sandfield Macdonald at this time offering
him three seats in the cabinet for Reformers who were "not Grits"
were less successful. The reply was another cryptic telegram: "No go."

Meanwhile party politics made havoc of traditional political principles. In the election of 1857 there is no doubt that John A. Macdonald, who had joined the Orange Order in 1843, owed much in

[1]See above, pp. 232 ff., 234 n. 1.

Canada West to the party loyalty of the Grand Master, Ogle Gowan, who was ready to condone even Taché's separate school legislation in order to neutralize the covenanting crusade of George Brown and the *Globe* against "the encroachments of popish politics." For the election of 1861 another Orange Conservative stalwart, J. Hillyard Cameron, more resourceful and still more successful than Ogle Gowan, avowed even "rep. by pop." in order to counter the Clear Grit monopoly of that unanswerable issue in Canada West. Secure in the confidence of Cartier and the Bleus of Canada East Macdonald once offered a portfolio to the Rouge chieftain A. A. Dorion himself who declined after some hesitation. Many of Macdonald's enemies were probably chosen with the same fastidiousness that he exhibited with his friends. The most valuable of these was, of course, George Brown whose bitter and uncompromising temper at this stage was a perfect foil for his rival's managerial technique. To both wings of the Reform party it became obvious that some accommodation between them was indispensable.

In October, 1859, the Rouges of Canada East held a caucus and reaffirmed Dorion's old proposal for a dual federation of the Canadas: "the true and statesman-like solution is to be sought in the substitution of a purely federative for the present legislative union." This manifesto bore the names of A. A. Dorion, Thomas D'Arcy McGee, L. T. Drummond, and L. A. Dessaulles. Meanwhile in Toronto a Clear Grit convention was being organized which was to prove a milestone in Canadian federalism. In November, 570 delegates assembled to deliberate upon the problems of Canada West. For a time it seemed that the sectional strife involved in establishing "rep. by pop." and in making it function was so forbidding a prospect that the convention might be induced to advocate a "simple dissolution" of the Canadian union. George Sheppard, then on the staff of the *Globe*, and a few others, were advocating the same course in the interests of a more devious policy—the detachment of Canada West from the union and its annexation to the United States. Whatever premonitions Brown may have had at this stage of Sheppard's ulterior views[1] there were two causes to which he himself never ceased to bear unwavering allegiance. One was the British connection and the other was the westward expansion of Canada. For both of these the continued association of the Canadas in the St. Lawrence system was imperative. The decisive resolution of the convention on the issue of "simple

[1]Sheppard's relations with the *Globe* were severed almost immediately after the convention of 1859. In 1867 he became an editor of the *New York Times.* His influence during the Civil War must have been far-reaching.

dissolution" was finally moved by William McDougall but it was George Brown's eloquence which carried it in the convention and committed the Clear Grit party to the cause of federalism for the Canadian provinces:

Even Mr. Sheppard admits that if the question is to be placed on the ground of nationality he must go for federation—but a Federation of all the British North American Colonies. Now, Sir, I do place the question on the ground of nationality. I do hope there is not one Canadian in this assembly who does not look forward with high hope to the day when these northern countries shall stand out among the nations of the world as one great Confederation. (Cheers.) What true Canadian can witness the tide of immigration now commencing to flow into the vast territories of the North-West without longing to have a share in the first settlement of that great and fertile country . . . and making our country the highway of traffic to the Pacific? (Cheers) . . . Is it not clear that the former ["simple dissolution"] would be a death-blow to the hope of future union while the latter [a dual federation of the Canadas] might at some future day readily furnish the machinery of a great Confederation? (Cheers.)[1]

During the ensuing session of the House and on the hustings of 1861 this constructive programme was not always in evidence in the counsels of the Clear Grit party. Had the short-lived Brown-Dorion Government of 1858 survived they might have developed a cohesiveness and sense of responsibility to match the weight of their undoubted abilities. It is doubtful if an abler group of Reformers ever held office under the Canadian union than George Brown, A. A. Dorion, John Sandfield Macdonald, Oliver Mowat, Luther Holton, William Mc-Dougall, and L. T. Drummond. But the fiasco of the two-day government was only less devastating to their prestige than the uncanny skill of John A. Macdonald in exploiting their differences and appropriating the malcontents for his own party. In its denunciation of "unprincipled corruptionists" the *Globe* ranged from the "double-shuffle" of the ministry to the "perfidious conduct" of Sir Edmund Head himself. Galt was a "jobber at heart." The governor was an "unscrupu-

---

[1]The fifth resolution as finally carried stated that "the best practicable remedy for the evils now encountered in the Government of Canada is to be found in the formation of two or more local governments, to which shall be committed the control of all matters of a local or sectional character, and some joint authority charged with such matters as are necessarily common to both sections of the province." The sixth resolution "deems it imperative to declare that no Government would be satisfactory to the people of Upper Canada which is not based on the principle of representation by population."

It was Brown's contention throughout that "rep. by pop." would be established automatically by the process of federation.

lous partisan." Dissensions within the party were not healed by the resolutions of the convention of 1859.

Brown followed them up nevertheless by an address from the Constitutional Reform Association to be forwarded to the Colonial Secretary through the governor-general. Head complied with caustic alacrity, accompanying the address by extracts from the Journals of the House which had debated in the meantime the contentious resolutions of the Clear Grit convention. The debate had remained on the order-paper of the House from April 16 to May 8, 1860. The resolution "that the Union, in its present form, can no longer be continued with advantage to the people" was overwhelmingly defeated by a vote of 66 to 27. The second resolution was offered to the House in the wording of the fifth resolution of the Clear Grit convention: that "the best practical remedy for the evils now encountered in the Government of Canada is to be found in the formation of two or more local Governments, to which shall be committed the control of all matters of a local or sectional character, and some joint authority charged with such matters as are necessarily common to both sections of the Province." This too was lost by a vote of 74 to 32. Only two French-Canadian members voted for the first and only four—A. A. Dorion among them—for the second. Head forwarded the extracts from the Journals of the House to Newcastle with the complacent comment: "After this action of the Legislative Assembly on the Resolutions, I do not know that it is necessary for me to trouble Your Grace with any remarks on the paper forwarded by Mr. Brown."

II

The truth was that the divergencies within the Reform party were now so alarming that the most irresponsible "ultras" were compelled to count the cost of sectionalism. When Thomas D'Arcy McGee, the champion of the "Irish Catholics of Canada," and George Brown, the covenanting zealot of the *Globe*, could unite against J. Hillyard Cameron, the "Orange henchman" of John A. Macdonald in Canada West, and Cartier with his disciplined cohorts of clerical Bleus in Canada East, it was obvious that party lines were no longer following conventional antipathies. There was nothing like office or the prospect of office to soften these unruly asperities. After the first taste of office in 1862 William McDougall was known to avow a measure of compromise and accommodation: "In opposition every man is at liberty to urge his own views as to the best remedy for the political ills of the country; but when he comes to take part in administration, he must adopt the remedy which is found to be practicable—that which he can induce his colleagues to adopt—even though not the best in theory or not in exact accord with his previously expressed views." Organic changes like "rep. by pop." or dual federation or both—Brown maintained that it would be easier to win both together than either one without the other—may have been in theory "the best practical remedy" for the ills of the Canadian union; but few members of the House could see any prospect of forcing either without a commanding majority in the House, and fewer still believed that a commanding majority in the House, if it could be won by any other means, should be sacrificed to the cause of remote and hypothetical organic changes.

For Brown himself the brief glimpse of office in 1858 and the exigencies of the party in 1859 and 1860 must have brought much salutary reflection. In his correspondence and in the *Globe* alike during these years there is a new sense of direction, a maturing political sagacity, a novel capacity for compromise and accommodation, in marked contrast to the sheer censoriousness of irresponsible opposition. He deplored to Mowat the Government's success in reviving and exploiting on the hustings "the personal hostility against myself . . . inspired by the fierce party contests of the past." More than once he announced his "determination to retire from parliamentary life at the earliest possible moment." A dangerous illness, the result in some measure of overwhelming financial reverses, barred him for many months from the House and from his office at the *Globe*. His defeat in Toronto East and the loss of several other constituencies in Canada West in the elections of 1861 may have been due to this fact, though the exploits of Hillyard Cameron and his Orangemen after the "Newcastle incident"[1] must have contributed materially to the result.

During Brown's absence from the House after his defeat in 1861 and his absence altogether from Canada in 1862, the cause of organic reform was left in abeyance. A new master of Reform strategy in the person of John Sandfield Macdonald challenged—successfully for nearly two years—the resourcefulness of "John A." himself in the artifices of Canadian politics. When Brown returned to the House in 1863 "events stronger than advocacy, events stronger than men" were already beginning to dominate the scene. Brown's famous committee

[1]The Duke of Newcastle who accompanied the Prince of Wales, afterwards Edward VII, during his tour of Canada in 1860 had countermanded Orange processions in full regalia at Kingston, Macdonald's own constituency, and at several other points in Canada West. Hillyard Cameron afterwards carried 100,000 signatures of Canadian Orangemen to London and was received by the Queen at Windsor Castle.

of twenty on constitutional reform marked a revival of federalism which carried the issue, as we shall see, far beyond the exigencies of Clear Grit politics. The coercive factors abroad in America after Gettysburg in 1863 belonged to a new order, and Canadian statesmanship, Brown's included, met the challenge with a new magnanimity.

For many months the new master of reform was a match for his clansman John A. Macdonald in harmonizing the heterogeneous elements of his party and demonstrating his conviction that the union could be made to work without organic change. Roman Catholic in religion, cautious in temper, and endowed with a fund of pawky humour and patience beyond the normal lot of mortal man, John Sandfield Macdonald succeeded in carrying on the government after the fall of the Cartier-Macdonald administration in May, 1862, and in reasserting in the election of 1863 the Reform ascendancy which had seemed so imminent in 1857. The adroitness of his adversary left him as usual encumbered with unpopular and insoluble issues. John A. Macdonald in 1858 had bequeathed to the Brown-Dorion Government the stigma of flouting the Queen's choice of Ottawa as the provincial capital. Tottering again to its fall in May, 1862, the Macdonald-Cartier Government decided to resign on the *Militia Bill* thus branding the Reform party for the second time with imputations of disloyalty. Charges of sectionalism and even of "bad faith" were added at the "railway fiasco" of 1863 when Sicotte and Howland in London evaded on a transparent technicality the terms agreed upon at the Quebec conference of 1862 for the building of the Intercolonial.[1]

Again John A. Macdonald cast his encircling net and Thomas D'Arcy McGee, now a Grand Trunk stalwart in Watkin's train who had presided at the interprovincial railway conference at Quebec in 1862, found himself in the Liberal-Conservative party. Foley and Sicotte followed suit in 1863. But despite defections and frustration John Sandfield Macdonald continued to hobble forward on the twin crutches of "double majority," restricting government measures to those which could command a majority in both sections of the province. Even this failed him when it became necessary to carry separate school legislation for Canada West by an overwhelming majority from Canada East. For once Sandfield Macdonald's fund of patience if not of pawky humour was exhausted. "You may shipwreck the Government," he said to the Clear Grit mutineers. "I can swim—you may go to the devil for me." "Double majority" was federalism at its worst in a legislative union—the last stage before deadlock. Brown would have nothing to do

[1]See above, p. 232, and below, p. 288.

with it and reported from Edinburgh "a most satisfactory interview
with the Duke of Newcastle at his request. His scruples about representation by population are entirely gone. It would have done even
Sandfield good to hear his ideas on the absurdity of the double
majority."

For nearly two years nevertheless the resourcefulness of John Sandfield Macdonald rivalled that of his Conservative namesake in the
quicksands of Canadian politics. Even the *Globe* once conceded
grudgingly that "John S. has been a winner" against "John A." in the
devious manipulations that were becoming more and more difficult in
Canada East. As yet neither John S. nor John A. could afford to avow
"rep. by pop." in Canada East but the Reform ascendancy slowly rising
in Canada West survived Confederation and continued uninterruptedly in Ontario under Sandfield Macdonald himself, Blake, and
Mowat until the turn of the century. When the kaleidoscopic ingredients of Canadian politics during the half-decade before "the great
coalition" of 1864 come to be examined in convincing detail it is
possible that John Sandfield Macdonald the "mugwump reformer" may
be rated worthy of his clansman's steel. From Brown however the
crisis of 1864 brought a response of a higher order, with results that
were epochal for the cause of British American union.

III

This confused pattern of incipient federalism in the Canadas contrasted strangely with trends elsewhere in British North America after
the failure of the first "drive for federation" in 1858. Both east and
west across the continent there was an immediate return to the earlier
projects of regional unions. On the Pacific the organization of a new
province on the mainland was already under way, as we have seen,
when Cartier, Galt, and Ross reached London in 1858. On the Atlantic
a movement towards maritime union was also under discussion in at
least one of the provinces in 1858, and it developed so rapidly and so
far that it supplied at Charlottetown in 1864 the occasion if not the
inspiration for the larger union. "If it had not been for this fortunate
coincidence of events," said Macdonald in the Confederation Debates
of 1865, "never perhaps for a long series of years would we have been
able to bring this scheme to a practical conclusion."

Two months before the Cartier-Galt-Ross mission left Canada in
1858, Lytton had provided by statute (21 and 22 Vic., c. 99) for the
mainland province of British Columbia. With a detachment of Royal
Engineers under Colonel Moody and the beginnings of law and order

under Judge Begbie, Governor Douglas of Vancouver Island proclaimed the new colony on November 19, 1858. The name of the new
province, British Columbia, with its capital New Westminster, had
been selected by the Queen. Lytton's intervention had come barely in
time. As early as 1850 the prodigious expansion of the American
frontier had reached the vacant territories of the Hudson's Bay Company at half a dozen vulnerable points. Texas and the Alamo, the
Mexican War and the Treaty of Guadalupe-Hidalgo and the Gadsden
Purchase were soon to become familiar portents for the British
provinces.[1] The ominous slogan of Polk's election—"fifty-four forty or
fight," which would have carried the boundary northward to what is
now the "pan-handle" of Alaska—and the annexation of Oregon north
of the Columbia by the "Oregon Treaty" of 1846, still hung heavily
over the prospects of the Hudson's Bay Company as the twenty-one
year licence of 1838 for the territory beyond the chartered area of
Rupert's Land drew to a close in 1858. Although Vancouver Island had
been granted to the Company in fee simple to supply the vested
interest of settlement so fatally wanting in the contest for Oregon, the
failure of the Company to implement this policy now jeopardized the
whole area west of the Rockies at a time when gold on the Fraser and
the Cariboo threatened to set into motion another unpredictable impact upon British territory.

Lytton's concern for the Pacific coast thus became the first rather
than the last (or almost the last) link in transcontinental British union.
British Columbia joined confederation only in 1871 but for a decade
and a half its security had been a prime concern of colonial policy.
During the sessions of the Select Committee of 1857 a series of comprehensive resolutions proposed by Gladstone and "intended to apply
to the whole country, from east to west, now under the Hudson's Bay
Company, whether held by charter, statute, or the Vancouver grant,"
had been lost only by the casting vote of the chairman. The final
report drafted by the chairman, Labouchere himself, had advised the
termination of "the connexion of the Hudson's Bay Company with
Vancouver's Island as soon as it can conveniently be done," and the
"ultimate extension of the colony over any portion of the adjoining
continent west of the Rocky Mountains, on which permanent settlement may be found practicable."

This regional union was finally effected in the converse order. The
boundaries of the mainland province of British Columbia established
in 1858 were extended five years later (26 and 27 Vic., c. 83) north to

[1]See above, p. 241.

the 60th parallel of north latitude and east to the Rocky Mountains and the 120th meridian of west longitude. It was not until April 3, 1867, that the Company surrendered Vancouver Island for £57,500 and the regional union of British Columbia became the colony which made its own terms with Canada as the sixth province of the Dominion in 1871. Perhaps no stage in the expansion of Canada was preordained so early in the process of British American union or achieved, as we shall see, with more careful regard to the orthodox principles of confederation.

In the east a much more elaborate project was less successful. Here as on the Pacific tentative plans for regional union were already under way when the first "drive for federation" loomed out of the Canadas. Here too when general federation came to a standstill in 1858 there was a return, with added emphasis, to the intermediate plan, a regional reunion of the Maritimes.

When Newcastle took the seals of the Colonial Office in 1859 after Lytton's brief but meteoric administration he found Head's views on maritime union well known there but his memorandum written for Labouchere "when in England in 1857" was nowhere to be found. One of Merivale's confidential minutes was no doubt a correct interpretation:

It was Sir E. Head's opinion (founded on his knowledge both of N. Brunswick & Canada) that the best prospect for the so called Lower Provinces was an Union between them (legislative, as I think, and not federative) to the *exclusion* of Canada with which a subsequent *federal* union might or might not be formed.

Applying to Head for another copy Newcastle and Merivale gave unwavering support for five years to the cause of maritime union. The prevailing vogue of "Sir E. Head's opinion" may be inferred from the fact that the second copy of his memorandum on maritime union was also lost in circulation at the Colonial Office and remained undiscovered until 1945 when a third draft was found among the papers of the governor-general's office in Ottawa.[1]

In this memorandum of 1857 for Labouchere, Head was stirred for once from his usual cold-blooded empirical temper to a vigorous avowal of faith. The familiar principles of the 1851 memorandum had been sharpened by experience:

[1]See "Sir Edmund Head's Memorandum of 1857 on Maritime Union: A Lost Confederation Document," ed. Alice R. Stewart, *Canadian Historical Review*, Dec. 1945, pp. 407–19.

There are many statesmen who doubt the advantage derived by England from the possession of British North America. . . . According to the view of this school of statesmen they [British provinces] are a source of weakness rather than of strength to the Mother Country.

I dissent entirely. . . . I believe that the greatness of England rests quite as much on her moral supremacy as on her material superiority: anything which wounds the one impairs the other also. The honour of a nation is not a mere empty name, or phantom. . . . The British Colonies in North America could not be abandoned . . . without loss of honour. . . .

If we desire to keep the British Colonies apart from the United States of America, their sympathies must be in favour of British Parliamentary Government rather than of the pattern shewn them at Washington. . . . We must enable the people of Canada or the other Colonies to point to their own system and say "On the whole, we are satisfied. . . . We do not desire to quarrel about Kansas, or submit to the abominations of the fugitive slave law. We see our way clear before us to future progress."

On this hypothesis "the two essential points" were "the success of Parliamentary self government" and "a sense of self importance" among the colonies themselves. The case for maritime union is stated in terms which became familiar currency during the ensuing seven years of discussion—the poverty of public life as a "field of ambition" in small and isolated provinces; the necessity of applying "Parliamentary Government . . . on a certain scale"; the "complete failure" of the old "system of constant interference" which "did not govern well, and . . . satisfied no one"; the prevalence of log-rolling in a small Assembly where "unscrupulous men combine to carry each others' jobs" and where even responsible government failed to reconcile them to the "initiative of money votes" by a responsible executive council;[1] the impaired prospects for a general federation since intercolonial intercourse was still too scanty for "constant or beneficial action," and the "rapid growth of Canada is *westward*" away from the Maritimes; the feasibility on the other hand of one united maritime province where "the size . . . would not be enormous, and the form would be compact"; the fair prospect of "municipal and educational systems beyond the grasp of an Assembly with little aggregate sense of self importance or self reliance"; the value of "some external influence from a more extended circle" to dispel the tendency to "doze on content with the belief that each is too small or too poor" for municipal taxation or adequate provincial expenditure. "The assimilation of the laws" would be far simpler than current practice in "Canada," and customs tariffs and public debts were easily adjustable. "The expense of the three

[1]Head's comment here was critical: "Honesty of purpose may hold out for a time . . . but in the end the jobs will probably be carried."

Governments would, on the whole, be diminished by consolidation, but this is a secondary matter." A "seat of government" problem like that in Canada could be solved by selecting a new capital. "Even those who look to a more extensive union of the North American colonies might conceive it to be a stepping stone towards that end." The process would require time but "several years are a small portion in the future of British North America." "Familiarity . . . has given me a deep interest in their welfare." Such was Head's forecast of maritime· union a few months before the Canadian crisis precipitated the first "drive for federation" in 1858.

The most exhaustive project for maritime union after 1858 came from the Earl of Mulgrave, lieutenant-governor of Nova Scotia. In a confidential despatch of December 30, 1858, which Herman Merivale, Lord Carnarvon, then under-secretary, and Lytton himself all commended—"perhaps the cleverest despatch we have had on the subject" —Mulgrave rated "the advantages to be derived by the Lower Provinces" from a federal union with Canada as "very problematical." A few months later (March 1, 1860) he could see "no reason to change" his views on federal union with Canada; but, avowing a "very different feeling" with regard to the legislative union of the Maritimes, he drafted for Newcastle a case for maritime union which remained a classic until it was discarded in the reversal of British policy in 1864. One reflection of Mulgrave's retained, in retrospect, a curious poignancy after confederation was won: in case of federation with Canada —and "I cannot help feeling that the question of a Union with Canada will be pressed, and perhaps ultimately carried"—it was essential for the Maritimes to come in "on something like equal terms" and after being "thoroughly amalgamated" by a previous union among themselves. Upon the margin of Mulgrave's despatch is a minute by Fortescue of the Colonial Office: "this agrees with Sir E. Head's opinion." The papers on the union of the British provinces were printed for confidential use in London. The cause of maritime union was clearly in the ascendant.[1]

IV

The developments of the next four years are traceable from a variety of sources. In 1859 (September 29) Manners-Sutton, lieutenant-governor of New Brunswick, reported that while he had "no reason to change" his opinions of the Canadian plan of general federation,

[1]For Mulgrave's subsequent support for confederation and conflict with Howe, see below, chapter xviii, p. 359.

there were signs of an "organized movement" for maritime union, supported by "some of the most prominent men in each of the Provinces,
although belonging to different political parties, and hitherto opposed
to each other in general politics." The correctness of his information,
he added, could admit of no doubt. Blackwood in the Colonial Office
immediately collected all the relevant correspondence and Merivale,
as we have seen, added his recollection of "Sir E. Head's opinion . . .
that the best prospect for the so called Lower Provinces was an Union
between them (legislative, as I think, and not federative) to the
exclusion of Canada with which a subsequent *federal* union might or
might not be formed." With "all the previous Correspondence" before
him Newcastle now reached the decision which fairly held the field
at the Colonial Office for nearly five years:

My opinion is in favor of the Legislative Union of the Lower Provinces. I
believe it would be beneficial in itself, and so far from being an impediment
to any future Union with Canada it would place such a measure upon a
more just footing by rendering it more nearly a union of equals instead of
appending three weak Provinces to one strong one and *swamping* the
divided interests of the former by the united influence of the latter.

A year later (September 27, 1861) Manners-Sutton in compliance
with "a strong and growing opinion here in favor of the Union, Legislative, of the three Lower Provinces" reported a plan for free interprovincial trade in colonial produce and manufactures. Newcastle who
had just had a round with a "host of pedantic objections" raised by
the Board of Trade (the phrase is that of the Colonial Office itself)
cut the Gordian knot by conceding the right to "free Commercial
intercourse between the different Provinces" and thus confronting the
Board of Trade with a *fait accompli*. Even Galt, it is now known, had
a secret ally in Newcastle against the Board of Trade in the famous
tariff controversy of 1859.

British policy was further crystallized by Newcastle's visit to the
British provinces with the Prince of Wales in 1860 and by Howe's
resolutions in Nova Scotia for "mutual consultation" with regard to
union. Mulgrave's correspondence again provides the clue to official
policy. Elliot of the Colonial Office made a confidential minute upon
the despatch of May 21, 1862:

It appears to me that there are strong reasons for encouraging a Union,
both Commercial and Legislative, of all the Lower Provinces, but that
whether it would be advisable to promote . . . their Incorporation into
Canada is far more doubtful.

A despatch from Newcastle prescribed for the first time the official procedure by which union was to be (and was in fact eventually) carried—by resolution and address from the several provinces and consultation with the Colonial Office. A confidential minute by Newcastle charted the course with unmistakable assurance:

I have always been of opinion that the necessary preliminary to a Legislative Union of the Lower Provinces is an Intercolonial Railway, and that the completion of *both* these schemes must precede a Union with Canada. The latter event may be hastened by the present condition of the neighbouring Country, but I do not expect success to any project which attempts it without *settling* (if not *accomplishing*) both the smaller Union and the Railway. . . . I am well inclined to enter heartily into any well-considered plan which has the concurrence of all Parties concerned.

It is significant that the interprovincial conference which met at Quebec in September, 1862, waived for the time the discussion of union and addressed itself to the building of the intercolonial railway. Newcastle renewed with alacrity the imperial guarantee which had gone by the board in the imbroglio between Grey and Howe in 1852; while a virtual contract between the governments of Canada, Nova Scotia, and New Brunswick divided the prospective cost of the railway in the ratio of 10, 7, and 7. The necessary legislation was passed by both Nova Scotia and New Brunswick and delegates from all three provinces forgathered in London to implement the guarantee with Gladstone, Chancellor of the Exchequer. Newcastle however reported from London in the following January that Sicotte and Howland had unaccountably sailed for Canada leaving behind a statement "repudiating the terms which had been accepted by their colleagues" at Quebec. In view of the "character of some of the objections [Newcastle added ruefully], the tone in which they are urged, and the immediate departure of the writers from England, without seeking any further discussion . . . their letter must be viewed, as far as Canada is concerned, as a practical abandonment of the scheme." The result in both New Brunswick and Nova Scotia was a wave of resentment in the press against Canadian "duplicity" and open charges of selfishness and "bad faith" in official correspondence. This resentment against Canada lent momentum to the cause of "union among ourselves," and it was not until Canadian delegates appeared at Charlottetown advocating Intercolonial as one of the prerequisites of confederation that maritime antipathies against Canadian "perfidy" were effectually allayed. Even then a few sly references to "Greeks bearing gifts" remained to qualify the response to "a people so disinterested as those of Canada are."

Manners-Sutton, whose chief concern for maritime union was to forestall a general federation rather than to prepare for it, was succeeded in New Brunswick by Gordon, the youngest governor in the service, son of Aberdeen once prime minister. Gordon became the most enthusiastic if not the most discreet advocate of the new policy. "I shall be glad," Newcastle wrote confidentially on July 31, 1863, "to learn that you have taken all prudent means, without committing the home Government beforehand, to bring about a proposal from the Lower Provinces for a Legislative Union." By August Gordon reported "every reason to hope that . . . the Legislatures of New Brunswick, Nova Scotia and Prince Edward Island will concur during the next Session in an Address [the approved procedure] for the immediate union of the Lower Provinces." In September Tupper of Nova Scotia foreshadowed a "resolution in its favour . . . by the Legislature of Nova Scotia without a single dissentient vote." Tupper was also prepared to waive his own proposed procedure—"resolutions . . . empowering delegates from each Province to meet for the discussion and settlement of the details of the Union"—for that already prescribed by Newcastle and advocated by Gordon: simultaneous general resolutions in all three legislatures to be followed by an "Address to Her Majesty" and mutual consultation with the Colonial Office.

Blackwood in the Colonial Office now believed "the *principle* of the step . . . supported by apparent unanimity. Whether *details* will raise difficulties remains to be seen. I do not myself apprehend difficulties that cannot be overcome." General Doyle, who had succeeded Mulgrave in Nova Scotia, forwarded extracts from both the *Chronicle* and the *British Colonist*—the party newspapers of Howe and Tupper —to indicate that "all parties are apparently unanimous in favor of such a step." Fortescue, one of the under-secretaries, in commending Doyle's despatch to Newcastle, noted "the strong feeling of alienation from Canada caused in the Lower provinces by the 'perfidy' of the Canadian Govt." Newcastle in reply stressed his continued "satisfaction at the concurrence of sentiment." By December Gordon reported the project "favorably received" by the Executive Council of New Brunswick; there were differences of opinion on details but "no punctilio" was to interfere with "the end in view." Concurrent resolutions were drafted for the three legislatures. When Gordon returned to England on leave of absence in April, 1864, there were gathering difficulties only in Prince Edward Island where the "eternal land question" was still to cry in vain for solution until the province entered confederation in 1873.

Gordon returned in August in time to appoint delegates to the

Charlottetown conference, September 1, and to attend for several days in person. He afterwards reported that "the Delegates from Nova Scotia (representing both parties) were unanimous in favour of the immediate Legislative and administrative union of the Lower Provinces." Those from New Brunswick, though divided in opinion, registered no dissent from the avowed policy of Tilley and the majority. Prince Edward Island was to prove hostile to both forms of union pending a settlement of the land question, but the union of the other two (Gordon thought all too confidently) seemed "certain of adoption." To Cardwell, who had succeeded Newcastle in the Colonial Office, Gordon wrote ruefully a few days after the concerted speeches of Cartier, Brown, Macdonald, and Galt at Charlottetown and Halifax had made havoc of the smaller union:

But for the proposals from Canada, I have no hesitation in saying that the union of the Maritime Provinces would have been effected, for the Delegates both of Nova Scotia and New Brunswick were fully agreed on the determination not to permit the reluctance of Prince Edward Island to affect their determination. The ultimate concurrence of that Island was a matter of certainty and in the meantime a temporary delay on its part would have inflicted no real inconvenience on the two chief Maritime Provinces in the event of their Union.

V

Could maritime union have been carried had the vast resources of "the great coalition" from Canada, supported after December 3, 1864, by the forthright decision of the Colonial Office, not been marshalled behind a second (and this time successful) "drive for federation"?

It would be easy to qualify Gordon's exuberant estimate by evidences of inertia and cross purposes. Where local division had been deliberately planted and had thriven for three-quarters of a century, provincialism was only too apt to degenerate into sheer parochialism. In the Maritimes as in Canada "the seat of government question" could be relied upon to antagonize two if not all three of the rivals in the field. Economy in administration, simplification in function, and above all reduction in numbers of the civil service, like that for the legislature itself, were scarcely calculated to win the rank and file of local officialdom, though broader horizons and more adequate rewards for legitimate ambition, and prospects of public enterprise quite beyond the resources of the divided provinces, might command a response altogether unforeseen from the leaders of public opinion on both sides. There is little evidence in the local press, or in local associations for trade or politics, of discerning response to the challenge of a great crisis such as underlay the exploits of "the great coalition" in Canada.

Could maritime union have "just happened" by spontaneous generation through plausible arguments from newspaper editors and chambers of commerce and compliant politicians? Dr. Whitelaw has said truly that the "emotional dynamic" for maritime union was traceable less to the affinities of "union among ourselves" than to the antipathies towards Canada after the "railway fiasco" of 1863: "the movement was being swept along toward what appeared to be a successful conclusion on a wave of hatred of Canadian duplicity and domination, and it was to meet its doom . . . in the trough of that wave."[1]

Assuredly maritime union would never have "just happened." But on the other hand no union of peoples under parliamentary government ever has "just happened." It will be conceded that confederation did not "just happen." It was carried in Canada as in the Maritimes by abnormal pressure, by coercive factors on the administrative level; by "events stronger than advocacy, events stronger than men," reinforced by "means" in quotation marks. Some of the "means" were legitimate, like the "proper means" which Cardwell enjoined upon Gordon after the reversal of British policy in December, 1864. Some were more devious, like the "means" without the adjective which Monck and Macdonald and Galt and Brydges of the Grand Trunk brought to bear from Canada. Nova Scotia, as that province has never allowed its colleagues in confederation to forget, was carried into confederation without a popular mandate, by resolution of the Assembly which was reversed after the first election under confederation by a vote of 39 to 1. In New Brunswick confederation was overwhelmingly defeated at the polls in March, 1865, and it required all the resourcefulness of Gordon and Tilley, reinforced by "every proper means" from the Colonial Office and "the needful" from Canada, to reverse the verdict in 1866 in time for the London conference.

A more realistic index to the prospects for maritime union in 1864 would seem to be the attitude of those who were in a position to use "means"—even a fraction of the "means," "proper" and otherwise—for the smaller union which were afterwards applied to confederation. For six years every colonial secretary and under-secretary had given the cause of maritime union exemplary support without dictation. The range of nominal support in the Maritimes at one time or another is equally imposing. Nowhere else, perhaps, during the second empire is such unanimity in policy to be found on both sides of the Atlantic. The case for maritime union as a prerequisite for confederation "on something like equal terms" with the Canadas commanded the sober judgment of Head as well as Mulgrave, of Newcastle as well as Tupper.

[1] *The Maritimes and Canada*, p. 201.

Howe lectured in Saint John on maritime union in 1859, Tupper in the same city on a general federation in 1860, and on the following evening in the neighbouring town of Portland on maritime union. The one was advocated as the antecedent not the alternative to the other, and after the defeat of federation in New Brunswick in March, 1865, Tupper reverted to maritime union in the attempt to keep the cause of federation alive. "If adopted," he assured Macdonald on April 9, 1865, "it will promote the larger union and place it upon a better footing." Tupper's resolution, that "a legislative union of the Maritime Provinces is desirable, whether the larger union is accomplished or not," passed on April 21, 1865, but it was countermanded by the Colonial Office because at so critical a juncture it might "tend to delay the Confederation of all the Provinces" unless it "formed part of the scheme for general union."

After the Charlottetown conference Galt, Brown, and Cartier were Gordon's guests at Government House in Fredericton, and Gordon in reporting upon "the scheme of federation which had. been agreed upon by the Canadian Cabinet" conveyed to ˙Cardwell, the new colonial secretary, Galt's assurance that it "involved as an essential preliminary the entire Union of the three Maritime Provinces.—It was proposed on this being effected that Upper Canada, Lower Canada, and the Maritime Provinces should each possess a local Legislature,"[1] and that the legislative council (senate) of the new federation should have equal representation from these three sections. There is every reason to believe that Brown and Cartier acquiesced in these views. Brown's original resolution at the Quebec conference still indicated but three local governments for the federated provinces, and the "three divisions" for the Senate in the B.N.A. Act of 1867 (s. 22) are the vestigial remains of the project for maritime union as a preliminary to federation "on something like equal terms" with the Canadas.

VI

A chapter of accidents and coercive factors elsewhere of unforeseen urgency forced a decision in 1864 and 1865 which left maritime union a hopeless derelict in the wake of confederation. Few would now question the "imperative necessity" of that decision. But the inadvertent debts of "imperative necessity" are frequently the hardest to liquidate because they can seldom be paid in full. The Canadas in their determination to supersede their own "intolerable" union helped to forestall another which subsequent experience was soon to endow

[1]When this despatch was edited subsequently for publication, "involved as an essential preliminary" was changed to "appeared to involve as a preliminary."

with nostalgic reflections. The "might-have-beens" of history are sometimes as persistent as the facts, and there was scarcely a major coercive
factor for the larger federation which did not present the Maritimes
with a hypothetical margin of preference in favour of immediate
maritime union.

The form of union in itself was symptomatic. With the United
States embroiled in civil war by reason of "state rights" and a fatal
dualism within the union, federalism was everywhere on the defensive.
The well-known views of Macdonald and Monck and Johnston on the
functional superiority of legislative over federal unions were shared
in some measure in 1864 by the most inveterate sectionalists in British
North America. When Brown and Mowat and McDougall could carry
the Clear Grits of Canada West into the most strongly centralized
federation of its day, the case for the nebulous "joint authority" of the
Clear Grit convention of 1859 must indeed have been desperate.
Maritime union would have involved no "division of powers," no inveterate conflicts between federal and provincial rights, no delicate
"balances" to complicate the functioning of parliamentary government. One legislature instead of three, one governor instead of three,
would continue to function as before, and the union could be effected
by a single simple statute obliterating the boundaries. Compared to
this the *B.N.A. Act of 1867* with its 147 sections and elaborate division
of powers (ss. 91 and 92) assumed the misleading proportions of a
"written constitution." Gordon's interminable despatches on this theme
continued until Cardwell assured him it was quite unnecessary to
labour the point. The Colonial Office was well aware of the superiority
of a legislative over a federal union, but federalism was the price it
was necessary to pay if British North America was ever to be united.
Gordon bowed to the inevitable: "I shall act [he wrote] in conformity
with . . . commands therein signified to me."

In practice as well as precept there was a margin of preference.
Many of the familiar arguments for maritime union were stultified by
Confederation. For ten years colonial governors had been preaching
the poverty of public enterprise and the indignities of public life in
provinces too small to sustain the parliamentary system at its best.
Head attributed the tardiness of New Brunswick in adopting responsible government to the "log-rolling" of old colonial days when "unscrupulous men combine to carry each others' jobs" and no responsible
executive council could command the "initiative of money votes."
Adequate "municipal and educational systems" were impossible without some "aggregate sense of self importance or self reliance." Mulgrave reported from Nova Scotia in 1860 that corrupt "means were

undoubtedly used, on both sides, at the last election," and that "party spirit and animosity"—"personal attack and recrimination"—had reached a new nadir in the rivalry of William Young and J. W. Johnston, the party leaders, to succeed Sir Brenton Halliburton, then in his eighty-sixth year, as chief justice of the province. Gordon once described to Newcastle a conversation at his own dinner-table where he heard "a member of the Executive Council boast to one of his Colleagues that his supporters had cost him a guinea a-piece, and that their votes were not to be had at three and sixpence a-head, like those of the County which his colleague represented!" Instead of fusing the three provinces into one in the interests of "dignity and enterprise," federation without a preliminary maritime union would remove to Ottawa the overwhelming preponderance of national interests, leaving the meagre residue of parochial politics still distributed between three straggling provinces as before.

Popular preference as well as political theory favoured a maritime union. After the "railway fiasco" of 1862 it was easy for the Maritimes to build up a case for "union among ourselves" against a background of Canadian "duplicity" and "breach of faith." Even when "Greeks bearing gifts" appeared at Charlottetown, and George Brown himself expounded the necessity of Intercolonial, Tilley quickly discovered that there was a very lively interest in Canada in the contracts for that great enterprise, and that maritime interests served by Levesey and the International Contract Company, already hovering about the Charlottetown conference in the hope of completing the line from Truro to the Bend under the auspices of maritime union, were to have no share in the by-products of federation. In letters to both Tilley and Tupper (November 14, 1864) Macdonald lost no time in pre-empting that field:

I cannot too strongly impress on you the necessity of carrying out the policy of not in any way giving any party the slightest control over the construction of any portion of the Intercolonial Railway. . . . Were it suspected that any considerable portion of the Road for which Canada is going to pledge itself was given away to contractors without the consent and sanction of the Government a storm would at once arise which could not be allayed, and would peril the whole scheme.

The concern of Galt and Macdonald for the loaves and fishes in the Intercolonial continued to beset the maritime approach to confederation, and at one stage, as we shall see, it threatened to overshadow confederation altogether.[1]

In trade and commerce the margin between legislative and federal

[1]See below, p. 361.

union was equally provocative.[1] Maritime export trade was largely complementary rather than competitive: that of Prince Edward Island chiefly with the United States, that of New Brunswick, chiefly lumber, with Great Britain, and that of Nova Scotia, chiefly fish, with the West Indies. Tariffs were traditionally low. On the other hand the Canadas and the Maritimes were competitors in staples for export—fish and lumber—while Galt's differential tariff of 1859 for the expanding industries of the Canadas was highly protective. For a renewal of the Reciprocity Treaty with the United States any association with Canada was worse than useless. It was a threadbare axiom in the Maritimes that the Reciprocity Treaty had been bought with the inshore fisheries of the maritime provinces, "hook and line, bob and sinker." Reciprocity was now jeopardized by Canadian border relations with the United States during the Civil War, culminating in the St. Albans raid and Seward's passport system, the worst border relations since the War of 1812. Those of the Maritimes by comparison were far from hostile, and the inshore fisheries still remained the most alluring bait for a renewal of reciprocity. As late as 1868 two advocates of it from the United States Congress came to Prince Edward Island and Nova Scotia to explore the prospects until their mission was bluntly counteracted by the Colonial Office in favour of confederation. Two years later Sir Francis Hincks in preparing a memorandum for Macdonald as one of the British plenipotentiaries for the Treaty of Washington, cited reciprocity as the first desideratum of the hour, with the inshore fisheries of the Maritimes as bait for the negotiations with Hamilton Fish, the United States secretary of state.

The widest margin of preference between maritime and federal union, however, was to be found on issues that were still more coercive in the cause of British American security. After Gettysburg in 1863 the triumph of the North was assured, and relations with the United States—the problem of "defence" in all its bearings—assumed a new and menacing aspect. While Colonel Jervois reported to the War Office that Canada West was virtually indefensible, British naval resources, based on Halifax and Bermuda, were never more assured. Naval expenditures there for 1865 amounted to more than £550,000. With nearly half a million tons of shipping on the seven seas the commercial interests of Nova Scotia regarded British naval defence as imperative. The dearest interests of the Maritimes were maritime and Canada was powerless to defend them. Not three dozen merchants in Halifax and Yarmouth, Howe maintained, could be found to support confederation. Nova Scotia had called out the militia and voted

[1]See above, p. 238.

£100,000 for the defence of New Brunswick in the "Aroostook War" over the Maine boundary. Obligations for defence through confederation now meant the privilege of defending Canada. After the *Trent* affair when British troops had to reach Canada by an overland march from New Brunswick, even the Intercolonial took on the aspect of "defence" since Newcastle's guarantee was undoubtedly geared to that necessity. The "railway fiasco" which wrecked the plan, added to the defeat of the Canadian *Militia Bill* in 1862, provided maritime newspapers with another opportunity of acquiescing only too readily in the scathing but uninformed comments of the British press.

To all these margins of preference for maritime over federal union was added the suspicion that "Federal Union was only sought as a means of separating the Canadas," and that it was necessary "to force its immediate adoption upon unwilling communities" because it could not otherwise be represented "even speciously . . . to the Imperial Government as in any manner a scheme of Union." This was the view of the Executive Council of New Brunswick (July 12, 1865) after the ominous defeat of confederation in that province, and it continued to colour the outlook of the Maritimes long after the element of truth in it had been submerged by more coercive factors. The result—a riptide in the approach to confederation between a rising legislative union in the Maritimes and a Canadian legislative union fast ebbing into "intolerable chaos"—baffled the most resourceful navigators of their day. Let it be repeated that few would now question the wisdom of seizing with every available resource of "means" and skill the supreme moment of 1864 for the consummation of confederation. That was the tide in the affairs of men which taken at the flood led on to fortune. In the Maritimes as in the Canadas and Britain that decision came eventually to rank as statesmanship of the first order. But it was a hard decision to make, for it appeared to be one of the most violent reversals of British policy. It was also a costly decision. The cost of such a decision may not be in the end excessive but it can seldom be liquidated in the lifetime of those who questioned its justice or its necessity. In the case of one at least of the maritime provinces the cost has persisted unto the third and fourth generation, and the carrying charges are still discernible in Canadian politics. The younger Pitt, facing a far heavier legacy of misunderstanding, as we have seen, once said that "misfortunes of individuals and of kingdoms that are laid open and examined with true wisdom are more than half redressed." It may be the part of true wisdom to explore the redress which comes from an attempt at mutual understanding.

Chapter Sixteen

MAINSPRING OF FEDERATION:

THE GREAT COALITION

THE coercive factors in the Canadian federation may be simplified in an axiom which would seem to admit of no exceptions. Among self-governing peoples union has invariably been the result of pressure. Far from being an instinctive natural process it contravenes the normal processes of self-government at almost every point.

Robert Baldwin was accustomed to say that it was the genius of British communities to be concerned with the government of themselves. Whatever truth there may have been in that flattering unction it is reasonable at least to suppose that first loyalties are apt to be local in case of conflict—to the city as against the province, to the province as against the national state, to the nation as against the claims of a broader international polity. Nothing but a compelling necessity can reconcile self-governing provinces to the surrender of cherished rights to the exigencies of a distant national state.

The "pressure" under which that surrender is made may be supplied by a variety of exigencies, internal as well as external, economic as well as political; but it normally functions most effectively in the hour of national danger. From a wide range of modern examples—the United States, Brazil, Australia, and Canada among them—a still more apposite corollary may be formulated: the degree of centralization in the federal government usually stands in direct ratio to the pressure under which the central powers have been acquired by the national state. In the throes of a national emergency the most sluggish elements of local inertia may be moved to action. Like chemical reagents which are inert towards one another under normal conditions of pressure and temperature, the most disintegrated provinces may react in a national emergency with unpredictable responsiveness. That reaction at the time may be due to abnormal pressure and temperature but once it has resulted in organic federation, the product may be a permanent chemical compound capable of withstanding the stresses and strains of normal atmospheric conditions with complete organic stability.

It may be added that the Canadian federation was presided over by some of the most expert chemists who ever attempted such an experiment. John A. Macdonald never concealed his preference for legislative union—a downright preference shared in 1864 by Charles Tupper of Nova Scotia and Charles Fisher of New Brunswick—and though he found it necessary at last to accept federalism as the only feasible basis for British American union, he was able to utilize, at the crisis of the experiment, the most coercive factors since the War of 1812 in his search for the maximum of centralization in the function of the national state.

Nowhere were the problems of federalism more manifest at the time than in that other experiment which Macdonald, above every other Canadian observer, was following with penetrating insight. In the American union, convulsed in civil war, were to be seen not only infirmities of structure in its origin but signs of renewed vitality and strength in its survival. It was Macdonald's distinction, above all his contemporaries, that he studied the chequered history of federalism in the United States with keen appreciation as well as critical disapproval so easy at the time. "It has been said," he remarked in Halifax after the Charlottetown conference, "that the United States Government is a failure. I don't go so far. On the contrary I consider it a marvellous exhibition of human wisdom. It was as perfect as human wisdom could make it, and under it the American States greatly prospered until very recently; but being the work of men it had its defects, and it is for us to take advantage by experience, and endeavour to see if we cannot arrive by careful study at such a plan as will avoid the mistakes of our neighbours."

By the time of the Quebec conference many of these conclusions had been accepted as axiomatic: by Brown and Mowat as well as by Macdonald, Galt, and Tupper. The function of "pressure," or conversely the absence of it, in the early stages of the American union was as discernible as it afterwards became in the federation of Australia. The early "League of Friendship" of 1781, welded together in the crucible of revolution, had been improvised too hurriedly for the purposes of the revolution itself to admit of a centralized constitution while the pressure was still at its maximum. When independence was conceded, the tensions of war were relaxed, the separatist tendencies of the old provinces again emerged, and it required in the *Federalist* the most skilful and concerted effort ever developed in such a cause, exploiting every expedient from Shay's Rebellion to financial chaos, to concentrate for the federal government enough power to function effectively in the interests of the nation. The constitution of 1787, as one of its architects once remarked, was "extorted from the grinding necessities of a reluctant people." In the midst of civil war it was still doubtful whether it could survive. As late as August, 1862, John Rose reported confidently to Thomas Baring that "the *Union is gone*, and that the North are fighting only for a frontier."

In Australia the cause of colonial union was equally protracted. Antedating by far the Canadian federation, union simmered on for half a century before it was finally brought to pass by the *Commonwealth of Australia Constitution* Act of 1900; and even with the rise of Japan and German expansion in New Guinea federal powers in Australia remained notoriously weak. Compared to the "pressures" of 1787 in the United States or 1891 in Brazil or 1900 in Australia the coercive factors in British North American union from 1864 to 1867 were imperative—"stronger than advocacy . . . stronger than men." Nowhere were such factors directed more discerningly to create what Macdonald never ceased to advocate, "a strong central government" charged with "the destinies of a nation."

II

Goldwin Smith once wrote that "the real author of confederation, so far as British and French Canada was concerned, was deadlock." This aphorism has had a long vogue in the traditions of the Canadian federation. Half-true though it undoubtedly was for the acceptance of federalism rather than legislative union by the British North American provinces, it has tended to obscure the truly coercive factors in the process. There were ways of breaking deadlock. At least four were under discussion during the last decade of the Canadian union. Why did the final solution, a general federation, become imperative in 1864?

It is a fact that among peoples accustomed to the more or less automatic functioning of parliamentary government after the British model there is a notorious dislike for "weak" governments subject to the whims of narrow majorities and fluctuating loyalties. This impatience had reached a pitch of exasperation in Canada during the early sixties which threatened to bring the whole machinery of government to a standstill. In contrast, however, to the devices habitually resorted to in the third French republic, or even in the United States when the President finds himself confronted by a hostile Congress, the resort to "double shuffles" and "double majorities" and kaleidoscopic coalitions in Canada seldom jeopardized the actual administration of government. Deadlock was not endemic in the Canadian union. It was the unnatural and artificial equality of representation between the two sections of the province—"the intolerable inequalities of equal representation"—which unsettled the House and locked the two sections of the province in uncompromising conflict. Is it true that this conflict was unsolved and insoluble?

The shrewdest minds of that day did not think so. The solutions proposed varied widely from time to time but the problem itself was everywhere conceded, and the Cartier-Galt-Ross mission assured Lytton in 1858 it was "yearly becoming worse." Some way must be found sooner or later of removing the "inequalities of equal representation." To Dorion and Galt and Holton in 1856, to Brown in 1857 and 1859 and 1864, to Head and Galt and Cartier in 1858, to Macdonald in 1864, to Monck in 1866, various adaptations for this one sovereign remedy seemed feasible. What daunted them all was not the insolubility of the problem but the cost of the solution. In the end what daunted them most was the cost of not solving it—the cost not only to party advantage and material prosperity, but the ominous cost to national loyalties transcending both.

To George Brown "simple rep. by pop." was the obvious remedy and he never struck that flag from the masthead of the *Globe* until representation by population was accepted in the Quebec Resolutions (number 17, passed under Brown's own sponsorship) as the basis for the federal House of Commons. By the *Union Act* (3 and 4 Vic., c. 35, s. 26) any "new and different apportionment" of representation for the two sections of the province required a two-thirds vote. In 1853, when provision was being made for an elective council, this section of the *Union Act* was repealed (17 and 18 Vic., c. 118, s. 5) "through misapprehension or inadvertence," the French members of the House maintained, and "without the previous knowledge and consent" of the House itself. Thenceforth the deadlock of "equal representation" could be broken by a bare majority; and the perennial votes of the House began to register a steadily rising tide in that direction.

Brown himself conceded on several occasions that "simple rep. by pop." might require adaptation to make it acceptable to both sections of the province, either by a dual federation of the Canadas as proposed by the Clear Grit convention of 1859, or by a multiple federation of all the British provinces as sponsored by "the great coalition" of

1864. "Rep. by pop." remained nevertheless not only the most dynamic but in the end, as we shall see, the dominant issue of provincial politics. By 1861 even Conservatives of Canada West tried to leave it "an open question." After the general election of 1863 George Brown exulted in "the complete rout of the old corruptionists" in Canada West. "The vote for representation by population," he wrote to Holton, "will be almost unanimous." "All but two oppositionists returned are as earnest as we are in claiming the same reform." By the spring of 1864 the rising tide had reached spring-tide proportions. Dorion moved in the House for a gradual increase of membership for Canada West— two new members for Huron and Bruce to one for Canada East. A resolution for "rep. by pop." forthwith, moved in amendment to Brown's own resolution (the famous resolution for a select committee on federation) was lost by only nine votes; while another amendment to maintain equal representation "unimpaired and inviolate" was overwhelmed by a vote of 82 to 25. "No one," wrote Brown, "sees his way out of the mess—and there is no way but my way—representation by population." To Brydges, and through Brydges to John A. Macdonald, Brown hinted in no uncertain terms that "rep. by pop." if openly avowed by Sandfield Macdonald "would win" the day. John A. Macdonald, too, as we shall see, was prepared at last to concede this issue had not the happier solution of "the great coalition" for federation been propounded by George Brown.

But shrewder men than Brown, shrewder at least in political tactics, were being coerced by the same necessity towards the same conclusion. Sir Edmund Head, as we have seen, had detected this "vicious element in the constitution of the Union" from the beginning of his Canadian administration. "This unsound spot in the Union," he wrote, "cannot be passed by or overlooked: the difficulty must be faced." Ominous as it already was during the early fifties it was becoming chronic with the phenomenal growth of Canada West. "The crisis may come sooner or later but the dualistic relation, if I may so call it, of U. & L.C. will be in constant peril" despite "the greatest tact on the part of the Govt. & the utmost forbearance on the part of all." "The poison of disunion" was "ready at any moment to influence to the utmost the rivalry of race language and worship." "To do the best we can from day to day and delay this crisis" became the chief concern of the government. "Every day however tends to increase it" and the fear was that "unscrupulous partizans [meaning, no doubt, George Brown and the Clear Grits] will endeavour to force on this question before the country is ripe for its peaceable solution." Of all the "modes of escape" from this *impasse* an adjustment of representation was obviously the most logical and direct; and Head wrote that "if the Eastern townships were to advance very rapidly & if that district & the English population of Montreal and its neighbourhood were to feel strongly & unanimously the importance of the Western trade then they might thrown their weight into the side of U.C. and render resistance on the part of the French population impossible." By 1858 the "crisis" had come, an "occasion for action" at last presented itself, and the first drive for federation, as Head confessed to Lytton, was the "direction in which we were about to seek escape." When that failed, every resource of tact and forbearance was again called into play for three years to keep the precarious "dualistic relation" of east and west in equipoise.

Galt too, with his flair for "objects of material advantage," had been spurred to action by the infirmities of the Canadian union. Sharing with Dorion and Holton the frustration of a Rouge in the "domination" of the Bleus of Canada East over the phenomenal development of Canada West, he was content in 1856 with Dorion's suggestion of a dual federation. In 1858, in his famous resolutions of July 5 from the cross-benches of the House, he still advocated a dual federation to preside over the illimitable prospects opening up in the West after the report of the British Select Committee on the Hudson's Bay Company. But after his quarrel with Brown a general federation seemed to be "most desirable" (section 3 of Galt's resolutions); and it is clear that the federal solution, whether dual or multiple, was made imperative by "irreconcilable difficulties . . . to the maintenance of that equality which formed the basis of the Union of Upper and Lower Canada," an equality now jeopardized by "sectional jealousies and dissensions." "Half a continent is ours," said Galt in the House, "if we do not keep on quarrelling about petty matters and lose sight of what interests us most."

After becoming "true blue" in the Cartier-Macdonald government it was obvious to Galt that some form of escape more acceptable than the dual federation advocated by Brown and Dorion would be necessary from the spectre of "rep. by pop. pure and simple." A general federation under "true blue" auspices sponsored by the sagacious counsels of Sir Edmund Head thus became, for Galt as for Cartier and his Bleus, the avowed alternative to a dual federation dominated by Brown and Dorion and accentuated by a Clear Grit ascendancy armed with "rep. by pop." and the prospect of westward expansion to Rupert's Land. With the failure of the mission of 1858 the spectre of simple "rep. by pop." returned once more to haunt the Canadian scene. The two Macdonalds succeeded in exorcising it fitfully for five or six years—John A. from 1858 to May 1862, John Sandfield from 1862 to March 30, 1864, and John A. again for two months longer until "the great coalition." By this time, however, the demand for "rep. by pop." was fairly unanswerable. At the Quebec conference the ratio of representation for Ontario and Quebec in the proposed federal House of Commons on the basis of "rep. by pop." was found to be 82 to 65. In the end the shrewdest political opportunist of his day was prepared to interpret the handwriting on the wall. In the Confederation Debates John A. Macdonald conceded that in Canada West the demand for "rep. by pop." was "daily augmenting"; that "if some such solution of the difficulties as Confederation had not been found, the representation by population must eventually have been carried." "It is certain that in the progress of events representation by population would have been carried." The effect upon the Liberal-Conservative party was easily foreseen. To one of his own supporters Macdonald afterwards added a singularly realistic forecast following the defeat of the Conservative Government on June 14, 1864: "As the leader of the Conservatives in Upper Canada, I then had the option either of forming a coalition government or of handing over the administration of affairs to the Grit party for the next ten years."[1]

Thus to Macdonald as to Brown and Galt and Head the real peril was not "deadlock" but what lay beyond. For Macdonald the choice was easy, but what lay beyond "deadlock" to induce George Brown to forgo the steadily mounting prospects of "rep. by pop.," the growing ascendancy of Canada West in wealth and population, the prospect of adding to the Canadian frontier the illimitable frontiers of Rupert's Land?

III

Brown's long illness in 1861 followed by his own defeat and the temporary setback to the Clear Grit wing of the party in the general election of that year, opened the way, as we have seen, for the conciliatory counsels of John Sandfield Macdonald and the integration of the Reform party. Brown returned from Scotland "a new man in mind and body" but there were new perils abroad in America more alarming

[1]The Reform ascendancy in Ontario after confederation would seem to vindicate this forecast. In the federal House of Commons the Liberals held 50 seats out of 88 in 1872, and 64 out of 88 in 1874; while the provincial governments of Sandfield Macdonald, Edward Blake, and Oliver Mowat held office continuously from confederation until 1896.

than the "inequalities of equal representation." By 1863 the American civil war had reached a stage which jeopardized the deepest convictions of his political life.

For many years the westward movement of population in the United States—more than two millions in a single decade—around the Great Lakes towards Rupert's Land had been followed in the *Globe* with grave concern. In its early stages there was little in this development but healthy rivalry and incentive for a Canadian type of "prairie fever" instead of the movement from the Canadian frontier into Iowa, Indiana, Illinois, Michigan, and Minnesota. Horace Greeley's familiar slogan "Go west, young man, go west" was already known in Canada. Greeley himself was brought to Toronto to lecture in St. Lawrence Hall with George Brown in the chair. By 1859 the fame of the Illinois Central, prototype of "land-grant railways" in America, was well established. The Hannibal and St. Jo line had reached the Missouri. The same year two young Canadians, Buckingham and Caldwell, founded the *Nor'-Wester* at Red River and began to advocate annexation to Canada. The *Globe* commended their enterprise and the *Nor'-Wester* reciprocated by commending the *Globe*. The report of the British Select Committee of 1857 was appropriated by both with conspicuous disregard for the "equitable principles" recommended for the interests of the Hudson's Bay Company.

After Lytton's failure to liquidate those interests in 1858 the concern of the Canadian government for the hinterlands of the continent was never relaxed. A policy of accommodation with the Company instead of the frontal assault advocated by Brown so far succeeded that Grand Trunk and the International Financial Society, under Watkin's mercurial enterprise, aspired between them to function through the Company itself. Head, at Newcastle's suggestion, was selected for the governorship of the Hudson's Bay Company in London. For Galt as for George Brown a new frontier beyond the Great Lakes seemed but the counterpart of the Mississippi and Missouri prairies in the phenomenal expansion of the United States. Hitherto the survival of British territory west of the Great Lakes had been due to good fortune rather than to foresight. Without the vested interest of settlement planted by Selkirk in Assiniboia during the second decade of the century it seems probable that Red River would have shared the fate of Oregon. It was Macdonald's opinion that even the Red River Settlement could not have safeguarded British interests in the West had it not been for the distractions of the Civil War. The free homestead system, vetoed by President Buchanan in 1860, was launched by Lincoln in 1862 as an instrument of policy to forestall the South in the race for free land in the West. The charter of the Union Pacific in 1862, followed by that of the Northern Pacific in 1864, canalized this movement, and threatened to dwarf the immigration into Canada by way of the St. Lawrence and the Grand Trunk, or lure it bodily across the border into the expanding frontier of the republic.

By 1863 British interests not only in the West but in Canada itself were in jeopardy. From the beginning of hostilities Brown had never concealed his sympathies with the North, his abhorrence of slavery. His chief concern, however, was to keep the peace. He deplored the caustic temper of the London *Times*, the truculence of the New York *Herald*, the "insolent bravado of the Northern press towards Great Britain." Even after the *Trent* affair the *Globe* maintained that "there would be no talk of war but for the mischief-making of newspapers in England and America." But the despatch of British troops overland on sledges to Canada brought home stark possibilities of war never seriously contemplated for nearly half a century. When the *Militia Bill* was thrown out in 1862 there was a revulsion of uninformed opinion in the British press against colonies too craven or apathetic or "degenerate" to defend themselves. The *Globe*—Howe too in Nova Scotia—resented these "diatribes of the newspaper press": "our duty has been laid down for us, chapter and verse, by gentlemen three thousand miles off, who know very little of our circumstances, and yet venture to tell us the exact number of men we are to drill and the time we are to drill them."

The steady deterioration of relations with the United States, nevertheless, soon created in Canada West a tension almost incredible to succeeding generations who contemplated it only in retrospect. The cumulative effect of the *Trent* affair, the *Chesapeake* incident, the depredations of the *Alabama* on Northern shipping, the threatened abrogation not only of the Reciprocity Treaty but of the Rush-Bagot convention, the crisis of the St. Albans raid at the time of the Quebec conference, Seward's passport system against the Canadian border, and a host of minor border incidents, daunted even Brown's "faith in the good sense of our neighbours." Galt returned from an interview with Lincoln with profound admiration for the president's "straightforward strong commonsense" but with the conviction that "the policy of the American government was so subject to popular impulses that no assurances can, or ought to be, relied on." Whatever complacency remained was shattered by the guns of Gettysburg in July, 1863. The largest armies in history, equipped with the most modern weapons, were in bivouac across the border. The Sandfield Macdonald government which had thrown out the *Militia Bill* in 1862 hastened to pass an improved *Militia Act*, and "the great coalition," as we shall see, was ready to spend $1,000,000 at once on the militia and to fortify Montreal. "I am not one of those [said George Brown in the Confederation Debates of 1865] who ever had the war-fever. . . . But it must be admitted—and there is no closing our eyes to the fact—that this question of defence has been placed, within the last two years, in a totally different position from what it ever occupied before." The plausible report of the British military commission of 1862 was now obsolete. In February, 1864, Colonel Jervois of the War Office reported that Canada West was indefensible and advised the withdrawal of British troops to Quebec. *The Times* added that nine or ten thousand British redcoats would only be bait "to allure the American army across the Great Lakes."

Brown returned from Scotland and re-entered the House for South Oxford in a by-election in the spring of 1863. By the time of the general election later in the summer it was clear that Grits and Tories were no longer free to fight out their quarrel, as Sir Lucius O'Trigger said, "in peace and quietness." In 1857 Brown had welcomed the prospect of annexing Rupert's Land to the frontiers of Canada West. In 1859 he was prepared to retrieve the West under "some joint authority" of a dual federation of the Canadas. After 1863 it was obvious that it would require all the resources and resourcefulness of all the British provinces and of Great Britain herself to safeguard British interests in North America:

The Americans [said Brown] are now a warlike people. They have large armies, a powerful navy, an unlimited supply of warlike munitions, and the carnage of war has to them been stript of its horrors. The American side of our lines already bristles with works of defence, and unless we are willing to live at the mercy of our neighbors, we, too, must put our country in a state of efficient preparation. War or no war—the necessity of placing these provinces in a thorough state of defence can no longer be postponed. Our country is coming to be regarded as undefended and indefensible.

IV

Head's shrewd memorandum on the "vicious element" in the Canadian union, as we have seen, had closed with the fear that "unscrupulous partizans will endeavour to force on this question before the country is ripe for its peaceable solution." In June, 1864, after "the great coalition," Lord Monck announced at last, in the Speech from the Throne, that the "constitutional question which has for many years agitated this Province, is ripe for settlement."

During that interval none had forced on the issue of "rep. by pop." in season and out of season more consistently and insistently than George Brown, but after his return to the House in 1863 the charge of unscrupulous partisanship in Head's indictment may fairly be withdrawn. Reluctant at all times to surrender the independence of the journalist for the accommodations of parliamentary life, Brown found himself in a position of unusual influence for the coercion of both parties. From his private correspondence there can be no doubt that his detachment from office under all the kaleidoscopic adjustments of the Sandfield Macdonald administration was instinctive and deliberate. This in itself was an element of strength. A turn in his private fortune, too, had not only repaired the financial losses of 1861 but left a margin of affluence in a wide variety of enterprising interests. There was truth in his boast to his wife that he "would rather be proprietor of the *Globe* newspaper . . . than be governor-general of Canada"; and next to the *Globe* it is probable that his farm at Bothwell was his most congenial refuge from the distractions of party politics. Moreover, in Great Britain his interview with Newcastle at Newcastle's own request had convinced him that "both the government and the leaders of the opposition perfectly understand our position" and that "scruples about representation by population are entirely gone."

In Canada both leaders, clinging desperately to the shreds of political power, tried in vain to escape the inevitable. In January, 1864, Sandfield Macdonald, not perhaps without guile, begged Brown to undertake a mission to Washington as "a quasi political agent . . . for some months" to forestall the threatened abrogation of the Reciprocity Treaty. A few months later John A. Macdonald in turn authorized Brydges, the ubiquitous general manager of the Grand Trunk—general manager, too, of many a devious design in Macdonald's political necromancy—to approach Brown with a still more alluring sop for Cerberus. Brydges reported under cover to Ferrier[1] that Brown had not given him "an opening to go *very* far."

I offered him the chair of the Canada Board of Hudson's Bay at which I think he was a good deal impressed. . . . I shewed him that nothing could be done about Northwest without the Intercolonial—On the latter point he is *much* mollified—Thinks that the action of the Yankees about reciprocity & bonding has put an entirely new phase on the question. . . . He does not object I think to the marrying of Northwest & Intercolonial but

[1] "I am afraid letters where the handwriting is known are tampered with."

. . . wishes an omnibus arrangement to include Northwest, Intercolonial, Representation, and change of tariff by lowering duties—He would support such a programme & thinks it could be carried.[1]

Brown conceded that the Sandfield Macdonald government was losing ground but added significantly "that he could propound a policy that would save them." It is safe to say that for George Brown the most important cargo in this "omnibus arrangement" was Northwest and Representation. The coercion of both the Macdonalds, still grasping at office by every device of political manipulation, by this ineluctable factor of "rep. by pop." in Canadian politics was the work of the next four months.

V

On October 12, 1863, after consultation with Thomas D'Arcy McGee, Brown moved in the House a resolution which may be regarded as the genesis of "the great coalition" for confederation.

During the previous July, within a few days of Gettysburg, McGee had published a series of letters in the Montreal *Gazette* on the portentous question which came to haunt the era of confederation: "What is to become of Canada and her sister provinces in the new arrangement of these times?" "The whole of British North America, from Atlantic to Pacific," wrote McGee, "should form one nation, and our safety lies in the growth of the national sentiment." Early in October Brown approached McGee, now bitterly critical of his old associates in the Sandfield Macdonald Government, with the assurance that he "would approve of a federal union of the two Canadas, or of all the provinces, or any other constitutional change which will eliminate the present sectional antagonism." The House was to prorogue on October 15 and Brown's resolution at this stage was little more than advance notice of a plan slowly maturing into deep conviction that the crisis now required a radical and permanent remedy. "Wearying to be back" at home as usual, Brown introduced his resolution only to withdraw it with a promise of re-introducing it during the next session. On March 14, 1864, he was as good as his word.

Brown's resolution of October 12, 1863, and March 14, 1864, struck a new note of conciliation and compromise in Canadian politics. With unwonted magnanimity he appealed in the preamble to the despatch which Galt and Cartier had addressed to Lytton during their mission of 1858: that the "views of the two sections" of the province were

[1]Brydges to Macdonald, Confidential, Feb. 24, 1864, Macdonald Papers, 191. 34 ff.

incapable of "complete assimilation"; that the rapid "progress of population" in Canada West had already given rise to claims of "representation . . . in proportion to their numbers"; that the agitation was "fraught with great danger which was yearly becoming worse"; that the time was come for "seeking such a mode of dealing with the difficulties as may forever remove them." To that end Brown moved for a select committee of twenty to "enquire and report on the important subjects embraced in the despatch." The committee was to include Sandfield Macdonald, then Prime Minister, and John A. Macdonald, Dorion (then Attorney-General East) and Cartier, Galt and Holton, McDougall and McGee and Dunkin, and eleven other members from both sides of the House. "I have determined," said Brown, "that I will take ground that cannot be assailed. . . . I ask my honourable friends opposite to take that course now which they considered it desirable to take five years ago."

Brown's resolution ran the gauntlet of debate until May 19 before the select committee was finally appointed. The amendments which were moved in the desperate attempt to halt or deflect its purpose were perhaps the most significant which had ever gone to the vote since "rep. by pop." became an issue in the Canadian union. An elaborate amendment by Perrault stipulating that "the principle of Equality in the Representation of the two Sections of the Province . . . may be maintained unimpaired and inviolate" was lost by an overwhelming majority of 57 votes, 82 to 25.[1] Not a single vote in its favour could be found from Canada West. Dorion and both the Macdonalds, Sandfield and John A., voted against it. Less than four years had passed since Brown's own resolution of May 8, 1860, "that the Union, in its present form can no longer be continued with advantage to the people" had been lost by a vote of 66 to 27. There was obviously "a sound of going in the tops of the mulberry trees." Another amendment, this time from Jackson, a Clear Grit from Grey, after the Sandfield Macdonald Government had left the helm on March 21, that the representation of Canada West "should be increased" forthwith, was lost by a margin of only nine votes. The last attempt to escape from Brown's motion came from Dorion who proposed to add two new members for Huron and Bruce and one new member from Canada East. This amendment too was lost, 32 to 74. The constriction of "rep.

[1]Perrault's amendment was doubly significant for in it he had protested against the "inadvertent" repeal of the "two-thirds" majority proviso in the original *Act, of Union*, by the Act of 1853 providing for an elective council. "Rep. by pop." could now be carried by a bare majority, and Dorion himself, as we shall see, was ready to act upon this hypothesis.

by pop." was now fairly inescapable. "There is no way," Brown wrote evenly on May 16, "but my way—representation by population." When Brown's original resolution for the select committee finally went to the vote on May 19 it was carried by a majority of eleven votes, 59 to 48, after what Brown pronounced to be "the best debate on the question we ever had in parliament—calm, temperate, and to the point." It was "the first vote," he added, "ever carried in parliament in favour of constitutional change." The names of John A. Macdonald, Galt, and Cartier, however, were still recorded among the "nays": Macdonald's after opposition to the whole principle of federation so openly avowed that it drew a sarcastic inquiry from Brown and disclaimer from Cartier with regard to the real policy of the government in 1858.

On May 20 Brown reported that "my committee had its first meeting at noon to-day." There was much banter about the origins of the plan but it is related that when the decision was reached to "sit with closed doors" in order to allay all inhibitions arising from inconsistency or partisanship, Brown himself strode to the door, turned the key in the lock and put it into his pocket. "Now gentlemen you must talk about this matter, as you cannot leave this room without coming to me."

Within a little more than three weeks no fewer than eight sessions of the select committee discussed their problem in an atmosphere of impending crisis. The secret and confidential nature of these discussions proved to be an asset of the first importance and the lesson was afterwards applied, as we shall see, with telling effect to the Charlottetown and Quebec conferences. All the surviving evidence indicates "useful and harmonious discussion," "calm and full deliberation" conducted "frankly and in a spirit of compromise." The Sandfield Macdonald Government, bogged down by intolerable infirmities, had resigned on March 21, still however without a direct vote of no confidence. The Taché-Macdonald Government with scarcely more cohesion within their ranks lost a division by a margin of two votes on June 14. The same day Brown as chairman of the select committee reported to the House "a strong feeling . . . in favour of changes in the direction of a Federative system applied either to *Canada* alone, or to the whole British North American provinces." Three votes only were recorded in the committee against this report but it is still significant that two of the three were the fellow-clansmen John A. and Sandfield Macdonald.

The *dénouement* to "the great coalition" now followed rapidly. The Taché-Macdonald Government met the adverse vote of June 14 by unanimous advice to the governor-general to dissolve the House for a third election within the span of a little more than three years. Had Monck acted upon this advice it is probable that "rep. by pop." would have dominated the hustings and the new House. This was conceded by John A. Macdonald himself after the crisis was over.[1] Fortunately Lord Monck determined to act upon his own initiative and redoubled his efforts towards a broader coalition which he had sought in vain at the fall of the Sandfield Macdonald Government in March. After two days of "constant interviews with gentlemen representing the different parties in Canadian politics" he replied to Taché by a formal written memorandum urging with all the suasion at his command another effort at coalition and compromise. A government caucus was held in John A. Macdonald's office and the party agreed to waive their advice for a dissolution. "The result," Monck reported on June 30, "was that on Wednesday the 22nd an arrangement was made satisfactory to both parties by which three gentlemen who have hitherto been prominent members of the opposition are to enter the Cabinet." The three members were George Brown, Oliver Mowat, and William McDougall; and "the great coalition" thus formed was probably the most dynamic group of men ever assembled in Canadian politics.

VI

The play of forces behind the scenes can scarcely yet be traced with complete certainty. Several members of the House who had long been advocating federation on the lecture platform and in the press had joined the search for compromise and coalition. Alexander Morris had been advocating British American union since the days of the British American League in 1849. His lecture on *Nova Britannia*, four months before Galt's original resolutions of July, 1858, had been published in pamphlet form and sold out within ten days. His first speech in the House in 1862, recognizing the dangers of "Representation by Population, pure and simple," as a remedy for the chronic infirmity of the Union, had foreshadowed a happier solution by the union of the British provinces and the "consolidation of the Britannic power on this continent." Though not a member of Brown's select committee Morris believed it would be "looked back to as an era in the history of this country," and Brown's report in favour of "changes in the direction of a Federative system applied either to *Canada* alone, or to the whole British North American provinces" opened up dynamic possibilities. "Without conferring with any one on the subject" Morris

[1]See above, p. 303.

sought an interview with Brown which may be regarded as the immediate prelude to "the great coalition." There was spontaneous agreement between these two men on a level of national statesmanship that the ministerial crisis,[1] instead of being allowed to degenerate into hopeless chaos in the House and on the hustings, might be utilized "in settling forever the constitutional difficulties between Upper and Lower Canada." Brown stated that he was "prepared to co-operate with the existing or any other Administration that would deal with the question promptly and firmly, with a view to its final settlement." The same assurance was given by Brown to J. H. Pope; and both Morris and Pope were authorized by Brown to convey these views to John A. Macdonald.

In this determination Morris received the approval of more than one of Macdonald's own stalwarts in the House. The Hon. James Ferrier, a life member of the Legislative Council, afterwards reviewed these approaches to the "political millenium" with much shrewd humour: "The Hon. George Brown—I speak it to his honor—was the first to declare what he was ready to do." Commending Brown's proposal and Morris's mission as "a deliverance from the dilemma we were in," Ferrier accompanied Morris to at least one of the ministers and no doubt reinforced the advice of both Morris and Pope to others. The result was a scene which filled the lobbies of the House with astonishment and anticipation. As the House was assembling on June 16 Macdonald and Brown were to be seen in the middle of the chamber in unprecedented and friendly conversation.[2] Acknowledging the messages relayed by Morris and Pope, Macdonald inquired if Brown had any objection to a meeting with Galt to explore the prospects. Brown's carefully recorded reply was "Certainly not." What happened

[1]The adverse vote of June 14 had taken place but a few hours after Brown's report from the select committee.

[2]It is possible that the secret interview between Brown and C. J. Brydges may have had something to do with these improving relations. See above, pp. 307 f. It will be recalled that Brydges had reported considerable progress in exploring the measure of Brown's co-operation: he "wishes an omnibus arrangement to include NorthWest, Intercolonial, Representation, and change of tariff by lowering duties. He would support such a programme & thinks it could be carried. You can judge from this if it is desirable for me to press him further at present." Brydges to Macdonald, Confidential, Feb. 24, 1864. Macdonald Papers, 191. 34 ff. A similar report (*ibid.*, p. 28) had been sent "under cover to Cartier by Monday night's post [Feb. 22]—I am afraid letters where the handwriting is known are tampered with." This of course was in February before Sandfield Macdonald's resignation and there was no suggestion, at that stage, of political coalition. Brydges had "offered him the chair of the Canada Board of Hudson's Bay."

at the famous meeting in Brown's quarters at the St. Louis Hotel has survived in Ferrier's account in the Confederation Debates of 1865:

I do not know that I ought to repeat what was the *on dit* of the day with reference to it . . . that when Hon. Mr. Galt met Hon. Mr. Brown, he received him with that manly, open frankness, which characterizes him; and that, when Hon. Mr. Cartier met Hon. Mr. Brown, he looked carefully to see that his two *Rouge* friends were not behind him—(laughter)—and that when he was satisfied they were not, he embraced him with open arms and swore eternal friendship—(laughter and cheers).

Two days later (June 18) Brown wrote to his wife of "great times" at Quebec:

At the Governor's suggestion they applied to me to aid them in reconstructing the government *on the basis of settling the constitutional difficulties between Upper and Lower Canada.* I refused to accept office, but agreed to help them earnestly and sincerely. . . . The facts were announced to the House to-day by John A. Macdonald, amid tremendous cheering from both sides of the House. You never saw such a scene.

Brown's own refusal to take office which had become almost an obsession with him and his family since his marriage in Scotland in 1862 was overcome at last only by the patient goodwill of the governor-general and by convincing evidence that nothing less could prevent the collapse of all their hopes for a permanent settlement. A caucus of the Reform party urged him "almost unanimously" to take office: the resolution was moved, not perhaps without guile, by Sandfield Macdonald. "Private letters from many quarters," wrote Brown, "did something more, and the extreme urgency of the Governor-General did still more. His Excellency sent a very kind letter, urging me to go in. . . . The thing that finally determined me was the fact, ascertained by Mowat and myself, that unless we went in the whole effort for constitutional changes would break down." Brown's final consent was given at three o'clock on June 22, and Macdonald's immediate announcement to the House was followed by scenes which taxed the resources of the press to describe.

The unanimity of sentiment [wrote Brown] is without example in this country: and were it not that I know at their exact value the worth of newspaper laudations, I might be puffed up a little in my own conceit. . . . I had to make a speech, but was so excited and nervous at the events of the last few days that I nearly broke down. However, after a little I got over it, and made (as Mowat alleges) the most telling speech I ever made. There was great cheering when I sat down, and many members from both sides crowded round me.

Many years afterwards (January 20, 1906) Sir Richard Cartwright, member for Lennox and Addington in 1864, recalled an incident which must have supplied a touch of catalytic humour:

When Mr. Brown, not without emotion, made his statement to a hushed and expectant House, and declared that he was about to ally himself with Sir George Cartier and his friends for the purpose of carrying out Confederation, I saw an excitable elderly little French member rush across the floor, climb up on Mr. Brown, who, as you remember, was of a stature approaching the gigantic, fling his arms about his neck and hang several seconds there suspended, to the visible consternation of Mr. Brown and to the infinite joy of all beholders.

The *Globe* reported the concluding statement of its chief with appropriate veneration: "I wish no greater honour for my children, no more noble heirloom to transmit to my descendants, than the record of the part I have taken in this great work."

The terms of coalition had been reduced, through Brown's insistence, to a precise and definitive compact in writing. The original memorandum, approved by the government and the governor-general, committed the coalition

in the most earnest manner to the negotiations for a confederation of all the British North American provinces. . . . Failing a successful issue to such negotiations, they are prepared to pledge themselves to legislation during next session of parliament for the purpose of remedying existing difficulties, by introducing the federal principle for Canada alone, coupled with such provisions as will permit the Maritime Provinces and the North-West Territory to be hereafter incorporated into the Canadian system. . . . For the purpose of carrying on the negotiations, and settling the details of the proposed legislation, a royal commission shall be issued, composed of three members of the government, and three members of the opposition, of whom Mr. Brown shall be one, and the government pledge themselves to give all the influence of the administration to secure to the said commission the means of advancing the great object in view.

This, however, was not explicit enough for Brown's forthright purpose, and the final compact was imperative for immediate action:

The government are prepared to pledge themselves to bring in a measure next session for the purpose of removing existing difficulties by introducing the federal principle into Canada, coupled with such provision as will permit the Maritime Provinces and the North-West Territory to be incorporated into the same system of government.

And the government will seek, by sending representatives to the Lower Provinces and England, to secure the assent of those interests which are beyond the control of our own legislation, to such a measure as may enable all British North America to be united under a general legislature based upon the federal principle.

It was already determined to send a Canadian delegation to the approaching conference on maritime union at Charlottetown and also "to England . . . to the Imperial government."

VII

The dramatic decisions of that sweltering June day of 1864—the weather was "fearfully hot" and Brown "got home at 2.30" in the morning—warranted the conviction which he committed at the time to the intimacies of a hurried letter to his wife: "The whole movement is a grand success, and I really believe will have an immense influence on the future destinies of Canada."

Following two months of meticulous preparation and in defiance of specific instructions to the contrary from the Colonial Office as late as August 9, "the great coalition" projected their case for a general federation into the Charlottetown conference on September 2. After a whirlwind tour of Halifax, Saint John, and Fredericton they reconvened with maritime delegates in Quebec on October 10, and within three weeks the Quebec Resolutions laid down the framework for one of the most difficult and complicated and successful systems of federal government in modern times. A few weeks later (December 3, 1864) the Colonial Office endorsed the "patient sagacity" and apparently "unanimous conclusions" of the Quebec Resolutions as the best possible "framework of a measure to be passed by the Imperial Parliament." The plan was "in the highest degree honourable to those who have taken part in these deliberations," and Cardwell, the Colonial Secretary, after "the most deliberate consideration," announced that "Her Majesty's Government will render you all the assistance in their power for carrying it into effect." How decisive and indispensable that "assistance" was to be could scarcely have been foreseen on December 3, 1864. From that point the tide moved irresistibly forward, submerging shoals and many a headland too in its flow. It would be hard to match this record of high-pressure statesmanship even in the achievements of the federalists of 1787 in the constitution of the United States.

But while "the great coalition" may truly have been the mainspring of federation, and while the key that wound up that clock may have been in a narrower sense the ineluctable issue of "rep. by pop." in the hand of George Brown, let it be repeated that there were coercive factors behind "the great coalition" itself—"events stronger than advocacy, events stronger than men"—which continued to function increasingly until confederation was won. Prodigious as the exploits of "the great coalition" proved to be, the circumstances themselves were scarcely less so. If the Canadian confederation was not a miracle, assuredly in any other circumstances it would have been; and even in the circumstances of 1864 it might have been, without "the great coalition." The temperature and pressure, so to speak, under which "the great coalition" thus came to function had almost the effect of cosmic phenomena upon the destinies of the British provinces. No experts in politics, on the other hand, could have guided those destinies with a surer touch. The miracle of confederation was the conjunction of men and circumstance; the combination of discerning statesmanship with "the contingent and the unforeseen." Had R. J. Uniacke been still alive he might have found in the miracle of 1864 the vindication of his faith: "Providence has destined such a Country for some great and mighty purpose. . . . The time is come for laying its foundations."

Chapter Seventeen

UNION "A FIXED FACT":

FRAMEWORK OF FEDERATION

HOW delighted we were to find that political bitterness had ceased. We all thought, in fact, that a political millennium had arrived. . . . Immediately after the close of the session, the agreement entered into was fully carried out." Thus spoke James Ferrier in the Canadian Legislative Council eight months after "the great coalition."

On the surface there was scarcely a sign of the ferment of constructive statesmanship which filled the summer months of 1864. It was well known in Canada that a conference on maritime union was in the offing with unprecedented unanimity on both sides of the Atlantic. As late as August, long after the framework of federation had taken form under the handiwork of "the great coalition," the other parties to confederation, the Colonial Office included, remained in almost complete ignorance of the Canadian strategy. When permission was sought for Canadian delegates to attend the Charlottetown conference it was intimated to them that "as the Delegates were appointed solely for the purpose of considering the Legislative union of the Lower Provinces, it would not be competent for them officially to discuss the larger and more novel proposal now made by Canada"; and when the Colonial Office finally heard, by way of Nova Scotia, of the proposed Canadian delegation, Cardwell addressed to Monck a curt request for an explanation. Monck's reply was a laboured apology for the intrusion into what was conceded to be "the primary object of the conference." On August 9 Cardwell himself wrote that "the official Mission of the Delegates should be limited to the Union of the Lower Provinces."

During the summer of 1864 an unofficial delegation from Canada including fifty-three from the legislature and a group from the Canadian press toured the Maritimes under the genial direction of Thomas

D'Arcy McGee. Reaching Portland over the Grand Trunk in a deluge of rain on August 4 the party ran the gauntlet of Confederate gunboats to attend "banquets" at Saint John and Halifax.[1] McGee "the orator of confederation" appealed for a general union of the British provinces, only however "to find the mass of the people opposed to the scheme." Later in the month the official Canadian delegation to the Charlottetown conference sailed down the St. Lawrence in the *Queen Victoria*. Ferrier afterwards recalled "standing on the bank of the river at Rivière du Loup, seeing the steamer pass down, and I wished them God-speed." More than one observer at that moment shared Ferrier's concern for the doughty argonauts on board the *Queen Victoria* with the destinies of Canada in their keeping. The golden fleece which inspired their mission presented a challenge to every resource of Canadian statesmanship. Less than two weeks later, in Halifax, the shrewdest opportunist of Canadian politics made a forecast which subsequent events were to endow with prophetic sanctions:

There may be obstructions [said Macdonald], local difficulties may arise, disputes may occur, local jealousies may intervene, but it matters not—the wheel is now revolving, and we are only the fly on the wheel, we cannot delay it—the union of the colonies of British America, under one sovereign, is a fixed fact. (cheers.)

I

For this new and dynamic outlook it would not be amiss largely to credit Macdonald himself. Up to "the great coalition" his record on confederation is so meagre that his official biographer is hard put to it to assemble any evidence at all. In the first "drive for federation" in 1858 Macdonald's views are passed over in ominous silence. His name is scarcely mentioned in the official correspondence, though it is a safe guess that the resignation on "the seat of government question" in 1858, leaving George Brown and the Clear Grits stigmatized by imputations of disloyalty in flouting the Queen's choice, was part of Macdonald's wily strategy. The "double shuffle" after the fall of the two-day Brown-Dorion Government and the silence on confederation once "the seat of government question" was settled in 1859 would be in keeping with this surmise. In 1861, in the debate on "rep. by pop.,"

[1]Many on shipboard "were compelled to sleep on the bare floor. To their complaints, Mr. McGee said, laughingly: 'Besides your transportation, you were only promised your *board*.' . . . The trip was made in safety and comfort, Mr. McGee . . . being the life of the party." Cameron, *Memoirs of Ralph Vansittart*, 172 f.

Macdonald appears for once to have discussed federation in some detail in the House, in terms which he was careful to recall in the Confederation Debates of 1865. Let the Civil War in the United States, he said, "be a warning to ourselves that we do not split on the same rock":

The fatal error which they have committed . . . was in making each state a distinct sovereignty, and giving to each a distinct sovereign power, except in those instances where they were specially reserved by the Constitution and conferred upon the General Government. The true principle of a Confederation lay in giving to the General Government all the principles and powers of sovereignty, and that the subordinate or individual states should have no powers but those expressly bestowed on them. We should thus have a powerful Central Government, a powerful Central Legislature, and a decentralized system of minor legislatures for local purposes.

"As to my sentiments on Confederation," Macdonald affirmed during the Confederation Debates of 1865, "they were the sentiments of my life, my sentiments in Parliament years ago, my sentiments in the [Quebec] Conference, and my sentiments now." The fact remains, nevertheless, that Macdonald had opposed the appointment of Brown's select committee of twenty in terms so hostile to federalism in any form that Cartier in the House had been driven to dissociate himself from them: "That is not my policy." Though a member of Brown's committee Macdonald voted in a minority of three against its report "in favour of changes in the direction of a federative system." His approach to "the great coalition" was equally reluctant. To one of his own party stalwarts, as we have seen, he once wrote bluntly that "as leader of the Conservatives in Upper Canada" in June, 1864, he "then had the option either of forming a coalition government or of handing over the administration of affairs to the Grit party for the next ten years." To another, equally critical of coalition, he added the convincing commentary that "if the Conservatives have not sense enough to see that the coalition must be carried through and supported, the consequences must be that the whole Government will be handed over to the Grits." "I am so strong a party man, and as a general principle so opposed to Coalition," he reminded yet another party stalwart, "that I strained every effort to form a Government . . . on purely Conservative principles." After the adverse vote of June 14, 1864, as we have seen, Macdonald had advised a dissolution and a third election in three years. But the fact that the caucus of the party which responded to the Governor-General's appeal to reconsider this advice was held in Macdonald's own office would seem to indicate that the supreme moment of decision was approaching. At this stage, said

Ferrier in the Confederation Debates, Macdonald "at a very quick glance, saw there was an opportunity." To which a critic in the House retorted "Saw his advantage." "Saw there was an opportunity," resumed Ferrier, "of forming a great and powerful dependency of the British Empire." Somewhere probably within the *nuances* of those lines lies one of the most dynamic decisions in Canadian politics.

Once Macdonald had put his hand to the plough however he drove forward to the end with incomparable steadiness. Almost alone among the fathers of confederation he followed a consistent course of action attended by increasing power until his ascendancy was unquestioned. Cartier, who staked his political fortunes more precariously upon the outcome, shared Macdonald's ascendancy but with much less to gain and much more to lose.[1] The maritime leaders, as we shall see, took still graver risks and paid a much heavier price. Tilley, who staked his government and his name on the same cause, went down at first to defeat and obloquy but emerged at last in the same august company. Tupper, whose indomitable courage and sagacity in the cause of confederation will stand comparison with any, stood loyally aside, like McGee, at the end in the interests of harmony and conciliation. Brown resigned from "the great coalition" in December, 1865, after confederation seemed assured, and Galt in August, 1866. Neither was a member of the government when the *B.N.A. Act of 1867* was passed.

Macdonald, on the other hand, established over both the substance and the method of confederation an early mastery that grew steadily without eclipse. How far and fast it was necessary for him to travel may be seen from the signposts along the way. In June, 1864, his group of 22 Conservatives from Canada West had been the smallest of the four main groups in the House. It was clear that no coalition could function without the Clear Grits (39) and the Bleus (38); and conversely that a coalition between Brown and Cartier could command the voting power in the House. From this *impasse* Macdonald emerged with easy and sustained assurance until in the end he stood incontestably first among them all. At Taché's death it was agreed to continue the coalition under the unobjectionable premiership of Sir Narcisse Belleau. With Sir Narcisse in the Legislative Council—a life member from Quebec—and Macdonald as the recognized leader of the

---

[1]Cf. McGee's impulsive opinion at the time of "the great coalition": "Brown has given the greatest exhibition of moral courage I ever knew or read of in political history. . . . Next to Brown, the man who has taken the greatest risks to his political future by his course in this matter is Cartier. . . . He must make it a success or give up his political power forever. He has put his all to the hazard." Cameron, *Vansittart,* 168 ff.

coalition in the House, this meant that Macdonald himself took the helm. Politics, Lord Morley once said, is "the art of the possible." Measured by any standard of his day Macdonald's artistry from "the great coalition" to confederation was politics upon the highest level. From the Colonial Office and from the Queen he then received a K.C.B., with more than one tribute to his amazing skill and versatility. Galt and Cartier were offered C.B.'s which both declined, justifiably, as incommensurate with their services. It is not on record that George Brown expected or received anything. There was a time in 1866 when the Governor-General, doubting Macdonald's goodwill and perhaps even his good faith in implementing the solemn pact of "the great coalition," was on the point of asking for his own recall in protest. Macdonald's reply may stand as the epitome of assured mastery:

No one is more anxious than I am that the event which will make us historical should be carried to completion with as little delay as possible. We do not know what a day may bring forth, and not with my will would another person take my position in completing the scheme for which I have worked so earnestly.

But, my dear Lord Monck, the proceedings have arrived at such a stage that success is certain and it is now not a question even of strategy. It is merely one of tactic. . . .

With respect to the best mode of guiding the measure through the House, I think I must ask Your Excellency to leave somewhat to my Canadian Parliamentary experience. . . . To you belongs, as having initiated, encouraged, and I may now almost say completed, the great scheme of Union, all the κῦδος . . . which must result from being the founder of a nation. . . . It is my greatest pleasure to believe that with your support and under your sanction I have not been uninfluential in carrying to completion the union of British North America.

II

There is every evidence that the argonauts on board the *Queen Victoria*, to whom Ferrier wished God-speed at Rivière du Loup on their way to the Charlottetown conference, had by that time charted their course with great accuracy. This was true not only for the measure itself but for the method.

On August 26 Brown as President of Council was still "hard at work with our constitutional discussion" and reported that "everything goes as well as we could possibly hope for. I do believe we will succeed. . . . It will be an immense thing if we accomplish it. . . . There is no other instance on record of a colony peacefully remodelling its own constitution." Thenceforth this readiness and resourcefulness became apparent at every stage. A few days after the visit of Galt, Brown, and

Cartier to Government House in Fredericton Lieutenant-Governor Gordon was referring (September 12) to "the scheme of federation which had been agreed upon by the Canadian Cabinet." Already Gordon was grudgingly impressed by it, though he little thought how triumphantly "the erratic course of this ambulatory conference," as he derisively called it at that stage, was to culminate at Quebec. A few days later, after much ingratiating discussion with Galt, Gordon was able to relay to Cardwell the most advanced forecast of Canadian federalism yet to be found in the official despatches of that time—a circumstance which may help to explain Cardwell's alacrity more than two months later in accepting without delay the Quebec Resolutions as the "framework" of confederation. Even the division of powers (ss. 91 and 92) in the final Act is forecast in convincing detail.[1] The overwhelming strength of the central government in finance, transportation, and the military and naval powers of the nation; the priority of the central government over the provinces not only in the creation of the new federation[2] but in the allocation of residuary powers; the care taken to safeguard the conventions of the British parliamentary system in both federal and provincial spheres of government; the acceptance of representation by population in the lower House, and of sectional appointments in the upper; all these and many other details at that stage reflect the thoroughness with which "the great coalition" had done its work. When the "ambulatory conference" finally reached Quebec the pace at which it was moving towards the Quebec Resolutions was such that the Canadian delegation was requested to forecast a day in advance the resolutions that were to come up the following day in order to enable the breathless delegates from the Maritimes to keep up with the discussion. The whole list of seventy-two Quebec Resolutions was completed, as we shall see, in less than three weeks.

With this body of doctrine already woven into a concerted plan the immediate task before the argonauts on the *Queen Victoria* was one of advocacy. No better team could have been chosen for the purpose. By September, 1864, they had been functioning for two months as a cabinet with long sessions of secret and constructive preparation behind them. Nothing contributed more in the long run to the success of this second foray into federalism than the secrecy and speed of all the

---

[1]One curious and interesting exception: education which was assigned to the provinces carried the proviso "with the exception of Universities."

[2]Cf. *B.N.A. Act of 1867*, ss. 3 and 5: "The Provinces of Canada, Nova Scotia, and New Brunswick shall form and be one Dominion under the name of Canada. . . . Canada shall be divided into four Provinces, namely Ontario, Quebec, Nova Scotia, and New Brunswick."

conferences. Brown's select committee with the door locked and the key in the chairman's pocket had been a foretaste of this ingratiating procedure. The exclusion of the press was irksome of course to newspaper men and costly in terms of public opinion since it left uninformed critics of federation in possession of the field until the conference reached Toronto where Brown for the first time was able to divulge the main outlines of the scheme. Within doors, on the other hand, at Charlottetown and Quebec and later on with the Colonial Office where the lessons of 1858 had already been well learnt, the gain in mutual confidence and responsiveness proved invaluable. The speed too was phenomenal. One of the maritime delegates confessed that at Quebec "where they kept us for sixteen mortal days . . . they treated us well, they, however, worked us well too. (Cheers and laughter.)" Few could stand the pace without faltering. At Quebec moreover the whole Canadian cabinet was in session, moving in high gear, and the deliberations reflected the confidential usages and conventions familiar to executive councillors from all the provinces when projecting government measures on the administrative level for subsequent action through normal channels of legislation. The most active delegates were men at this time in the prime of life, endowed with unique and varied gifts. Macdonald in 1864 was 49, Galt was 47, Cartier barely 50, Brown 46, McGee 39, Tupper 43, Tilley 46. The Canadian quartet whose performance at Charlottetown and Halifax first won their maritime colleagues to the plan for federal union were singing not only in close harmony but in parts for which they were ideally cast.

Macdonald's uncanny skill in political improvisation was already well known at Halifax. This prince of political opportunists, for the first time, recorded his verdict on the feasibility of federation, and it lost nothing in its effectiveness from Macdonald's openly avowed preferences for legislative union. If politics was in truth "the art of the possible" here was the word of the most consummate artist of his own day or of any other in British American politics: "We must consider what is desirable and practicable. Everybody admits that Union must take place sometime. I say now is the time." This unremitting stress upon the hour and the perils of the hour was reinforced by a body of doctrine which Macdonald made peculiarly his own. The need of a "strong central government" with "rights of sovereignty" to forestall the fatal defects of "state rights" in the United States was an obvious corollary of federalism at that moment fighting for its life, "not without dust and heat," across the border. This doctrine Macdonald never ceased to avow as long as he lived: in the expansion of Canada after

1867, in the *B.N.A. Act of 1871*, in the federal control of "Dominion lands" in the West, in the building of the C.P.R., and in many other aspects of national policy. But the lesson was easily taught in 1864 when Oliver Mowat, the apostle of "provincial rights" for thirty years afterwards in Ontario, and George Brown who had been satisfied with the nebulous form of "some joint authority" in the Clear Grit resolutions of 1859, and Cartier the guardian of all the cherished rights of French Canada, could all underwrite the *B.N.A. Act of 1867*. Next to Macdonald's assertion that "now is the time," no more skilful exploit of political opportunism could have been devised for the tensions of 1864 than Macdonald's doctrine that this was to be the pattern of Canadian federalism.

The other parts in the Canadian quartet were equally appropriate. After Macdonald and "Colonial Union" the next toast on the list at Halifax was "British American Commerce" coupled with the name of Galt. Concerned as always with "objects of material advantage" Galt represented to the Maritimes in 1864 the most spectacular features of Canadian economic development for more than a decade—the big land companies, the Grand Trunk, the rise of Canadian industry, its vindication against the Sheffield manufacturers in 1859, above all the drive for the Intercolonial. To Gordon who had "a good deal of conversation with the Canadian ministers" Galt appeared to be "by far the ablest of their number. . . . He developed to me at considerable length the details." By the time of the Quebec conference Galt's polished address and resourcefulness had won a commanding place. McCully of Nova Scotia afterwards referred to his appearance at Charlottetown in terms of facetious respect: "mighty in finance, great in statistics, and wonderful in political skill—(cheers)—he charmed us for another half day." The Canadian expert on "material advantage" could demonstrate that federation was economically and fiscally sound and feasible.

George Brown, according to the same shrewd witness, appeared at Charlottetown as an expert of another order. "Last but not least," said McCully, "followed my honorable friend from Upper Canada, Mr. Brown—(cheers)—enlightening us, and producing sensations so overwhelming that we almost forgot where we were. (Great cheering and laughter.)" Brown's role at Charlottetown must have been notable at least for its novelty. By the Conservative press and by the *Globe* itself the Maritimes had been taught for ten years to regard him as the troubler of Israel. Here was the arch-sectionalist of Canadian politics, the inveterate foe of Grand Trunk, the factious censor of the Queen's choice of Ottawa as the capital of the province and the *Militia Bill* of 1862, the covenanting zealot of the Corrigan trials, the adversary of the Hudson's Bay Company and of Intercolonial, the apostle of westward expansion into Rupert's Land, the uncompromising champion of "rep. by pop." for the Canadian union. Every one of these issues except the last two was now waived in the interests of confederation. The results of the Quebec conference were announced for the first time by Brown himself in his own bailiwick at Toronto, and it was there that the Charlottetown conference for maritime union was formally adjourned "sine die" in favour of the larger federation.

The fourth in the Canadian quartet at Charlottetown was undoubtedly Cartier; and in one sense his case for confederation was not only the first there in point of time but the most distinctive in counterpoint and harmony. The guardian of French interests in the Canadian union and the bulwark for ten years of the Conservative party, Cartier now advocated federation with four English-speaking provinces of the Atlantic seaboard and with the unpredictable regions of the West. "What was required to make a great nation," Cartier said at Charlottetown, "was the maritime element." Canada already had the territorial range and population. A British American nation required assured access to the sea. With this national comprehensiveness and power without must be combined the preservation of historic rights and interests within. Cartier's resolute purpose here was acclaimed at Quebec. "They would all have desired to effect a legislative union had it been possible," said Galt at Toronto, "a central government extending its aegis over all interests."[1] What "rendered this impossible" was the historic role of Lower Canada. Federalism was the price of this diversity. Cartier's support, nevertheless, for "strong central government" was an object lesson in courage and statesmanship. "Cartier was as bold as a lion," Macdonald once said, "and but for him Confederation could not have been carried." It was McGee's opinion, as we have seen, that next to George Brown, Cartier had "taken the greatest risks" for confederation. He had "put his all to the hazard." Galt, too, after a longer and closer association with Cartier than McGee's, added the same tribute on behalf of Canada East at the conclusion of the conference at Toronto: "There was no man in the whole length and breadth of British North America who had shown a greater degree of self-sacrifice than his friend Mr. Cartier."

To this key-note of courage and statesmanship the Canadian quartet presented their case at Charlottetown with inimitable harmony. Without abusing the metaphor unwarrantably it may be added that McGee's classic diction supplied an appropriate accompaniment. Mc-

---

[1] An anthology could be compiled on this theme from Monck and Gordon, from Tupper and Tilley and Fisher, and of course from Macdonald.

Gee was already known in the Maritimes from the excursions both west and east which he had organized under the auspices of the Grand Trunk in 1861, 1862, and 1864 in the interests of Intercolonial and confederation. The appeal to racial and religious toleration for which he was soon to give his life came with telling effect from a "Young Ireland" exile who had explored the wiles of Fenianism in Boston before embracing the cause of "a new nationality" for British North America. It was in McGee's fiery diction, too, that the overtones of tension with the United States, already audible at Charlottetown and Quebec, reached their most strident pitch: "Canadian vigilance must sleep no more except upon its arms. We have burst into a new era . . . the storm and peril are daily visible in our horizon."

To this accompaniment the solid work of federation began at Charlottetown in unprecedented harmony and goodwill. When the conference reached Halifax Tupper stated publicly that this unanimity applied to every member of it "without a single exception." With oppositions as well as governments represented in the maritime delegations and paced by the "great coalition" from Canada personifying by their very presence their dedication to the cause of federation, the "ambulatory conference" began to move with accelerating momentum. The impact, as Gordon himself was soon to discover, was to be felt not only in Halifax, Fredericton, Quebec, Montreal, and Toronto but in the inner counsels of the Colonial Office. The tensions, too, from the Civil War were to reach in October, 1864, as we shall see, the gravest stage since the War of 1812. "We have been united as one man," said Macdonald in Halifax. "We all approached the subject . . . feeling that in our hands were the destinies of a nation."

III

There were other elements of good fortune in addition to the men and the times. The first "drive for federation" in 1858 had blazed a procedure which enabled the fathers of confederation this time to drive through to spectacular success.

Head's original plan in 1858, more advanced than Galt's, was a conference of delegates from all the British provinces to "meet in Toronto in the month of October next" in order to prepare "the draft of a definite scheme or plan of Confederation."[1] In default of any

---

[1]Galt's resolutions, it will be recalled, had proposed only "a Committee of nine members . . . to report on the steps to be taken for ascertaining without delay the sentiments of the inhabitants of the Lower Provinces and of the Imperial Government on this most important subject."

formal resolution from the House, however, Head's final minute of council proposed only a "meeting of delegates on behalf of each colony, and of Upper and Lower Canada respectively" to explore "with as little delay as possible" the prospects of a "federative union." Even for this the other provinces were not then ready, and the whole scheme incurred, as we have seen, the officious censure of a new administration in Great Britain unfamiliar with the initiative entrusted confidentially to Head by Lytton's predecessors in the Colonial Office. Fortunately the good offices of Lord Carnarvon as under-secretary with Newcastle and Stanley had stood between Head and the censorious wrath of his chief on that occasion. It was equally fortunate that Lord Carnarvon, with that range of interest and experience behind him, was himself to be Colonial Secretary when the Westminster conference assembled to carry the second "drive for federation" through to completion in 1866–7.

For many reasons it was perhaps fortunate too, paradoxically, that the first "drive for federation" in 1858 had not succeeded. One reason alone in retrospect would seem to be conclusive. Without the fierce tensions of the Civil War the powers conceded to the federal government would have been incomparably weaker. The timid concession of "some joint authority" by the Clear Grit convention of 1859 could never have been extended to the design forecast with unanimous approval by Macdonald in 1864: "strong central government—a great central Legislature—a constitution for a Union which will have all the rights of sovereignty except those that are given to the local governments." Despite immediate failure nevertheless the procedure explored by Head in 1858 proved indispensable in 1864 for it was authorized by Newcastle in 1862 and it was substantially implemented afterwards in London in 1866. For the Quebec conference in particular it was invaluable since Head's problem in 1858 of convening a conference "in Toronto in the month of October next" could now be solved by carrying off the Charlottetown conference almost bodily on the *Queen Victoria* to Quebec in October, 1864. "If it had not been for this fortunate coincidence of events," Macdonald afterwards reflected, "never, perhaps, for a long series of years would we have been able to bring this scheme to a practical conclusion."

But it was within the conference itself that Head's sagacity and courage in 1858 were most effectively vindicated. Elliot of the Colonial Office had been quick to see in 1858 the advantages of an immediate conference "with as little delay as possible" before partisanship and local prejudices could play havoc with their outlook. Such a conference "might prevent or postpone general excitement" since "the best men would be selected from each Government, and would go un-fettered to the preliminary examination of the subject." This initial advantage was secured at Charlottetown and Quebec by the mag-nanimous policy of Tupper and Tilley in including opposition as well as government members in the delegation—a stroke of statesmanship already functioning in Canada in the "political millennium" of "the great coalition." The decision to protect the proceedings of the con-ference behind closed doors where discussion could be kept confi-dential and informal was the logical outcome of this procedure. This in turn was probably inspired, as we have seen, by the happy results of Brown's select committee which had not only sponsored for the first time "a federative system" from both sides of the House but supplied a foretaste of "the great coalition" itself in the freedom and candour of its discussions. Macdonald afterwards added a tribute to this "wise provision" during the critical days of May and June, 1864:

the committee . . . in order that each member of the committee might have an opportunity of expressing his opinion without being in any way com-promised before the public, or with his party, in regard either to his political friends or to his political foes,—agreed that the discussion should be freely entered upon without reference to the political antecedents of any of them, and that they should sit with closed doors, so that they might be able to approach the subject frankly and in a spirit of compromise.

Thus was that "hobgoblin of little minds," the fear of political inconsistency, to be exorcised, all too briefly, from the cause of British American union. Under these auguries, favourable and otherwise, the *Queen Victoria* steamed into Charlottetown harbour on the morning of September 1, 1864. Next day, Friday, September 2, the Canadian delegates were invited to present their case for a general federation.

IV

The details of the "ambulatory conference" from Charlottetown and Halifax to Quebec, Montreal, and Toronto have been pieced together from sources so meagre that the record still remains fragmentary and incoherent.[1] Some of the preliminaries at Charlottetown were incon-gruous to the point of anticlimax. A circus had come to town and

[1]Pope's *Confederation Documents*, and the Macdonald Papers from which they were culled, a few notes by A. A. Macdonald of Prince Edward Island edited by Dr. Doughty in 1920, Gray's *Confederation* by one of the "fathers," a few random reports of the contemporary press compiled by guess-work from the public gatherings at Charlottetown, Halifax, St. John, Quebec, Montreal, Ottawa, and Toronto, a more formal record of speeches on these festive occasions compiled

accommodation for the delegates was disputed with the crowds "who had poured in from the country to see not the Conference but the circus."[1] The maritime delegates had assembled on September 1 to elect their chairman—Col. J. H. Gray, prime minister of Prince Edward Island—and to pay their respects at Government House where Lieutenant-Governor Gordon of New Brunswick was already a guest of Lieutenant-Governor Dundas. When the *Queen Victoria* with the Canadian delegates on board came to anchor in the harbour about noon, the provincial secretary of Prince Edward Island, W. H. Pope, summoned "all the dignity he could" and rowed out in solitary state to meet them. The delegation from Canada was twice as large as Monck had indicated—McGee, Campbell, McDougall, and Langevin as well as the famous quartet. Pope succeeded in bestowing a few of them in the Franklin House on shore but the big four whose impact was soon to dominate the scene remained with three secretaries on board the *Queen Victoria*. The Canadian mission thus began on September 2 under advantages of timing and procedure that were never relaxed until their task was done.

The decision at the outset to meet behind closed doors was of the first importance, for though no formal oath like that of executive councillors was imposed upon the delegates Taché afterwards made it clear at Quebec that "they were bound in honor as gentlemen to preserve secrecy." This in itself may account in part for the paucity of evidence. In this too the conferences from beginning to end ran the gauntlet of an uninformed and critical press, and of all the maritime governors who remained almost equally uninformed in covert opposition until the Quebec Resolutions were placed in their hands. Tupper defended this procedure from the outset "not because there was any desire to conceal its proceedings, but in order that the confidential character of the Delegates might lead to speedier results." At Halifax Cartier and Brown and Tilley all replied with growing assurance to the restiveness and criticism of the press. Deliberations had been "carried on with closed doors" confidentially and "secretly" and in a "conversational manner," but their task had been nothing less than welding "fragments . . . into a great nation." They were "right in studiously refraining at present from all public discussions." From

by the Hon. Edward Whelan of P.E.I. (*The Union of the British Provinces*: new edition ed. by D. C. Harvey in 1927) and *obiter dicta* of the fathers of confederation from the voluminous debates of the ensuing two years. See Whitelaw's scholarly research in *The Maritimes and Canada before Confederation*, chaps. x and xi.

[1]*Id.*, p. 220.

the "delicacy of our mission [this from Tilley] it was absolutely necessary that such informal discussions should be carried on with closed doors." At Quebec, where the rule of secrecy was formally moved and seconded by Macdonald and Tilley, Taché, now chairman of the conference, still defended their procedure with uncompromising candour. The Board of Trade, he said, "might expect something from him as to the secrets of the Conference; but if they did they were much mistaken. (Laughter.) The members were not sworn; but they were bound in honor as gentlemen to preserve secrecy." Nobody knew "what modifications or changes might become necessary."

At the Montreal banquet a few days later Lieutenant-Governor MacDonnell of Nova Scotia who happened to be present referred pointedly to "the mist of secrecy which has hung over their proceedings" and suggested that "the hour has come when public opinion should be brought to bear a little on matters in which the general public is so deeply interested." It fell to Cartier and McGee in no uncertain terms still to defend the "confidential" relations of the delegates and "the delicacy of the trust reposed" in them against uninformed criticism, gubernatorial and otherwise. In the midst of tension over the St. Albans raid McGee's calculated indiscretion could scarcely have been absent from many minds: "If you ask, wherefore this Conference with closed doors at Quebec, why all this mystery, why this assembling together of their Excellencies' advisers at Quebec, leaving Governors and Lieutenant Governors in the meantime deprived of their counsels ... he would give the answer in one word, *circumspice*. . . . Look around you to the valley of Virginia . . . to the mountains of Georgia. . . . They found their justification in the circumstances of British North America, and of Republican North America."

At Toronto after the completion of the Quebec Resolutions and the formal adjournment ("sine die") of the maritime conference McCully of Nova Scotia could speak with less restraint of the Canadian mission. There is general agreement that at Charlottetown Cartier with his plea for a "maritime element" and "a great nation" opened the case for a general federation. Macdonald "in that pleasing, chaste, and classic style for which he is distinguished . . . spoke to us half a day," adds McCully, "on the subject of government and governmental institutions," the defects of federalism in the United States and the paramount necessity for strong central government in order to "build up a great empire of these Provinces." In the "conversational" discussion which ensued Macdonald took high ground from which the conference never afterwards retreated, exploring no doubt the preferences which he shared with the Maritimes for the maximum of legislative union. "Close upon him," continued McCully, "came Mr. Galt, mighty in finance, great in statistics, and wonderful in political skill—(Cheers)—he charmed us for another half day." "Last but not least" came George Brown, a sinister figure to maritime interests but now the apostle of "rep. by pop." for the federal House of Commons and of maritime union as the basis of sectional representation in the upper house: "enlightening us," said McCully, "and producing sensations so overwhelming that we almost forgot where we were. (Great cheering and laughter.) I suppose you will hardly believe me when I tell you that the representatives of the Maritime Provinces, who had been convened for the purpose of securing a particular constitution for themselves, having heard your Delegates, adjourned with their work unfinished, if I may perhaps coin a word, unbegun. (Cheers.)"

Already rumours were in the air for a plenary conference on federation at Quebec—a project forecast by Canadian minute of council as early as August 29. On September 7 the conference formally adjourned for Halifax, and two days later, after the usual "banquet" and a ball at Government House, all the delegates, maritime and Canadian alike, left Charlottetown on the *Queen Victoria*. Nothing could have symbolized more aptly the results of that historic week.

On September 10 the delegates reconvened in the old Province Building in Halifax. On Monday the twelfth the invitation of the Canadian delegates for a special conference on federal union at Quebec was formally accepted. By this time it was clear that the initiative had passed beyond the control of obstructive governors in the Maritimes, and a fortnight later Blackwood in the Colonial Office noted that it also was "getting beyond the scope of Secretaries of State." Alexander Campbell, Macdonald's old law partner, had already left Charlottetown for Quebec in order to make the necessary arrangements. Macdonald was able to confirm the plan by telegram to Taché on the twelfth while another telegram to the prime minister of Newfoundland (the formal invitation through the governor could follow later) invited a delegation from that province also to Quebec. The public "banquet" that evening in Halifax, in the opinion of Galt and of many another then and since, marked "an era in the history of British America." Both Tilley and Tupper here announced their support of a general federation as well as the preliminary legislative union of the Maritimes. This was the first impact of confederation upon the public—the most "momentous gathering of public men" which had "ever taken place in these provinces." Lieutenant-Governor MacDonnell still entered a plea for "a worthy and adequate position" for the Maritimes—"some more intimate union among themselves . . . in the first instance . . . which could not but have an effect even with a people so disinterested as those of Canada are. (Cheers and laughter.)" Cartier countered by deprecating the old quotation "Timeo Danaos, et dona ferentes": "the promises we make are made in all sincerity and good faith." After the "railway fiasco" of 1862 the public avowal of Intercolonial and Brown's candour in expounding "the great coalition" must have been a revelation to a Nova Scotian audience. For the first time a "unanimous conclusion" for union was announced if terms "fair to all and acceptable to all could be devised." From Macdonald, as we have seen, came the historic forecast of "Colonial Union" which proved to be not only the first but also the last public statement to be made by him until that prophecy was potentially fulfilled by the decision of the Colonial Office in December:

The question of "Colonial Union" is one of such magnitude that it dwarfs every other question on this portion of the continent. It absorbs every idea as far as I am concerned. For twenty long years I have been dragging myself through the dreary waste of Colonial politics, but now I see something which is well worthy of all I have suffered in the cause of my little country. This question now assumes a position that demands and commands the attention of all the Colonies of British America. . . . There may be obstructions, local difficulties may arise, disputes may occur, local jealousies may intervene, but it matters not—the wheel is now revolving, and we are only the fly on the wheel, we cannot delay it—the union of the colonies of British America, under one sovereign, is a fixed fact. (Cheers.) Sir, this meeting in Halifax will be ever remembered in the history of British America. . . . We have arrived unanimously at the opinion that the union of the provinces is for the advantage of all. . . . Everybody admits that Union must take place sometime. I say now is the time. . . . If we allow so favorable an opportunity to pass, it may never come again. . . . I may state without any breach of confidence—that we all unitedly agree that such a measure is a matter of the first necessity.

The discretion with which this plea of "necessity" was urged in public may well have been discarded behind the closed doors of the conference.[1] For purposes of defence in the presence of unprecedented "military power" across the border, the British provinces despite their "common allegiance . . . were as wide apart as British America is from Australia." Intercolonial must provide "greater security . . . in the hour of danger. . . . This Railway must be a national work." After the War of 1812, "the Oregon question, the Trent difficulty, question after

[1]The Jervois report on the defencelessness of Canada had been under discussion at Quebec just before the delegates left for Charlottetown.

question in which the Colonies had no interest," everything was "to be gained by Union, and everything to be lost by disunion." "We were liable," added Macdonald, "in case England and the United States were pleased to differ, to be cut off one by one, not having any common means of defence. . . . Look at the gallant defence that is being made by the Southern Republic—at this moment they have not much more than four millions of men—not much exceeding our own numbers. . . . We will become a great nation." The corollary of all this was Macdonald's favourite theme, a "strong central government" with "all the rights of sovereignty except those that are given to the local governments."

After the decision at Halifax "the ambulatory conference" at Saint John and Fredericton was now merely preparatory to the plenary conference at Quebec on October 10.[1] Once again the *Queen Victoria* "most abundantly provided with every comfort and luxury that could be desired," and graced this time by the presence of Sir Richard and Lady MacDonnell, was the argosy for gathering maritime delegates from Pictou, Charlottetown, and Shediac on October 5, 6, and 7. On the ninth they reached Quebec and the St. Louis Hotel became the headquarters for all the maritime delegates "as the guests of the Canadian Government."

V

The stream-lined procedure already foreshadowed at Charlottetown functioned at Quebec with speed and precision. Even the weather seemed to conspire to drive the delegates together. It rained almost incessantly during the conference: never surely "since Noah's flood" had they known such a deluge. Since the purpose of the conference was to explore the Canadian plan the Canadian cabinet found itself acting concurrently as executive councillors in preparing their own

[1]While the decision to invite a general conference to Quebec had been reached as early as August 29 before the Canadian delegation left for Charlottetown it was not until September 23 that formal action was taken and a statement (prepared by Brown) issued to the Canadian press. Monck then issued formal invitations through the maritime governors and formal notification to the Colonial Office. The unofficial delegate from Newfoundland had already left on September 21. The delegation from New Brunswick, delayed perhaps by Gordon's fussiness or worse, was forced to leave for Quebec without written credentials. The Colonial Office, hearing of the proposed conference only by way of Nova Scotia, hastened to approve the conference in advance: "as time is important," noted Cardwell, "I have no hesitation in giving the required permission." Blackwood, though still committed to maritime union, added a minute that "this federation movement is getting beyond the scope of Secretaries of State . . . it is of no use to impose restrictions."

policy and as delegates in expounding it on the floors of the conference. Behind the scenes too, as we shall see, Canadian defence was being discussed with Colonel Jervois in person. On October 12 three representatives of the British and Canadian press sought some sort of "compromise between absolute secrecy and unlimited publicity," but the official joint secretariat made up of all the provincial secretaries still met the request with a firm refusal,[1] and the appointment of Major Hewitt Bernard, chief clerk of Macdonald's own department, as executive secretary ensured a methodical attempt to keep pace with the rising *tempo* of the conference. From this fortunate circumstance came such records as Pope was able to compile from the Macdonald Papers for his invaluable *Confederation Documents*.

It was settled also on October 11 that each province (counting Canada as two provinces) should have one vote; that free discussion "as if in Committee of the Whole" should prevail, but that "after vote put no discussion be allowed"; that "each Province may retire for consultation after vote put" but that "after the scheme is settled in Committee of the Whole, all resolutions be reconsidered, as if with Speaker in the chair." At the conclusion of the conference the minutes were to be "carefully gone over and settled, with the view of determining what is to be submitted to the Imperial and Provincial Governments, and what to be published for general information." The fact that "the proceedings of the Conference towards the close of its deliberations were very much hurried," as McDougall, the Canadian provincial secretary, afterwards conceded, complicated this record. Macdonald, whose general supervision over the secretariat had been invaluable, was absent altogether from the last sessions at Montreal and Toronto, through illness and over-work.[2] A letter of George Brown's on October 17 outlined the routine: "Last week the council met at 9 o'clock and sat till 11; the conference from 11 o'clock to 4. Council again from 4 o'clock to 6 or later, and after dinner came letter writing, resolutions, drafting till all hours in the morning. This week we have council from 9 to 10 o'clock; conference from 10 to 2; council from 2 to 6; and conference from 7.30 as long as we like to sit." Even Brown's herculean physique could scarcely withstand this. "I have

---

[1]"It is inexpedient, at the present stage of the proceedings, to furnish information which must, of necessity, be incomplete."

[2]At Ottawa (November 1) Macdonald's "illness excited deep sympathy, and when he resumed his seat after the brief expression of his thanks, he was applauded as if he had made the most brilliant oration ever delivered—thus manifesting the profound respect entertained for him." Whelan, *The Union of the British Provinces*, 130 f.

come to my quarters," he noted on the fifteenth, "weary and worn and with a shocking headache." McCully's rueful report at Toronto has already been noted: "They kept us for sixteen mortal days. Though they treated us well, they, however, worked us well too. (Cheers and laughter.)"

On the third day (October 12) the conference went into high gear with the agreement that "it would tend to the despatch of business before the Conference if the several resolutions intended to be moved were prepared in advance by a committee composed of the delegates of Canada." It would be hard to devise a better background than this for Macdonald's skill as the first parliamentarian of his day. The substantive first resolution for a "Federal Union" passed with the same unanimity which Macdonald and Tupper had asserted in Halifax. Once only—on an inconsequential detail—were the Canadas outvoted by the other provinces and never were the two Canadian votes divided. Many of the most distinctive features of the Canadian federation passed with surprisingly little controversy. To Brown fell the task of sponsoring a "General Government, Local Governments for each of the Canadas and for the Maritime Provinces . . . provision being made for the admission into the Union on equitable terms of the North-West Territory, British Columbia and Vancouver." This too was carried unanimously (October 12).

It is clear that at this stage maritime union (including Newfoundland) was still regarded as an antecedent to the larger federation. This, however, became manifestly impossible when the details of a bicameral federal system came up for discussion. Brown had little difficulty in carrying representation by population for the House of Commons, Prince Edward Island alone dissenting: the historic significance of this for the Canadas had already been explained at Charlottetown. But the problem of the second chamber nearly wrecked the conference. Macdonald and Mowat suggested "three divisions," Upper Canada, Lower Canada, and "the four Maritime Provinces," each division to be represented "by an equal number of members." By this time it was clear that Prince Edward Island would be a chronic dissentient. In vain Tilley proposed twenty-four each for the Canadas and thirty-two for the Maritimes. On the seventeenth the final numbers were fixed at twenty-four for each division, ten each from Nova Scotia and New Brunswick and four from Prince Edward Island. Newfoundland was "now invited to enter" with four members. By this time too it was clear that local governments must be left for each of the Maritimes, and Brown's original plan was amended accordingly. Appointment by the Crown was conceded unanimously in principle but the initial appointments raised spectres of provincial politics which threatened to wreck not only the conference but the Canadian coalition. All agreed that senators, except for Prince Edward Island, should "in the first instance, be selected from the Legislative Councils of the various Provinces," but for once the Canadian suggestion, sponsored by Galt, that they should be chosen in the first instance by lot was overwhelmingly defeated. Brown's remark (October 19) that "a conflict might arise in the Cabinet before the choice was made, and a party administration might be formed" had a familiar ring about it which already belied the harmony of the "political millennium." McCully of Nova Scotia finally hit upon an acceptable formula for initial appointment by the Crown: "the Federal Executive Government upon the nomination of the respective Local Governments," with an injunction that "all political parties be as nearly as possible fairly represented."

With this portent of stormy weather to come the conference moved on rapidly to underwrite the most distinctive features of the Canadian federation. Macdonald's familiar thesis was acclaimed on all sides: "the primary error" in the United States was that "each state reserved to itself sovereign rights, save the small portion delegated. We must reverse this process by strengthening the General Government":

Our present isolated and defenceless position is, no doubt, a source of embarrassment to England. If it were not for the weakness of Canada, Great Britain might have joined France in acknowledging the Southern Confederacy. We must, therefore become important, not only to England, but in the eyes of foreign states, and especially of the United States, who have found it impossible to conquer four millions of Southern whites. Our united population will reach that number. For the sake of securing peace to ourselves and our posterity we must make ourselves powerful.[1]

Macdonald carried unanimous resolutions that the executive authority including authority over all land and naval forces be vested in the Crown to be "administered according to the well understood principles of the British Constitution";[2] that the federal government should "make laws for the peace, welfare and good government of the Federated Provinces . . . and especially laws respecting" no fewer than thirty-two categories of powers, including "trade and commerce," customs and excise duties, "all or any other modes or systems of taxation," "military and naval services and defence," railways and canals,[3] and "generally

[1]Pope, *Documents*, pp. 54 ff.
[2]*Id.*, p. 21, October 20.
[3]Macdonald's stipulation in ss. 28 to include even those "wholly within one Province" if declared "to be for the general advantage" was dropped in Quebec but reinserted under s. 92 of the *B.N.A. Act of 1867* in London.

. . . all matters of a general character, not specially and exclusively reserved for the Local Governments and Legislatures." With the concurrence of the respective provincial legislatures the federal legislature was to "have power to pass statutes for rendering uniform all or any of the laws relative to property and civil rights," except for Lower Canada.[1] Oliver Mowat's support for this was enthusiastic: "I quite concur in one uniform system. It would weld us into a nation."[2]

It is remarkable that even during the bitterest exchanges over the Upper House no appeal[3] was made to United States precedent to claim equality for all the provinces, or to stipulate election, either secondary or primary, for the Upper House, or to emulate the functional powers of the United States Senate. The principle was adopted at the outset (October 13) "that in framing a Constitution for the General Government, the Conference, with a view to the perpetuation of our connection with the Mother Country, and the promotion of the best interests of the people of these Provinces, desire to follow the model of the British Constitution, so far as our circumstances will permit."[4]

The financial resolutions for federation were sponsored (October 22) by Galt, "mighty in finance, great in statistics," whose mastery in that field had already been established at Charlottetown. The intricate regulations of debt adjustment, public works and property, subsidy grants to the provinces "in consideration of the transfer to the General Legislature of the powers of taxation," were all passed with surprisingly little discussion in a single day's session. Since Tilley of New Brunswick was the only other finance minister present Galt had no difficulty in establishing the fiscal preponderance of the federal government in overwhelming detail. The federal subsidy of eighty cents per head was based upon the most modest estimate of local expenditures among the provinces, that of Nova Scotia, and it was not long before the surrender of provincial rights for "the price of a sheepskin" was reverberating ominously from the hustings of that province. An allowance of $63,000 a year for ten years to New Brunswick to meet "large additional charges upon her local revenues" was the first of those interminable adjustments which were soon to vex the resources of national finance. Nowhere was the trend towards "strong central government" more clearly manifest than in the financial schedules of the Quebec Resolutions. During the first "drive for federation" in 1858

---

[1]Pope, *Documents*, p. 33.
[2]*Id.*, p. 82.
[3]Except by A. A. Macdonald of P.E.I. See below, p. 402.
[4]Pope, *Documents*, p. 9.

Galt had been content to see the "general revenue," after paying costs of collection and government, and interest on the funded public debt, redistributed to the provinces: "the surplus to be divided each year according to population."[1] The federal government was now to be endowed with overwhelming powers and priorities in taxation—"the raising of money by any mode or system of Taxation."[2]

How far the St. Albans raid and other tensions of the Civil War in October, 1864, influenced directly the deliberations of the Quebec Conference can only be surmised. Colonel Jervois who had been inspecting Canadian defences on behalf of the British War Office after Gettysburg and Vicksburg presaged the final triumph of the North, and whose report was under discussion in Quebec just before the Canadian delegates left for Charlottetown, arrived in person in Halifax on September 14, 1864, before the "ambulatory conference" had left the Maritimes. At Quebec, behind the scenes, he was discussing revised estimates for the defence of Canada with the governor-general and cabinet, and he returned to Great Britain on the same ship as George Brown in November, 1864, a few days before the reversal of British policy on December 3. A schoolmaster more persuasive than Macdonald or Galt or Jervois may have been abroad to teach the lesson of "strong central government" in 1864.

To Oliver Mowat fell the task of sponsoring (October 24) the powers of the provinces. These resolutions, too, were completed in short order, on the following day. The provincial control of education carried the well-known proviso, sponsored by McGee, "saving the rights and privileges which the Protestant or Catholic minority in both Canadas may possess as to their Denominational Schools at the time when the Union goes into operation." To Mowat also fell the sponsorship of resolutions relating to concurrent jurisdiction[3] and additional powers for the federal government—the appointment of lieutenant-governors by the governor-general in council, the payment of their salaries by the federal government, and the right of reserving or disallowing provincial legislation. That these and other aspects of provincial subordination were sponsored at Quebec in 1864 by Oliver Mowat, the champion of provincial rights for a whole generation after confederation, was also a sign of the times.

[1]Memorandum to Lytton, October 25, 1858, Skelton, *Galt*, p. 243.
[2]*B.N.A. Act of 1867*, s. 91 (3).
[3]Mowat and Tupper were in complete agreement that concurrent jurisdiction over agriculture and immigration would diminish rather than increase the danger of conflict, and that "a common system of jurisprudence" except for Lower Canada would be advisable. "One uniform system," in Mowat's opinion as we have seen, "would weld us into a nation."

From the meagre notes of discussion left by Bernard at Quebec it is obvious that the general principle of a strong central government with residuary powers had been so firmly established from the outset at Charlottetown that it was never seriously disputed. "Consider how insignificant," said Brown on one occasion at Quebec, "are the matters agreed at Charlottetown, to be left to the Local Governments." "Those who were at Charlottetown," Tupper reminded the delegates, "will remember that all the powers not given to Local should be reserved to the Federal Government. . . . It was said then that it was desirable to have a plan contrary to that adopted by the United States. It was a fundamental principle laid down by Canada, and the basis of our deliberations. . . . If it were not for the peculiar conditions of Lower Canada, and that the Lower Provinces have not municipal systems such as Upper Canada, I should go for a Legislative Union instead of a Federal." Fisher of New Brunswick too once declared roundly for "a legislative union if it were feasible."[1] It would be hard to find a better illustration of timing and relativity in politics than the settlement of these basic principles of the Canadian federation during the crucial months of 1864.

As the Quebec conference drew to a close (it moved on to Montreal on October 27, to Ottawa on October 31, and to Toronto on November 2) resolutions to "secure, without delay, the completion of the Intercolonial Railway" and "communications with the North-Western Territory . . . at the earliest possible period" found their way into the seventy-two Quebec Resolutions, but others were crowded out in the haste and confusion of departure. To the last the conference refused to issue even "a synopsis of the scheme" to the press. For the maritime delegations storm clouds were already visible on the horizon, but every local consideration was now subordinated to the imperative necessity of securing the sanction of the Colonial Office. To that end the Quebec Resolutions, duly "authenticated," were to be submitted by the chairman "to the Governor General for transmission to the Secretary of State for the Colonies."

VI

The *imprimatur* of the Colonial Office was now the next step in the cause of British American union, and that sanction, as we shall see, proved to be the determining factor in its consummation. In this respect at least the contrast with 1858 was complete.

The alacrity with which Cardwell had sanctioned in advance the conference in Quebec was a sign of something more than acquiescence.

[1]Pope, *Documents*, pp. 77, 84 f., 59.

Whatever the reluctance of the under-secretaries Blackwood and Rogers to jeopardize maritime union, to which the Colonial Office had been committed for six years, Cardwell's decision in advance[1] bears every mark of spontaneity: "As time is important I have no hesitation in giving the required permission." For reasons which are not far to seek the reversal of British policy, violent and sudden though it seemed to the Maritimes, was already in train, and it proved to be the pivot of confederation.

Monck's first despatch transmitting the Quebec Resolutions was dated November 7, and it was accompanied by a confidential despatch —twenty-four pages in the original draft—which must have exhausted every resource at his command to procure Cardwell's approval. It was necessary at the outset to supplant the universal prejudice of British opinion, and of provincial opinion at this time, against federalism in all its forms, and particularly against the fatal aspects of federalism in the American civil war. Monck insisted, aptly enough, that "confederation" was an "entire misapplication of the term" for the Quebec plan. Instead of "a union of independent communities bound together by a treaty or agreement entered into in their quality of sovereign states," the proposed union would be "expressly conferred upon them by an Imperial Act of Parliament." This, after the sagacious counsels of Head and Galt in 1851 and 1858, was no new doctrine, but there was a corollary which was not without its bearing, then and later, upon the true nature of Canadian federalism. The federal government, dealing not with provinces as such but with individuals everywhere throughout the union, was clothed with authority through its own officers to enforce its own predominant powers: "to the extent of that authority, the Union is not Federal, it is Legislative—Whatever the Union may be called the central government under such a system possesses to the extent of the powers given to it, and for the purposes of the execution of those powers, all the characteristics of a government representing a Legislative consolidation. . . . It secures to the central government . . . the elements of strength and stability."

A second chamber to be appointed by the Crown (preferably, thought Monck, for eight years), a House of Commons elected by uniform representation ("very ingenious and in my opinion unobjectionable"), the appointment of lieutenant-governors by the federal government together with its powers of reserving and disallowing provincial legislation, all reinforced the preponderance of federal

[1]The official Canadian invitations to the provinces and notification to the Colonial Office had been issued only on September 23. See above, p. 323 n. 1.

powers. "My excuse for the length of this despatch," Monck concluded, "must be my earnest desire for the success of this important movement, and my sincere wish to give my humble aid in the furtherance of their object to the public men of these Provinces, who I am convinced have embarked on this great undertaking with the most patriotic motives and the most complete honesty and singleness of purpose."

There were other arguments, however, more convincing to Cardwell in 1864 than abstractions about federalism. After the tensions of the *Trent* affair Newcastle, Colonial Secretary until April, 1864, had been deeply concerned for the defence of the British provinces. The military commission of 1862 which had reported at that stage of the Civil War that Canada was defensible but at a formidable cost in men and money; the necessity for renewing the guarantee for the Intercolonial, whatever Watkin's Italian hand might have extracted for the Grand Trunk; the defeat of the *Militia Bill* in 1862 together with the abrogation of the Quebec agreement of that year for the building of the Intercolonial—all these must have clouded Newcastle's closing months at the Colonial Office with grave perplexity.

But if Newcastle was deeply concerned with defence, Cardwell was obsessed by it, and with the best of reasons. He was in a position to know—better than McGee or Macdonald or Galt—that the outcome of the Civil War was now no longer in doubt. As late as August, 1862, John Rose, as we have seen, had written to Thomas Baring that "the *Union* is *gone*, and that the North are fighting only for a *frontier*." After Gettysburg and Vicksburg in July, 1863, it was clear that the Union was to survive, safe and strong, and that the torrent of anti-British resentment in the triumphant North might soon be freed from the restraints of that desperate struggle. Colonel Jervois had been sent out by the War Office to observe at first hand these rapidly changing conditions in North America, and had visited Canada and the northern states just after the news of Gettysburg foreshadowed the triumph of the North. He had reported that Canada West was now virtually indefensible and that the only sound strategy in case of war was to fortify Quebec and withdraw imperial troops thither until sea power could be brought to bear elsewhere from Halifax and Bermuda in order to readjust the balance.

In the midst of negotiations for "the great coalition" Monck had protested bitterly against this devastating conclusion. A debate in the British House of Commons on June 27, 1864, littered again the press and public opinion in Great Britain with scathing comment. Resentment spread like wildfire in Canada West. A vehement private memorial from Toronto bore the name of "practically every man of any public prominence in the Toronto district without distinction of party"—the Anglican and Roman Catholic bishops, the Chief Justice and Chancellor, the Mayor, the chief dignitaries of the bench, the university, and the militia. In phrases smacking strongly of Principal McCaul's classic diction, "the apprehension of present danger" was disputed as "a sufficient reason for leaving the most populous, the most fertile, and the most extensively cultivated portion of Canada without a British Soldier." Could it be that Canadians were soon to

hear from these same Statesmen, the language which an eminent Historian tells us the Romans used when they withdrew from Britain. They "informed the Britons they must no longer look to them for succour, exhorted them to arm in their own defence, and urged that as they were now their own Masters it became them to protect by their own valour that independence which their ancient lords had conferred upon them". . . .

Alarm . . . is the more lively because they fear it will be regarded as the first step to an end to which no consideration can reconcile them, and which . . . they must view as an unmitigated calamity. They may be told coldly if not insultingly that "Canada can no longer rebel for this simple reason that she has nothing to rebel for"; their loyalty . . . may be a matter of contemptuous surprize to some whose only idol is a cold-blooded utilitarianism. It nevertheless continues to exist in undiminished force,—and it will not be the least painful part of what the People of Canada may be called upon to undergo that they should be treated as Outcasts from the Country which they have ever called their "Home."[1]

Less than a fortnight before the Canadian delegation left for Charlottetown the Jervois *Report*, printed for confidential use in London in February, 1864, officially reached Quebec (August 20) and rumours with regard to its contents were only too grimly confirmed. Colonel Jervois himself, as we have seen, arrived in Halifax on September 14, before the "ambulatory conference" had left the Maritimes, and the Canadian executive council at the Quebec conference was carrying on concurrently the most anxious consultation with regard to the defence of Canada based upon a new plan by Colonel Jervois to include not only Quebec and Montreal but Kingston and Lake Ontario. This undercurrent together with the details of federation itself remained discreetly concealed from the public view, but Macdonald as well as McGee, Whelan, Cartier, and others referred openly to it at public gatherings in Halifax, Montreal, and Toronto. After the St. Albans raid the United States gave notice, effective November 23, 1864, for the abrogation of the Rush-Bagot convention relating to armed vessels on the Great Lakes, though this notice, unlike that

[1]Stacey, *Canada and the British Army, 1846–71*, p. 159.

relating to the Reciprocity Treaty, was subsequently rescinded. The Canadian correspondence with Colonel Jervois, an urgent memorandum by the governor-general to his executive council, and the subsequent minute of council (November 16) after consultation with Colonel Jervois, all attest the tension at this time. Cardwell's thesis to Monck that the time had "arrived when the whole question respecting the relative responsibilities of the Mother Country and the Provinces in the matter of defence should be frankly and freely discussed and determined" was accompanied by the stringent comment that the defence of Canada "must ever principally depend upon the spirit, the energy and courage of her own People." On November 16 Monck was able to assure Cardwell that the executive council underwrote his main "proposition" and were prepared to recommend to the Canadian legislature the fortification of Montreal and a vote of a million dollars for the militia.

To Macdonald and to more than one of his colleagues this compliance concealed a measure of resentment not only at the rankling comments of the British press but at the official policy of the government. Four months later as a desperate Canadian mission was about to leave for London to resume the discussion of defence after the overwhelming defeat of confederation in the New Brunswick elections of March, 1865, Macdonald wrote to Colonel Gray of New Brunswick:

The indiscreet publication of Col. Jervois' report in England has at present caused a panic in Western Canada, as it shows the defencelessness of most of our provinces, unless protected by permanent works; and the wretched debate in the House of Lords has not diminished the dread of forcible annexation, and abandonment by Great Britain. Fancy the British Empire, for the purpose of defending Canada and the British flag from an impending war, voting £200,000 in all, to be expended at £50,000 a year! . . . In order to shame them we carried the vote for a million of dollars, to be immediately expended, and we go home with that sum in our hands.

Monck observed pointedly to Cardwell (November 16, 1864) that "this is the first instance in which a Colony has offered at its own expence to erect permanent defensive works"; and the strongest argument he could muster in support of federation was the improved prospect for defence. The Quebec Resolutions had provided (s. 67) that "All engagements that may, before the Union, be entered into with the Imperial Government for the defence of the country shall be assumed by the General Government." This in itself was an argument for speeding up federation since Canada alone would be "scarcely justified in concluding single handed final arrangements with Her Majesty's Government which would bind the other provinces" and "exercise an injurious influence upon the chances of carrying into effect the proposed Union." "There is no doubt," added Monck, "that should the Union take place those who are likely to compose its Executive will be animated by the strongest desire to meet the views of Her Majesty's ministers."

VII

This argument, plied with great skill and conviction, must have converged upon the Colonial Office from many quarters as British policy came under discussion during the closing days of November, 1864. The Quebec Resolutions reached the Colonial Office on November 22 and the printing of the despatches presaged at last a full-dress cabinet decision on British North American union. George Brown, the only Canadian behind the scenes when the great decision was announced on December 3, had sailed from New York on November 16 charged with the twin problems of defence and the safeguarding of Hudson's Bay territories for the future federation. No more convincing emissary could have been found to repair the ravages of the lost *Militia Bill* of 1862 than the editor of the *Globe* who had exchanged many a Roland for an Oliver in that bitter controversy. On the same ship and returning to England on the same mission was Colonel Jervois himself whose "great tact and ability which have marked his intercourse with the Canadian authorities" were warmly commended by Monck. This joint influence in reinforcing Cardwell's own views can only be surmised, but Brown discovered that the scheme of confederation gave "prodigious satisfaction." A "private and confidential" report from Brown to Macdonald must surely rank among the "museum pieces" of Canadian politics:

The Ministry, the Conservatives, and the Manchester men are all delighted with it, and everything Canadian has gone up in public estimation immensely. . . .

From all classes of people you hear nothing but high praise of "Canadian statesmanship," and loud anticipations of the great future before us. I am much concerned to observe, however, and I write it to you as a thing that must seriously be considered by all men taking a lead hereafter in Canadian public matters—that there is a manifest desire in almost every quarter that, ere long, the British American colonies should shift for themselves, and in some quarters evident regret that we did not declare at once for independence. I am very sorry to observe this, but it arises, I hope, from the fear of invasion of Canada by the United States, and will soon pass away with the cause that excites it.

The mission of Macdonald, Cartier, Galt, and Brown to London in April, 1865, as we shall see, was charged with the problem of defence in a still more acute form. The death of Lincoln was in itself an ominous portent. It will be recalled that Galt, whose interview with that great man just after the *Trent* affair had left him profoundly impressed with Lincoln's "straight-forward strong common-sense," hastened to add that "the policy of the American government is so subject to popular impulses that no assurance can be, or ought to be, relied on." In the midst of the defence mission of 1865 Galt wrote to Tilley from London (April 29) that "the means and cost of defending the Colonies now occupy such a prominent position before the public that our Union is regarded rather as an accessory to that more urgent question than purely in its public aspect." A few months later General Michel, administrator during Monck's absence and in command of British forces in North America, wrote roundly to Cardwell (October 30, 1865) that without iron-clads on the Great Lakes "Canada is utterly defenceless"; that without control of the French River route to Georgian Bay "England's peril is great. . . . *Western Canada aided by all the power of England, and the whole armed might of Canada would only be defensible for a short time, and must eventually fall.*" In the "pecuniary difficulties of the case," he added, "it may be well to settle first the Federation and Intercolonial Railway questions, although every day lost is one day of peril for England."

It would seem to be unnecessary to explore further the dominant influence of defence in British policy at this time. There is little evidence that Cardwell had any abiding interest, compared with Newcastle's or even with Lytton's after the arrival of the Canadian mission of 1858, in British North American union as such, either maritime or federal. On the other hand his subsequent career in the War Office bore out his dominant interest and success in "calling home the legions" and curtailing expenses to the British taxpayer.[1] Among the motives of the Colonial Office in sponsoring federation and in bearing down relentlessly all opposition to it in the Maritimes, Cardwell himself gives first place to the fact that "it was eminently calculated to render easier and more effectual the provisions for the defence of the several Provinces."[2] A few months later this decision, as we shall see, was stated to the loyalist province of New Brunswick in terms which may well have appeared mandatory:

There is one consideration which Her Majesty's Government feel it more especially their duty to press upon the Legislature of New Brunswick. Looking to the determination which this Country has ever exhibited to regard the defence of the Colonies as a matter of Imperial concern—the

---

[1]See Stacey, *Canada and the British Army*, pp. 206 ff.
[2]To Gordon, April 12, 1865.

Colonies must recognize a right and even acknowledge an obligation incumbent on the Home Government to urge with earnestness and just authority the measures which they consider to be most expedient on the part of the Colonies with a view to their own defence.[1]

On December 3, 1864, a despatch left the Colonial Office which in Brown's enthusiastic report two days later "outdoes anything that ever went to any British colony."[2] Measured by its historic phrases and also, as we shall see, by its results, this must have been literally true. "Her Majesty's Government" had received the Quebec Resolutions "with the most cordial satisfaction." Every appropriate sanction had been met:

With the sanction of the Crown—and upon the invitation of the Governor General—men of every Province, chosen by the respective Lieutenant-Governors without distinction of party, assembled to consider questions of the utmost interest to every subject of the Queen, of whatever race or faith, resident in those Provinces; and have arrived at a conclusion destined to exercise a most important influence upon the future welfare of the whole community.

They had "conducted their deliberations with patient sagacity" and had "arrived at unanimous conclusions on questions . . . calculated under less favourable auspices to have given rise to many differences of opinion." The outcome was "in the highest degree honourable to those who have taken part in these deliberations," and inspired "confidence in the men by whose judgement and temper this result has been attained." Her Majesty's Government, wrote Cardwell, pronounced the Quebec Resolutions "as complete and perfect an union of the whole into one Government, as the circumstances of the case and . . . existing interests would admit," and accepted them as "the best framework of a measure to be passed by the Imperial Parliament." The Governor-General was urged to take "immediate measures" to implement the "project of the Conference," and "Her Majesty's Government will render you all the assistance in their power for carrying it into effect." "A deputation of the persons best qualified" was invited to London to be "present during the preparation of the Bill" and the "passage of the measure through the two Houses of Parliament."

Cardwell little suspected how soon this pledge of "all the assistance in their power" was to be put to the test. Storm signals were already aloft in the Maritimes.

[1]Cardwell to Gordon, June 24, 1865, C.O. 188, vol. 45.
[2]"Nothing could be more laudatory. It . . . praises our statesmanship, discretion, loyalty and so on." At what stage Brown was consulted it is impossible to say but it is reasonable to suppose that he was shown the despatch before it was sent.

Chapter Eighteen

CARRYING CONFEDERATION

THE opposition to federation which developed in the Maritimes —in each of the four provinces—was too general to be the result of personalities or sheer parochialism. The factual record in itself is remarkable for its uniformity.

In Prince Edward Island a series of resolutions was submitted to the Assembly (March 24, 1865) approving the Quebec Resolutions as a "declaration of principles . . . which the House considers just to the several provinces." Neither the mover nor the seconder of the resolutions—W. H. Pope and Colonel J. H. Gray—was by this time a member of the government, and an amendment moved by the new prime minister was carried by an overwhelming vote of 23 to 5 condemning the terms of the Quebec Resolutions as "politically, commercially, and financially disastrous to the rights and interests" of Prince Edward Island. An Address to the Queen (April 3) reaffirmed this uncompromising opposition. The disastrous election in New Brunswick in March, 1865, may have influenced this debate but no inducement from the Colonial Office could mitigate the verdict. Not until 1873, six years after confederation, did Prince Edward Island become the seventh province of the Dominion, three years after Manitoba and two years after British Columbia.

Newfoundland, which was the last of the present Canadian provinces to join the union, shared with Prince Edward Island initial exclusion from federation. By a curious coincidence both had distinguished themselves by responding affirmatively to Head's overtures of 1858. The two Newfoundland delegates at Quebec, F. P. T. Carter, Speaker of the House, and Ambrose Shea, leader of the opposition, returned to Newfoundland convinced if not enthusiastic supporters of federation, but following the reorganization of the coalition government in the spring of 1865 with Carter as prime minister and Shea as a colleague it was decided to defer a vote on the Quebec Resolutions until after a general election. The government was returned but re-

347

mained divided on the issue of federation. The House was prorogued at last in May, 1866, too soon to be swayed by "the great election" which carried New Brunswick into confederation in June. New-foundland remained altogether unrepresented at the London confer-ence which finally launched the *B.N.A. Act of 1867*. For a time, however, it seemed that Newfoundland might be the first of the recalcitrants to follow the original provinces into the union. Terms of union were successfully negotiated in 1868 and embodied, as pre-scribed by the *B.N.A. Act of 1867*, section 146, in addresses to the Queen, only to be overwhelmed by an adverse vote at the polls in 1869. Two at least of the Maritimes were not to be charter members of confederation.

The factual record in New Brunswick and in Nova Scotia is equally emphatic. Instead of submitting the Quebec Resolutions immediately to the New Brunswick legislature as prescribed at Quebec, Gordon and Tilley decided to dissolve the House, which was to expire in any event in June, in order to carry confederation at the polls in March. The result was an overwhelming defeat which was to reverberate through all the other provinces until the verdict was reversed by "the great election" of June, 1866. In Canada, where the Confederation Debates on the Quebec Resolutions were approaching a vote when the news of the New Brunswick *débâcle* arrived, the recalcitrance of the Maritimes served only to confirm "the great coalition" in their determination to succeed. Within a week the same veteran quartet which had carried all before them at Charlottetown and Quebec had decided upon a still more desperate mission to London "to *take stock* of the situation" with the Colonial Office.

Meanwhile the storm of opposition in Nova Scotia was rising to hurricane velocity. The result of the New Brunswick election in March, 1865, even in the opinion of the redoubtable Tupper, seemed to demonstrate that "an immediate Union of the British North Ameri-can Provinces has become impracticable." Tupper, like Macdonald, however, was fortunate in dominating a legislature with two years yet to run. In an attempt to salvage some measure of union from the general *débâcle* Tupper carried joint resolutions in favour of maritime union as a preliminary of the larger federation, only to discover that the Colonial Office would no longer support the policy they had sponsored from 1858 to 1864 except as an integral "part of the scheme for general union": "Her Majesty's Government can give no counte-nance to any proposals which would tend to delay the Confederation of all the Provinces." In the end Nova Scotia was voted into federation by an Assembly which had never discussed the issue on the hustings, which never approved the Quebec Resolutions, and which authorized even the London conference only in the general resolutions of April, 1866, without subscribing to any fixed terms of reference.[1] As a matter of fact neither the Quebec Resolutions nor the London Resolutions were ratified by a Nova Scotian legislature either before or after the *B.N.A. Act of 1867*. The first federal election in Nova Scotia sent 18 out of 19 members to Ottawa pledged to the repeal of federation. The provincial elections, held the same day, returned but two members in favour of federation in a House of 38, and one of the two was almost immediately unseated and replaced by an anti-federalist.

It will be conceded that this record of opposition in the Maritimes is too nearly uniform to be attributable to the perversities of parochial politics. How was it overcome in time for the London conference of 1866 and the *B.N.A. Act of 1867*?

II

New Brunswick, which happened to be the only one of the provinces under a Liberal administration at the time of the Quebec conference, was the only province to submit the issue to a general election. This, however, was due to no excess of "liberal" principles. By the terms of the Quebec Resolutions (number 70) it was provided only that "the sanction of the Imperial and Local Parliaments shall be sought for the Union of the Provinces, on the principles adopted by the Conference." The decision to submit the issue not to the legislature which was due to expire in the following June but to the electors of the province at the approaching elections was scathingly condemned by other parties to the Quebec conference. As early as December 13, 1864, Tupper in Nova Scotia wrote apprehensively to Macdonald of the decision in New Brunswick to defer ratification of the Quebec Resolutions "until after an appeal to the people. . . . Not much time would be lost but the precedent is a bad one." The prospect of a general election in itself inspired latent hopes of obstruction to federation in all the Maritimes, and the hapless results of the election of March 3, 1865, in New Brunswick seriously impaired the prospect of ratifying the Quebec Resolutions elsewhere without an election. When the news reached Quebec in the midst of the Confederation Debates Dorion roundly asserted that "this scheme is killed. I repeat that it is killed," and he redoubled his demand for a Canadian election. Mac-

[1]"In the Legislature of Nova Scotia it was understood that all matters should be entirely open." Ritchie at the London conference. Pope, *Documents*, p. 121.

donald on the other hand recognized "an additional reason for prompt and vigorous action." A fortnight later he wrote bluntly to Gray of Prince Edward Island:

The course of the New Brunswick government in dissolving their Parliament, and appealing to the people was unstatesmanlike, and unsuccessful, as it deserved to be. Mr. Tilley should have called his Parliament together, and, in accordance with the Agreement of the Conference at Quebec submitted the scheme. . . . If he had been defeated, he then had an appeal to the people. As it is, the scheme was submitted without being understood and appreciated, and the inevitable consequences followed.

I regret to find that the course of events in New Brunswick has frightened the Legislature in Nova Scotia. In Canada you see that we carried the Address in both Houses, by majorities of nearly 3–1, and we now send four of our Ministers to England to *take stock*. I quite agree with you that the British Government will carry their point if they only adopt vigorous measures to that end, and we shall spare no pains to impress the necessity of such a course upon them.

But this criticism at long range and after the fact was less warranted on the spot in 1865. The truth was that Tilley had very little choice in the matter. How could a House committed to maritime union and with but six months to run sanction a general federation? An election in any event was inescapable. Tilley quickly discovered that defections not only in his party but in his cabinet would command "a large majority of the members of the Old House." Every newspaper in the province except two opposed "legislating upon the subject previous to a General Election." Any attempt to ratify the Quebec Resolutions, wrote Tilley, "would have been of no avail, as our Governor informed me shortly after our return, that he would not consent that the measure or address should be submitted to the House for their action until after an Election: *and that he had ascertained that he could find a Ministry who would take the responsibility of advising that course*."[1] The only range of choice was the time and manner of the appeal.

Here again the responsibility for an immediate election must rest with Gordon, under private instructions from the Colonial Office to expedite enactment by the British Parliament if possible during the session of 1865. Gordon too had little choice in the matter after Cardwell's official despatch of December 3, 1864, though Tilley and Fisher and many others came to suspect that there was still ample range for indulging his prejudices. By November 21 Gordon was prepared to concede that the Quebec plan "has many merits and is by no means unskilfully constructed," but interminable despatches from

[1]Tilley to Galt, Macdonald Papers, 6, 83. Italics are Tilley's.

Gordon in favour of maritime union or at any rate of a legislative union of all the provinces continued to reach the Colonial Office until the torrent was abruptly stopped by the official decision of December 3.[1] "I need not say," Gordon replied, "that I shall act in conformity with Her Majesty's gracious commands therein signified to me." He immediately offered to place his resignation in Cardwell's hands but the despatch of December 3, according to Tilley, was followed a few days later by urgent "private letters . . . from Mr. Cardwell" forecasting early legislation in London. "These," added Tilley, "placed us in a dilemma . . . sooner than assume the consequences of delay . . . for a year, we reluctantly advised the dissolution."

There can be no doubt that Tilley counselled delay as long as possible in order to dispel ignorance and apathy on the one hand and a whole series of active antipathies to federation on the other. The cabinet was still divided on the issue and Tilley recorded for Cardwell's benefit[2] his formal protest against an early dissolution unless "delay on our part . . . would prevent any action of the Imperial Parliament until the session of 1866."

Tilley's advice might have forestalled more serious delay than this, for the results of the New Brunswick elections jeopardized for a time the whole cause of federation. The House was dissolved on February 8 and the other provinces awaited the outcome with ominous foreboding.

III

The results of the election were unforeseen but many of the factors were unpredictable. It was Gordon's view—and despite his violent prejudices there is no reason to doubt his good faith—that Tilley would be returned to power. "I have no doubt of the triumph of the Government," he wrote on January 30. "At St. John and in the Counties of Westmorland and York the question of Confederation will in some degree affect the result: but in other quarters local interests and local partialities will be almost exclusively considered." Whatever reason there may be to credit Gordon's good faith and goodwill at this stage, there can be less defence for his judgment. The government was overwhelmed 30 to 10. Tilley, Gray, and Fisher were all defeated in key constituencies of the province. "We have been pounded," Gray wrote to Macdonald, "infernally pounded." Gray's own constituency which he had represented for fifteen years went to one of the most violent

[1]Gordon's "confidential" despatch of October 11 filled more than seventeen pages in the N.B. Letter Books.
[2]Enclosed in Gordon to Cardwell, Confidential, Jan. 30, 1865.

opponents of confederation. "Send me a line," he implored Macdonald, "as living proof that the dead upon the field of battle are not forgotten by the friends who survive." What was the reason for this *débâcle*?

"Ignorance and suspicion" would explain much in the rural constituencies but there were formidable factors in active opposition. The clangour about higher taxation, higher tariffs, higher expenditures for Canadian canals, Canadian defence, and Canadian railways had a familiar ring in the Maritimes. A railway to the Pacific, said one enterprising editor, was "a project on which old George Brown has breakfasted, dined, and supped for the last twenty years."[1] In opposition to these hypothetical prospects of westward expansion across the continent was a group of merchants and bankers in New Brunswick advocating "westward extension" of another sort—the extension of the Saint John–Shediac line to the Maine boundary to link up the Maritimes with American commerce to the south. After Earl Grey's withdrawal of the imperial guarantee for the Intercolonial in 1852 New Brunswick had built its own railways, with results that were regarded in 1865 with some pride. The Saint John–Shediac line had a surplus in that year of $40,738 and Gordon referred to it as "a work of which the Province has good reason to be proud"—in construction "inferior to none in North America and certainly far superior to any other in the British Provinces including the Grand Trunk Railway of Canada." Tilley reported to Galt that "the People of St. John have been so wild about the Western Extension question, that any . . . showing indifference upon it was almost certain of defeat." The government had offered a bonus of $10,000 a mile to any private company for the completion of the line to the Maine boundary but "the friends of Western Extension, who are mostly the enemies of Confederation" demanded nothing less than the completion of the line by the government. It was Tilley's opinion after the election that the defeat of all the union candidates for Saint John was due to "western extension" together with "the all but unanimous vote of the R. Catholics." "Had we carried the six members for the City and County of St. John we could have put the address through." It was "western extension," as we shall see, which fought "to the last ditch" against federation in 1866, with resources both from the United States and from New Brunswick which rivalled "the means" forthcoming from Canada for that crucial contest.

[1]A. G. Bailey, "The Basis and Persistence of Opposition to Confederation in New Brunswick," *Canadian Historical Review*, 1942, p. 378.

In the northern and eastern constituencies the deciding factors, wrote Tilley, were "the united Catholic vote" and the "uncertainty . . . in relation to the Intercolonial Railway." The bogey of "the railway fiasco" of 1863 was easily raised. Tilley's scathing comments on Canadian perfidy still rankled in the dour highland temper of Sandfield Macdonald,[1] and they were not yet forgotten in New Brunswick. The anti-unionist press seized upon a remark by John A. Macdonald during the Confederation Debates then approaching a final vote at Quebec to the effect that "the Intercolonial Railway would not form part of the Constitution." Three weeks before the election Tilley begged Macdonald frantically to contradict this impression: "We have always regarded it as the policy of the conference that the subsidy to the Local Governments and the building of the Intercolonial Railway, would be secured to us by Imperial Act. The Delegates from the Lower Provinces could never have consented to the Union on any other terms. . . . No Delegates from this Province will consent to Union unless we have this guarantee and we will certainly fail in all our Elections. . . . Great alarm and anxiety has been created." Macdonald's reassuring telegram that Intercolonial was "one of the conditions on which Constitution was adopted" and that "such conditions will of course be inserted in the Imperial Act" arrived (February 20) too late to allay the suspicions of a second "railway fiasco." Even after the election Gray was still dubious about Canadian policy. "If you withdraw your propositions about the Intercolonial which I gather from some of your observations may be the Case," he wrote desperately to Macdonald on March 13, "I feel the doom of this Province is settled for many a long day." The uncertainty over Intercolonial was apparent on the hustings and at the polls on March 3. When the Canadian delegates got to London a few weeks later to "take stock" with the Colonial Office after the *débâcle,* they found Cardwell in receipt of private letters attributing the defeat in no small measure "to a doubt on the part of the people there as to the sincerity of the Canadians on the subject of the Railway."

A third aspect of the ubiquitous "railway question" probably lost the key constituency of Westmorland County to A. J. Smith, the new anti-unionist prime minister. The gap between Truro and the Bend

[1]"I have a pleasure—a mischievous pleasure—(hear, hear, and laughter) . . . in knowing that the Hon. Mr. Tilley has been defeated . . . the man who went throughout the length and breadth of his province crying out against the good faith of the then Canadian Government." Sandfield Macdonald, March 6, 1865.

(Moncton) was to have been filled in as one of the by-products of maritime union. At Charlottetown the Levesey interests with contracts in prospect were already hovering in the background. After the Quebec conference, as we have seen, Macdonald lost no time in pre-empting the line from Truro to the Bend for the Intercolonial. "I cannot too strongly impress on you," he wrote to Tilley and to Tupper on November 14, 1864, "the necessity of . . . not in any way giving any party the slightest control over the Construction of any portion of the Inter-colonial Railway. . . . Were it suspected that any considerable portion of the Road for which Canada is going to pledge itself was given away to contractors without the consent or sanction of the Govern-ment a storm would at once arise which could not be allayed and would peril the whole scheme." Tupper was prepared to await, with what patience he could command, some reassuring "letter from Mr. Brydges [of the Grand Trunk] telling me that he is prepared to build the Truro and Moncton section of the Intercolonial with the sanction of the Canadian Government. *This is indispensable.*" Tilley, however, was not so happy in this prospect, and Macdonald reported ruefully to Galt his fear that the Maritimes meant "to go on with the R.R. contract" from Truro to the Bend. Meanwhile Smith, in collusion with "western extension," won his seat so handily in the election of March 3 that his by-election as prime minister was conceded by acclamation.

A final complication in the election of 1865, and perhaps the most baffling to account for, was the religious factor. It was conceded on every hand that the Roman Catholic vote was overwhelmingly hostile to confederation. "The Catholic vote," wrote Gray, "led by their Bishop and Clergy went against us almost to a man. What will our friend Cartier say to that?" Tilley was equally mystified. On his return from Quebec he had discussed the prospects with Bishop Sweeny of Saint John who "appeared to fear the large influence of Western Canada. . . . At the conclusion of the conference he was pleased to say that I had removed many of his objections." But the Roman Catholic vote on March 3 was too uniform and uniformly hostile to be the result of local prejudices. "I have not yet been able to discover," added Tilley, "what it was that produced so great a change with the Bishop and People in so short a time—It would have carried nearly every con-stituency in the Province had the Catholic vote been divided, certainly all except York and Kent." Can it be that the covenanting zeal of George Brown and the *Globe* in the bad old days of the Gavazzi riots and the Corrigan trials still re-echoed from the banks of the St. Lawrence?

IV

In Nova Scotia the opposition to confederation came to be over-shadowed by the gargantuan figure of Joseph Howe. Here too, how-ever, as in New Brunswick, there were solid reasons for resistance based upon conflicting interests and a long train of policy.

The myth that Nova Scotian opposition, the most deliberate and implacable of all, sprang from Howe's repugnance to "play second fiddle to that damned Tupper" has had a long vogue in the credulity and partisanship that closed in upon a lost cause and finally submerged it in a grudging acceptance of confederation.[1] It is hard to believe that petty jealousy on the part of one man could have been shared by a whole province to the point of electing, at their first access to the polls, a solid phalanx of 18 out of 19 federal members and 36 (eventu-ally 37) out of 38 provincial members pledged to the repeal of federation.

On behalf of the Anti-Confederation League Howe once recorded for an old friend in the British House of Commons his early reluctance to join the forces of opposition and resistance: "The opposition to Confederation in Nova Scotia did not originate with me. For weeks after the convention broke up in Quebec I took no part in the contro-versy, nor did I express any opinion, even to my personal friends, until the delegates set systematically to work to make the people of the Province believe that I was in favour of their scheme. I then wrote just what was necessary to disabuse the public mind upon that point."[2]

Between Howe and Tupper the rift on federation came early despite their common ground on maritime union and the preference of both for a legislative rather than a federal union. A chapter of accidents had barred Howe altogether from the Charlottetown and Quebec conferences. On August 16, the day on which he sailed for Newfound-land as fisheries commissioner, a letter from Tupper informed him that his name had been "this morning submitted by the Executive Council . . . as one of the delegates to the conference upon the union of the Maritime Provinces." Howe's course had he been able to accept can only be conjectured. Three days before Tupper's invitation Mc-Gee's excursion from Canada had reached Halifax. Howe took them for a trip to Bedford Basin in the *Lily* and made a speech to them at Prince's Lodge which was quoted more than once in the ensuing

---

[1]See L. J. Burpee, "Howe and the Anti-Confederation League," *Transactions of the Royal Society of Canada*, 1916, section II, pp. 409–73.
[2]"The Botheration Scheme," *Morning Chronicle*, Jan., 1865.

controversy. But the quotations were garbled out of their context, for his counsel to the Canadians ran counter to the fundamental pact of "the great coalition." Howe begged them to "take in good part" his appeal to preserve at all costs the Canadian union:

I have always been in favour of uniting any two, three, four, or the whole five of the Provinces. . . . There now come rumours across the land that they are going to split Canada into two parts again. . . . There is at least one Nova Scotian honest enough to say to you this,—that if you do that, you will commit an act of political suicide. . . . I would rather see every public man upon both sides of politics crucified, than I would divide Canada now that Canada is united. Join the Maritime Provinces if you can; but at any rate, stick together. . . . The day is rapidly approaching when the Provinces will be united, with one flag above our heads, one thought in all our bosoms, with one Sovereign and one constitution.

As fisheries commissioner under the expiring Reciprocity Treaty Howe was absent from Nova Scotia for seven months in 1865, ten weeks being spent in Washington. He returned to Nova Scotia to find that the shipping, mercantile, and banking interests of the province were thoroughly alarmed. Along the whole waterfront in Halifax "barely seven merchants," he asserted, "are in favour of the Scheme." In Yarmouth, the second port in the province, "not twenty persons of any position in business or social life" could be found to support it, and old Enos Collins, "the wealthiest man in British America," declared roundly that if he were twenty years younger he would "take up his rifle and resist it." "With an enormous amount of shipping at sea," Howe added, "Nova Scotia must belong to a great Naval Power." The Nova Scotian flag was on all the seven seas and she could not be expected to "commit the care of her commerce to the Canadians who have one paltry steamer in the Gulf in Summer and are frozen up for half the year." Impending conflict with the United States, after Gettysburg and Vicksburg, made British sea power indispensable. British naval expenditures at Halifax were impressive, and there can be no doubt that in the event of war naval operations from Halifax, and Bermuda were relied upon by the War Office to counterbalance the defencelessness of the Canadas. Writing privately to an old admiral who had served his round at the Halifax station and who now sat for Stamford in the House of Commons Howe could indulge both pride and prejudice without restraint: "Our only chance of remaining British is to preserve our old institutions and stay within the Empire. You would not take a Ten Gun Brig into action against an Eighty Gun Ship and you would be dismissed the service, for wasting men's lives, if you did." After "full fraternity with a great British Community, who have an army and navy and are afraid of nobody," why "embark in this crazy Confederacy with a mongrel crew half French and half English and certain to be sent to the bottom at the first broadside"?[1]

By this time it was clear that opposition in Nova Scotia was implacable. Two circumstances brought Howe himself upon the stage. McCully, who had shared with Archibald the chief responsibility for committing the liberal wing of the Nova Scotian delegation to the cause of federation at Charlottetown and Quebec, returned to his post on the *Morning Chronicle* to find the publisher William Annand deeply critical of the plan and openly sympathetic with the banking and mercantile interests of Halifax in opposing it. Howe's financial interest in the *Chronicle* was still very considerable and McCully's attempts to expound federation by citing Howe's magniloquent references to British American union at various stages of his career brought speedy and summary retribution. Howe's published letters on the "Botheration Scheme" were enough to "disabuse the public mind upon that point" with a vengeance, and McCully's relations with the *Morning Chronicle* came speedily to an end.

Meanwhile the decision in New Brunswick to submit the issue to a general election reinforced the same demand for Nova Scotia. It was Archibald's refusal to guarantee any such procedure which brought Howe himself into the field, horse, foot, and artillery. The Anti-Confederation League, organized by Annand and Stairs and the merchants and bankers of Halifax, quickly commanded financial resources that enabled them to carry the fight to every avenue of British politics. It was beyond dispute, the League maintained, that the Quebec Resolutions "could not be presented and carried in any one of the four Legislatures then existing" in the Maritimes. They were never so ratified, and the resort to the *brutum fulmen* of an imperial statute after the stark refusal to submit the issue to the electorate was calculated to fuse the elements of frustration in Howe's vehement career into incandescent fury. A series of baffling rebuffs—from the bitter feud with Hincks and Grey over the imperial guarantee for the Intercolonial to the quixotic recruiting campaign in the United States for the Crimean War—had by this time revealed infirmities of temper peculiarly vulnerable to such "slings and arrows of outrageous fortune." With prodigious powers of appealing to his countrymen still unimpaired, Howe flung himself into a movement which he could not control, and found himself carried by it at last to the brink of a

[1]Howe to Sir John C. D. Hay, Nov. 12, 1866, Burpee, "Howe and the Anti-Confederation League," p. 438.

destiny which of all others he least desired for his native province. He surrendered at last to federation in order to forestall annexation to the United States.

Something of the deadly seriousness of this struggle is to be found in the papers of the Anti-Confederation League and in the interminable polemics of the Howe Papers. For days on end in London Howe toiled with demonic energy upon his "Case" for Lord Carnarvon, upon a new paper on the organization of the Empire for Earl Russell, upon letters by the score for British journals and parliamentarians. In the House of Commons John Bright secured eighty-seven votes for an inquiry into the resistance of Nova Scotia. At one point when it became clear that both government and opposition leaders in Great Britain had committed themselves to federation, Howe girded himself to stand alone if necessary for a final quixotic appeal at the bar of the House. Though the "Case," as he afterwards wrote, was "backed by petitions from thirty-one thousand of our people, and though we prayed but for a few weeks' delay, the British North America Act was passed." With the loyalties of a lifetime torn from their moorings, the Anti-Confederation League's last hope was now the still more desperate expedient of repeal. In some quarters the effect of this futile gesture was more successful than it seemed. When Tupper reached London in 1868, the accredited agent of the new Dominion, he found that "the matter was more serious than we supposed. The duke[1] told me that five of his colleagues . . . were satisfied that Nova Scotia had strong grounds for complaint." There was a time, as we shall see, when even Galt was ready to despair of Nova Scotia, forgo federation altogether, and rely upon a legislative union of the Canadas with New Brunswick to secure "the objects of material advantage" so vital to Galt's conception of British American union.

The measure of Howe's desperation at this time may be surmised both from his sober counsels to his friends and from his reckless prophecies to his critics. After reminding his followers that Nova Scotians had "established some reputation for common sense" and that his own "public life for forty years" had not been "remarkable for reticence when the interests of our country require candour and plainness of speech," he rejected armed resistance or annexation to the United States as "follies akin to madness." His forecast for confederation was equally gloomy. Turning from his own vision of Nova Scotia and the sea—a vision of maritime expansion, then at its peak, in closest association with an imperial sea-power—Howe found the prospect of

[1]Buckingham and Chandos, now Colonial Secretary.

consolidating a transcontinental British nationality in North America uncertain and perhaps forbidding. As the provincial delegates were assembling in London for the final conference of 1866, the Marquis of Normanby, who as Lord Mulgrave had been Governor of Nova Scotia during Howe's own premiership, tried to reconcile these two destinies for the British provinces. Without surrendering his early preference for maritime union he sought to win Howe to the more precarious venture of a general federation. Howe was duly grateful as "an old friend who will ever attach great weight to your Lordship's opinions," but he added a prophecy which was probably the worst and the most reckless of his career:

I have bet four baskets of Champagne—one that Confederation will not be carried—another that, if it should be carried, in a Year after we shall elect our own President and send our Minister to Washington—and two that in less than five Years after this new Nationality is set up, the frontier will be rubbed out, and British America will be incorporated with the Republic. I hope Sincerely that I may win the first, if not, I am sure to win the other two.

There were truer prophecies and profounder convictions than this abroad in British North America. Even for Nova Scotia there was to be "a new and untried destiny" which Howe himself came at last to share. He lived as lieutenant-governor of his native province to preside in the same council chamber where Sir John Harvey had proclaimed the first responsible government overseas in 1848, and he died in Government House within a few yards of the spot where his "honest hand-shake" with old Sir Colin Campbell had closed one of the most brilliant passages of that great achievement.

V

The "new and untried destiny" for Nova Scotia in a British North American nationality was personified in the indomitable figure of Charles Tupper. Tupper's declaration in Halifax after the Charlottetown conference may rank with Macdonald's on the same occasion as the portent of a "fixed fact." "No more momentous gathering of public men," said Tupper, "has ever taken place in these provinces. . . . The great question in which they are engaged will receive at no distant day a satisfactory solution at their hands." The political alliance between these two men was to form for many a day the axis of Canadian politics.

As a discerning act of faith in the destiny of British North America it would be difficult to equal Tupper's decision at Charlottetown to join the Canadian argonauts in their quest for the golden fleece. In one respect the metaphor is singularly inappropriate. Nearly half a million tons of shipping were on the provincial registers of Nova Scotia, but it was Howe rather than Tupper who thought of the future in terms of maritime adventure and naval power. It was Tupper's lot to carry his native province into an era of expansion into the illimitable hinterlands of the continent. Under his administration as minister of railways the Canadian Pacific Railway was organized to reach the Pacific, and the territories of Canada were to be rounded out (1880) to include the remotest British territory in the Arctic. Macdonald's decision on June 14, 1864, had been equally crucial, but Macdonald "saw his advantage" and knew at least what the alternative was likely to be. Tupper's decision at Charlottetown was the sacrifice of an assured prospect as prime minister of Nova Scotia for something which no man in 1864 could foresee, for like Abraham he accepted on faith the place he should after receive for an inheritance and went out knowing not whither he went.

There is every evidence that Macdonald and Tupper fell into step on the issue of confederation with instinctive mutual confidence. Galt and Sidney Smith, McGee and McDougall, Tilley and Peter Mitchell had all to be won from the ranks of reform to the "true blue" of Macdonald's liberal-conservatism. There was never a "reddish tinge," a touch of "the dying Dolphin," in Tupper's political allegiance. In the first exchange of letters between them after the Quebec conference Macdonald confirmed their alliance with spontaneous assurance: "I have not forgotten," he wrote, "the compact we made here and shall act strictly and cordially up to it."[1]

Tupper's contribution to this remarkable partnership was equally distinctive. Lord Morley once remarked at the end of a long association with many of the greatest names of British politics that the rarest attribute in public life was simple courage. In Canadian politics it would be hard to match the record of that sublime attribute in the career of Charles Tupper. From 1864 at Charlottetown where his decision was irrevocably made on confederation to 1896 in Winnipeg where he carried the citadel of the "Manitoba school question" by

[1] It is possible that more tangible resources were involved in this cryptic assurance than Macdonald's official biographer afterwards detected. Pope, *Memoirs*, I, 271, 273. Tilley afterwards referred to "the arrangement . . . that was talked of when I met you in Quebec" when applying for "the needful" for the crucial election of June, 1866, in New Brunswick: "Telegraph me in cypher saying what we can rely upon. . . . It will require some $40,000 or $50,000 to do the work." Tilley to Macdonald, April 17, 1866.

assault almost single-handed while the government of which he was prime minister went down to defeat on every other front, Tupper was "the Cumberland war-horse" of Canadian politics. It is not on record that his decision on confederation or any other issue ever suffered from squeamishness or scruple or any other infirmity of purpose. He followed Howe to London, he spent a week-end at Stowe with Howe and Mrs. Howe as the guests of the Duke of Buckingham and Chandos, he drove home from the Lyceum with Howe himself, and he breakfasted with the Howes the next morning. Mutual tributes are not wanting to courage and magnanimity. Neither was surprised to find the other in London, and Tupper reported that Howe "said a great many civil things" not only to him but about him. They were "both too old soldiers," Howe observed, "to play tricks on each other." They returned to Nova Scotia on the same boat, and when it became obvious that "the game was up" for repeal, Tupper stood loyally aside in order to commit his rival and his rival's followers to the cause of confederation.

Tupper's impact on Canadian politics was quickly seen. In due time he crossed swords with Brydges on the Intercolonial and Macdonald was constrained to find a refuge for that doughty partisan in the land department of the Hudson's Bay Company. In the end it was Tupper and not Galt who exploited the Canadian High Commissionership on a permanent basis in London and built the C.P.R. There was a time in 1866 when Tupper's vehemence in the cause of federation threatened to complicate Macdonald's shrewd calculations in the Canadas. Galt was inclined to be equally critical of Tilley, "considering he owes everything to us. As regards Tupper I do not care—nor much as respects Nova Scotia—indeed I should not grieve greatly if that Province were not to come in *now*—as we could then make a Legislative Union with New Brunswick and save all the trouble about Local Governments and guarantees."[1] Fortunately for the cause of confederation such vicissitudes of opinion were not shared by Macdonald and Tupper. The "compact" between them was honoured "strictly and cordially" to the end.

Tupper's surrender to federalism, like Macdonald's and in the end Howe's too, was reluctant even after the Quebec conference.[2] It was not long (January 4, 1865) before he was reporting "hard work here.

[1]Galt to Macdonald, Aug. 31, 1866. Confidential, Macdonald Papers, 191. 321.
[2]"Would it be practicable to provide for surrendering local Governments? I suppose not altho I think it very desirable." Tupper to Macdonald, "Private," Dec. 13, 1864.

A great body of the leading men, comprising the most wealthy merchants in the city are exerting themselves to the utmost to defeat the scheme. Archibald and McCully have stood by me like trumps." Surmising that Howe was "at the bottom of the opposition" he chose the short cut as usual as the nearest way home for both Nova Scotia and New Brunswick. He wrote desperately to Macdonald: "I wish Lord Monck would write to Earl Russell to choke him off as his action may endanger the passage of the measure here. I would not trouble Lord Monck if I could avoid it. I hope you will assist me in pressing Tilley to put it through without first going to the people." "You can at all times rely upon me to any extent." Here was an ally after Macdonald's own heart.

After the *débâcle* in New Brunswick Tupper fell back upon maritime union as the only device for advancing the cause of union in any form. Joint resolutions passed the Assembly and Legislative Council (April, 1865) that "an immediate Union" of all the provinces had now "become impracticable." A legislative union of the Maritimes was "desirable, whether the larger Union be accomplished or not." Negotiations therefore for maritime union "should be renewed in accordance with the Resolutions passed at the last Session of the Legislature." Tupper's own explanation to Macdonald at this stage is illuminating. His sanguine hopes at Quebec had been built upon the fact that with the *Colonist* committed to the plan on behalf of the government and McCully in the *Morning Chronicle* on behalf of the opposition (the "two leading journals which influence public opinion"), and with both "Archibald and McCully in favour, and Mr. Howe neutralized as an Imperial officer . . . I knew no effectual opposition could be raised to our arrangements." The prospects even in the legislature, however, rapidly deteriorated. McCully was "deposed" from the *Morning Chronicle*. Both Archibald and McCully "remained as true as steel, but it is doubtful if they could bring over two votes in the Assembly." How could they counteract an "appeal to the people . . . as a war cry" and Tilley's surrender to that appeal in New Brunswick as a precedent? Tupper found all his "ingenuity . . . required to avert the passage of a hostile resolution" in the Assembly. A general election in Nova Scotia, he conceded, would be "most disastrous to Confederation and probably defeat it altogether."

For the information of the Colonial Office Tupper expounded still more bluntly to the lieutenant-governor his attempt to escape the fate of New Brunswick. "There can be no doubt," he wrote, "that an appeal to the people here . . . would have resulted as it has in that Province in placing the opponents of Confederation in power and affording them the means of obstructing that great measure."

VI

The steps taken to dispel these portents of defeat and to carry confederation must be set down without extenuation. Neither in Canada nor in London was the plan devised at Quebec and ratified at the Colonial Office on December 3, 1864, for a moment abandoned or compromised.

The reaction to Tupper's own plausible plan for maritime union was characteristic. During the summer of 1865 Tupper and Henry, at Cardwell's invitation, found themselves in London heartened and convinced by the forthright assurances of the Colonial Office. In due time Cardwell relayed to Monck "the purport of the interviews" in London not only with the co-operative delegates from Nova Scotia but with a hostile delegation in a vastly different temper, as we shall see, from New Brunswick. "I have . . . spoken with them," he wrote, "on the proposed Union of the Maritime Provinces,—and have taken the opportunity of expressing myself on the subject of Confederation in accordance with the despatches in your possession":

I have stated that Her Majesty's Government can give no countenance to any proposals which would tend to delay the Confederation of all the Provinces, which they are so desirous to promote: and can only aid in the promotion of a closer union between Nova Scotia and New Brunswick if that closer union be ancillary to and form part of the scheme for general union.[1]

In this there can be no doubt that the advocates of confederation at the Quebec conference sought to enlist the aid of the Colonial Office without compunction in quelling the rising storm of opposition. Long before the despatch of December 3, 1864, reached the provinces Tupper was speculating upon their chances "if properly sustained by the British Government." Lord Monck might "induce the Colonial Secretary to authorise our Lieut.-Governor to appoint two or three additional Legislative Councillors if found necessary." At the same time Tupper knew the spirit of his countrymen too well to rely upon the intervention of the Colonial Office alone. Any appearance of "coercive measures on the part of the Imperial authority" would only be "likely to be prejudicial to the cause." With regard to Howe, as we have seen, there was less compunction. He could "wish Lord Monck

[1]The same reply was made to Smith and Allen of New Brunswick.

would write to Earl Russell to choke him off. . . . I would not trouble Lord Monck if I could avoid it."

The reliance of the federalists from New Brunswick upon the Colonial Office was equally ingenuous. As early as December 6 Charles Fisher hoped that Lord Monck whose "heart is in this work" might "induce the Colonial Secretary to send out a Despatch" to all the maritime governors who were notoriously "against this scheme," directing them "to aid and assist in the movement." Macdonald agreed with Colonel Gray of Prince Edward Island that the Colonial Office could "carry their point if they only adopt vigorous measures to that end." Before leaving for London to "take stock . . . with the British Government" after the New Brunswick election of March, 1865, Macdonald assured him "we shall spare no pains to impress the necessity of such a course upon them." Tilley implored Galt to "take no step that will leave us entirely 'out in the cold.' " "If you should find when in England," he added, "that there is to be a change [of governors] soon, ask the Government to *send us a Man who is heartily in favour of the Union and none else. Pray do not forget this.*" Fisher repeated this plea to Macdonald for a governor who is "honestly and faithfully at heart in earnest to carry Confederation."

The most resolute move for federation, however, had already come from the Canadian legislature. In accordance with the basic pact of "the great coalition" and the procedure prescribed by the Quebec Resolutions (number 70) the Government lost no time in sponsoring "the Union of the Provinces, on the principles adopted by the Conference." On February 3, 1865, Taché in the Legislative Council moved his address to the crown for union "based on" the Quebec Resolutions. This was carried on February 20 by a vote of 45 to 15. In the Assembly the address moved by Macdonald on February 6 was finally carried on March 10 after more than four weeks of almost continuous discussion—probably the most voluminous and exhaustive and crucial debate ever held in the Canadian legislature. With a sense of history steadily rising to envisage a national destiny the debates of both Houses were printed verbatim in a ponderous tome of more than a thousand pages, in double column, nearly a million words of exposition and invective, of parliamentary fence and cool statesmanship. The Confederation Debates thus became a classic in which no fewer than 37 councillors and 76 assemblymen recorded for posterity in imperishable print their convictions on the greatest political issue of their day.

Macdonald proposed at the outset that the debate "should continue day after day, and that for the purpose of greater regularity the

Speaker should remain in the chair." At the same time the procedure which had proved so useful at the Quebec conference was retained "in order that every member might have the same liberty of discussion as he would have in Committee of the Whole." The distinguished quartet whose exploits behind closed doors at Charlottetown and Quebec were already passing into a legend now completed one of the most impressive performances in Canadian politics. McGee, as before, made (February 9) his impassioned plea for "a new and vigorous nationality," destined by "events stronger than advocacy, events stronger than men" to surmount sectional difficulties and to unite "for nobler and more profitable contests." Much of the opposition was equally formidable—the pawky obstructiveness of Sandfield Macdonald, the uncompromising resourcefulness of Holton, the cynical hostility of Dorion, the methodical and closely reasoned case of Christopher Dunkin, in its comprehensiveness and certainly in its inordinate length perhaps the ablest single speech in the Confederation Debates. But none of these could withstand the ascendancy of "the great coalition." The final vote stood at 91 to 33.

When the news of the *débâcle* in New Brunswick reached Quebec Dorion boldly claimed: "this scheme is killed. (Hear, hear, and derisive Opposition cheers.) I repeat that it is killed." But Macdonald rejected without hesitation "any signs of weakness, any signs of receding on this question." The New Brunswick election was "an additional reason for prompt and vigorous action." By moving "the previous question" he restricted debate to the substantive resolution without further amendment. The same day (March 7) news of the deplorable debate in the House of Lords on the defence of Canada reached Quebec and Macdonald lost no time in forcing the issue: it was "of the greatest possible importance that Canada should not be unrepresented in England at the present time. (Cheers.) . . . The two questions of Federation and Defence should be discussed at the same moment." Defence was "the most imminent necessity. (Hear, hear.) No one can exaggerate the necessity." To Watkin in London Macdonald could describe (March 27) the Canadian mission of April, 1865, in less guarded terms:

We have carried the scheme through both Houses by majorities of about 3 *to 1*. We have voted a million of dollars for permanent defences and we send a mission to England to *take stock* of the situation, to ascertain exactly where we are in our relations with the Home Government and to concert measures in case of war, which, on this side of the water, we think imminent. . . .

You say that you have been snubbed for interfering in Canadian affairs.

I hope that you will disregard the snubbings and continue. . . . We must make up our minds to fight it out. But if England can do nothing better for us than to vote £ 50,000 a year for four years to fortify Quebec we may give up the idea of resistance as hopeless.

Two other letters, already cited, from Macdonald during that same hectic week—one of March 24 to Colonel Gray of Charlottetown and the other of March 27 to Colonel Gray of New Brunswick—put the desperate mission from Canada in 1865 in convincing perspective. To the latter he wrote that

the indiscreet publication of Col. Jervois' report in England . . . caused a panic in Western Canada as it shows the defencelessness of most of our Province . . . and the wretched debate in the House of Lords has not diminished the dread of forcible annexation and abandonment by Great Britain. Fancy the British Empire for the purpose of defending Canada and the British Flag from an impending War voting £ 100,000 in all, to be expended at £ 50,000 a year! . . . In order to shame them we carried the vote for a million of dollars to be immediately expended, and we go home with that sum in our hands.

With regard to union, he added discreetly, "we will not however in any way attempt to induce the Imperial Government to force the Maritime Provinces into Federation." To Gray of Charlottetown he wrote with less restraint: "I do not at all despair of carrying out our great project. . . . I quite agree with you that the British Government will carry their point if they only adopt vigorous measures to that end, and we shall spare no pains to impress the necessity of such a course upon them."

A hurried conference *en route* with several of the maritime leaders and confidential counsels in writing from Tupper, Tilley, and Fisher charged the Canadian argonauts a second time with "the fortunes of their cause."

VII

The success of Macdonald, Cartier, Galt, and Brown in London in April, 1865, was scarcely less spectacular than the exploits of the same quartet at Charlottetown and Quebec. There were three objects of their mission, defence, federation, and the accession of the West, but the greatest of these was federation for in it was comprehended the only means of safeguarding the other two. In that respect at least the Canadians quickly discovered that their anxious concern to *"take stock"* with the Colonial Office had already been anticipated. Cardwell himself had already "taken stock of the situation" in New Brunswick, and had begun with patient sagacity to repair the ravages of the March election. The "vigorous measures" advocated by Gray and Macdonald were already in train, attested not only by Galt's memorandum in the Macdonald Papers but by a series of forthright despatches which in the end bore down all before them in Nova Scotia and New Brunswick. The first of these was already on its way a fortnight before the Canadian delegation reached London.

The Canadian mission arrived a few days after the assassination of Lincoln. It is possible that the revulsion from the death of that great man was deeper than the impact of the living statesman upon the British public. From the careful memoranda in the Macdonald Papers it is clear that defence was now, more than ever, the open sesame of British policy. Galt took the precaution of exploring the prospects in an informal round with Cardwell before the appearance of his colleagues. An imperial loan of £9,000,000 would be necessary for the permanent works stipulated by Colonel Jervois for the security of central Canada. Meanwhile Canada was "obliged to urge such measures as if war were immediate and certain"—defence of inland waters and the protection of British regulars. After consultations with Cardwell, de Grey of the War Office, Gladstone for the Exchequer, and the Duke of Somerset, it became obvious that the soundest procedure would be to complete federation as soon as possible and to devolve upon Canada in the meantime the task of dealing with Fenian raids and border incidents of unusual gravity. The formal report of Cardwell to Monck is a record of clear and definitive policy. "We repeated," wrote Cardwell, "on the part of the Cabinet the assurances which had already been given of the determination of Her Majesty's Government to use every proper means of influence to carry into effect without delay the proposed Confederation" and that "priority in point of time should be given to the Confederation of the Provinces." In conclusion there were "assurances given by the Canadian Ministers on the part of Canada that that province is ready to devote all her resources both in men and money to the maintenance of the connection with the Mother Country," and assurances in return "that the Imperial Government fully acknowledged the reciprocal obligation of defending every portion of the Empire with all the resources at its command." An equally definitive conclusion was reached on the Hudson's Bay territories. In case of transfer to the Canadian federation "the indemnity, if any, should be paid by a loan to be raised by Canada under the Imperial Guarantee. With the sanction of the Cabinet, we assented to this proposal."

With these reciprocal assurances the success of the Canadian mission seemed assured. It is doubtful if "the great coalition" ever functioned more smoothly than during these crucial months from the St. Albans raid to the death of Lincoln and the conclusion of the London mission. "We acted together," Macdonald afterwards recalled, "dined at all public places together, played euchre in crossing the Atlantic, and went into society in England together. And yet on the day after he [Brown] resigned, we resumed our old positions and ceased to speak." It would be hard to find a more whimsical passage in that strange association than the incident which Sir John in a reminiscent mood once related to his secretary in 1889. "They all went down to Epsom in company with Russell of the 'Times'" to see the races—"the only one [added Sir John] I ever bet on":

A lot of us got up a pool of a guinea a draw; Galt drew the favourite Gladiateur, I drew the field. You are a lucky fellow said I to Galt. I do not know about that replied he. . . . Well, said I, I will swop and give you a guinea to boot. Done said Galt, we swopt and Gladiateur won. . . . Coming home they had lots of fun, even George Brown, a "covenanting old chap," caught the spirit. I bought him a peashooter and a bag of peas, and the old fellow actually took aim at people on the tops of busses, and shot lots of peas.

This exemplary association came to an end all too soon, as we shall see, but the report which the Canadian argonauts brought back from London was now confident and assured. Scarcely ten months had passed since the *Queen Victoria*, with Ferrier's blessing, had set out like another *Argo* in search of the golden fleece.

But whatever the harmony and resourcefulness of British and Canadian policy, there still remained in New Brunswick and Nova Scotia resources of opposition which taxed "every legitimate means"—"every proper means," "every means in his power"—pledged by the Colonial Office to carry "without delay the proposed Confederation." A fortnight before the Canadian delegates arrived in London Cardwell had pointed out for the benefit of Gordon's "new Advisers" the "intimate connection . . . between the numbers of the population and the measures proper to be taken for the defence of the Province." "It will only be right [he added] for New Brunswick to bear in mind" that as a separate province it could "make no adequate provision for its own defence," and would therefore depend "upon the defence which may be provided for it by this Country. It will, consequently, be likely to appear to your Advisers reasonable and wise that, in examining the question of the proposed Union, they should attach great weight to the views and wishes of this Country . . . and to the reasons on which these views have been based." A few days after the departure of the Canadian mission Cardwell repeated in its final form, and in stereo-typed terms which found their way in due time to Halifax and Charlottetown, the "strong and deliberate opinion" of the British government. He wrote to Gordon:

There is one consideration which Her Majesty's Government feel it more especially their duty to press upon the Legislature of New Brunswick. Look-ing to the determination which this Country has ever exhibited to regard the defence of the Colonies as a matter of Imperial concern,—the Colonies must recognize a right and even acknowledge an obligation incumbent on the Home Government to urge with earnestness and just authority the measures which they consider to be most expedient on the part of the Colonies with a view to their own defence.

The reply of the New Brunswick cabinet to this exhortation was perhaps the most spirited and incisive rejoinder of the entire con-troversy. The whole "motive and groundwork of the scheme" was to be found in the "local exigencies" of Canadian politics. "Federal Union," observed the executive council sardonically, July 12, 1865, "was only sought as a means of separating the Canadas," and "the eagerness with which they seek to force its immediate adoption upon unwilling communities" was due to the fact that the alternative, a dual federation of the Canadas, could not be represented "even speciously . . . to the Imperial Government as in any manner a scheme of Union." But the patient importunity of the Colonial Office was not to be denied. The reception which awaited A. J. Smith, the new prime minister, and J. C. Allen, attorney-general, on their mission to the Colonial Office a few weeks later was relayed resolutely in due time to Monck and Gordon. It is fair to surmise from Gordon's confidential despatches that both Smith and Allen were duly impressed. Upon Gordon and MacDonnell of Nova Scotia the pressure was less complaisant. The Canadian delegates, charged as we have seen by Tilley and Fisher and Tupper, had suggested bluntly to Cardwell that "the action of the Lieut.-Governors both of Nova Scotia and New Brunswick had been calculated to defeat the measure." Both Gordon and MacDonnell found themselves on leave of absence in London during the autumn of 1865. The latter was transferred forthwith to Hong Kong. Gordon too was soon to leave the Canadian scene—he was appointed in May, 1866, to Trinidad. Meanwhile he returned to New Brunswick under instructions to secure if possible the support of the New Brunswick legislature in time to permit of British legislation during the ensuing session of Parliament. To Macdonald Lord Monck, then in London

(October 26, 1865), described Gordon's return to New Brunswick in less guarded terms: "Mr. Gordon has gone out under instructions from Mr. Cardwell to further the cause of union by every means in his power."

The "means," both "legitimate" and "proper" (as Cardwell had enjoined) and otherwise, by which New Brunswick was finally committed to confederation are not altogether pleasant to reflect upon. For a time after the return of Smith and Allen there was a prospect of inducing the Government itself to permit a general resolution sanctioning union without a second election. Anglin, the "most determined isolationist," left the Government and others, wrote Gordon, were ready to accept "any loop hole for escaping from the reproach of inconsistency." Smith professed himself a convert and might have carried his party into acquiescence had not some of the advocates of federation (as Gordon thought) been "less anxious for the success of a scheme of union than for the return of their own particular party to office." At one stage Gordon reported that Smith and his colleagues "fully recognize the necessity for the adoption of an union policy, an avowal . . . which does that gentleman much credit." Gordon's memorandum for Cardwell was shown in advance to Smith for his approval. Cardwell in reply (March 31, 1866) ventured to express "great satisfaction" at last in "the prospect . . . of the success of the Confederation." But Gordon was too sanguine. The long train of coercive factors underlying "the political millennium" of "the great coalition" in Canada was scarcely to be expected over the week-end in New Brunswick. Tilley and Gray were no longer in the House and the opposition, wrote Gordon, instead of expediting "the adoption of Federation" were "determined to throw every obstacle in the way of the Government" in the hope of forcing them from office. The bitter debate on the Address in reply to the Speech from the Throne dragged on for six weeks and degenerated into "gross personalities and angry recriminations," sometimes without the formality of addressing the Speaker and accompanied on occasion by "unchecked applause or disapprobation of a numerous audience in the galleries."

Meanwhile by Gordon's own admission he was in constant collusion with Tilley against his constitutional advisers, and there were other tactics still more unconstitutional. The act by which at last he precipitated the election of June, 1866, was an outrage against the accepted practices of responsible government. Learning that the Legislative Council was prepared to present an address favourable to federation on the basis of the Quebec Resolutions, Gordon proposed to accept it with an avowal of policy both British and provincial so emphatic that there could be no retreat. Unfortunately Gordon's note to that effect to the Prime Minister did not reach him until 2.30 of the afternoon appointed for the Governor's reply. Smith drove to Government House where an unseemly wrangle delayed the ceremony for the assembled councillors. In the end Gordon defied his constitutional advisers and gave his own reply. "I knew," he afterwards conceded to Cardwell, April 23, 1866, "that I was rejecting the advice of my whole Council and must be prepared for the probable consequences of such a step."

Three days later Smith and his colleagues resigned in protest. Resolutions for the Governor's recall were forestalled by the prorogation of the House, though Gordon had the candour to forward the resolutions for Cardwell's information. Since Tilley was not a member of the House the Hon. Peter Mitchell, a legislative councillor, became prime minister and plunged immediately into the throes of a general election. "This transaction," Gordon confessed ruefully, "has throughout caused me the deepest mortification. It is mortifying to know that efforts to effect in a tranquil manner . . . a great object desired by the Imperial Government have proved wholly abortive."

VIII

With the approach of the New Brunswick election of June, 1866—the only general election in any province to ratify the Canadian confederation—the forces for union moved into the fray from all quarters with a sense of impending crisis.

In Nova Scotia Tupper carried his resolutions on April 17—still in general terms without formal ratification of the Quebec Resolutions —"to arrange with the Imperial Government a scheme of union which will effectually insure just provision for the rights and interests of this province." The vote in the Assembly stood thirty-one to nineteen. The timing was calculated to encourage hard-pressed allies in New Brunswick. The Colonial Office was equally apprehensive. Whoever was to supply the "means," Cardwell may be said to have supplied the election. He plied Gordon with encouraging exhortations, concurred in his "views as to the consequences which might follow a dissolution if injudiciously resorted to," enjoined upon him the most pious counsels "that in giving just effect to the instructions you have received on the subject of the union of the Provinces, you will be guided by a prudent regard to what you believe to be the real public feelings of the Province," and when the worst came to the worst assured him of "Her

Majesty's gracious decision" to approve his appointment "in accordance with your own wishes" to the government of Trinidad.

Fortunately for the cause of federation the constitutional issue was too awkwardly handled to be dangerous. Had Howe instead of Smith been prime minister the "mortifying" consequences of the Governor's tactics might have been more costly to the cause of federation. But it would have required more than a good case for responsible government after the manner of Howe's great "Case" for Lord Carnarvon to win the election of June, 1866. The politics of New Brunswick have seldom responded to abstract principles. Even during the catalytic contest for responsible government the amorphous state of New Brunswick politics had more than once mystified its neighbours. "You say you do not understand our political parties," Wilmot once wrote to Howe, "I am not surprised at this when I cannot understand them myself—Our People are running wild."[1] With the leading reformers themselves now committed to confederation it is doubtful if Howe in person could have turned the tide in New Brunswick, for despite all the gaucheries of Gordon's management and the "means" from Canada and elsewhere unsparingly used at the polls, it may fairly be said at the end of the day that confederation in New Brunswick was carried on its merits.

Beyond a doubt the "means" (in quotation marks and without the pious adjectives) from Canada were regarded at the time as indispensable. The evidence for this is all too clearly traceable and must be set down without palliation. As early as the Quebec conference there are signs of an understanding that Canadian resources were to be forthcoming for the contest in New Brunswick and Nova Scotia. The by-election in York County in October, 1865, which was interpreted as the turning of the tide, is the subject of some interesting correspondence in the Macdonald Papers. "I am quite certain," wrote Tilley, "Fisher can be returned under any circumstances with an expenditure of 8 or ten thousand Dollars. . . . Is there any chance of the friends in Canada providing half the expenditure?" Upon the back of this letter is a memorandum in Macdonald's handwriting: "My dear Galt Read this. What about the monies?" "Do not allow us to want now," implored Fisher, "[or] we are all gone together." The Governor-General, then in Britain, regarded the York by-election as "the most important thing that has happened since the Quebec Conference, and if followed up judiciously affords a good omen of success in our spring campaign." "It has cost very much more than we

[1]See above, p. 65.

expected," Fisher afterwards reported, "and if every dollar is not paid it will kill us at the General election," for the contest "was looked upon as the turning point in the great Confederation struggle." In due time Brydges of the Grand Trunk assured Macdonald that he had "sent the needful to Tilley and kept all our names here off the document." Perhaps the most grotesque commentary upon this supply of "the needful" from Canada is a postscript from George Brown, of all people, at the time of his resignation in December, 1865. "I pray you not to commit any mistake in that New Brunswick matter," he wrote to Cartier, "but we are pledged of course by Macdonald's letter. . . . What is proposed would be wrong and most hurtful hereafter. However, I am ready to give a cheque for $500 towards the fund, and will not be behind if further aid is required." If anything could sanctify "the needful" to the cause of federation in 1865 it must surely be a cheque from George Brown, after his resignation, to the "corruptionist" wing of "the great coalition."

For the election of June, 1866, "the needful" from Canada was more substantial. Tilley wrote to Macdonald:

We must have the arrangement carried out and without delay that was talked of when I met you at Quebec. . . . Telegraph me in cypher saying what we can rely upon. . . . The election must be carried at all Hazards. . . .

We can send a respectable man . . . to Portland where he might [meet] Brydges or some other person to arrange Finances. It will require some $40,000 or $50,000 to do the work.

A few days later he added:

To be frank with you the election in this Province can be made certain if the *means* are used. . . . If you give us aid as indeed you must to ensure success, you can arrange details as you think best.

The Governor-General recorded his own appeal and Gordon's for prompt measures. He telegraphed to Macdonald:

I have seen Galt and I think it very desirable that he should undertake the journey to Portland.

The counterpart to this is a note from Galt in the Macdonald Papers:

I saw Lord Monck today. . . . He agrees . . . that *means* had better be used —I think we *must* put it through cout que cout [*sic*]—and that I had better discuss it in this sense with Tilley—I should like to take Brydges to Portland with me.

But even when the worst has been set down without extenuation in this desperate *impasse* it would be a monstrous perversion of the truth to attribute the overwhelming victory at the polls in June, 1866, primarily to these "means." It is true that the Canadian interests who purveyed "the needful" were not disposed to minimize their contribution. Galt wrote complacently that Tilley "owes everything to us," and one of the Barings who happened to be in Canada after the disastrous election of March, 1865, reported to his uncle his surprise "to find how little importance the Canadians attach to the apparent unwillingness of the three lower provinces to accept the proposed union. They seem to think that the members of the New Brunswick and Prince Edward Island legislatures only require a little pecuniary persuasion and a promise of a place or two to change their minds, and there is some talk of Lord Monck making a tour through the provinces to apply the necessary means." But this was neither the chief cause nor the main purpose of the "means" of 1866. The "means" for Grand Trunk and Intercolonial were necessary chiefly because rival "western extension" interests were being supplied from the United States with "means" in abundance from more sinister quarters. It was "western extension" more than any other interest which had won the election of March, 1865, and it was still "western extension" which fought federation "to the last ditch" in 1866. "I know that our enemies will have aid from abroad," wrote Tilley, "and we must be in a position to meet them." If one set of "means" was less reprehensible than the other it was because the Intercolonial had now become the cornerstone of maritime policy.[1]

The truth was that there were reasons more convincing than "a fair share of the needful" for the overwhelming reversal of June, 1866. The building of the Intercolonial was now assured. "The great coalition," responding no doubt to Cardwell's broad hint in London that "Canada had herself the means" of dispelling the doubts of the Maritimes "as to the sincerity of the Canadians on the subject of the Railway," reaffirmed in a formal minute of council (August 14, 1865) their pledge for the Intercolonial as a "necessary accompaniment and condition of Confederation." Not a day would be "unnecessarily lost after the accomplishment of Confederation in commencing the work and prosecuting it to completion." Even the cost of the line from Truro to the Bend was eventually to be assumed by the Intercolonial.

By June 1866, too, the fiscal case for confederation had been so convincingly expounded by Tilley and Botsford that the unionists in this respect remained virtually masters of the field. In due time Tilley

[1]See A. G. Bailey, "Railways and the Confederation Issue in New Brunswick, 1863–5," *Canadian Historical Review*, Dec., 1940, pp. 367–83.

was to inherit Galt's own mantle as the architect of Canadian fiscal policy. The sponsor of the National Policy of 1878 was already demonstrating in New Brunswick his mastery of federal finance on the hustings for confederation in 1866.

Other factors in "the great election" of 1866 were less ponderable. It happened that the major concern of British policy—the problem of defence in all its implications—received its greatest impulse in New Brunswick during the months of 1866 when the Fenian movement was known to be organizing forays into British territory. Local panics in Canada West were followed by threats of local raids across the boundary into New Brunswick. Reinforcements of two British regiments were sent again to Canada, and the transfer of British regulars from Halifax to the Maine boundary was accompanied by the mustering of militia on both frontiers. The Fenian raid into Canada in June, 1866, was more serious than the fiasco on the Maine boundary but the New Brunswick volunteers remained under arms and the campaign for confederation went forward under the stimulus of rising concern for national defence. During the election Gordon, who conceded that the reports from the frontier were "very much got up for election purposes," replaced the militia at the border by British regulars in order that the "Volunteer Battalion should be at St. John during election. Nearly all are voters and a majority favourable." The Fenian brotherhood may be entitled to unsuspected credit in the federation of the British provinces.

And finally there was one other factor in "the great election" of 1866 which was so characteristic of the prevailing temper of New Brunswick at that time that it must be credited with a very strong if somewhat inscrutable influence at the polls. The patient but inflexible approval of British North American union by both parties in Great Britain commanded much respect in New Brunswick. Without overstepping the bounds of "earnestness and just authority," Cardwell could remind the "province of the loyalists" with deep concern of the "determination which this Country has ever exhibited to regard the defence of the Colonies as a matter of Imperial concern." These exhortations would have been destroyed by a touch of arrogance or of justifiable impatience. But it is not to be found. The spirited minute of council of July 12, 1865, is scathing to the point of disrespect. It is answered with patience and forbearance, with "earnest and friendly suggestions" unmarred by resentment or false dignity. By June, 1866, even the Roman Catholic vote which had gone so unaccountably against confederation in 1865 responded in some degree to these ingratiating sanctions. During the Confederation Debates in Quebec in 1865 Thomas D'Arcy McGee had read into the record the forthright appeal of Archbishop Connolly of Halifax, a "mitred statesman" whose plea for "Confederation at all hazards and at all reasonable sacrifices" had probably inspired McGee's own impassioned plea to "prepare . . . prepare . . . prepare." Archbishop Connolly's appeal must have found its way into many hidden quarters in New Brunswick:

Whenever the present difficulties [the Civil War in the United States] will terminate . . . we will be at the mercy of our neighbours. . . . They more than quadrupled their territory within sixty years. . . . I now state it, as my solemn conviction, that it becomes the duty of every British subject in these provinces to control that power, not by the insane policy of attacking or weakening them, but by strengthening ourselves. . . . The sort of preparation I speak of is utterly hopeless without the union of the provinces.

During "the great election" of 1866 it could scarcely have been a coincidence that Bishop Rogers of Chatham, N.B., after a visit to Halifax responded to an appeal by the new solicitor-general of the province "on behalf of Confederation." The timely reply of Bishop Rogers, published in the form of a campaign pamphlet, must have expressed the conviction of many a baffled patriot in New Brunswick:

Among the reasons which convince me of the benefit of the proposed Union, there is one entirely independent of the intrinsic merits of the question; it is, that this measure is earnestly recommended to us by the British Government—not by this or that particular Statesman or Party—but by the great Statesmen of all Parties. . . . Nay, I go further and say, that, considering the past and present relationship between us and the Mother Country, *it is our duty* to acquiesce. . . .

Are we, in return, to thwart and oppose British policy, to stickle for our opinions? . . . While Great Britain wishes us to unite, the Fenians have avowed it to be their policy to prevent such union. Which of these two should we try to please? *Fas est ab hoste doceri*—Should we not do the opposite of what the enemy wishes? . . .

But besides the argument [of] honor and duty . . . that of self-interest . . . would make it the most preposterous folly for us obstinately to persist in refusing to take part in the benefits of the proposed union.

This twin appeal to "duty" and "self-interest" in a federation already regarded as predestined and inevitable may well have caught the prevailing temper of New Brunswick in 1866. As Gray and Macdonald had predicted, "the British Government will carry their point if they only adopt vigorous measures to that end." It is true that the fathers of confederation themselves spared "no pains to impress the necessity of such a course" upon the Colonial Office[1] and supplemented the "legitimate" and "proper" means to that end by "means" of their own deemed "needful" for the desperate emergency of 1866. It is equally true that for two at least of the Maritimes—Nova Scotia and Prince Edward Island—the most "decided expression" of British policy would have been unavailing at this time to carry confederation at the polls. Tupper who knew his countrymen better than Macdonald or Galt or Cartier shrewdly deprecated, as we have seen, "coercive measures on the part of the Imperial authorities" as "prejudicial to the cause."

But for New Brunswick, "the province of the loyalists," the background in the chaotic politics of 1866 was different, and it may be that the temper of the province, like the election itself at that time, was unique. This was the only election which attended the achievement of confederation and despite the sinister evidence to the contrary the unionists could claim with some pride that it was won on its merits. In truth the margin of success was unexpected and overwhelming. Midway through the contest Gordon reported elatedly that "sixteen Gentlemen favorable to Confederation . . . have already been returned to the new Parliament whilst not a single member or supporter of the late administration has as yet succeeded in securing his re-election." The final returns stood four to one, and the resolutions modelled on those of Nova Scotia for "the Union of British North America, upon such terms as will secure the just rights and interests of New Brunswick" passed the House by a vote of 31 to 8. One added stipulation was characteristic: there was to be unequivocal "provision for the immediate construction of the Inter-Colonial Railway."

With "the great election" of 1866 in New Brunswick safely won the most formidable barrier to confederation was removed and the remaining complications were to be found in Canada and in London. In Canada Fenian raids and finance and the organization of provincial governments for the new provinces of Ontario and Quebec continued to delay the process of federation, and Galt, like Brown and Mowat, found himself out of office before it was completed. In London no

---

[1]"Believing that the Defence of the Country was most intimately connected with the Union," Cartier suggested to Cardwell that "the Imperial Government who were charged with the responsibility . . . might properly exercise a very great influence thro' a decided expression of their views." Galt added his opinion that "a decided expression" of British policy would have "a most marked effect on the loyal and high-spirited people of the Maritime Provinces," in favour of "a plan which will assure to them the continuance of the British connection."

fewer than three colonial secretaries held the seals from March, 1864, to the passing of the *B.N.A. Act of 1867* in March of that year. It was fortunate that the closing phases of federation fell to Lord Carnarvon whose services as under-secretary at the Colonial Office had proved so timely under Newcastle and Stanley, and so effective in the defence of Sir Edmund Head against Lytton's censorious criticism during the first "drive for federation" in 1858. With Carnarvon now in control at the Colonial Office the London conference could rely upon a more favourable reception than Galt and Cartier and Ross experienced in 1858. The union of British North America, as Macdonald had predicted in Halifax, was soon to be "a fixed fact."

Chapter Nineteen

CONFEDERATION AND ITS COROLLARIES

THE carrying of confederation in the British provinces had involved three far-reaching reversals of policy. "The great coalition" had supplanted the official advice of the Government for a new election on the old party lines; the despatch of December 3, 1864, reversed the official policy of the Colonial Office after six years' support of maritime union; "the great election" of June, 1866, in New Brunswick reversed the ominous verdict of March, 1865, and opened the way to the *B.N.A. Act of 1867*. To all appearances Macdonald's forecast of federation as a "fixed fact" in Halifax in September, 1864, was now, it seemed, in everything but legislation a *fait accompli*. But appearances were deceptive. There were grave differences of opinion —the gravest which ever divided the fathers of confederation—grave enough, it seemed at one stage, to disrupt the cause of federation altogether. The final Act was above all a matter of timing, and the *B.N.A. Act of 1867* was a masterpiece of that art in the hands of the shrewdest opportunist of his day, John A. Macdonald.

For the Maritimes speed was now a prime necessity. Howe was in London bending every energy towards one plausible objective—delay if only for a few months until a provincial election in Nova Scotia could demonstrate the overwhelming opposition of that province. As the term of the House elected in 1863 drew to a close the Anti-Confederation League began to focus its opposition upon the impending "May (1867) election." The prospective result was everywhere conceded. "We must obtain action," Tupper wrote to Macdonald, "during the present session of the Imperial Parliament, or all may be lost. Our House expires by law in May next, when a general election must be held. . . . The result would be most disastrous to Confederation and probably defeat it altogether."

On the other hand the Quebec Resolutions had not been ratified in any of the maritime provinces and it was necessary therefore not only to meet soon in London but to meet soon enough to permit time for discussion *de novo* if necessary before the impending election in Nova Scotia could imperil the whole cause. Tupper and Archibald hurried to Ottawa to explain their predicament, and the two maritime delegates secured an agreement from the Canadians to leave for London in July, 1866. On July 14 Tupper telegraphed desperately to Macdonald: "Any delay on the part of Canada . . . will undoubtedly be fatal to Confederation. This province is convulsed by Canadian policy on fisheries. Petitions against Union being signed all over the country." On the nineteenth Tupper and Tilley sailed together from Halifax relying to the last "upon Canadian delegates meeting them promptly in London as agreed on. We speak advisedly," they wrote to Macdonald, "when we say that any further delay would be most dangerous to Confederation."

Cardwell too had the best of reasons for expediting the bill if the whole plan was not to risk shipwreck in the shoals of British politics. The Palmerston Government was sustained in the elections of 1865 but the aged Palmerston died in October and Earl Russell resigned in June, 1866, to avoid a dissolution on parliamentary reform. There were unpredictable issues at stake in Europe and America but fortunately the Derby-Disraeli Government brought Lord Carnarvon to the Colonial Office, and by this time both parties had reached common ground on the problem of British North American union.

Lord Monck in Canada, too, had the best of reasons at this stage for advocating speed. "The great coalition" was still functioning in spirit but it was already doomed in formal administration. Taché was dead, Brown had seized a technical controversy over reciprocity as a convenient opportunity of resigning in December, 1865, and Galt was soon to follow him out of office on issues of educational policy for the new provinces of Ontario and Quebec. Monck whose good offices had been pledged to Brown and the Clear Grits in the formation of "the great coalition" now found the administration slipping ominously towards the old party lines and called upon Macdonald to implement loyally the basic pact of June, 1864, while there was yet time. Macdonald's reply, as we have seen, was a letter which demonstrated not only his assured mastery of the situation in Canada but his assured faith in federation: "But, my dear Lord Monck," he concluded, "the proceedings have arrived at such a stage that success is certain and it is not now a question even of strategy. It is merely one of tactic." The truth was that Macdonald was having his own troubles in restraining some of his followers from seizing power boldly in the interests of the Conservative party. He reminded one of his party stalwarts of his own unavailing efforts to avoid coalition altogether: "I am so strong a party man, and as a general principle so opposed to Coalition that I strained every effort to form a Government . . . on purely Conservative principles." To another he had written reassuringly (September 28, 1864), "you may be assured that the Conservative cause won't suffer in my hands." Another exuberant partisan he upbraided reproachfully with altogether unwonted impatience: "If the Conservatives have not sense enough to see that the coalition must be carried through and supported, the consequences must be that the whole Government will be handed over to the Grits. I have been strongly tempted, several times, to do so, from the inconsiderate folly of my own friends." Partisanship must have been black indeed to merit this reproof from John A. Macdonald.[1]

Macdonald's tactics at this stage were more subtle than Tilley's or Tupper's and in the end they were openly avowed to his maritime colleagues. Every precaution had been taken to keep the Quebec Resolutions in focus as the basic "framework" of federation. They were to be "carried en bloc and without alteration lest any alteration should create the necessity for a new Conference." These tactics had received unwavering support during the Confederation Debates—from Brown and McGee as well as from Galt and Cartier and Macdonald. Monck after an initial *faux pas* which threatened to open the Quebec Resolutions to endless wrangling and delay in every legislature[2] countermanded his mistake by telegram to all the provinces and drafted in due time for Carnarvon the classic case for regarding the Quebec Resolutions as the "groundwork of the Act for the Union of the Provinces."[3] This was the nearest approach hitherto achieved to technical unanimity among the provinces. Whatever defects in popular sanction may have attended the Quebec conference, this at least could be said that all delegations except that from Newfoundland had been

[1]To a congenial party audience in Montreal Sir John in 1875 described George Brown's share in "the great coalition": "The only patriotic thing that man ever did in his life—impelled by a sense of fear for the consequences he had himself rendered imminent by his course—was to coalesce with me for the purpose of forming a larger union, and carrying out the Confederation of all the British American provinces. To be sure, gentlemen, he deserves the credit of joining with me; he and his party gave me that assistance in Parliament that enabled us to carry Confederation, and if we now are a Dominion, we must not forget that it was owing in great measure to Mr. Brown's momentary feeling of patriotism, of which, however, he soon repented."

[2]"The resolutions adopted by the Conference will be subjected to the action of many minds before they shall have become embodied in addresses from the legislatures of the several Provinces." Monck to Cardwell, Dec. 23, 1864.

[3]Confidential, Sept. 7, 1866.

duly appointed by governors acting on the advice of their constitutional advisers and had included to a degree unprecedented in previous projects the views of oppositions as well as governments in order to broaden to the utmost the basis of concurrence and co-operation. Macdonald was careful to see that the addresses which emerged from the Confederation Debates in Canada authorized the Canadian delegation to London to negotiate only on those terms, and it is clear that any deviation was to be permitted only through the plenary authority of the Colonial Office. "The Imperial Government is now the arbiter."[1] Macdonald's tactics therefore were in many respects the opposite of Tupper's and Tilley's. Theirs called for an early conference and time for better terms before any fatal "May election" could intervene in Nova Scotia. Macdonald sought to defer the conference until statutory implementation was clearly in sight and then to act with the utmost despatch in order to forestall public discussion and ensure the maximum sanctions for the Quebec Resolutions.

As the two lines of policy diverged the rift between them began to assume a serious if not menacing aspect. Tupper's importunity, in his desperate race for time against Howe and the Anti-Confederation League, was expressed with characteristic frankness and assurance. "We must obtain action," he reiterated, "during the present session of the Imperial Parliament, or all may be lost." "I wish to impress upon you the urgent necessity of *immediate* action." Tilley's protest to Galt (from London, August 9) was still more incisive. It was forwarded to Macdonald for reply but remained unanswered until October 8. Galt's comment, as we have seen, was ominous not only for Tilley's plea but for the whole cause of federation. Galt was "exceedingly disappointed at his tone considering he owes everything to us. As regards Tupper," added Galt, "I do not care—nor much as respects Nova Scotia—indeed I should not grieve greatly if that Province were not to come in *now*, as we could then make a Legislative union with New Brunswick and save all the trouble about Governments and guarantees." Tilley had written apprehensively of Howe's tactics in London "hoping and praying for delay, that a general election in Nova Scotia may destroy all our prospects for Union. . . . Your inability to accompany us may turn out to be a sad calamity. . . . If it is your determination to delay your visit until November we must return . . . leaving the object of our mission postponed indefinitely. I will not believe that you will drive us to this course." Brydges, too, forwarded to Macdonald

[1]Macdonald to Mitchell, April 10, 1866.

(October 8) extracts from "my latest English letter"—probably from Watkin—which must have brought the seriousness of the *impasse* in London home even to Macdonald. Charges of "indifference, if not bad faith" on the part of Canada "might be fanned into such a flame as would put an end to the whole matter for the present. . . . You may depend upon it that the position is serious, and that the Canadian Government are making a serious mistake." There was a possibility that the maritime delegation might "throw up their cards, and return home, "functus officii" . . . I should not have written you if I did not believe the position to be critical." And finally Carnarvon himself in London added his importunities (August 31) to Tupper's and Tilley's against "any unnecessary delay in the settlement of this question." "The prolonged detention of the delegates now in England is attended with much inconvenience." Even if Monck and his ministers were delayed by the "impending Fenian disturbance . . . it might deserve their consideration whether some of their number could repair at once to England."

There were solid reasons as well as plausible excuses for the timing upon which Macdonald had now set his mind. As his plan developed he found his staunchest ally in Lord Monck whose conversion to the new tempo was now complete. At the change of government in London in June, 1866, the Governor-General resolutely refused to move until the co-operation of the new Colonial Secretary, Lord Carnarvon, could be assured.[1] One of the most elaborate confidential memoranda of Monck's whole term of office—twelve folio pages in the original draft —was prepared for Carnarvon's information. There were valid local reasons too for delay. Reports of Fenian raids, which could be much "got up for election purposes" in New Brunswick, were only too well founded in Canada. Reinforcements were hurriedly summoned from Great Britain and Macdonald, who had taken over the Department of Militia in order to allay the fears of the public, encountered perhaps the most scathing criticism of his career when he surrendered, in the midst of so grave a crisis, to one of those devastating interludes which sometimes marred his administration. Comment from the Canadian press, on both sides of politics, multiplied until it reached the British press and the Colonial Office. "We do not speak," wrote the editor of the *London Daily Telegraph* (September 29, 1866) "till silence has become affectation." "Whether these charges be true, or false," wrote

---

[1]"A chief whom I do not know personally and of whose habits of mind I am equally ignorant." Monck to Macdonald, private, Oct. 12, 1866.

Carnarvon to Monck,[1] "I cannot disguise the sorrow with which I read them."[2]

By October 8, however, Macdonald was again master not only of the situation but of himself, and the reply which he finally wrote to Tilley on that date was a masterpiece of adroit advocacy intended originally for Carnarvon's eye as well as Tilley's.[3] This letter which was drafted with great care may stand as the classic case for "Old Tomorrow" and "Canada's conduct with respect to Federation." "We Canadians think that Canada is the only Province that carried out its engagements" to submit the Quebec Resolutions to the provincial legislatures. The Maritimes "did not even *attempt* to pass them," though Macdonald conceded that they "were never in a position to go to the polls on those resolutions." The agreement with Tupper and Archibald to meet in London in July was followed almost immediately by news from Cardwell that "there was no chance of a Bill being passed" that session, and by "the defeat of the ministry." The maritime delegates were informed by telegram that "Lord Monck could not go and would not allow any of his ministers to go to England" pending instructions from the new Colonial Secretary. "The delegations from N.S. and N.B. therefore went at their own risk." With a new Fenian invasion expected in September Lord Monck, whose presence in London was indispensable,[4] would never have been justified in "abandoning his post or allowing his principal advisers to leave Canada." "Even had we sailed on 21st July," Macdonald concluded, "I do not believe that Confederation could have been carried. The settlement of the terms of the Bill is not the work of a day—it must take weeks of anxious and constant labour. The measure would have been easily drafted had the Quebec Resolutions been carried—but we are all at sea and obliged to commence de novo."

And finally the real secret of Macdonald's timing is stated with convincing frankness:

The Bill should not be finally settled until just before the meeting of the British Parliament. The measure must be carried per saltum—with a rush,

[1]"Confidential," Oct. 18, 1866.

[2]"The correspondent of a leading London paper repeats a casual joke of the Fenians that, in view of the next invasion, agents will be appointed to see that the Minister of Militia is 'gloriously tight' again." *London Daily Telegraph*, Sept. 29, 1866.

[3]"I think on consideration I had better not send your letter to Tilley to Lord C.—I will tell you my reasons when we meet." Monck to Macdonald, private, Oct. 12, 1866.

[4]"He will be the Solvent and the intermediary between the paramount power and the Provinces."

and no echo of it must reverberate through the British provinces until it becomes law. . . . There will be few important clauses in the measure that will not offend some interest or individual, and its publication would excite a new and fierce agitation on this side of the Atlantic. . . .

The Act once passed and beyond remede, the people would soon learn to be reconciled to it. . . . It is our intention to sail D.V. on the 7th Nov[r]. for England and I hope to find you all in good health and spirits—ready to tackle to the work and in no degree enervated by the dissipations of London.[1]

With this ingratiating but somewhat superfluous admonition to Tilley—"a good man in the very best meaning of the word," according to Macdonald's official biographer—the Canadian delegation arrived at last in November and took up unpretentious quarters in the Westminster Palace Hotel for the final conference on confederation.

II

The timing of the London conference—only less adroit and successful than the miracle of Charlottetown and Quebec—proved to be a convincing demonstration of Macdonald's uncanny sense of politics as "the art of the possible." By the time of the first meeting on December 4 it was obvious that his letter to Tilley, reinforcing an exhaustive minute of the Canadian Executive Council (September 24) for Carnarvon, had won its way with both the maritime delegations. It was Tupper who moved and Tilley who seconded the unanimous choice of Macdonald as chairman of the conference.[2] Monck's best

[1]A carefully marked "Copy" in Macdonald's immaculate handwriting is preserved in the Macdonald Papers, vol. 51, 342 ff., together with Tilley's original letter of Aug. 9 to Galt and Galt's original letter of Aug. 31 (marked "Confidential") to Macdonald enclosing Tilley's letter, "to which I presume you will wish to reply." Macdonald enclosed to Tilley a copy of Galt's letter, with apologies for the long delay of "some six weeks" in answering it, "as I fancied from his state of feeling that its tone would not be conciliatory."

[2]For the joint conferences with the Colonial Office Carnarvon was in the chair. In a later memorandum for Lord Dufferin Macdonald has the statement: "I acted as Secretary to the delegates from the various Provinces which met in Quebec in October 1864 who then passed the resolutions which, with some subsequent alterations, formed the germ of Confederation.

"And I acted in the same capacity at London in 1866–67 when resolutions were made on which was passed the B.N.A. Act of 1867, by which Confederation was accomplished.

"But on these occasions it was determined that no minutes of the various discussions should be taken, and no record, therefore, exists of them."

The "executive secretary" on both occasions was of course the deputy minister of Macdonald's own department, Lieut.-Col. Hewitt Bernard, soon to be his brother-in-law (Feb. 16, 1867). Macdonald may have "acted as Secretary" for the joint sessions with the Colonial Office.

offices too were now in complete accord. By October 12 he had become an enthusiastic convert to Macdonald's shrewd tactics. "To tell you the truth," he wrote, "my fear is that you will be ready too soon for your conferences with Lord C. I should wish that *these* should not take place till *after* Christmas. . . . This mode of arrangement would bring you very near the opening of the Session before any definite plan could be decided on and this I look upon as a great desideratum." This proved to be the programme of the London conferences.

In truth Monck's share in confederation, while no longer dominant like Head's in the first "drive for federation" in 1858, supplied indispensable factors in the process, and it would not be amiss to recount them here. Many of the adjustments, devious and otherwise, which became necessary are traceable in no small measure to Monck's goodwill and resourcefulness behind the scenes. It will be recalled that "the great coalition" itself might never have come to pass without his resolute initiative in contravening the unanimous advice of his constitutional advisers in order to forestall another election on the old party lines. From that point his dedication to the cause of union was never belied by squeamishness or self-interest. In June, 1866, he reached the desperate pass of suggesting his own recall unless the basic pact of the coalition to which he had pledged his support could be honoured forthwith. Macdonald himself in reasserting, as we have seen, his own mastery of that situation could not withhold a tribute which with all its fulsomeness was measurably true: "As to the personal portion of your note," he wrote, "all I can say as a sincere friend of Your Excellency, is that you must take no such step as you indicate. To you belongs, as having initiated, encouraged, and I may now almost say completed, the great scheme of Union, all the κῦδος, and all the position (not lightly to be thrown away) which must result from being the founder of a nation."

The goal was now in sight. The London conference, despite the priority claimed for it in the traditions of the Maritimes, was far less crucial however than that of Quebec, and the meagre record of the sessions in the Westminster Palace Hotel warrants the Canadian view that the Quebec Resolutions remained the "framework" of federation. At one stage of the conference there was much frank talk about this contrast in approach and emphasis. Macdonald who had stressed unerringly from beginning to end the sanctity of the Quebec Resolutions as the only hope of avoiding controversy—"we did not feel at liberty ourselves to vary those resolutions"—conceded that it was "quite understood in Canada, though never reduced to writing, that if any serious objection should be made by the Maritime Provinces, we should be prepared to listen and consider." Ritchie, on the other hand, stated bluntly that "in the Legislature of Nova Scotia it was understood that all matters should be entirely open." Mitchell too could cite "certain and specific objections to that scheme" on behalf of New Brunswick, "having gone twice to the people on the Quebec scheme." The resolution of the New Brunswick Assembly (June 30) had stipulated with the utmost finality "provision for the immediate construction of the Inter-Colonial Railway." McCully of Nova Scotia whose conciliatory counsels had oiled the troubled waters more than once at Quebec supplied once again a sensible compromise which was probably as near to consensus as the conference could expect to get: "We have adopted the Quebec scheme as the backbone, but I think we are here to bring our judgment and maturer reflections to bear upon it. We are tied down to nothing, but should not depart unnecessarily from the Quebec Scheme. I will act with the majority of the Conference, although contrary to my own opinion." Macdonald in the chair closed the discussion with a characteristic comment somewhat at variance with the version which his biographer afterwards published in *Confederation Documents*: "Conference can now quite understand position and we may now go on. It is a matter for ourselves to discuss points, as if they were open, altho' we may be bound to adhere to Quebec Scheme."

From the fragmentary notes in Macdonald's handwriting it would appear that no fewer than 29 of the Quebec Resolutions were reviewed on December 4, the first day of the conference. On December 5 twelve more—31 to 42—were summarily dealt with, together with 18 subsections of number 43 relating to federal powers. The rest of the list was reviewed on December 6. On December 13 the conference reverted to details marked "stand over" from the first survey. It was at this stage that the term "confederation" was agreed upon, and the term "Parliament" reserved for the federal government. The term "House of Commons" was in current use from the outset. As late as the draft bill of January 23 the term "Legislative Council" was still applied to the "Upper House"—the word "Senate" finally appeared in the draft bill of February 2. While the notes afterwards published in Pope's *Confederation Documents* are in Macdonald's handwriting it is clear that much of Macdonald's own comment is omitted. With Macdonald himself in the chair the technique developed at Charlottetown and Quebec functioned with great smoothness and despatch. The vote was taken by provinces and the London Resolutions, 69 in number, were finally "adopted by the unanimous vote of the Provinces."[1]

The secrecy and informality so valuable at Charlottetown and Quebec were more easily safeguarded in London. Macdonald's note to Carnarvon on Christmas day in advance of the formal resolutions contained the same stringent precaution. Having "sat steadily from the 4th to the 24th inst. . . . the Delegates desire me to convey to you their opinion that it is expedient to avoid any publicity being given to the resolutions until the Bill is finally settled and ready to be laid before Parliament. They think that their early publication would answer no good purpose, and might tend to premature discussion on imperfect information of the subject both in this country and America." Carnarvon too commended (December 28) "the expediency of considering the resolutions private for the present." He had been far from well,[2] and when the time came to distribute the draft bill to the delegates on January 23, he sent eighteen copies to Macdonald "under a cover marked private" for distribution "with a caution as to the importance of treating them as confidential."

Meanwhile Monck behind the scenes was arranging the plenary conferences between the Colonial Office and the delegates. Macdonald's own relations with Carnarvon, enhanced by hospitality at Highclere, quickly reached a stage of great mutual confidence. By this time the machinery of federation was moving smoothly and swiftly, not without lubrication. Senators, Macdonald explained, were not to be named until the old provincial legislatures had met for the last time: "If the Lists were settled now, every man in the Upper Houses . . . who is omitted rightly or wrongly, would vote against the Government." Howe discovered to his dismay that a private member who had undertaken to move an investigation in the House of Commons on behalf of Nova Scotia flinched from the ordeal through Carnarvon's own intervention. Both Government and Opposition were now committed to a fair trial for the new federation.

By February 9 "the seventh and last draft" of the bill was ready. As late as the sixth draft Macdonald's preference for the title "Kingdom of Canada" was stoutly maintained, until it encountered Lord Derby's concern lest so frank an avowal of monarchy in North America might "wound the sensibilities of the Yankees." By a final perversity of domestic politics Carnarvon was denied the role of seeing the bill through. He had " 'sat at the cradle' of the new Dominion" but his

---

[1] Macdonald to Carnarvon, Dec. 25, 1866.
[2] "I have been and still am so far from well that I cannot leave my room."

"ill-omened resignation" on March 4 over his party's policy on reform left the final phases of the Act in the hands of the Duke of Buckingham. The *B.N.A. Act of 1867* finally passed (March 29) without fanfare. A voluminous and by no means ill-informed anthology on the Canadian federation could be compiled from the British press but the last scene in the House was anti-climax. Garvie of the Nova Scotian Anti-Confederation League was in the gallery and wrote scathingly of the utter indifference of "the great body of the House . . . even the delegates seemed chagrined at the lazy contempt with which a thin House suffered their bill to pass." Carnarvon alone seems to have caught something of the vision of the Canadian fathers. In the exchange between Macdonald and Carnarvon at the end there is a note of deep regard which proved to be mutual. Macdonald wrote:

I can scarcely tell you the regret with which I learnt yesterday that you had given up the seals of office and that our official relations were to cease for the present.

I say "for the present" as I feel that ere long when the ship rights itself again . . . your services to your party and the Country will be eagerly sought for—and I hope not in vain.

I hope too . . . and I confess to a little selfishness . . . the Colonial Office may be the field of your labours.[1]

Carnarvon in reply (March 6) was "very grateful for the official duties" which had "changed political into personal relations of so pleasant a kind to me. I hope much that when the sea is between us we shall not wholly lose sight of each other. You have made my work so easy to me that I shall always look back with pleasure upon it."

Upon this kindly note and the more intimate felicitations of friends upon his marriage (February 16) the "London mission" of Macdonald closed with phenomenal success. His official biographer has recorded his oft-repeated dictum that his "greatest triumphs were won before Confederation." In that sense the climax of a career may be regarded also as the climax of Canadian politics. But it was not far removed in either case from anti-climax. With Monck's appointment as the first governor-general and his charge (privately conveyed as early as

---

[1]Carnarvon's son had been in Quebec during the Quebec conference. Whitelaw, *The Maritimes and Canada before Confederation.* The good offices of Carnarvon in support of Head and the first "drive for federation" in 1858 had been shared by Elliot and others who were still in the Colonial Office at this time. Sir Frederic Rogers (later Lord Blachford), permanent under-secretary in 1867, afterwards wrote of the London conference: "Lord Carnarvon was in the chair, and I was rather disappointed in his power of presiding. Macdonald was the ruling genius and spokesman, and I was greatly struck by his power of management and adroitness." *Letters,* p. 301.

March) to Macdonald as prime minister "to put in motion the machinery we have created," the federation of Canada began unostentatiously to function on July 1, 1867. The ceremony at Ottawa— "for business only" as the governor-general deprecatingly suggested to Macdonald—was characteristically phlegmatic and practical. At various points in the new provinces of Quebec and Ontario there were salvos of artillery and military parades, bonfires, and fireworks. Here and there in New Brunswick there was black crepe on the doors, and the flag of Nova Scotia flew at half-mast on many a ship. But "the new coach" was at last ready to start. Meanwhile two of the stoutest advocates of confederation, Tupper and McGee, stood loyally aside to expedite the formation of the first "tessellated cabinet" of Canada.

III

The instrument which emerged from the British Parliament on March 29, 1867, for the federation of Canada has had a long tradition of criticism as well as veneration, and it can scarcely be said to this day that its true nature has settled acceptably into a consistent body of doctrine. In Great Britain where federalism in all its forms was suspect in 1867 and where the techniques of federal government have not always been appreciated even in the sacred precincts of the Judicial Committee of the Privy Council there has always been a tendency to interpret the *B.N.A. Act of 1867* for what it was and still is, a statute of the British Parliament subject only to the accepted principles of statutory interpretation. This in itself is a salutary safeguard against some of the traditions which have flourished, on occasion, in self-interested quarters in Canada and elsewhere.

The *B.N.A. Act of 1867* is not in any sense whatever a "written constitution" comparable to that of the United States or Brazil. The temptation to regard it as such has been sanctioned on occasion by eminent authority. Lord Bryce in his *Modern Democracies* refers to "the Canadian Constitution" as "prepared by a group of colonial statesmen in 1864 and enacted in 1867 by a statute of the British Parliament." Professor Dicey in a lecture to undergraduates at Oxford is said to have referred facetiously to the preamble of the *B.N.A. Act of 1867* with its emphatic avowal of "a Constitution similar in principle to that of the United Kingdom" with the observation that in the interests of accuracy "Kingdom" might well be changed to "States." Perhaps the boldest claims ever made for the Act were advanced by Sir Clifford Sifton in 1922:[1] Canada was "given the right to govern

[1]In advocating a constituent convention with parliamentary sanctions to remove anomalies by drafting an "amended constitution."

itself by the B.N.A. Act of 1867. . . . We started with the B.N.A. Act. On the date when the B.N.A. Act was passed it represented all the rights of self-government which Canada possessed. This statement must be understood to be without any qualification whatever."

On the other hand it was recognized from the outset in Charlottetown, Quebec, and London that the most vital part of the "constitution" had never been written at all. The accepted practice and procedures of parliamentary government after the British model had been introduced into the British provinces by no statute, had never been defined by statute, and were to continue unimpaired and almost unchanged by the *B.N.A. Act of 1867*. Had a legislative instead of a federal union been feasible in 1867 the function of the Act would have been merely to obliterate interprovincial boundaries, to substitute one capital and one governor for three or four and to carry on the conventions of responsible government exactly as before. Since federalism, the price of sectionalism and distance, was inescapable it became necessary to leave certain fields of government to the provinces and to concentrate all those that could be exercised in common. Within both fields, nevertheless, the unwritten conventions of responsible government continued to function as before, and the legal fiction which was employed to vindicate this doctrine was so characteristic that it still impresses the Japanese or American observer as a meaningless anachronism: "the Executive Government . . . is hereby declared to continue and be vested in the Queen" (s. 9); "the Command-in-Chief of the Land and Naval Militia, and of all Naval and Military forces, of and in Canada, is hereby declared to continue and be vested in the Queen" (s. 15). If this were to appear in the constitution of Brazil or the United States it would presumably mean what it says. In the *B.N.A. Act of 1867* it means that the long tradition of parliamentary government from Pym and Hampden to Baldwin and Durham and the third Earl Grey remains unbroken, and that the same flexibility and adaptability in the name of the crown may be expected to continue in the evolution of parliamentary government in Canada. This has been as pronounced in the provincial as in the federal field, and it is a remarkable fact that the most venturesome experiments in Canadian government—"social credit" in Alberta or provincial socialism in Saskatchewan—have employed these unwritten "conventions" as a matter of course.

It is from this source that many of the most distinctive and valuable differences between the Canadian parliamentary system and the congressional system of the United States took their rise and still survive in North America. The flexibility of the parliamentary system for purposes of adaptation or improvisation depends upon no statute, no nice balance of functions, in a written constitution. The sanctions of cabinet government, the commanding position of the prime minister, the responsibility of prime minister and cabinet alike to the House of Commons, the invaluable integration of legislative and executive functions, had already been evolved in the practice of responsible government and were left unimpaired by confederation. The division of powers that then became necessary between the provinces and the federal government required a written "fedes" or bond to delimit the boundaries but within those boundaries the old functions of responsible government continued as before. Between federal and provincial government there is a division not of function but of "powers" or fields of administration. Instead of dividing and balancing functions of government in written "constitutions," either federal or provincial, all the usual conventions of parliamentary government remain paramount in each. Thus it came to pass that Sir Robert Borden could underwrite with authority on behalf of Canada the acceptance of the League of Nations which President Wilson himself failed so disastrously to secure from his own country. This integration of function and responsibility continues to simplify external relations for the Canadian federation; the contrast in that respect with the checks and balances of a "written constitution" remains one of the most baffling problems of association with the United States. A record of the treaty negotiations, abortive and otherwise, between the two from the Reciprocity Treaty of 1854 to the Alaska boundary and the development of the St. Lawrence seaway would illustrate some of the complications arising from these distinctive differences in government.

While the integration of function and responsibility continues to mark the unwritten part of the Canadian constitution, both federal and provincial, the written part of it also—the statutory division of federal and provincial "powers"—has been marked by a similar concentration of power in the hands of the national government. From Charlottetown to Quebec and London this objective was never lost to sight. This is true of the process as well as the form of the Canadian federation. Without the tensions of the Civil War, jeopardizing the West and after Gettysburg even the security of Canada, it would be hard to account for many of the most coercive factors in confederation, including "the great coalition" itself without which it would be hard to account for federation at all at that time. Without the great "necessity" which Macdonald expounded at Halifax and which must have been a commonplace of the discussion behind closed doors at Charlottetown and Quebec it would be hard to account for the easy abrogation of maritime union, for the specious "unanimity" of the Quebec Resolutions, for the precipitate accession of Cardwell, for the deliberate decision to bring "means" to bear upon the Maritimes, and for the overwhelming support of both parties in Great Britain.

The form no less than the process of the Canadian federation reflected the proximity of the Civil War and the consistent aim to protect the Canadian federation as far as possible from the infirmities which seemed at that time to be jeopardizing the American union. This theme is unanswered and is regarded as unanswerable in the press and official correspondence and political discussion at that time. None of the fathers of confederation had a deeper appreciation than Macdonald for the virtues as well as the defects of the American union but his doctrine of "a powerful Central Government" was so generally conceded at Charlottetown at the outset that by the time of the Quebec and London conferences it was accepted as axiomatic.

When the division of "powers" in the Canadian federation is examined in detail this contrast with the United States becomes unmistakable. In the preamble of section 91 appears the comprehensive phrase "laws for the peace, order, and good government of Canada, in relation to all matters not coming within the classes of subjects by this Act assigned exclusively to the Legislatures of the Provinces." To the national government fell the "exclusive legislative authority" over "the regulation of Trade and Commerce" (subs. 2), *carte blanche* for the raising of money for federal purposes "by any mode or system of Taxation" (subs. 3), "Militia, Military and Naval Service, and Defence" (subs. 7 forestalling altogether the state militia which made possible the Civil War), "Navigation and Shipping" (subs. 10), "Sea Coast and inland Fisheries" (subs. 12), "Banking, incorporation of banks, and the issue of paper money" (subs. 15, in contrast to the banks with state charters in the United States), "Savings Banks" (subs. 16), "Bankruptcy and Insolvency" (subs. 21), "Marriage and Divorce" (subs. 26), "the Criminal Law, except the Constitution of Courts of Criminal Jurisdiction, but including the Procedure in Criminal Matters" (subs. 27) and including the prerogative of pardon in criminal cases,[1] "Lines of steam or other ships, railways, canals, telegraphs, and other works and undertakings connecting the Province with any other or others of the Provinces or extending beyond the limits of the Province" (s. 92 (10a)), "Lines of steam ships between

[1] In contrast to the well-known range of pardon by forty-eight elective state governors in the United States.

the Province and any British or Foreign Country" (s. 92 (10b)), and "such works as, although wholly situate within the Province, are before or after their execution declared by the Parliament of Canada to be for the general advantage of Canada or for the advantage of two or more of the Provinces" (s. 92 (10c)).

In view of this impressive array of federal "powers" it is still possible to argue, as Monck and many of the centralists maintained so emphatically in 1864, that, within the range of section 91 of the Act, the B.N.A. *Act of 1867* is strictly not a federation at all but a legislative union. In some respects this is literally true. By section 3 of the Act "the Provinces of Canada, Nova Scotia, and New Brunswick shall form and be one Dominion under the name of Canada." Only after this union was it provided (s. 5) that "Canada shall be divided into four Provinces, named Ontario, Quebec, Nova Scotia, and New Brunswick." Monck insisted throughout, aptly enough as we have seen,[1] that "confederation" was an "entire misapplication of the term." Canada was not "a union of independent communities bound together by a treaty or agreement entered into in their quality of sovereign states," but a union "expressly conferred upon them by an Imperial Act of Parliament." Within the range of its own predominant "powers" the central national government deals not with provinces as such but with individuals everywhere throughout the union, and it is equipped to enforce its own legislative authority by its own officers in their national capacity. In national emergencies the federal "powers" have been more than once still further enlarged in order to command discerningly the maximum of national co-operation. Monck's insistence on this doctrine has already been noted:

To the extent of that authority the Union is not Federal, it is Legislative— Whatever the Union may be called the central government under such a system possesses to the extent of the powers given to it, and for the purposes of the execution of those powers, all the characteristics of a government representing a Legislative consolidation. . . . It secures to the central government . . . the elements of strength and stability.

IV

Next to the unwritten parliamentary system "similar in principle to that of the United Kingdom," the most deliberate departure from American models was the attempt to reverse the bias of the "residuary powers" of the federation and to vest not only the overwhelming preponderance of powers specifically divided but residuary powers, un-

[1]See above, p. 340.

specified in sections 91 and 92 of the Act, in the central national government. In the United States "the powers not delegated to the United States by the Constitution (nor prohibited by it to the States) are reserved to the States respectively or to the people." By the *B.N.A. Act of 1867* the federal government is empowered "to make laws for the peace, order, and good government of Canada, in relation to all matters not coming within the classes of subjects by this Act assigned exclusively to the Legislatures of the Provinces"; and even the federal powers listed under section 91 were specified "for greater certainty, but not so as to restrict the generality of the foregoing terms of this section."

It is true that this indubitable purpose of the fathers of confederation has had a strange and chequered history at the hands of reinvigorated provincialism in Canada and above all at the hands of the Judicial Committee of the Privy Council who conceived, not without reason, under Lord Watson and Lord Haldane, that they were interpreting the prevailing temper of the Canadian people at that time. The attempt to avoid conflict by listing "for greater certainty" the 29 federal powers in section 91 as well as the 16 provincial powers in section 92, has proved a delusion, for it opened the door to a long train of conflicts over "provincial rights," and no provincial prime minister with the legal sagacity and resourcefulness of Oliver Mowat could be expected to forgo the temptation to exploit them to the magnification of his office and the advantage of his party. But the attempt to reserve residuary powers for the federal government was not altogether unsuccessful, nor did it come to an end in 1867. Perhaps the most extensive residuary powers ever exercised by the federal government were acquired after that date.

The original union of 1867, as we have seen, was a federation of provinces each endowed (s. 109) with control of "all lands, mines, minerals, and royalties" within their boundaries, and the "management and sale of the Public Lands" (s. 92 (5)). In this respect the federation of the original thirteen states of the American union had followed the same pattern. But when seven of the states ceded to the federal government their claims to 400,000 square miles of disputed territory in the hinterlands as a "public domain," one of the profoundest policies in the unity and expansion of the republic began to dominate their politics. Within sixty years a vast area of nearly 2,500,000 square miles was acquired by treaty or purchase or conquest and added to the "public domain." Even when organized into territories and admitted as states into the union, these vast territories remained under "the absolute and complete proprietary power" of the federal government. With the exception of Texas, which retained control of its "public domain" when it joined the union, these "public land states" endowed the federal government with resources and prospects beyond the dreams of the primitive union of 1781. In the conflict between the industrial North and the agrarian South the prospective control of these resources and the prospective role of states created from them became the prime concern of the republic. From the time of the Missouri compromise the hope of settling these dynamic issues receded until war itself became the only resort in order to save the union. The free homestead system and the transcontinental railways were phases in this fundamental conflict, and the triumph of the North opened up for a whole generation an era of unprecedented expansion and exploitation.

This basic conflict in the American union was already clear enough to Canadian observers during the discussion of their own federation in 1864, and it is interesting to note that Galt would have vested the control of all public lands in the federal government in the first "drive for federation" in 1858. By the time of the Quebec conference, however, it was clear that the provinces would never relinquish their public lands. This was one of the penalties of sectionalism and distance in the federal system. For a time too it seemed that the new provinces already contemplated in the *B.N.A. Act of 1867* (s. 146) were to conform to the same pattern: the admission of British Columbia, Prince Edward Island, Newfoundland, and "Rupert's Land and the Northwestern Territory" was to be "subject to the provisions of this Act." This, as we shall see, was easily effected for British Columbia, and in the admission of Prince Edward Island the Dominion explored every resource to compensate that province for the ravages of "the eternal land question." But the first stage of expansion was the transfer of Rupert's Land from the Hudson's Bay Company to Canada, and in this process a whole new range of federal powers came into view. The phrase "subject to the provisions of this Act" was omitted in the provisions of the *Rupert's Land Act* of 1868 and the vast area from the Great Lakes to the Rocky Mountains and from the United States boundary to the Arctic Ocean was admitted as a territory. Canada was thus transformed, as we shall see, from a federation of equal provinces, each endowed with the administration of its own public lands, into an empire in its own right with the widest range of unalienated public lands directly under federal control to be found at that time in the British Empire. When the little province of Manitoba was organized in 1870 as a result of the Riel Insurrection the lands were still to be "administered by the government of Canada for the purposes of the Dominion." When Saskatchewan and Alberta were organized as provinces in 1905 the same proviso appeared in the *Saskatchewan* and *Alberta Acts*. American precedents in this respect were openly avowed. In 1882 the federal government asserted that Manitoba stood "in the same position as lands in the Territories of the United States which are not given to new States as these new States are created but remain the property of the United States." Two years later "the procedure of the Federal Government of the United States" which "rigidly retains the public lands" was still avowed at Ottawa. As late as 1905 Sir Wilfrid Laurier appealed for precedents to the United States where "the Federal Government has always retained the ownership and management of the public lands."

It was not until the two chief "purposes of the Dominion"—settlement based upon the free homestead system and a transcontinental railway based upon the railway land grant system—were effectually achieved that the remaining resources of the prairie provinces were restored in 1930 to provincial control with compensation for those alienated "for the purposes of the Dominion." If this long cycle of sixty years can be credited in any sense to "residuary powers" accruing to the new Dominion in the interests of "peace, order, and good government," it will be conceded that the attempt of the fathers of confederation to pre-empt residuary powers for the nation was not in vain. Probably the most effective era of federal control for "Dominion lands"—the first decade of the twentieth century—accrued long after the provinces had won back an impressive array of "provincial rights" and the Judicial Committee of the Privy Council had succeeded in devising certain "residuary" powers also for those categories listed for the provinces under section 92 of the *B.N.A. Act of 1867*.

V

This triple combination of power in the hands of the federal government—the unwritten conventions of parliamentary government, the formidable array of powers specifically assigned to the federal government, and the attempt, not altogether unsuccessful, to pre-empt residuary powers for the national government—have endowed the Canadian federation with the strongest powers, by comparison with those of provinces or states, to be found among democratic federations of the modern world. South Africa, to be sure, has gone farther towards centralization in a union rather than a federation. Nor must it be

assumed that such concentration of power is desirable for its own
sake apart from the purpose which it was designed to serve. In fact
this age-long controversy has passed through many vicissitudes in
Canada as well as in the United States, and federal-provincial conflict,
while less spectacular than that which culminated in civil war, has
been serious enough at times to dominate provincial and even federal
politics, and to cause grave concern for the future.

Whatever may be said of the relative powers vested initially in the
respective federal governments, or the relative balance between federal
and state or provincial powers at the present time, the trends in the
two federations have been remarkably different. In the United States
the long-range trends would appear to have been set with great consistency towards repairing the defective initial powers of the union.
Since the day of Chief Justice Marshall the judicial interpretations of
the Supreme Court have steadily reinforced this tendency while the
Judicial Committee of the Privy Council, with a few conspicuous
exceptions, has veered notoriously towards provincial rights until the
demonstrable designs of the fathers of confederation have been substantially undermined. It would almost seem that the American union,
beginning with the infirm "League of Friendship" in 1781 and in-
adequately reinforced even in the constitution of 1787, has employed
discerningly every device of statesmanship and judicial interpretation
—even war itself—to safeguard the union and its powers in the interests
of the republic. The Canadian federation, on the other hand, utilizing
skilfully and deliberately the phenomenal pressures under which confederation was achieved during the sixties, went farther towards
centralization than public opinion was sometimes prepared to sanction
after those pressures were removed. Thus while readjustment in the
United States has tended over the years with great consistency to
increase the federal powers of the republic, readjustment in Canada,
with conspicuous exceptions, has come in the direction of "provincial
rights."

How far these readjustments have impaired the original strength of
federal powers may be open to question. Much of the long tradition
of provincial rights in Ontario was built upon law cases like the St.
Catharines Milling Company case or the Manitoba Boundary dispute
in which Oliver Mowat's litigious skill and resourcefulness became a
familiar feature of provincial politics. In Quebec the deliberate estimate of Sir Etienne Taché in the Confederation Debates has been
underwritten ever since, it is safe to say, by every provincial government in that province:

If a Federal Union were obtained it would be tantamount to a separation of the provinces, and Lower Canada would thereby preserve its autonomy together with all the institutions it held so dear, and over which they could exercise the watchfulness and surveillance necessary to preserve them. (The honorable member repeated this portion of his speech in French, for the express purpose of conveying his meaning in the clearest and most forcible manner to his fellow-members for Lower Canada, who might not have apprehended so well the English.)

It was not by chance that the first interprovincial conference in 1887 was invited to Quebec by Honoré Mercier with Oliver Mowat in the chair.

In the prairie provinces much of the tradition of provincial rights may be traceable to nothing more sinister than the fact that it required a whole generation of controversy to restore those provinces to the status enjoyed by their colleagues in control of their public lands. In this controversy over the "Natural Resources Question," moreover, the wisdom of the federal government in retaining "Dominion lands" for national purposes of railways and immigration was never called in question, and it was only after those purposes had been achieved, so far as public lands could help to achieve them, that the transfer of the remaining resources to provincial control took place in 1930. It is remarkable too how quickly other provinces can develop provincial rights when one or two of them seem to be succeeding in that respect. When the Manitoba boundaries were extended in 1912 to equal those granted to Alberta and Saskatchewan in 1905 it was necessary to compensate Ontario and Quebec by extending their boundaries from the historic height of land to Hudson Bay and the distant shores of Davis Strait. In the long tale of fiscal readjustments the clamour of indigent provinces has been not only incessant but on occasion (as in 1907) successful. Fiscal claims against the provinces, on the other hand, do not make good federal politics. Provincial political parties can afford to be much more assertive and articulate in exploiting provincial rights. Since the Manitoba School Question, where the basis of provincial rights avowed in the Laurier-Sifton settlement seemed to make that doctrine unanimous, federal governments have been notoriously chary about burning their fingers in that particular fire.

It may still be true that a serious conflict with any one of the provinces could be relied upon to stir the embers of provincial rights in all of them. The Venetian ambassador once referred to the gregarious propensities of the Netherlands during the sixteenth century: "they are like a herd of pigs, pull the ear of one and they all squeal." The chorus of provincial rights in Canada has been less discordant than the clamour of the Dutch provinces under Charles V but it can scarcely be called a symphony. It has never approached the concerted action of the seceding states during the American Civil War. There has never been a civil war in Canada. Had federal powers, military, naval, and fiscal, been as paramount in the United States as in Canada it is hard to believe that secession could so far have jeopardized the American union. In any event the real peril in that desperate struggle arose less from cumulative "state rights" than from a fatal dualism among the states themselves. Such dualisms, east *versus* west, agriculture *versus* industry, French *versus* English in language and culture, are not unknown in Canada; though Canadian statesmanship must be bankrupt indeed to despair of reconciling these varied and invaluable interests. There are other aspects of dualism, however, which are not so easily reconciled, and in one respect at least the Canadian federation presents a contrast with the United States which appears to be permanent and irremediable.

VI

There is an element of stolidity if not of stability in the very number of constituent states in the American union. In Canada the provinces are much fewer in number. The big provinces are much bigger, the small provinces are relatively smaller, and the clash between the big provinces on the one hand and the smaller provinces on the other has been known to reach dangerous proportions.

There are big states too in the United States but there are more than two of them. New York and Pennsylvania, Texas and California, to name but four of them, wield inordinate power in presidential elections and in congress, but there are so many big states and so many relatively small ones that the clash of interest between big and small is lost in the mass and complexity of forty-eight states in every stage of development. A simple experiment in physics to illustrate the parallelogram of forces may be carried to the point where the result is almost incredible to the uninitiated observer. Two men can thrust a vertical staff downwards towards the floor against the power of any one man of equal strength to sustain it. But twenty men cannot do so if the one man knows the knack of diffusing and neutralizing the resultant diagonals from the downward thrust of the twenty into such a series of horizontal thrusts and tensions that the single undivided thrust upward can appear to sustain the vertical staff in equipoise. There may be not only mass and inertia but an element of safety and stability in sheer numbers.

In Canada the two big provinces of Ontario and Quebec have exerted from the beginning an inordinate influence upon the form and function of the Canadian federation. An Ontarian or a Québécois could retort without false modesty that this inordinate influence has been used on more than one occasion to meet national emergencies and to ballast the ship of state with stabilizing resources. In many respects, too, the big provinces provide balance as well as ballast in the Canadian lading.

It would be easy on the other hand to cite instances in which the two big provinces have used their preponderance in population and resources with something less than disinterested benevolence. In the fiscal adjustments of 1907 the old subsidy of 80 cents per head up to 400,000 of population was changed to 80 cents per head up to 400,000 and 60 cents per head thereafter. The result was an immediate increase of nearly 60 per cent in the provincial subsidy of Ontario and an increase of 41 per cent in that of Nova Scotia. By 1951 this subsidy had increased by some $145,500 per annum for Nova Scotia, more than $2,500,000 for Ontario and nearly $2,200,000 for Quebec. In 1912 the boundaries of Manitoba were extended, as we have seen, to equal those of Saskatchewan and Alberta in accordance with Sir Wilfrid Laurier's promise in 1905. Ontario secured her equivalent in the extension of her boundaries to Hudson Bay, and Quebec twice as much in the extension of that province to Davis Strait. The balance between Ontario and Quebec was readjusted when Ontario received a five-mile strip of territory through the province of Manitoba to York Factory which was regarded at that time as the terminus of the Hudson Bay Railway. It is not on record that the boundaries of the Maritimes were readjusted by "five-mile strips" in Ontario and Quebec.

In the original plans of Head and Mulgrave and MacDonnell as well as Tupper and Tilley a union of the Maritimes was intended, as we have seen, to precede and accompany the federation with the Canadas "on something like equal terms." The twenty-four senators from the Maritimes (with four more from Newfoundland) were intended to balance the twenty-four senators each from Ontario and Quebec. The defection of Prince Edward Island and other intractable problems so far complicated the issue of maritime union that it never recovered its place in the scheme of British American union. Tupper's makeshift plan of 1865 after the disastrous election of March in New Brunswick was countermanded by the Colonial Office unless it could be made at once "ancillary to and form part of the scheme for general union." Probably the last serious consideration of maritime union was

Howe's desperate plan to exact it as an alternative to outright repeal of federation for Nova Scotia. By that time it was clear that Prince Edward Island would accede to neither union, while New Brunswick had already crossed the Rubicon towards confederation. It was too late to stipulate maritime union as a guarantee of "something like equal terms." The device of equalizing all the states big and small in the senate of the United States by conceding two senators from each state—the same from Rhode Island or Delaware or Connecticut as from New York or Pennsylvania or Virginia—was once suggested at Quebec by A. A. Macdonald of Prince Edward Island after maritime union had gone by the board, but precedents from the United States were not in high esteem at that time and the suggestion was never seriously considered. In any event the inequality between big and small provinces in Canada was scarcely to be redressed by egalitarian representation in a Canadian senate. Thus two of the original four provinces had more than 76 per cent of the population of the Canadian federation. The provinces have since increased in number from four to ten but the disparity still remains. Ontario and Quebec still contain (1951) 61.77 per cent of the total population and 887,000 out of 2,151,000 square miles in area under provincial organization in Canada.

Could federation "on something like equal terms" still be attained by dividing the two big provinces or uniting the smaller provinces into regions more nearly equivalent in population and resources? Both devices have commanded a measure of academic interest, though it is doubtful if mere disparity is the real problem or an artificial equalization the real remedy. The Canadian federation is a family or a clan rather than an aggregation of territory or population. In any event the reception may be imagined which any serious proposal to subdivide Ontario or Quebec would receive at Queen's Park or on the Grande Allée. What political party, federal or provincial, would undertake to bell the cat? Inducements of considerable attractiveness might be brought to bear. Two completely bilingual provinces instead of one—bilingual in both federal and provincial fields as provided for Quebec alone by section 133 of the B.N.A. Act of 1867—might appeal to ardent nationalistic circles in Quebec. Manitoba from 1870 to 1889 has been the only other province in Canada similarly bilingual. The separation of northwestern Ontario could scarcely be expected to appeal to Bay Street, or the division of Quebec to St. James Street. Equality would still be illusory, while the stabilization derived in the United States from many states, both big and small, indistinguishably integrated, would still be far from won. There are not enough Rhode Islands and

Californias in Canada to obliterate the distinction between big and small or at any rate to make it impossible to gauge disparagingly the balance between them.

Could a series of regional unions readjust the balance in the other direction? The regional unions advocated by Sir Edmund Head and others after the failure of the first "drive for federation" in 1858 would have gone far towards this solution. Vancouver Island and the mainland west of the Rocky Mountains could be enlarged to include the Yukon. Head's project for "Saskatchewan" from the Rocky Mountains to Lake Nipigon would now include one of the most varied aggregations of potential wealth in Canada—coal and oil, mining and water-power, grazing and agriculture in unpredictable profusion. The project of maritime union, left derelict after the Quebec conference, has never been seriously revived, and it must be conceded that attempts to revive it have no such prospect as that of 1864 to warrant the attempt. Measured by the tonnage on provincial registers and the range of maritime trade the expansion of the Maritimes at that time was imposing and there was little to show that it had already passed its peak. Newfoundland, to be sure, is now at last a member of the Canadian Maritimes, with resources of iron in Labrador greater than the Mesabi range and of water-power on the Hamilton greater than Niagara, but it is doubtful if the Maritimes could be induced to forgo the atavistic parochialism so prevalent since the division of the old maritime province in 1769 and 1784. It would require pressures of inordinate strength and attractiveness to carry these counsels of perfection beyond the stages of academic speculation.

Meanwhile it is possible that the remedy for the glaring contrasts in size and resources among the Canadian provinces is to be found in the spirit rather than in the statistics of Canadian nationhood. A pan-Canadian approach in Canadian statesmanship may be more potent than all the calculations of the counting-house to unify and inspire the nation. A homely parable has survived from the era of utopian peace before the world wars. An Australian, a South African, and a couple of Canadians were congratulating a New Zealander upon the harmony which seemed to prevail in that idyllic community—an equable climate, a homogeneous population, an isolation which seemed at that time to amount to insulation from the stormy issues which beset the rest of the British dominions. The modest retort of the New Zealander was a compliment—perhaps an undeserved compliment—to the achievements of Canadian politics. How does it happen, he replied, that so many of the most constructive issues of the second empire were settled first in Canada: the problem of colonial administration by responsible government, the problem of regional disintegration by the Canadian federation, the problems of race and expansion and transcontinental transportation by prodigies of statesmanship and resourcefulness. The truth is, he concluded modestly, we have not enough difference of opinion in New Zealand to engender energetic statesmanship. It may be conceded without false modesty that Canadian politics are never likely to go bankrupt for want of issues to challenge the resourcefulness of Canadian statesmanship. A pan-Canadian approach may be the response to such a challenge and Canadian nationhood may emerge the stronger for the ordeal. A pan-Canadian nationhood rising above the miasma of parochialism is warranted by the best traditions of Confederation. It is equally warranted now. "Magnanimity in politics," said Burke, "is not seldom the truest wisdom. . . . We ought to elevate our minds to the greatness of that trust."

IV

EXPANSION

Chapter Twenty

POLITICAL EXPANSION:

"THE KEYSTONE OF THE ARCH"

THE original three provinces of the Dominion, becoming four in the process of federation, comprised less than one-sixth the present area of Canada. The rest of British North America was still in jeopardy though its ultimate destination in the design of the fathers of confederation was no longer in doubt. At least one of the provinces contemplated in 1867 reached that destination only in 1949 after no fewer than three abortive attempts at union. The rest of British North America entered federation within a single decade, much of it, however, in a status so primitive that a cycle of sixty years of development was required to bring it into conformity with the original design of 1867. The Riel Insurrection which thwarted for a time, as we shall see, the first major impact of the political expansion of the new Dominion, threatened to infect that process from the outset with the bitter strife of the Canadas.

The thirteen states of the American union had begun with much more precarious prospects of westward expansion. Franklin had set the South Sea as the ultimate destination of the undivided empire. For a divided empire the physical barriers were more hazardous. Knox consoled himself with the reflection that the rebellious states would lose themselves in the illimitable hinterlands of the continent. The political and diplomatic problems were still more formidable. But Knox "knew not the stomach of that people," the resourcefulness of the American pioneer. It required every official device from purchase and diplomacy to war itself to keep pace with the westward march of the American frontiersman. For two generations the task of supplanting Spain in the Floridas, France in Louisiana, Mexico in Texas and beyond to the Pacific, Britain in Oregon, and Russia in Alaska, was pursued with unwavering assiduity. The purchase of Alaska within a few months of the Canadian federation completed an era of territorial expansion which rivalled the colonial expansion of Spain in the new world or of Russia in the old.

Compared with this ubiquitous growth the political expansion of Canada from sea to sea was a forthright and simple process, and it was substantially achieved within less than a single decade. In the Quebec Resolutions of 1864 (section 10) the Pacific was already in view. The B.N.A. *Act of 1867* supplied at once the statutory basis for a transcontinental Dominion. By section 146 of that Act both Newfoundland and Prince Edward Island on the Atlantic and British Columbia beyond the Rockies were foreordained to union with Canada "on Addresses from the Houses of Parliament of Canada, and from the Houses of the respective Legislatures" of those provinces. For Rupert's Land and the North-Western Territory—the chartered territory of the Hudson's Bay Company and the vast regions beyond formerly held by the licences of 1821 and 1838—a less orthodox procedure was necessary. Since there were no "legislatures" to sponsor the views of the inhabitants, the "terms and conditions" of union were to be left to the Canadian Houses of Parliament on the one hand and to such considerations on the other "as the Queen thinks fit to approve, subject to the provisions of this Act." Before the process was over the constitution of Canada, as Lincoln once remarked of that of the United States during the Civil War, was to have a "rough time of it." In the central regions of the West as in the Canadas before Confederation two uprisings were to mar their peace and harmony. The first "new province" of Manitoba in 1870, British Columbia in 1871, and Prince Edward Island in 1873 completed, except for Newfoundland, the tale of provinces projected by the B.N.A. *Act of 1867.* By this time a new B.N.A. *Act of 1871* had validated the irregularities of the transfer of Rupert's Land "for all purposes whatsoever," and provided a technique for territorial government and for the admission of new provinces to keep pace with the settlement of the West. This process was completed in Canada in 1905 with the organization of Alberta and Saskatchewan and in 1930 when all three of the prairie provinces like the other provinces of confederation were endowed with their public lands.[1]

Canada far outdistanced the United States in the speed and simplicity of her political expansion—a consummation directly due, of course, to the fact that the whole region from Newfoundland to Vancouver Island was already British and required for its political consolidation only a transfer from one administration to another. The process of state organization in the mainland area of the United States

[1]See Figs. 1 to 4 following p. 508.

was completed only in 1912 with the admission of Arizona and New Mexico to the union. Much of the area which still remains under territorial organization north of the sixtieth parallel in Canada may yet reach provincial status when the unpredictable resources of the north are systematically explored. It is in this aspect of their history, the appropriation and organization of the frontier, that the two nations come closest together in association and environment. In many respects the experience of the United States has been invaluable. A series of regulations in territorial organization, valuable not only for their intrinsic worth but for the lessons to be drawn from a few costly and avoidable mistakes, were adapted to Canadian needs with phenomenal ingenuity and success.

I

When the Select Committee of the British House of Commons brought in their famous *Report* in 1857, the Hudson's Bay Company controlled more than a quarter of the North American continent, nominally the largest area ever administered under one government in America. Within five years this vast area had been broken into fragments. Two of these, west of the Rocky Mountains, had been organized to form eventually the province of British Columbia. Two others—Rupert's Land, the original chartered territory of the Company, and the North-Western Territory which lay between Rupert's Land and the Arctic—still awaited the outcome of British policy in the eastern provinces. It was this vast intermediate area—"the keystone of the arch," as Lord Dufferin once called it—which left the rest in such precarious isolation. Without it union with British Columbia was of course impossible. Without it even the massive abutments of that arch in the east, in George Brown's opinion (1862), could scarcely have remained intact. When the hour at last struck, the sequel in British policy was very rapid. Within fifteen years all the Hudson's Bay territories of 1857 had found their way piecemeal into the Canadian federation.

This disintegration of Hudson's Bay rule was a very deliberate as well as a very rapid process. It followed upon the profoundest change in British colonial policy—the concession of responsible government—and it culminated in a transcontinental British Dominion. It marked a turning-point in imperial as well as Canadian policy, a definite project of devolving responsibility for British interests in North America upon the shoulders of the young Dominion; and in accepting that responsibility Canada was transformed, as we shall see, from a federation of equal provinces into a veritable empire, with a vast domain of subordinate colonial territory under its control. The spirit in which Canada then proceeded to deal with this "colonial" territory affords a curious parallel to British colonial policy at that time. Scarcely emerging as yet from adolescence under the parental eye of the Colonial Office, Canada found itself within four years *in loco parentis* to all the orphan children of the Hudson's Bay Company across the continent. The discharge of those parental duties confronted the new Dominion with the first major crisis of its existence, and the results of that experiment are still discernible in Canadian politics.

There were four distinct areas involved—two on either side of the Rocky Mountains—and the inconsistency in dealing with these was responsible for much mischief. That inconsistency was inescapable in 1870 and 1871. Rupert's Land, the terrain draining into Hudson Bay and Strait, on the extreme east and Vancouver Island on the extreme west were both proprietary areas held by the Company in fee simple, the first by the Charter of 1670, the second by Letters Patent of 1849. Without discussing here the controversy between Canada and the Company with regard to the chartered rights of 1670 it will be sufficient to state that the *Rupert's Land Act of 1868* which provided for the final transfer to Canada in 1870 was based upon the amplest recognition of the Company's proprietary rights and government. "Eminent law officers, consulted in succession," wrote the Colonial Secretary, "have all declared that the validity of the Charter cannot justly be disputed by the Crown."

Between Rupert's Land and Vancouver Island lay a vast territory held since 1821 by twenty-one year licences and divided by the watershed of the Rocky Mountains into New Caledonia on the west and the North-Western Territory on the east. These four districts were to go into confederation as the living creatures went in two and two unto Noah into the ark. The two areas west of the Rockies, one "chartered" and one "licensed," went in as the Province of British Columbia. The other pair, Rupert's Land and the North-Western Territory, passed through a vastly different process. The legal and constitutional preliminaries were the same and might have been expected to lead to the same result. Both "licensed" areas reverted to the crown in 1859 at the expiration of the licence of 1838. There was no difficulty here. In both "chartered" districts too, east and west, the process of extinguishing the Hudson's Bay title was the same—by compensation to the Company for the surrender of proprietary rights to the crown. The subsequent transfer to Canada in all four areas presented no difficulty. This took place like confederation itself by free grant from the crown. What complicated the whole process was the compensation to the Company for the surrender of the ancient and venerable proprietary rights in Rupert's Land.

The compensation of £57,500 for Vancouver Island was paid by the British government; the old "chartered" and "licensed" areas were united under the name of British Columbia, and British Columbia could thus make its own terms with Canada. Those terms were so magnanimous that a Manitoban or Nova Scotian can only contemplate them, like the gargantuan prodigies of nature that abound in that happy province, with wonder and admiration. The spirit in which they were offered seems almost as exotic in Canadian politics as Douglas firs and salmon runs and totem poles in the more sombre background of Canadian pioneering.

The contrast in this respect between the two western districts under British tutelage and the two corresponding eastern districts under Canadian is too striking to be accounted for by infirmities of temper. With a population half as large again as that of British Columbia, Rupert's Land found itself between the upper and the nether millstone. For reasons which are still defensible for their sagacity and courage the attempt was made to acquire this whole area from the Great Lakes to the Rockies not as a province but as a subordinate territory; and even when the Riel Insurrection played havoc with that calculation and made it necessary at the outset to create the Province of Manitoba, the same valid reasons prevailed to restrict its status. "The land could not be handed over to them," said Sir John A. Macdonald in discussing the *Manitoba Act*, "it was of the greatest importance to the Dominion to have possession of it, for the Pacific Railway must be built by means of the land through which it had to pass." Rupert's Land lay in the pathway to the Pacific, and a primitive population there awaited the transfer with foreboding. What were to be the fortunes of the Métis whose forbears, the French *voyageurs*—the "freemen" of the old North West Company—and their dusky progeny, had roamed the *pays d'en haut* for three generations? Above all what were to be the rights of the little Quebec which men of French race had founded and a devoted clergy had cherished on the banks of the Red River? In its immediate results the Riel Insurrection was almost completely successful. Its ultimate results have not been so clear. Some of the most poignant reflections not only upon the process of confederation but upon the subsequent relations between the two historic races of Canada have come to be associated with the name of Louis Riel.

There were four alternatives before the Red River district during the decade before confederation. The first of these was the recommendation of the Select Committee of 1857. British policy had not as yet risen to the task of integrating a transcontinental Dominion. Without surrendering the prospect of ultimate federation Sir Edmund Head had been forced, as we have seen, by the exigencies of Canadian politics to forgo anything like the project of 1851 which he had drafted for Lord Grey from the placid province of New Brunswick, and to recommend (1856) for Labouchere a series of preliminary regional unions across the continent. After the failure of the first "drive for federation" in 1858 there was a return with renewed emphasis to these regional projects. For the central regions of the continent the existing union of the Canadas formed the obvious nucleus, and the Select Committee had advised that the "districts on the Red River and the Saskatchewan" should be "ceded to Canada on equitable principles." Had this taken place in the fifties a decade of settlement might possibly have warranted another province in 1867.

A second alternative—annexation to the United States—was long regarded in many quarters as the "manifest destiny" of the Red River district. In a single decade the current of population through Iowa, Illinois, Wisconsin, and Minnesota had reached the proportions of a Gulf Stream in direction and momentum. This movement of more than two millions of resourceful settlers south of the Great Lakes was already approaching the upper reaches of the Red River when Canadian opinion in 1856 suddenly awoke to the danger. Except for the Hudson Bay route the only access from Red River to the outside world now lay through the United States. Red River carts were soon plying regularly to St. Paul. Steam navigation began in 1861 with the old *Anson Northrup,* renamed the *Pioneer,* and the Hudson's Bay Company soon supplanted it with their own *International.* A resolution of the Minnesota legislature, framed in language which would now invite an international crisis, demanded the annexation of Assiniboia. The gesture was interpreted at Red River as "the highest tribute yet paid to this country." An American agent—afterwards Consul "Saskatchewan" Taylor—reported in 1865 that without prompt action on the part of Great Britain "the speedy Americanization of the fertile district is inevitable." As late as 1869 Governor McTavish of the Hudson's Bay Company wrote from Fort Garry that the annexation of Assiniboia to the United States would be its "ultimate destiny" and the sooner it could take place the better.

More than one American observer has been inclined to regard

annexation as a major issue in the Riel Insurrection. But the truth was that American opinion at Red River was more sanguine than influential. O'Donoghue, whom Riel used for his own purposes throughout the insurrection—it may be to his own undoing—was of course an incorrigible Fenian, and this fact lent an altogether fictitious tinge to the movement. Major Robinson, too, who edited the *New Nation* for a time during the insurrection ventured to print one issue which was called an annexation number; but it proved to be the last to advocate that cause, for of all the eventualities of that time, annexation to the United States must have been the least attractive to Louis Riel. For the little Quebec at Red River, even the Canadian federation, with Quebec as a powerful partner, seemed a precarious venture in 1869. Annexation to the United States would have exterminated every major safeguard which the Riel Insurrection was designed to establish. The traditional role of Quebec in Canadian history is a commentary upon this theme.

The third alternative was the creation, as in British Columbia, of a crown colony capable of making its own terms with Canada. There were many advocates of this course both within and without the Hudson's Bay Company. When the control of the Company passed to the International Financial Society in 1863 this became the official policy of the directorate. Even before Sir Edmund Head left Canada there were signs of this plan in the relations between John Ross of the Grand Trunk, Sir George Simpson in Montreal, and Cartier in the shoals of Canadian politics. With Head translated to the governorship of the Hudson's Bay Company in London "at the suggestion—almost the personal request—of the Duke of Newcastle" (according to Watkin) this policy was openly avowed until it came to grief upon the ugly problem of compensation to the Company. Newcastle and Head must have fallen instinctively into step with mutual confidence and assurance. Had Newcastle lived to authorize a crown colony at Red River it is conceivable that like British Columbia it might have made its own terms with Canada and forestalled the long record of insurrection and turmoil in Manitoba. But there were obstacles well nigh insuperable in 1863. To begin with, Watkin's chimerical schemes for coping with a Clear Grit ascendancy in Canadian politics after May, 1862, may well have become as dubious to Head as Watkin's equally chimerical finance to the house of Baring. Both confronted Watkin in the end with a polite but realistic *non possumus*. The truth was that even Head and Newcastle, with the best of goodwill on both sides, were unable to devise mutually acceptable terms in 1863. Compensation in "hard money," so dear, as we shall see, to the old shareholders of the Company, was out of the question from the Colonial Office; while the Company's alternative, a proprietary interest in the land, was not calculated to appeal to the Colonial Office at a time when the Howe-Gray-Ritchie imperial commission on "the eternal land question" in Prince Edward Island had just exhumed in all its ugliness the record of absentee proprietorship in that province:

In an unsettled colony . . . the whole progress of the Colony depends on the liberal and prudent disposal of its land. These considerations afford decisive reasons against leaving that land in the possession of a corporation. . . .

In Prince Edward Island . . . the result has not been such as to invite imitation. . . .

Colonists of the Anglo-Saxon race look upon the land revenue as legitimately belonging to the community.

The fourth alternative was that which eventually came to pass: transfer Rupert's Land "on equitable principles" not to the old province of "Canada" but to the Canadian confederation. Two steps were obviously necessary. The Company must be compensated for surrendering its proprietary rights to the crown, and the whole vast area of Rupert's Land and the North-Western Territories beyond must be organically incorporated into the structure of the new Dominion. The first step taxed the ingenuity of the Colonial Office to the utmost. The other was still more difficult. In what capacity was the new district to enter confederation? It was this second problem which led to the Riel Insurrection, raising issues which have never yet been completely solved in Western Canada, and in a very real sense changing not only the scope and function but the very nature of the Canadian confederation.

II

The statute which finally dealt with these problems was the *Rupert's Land Act* of 1868—next to the *B.N.A. Acts* themselves the most important imperial Act of the nineteenth century in its bearing upon the destinies of Canada.

Two decisions of prime importance were finally registered by this statute. The first was the surrender of Rupert's Land to the crown with compensation to the Hudson's Bay Company. For this at least there was a salutary precedent, as we shall see, in British Columbia. The terms, as for Vancouver Island, were to be "agreed upon by and between Her Majesty and the said Governor and Company." Overtures to that effect had been opened, as we have seen, by Lytton as

early as 1858. Six years later George Brown, the lone Canadian behind the scenes in London when the great decision of December 3,
1864, was announced for a general federation to supplant the preliminary regional unions across the continent, had been specifically
charged by the Canadian cabinet with the problem of the West. The
Canadian delegation to the Colonial Office in the following April,
though concerned primarily with defence and the carrying of the
Maritimes into confederation, brought the influence of that famous
quartet under Brown's enthusiastic enterprise to bear also upon the
problem of Rupert's Land. An agreement was reached that in case of
transfer to Canada "the indemnity, if any [to the Hudson's Bay
Company], should be paid by a loan raised by Canada under the
Imperial Guarantee."

The presence in London in 1865 of Sir Edmund Head, now Governor
of the Hudson's Bay Company, was more than a coincidence. It would
be interesting to speculate upon the reflections which must have been
his as the long journey in the cause of British American union drew
to a close. What would Head and Cartier and Galt have had to say
to each other over the port and walnuts had it been possible for them
in 1865 to renew the confidences of the first "drive for federation" in
1858? Head lived only long enough—January, 1868—to see his dream
of federation taking tangible form on foundations deeper and stronger
than he had ever dared to hope for during the two decades of his
administration over British North America. The terms of the transfer
were drawn up in the end by the Colonial Office and forced upon the
Company under considerable pressure after Head's death. Cartier and
McDougall, sent to London (1868) to supervise the transfer, were
warranted by the Act in disclaiming responsibility not only for the
terms of surrender to the crown but for the payment of the compensation to the Company. *The Rupert's Land Act*, they wrote, "was not
introduced at the instance or passed in the interest of the Canadian
Government," and it "placed the negotiation of the terms of surrender
by the Company to the Crown in the hands of Her Majesty's Government where . . . we are of opinion it must remain."

This aloofness, as we shall see, could scarcely be maintained, but
the terms proposed by the Company in 1868 by comparison with those
eventually conceded by Canada are apt to impress a Canadian minister
of finance at the present time with rueful reflections. The Company
was prepared to surrender its proprietary rights for "a sum of hard
money," "one million sterling, in bonds" being stated by the Company

as a settlement "acceptable to our proprietors."[1] The final terms were £300,000 "in hard money" and one-twentieth of the "fertile belt"[2] together with certain other specified blocks adjoining Hudson's Bay posts. This resulted in the grant of some 6,630,000 acres of land in lieu of the £700,000 "in hard money" which the Company was induced to forgo—a valuation of £700,000, it would seem, for one-twentieth of the "fertile belt." The proceeds from this princely patrimony have dwarfed the most fantastic price "in hard money" that could have been conceived by the Company in the impecunious era of 1868. The gross sales of Hudson's Bay lands in Western Canada to 1930, without cancellations and revestments, amounted to about $60,000,000. Moreover, the shrewd policy of the Company in retaining mineral rights at the sale of their lands has endowed the Company, in sections 8 and 26 of every township, with fabulous reserves within a distance of three miles of every oil well in the fertile belt.[3]

Fiscal poverty, of course, was not the only motive of Canadian policy. The active co-operation of the old Company was sought in the form of a vested landed interest in the settlement of the West. But the compensation to the Company even to the extent of £300,000 "in hard money" was still a problem. It could scarcely be expected from the United Kingdom without setting a disastrous precedent for crown grants all over the British Empire. When the *Rupert's Land Act* came from the House of Commons it was found to contain an amendment "that no Charge shall be imposed by such terms upon the Consolidated Fund of the United Kingdom." It became necessary therefore for Canada either to compensate the Company for the surrender to the crown or to forgo the subsequent free transfer to Canada. This was agreed to by Cartier and McDougall in London[4] under protest as a sort of settlement out of court, though interested parties in Canada

[1]Lord Kimberly to Colonial Secretary, Oct. 27, 1868, *Correspondence Relating to the Surrender of Rupert's Land*, p. 25.

[2]The "fertile belt" was bounded "on the south by the United States boundary; on the west by the Rocky Mountains; on the north by the northern branch of the Saskatchewan; on the east by Lake Winnipeg, Lake of the Woods, and the waters connecting them." See Fig. 2.

[3]The one-twentieth was allocated in section 8 and three quarter-sections of section 26 in each township for four townships, and the whole of section 26 in every fifth township. Of the 720 quarter-sections in every five townships the Company thus received 28 in four townships and 8 in the fifth or a total of 36/720. See Plan of Township, Fig. 3.

[4]Ratified by Joint Address of the Canadian Houses of Parliament, May 29 and 31, 1869.

did not hesitate in later years to maintain that Rupert's Land had been "purchased" by Canada and was therefore "owned," "possessed," and "administered [as the *Manitoba Act* stated] by the Government of Canada for the purposes of the Dominion." The "hard money" was raised by loan guaranteed by the imperial government[1] and retired only in 1904. The rest of the compensation to the Company—the twentieth of the fertile belt and certain blocks of land near Hudson's Bay posts—was still more protracted. Allocated evenly in sections 8 and 26 in every township the area which finally accrued to the Company was about 6,630,000 acres, nearly six times the area of Prince Edward Island. Of this more than 2,600,000 remained unsold in 1930.

The second provision of the *Rupert's Land Act* was more revolutionary for it transformed not only the size but the nature of the Canadian confederation. The original Dominion was a federation of equal provinces each endowed with its public lands. For British Columbia, Prince Edward Island, Newfoundland, and even for Rupert's Land and the North-Western Territory, section 146 of the *B.N.A. Act of 1867* prescribed the organization of similar provinces "subject to the provisions of this Act." In the *Rupert's Land Act*, however, this phrase was significantly omitted and the whole area from the Ontario boundary to the Rocky Mountains and from the original Quebec and Ontario boundaries northward to Hudson Bay and the Arctic could now be appropriated not as a province but as a subordinate territory. Canada thus ceased to be a confederation of equal provinces and became a veritable empire in its own right endowed with the widest range of unalienated public lands to be found at that time under one administration in the British Empire. The various stages through which the central provinces had passed from the *Quebec Act* to confederation were now prescribed for these primitive Canadian colonies in the West. An *Act for the Temporary Government of Rupert's Land and the North-Western Territories when United with Canada* was hurriedly passed in 1869 (32 and 33 Vic., c. 3) providing for the government of this whole vast area by governor and council both to be appointed from Ottawa. With no representative institutions whatever and no statutory safeguards for the French population at Red River, whose compatriots even in Quebec were still restive under the safeguards of confederation, the new Canadian colonial system began at a stage more primitive than the old colonial system at its worst. It became apparent that the population at Red River had been too

[1]*Rupert's Land Loan Act.* 32 and 33 Vic., c. 101.

casually overlooked in the desperate hurry to appropriate the West. One group in particular, for reasons we must now examine, objected to being "bought like the buffalo."

III

The little community at Red River contained at this time a white and mixed population of about eleven thousand, exclusive of the native Indian. All but a few hundred of these represented the second or third generation in Rupert's Land. The responsibility for the insurrection of 1869 may be narrowed by a simple process of elimination.

The American element, though exploited by Riel wherever it could fortify his cause, never comprehended, it would seem, the dominant motives of the French Métis and their trusted leaders at Red River. Stutsman at the boundary, O'Donoghue, Riel's Fenian ally, at Fort Garry, Major Robinson and others were intent upon making trouble between the Settlement and the Canadian or British authorities. The shamrock appeared upon the flag of the provisional government. One of the three delegates appointed to discuss terms at Ottawa was Alfred Scott, an American citizen. But Scott's influence was negligible, and O'Donoghue discovered in good time that his Fenian projects were not to be served by the French Métis at Red River. O'Donoghue's Fenian raid of 1871 was easily scattered by Captain Wheaton of the United States army, and his attempts to involve Riel and the French cause were easily frustrated. "I perceived at once," wrote Archbishop Taché of St. Boniface at a later date, "that he was endeavouring to deceive me."

The Hudson's Bay interests may be more easily absolved from any direct share in the insurrection. None, it is true, had more to lose by the transfer to Canada than the sedate officials in Rupert's Land. Men like Governor McTavish of Rupert's Land and Dr. Cowan, Chief Factor at Fort Garry, were to be transformed by it from veritable "nabobs" to local shopkeepers. For generations the staid officials of the Company at Fort Garry had set the standards of deportment and private integrity at Red River. Now they were ignored alike by the directors of the Company in London who were "little better than greenhorns" in the fur-trade, and by the Canadian government at Ottawa. They were not consulted upon their claim to a share in the compensation for the surrender to the crown; and when Governor McTavish of Rupert's Land stopped off at Ottawa on his way to Red River he reported that "these gentlemen are of opinion that they

know a great deal more about the country than we do." Had the
Canadian government appointed Governor McTavish of the Hudson's
Bay Company as the first governor of the territory, much might have
been done to "smooth" the transfer in the traditional "Hudson's Bay
manner." But on the other hand it may be stated with certainty that
no such appointment would have removed the real causes of the Riel
Insurrection. Meanwhile the aspersions showered upon the Hudson's
Bay officials by McDougall and the Canadian party at the Settlement
were singularly gratuitous. No man perhaps was better informed than
Archbishop Machray with regard to the temper and opinion of the
old settlers at Red River. In a confidential memorandum which must
be regarded as one of the most judicious and convincing records of
that day the Archbishop deplored the "most undeserved suspicion . . .
thrown out upon Gentlemen whose reports could have been thoroughly
relied upon. . . . I am perfectly sure that no dissatisfaction of the
employees of the Hudson's Bay Company had anything to do with
these troubles."

One other group, by far the most considerable in numbers and
affluence in the immediate vicinity of Fort Garry, may be eliminated
with equal certainty. From 1821 to 1850 the Selkirk settlers had their
own battles with the Company but the influences which reached the
Settlement from without during the fifties and the sixties served to
identify their interests. The instinctive conservatism which they had
in common was fortified by deliberate policy, by intermarriage, by
the increasing numbers of retired officials of the Company at Red
River, and by a growing tradition enshrined in the classic pages of
Ross's *Red River Settlement*—a tradition surviving to this day in the
intimate and closely knit coterie of the Lord Selkirk Association. The
gaucheries of the Canadian party aroused much resentment in these
reserved and sedate circles, but the old settlers, wrote Archbishop
Machray, "never had any doubt that the matter would soon right
itself. . . . They certainly never did anything to give a beginning to
the French action." Their attitude, however, for many years was
gravely misunderstood. The Canadians accused them of "disloyalty,"
and in addition to that monstrous imputation charged them with
cowardice in not taking arms against their kindly French neighbours
across the river. "Take down my old musket and shoot Louis Riel?"
retorted old McBeth. "Why, he cuts my wood for me in the winter."
The French in turn reproached them with a betrayal of that "neighbourliness and good feeling" so long traditional between them. A few
of the old settlers acquiesced in Riel's ascendancy in the interests of

peace, but the truth is that they had no reason to share the worst fears of the French clerical interests at Red River. "The originating causes of those troubles," wrote Archbishop Machray, had "arisen entirely from the French and Roman Catholic Section of the Community."

There remain the two antagonistic groups of the insurrection. For ten years the Canadian party, supported by the *Nor'-Wester*, the only newspaper in the Settlement, had advocated union with Canada, but frequently in a manner which antagonized many of the most influential among the old settlers, and filled the clerical guardians of the French Métis with alarm. Improvident, good-natured, credulous, the Métis were easily stirred to suspect that "they would probably be crowded out." "The indolent and careless," proclaimed the *Nor'-Wester* "like the native tribes of the country, will fall back before the march of a superior intelligence." It would be easy to multiply instances of tactlessness, of blundering mismanagement and worse on the part of the Canadian party. Their most aggressive champion, Dr. Schultz, was once committed to jail by the sheriff and forcibly liberated by his friends. It was Dr. Schultz, jailed a second time by Riel during the insurrection, who escaped to Canada on snowshoes and set the heather on fire in Ontario after the barbarous death of Scott in March, 1870.[1]

The French Métis who supplied the brawn though not the brain behind the Riel Insurrection were disposed by the rude discipline of the buffalo hunt to obey their chosen leaders with credulous self-confidence. Like the Dutch in South Africa they represented generations of skilful adaptation to a strange and exotic environment. The buffalo hunt of the Red River Métis had long been famous. Ross describes the pandemonium of discordant noises as the buffalo hunters, all "crack shots" and mounted on their well-trained ponies, left the Settlement for the plains accompanied by their dusky progeny in Red River carts equipped at Fort Garry for the preparation of the season's pemmican. The prodigious numbers of the buffalo were as yet scarcely diminished from the myriads which the younger Henry had described at Pembina, in the early days of the fur-trade. The danger and wild excitement of the stampede in which hunters fired and reloaded in full career, followed by the preparation of the pemmican in their disciplined encampment after the hunt, developed a primitive skill and resourcefulness which was not to be gainsaid when the occasion

---

[1]Dr. Schultz lived to be Lieutenant-Governor of Manitoba and to give assent to the legislation deleting separate schools and the French language from the *Manitoba Act*.

arose to use it for other purposes. Ambroise Lépine who was master of the buffalo hunt in 1869 had only to lead his well-trained and well-armed cohorts into Fort Garry after the autumn buffalo hunt to establish there, under the vainglorious leadership of Louis Riel, a force which easily dominated the Red River Settlement until the arrival of the troops in the following August.

The fears of the Métis are easily understood. They had no title to their rude little farms on the river-banks, and it was easy to play upon their credulity. The rough horse-play of a "chain-man" on the Dawson road who pretended that he was surveying a farm for his brother in Ontario could do irreparable damage to the goodwill of these simple but resentful people, and those who could have reassured them had no interest in allaying their resentment. Riel himself, who protested before the Council of Assiniboia that the Métis were "uneducated and only half-civilized," admitted that he had done nothing to reassure them. In their ignorance and simplicity they were inclined to magnify their own prowess as well as their grievances. An authentic instance is attested by an eye-witness. One of the Canadian "prisoners" in the jail during the insurrection sought to impress the Métis on sentry-go with the might of Canada and the British Empire. The Métis remained unimpressed. The savage Sioux whose long feud with the American outposts was to culminate in Custer's Massacre had always given a wide berth to the well-trained buffalo hunters at Red River. "We beat de Sioux," replied the sentry. "De Sioux dey beat de Yankee, de Yankee dey beat de British. . . . We beat de British." The immediate aims of the Métis were equally naïve and equally impossible. "Reserves" of land appeared early in their demands, and 1,400,000 acres were set aside for them in due course by the *Manitoba Act*. But the land was granted in the form of negotiable scrip and the improvident Métis all too often sold it for a pony or a few dollars and moved off to the Saskatchewan where a more serious uprising under their old leader challenged the militia of the young Dominion in 1885. Whatever the value of "reserves" of land for the Métis there could be no reserves for the buffalo; and the "freighting" of the Red River cart was already doomed by the steamboat on the Red River, to be followed by the railway from St. Paul in 1878. Meanwhile the Canadian surveyors at Red River during the summer of 1869 were themselves harbingers of change. They were operating, it is now known, under permission of the Company in London when a survey party was stopped by a band of Métis under Louis Riel who resented their "intention to ride roughshod over everything and everybody."

IV

The roots of the Riel Insurrection, however, go much deeper than this, and both the French cause and in the long run Riel himself have suffered through the tactics of his apologists in seeking to justify every act of violence by citing piecemeal the stupidity or folly of his antagonists. No amount of special pleading can legalize by these methods the expulsion of McDougall, the prospective lieutenant-governor of the territory, while yet a private citizen; the seizure and appropriation of his furniture; the opening of the mails; the occupation of Fort Garry; the expropriation of the private quarters of Dr. Cowan the Chief Factor; the opening of the safe; the seizure of arms, ammunition, and provisions; the declaration of November 24, a week before government by Canada was even contemplated, that the Métis were "free and exempt from all allegiance" to the Hudson's Bay Company and that they had "on the said 24th of November, 1869, above mentioned, established a Provisional Government and hold it to be the only and lawful authority." The subsequent blunders of McDougall in issuing the spurious proclamation of December 1 and a commission to Colonel Dennis to raise a force to overthrow the French party were no less illegal. Reprisals on both sides became inevitable, and the virtual imprisonment of Governor McTavish, already mortally ill, and of Donald Smith, the subsequent capture of the Portage party, and the cold-blooded execution of Thomas Scott by a firing-party outside the walls of Fort Garry, mark a steady and rapid descent into Avernus.

But those who find in these surface indications the full story of the Riel Insurrection and the creation of a new province under the *Manitoba Act* must be singularly undiscerning. There is method in all this, but its justification is not to be found in piecemeal extenuation. For Canadians of French origin, at least, there are higher grounds which might dignify not only the cause but the part which Riel played in it beyond the power, it may be, of his most costly blunders, his most egregious defects of temper and of character, altogether to destroy. The trusted guardians of the French population of Assiniboia, Bishop Taché and Father Ritchot among them, claimed the rights of their compatriots in the province of Quebec. Their history at Red River for two generations, they believed, justified those claims. A Canadian governor and council appointed from Ottawa might have jeopardized their "rights" at every point. Nothing but their admission as a province, with statutory safeguards for separate schools, the French language, and a second chamber for the protection of minorities, could supply adequate guarantees. In 1869, with both imperial and Canadian statutes about to be implemented at Red River, the situation seemed irremediable; and so indeed it was without drastic action to prevent the transfer until satisfactory "terms" could be made.

That drastic action was largely the work of one man. We are here concerned not with the later phases of Riel's wayward and tragic career which was in the nature of anti-climax but with the expansion of Canada in 1870 and the demonstrable origins of the *Manitoba Act*. There were others such as Father Ritchot and Bishop Taché who were wiser in counsel, and others such as Ambroise Lépine who were equally resolute in the use of force. But none at Red River combined the will to use both more successfully than Louis Riel, and so long as French rights are cherished it will stand to his credit among his countrymen in Western Canada that he saw what had to be done and had the courage to do it. When M. Provencher, nephew of the first bishop at St. Boniface, was sent by McDougall in October to reassure the Métis, "they uniformly answered," he reported, "that . . . the insurrectionary movement had taken such precautions as to prevent any peaceful settlement at present." The price of peaceful settlement was to be the *Manitoba Act* which created the province of Manitoba, and the name of Louis Riel can never be dissociated from that achievement.

It must be added that the results of the insurrection were jeopardized chiefly by Riel's own infirmities of temper—his "insensate pride," as Archbishop Taché afterwards wrote, his "unquenchable thirst for power" degenerating at last into arrogance and bloodshed. Without this it is conceivable that the immediate success of the insurrection might never have been reversed by the whirligig of time. Beyond a doubt, too, many of Riel's followers were but imperfectly initiated into the *arcana* of the movement. The French language and separate schools, enshrined in the ark of the covenant, a statute of the Canadian Parliament, were strange objectives to be won by many who habitually spoke Cree and had never gone to school in their lives. In truth it is not hard to trace behind Riel himself a surer touch, a more discerning influence in all that was sustained and well ordered in the insurrection. In the hands of Father Ritchot and of Bishop Taché the negotiations of 1869–70 transcended the events at Red River and challenged the dictates of Canadian statesmanship.

The natural guardian of French rights at Red River was Bishop Taché. The throng of visitors, French-speaking and English alike, at Bishop's Palace in St. Boniface every *Jour-de-l'An* was a tribute to his kindly and beneficent relations with the whole community. Governor McTavish at Fort Garry, Archbishop Machray at old St. John's, even the dour Presbyterian Selkirk settlers at Kildonan, shared in the deep respect inspired by this kindly man. Had he shown no concern for the prodigious changes in store for his primitive flock at Red River few would have failed to hold him derelict in his duty.

Bishop Taché had set out for Ottawa, ostensibly on his way to Rome, in June, 1869, before serious trouble had developed between the Métis and the Canadian surveyors at Red River. He was implored by Governor McTavish of the Hudson's Bay Company and by Hector Langevin in the Canadian Government to return to the Settlement but the Government of that day was not prepared to authorize, as he invoked at the time, a "reply which could satisfy the people." What such a "reply" must have included may be inferred from the consistent objectives afterwards pursued unwaveringly not only by Bishop Taché himself but by Father Ritchot and by Louis Riel in Bishop Taché's absence. There was a little Quebec on the banks of the Red River, and the immemorial objectives of separate schools and the French language, and the more immediate objective of reserves of land for the semi-nomadic Métis, were to be secured only by the creation of a province embodying by statute those safeguards in the basic Act of its incorporation. Had Bishop Taché been able to secure these safeguards in July, 1869, instead of February, 1870, with the attendant turmoil and bloodshed at Red River, a happier if not a serener day might have dawned for Western Canada. But Sir George Cartier, for some inscrutable reason, failed to respond, and Bishop Taché continued reluctantly on his way to Rome. "J'ai toujours redouté l'entrée du Nord-Ouest dans la Confédération," he wrote bitterly to Cartier on October 7, "parce que j'ai toujours cru que l'élément français catholique serait sacrifié; mais je vous avoue franchement qu'il ne m'était jamais venu à la pensée que nos droits seraient si vite et si complètement méconnus. Le nouveau système me semble de nature à amener la ruine de ce qui nous a coûté si cher."

Had the transfer now taken place as originally planned, the French-Canadian cause might have been irretrievably lost. The transfer had to be staved off at any cost until "safeguards" could be obtained. The absence of Bishop Taché was a circumstance of the first importance. The insurrection took form under Riel's vainglorious leadership, guided and sustained by the resourceful and subtle intellect of Father Ritchot.

V

In October, 1869, Joseph Howe, now secretary of state in Sir John A. Macdonald's Government, set out to prepare the most distant outpost of the Dominion for the coming transfer. Beyond a doubt Howe's bitter resistance to confederation and his final acquiescence in "better terms" for Nova Scotia were well known at Red River. He assured them that "the same Constitution as the other provinces possessed would ultimately be conferred upon the country," and there is no evidence that he anticipated any serious resistance to the transfer or surmised the measures that were already in train to secure the necessary "terms" at Red River. On the way south to St. Paul he met McDougall *en route* to his prospective bailiwick. The environment was not auspicious. In the midst of a prairie blizzard which must have daunted them both, Howe welcomed the governor-elect to a "God-forsaken country": "it took two men to hold one man's hat on." Meanwhile Ambroise Lépine, master of the buffalo hunt that year, was marshalling his trained buffalo hunters, just in from the prairie. Without resistance (November 2) they rode into the courtyard of Upper Fort Garry. Louis Riel and his council established themselves in the counting-house where their accoutrements were found by the troops in the following August. The quarters of Dr. Cowan, the Chief Factor, were appropriated. Governor McTavish, too ill to leave his room, was "hors de combat personally and officially," and nearly "choked with mortification" to see the flag of the old Company replaced on the great flag-staff of Fort Garry by that of the "provisional government," with *fleur-de-lis* and shamrock wrought by the sisters at St. Boniface.

The appearance of Dr. Tupper on a private mission—his son-in-law was one of McDougall's aides—was a sign that one redoubtable Canadian at least had anticipated trouble at Red River. He set out for the Settlement only to find that McDougall's party had been met at the Rivière Sale barricade and resolutely escorted back to the United States boundary. A guest for the night with Father Ritchot at St. Norbert, Tupper quickly discovered that no immediate settlement was likely at Red River. Two semi-official commissioners from Canada— Colonel de Salaberry, son of the victor of Chateauguay, and Grand Vicar Thibault who had spent more than thirty years in Rupert's Land —reached Red River on a mission of "peace and conciliation," but Riel seized their papers and quickly discovered that they lacked "any requisite powers to treat . . . with the people." "The Very Reverend gentleman and his associate were politely bowed out and lost sight of." The appointment, however, of Donald A. Smith, afterwards Lord Strathcona, brought the ulterior aims of Riel and his associates into sharp relief. Smith was charged vicariously with powers from both Canada and the Company to "smooth" the transfer in characteristic

Hudson's Bay manner. As an officer of the Company he was authorized "to assist, or, in case of emergency, replace Mr. McTavish." As a Canadian commissioner he was authorized to expound the "most liberal policy" already foreshadowed by Howe.

But "smoothing" was no longer in fashion at Red River. Smith was kept "virtually a prisoner within the fort," though Riel's attempt to seize his papers was foiled by Smith's customary caution in leaving them in safe keeping in Pembina until they could be brought in by a trusty "well-affected party" of fifty men under Richard Hardisty, his brother-in-law. The papers were delivered to Judge Black, and it was under their joint auspices that the famous convention of January 19, 1870, took place in the courtyard of Fort Garry. The temperature was twenty degrees below zero. At the subsequent Convention which met from January 25 to February 9 Riel's ulterior design became at last apparent.

It is clear that this master plan was still unknown to the inhabitants of Assiniboia. Two lists of "rights" were drafted by a committee, the one for admission as a territory, the other as a province. Riel demanded categorically "if the Canadian Government will consent to receive them as a Province." Donald Smith replied that "it had not been referred to when I was at Ottawa." To Riel's chagrin the Convention, ignoring the "provincial" list, voted overwhelmingly for admission as a territory. Riel's demeanour at this stage showed symptoms of the paranoia which afterwards played so controversial a part in his stormy career: he called out the guard, "behaved altogether like a madman" (Alexander Begg) and declared roundly, "devil take it . . . the vote may go as it likes": the West was to enter as a province. Riel's prediction, as we shall see, was to prove as valid as his imprecation. The overwhelming vote of the Convention for admission as a territory remained a dead letter at Ottawa, and the long "list of rights" discussed in detail with Donald Smith on that basis at Fort Garry was never even submitted by the three delegates from Red River, Judge Black, Father Ritchot, and Alfred Scott, who were afterwards supposed to concert the terms of union with Canada. It is safe to say that the English-speaking inhabitants at Red River and probably the great mass of their Métis neighbours long remained in ignorance of the subtle influences which resulted in provincial status under the *Manitoba Act.*

With the news of organized resistance at Red River these influences began to converge on Ottawa with compelling force. Canada declined (November 27) to "accept transfer unless quiet possession can be given." The Colonial Office sent to Ottawa Sir Clinton Murdock, a veteran in Canadian affairs, to sponsor (as prescribed by the *B.N.A. Act of 1867*, s. 146) such terms for the transfer of Rupert's Land "as the Queen thinks fit to approve." Scarcely thirty years had passed since Murdock as the indefatigable secretary to Sydenham during the inception of the Canadian union had drafted for his daemonic chief a memorandum for dealing with Howe and his famous resolution of no confidence in Nova Scotia. It was Murdock in 1838 who had taken Howe in to see Glenelg at the Colonial Office for a secret interview, too confidential, as Howe noted at the time, even for the intimacies of his secret diary. Howe was now secretary of state in a federated Dominion, advancing with seven-league boots across the continent. What must have been Sir Clinton Murdock's reflections in 1870? Accord was quickly reached with the Canadian Government. Thus while the Convention in Fort Garry wrangled over hypothetical "rights" in a temper which bordered upon "a purely lunatic atmosphere"[1] of unreality, the vital decisions were being made at Ottawa. Bishop Taché had been summoned back from Rome and his counsels in February, 1870, unlike those in the previous July, were now eagerly sought. More than a month and a half afterwards (April 11, 1870) the Governor-General informed the Colonial Office that "Bishop Taché before leaving Ottawa [February, 1870] expressed himself quite satisfied with the terms accorded to himself and his church." This illuminating comment, be it noted, was dated more than a month after Bishop Taché had returned to Red River and fifteen days before the three delegates from Red River opened at Ottawa the negotiations which are usually credited with the *Manitoba Act*.

The truth was that none of the three "lists of rights" drafted at various times at Red River contained the basic stipulations, the French language and separate schools "according to the system of the Province of Quebec," which mysteriously found their way into the *Manitoba Act*. It was Bishop Taché himself who placed in the hands of Father Ritchot in Bishop's Palace, St. Boniface, on the departure of the delegates for Ottawa, the so-called "secret list" containing the famous clauses already, no doubt, "accorded to himself and his church." Fantastically remote sometimes are the plausible appearances of the day from the secret springs of state policy. The addition in Bishop Tache's "secret list" of a second chamber as the bulwark of minorities and of land reserves for the Métis marked a further de-

[1]Judge Black from the chair. Cf. his retort to Riel: "arrangements made in a quarter where, I rather think, higher authority is held than you can touch."

parture from the "lists of rights" drafted for the Convention at Fort Garry.[1] The land reserves for the Métis in the form of negotiable scrip were forthcoming in section 31 of the *Manitoba Act,* but "full control of all the public land" was not to belong to Manitoba for more than sixty years. Section 30 of the Act contained the revolutionary provision which required the *B.N.A. Act of 1871* to establish its validity "for all purposes whatsoever": "all ungranted or waste lands in the Province shall be, from and after the said transfer, vested in the Crown, and administered by the Government of Canada for the purposes of the Dominion."

VI

The terms negotiated by Bishop Taché and "accorded to himself and his church" in Ottawa in February, 1870, were never to have a fair chance of acceptance at Red River. Bishop Taché was known to be within a few days' journey of Red River, armed with tentative indemnities and every ingratiating attribute of peaceful authority, when an act of wanton bloodshed destroyed forever the prospect of a peaceful settlement. The cold-blooded execution of Thomas Scott, an Ontario Orangeman, by a firing-party of Métis on March 4 without "even the decencies of an ordinary drum-head courtmartial" (Lord Dufferin) was attended by circumstances of almost incredible brutality. Riel "did not hesitate to throw a dead body between his brother half-breeds and the conciliation which the holy missionary was bringing with him."[2] Lord Dufferin's deliberate verdict after a review of the evidence for the pardon of Lépine was that "all the special pleading in the world will not prove the killing of Scott to be anything else than a cruel, wicked and unnecessary crime." It was the "slaughter of an innocent man, aggravated by circumstances of extraordinary brutality."[3] The Fenian motives of O'Donoghue in the death of Scott

[1]Though the "territorial" list discussed with Donald Smith had stipulated (clause 17) "that the Local Legislature of this Territory have full control of all the public land . . . inside a circumference, having Upper Fort Garry as centre; and that the radii of this circumference be the number of miles that the American line is distant from Fort Garry"

[2]Statement of Hon. J. A. Chapleau who defended Lépine in the subsequent trials and did not hesitate to pronounce the real authors of this brutal crime "guilty of . . . murder."

[3]The manner of Scott's death like Riel's fifteen years later was probably responsible for much of the havoc in Canadian politics. Though ostensibly buried in the court-yard at Fort Garry the body was never found. When the grave was opened after the arrival of the troops it was found to contain only a rough coffin with a rope and some blood-stained clothing.

are easily surmised, but Riel (wrote Begg) "could not have taken a surer step to give his enemies a victory over him than when he committed this vile deed."

The departure of the three delegates on March 23 and 24[1] transferred the issues of the Riel Insurrection to Ottawa where the *Manitoba Act* on May 12, after a month of turmoil in Ontario, finally created the first new province of the Dominion under circumstances which were to reverberate through Canadian politics for many a day. Judge Black, who had been induced by Donald Smith to act at Ottawa as the representative of the Selkirk settlers and the Company, submitted the "provincial list" of rights drafted at the Convention at Fort Garry but not discussed at that time. This was afterwards published in the British blue-book as the "terms and conditions . . . which have formed the subject of conference."[2] Alfred H. Scott, a second delegate, was an American whose influence both at Fort Garry and at Ottawa was negligible. The third delegate, however, was Father Ritchot, armed by Bishop Taché with the "secret list" containing for the first time the demands for the French language and separate schools "according to the system of the Province of Quebec." It is reasonable to suppose, as has been suggested above, that these had already found a place in the terms "accorded to himself and his church" in Ottawa in February, 1870, and that a place had therefore to be found for them in any "provincial list of rights" which Father Ritchot was supposed to purvey to Ottawa. It was nearly twenty years before this list was published (December 27, 1889, and January 16, 1890), by Bishop Taché himself in the *Free Press* and the English-speaking population of Manitoba then discovered these mysterious origins of the "Manitoba School Question." Neither the "complete amnesty" which Bishop Taché promised even for the death of Scott, nor the recognition of the so-called provisional government which Riel stipulated in writing to the delegates could of course be conceded either in Ottawa or in London,[3] and even yet the real facts about "the amnesty question"

[1]"It was through me that they received the money for their travelling expenses." Archbishop Taché.

[2]Young to Granville, April 29, 1870, *Recent Disturbances*, p. 130.

[3]"The reply made by Sir John A. Macdonald and the undersigned [to the delegates regarding an amnesty] was to the effect that the Canadian Government could not advise upon or in any way deal with that question inasmuch as the acts and offences intended to be covered by it had taken place during a period of time when the Canadian Government had no authority over that territory." Cartier to the Governor-General, July 27, 1870. Cf. the decision of the Colonial Office, Jan. 7, 1875: "It is impossible to admit that he [Bishop Taché] had any sufficient

and the *Manitoba Act* can scarcely be cited without stirring embers still smouldering in the ashes of the past.

By a curious coincidence a joint British and Canadian force to restore order at Red River had been decided upon on March 5, the day after the death of Scott. In April Governor McTavish, mortally stricken at Fort Garry, virtually surrendered at discretion to the armed forces bivouacked within the gates. A "loan" of £3000, stores to the value of £4000 carried off "in vast quantities without let or hindrance," and the threat of intercepting the "returns of the Athabasca and Mackenzie River districts and of plundering every Fort along the route," marked the closing chapter of the Company's rule in Rupert's Land. With the approach of spring the buffalo hunters once again took to the plains leaving Riel and a corporal's guard in control at Fort Garry. On the morning of August 25 when the British regulars under Sir Garnet Wolseley moved in from Point Douglas through a deluge of rain to Fort Garry, it was found that Riel and his followers had fled.

Meanwhile the transfer had at last taken place by bell, book, and candle. The surrender of Rupert's Land from the Company, though dated November 19, 1869, was formally accepted by imperial order in council only on June 22, 1870. By a second order in council on June 23, 1870, both Rupert's Land and the North-Western Territory were to be "admitted into and become part of the Dominion of Canada" on July 15, 1870. Thus the young Dominion, scarcely emerging from adolescence itself, assumed parental responsibilities over an appanage of colonial territory which for a generation and a half was to tax the Canadian federation to the limits of its resources.

For more than a decade Manitoba remained the "postage-stamp province" of 1870, scarcely one-tenth the present area of the province. The organization of the territories beyond was a formidable task which still challenges, north of the sixtieth parallel, the ingenuity of Canadian colonial policy. The complexities of frontier administration,

---

ground for believing that the Crown, or the Colonial Government acting for the Crown, did or could delegate to him . . . or indeed to any one . . . an unlimited power of pardoning crimes of whatever atrocity not even known to have been committed."

Sir Clinton Murdock, the British commissioner, stated that Riel's attempt to make the negotiations "subject to confirmation by the Provisional Government . . . would have involved a recognition of Riel and his associates. . . . There was no choice but to reject these terms."

the extinguishing of the Indian title, the spectacular exploits of the "mounties," the herculean labours of the railway builders, merging at last into the grim story of permanent settlement, were yet to repeat on Canadian soil the historic role of the frontier in the expansion of the United States.

For the little province of Manitoba a strange fatality seems to have hounded the achievements of 1870. Born out of due season and bundled into provincial government from the most primitive colonial status since the *Quebec Act*, the province faced from the outset an era of "great and melancholy privation." The Riel Insurrection to all appearances had been immediately and completely successful. To this resolute resistance must be attributed the difference between Bishop Taché's failure in July, 1869, and his success in February, 1870. But almost every aspect of the Riel Insurrection met its nemesis in the years to come. A melancholy fate overtook the semi-nomadic and improvident Métis whose daring exploits had subserved the interests of a subtler policy. The "reserves" of land for which they had fought were granted in the form of negotiable scrip which all too often found its way at trifling cost into the hands of the speculator and defeated any prospect of contiguous settlement in "reserves" of their own for mutual protection. Retreating with the buffalo before the march of the land-surveyor and the railway they made their last stand on the Saskatchewan in 1885 under Gabriel Dumont and their old chief of 1870, but this time in defiance of church as well as government and in league with Poundmaker, one of the noblest chiefs who ever sought to restrain his braves from the slaughter of the white man. A new age had indeed come for "the native tribes of the country." Riel himself, gifted with "brilliant qualities of spirit and of heart" but cursed with a "diseased vanity" and an "unbridled ambition which poisoned his intelligence" (Archbishop Taché) ended his turbulent career on the scaffold at Regina. A shaft of granite in the St. Boniface churchyard inscribed with the single word "RIEL" marks the spot where his devoted followers resolutely buried him in consecrated ground. Not only the "separate school" clause but the French language (ss. 22 and 23) was torn out of the *Manitoba Act* in the throes of the Manitoba School Question, leaving Quebec the only completely bilingual province of Canada. The embers of that controversy still smoulder in both provinces. The legislative council (s. 10), which was supposed to protect the rights of minorities, was abolished in 1876 in order to save the paltry salaries of six councillors at $300 apiece. In 1896 the federal party which had passed the *Manitoba Act* was driven from office on the Manitoba School Question. The train of events started by the Riel Insurrection has been one of the most intractable elements in the religious and racial harmony of Canadian politics.

VII

There was one feature of the transfer of 1870 which paralleled the expansion of the United States more closely perhaps than any other aspect of federal policy. When the original states of the union dedicated to the national government of the republic their claims to the hinterlands they endowed the federal government with the task of acquiring and consolidating their destiny across the continent. The nucleus of the "public domain" of the United States was the cession to the nation of over 400,000 square miles of territory by the states of New York, Virginia, Massachusetts, Connecticut, South Carolina, North Carolina, and Georgia, ranging in date from 1781 to 1802. Virginia alone ceded 265,562 square miles. The "legislative states" afterwards created out of this area—Kentucky, Vermont, Tennessee, Maine, West Virginia—were endowed with the same title to their "public domain" as the original states of the union. This was true also of Texas which was annexed in 1845 and of West Virginia which came into the union under that name only in 1862. In the vast area of nearly 2,500,000 square miles, however, which the republic afterwards acquired by purchase, conquest, or treaty, it scrupulously retained the "public domain" for the federal government, and the "land states" later created from these territories have never made good their claims to the "public domain" within their boundaries except in the form of school lands, university lands, swamp lands, etc. given to them on reaching statehood within the union. This is true of the whole vast area west of the Mississippi.

Had the Mississippi instead of the Pacific been the westward goal of the republic it is conceivable that the rivalry between slave and free might have been resolved as in Jamaica or Barbadoes by piecemeal emancipation from the *status quo* instead of by ineffectual compromises over prospective territory which for a time postponed but in the end precipitated the armed conflict. The northern transcontinental railways and the revolutionary change in the administration of the "public domain" from the lucrative land sales system to the free-homestead system were both dictated by this rivalry, and the whole process of expansion, both north and south, bore the scars of that deadly conflict.

The conflict between slave and free never emerged on Canadian soil. Slavery came to an end by the prosaic but peaceful process of British law, and it was not by chance that both Metcalfe and Elgin brought to Canada from Jamaica the reputation of statesmanship won in that difficult task. But the dynamic function of the "public domain" in the unity and expansion of the republic during the following decades was too convenient a resource to be lost on the Canadian federation. "Such a thing had never yet occurred to any people," said Galt in 1858, "as to have the offer of half a continent. . . . Half a continent is ours if we do not keep on quarrelling about petty matters and lose sight of what interests us most." Among the "objects of material advantage" which engaged at one time or another the energies of that versatile *entrepreneur*, the West grew steadily in importance. It inspired the second of his resolutions on federation in 1858 and it proved in later years to be the setting for many of his most lucrative enterprises.

But to George Brown and the *Globe* the West was an article of irredentist faith. It inspired his first speech in the Canadian legislature and it formed the text for editorials without number on its function in the Canadian economy. "A great empire," he wrote, "is offered to our ambition." In the race for the Pacific "we can beat the United States if we start at once." "If we let the West go to the United States," he wrote in 1862, "our ultimate absorption will be inevitable." Old Simon Fraser who had reached the Pacific in 1808 was still living at eighty-six years of age. "Is it not disgraceful to us as a people that in the year 1862 we should have advanced so little beyond the steps taken by the bold fur-trader? . . . How long are we to hear this reproach upon the enterprise of our race?" The West, together with the problem of defence, formed the chief issue entrusted to Brown on his lone mission to the Colonial Office after the Quebec Conference. "There is yet time," he wrote in 1864, "to make up in great measure for that which has been lost. And if we are not the most supine of any people in existence, we shall prove equal to the occasion."

While the "public domain" of the United States supplied the historic analogy for "Dominion lands" in the West there was one fundamental difference which resulted in 1930 in a vastly different outcome. In a very literal sense the "public domain" of the United States was "owned" and "possessed" by the national government since all of it had been acquired by purchase or war or diplomacy by the republic, and the "land states" of the union unlike the prairie provinces of Canada have never established their claim to its administration. For many years in Canadian policy the temptation to exploit the transfer of 1870 on the American analogy was too strong to be resisted. "It was worthy of attention," said Sir John A. Macdonald in discussing the *Manitoba Act* and the claims of the new province to their public lands, "how carefully the interest of the Dominion had been looked to in the reservation of all lands for all purposes. . . . They wished Rupert's Land made into one Province and to have all the land within the boundary as in other Provinces. . . . The land could not be handed over to them, it was of the greatest importance to the Dominion to have possession of it." The purposes of the Dominion could be achieved "only by carrying out that policy of keeping the control of the lands of the country, and . . . they had determined to do so." Sir George Cartier on the same occasion added that the public lands of the West had been "given up for nothing." In 1882 it was stated bluntly by the federal government that Manitoba had been "acquired . . . by purchase . . . and thus became the property of the Dominion." Sir Wilfrid Laurier in introducing the *Alberta* and *Saskatchewan Acts* referred to the public lands as "bought by the Dominion Government and they have remained ever since the property of the Dominion Government."

It was not until April 21, 1922, that the federal government brought the long era of litigation and controversy to an end by conceding to the prairie provinces "full recognition to the principle that in this respect they are entitled to be placed in a position of equality with the other provinces of Confederation"; and it was not until July 3–4, 1928, that Manitoba established its constitutional right to this equality "as from its entrance into Confederation in 1870." The settlement of the "natural resources question" for all three prairie provinces in 1930 was the outcome of this statesmanlike concession. In the historic words of the Turgeon-Crerar-Bowman Commission, "the lands of Manitoba were retained in 1870, without any recognition being given to what may now be called the rights of the Province." "The Crown Lands of the Province remaining unalienated, will be transferred to the Provincial Government as a matter of course," and compensation was provided for those alienated since July 15, 1870, "by the Government of Canada for the purposes of the Dominion."

The historic "purposes of the Dominion" during this cycle of sixty years of "Dominion lands" (1870–1930) reflected the national emergency, and there has never been, then or since, any difference of opinion with regard to this paramount necessity. The bitterest of controversy over the "natural resources question" never obscured this national tradition. The Prime Minister of Manitoba wrote in 1918:

We do not disparage the work of the early builders of the Dominion in a task which must have been as formidable as any which has ever been surmounted in such a cause. Their courage in achievement has always commanded admiration, and the Prairie Provinces are not without pride in having been able to lend, so to speak, to the Dominion, the immediate resources without which these great national enterprises could never have been effected.

The first in point of time and importance among the historic "purposes of the Dominion" in 1870 was the building of a "Pacific Railway" on Canadian soil to counterbalance the transcontinentals south of the boundary. In 1869 the Union Pacific, chartered in 1862, had just reached the Pacific. The Northern Pacific, chartered in 1864, was following a more northerly route which filled Canadian observers with apprehension. In the midst of the Riel Insurrection Brydges of the Grand Trunk reported to Macdonald a conversation with Governor Smith of Vermont, then president of the Northern Pacific: "He made no secret . . . of the fact that in their arrangements . . . they hope to carry the line so near the boundary, that drop lines into the territory may be constructed, and thus injure, if not prevent, the construction of an independent line in British territory." Macdonald replied: "It is quite evident to me, not only from this conversation, but from advices from Washington, that the United States Government are resolved to do all they can short of war, to get possession of the western territory and we must take immediate and vigorous steps to counteract them. One of the first things is to show unmistakably our resolve to build the Pacific Railway."

In 1870, as we shall see,[1] the railway land grant system was already under fire in the United States, but for Canada the necessity for it was imperative and there was no other resource. Macdonald stated this purpose of the Dominion very frankly in discussing the *Manitoba Act*: "The land could not be handed over . . . for the Pacific Railway must be built by means of the land through which it had to pass." A transcontinental railway was to be the chief of the "terms of union" designed, as we shall see, to bring British Columbia into confederation and to commit Canada irretraceably to that national enterprise. For the building of the C.P.R. and nearly a dozen "colonization railways"

[1] See chap. xxii.

in the West the railway land grant system remained the staple of "Dominion lands" policy until 1894, and long after the system had been abrogated the Hudson Bay Railway was to be built from the proceeds of "pre-emption" and "purchased homestead" land sales. The paramount national "purposes of the Dominion" in the building of the C.P.R. were avowed with characteristic courage and candour by the minister of railways, Sir Charles Tupper himself: "The interests of this country demand that the Canadian Pacific Railway should be made a success. . . . Are the interests of Manitoba and the North-West to be sacrificed to the interests of Canada? I say, if it is necessary, yes."

The second of the historic "purposes of the Dominion" reflected even more directly the neighbourhood of the United States. "It would be injudicious," said Macdonald, "to have a large province which would have control over lands and might interfere with the general policy of the Government. . . . The land regulations of the Province might be obstructive to immigration. All that vast territory should be for purposes of settlement under one control and that the Dominion legislature." In the free-homestead system, adopted from the United States but shrewdly adapted, as we shall see, to meet the requirements of dry-farming in a Canadian environment, the Dominion developed a policy of land settlement which provided homes for a million new settlers in Western Canada in a single decade. By 1930 the Turgeon-Crerar-Bowman Commission was able to report that "the purposes for which the Dominion retained the agricultural lands of the Province have been achieved; the railways have been built and the lands settled."[1] With the return of the remaining public lands to provincial control the free-homestead system like the railway land grant system before it (1872–94) came to an end. Though the origins of both were to be found in the United States there were many distinctive adaptations to meet Canadian conditions. Many of the worst features of both systems south of the border were successfully forestalled. By virtue of these adaptations not only the political expansion of Canada "from sea to sea" but the physiographical expansion in the

---

[1]There were of course other "purposes of the Dominion" in 1870 which could scarcely be avowed in 1930. The compensation to the Hudson's Bay Company had been paid by Canada, both the £300,000 "in hard money" and the twentieth of the fertile belt and blocks of land about the Hudson's Bay posts. This land could best be administered by a government with undivided authority over the whole area. Then too the Dominion "would be in a position to obtain repayment of the disbursement of the £300,000. . . . The expense would be defrayed by that means instead of being charged against the people of the Provinces of Ontario, Quebec, Nova Scotia and New Brunswick."

building of the transcontinental railways and the demographic expansion in the process of land settlement will be found to follow distinctively Canadian patterns. The last of these was of course the ultimate objective of both the others, for without prosperous and permanent settlement the builders of railways and the builders of political dominion "from sea to sea" alike labour in vain. The surest foundations of Canadian nationhood are to be found in the Canadian people, the tough and indomitable tradition of their survival, their fortitude, their competence, and their character.

Chapter Twenty-One

DOMINION FROM SEA TO SEA

THE PACIFIC

THE distant province of British Columbia was an exotic element in the pattern of British North American union. Its impermeable distance beyond the Rocky Mountains, its orientation on the Pacific, its unpredictable politics like the tales of the prodigies of nature there which attended the news of the Cariboo gold-rush in the eastern press, all lent a fantastic element of novelty to the Canadian scene. Though not the first of the new provinces of the Dominion, it had been the first to achieve a regional union of its own. Unlike the central regions of Rupert's Land and the North-Western Territory with their "rough time of it" in acquiring full provincial status in confederation, British Columbia became at once an orthodox province in 1871 "as if the Colony of British Columbia had been one of the Provinces originally united." The terms of union included the most formidable enterprise ever undertaken by the Dominion in relation to its immediate resources—the building of a transcontinental railway within ten years. That enterprise dominated Canadian policy for the rest of the century. The western terminus of the C.P.R. is now the largest seaport in Canada, and a British Columbian has predicted that the outlook on the Pacific will yet again dominate Canadian policy.

After the loss of Oregon the chief concern of British policy on the Pacific was never seriously in doubt. Its main features have already appeared more than once in the course of these studies.[1] Vancouver Island had been ceded to the Hudson's Bay Company in fee simple in 1849 in order to supply the vested interest of settlement so fatally wanting in the contest for Oregon. The Select Committee of 1857 recommended (section 10) the resumption of Vancouver Island by the crown and the "extension of the colony over any portion of the

[1]See above, pp. 229, 271, 282 ff.

adjoining continent, to the west of the Rocky Mountains, on which permanent settlement may be found practicable." Lytton in the Colonial Office had already begun to implement the *Report* of 1857 by the creation of the mainland province of British Columbia (21 and 22 Vic., c. 99) when Cartier, Galt, and Ross appeared upon the scene in London to urge Head's first "drive for federation" in 1858. This mainland province was enlarged in 1863 (26 and 27 Vic., c. 83) to the Rocky Mountains and the 120th meridian on the east and to the 60th parallel of latitude on the north—a line which was to be projected eastward for the northern boundary of Alberta and Saskatchewan in 1905 and for the enlarged province of Manitoba in 1912. Though administered by the same redoubtable officer—Governor Douglas—in 1858, the two districts of Vancouver Island and "British Columbia" were united under the same government only in 1866 (29 and 30 Vic., c. 67). In the following year, on April 3, 1867, a few days after the passing of the *B.N.A. Act of 1867*, the Company formally surrendered its rights in Vancouver Island, with compensation of £57,500 paid in this instance by the United Kingdom. Had the same procedure been followed for Rupert's Land east of the Rockies, that region also might have been organized to make its own terms with Canada. Since this intervening territory was to be ceded to Canada only "on equitable principles," it was obvious that the union of British Columbia must await the outcome of that bitter controversy. With the transfer of 1870 this gap was spanned by an arch of Canadian territory, if not, as yet, of Canadian provinces. Union of British Columbia with Canada became at last feasible.

Behind this procedure, preordained since 1849 and confirmed, as we have seen, by the *B.N.A. Act of 1867* itself, lay many vicissitudes of local fortune as spectacular perhaps as any in the course of British North American union. The discovery of gold in the sand-bars of the Fraser river, and a few months later on the Cariboo, four hundred miles inland, brought a gold-rush from California which threatened to engulf the staid little town of Victoria and turn the whole economic outlook of both sections of the province southward to San Francisco. The newspapers, the supplies for the mines, the first independent bankers and merchants, the steamboats, the prevailing currency, the mails, were American. Many of the miners went to California for the winter and brought back the news of civil war and the pandemonium of enterprise—and of vice—so characteristic of the gold-rush in every quarter of the world.

The varieties of local opinion generated in this atmosphere were fiercely antagonistic. The mainland province built the Cariboo road at a cost of a million and a half, nearly half of which was borrowed at ruinous rates of interest. Tolls on the Cariboo road and heavy customs duties added to the distress as the golden mirage of the Cariboo rush began to fade into the commonplaces of frontier settlement. Meanwhile the island colony which monopolized most of the jobbing business for the mines flourished under free trade and operated a smugglers' paradise in both directions. Here developed a new generation of "forty-niners," sharing with San Francisco the seasonal lay-off from the mines and predisposed by every consideration of interest and environment towards annexation to the United States. This was the "bogey of the politicians" which brought the mainland colony into the field in favour of the Canadian federation. The feud between the two soon reached an incredible stage of rancour and irresponsibility.

When these two communities were united under the same government in 1866 (29 and 30 Vic., c. 67) the name of British Columbia only served to cloak their antipathies. The mainland customs tariff which was now applied to the whole united province left the enterprising merchants—to say nothing of the adroit smugglers—of Victoria stranded by a receding tide. Governor Seymour, obsessed by the cross purposes of a primitive economy, once described the province as a road with a gold mine at one end and a seaport town at the other. Moreover the road had not been paid for, and a transient population had scarcely as yet begun to supplant, from the immense potential resources of fish and minerals and lumber, the waning resources of the placer gold mines. The economies that were anticipated from union failed to materialize under Seymour's kindly but complacent administration. By 1867 the population, now less than 10,000, was losing not only numbers but faith in their star when the new day-star of their destiny arose in the east. The Canadian federation appeared upon the horizon charged with its mission of expansion across the continent.

The reputations which emerge from this early period of isolation bear all the marks of their exotic environment. Governor Seymour whose complacency was berated by extremists on all sides was nevertheless probably a better realist than many of his critics. Separated still from the Canadian federation by two thousand miles of prairie wilderness and mountain ranges, and by the immortal charter of the Hudson's Bay Company in Rupert's Land, the Legislative Council could afford to pass unanimous resolutions (1867) for union with

Canada and a call upon the governor to do the impossible.[1] A convention in Victoria (January, 1868) claimed popular support for union, and suggested terms as prescribed by section 146 of the *B.N.A. Act of 1867*. But the "legislature" of British Columbia was still a composite body in which the appointed members outnumbered the elective members nearly two to one: it could scarcely qualify as the "legislature" of British Columbia under the Act. In Governor Seymour's opinion the resolutions of the council were more concerned with escape from the past than provision for the future—"the expression of a despondent community longing for change." Relief from the public debt on which the carrying charges absorbed a third of the provincial revenue, a subsidy from the Dominion for purposes of local government, and a wagon road through the Rockies and across the trackless domain of the Hudson's Bay Company, were still utopian dreams in 1867. With the *Rupert's Land Act* of 1868 the day-star from the east took on a new lustre but the Legislative Council were still far from unanimous on the precise details of "advantageous terms" of union. It is possible that the headlong tactics of the unionists had something to do with the growing reluctance of the council, and it was not long before the Confederation League (May, 1868) was impugning the Governor and his "sham legislature" for their apathy. A convention at Yale, supported by an exuberant press, demanded responsible government and purveyed a score of resolutions which Governor Seymour undertook to forward to the Colonial Office "with perfectly respectful comments." The truth was that the three-cornered contest which now developed between the *status quo*, union with Canada, and annexation to the United States, was almost as remote as the rugged regions of British Columbia itself from the setting where the real decisions on British American union and expansion were already being made.

In British Columbia as at Red River the cause of union with Canada suffered from the immoderate counsels of some of its advocates. Few more colourful characters even in that fantastic place and time are to be found than Amor de Cosmos. Born William Alexander Smith within a few yards of Thomas Chandler Haliburton's house in Windsor, Nova Scotia, he reached Victoria by way of California in the gold-rush of 1858, changed his name with a versatility worthy of

[1]"To take . . . steps, without delay . . . to ensure the admission of British Columbia into the Confederation on fair and equitable terms, this Council being confident that in advising this step they are expressing the views of the colonists generally." March 19, 1867.

Sam Slick himself, and led in the columns of the *British Colonist* and elsewhere a campaign for union with Canada which antagonized many less sanguine supporters by its self-centred strictures on the old order. It was Amor de Cosmos who moved the resolutions of the Victoria convention in January, 1868, but he could muster but three supporters in the council in March for immediate action. The council, "while confirming their vote of the last session in favour . . . of the union of this Colony with the Dominion of Canada to accomplish the consolidation of British interests and institutions in North America, are still without sufficient information and experience of the practical working of Confederation . . . to admit of their defining the terms on which such a union would be advantageous to the local interests of British Columbia."

To Amor de Cosmos the council's wary approach was arrant opposition to confederation. Thenceforth both governor and council were guilty of staving off the inevitable in order to retain office. There can be no doubt that encouragement from Ottawa inflamed and magnified this campaign and probably confirmed the opposition. Macdonald himself wrote that it was time to put "the screws on at Vancouver Island" and to recall Governor Seymour. The terms of transfer for Rupert's Land would predispose the Hudson's Bay Company to "instruct their people to change their anti-Confederate tone. We shall then have to fight only the Yankee adventurers, and the annexation party proper, which there will be no difficulty in doing, if we have a good man at the helm." Tilley suggested to a friendly councillor[1] "immediate action by your legislature and passage of an address to Her Majesty regarding union with Canada. Keep us advised of progress."

This inordinate haste was probably reflected in the changing temper of the council. Reversing (February, 1869) the resolutions of the two previous sessions in the "conviction that under existing circumstances the Confederation of the Colony with the Dominion of Canada would be undesirable, even if practicable," they urged "Her Majesty's Government not to take any decisive steps towards the consummation of such a Union." The death of Governor Seymour in the following June, however, opened the way for "a good man at the helm" in the person of Governor Musgrave whose record in Newfoundland had already impressed Macdonald with his "prudence, discretion and loyalty to the cause of Confederation."

Meanwhile "the bogey of the politicians," the cause of annexation

[1]H. S. Seeley, March 25, 1868.

to the United States, though dignified by the traditional support and sagacious counsels of Dr. J. S. Helmcken, suffered like the cause of Canadian union by the excesses of its immoderate allies. In July, 1866, news of the famous Banks bill in Washington "for the admission of the States of New Brunswick, Nova Scotia, Canada East and Canada West, and for the organization of the territories of Selkirk, Saskatchewan, and Columbia" made the rounds of the British provinces. The death of Lincoln which had shocked for a time the fiercer antipathies of the day into a common sorrow was followed by half a decade of tension during which the wildest rumours circulated freely on both sides of the border. The American press, east and west, teemed with manifestations of "manifest destiny." It was a "fiat which has the potency of irrevocable law." British Columbia was to be annexed in liquidation of the Alabama claims. In 1869 a petition to President Grant for annexation to the United States encountered so spirited an opposition in British Columbia that the neighbouring press threatened dire reprisals and "a force of filibusters" to "seek the overthrow of the British Dominion upon this coast."[1] It was then found that the petition to President Grant bore fewer than fifty signatures. These excesses, however, could not conceal the solid advantages which annexation might offer to a bankrupt and expectant community. When sagacious observers like Dr. Helmcken could argue that "it would be absurd for us to sacrifice our interests" and that "it cannot be regarded as improbable that ultimately, not only this Colony but the whole Dominion of Canada will be absorbed by the United States," the annexation movement in British Columbia can scarcely be dismissed as a meretricious device to extort better terms from Canada. "No union," added Helmchen, "on account of love need be looked for. The only bond of union . . . will be the material advantage of the country. . . . Love for Canada has to be acquired by the prosperity of the country, and from our children."

The cause of union with Canada, however, no longer lacked "a good man at the helm," to interpret chart and compass and the sailing orders of the day. Armed with despatches from the Colonial Office "for the consideration of the community and the guidance of Her Majesty's servants" Musgrave moved in without compunction to carry the union. "The constitution of British Columbia," wrote Granville to Musgrave (August 14, 1869) "will oblige the Governor to enter personally upon many questions . . . with which, in the case of a negotiation between two responsible governments, he would not be bound

[1]Quoted by Keenleyside, *Canadian Historical Association Report*, 1928, p. 38.

to concern himself." Magistrates in the council were provided with safe retreats on the bench. Others were mollified by pensions. Above all, the project of a wagon road within three years and a million a year thereafter for railway construction, with the prospect of generous debt allowances and subsidies for local government, wrought miraculous changes in the council. "It was thumbs down on Confederation last session," wrote Robson in the *British Columbian*,[1] "because Simon said 'Thumbs down'; but if Simon says 'Thumbs up', up the official thumbs will go." The same council, with three exceptions, which had rejected confederation under Governor Seymour now carried new terms for union with Canada without a dissenting vote.

The terms finally carried to Ottawa by J. S. Helmcken, R. W. W. Carrall, and J. W. Trutch—the first two being elective members of the council from Victoria and Cariboo respectively—were not wanting in acquisitiveness but it is well known that the bounty of Macdonald, Cartier, and Tilley in the tense political atmosphere of 1870 exceeded their liveliest expectations. Instead of a wagon road they returned with pledges of a railway to be begun within two years and completed in ten. There could now be no retreat from a Pacific railway. The public lands of the province were to remain, as a matter of course, under provincial control. For the railway belt, to be transferred to the Dominion "in trust" and not to exceed twenty miles on either side of the railway, the Dominion agreed (clause 11) to pay $100,000 per year in perpetuity "from the date of the union." The sequel to this arrangement was in keeping with its inception. In 1883 the province agreed to transfer the "Peace River Block" to the Dominion in lieu of lands that were "unfit for settlement" in the railway belt; but since the railway belt had been ceded "in trust . . . in furtherance of the construction of the said Railway," the province, as the *cestui que trust*, succeeded more than forty years later in recovering from the Dominion not only the unalienated lands in the railway belt but the Peace River Block, on the grounds that it had not been used for the purposes of the trust. The $100,000 per year "from the date of the union" is still paid "in half-yearly payments in advance."

The evolution towards responsible government had been hastened by the process of union. In the terms proposed by the province appeared for the first time (clause 14) "the introduction of responsible government when desired by the inhabitants of British Columbia." In preparation for this it was "the intention of the Governor of British Columbia, under the authority of the Secretary of State for the

[1]See Howay in *Canadian Historical Association Report*, 1927, p. 73.

Colonies, to amend the existing constitution of the Legislature by providing that a majority of its Members shall be elective." Every elective constituency in the province (November, 1870) supported confederation, and it was the reformed council in which for the first time the elective members outnumbered the appointed members, nine to six, which approved the provincial terms of union (January, 1871) without a dissenting voice. With generous pensions to retiring officials and with three senators and six members of the House of Commons at Ottawa, British Columbia formally entered confederation on July 20, 1871. On July 25 Governor Musgrave sailed for home on H.M.S. *Sparrowhawk*. At the time of the Pacific Scandal the Macdonald-Cartier Government held office by a margin of six votes, the representation of British Columbia in the House of Commons. It may be that considerations less ponderable than debt allowance and provincial subsidies and railways entered into the bountiful terms granted to British Columbia in 1871.

THE ATLANTIC

The cycle of federation which began in Charlottetown in 1864 closed in Charlottetown in 1873. The overwhelming vote of the legislature against confederation in April, 1865, though repeated with an added note of "finality" in 1866, was not to be the ultimate verdict of Prince Edward Island. The statutory basis for union, like that of Rupert's Land and British Columbia, was preordained by section 146 of the *B.N.A. Act of 1867*, and no attempt to read "finality" into the rejection of the Quebec Resolutions could prevail in the end against the spirit of 1867.

There were two proprietary provinces in the second empire in America, Rupert's Land and Prince Edward Island, and nothing less than a caesarean operation could be expected to bring either of them to function as a normal province of the Dominion. For Rupert's Land, as we have seen, the compensation to the Hudson's Bay Company challenged the ingenuity of Canadian statesmen for a whole generation, and the price has yet to be paid in full in the settlement of Western Canada. In Prince Edward Island "the eternal land question" dragged its serpentine length through nearly a century and a half of controversy. Its settlement was indispensable for union in 1873, and even the great *Land Purchase Act* of 1875 with its amendments continued to grind out its piecemeal solution into the twentieth century before the last holdings of the absentee proprietors were finally expropriated.

The Howe-Gray-Ritchie imperial commission of 1860–61[1] brought "the eternal land question" into focus for a final settlement after ten months of investigation into a "controversy unexampled, perhaps, for length and virulence, in the history of colonization." A proposed imperial guarantee of £100,000 for a project of purchase, reinforced if necessary by compulsory arbitration, came to grief, like the compensation to the Hudson's Bay Company for Rupert's Land, upon the liability which such a settlement would have implied for scores of imperial land grants surviving from the first empire. One such precedent would have opened floodgates of compensation all over the empire.[2] In 1866 the Cunard estate of 212,000 acres was purchased for £53,000. By 1868 some 450,000 acres out of 1,400,000 in Prince Edward Island remained in the hands of proprietors. The Colonial Office in advocating federation with Canada hinted bluntly that in the event of failure "the Imperial Government would probably cease to concern itself" over the land question.

The maritime delegates to the London conference in 1866 while awaiting the belated arrival of their Canadian colleagues utilized their time to discuss prospective terms with Prince Edward Island. J. C. Pope, the Island prime minister, who happened to be in London, was favourably impressed by a plan of granting $800,000 in cash to liquidate the rights of the absentee proprietors. This proposal was embodied in a Canadian minute of council (December 14, 1869) but was declined by the Island Government as not "sufficiently liberal," though it was conceded that such "a free gift from the Dominion . . . from whom the Island has received no injury" would require the Dominion "to assume a duty which, clearly, is not hers." The final conference of March, 1873, nevertheless drew up "better terms" which brought "the eternal land question" at last into the realm of temporal solution. The Dominion agreed to pay Prince Edward Island $45,000 per annum in perpetuity in lieu of land revenue, and to advance as required the capital up to $800,000 "for the purchase of lands now held by large proprietors." This area, now reduced to 381,720 acres, was dealt with by a series of provincial *Land Purchase Acts* which

[1]See above, p. 108.

[2]The procedure in Vancouver Island was less vulnerable as a precedent since the grant "in free and common soccage" to the Hudson's Bay Company had been made only in 1849, and the Letters Patent (January 13, 1849) had specifically reserved the right "to repurchase and take from the said Company, the said Vancouver Island, and premises thereon granted" at the expiration of the Company's licence of exclusive trade with the Indians granted in 1838 for a period of twenty-one years.

escaped disallowance in 1875. Thenceforth until well on in the twentieth century the mortmain of absentee proprietary rights was slowly lifted from the land in Prince Edward Island.

As in British Columbia, however, there were other inducements, ponderable and otherwise, to speed the union. A committee from Congress, General Butler of Massachusetts, Mr. Beck of Kentucky, and Judge Poland of Vermont, had reached Charlottetown (August, 1868) to discuss the renewal of reciprocity. The Island Assembly in the following session advocated free trade with the United States "even if the same could not be secured for Her Majesty's other British North American colonies." To these overtures the Colonial Office replied pointedly that negotiations with Washington must now pass through the hands of the Canadian governor-general. The governor-general himself, with Cartier, Tilley, and Edward Kenny of Nova Scotia, discussed "better terms" at Charlottetown in 1869, and Sir John A. Macdonald spent a vacation on the Island in 1870, not without consultations, it may be assumed, with the Union Association and the exponents of a Prince Edward Island railway. Here was another appropriate addition to "better terms." The venture, begun "at railroad speed" in 1871, reached a stage by 1873 where the provincial railway debentures were beginning to require the good offices of Sir John Rose in London and of Tilley in Ottawa to ensure their solvency. The final terms of 1873 included not only the settlement of "the eternal land question" but a debt allowance of $50 per head of population, and the assumption of the sagging railway debentures by the Dominion. The final resolutions passed the Assembly by a vote of 27 to 2, and the Council without a dissenting voice.

A few weeks after the union on "Dominion day," 1873, Lord Dufferin wrote to Macdonald from Charlottetown of the "high state of jubilation" there and the "impression that it is the Dominion that has been annexed to Prince Edward Island." "In alluding to the subject," he added, "I have adopted the same tone."[1]

[1]See D. C. Harvey, "Confederation in Prince Edward Island," *Canadian Historical Review*, June, 1933.

Chapter Twenty-Two

CONSOLIDATION: THE C.P.R.

THE political expansion of Canada was so rapid that it required two whole generations of enterprise in transportation and settlement to catch up with it.

There were unforeseen advantages in this timing. An empire of "Dominion lands" had been transferred to Canada in a single day. A uniform and integrated system of survey thus became possible over a quarter of the continent, instead of the variety of base lines and more than a score of meridians that had been forced upon the United States in their piecemeal expansion to the Pacific. Confronted with the national necessity of a Pacific railway Macdonald could boast "the advantage of having one great country before us to do as we like," with "one vast system of survey, uniform over the whole of it."[1]

One of the most fantastic casualties of the Riel Insurrection was the system of survey which had contributed to the fiasco of 1869. More than a year before the transfer McDougall and Colonel Dennis had devised a rectangular survey for the West, 800 acres instead of 640 acres to each "section" and 64 sections instead of 36 to each township, in order to offer settlers from Canada "lots of a size to which they had been accustomed" and provide to each settler a margin of 40 acres above the normal quarter-section in the United States. Louis Riel and the Métis at Oak Point put an end, permanently as it proved, to this plan of survey, and after the insurrection was over the whole system came under review. By order-in-council of April 15, 1871, one of the most important decisions of Canadian administration was finally ratified: the square-mile "section" of 640 acres became the unit of administration for "Dominion lands." Sections, 36 to the township, were numbered from the lower right instead of the upper left as in the United States, and the townships were numbered horizontally into "ranges" westward from the principal meridian at Fort Garry, and vertically northward into "townships" from the international boundary

[1]See system of land subdivision, Fig. 7.

at the 49th parallel of latitude.[1] Road allowances, in contrast to American practice, were provided for every "section," and the use of the astronomical system instead of the magnetic or solar compass resulted in phenomenal accuracy as well as phenomenal uniformity for the Canadian survey.

There were unforeseen advantages too in the timing of the C.P.R. The long controversy over railway gauges in the United States—no fewer than six were in use during the fifties—with attendant rivalries in finance and sectional interest had been finally settled by the very size and national importance of the Union Pacific. When that great enterprise, and the Northern Pacific two years later, decided upon a gauge of 4 feet 8½ inches, they fixed, in effect, the standard gauge for the continent. The plague of conflicting gauges which became chronic in Australia and still survives in Newfoundland never complicated the problem of bringing the vast disintegrated regions of Canada into physiographical union. Canada, too, was spared much of the costly experimentation which attended the settlement and administration of the public domain in the United States. Interminable disputes about "graduation," "donation," squatters' rights, "commutation," and "pre-emption" in the United States could safely be by-passed for "Dominion lands." Even where the nomenclature was the same—railway land grants and free homesteads, swamp lands, school lands, the sectional survey, thirty-six to the township, and many other invaluable details of administration—the function in many instances was so modified by timely adaptation in Canada that the origins were almost unrecognizable.[2] Perhaps the greatest adaptations of all were made in the railway land grant and free-homestead systems which formed the staples of land policy in both countries.

I

Three aspects of Canadian expansion were inextricably bound together—the political expansion from sea to sea, the physiographical expansion to bring these disintegrated segments together, and the demographic expansion which could alone give permanence and soli-

[1] See Figs. 6 and 7.

[2] The "pre-emption" regulations, for instance, to safeguard squatters' rights in the United States had no counterpart in Canada where normal "pre-emption" was devised for the homesteader already established upon a contiguous quarter-section of free land in order to permit of the expansion necessary for the technique of dry-farming. The name was the same but it would be hard to find a greater contrast in purpose and function. Similar adaptations are traceable in almost every aspect of administration. See Chester Martin, "Dominion Lands" Policy, 228ff.

darity to the whole. The second of these was recognized, from the outset, as the most urgent and the most difficult. In the midst of the Riel Insurrection Macdonald had cited to Brydges "advices from Washington that the United States Government are resolved to do all they can short of war to get possession of the western territory and we must take immediate and vigorous steps to counteract them. One of the first things to be done is to show unmistakably our resolve to build the Pacific Railway." The most startling innovations in "Dominion lands" policy arose from this necessity.

Among the historic "purposes of the Dominion" avowed in 1870 for the administration of public lands in the West "by the Government of Canada," none was more immediately imperative than this project of a Pacific railway. "It must be in the contemplation of the Members of the House," said Cartier in discussing the *Manitoba Act*, "that these [lands] could be used for the construction of the British Pacific Railway from the East to the West." It would soon be necessary to construct a railway through Red River, and consequently the Dominion Parliament would require to control the wild lands." The land, added Macdonald, "could not be handed over to them, it was of the greatest importance to the Dominion to have possession of it, for the Pacific Railway must be built by means of the land through which it had to pass."

The national aspect of this enterprise—its "paramount national importance," in the historic words of the Turgeon-Crerar-Bowman commission—is traceable on every hand. Had there been no international boundary from the Great Lakes to the Pacific an accommodation between the Grand Trunk and the Northern Pacific might well have proved, on strictly economic grounds, the soundest project of transcontinental transportation ever devised for the Canada of that day. Watkin once outlined to the Barings the advantages of such a route. Avoiding the long unproductive haul north of the Great Lakes it would have tapped on both sides of the boundary the most lucrative areas of the prairies beyond. But national considerations were imperative, and if the gigantic stride of the United States across the continent filled Canadian statesmen with apprehension, it also supplied them with a challenge and an example.

It supplied them also with many a warning, for the heed which they gave to the warning signals of the Union Pacific and the Northern Pacific was the measure, in many respects, of the phenomenal success of the Canadian Pacific Railway. For twenty-two years, from the Illinois Central in 1850 to the Chicago and Northwestern in 1873, the railway land grant system in the United States wrought havoc with public finance and devastation in politics until it was swept away by a disillusioned frontier. In Canada the system was appropriated just as it was disappearing in the United States, and by a curious coincidence it lasted almost exactly the same length of time, from the abortive C.P.R. charter of 1873 to the last grant to the Pipestone extension of the C.P.R. in 1894. But the system was adopted in Canada neither in defiance nor in ignorance of the experience in the United States, and before it came to an end there were radical adaptations which fairly transformed its function. It was twenty years later in closing because it was twenty years later in beginning. In both cases the railway land grant system was a psychological phase in the development of the frontier.

In the early stages of the system in the United States every ambitious community plunged into railway projection with reckless prodigality. Missouri issued state bonds to no fewer than six railway companies. Minnesota, created a state in 1858, immediately authorized loans of $5,000,000 to be advanced $100,000 at a time for each ten miles of grading and for each ten-mile section completed. As the price of the bonds fell the railway for obvious reasons concentrated upon the grading, and "the only track in existence was a stretch of 1400 feet which the Minnesota and Pacific used to store its only engine."[1] In Western Canada, too, one searches almost in vain in the press of that day for the wisdom which became so articulate after the fact. "If we could get the railway and keep our public land," wrote the *Manitoba Free Press* (May 24, 1873) "we would prefer such a course, but that is impracticable." Seven years later the same views were held for the C.P.R. (March 17, 1880): ". . . beyond a doubt the only practicable mode of building the Pacific Railway is from the proceeds of the Crown lands."

The lessons learnt from the Union Pacific and the Northern Pacific went far beyond the old adage of making a virtue of necessity. There were altogether unsuspected virtues in the system itself which the C.P.R. developed with great skill and sagacity. The distinctive Canadian method of "indemnity selection" of railway land grants—in odd-numbered sections evenly distributed among the even-numbered homestead sections of the township[2]—was providential, as we shall see, for agriculture in Western Canada. Without it the whole technique of dry-farming might never have escaped the tragic consequences south

[1]Riegel, *The Story of the Western Railroads.*
[2]See plan of township, Fig. 6.

of the boundary where contiguous settlement in the semi-arid regions west of the 100th meridian doomed the homesteader to his quarter-section farm and strangled the expansion so necessary for summer-fallowing in the practice of dry-farming. Such adaptations were as fortunate for the C.P.R. as for the settler himself. Both the Union Pacific and the Northern Pacific passed into bankruptcy—one of them twice over—during the battle of giants for the control of the trans-continentals in the United States. The C.P.R. proved to be the only transcontinental of that era which has never gone into the hands of a receiver.

Beyond a doubt the area of railway land grants in Western Canada was prodigiously large. "My kingdom for a horse," was the king's price in *King Richard III*. By a curious coincidence the total area alienated in railway land grants in Western Canada, about 32,000,000 acres, was almost exactly the area of King Richard's kingdom. But the iron horse was well worth the kingdom, for without it the national emergency could never have been met. Without it, too, the phenomenal record of the C.P.R. in the building of Western Canada could never have been attainable. In both cases, as we shall see, certain elements of luck were only less important than the invaluable lessons derived for nothing from the grim experience of the United States. Thus while the railway land grant system disappeared in the United States after twenty-three years of disillusionment and frustration, the twenty-two years of the system in Canada left behind a legacy of unforeseen advantages which have scarcely yet been appreciated in the westward expansion of Canada. Before the Saskatchewan Resources Commission a C.P.R. witness once asserted roundly, "We built Western Canada." It may be that this is measurably true, and that the C.P.R. in adversity will stand even higher in popular esteem than in the day of its militant and unquestioned supremacy.

II

The use of the public domain for roads and canals was already a familiar practice in the United States—some 10,000,000 acres had been granted for these purposes—when the railway appeared and proceeded like Cronos to devour its children. The railway age was a prodigy of faith and enterprise. By comparison with this the conquest of the air by a later generation was slow and dubious. Every frontier town was a prospective metropolis. Local editors "took glimpses of the moon" and prophesied the millennium. In 1850 Congress for the first time endowed the public land states from Lake Michigan to the Gulf and from the mouth of the Ohio to the eastern boundary of Iowa with alternate sections of land in a twelve-mile "railway belt" for the construction of the Illinois Central. The states themselves were to apply these lands to the building of the railway. Since much of this vast area was already settled the public domain was to share in the adventure by the sale of the intervening sections at twice the normal minimum price—not less than $2.50 per acre. The uncanny success of Stephen Douglas in lobbying the land grants through Congress and the phenomenal sale of railway lands in an area already populated opened the flood-gates and deluged the public land states for twenty years with railway land grants. Within a decade every public land state on the Mississippi had received its quota from the public domain. State credits were flung recklessly into the flood. Missouri advanced $25,000,000 of state bonds to six railways. Minnesota, as we have seen, in the first session of statehood, authorized $5,000,000 of state bonds as loans for railway building. States which were sovereign bodies could repudiate these obligations but counties and municipalities were not so fortunate, and one enterprising county in Missouri retired the last of its railway bonds in 1918. Of the 155,000,000 acres of railway land grants in the United States nearly one-third belongs to this phase of railway projection through the public land states.

With the approach of civil war a new technique became imperative. A transcontinental railway and a free-homestead system to speed settlement and forestall the South in the race for the West became national necessities, and both came together under Lincoln in 1862. The admission of California into the union in 1850, like that of British Columbia into the Canadian federation twenty-one years later, had raised national emergencies which could not wait. Curious parallels abound. In the United States the name of Asa Whitney and in Canada that of Edward Watkin belong to the speculative, not to say chimerical, aspects of the project. By the early sixties the industrial North, traditionally wedded to orthodox views on the public domain, was in the throes of a revolutionary conflict of interests. Cheap land on the frontier would have encouraged migration, jeopardized the supply of industrial labour, and driven up wages; buoyant land sales too would have threatened the fiscal dependence of the nation upon the tariff. It was the agricultural South, traditionally wedded to low tariffs and cheap land, which long championed the cause of the frontier. For twenty years Benton bombarded Congress with "log cabin bills" in the interests of the "squatter." Calhoun went farther and advocated "retrocession" of land administration, still however under federal regulation, to frontier states—"the most splendid bribe that had ever yet been offered" to the West to throw in its lot with the South against the growing industrial power of the North. Henry Clay's ingenious compromise, to save the tariff by a policy of "distribution" to the land states of the "proceeds of the sale of Public Lands," was defeated only by the veto of President Jackson.

By 1860 these devices no longer availed to postpone the conflict. The industrial North, now won to the cause of cheap land by the prospect of forestalling the South in the settlement of the West, added to this the bold strategy of a transcontinental railway by a northern route. Since much of the territory was unorganized it was necessary for the government either to build the road itself, as Benton advocated, from the proceeds of the public domain or to deal with corporations sufficiently endowed in land and capital to carry so vast a project through to completion. The issue was vital for the nation and none but the nation could cope with it. In 1862, in the midst of civil war, Congress passed the Free Homestead Act and chartered the Union Pacific Railway. Two years later an amended charter underwrote the project to the accompaniment of influences at Washington which can only be surmised. Nearly half a million dollars went into the company's "expense account" for that year. Five years later, in 1869, the golden spike was driven in the first transcontinental railway to the Pacific.

The chief features of the Union Pacific, like those of the Northern Pacific and Great Northern of a later date, stand in such marked contrast to the C.P.R. that it is worth emphasizing from the outset the fundamental differences between them. The land grant to the Union Pacific, made for the first time not to the states but to the railway itself, included the odd-numbered sections in a belt forty miles in width; but there was no "indemnity selection" in lieu of lands already occupied or unfit for settlement, and railway lands remaining unsold three years after the completion of the road were to be open to actual settlement at $1.25 per acre. Mineral lands including coal and iron were expressly reserved. No cash subsidy was paid by the government, though the priority of the thirty-year 6 per cent first mortgage government bonds which the original charter had provided in 1862 was waived in 1864 in order to give right of way to the first mortgage bonds of the company. In the end the road was built as a contractor's job. Using a subsidiary company, the "Credit Mobilier of America," the Union Pacific contracted with themselves to build the road. "We were building it ourselves," one of the contractors testified before the

Committee of the House in 1873, "by ourselves and among ourselves. There was not $20,000 outside interest in it."[1] For the three chief contracts the cost to the company was over $93,500,000, and the cost to the contractors was less than $50,750,000—a clear profit of nearly $43,000,000. The actual construction was financed chiefly by $27,000,000 from government bonds—interest on which was never paid by the company—and by $23,700,000 from first mortgage railway bonds, negotiable only because the government had accepted a junior rating for its own debentures. The company's own land grant bonds—on the security of the land grant of over 12,000,000 acres—brought in scarcely more than $6,000,000. It is true that subsequent land sales amounted to nearly $7,500,000 up to 1880, and to nearly $22,500,000 within twenty years, but it is clear that land grants neither financed construction nor precluded bankruptcy in 1893. The chief function of the land seems to have been its attraction for promoters after the fabulous success of the Illinois Central. That railway by 1864 had sold over half its land grants at an average of $10.77 per acre, and the intervening sections of the public domain which had been almost unsalable at $1.25 per acre were selling at more than $2.50 in a buoyant market.

The land grant system was finally discredited not because it was unprofitable for the railways but because it created "fearful monopolies of the public domain," and "broke faith towards the landless" at a time when free lands and rapid settlement were coming to dominate land policy. The free homestead, though introduced with the Union Pacific in 1862 largely as a measure of high policy to meet a national emergency, fairly captured the imagination of that generation, not only in America but in the teeming population centres of Europe. For the railway land grant system, however, the cycle from extravagant faith to revulsion took place within a span of twenty-two years. The Canadian experiment was more fortunate. It is true that there were many superficial resemblances. It began just as its counterpart in the United States was coming to an ignominious end, and it passed through many of the same pathological symptoms of revulsion against "monopoly" and "land-lock" in almost exactly the same period of time. Moreover in Canada it fairly ran its course to the virtual exhaustion of eligible land reserves in the prairie provinces of Canada. But in the adaptation to Canadian conditions there was sagacity and even statesmanship of a high order, and in its ultimate effect, as we shall see, upon permanent and prosperous settlement it may fairly challenge comparison with any other major category of land policy.

[1]*Congressional Globe*, 1872–3, 3rd Session, Appendix, p. 108.

Two other analogies in the United States—the Northern Pacific and the Great Northern—add to the contrast with the C.P.R. It was expressly provided that "no money should be drawn from the treasury of the United States to aid in the construction of the Northern Pacific Railroad." The land grant, on the other hand, was the most lavish ever made to a single railway in North America—the odd-numbered sections in a belt of forty miles through public land states and eighty miles through the territories, amounting to 39,000,000 acres in its own right and a total of 43,000,000 by amalgamation with other land grant railways. Not even the necromancy of Jay Cooke and his "banana belt," however, could build the road "by means of the land through which it had to pass." Both the railway and his own firm went down in the crash of 1873. Land sales to 1880 produced some $9,000,000 and more than $27,750,000 by 1894, but the Northern Pacific went into bankruptcy a second time in 1893. Sales have since reached the total of $136,000,000,[1] confirming, no doubt, the early faith of Asa Whitney and Jay Cooke in the ultimate value of western lands. In early policy, nevertheless, as well as in the normal processes of bankruptcy the enormous land grants of the Northern Pacific seem to have been indistinguishable from other assets of the company. Nor were they responsible for restoring the Northern Pacific to solvency. It was not until 1883 that the line was completed to the Pacific.

The third analogy from the United States was the only one of the three transcontinentals to receive no federal land grant directly from the public domain though it inherited from its predecessor, the bankrupt St. Paul and Pacific, some 3,848,000 acres acquired under state auspices in 1857 and 1865. The reorganization of the defunct St. Paul and Pacific as the St. Paul, Minneapolis and Manitoba Railway—the first to make contact with Western Canada—brought into the field three or four men whose skill set a new pattern in the use of their limited land grants to produce not land revenues and dividends but permanent settlement and dependable traffic for the railway. Some of the soundest policies in American railroading may have originated with this remarkable group of men. The new president of the company was George Stephen of Montreal. The general manager was J. J. Hill who had been associated with the Dutch bondholders of the old St. Paul and Pacific. A third, Donald Smith of the Hudson's Bay Company, had already been "blooded" in Canadian politics in precipitating the collapse of the Government after the Pacific Scandal. From this "great divide" of enterprise and of politics two streams of railway

[1]Hibbard, *History of the Public Land Policies* (1924), p. 260.

projection eventually reached the Pacific. In the United States J. J. Hill became president of the company in 1883, reorganized it as the Great Northern in 1890, and reached the Pacific in 1893 after a titanic struggle with the Harriman interests of the Northern Pacific. Hill's doughty colleagues in the St. Paul, Minneapolis and Manitoba Railway fared forth to a still more spectacular achievement on Canadian soil. To George Stephen, Donald Smith, and R. B. Angus fell the organization and completion of the Canadian Pacific Railway.

III

With this background the new Dominion set itself to a problem of "paramount national importance," the building of a Pacific railway. Railway land grants were taken for granted. Galt thought "10 or 12,000 acres" and a subsidy of $15,000 per mile "would be a sufficient inducement." There was no counterpart here to Jay Cooke with his "banana belt" and the exuberant plans for the Northern Pacific. Cartier and Macdonald at the time of the *Manitoba Act* congratulated themselves that the lands had been "given up for nothing," and could be "used for the construction of the British Pacific Railway." "The Pacific Railway must be built by means of the land through which it had to pass." Six months before the transfer of 1870 Macdonald in a private letter to Brydges of the Grand Trunk had pledged the government to "most liberal grants of land in alternate blocks," with perhaps "a small pecuniary subsidy." The terms of union with British Columbia, as we have seen, were designed to commit the nation irrevocably to this project—a railway within ten years and a railway belt through British Columbia, not to exceed forty miles in width, to be transferred to the Dominion in trust for this purpose. An order-in-council of March 1, 1871, for Manitoba and the Territories authorized the withdrawal of "three full townships on each side of the line . . . for the Inter-Oceanic Railway." As late as April, 1882, Macdonald maintained that "not a farthing of money will have to be paid by the people of Canada."

The first C.P.R. charter of February, 1873, introduced startling innovations in the railway land grant system, many of which were fortunately eliminated after the Pacific Scandal. The first was the exceptional size of the land grant, 50,000,000 acres, half as large again as the maritime provinces, the largest hitherto projected for an American railway. The second innovation was the location of the grant, not in alternate sections as in the United States but in alternate blocks "twenty miles in depth on each side of the said railway" and ranging from six to twelve miles in width. The intervening government blocks containing from 76,800 to 153,600 acres were to be sold at $2.50 per acre. This second innovation was accentuated by a third, that if the railway blocks in the aggregate amounted to less than 50,000,000 acres, the residue might be taken up outside the forty-mile belt. A fourth innovation proved to be as permanent in the Canadian plan as it was revolutionary. The railway must "not be bound to receive any lands which are not of the fair average quality of the land in the sections of the country best adapted for settlement." A fifth was equally permanent and revolutionary—a cash subsidy not to exceed $30,000,000. Even the charter of the Northern Pacific had stipulated that "no money should be drawn from the treasury of the United States" for its construction. These terms to Sir Hugh Allen and his associates in the C.P.R. were contingent upon the exclusion of Jay Cooke and Northern Pacific interests from the Canadian enterprise. One month before the first C.P.R. charter, the last railway land grant in the United States had been made to the Chicago and Northwestern. As early as June 24, 1870, the New York *Tribune* had written the epitaph of the system in the United States: "the sooner this land-grant business for railroads is now stopped the better." Its adoption nevertheless in Canada was the measure of the emergency.

The Pacific Scandal destroyed both the company and the Government, but the Liberal programme of 1874 embodied no radical change with regard to land grants. The cash subsidy, $10,000 per mile, was to be less but the land grant in the railway belt was to be half as much again, still in alternate blocks as in 1873 alternating with government blocks for sale. With the Prime Minister himself sitting upon the treasury, as he once expressed it, "with a shot gun," neither the financial crisis nor the parsimony of the Government seems to have dispelled the delusion that the railway could still be built "by means of the land through which it had to pass." The St. Paul, Minneapolis and Manitoba Railway made contact from the south in 1878. Meanwhile the terms of union with British Columbia were to be met by an amphibious rail and water system carried forward, in default of private enterprise, by government contract.

After the return of the Conservative party to power in 1878 the railway land grant regulations passed through a bewildering variety of changes before the final incorporation of the Canadian Pacific Railway in 1881 brought into being the organization which carried the first Canadian transcontinental railway through to completion in 1885. The place assigned to land grants in the process at first reached astronomical proportions. At one stage in 1879 the House of Commons was prepared to grant "one hundred million acres of land, and all the minerals they contain . . . for the purpose of constructing the Canadian Pacific Railway." By 1881, however, certain basic principles began to emerge in government policy. The road was to be built by private enterprise. Its princely endowments in land, cash subsidies, and mileage already completed at the expense of the government, were intended to identify the railway with the national interests of Canada. The company reciprocated by conceding obligations to the settler and to the nation. In its own interest too as a "railroading proposition" it was already prepared to underwrite that partnership by far-sighted regulations which came to merit the verdict of statesmanship.

Three distinctive features of the C.P.R. charter of 1881 may be outlined without unnecessary detail:[1]

(i) Though projected and built as a private enterprise the C.P.R. was endowed with both land and cash in truly lavish proportions—a fair index of the national emergency. The land grant of 1881— 25,000,000 acres for the main line—was more than twice as large as the final grant to the Union Pacific (12,000,000 acres) though it was less than two-thirds of the grant to the Northern Pacific (39,000,000 acres) and exactly half the grant of 50,000,000 acres in the original project of 1873.

Of the main line grant of 25,000,000 acres to the C.P.R. some 6,793,014 were surrendered in 1886 to retire part of a government loan. Additional grants directly to the C.P.R. were made for the Souris branch (1890–1) and the Pipestone Extension (1894)—1,408,704 acres and 200,320 acres respectively. In addition to this principality in its own right the C.P.R. absorbed no fewer than six of the ten "colonization railways" which received land grants during the Canadian era of the system.[2] These brought the reversion of some 6,239,453 acres into the orbit of the C.P.R., making a total of 26,055,462 acres in all out of an area of 31,783,634 acres granted to railways from "Dominion lands" from 1881 to 1894.

This was by far the largest part of the C.P.R. endowment but there were other ingredients much more revolutionary. Land there was in abundance for the iron horse; the most serious problem in 1881 was

[1]See Chester Martin, *"Dominion Lands" Policy*, chaps. III, IV, V, and XIII.

[2]The Alberta Railway and Coal ("Irrigation") Company (1885–91) with original land grants of 1,101,716 acres; the Calgary and Edmonton (1890) with 1,820,685 acres; the Great Northwest Central (1886) with 320,000 acres; the Saskatchewan and Western (1894) with 98,880 acres; the Manitoba and North-Western (1885–6) with 1,501,376 acres; and the Manitoba and Southwestern Colonization Railway (1885, 1891) with 1,396,800 acres.

capital. Unlike the Union and Northern Pacific railways the C.P.R. received cash subsidies of lavish size for those days both in the form of direct subsidies and in the form of government loans. The original cash subsidy to the C.P.R. syndicate was $25,000,000. In addition to this the company was endowed with railway mileage already completed at a cost of $35,000,000, and surveys already made towards the Pacific at a cost of $3,500,000. Government loans of $29,880,000 in 1884 and a final loan of $5,000,000 in 1885 brought the total of government subsidies, cost of completed railway and surveys, and government loans to $98,380,000.

With this princely endowment of more than 26,000,000 acres of the best agricultural lands that could be selected in Western Canada and financial subventions of nearly $100,000,000, it is somewhat paradoxical to regard the C.P.R. as the norm of private enterprise. None, however, could impugn either the enterprise or the far-sighted efficiency of the C.P.R. as a "railroading proposition, first, last, and always." The final loan of $5,000,000 from the government which saved the company from bankruptcy in 1885 and "the country from catastrophe" may stand as the narrowest margin of national solvency in the expansion of Canada. Donald Smith had already thrown into the scales his last reserve, the secret "nest egg" saved up, with true Scottish thrift, for just such an emergency. The Minister of Finance was adamant that any further grant to the C.P.R. would be political suicide. George Stephen wrote ominously of despair and failing health: there were "warnings of which nobody knows but myself which I will fight against and conceal to the last." Tupper too had written desperately from London (February 24, 1885) that "the interests of the whole Dominion" were at stake and the "C.P.R. inseparably bound up with them. . . . I will, if needed, go back to Parliament as a private member, and sustain you all to the best of my ability" rather than "let the C.P.R. go down."

Stephen's conclusive appeal was probably a telegram in cypher which found its way to the Prime Minister: "Van Horne writes: 'Have no means paying wages . . . unless we get immediate relief we must stop.'" When the final loan of $5,000,000 was made at last it cost the resignation of the Minister of Finance and was carried through the caucus of the party by the threat of Macdonald's own resignation. Here was private enterprise at its best, with public enterprise at its best not far behind. The political courage of two men, the same two whose troth was pledged to each other and to their cause in Halifax in September, 1864, may fairly be linked with the enterprise of

George Stephen, Donald Smith, R. B. Angus, and William Van Horne in the building of the C.P.R. To Macdonald as prime minister and Tupper as minister of railways, high commissioner, and ubiquitous "Cumberland war-horse" of the party for every emergency, the success of this greatest of national achievements was chiefly due.

(ii) A second feature of the C.P.R. marked so radical a departure from the practice in the Union and Northern Pacific that the history of land settlement in the prairie provinces is scarcely more than a commentary upon it. The hope of building the railway "by means of the land through which it had to pass" proved to be a delusion. For Canada and for the C.P.R. alike the first need of the hour was rapid and permanent settlement, and this "paramount necessity" fused the interests of the railway and the nation into indissoluble partnership. Henceforth railway land grants and free homesteads were systematically interwoven into a pattern of land settlement which had no counterpart for the transcontinentals south of the border.[1]

The approach of the railway and the government *pari passu* to this pattern of land settlement was at first slow and halting. The delusion that the railway could be built "by means of the land through which it had to pass" died hard. As late as 1885 the government still professed to regard "the expenditure in construction and in cash subsidy . . . as an advance, to be repaid from the lands." The fabulous land sales of the Illinois Central probably sanctioned this delusion. Scarcely half its land endowment was sold at an average price of $10.77 per acre and the railway was still doing a "land office business," with the intervening sections of government land sharing in the rising prices.

But between the Illinois Central and the C.P.R. there was one incorrigible difference. The C.P.R. was building not through the Mississippi prairies with their buoyant enterprise and maturing economy but into a wilderness of unpredictable resources. Much of it was known to be a region of subnormal rainfall. Despite the enthusiasm of Macoun and the more measured confidence of Hind it was known that nothing like Jay Cooke's "banana belt" was to be found in the Canadian West. "Palliser's triangle" of semi-arid prairie was yet to take its toll of the unwary settler. West of the infant city of Winnipeg the railway was so far in advance of settlement that settlement itself was forced to wait upon the hazards of frost and rust and drought before it could trust the enterprise of the railway.

In these circumstances the joint decision of the government and the railway to pool their resources and to forgo land revenues in the

[1] See plan of township, Fig. 6.

interest of rapid settlement was national policy on the highest level. Thenceforth the interests of the government and the C.P.R. were so nearly indistinguishable that the Minister of Railways never ceased to identify their joint responsibility to the nation. Tupper avowed the consequences with characteristic candour: "the success of the C.P.R." was a national necessity. "Are the interests of Manitoba and the North-West [in their public lands] to be sacrificed to the interests of Canada? I say, if it is necessary, yes."

The technique by which this partnership was implemented was a radical departure from American policy. In the United States the land grants were located in odd-numbered sections in railway "belts" adjoining the railways—in the case of the Union Pacific in a "belt" of 40 miles, 20 on either side of the line. If certain odd-numbered sections were already occupied no "indemnity selection" was permitted. The railway lands were thus the "mine run" of the region "good, bad, and indifferent." Meanwhile the railways had insisted upon the sale of even-numbered sections by the government at prices that should not impair the market for contiguous odd-numbered sections owned by the railways.

In Canada a much wiser and more discerning policy prevailed. The prime necessity was to get permanent and prosperous settlers on the land. To that end the C.P.R., as its projectors never tired of repeating, was from the beginning to end a "railroading proposition"—not a contractor's road nor a speculator's road nor a land-jobber's road. In Canada the even-numbered sections throughout were reserved for free homesteads. The long-range advantages of this policy to the railway itself was of course easily predictable. By comparison with the prospective freight rates west on the settler's chattels and equipment and east to world markets on his wheat the initial price to be obtained from his land was trifling. Once their own land grants were securely located, therefore, the railway could afford to give right of way to the adjoining homesteads. Tupper himself expounded this policy with convincing courage:

We are free to give away every acre that remains in our possession should the public interest warrant it. No policy did the syndicate press more strongly upon us than that of settling the land as fast as we could. They said we should be only too glad to plant a free settler upon every acre belonging to the Government.

The result was an even pattern of free homesteads and contiguous railway land for sale, throughout the vast reserves set aside for the selection of land grants "earned" by railway construction in Western

Canada. Not only the odd-numbered sections of railway lands but school lands (sections 11 and 29 in each township) and Hudson's Bay lands in sections 8 and 26 provided the settler with a choice of several quarter-sections of land for sale contiguous to his homestead.[1] Of the eight quarter-sections contiguous to each homestead four were normally for sale, and in several cases five. An enterprising settler with capital could thus expand his holdings *ad libitum* and even the primitive settler could usually pre-empt at least one quarter-section contiguous to his homestead.

The significance of this for the technique of dry-farming may have been largely unforeseen in 1881 but its ultimate bearing upon the development of Western Canadian agriculture can scarcely be overestimated. Since two years' rainfall is usually necessary for one year's crop west of the 100th meridian, summer-fallowing for half the area under cultivation became standard practice. The half-section thus supplanted the quarter-section as the norm for successful agriculture. Contiguous settlement in eligible areas would have strangled this salutary expansion at the outset. The tragedy west of the 100th meridian in the United States where one homesteader usually devoured another—"dog eat dog"—or both fell a prey to the lurking speculator, was never repeated in Western Canada. The percentage of farms of over 200 acres in Saskatchewan rose steadily from 38.56 in 1901 to 67.45 in 1921 and over 70 in 1926. The average farm in Saskatchewan in 1926 was 389 acres of which 229 acres—all but the original homestead of 160 acres—must have been purchased.[2] From this pattern of free homesteads evenly interspersed with railway lands, school lands, and Hudson's Bay lands for sale arose untold advantages for all concerned. The fact that many of these were at first inadvertent does not impair the ultimate importance. "Man goeth out like Saul to find his father's colts and findeth instead a Kingdom."

(iii) A third variation of the system in Canada left its prototype in the United States almost unrecognizable. It was conceded that railway land grants must be "fairly fit for settlement," and before the system came to an end in 1908 the whole range of "Dominion lands" in Western Canada had to be exploited to provide such lands "earned" by the railways.

The rigid pattern of railway "belts" of fixed dimensions for the Union and Northern Pacific precluded "indemnity selection" for subnormal areas and left government and railways, both with land for

[1]See plan of township, Fig. 6.
[2]See Figs. 8, 9.

sale, locked inflexibly at cross-purposes in uncompromising rivalry. The decision to discard railway "belts" altogether in Canada was forced upon the government by the very size of its land grants. There can be no doubt that Ontario was originally expected (1872) to contribute 9,000,000 acres for mileage built in Ontario; and British Columbia, as we have seen, undertook to supply "a similar extent of Public lands . . . throughout its entire length in British Columbia . . . as may be appropriated . . . from the Public Lands in the North-West Territories and the Province of Manitoba." Neither of these provinces in the end contributed to the C.P.R. land grant,[1] for reasons that are easily surmised: "Dominion lands" could be used indiscriminately and with impunity for that purpose. With mileage of approximately 662 miles in Ontario, 208 in Manitoba, 419 in Saskatchewan, 336 in Alberta, and 268 in British Columbia, the railway eventually selected its main line grant in Manitoba (2,183,084 acres), Saskatchewan (6,216,784 acres, of which 6,128,000 were selected before the creation of the province in 1905), and Alberta (9,805,446 acres, of which more than 8,217,400 acres were selected before the creation of the province in 1905).[2] Of the total of 3630 miles of land grant railways in Western Canada, Saskatchewan secured less than 24 per cent of the mileage and contributed nearly half the acreage of land grants. Alberta with 22 per cent of the mileage contributed over 41 per cent of the land grants. Saskatchewan contributed 1,330,000 acres—almost the area of Prince Edward Island—to railways with no mileage whatever in that province.[3]

This was made possible only by a practice which filled the Canadian era of railway land grants with intractable controversy. With government and railway now indissolubly in partnership in the interests of rapid and permanent settlement, the range of selection of lands "fairly fit for settlement" was extended to vast "reserves" in which the acreage "earned" by actual railway construction could be chosen; and since time limits for the selection of lands "fairly fit for settlement" were seldom enforced or enforceable—"never in one single case lived up to"[4]—the process went on interminably until it was brought violently to an end by the government in 1908. The first Northern Reserve for the C.P.R. (1882), even after the surrender of nearly 7,000,000 acres to retire part of the government loan in 1886, endowed the railway

[1] Except for 1,300 acres in British Columbia.
[2] The balance, 6,793,014 acres, were surrendered in 1886 to retire part of the government loan.
[3] See map of land grant railways, Fig. 10.
[4] P. A. Gordon before the Saskatchewan Resources Commission.

with the odd-numbered sections all "fairly fit for settlement" in one of the most productive areas of Western Canada. Two reserves south of the main line in Manitoba (1882 and 1883), the Lake Dauphin Reserve (1895) and the second Northern Reserve (1896), added to the range of selection. Even this was not enough to supply the necessary acreage, and in the end the C.P.R. agreed to accept the solid block between Medicine Hat and Calgary for the vast irrigation project of 1903. Meanwhile no fewer than ten "colonization railways" had entered the field against the "monopoly" of the C.P.R. Rival "reserves" began to "blanket" the West with ungovernable rivalries. As the large companies began to devour the small ones their land grants fairly exhausted the range of odd-numbered sections "fairly fit for settlement." In the end Clifford Sifton's sardonic comment was measurably true: the railway land grant system came to an end because the government had come to the end of eligible land grants. The price of the iron horse in terms of land was half the land "fairly fit for settlement" in the prairie provinces.[1]

IV

Viewed in retrospect many features of this third aspect of the Canadian system are now less forbidding than they must have been to the generation which had to deal with them at close quarters. As the rivalry for eligible reserves "fairly fit for settlement" increased, hostile interests, sheltered behind the patronage of rival political parties, turned every frontier into a "battle-ground for giants."[2] Like the prehistoric dinosaurs whose bones are still to be found embedded in the banks of the Bow River, these predatory interests eventually toppled over into oblivion, while the regions over which they once ranged with such indomitable ferocity have blossomed into wheat farms and ranches. The key to this evolution in both cases has been adaptability.

The use which the Canadian railways, and particularly the C.P.R., made of their gargantuan land grants may fairly be taken into account in appraising the ultimate results of the system as a whole. Measured by these standards many advantages, unforeseen at the time, must be credited to it. Among the score or more categories of administration into which "Dominion lands" eventually found their way in Western Canada it is doubtful if any subserved the interests of permanent and prosperous settlement more effectually in the long run than the princely land grants to the C.P.R.

[1]See map of railway land grants, Fig. 11.
[2]See map of typical railway land reserves, Fig. 12.

It is true that "school lands" (sections 11 and 29 in each township) and in some respects the free homestead itself functioned admirably to focus the interest of the enterprising settler upon the frontier. The school lands, however, were merely a by-product of the system, while the free homestead, as we shall see, was never more than half the system at best, with devastating results, in many respects, upon the human material which went into the experiment. The railway land grants, on the other hand, in the very process of their selection and administration met the problem of permanent settlement at every point. They were all "fairly fit for settlement." In every section they were contiguous to the homesteader. Undoubtedly many of the "colonization railway" grants were exploited in the interests of speculators and speculative land companies. The land was frequently held for higher prices and sold for the highest price it would bring. Indeed the C.P.R. itself was not guiltless of such practices in the Northern Reserve remote from its own lines. But a comparison with Hudson's Bay lands which were in "mine run" sections (8 and 26) of the fertile belt or even with "school lands" (sections 11 and 29) which were also "mine run" in every township would provide some very conclusive evidence for the C.P.R.[1] The average price of Hudson's Bay lands was $12.10 per acre. School lands, sold at auction and administered avowedly for purposes of revenue, brought $9.79 per acre in Manitoba, $14.40 per acre in Alberta, and $16.85 in Saskatchewan. From 1893 to 1930 C.P.R. lands, all "fairly fit for settlement" and selected during the most favourable period of the railway land grant era from the widest range of "reserves" in Western Canada, were sold at an average price of $8.55. Excluding irrigation lands, which averaged more than $40 per acre, the price was $7.63 per acre, and excluding cancellations and revestments it was $7.37 per acre.

This remarkable disparity between C.P.R. lands and the "mine run" of other lands administered avowedly for revenue reflects the policy openly claimed by the company and pursued, on the whole, with great persistence and discrimination. From beginning to end the C.P.R. was a "railroading proposition." Land revenues were not its prime concern. These were systematically "ploughed back into development." The settler's ability to buy land at enhanced prices in the future was less important than his ability at once to get land cheaply, to get all he could successfully use, to get it into cultivation without loss of time, and to provide an export staple for world markets. This export staple for many years was one of the most lucra-

[1] See plan of township, Fig. 6.

tive commodities in the Canadian economy. The explanation for all this was of course very simple. Perennial freight rates for the settlers' wheat were more profitable than any prospect of inflated prices for his land.

For many years the C.P.R. sold land at $2.50 per acre with a rebate of $1.25 for every acre brought into cultivation. The 6,793,014 acres surrendered to retire government loans in 1886 were given up for $1.50 per acre. Up to 1906 the average price of C.P.R. lands was less than $5 per acre. By 1912, when the Natural Resources Department of the C.P.R. was organized, more than 13,750,000 acres had been sold and the company announced a "policy of selling lands to settlers only." To the Saskatchewan Resources Commission in 1934 the net proceeds of C.P.R. agricultural lands were given at less than $144,000,000 while the cost of administration, including townsites, irrigation, and "immigration and colonization," amounted to $94,000,000.

More convincing than this record of land prices was the concern of the C.P.R. throughout for the permanence and prosperity of settlement. It is true, as the company conceded, that C.P.R. lands were "seldom sold to new immigrants, but generally to those who have already established themselves on free homesteads," but by 1922 the company could claim no fewer than 54,000 families "placed upon its lands alone." The proof of their permanence and prosperity was the fact that the percentage of cancellations from beginning to end was phenomenally low, probably the lowest on record. In cycles of drought or depression this was undoubtedly due to the paternalistic policy of the company. When the tide of immigration began at last to flow towards Western Canada at the turn of the century the company began to reap the harvest cast upon the waters during the long years of adversity. Thus in 1922 the company could claim to have spent more on colonization than the government itself—"an amount in excess of the total expenditure of the Dominion Government for immigration during that period." "The Canadian Pacific for many years," wrote the president of the company, "has been the most active colonizing agency in Canada." In 1926 the C.P.R. was selling land on an initial payment of 7 per cent with no interest on deferred payments for the first year and with the balance amortised in thirty-four equal annual payments. "I know of no organization in any country," the president of the company stated, "which gives such terms to settlers. . . . At no time during the life of the contract is the purchaser called upon to pay more than $200 a year on each quarter section, except in the case of the higher priced irrigated land. In the United States and other

demand for land + surveys.

countries he would pay more than this amount in annual rental alone."

Beginning in 1910 the policy of ready-made farms—nearly a quarter of a million acres were developed in this way—resulted in more than 800 "improved farms" and 432 demonstration farms to raise standards of agriculture for the whole community. More than $20,000,000 were spent upon the 3,000,000 acre irrigation project in Alberta, with more than 4000 miles of canals and distributing ditches in "the largest private enterprise of its kind ever carried out."

The record of the C.P.R. as it was presented to the Saskatchewan Commission (1934) was probably the best of any category of land administration during the sixty-year cycle of "Dominion lands" from 1870 to 1930. The C.P.R., said one veteran in the company's service,[1] was a "paternal institution in Western Canada." The land policy of the company was "not a real estate proposition at all. It was the building up for an empire in the West." During the depression no cancellations were ever enforced against *bona fide* settlers. The partnership between the railway and the government was vital to both— "the homestead policy was the foundation on which we worked." "We built Western Canada." It was possible to qualify this *ex parte* evidence by resurrecting old traditions of "land-lock" and "monopoly," of land-use "prodigal and extravagant." In the battle for land "reserves" the largest of the dinosaurs was frequently the fiercest and most ruthless. The freedom of C.P.R. lands from taxation was systematically exploited by the purchasers of C.P.R. lands who by the simple expedient of deferring patent could evade municipal taxation and other obligations in a primitive community. Before the Dysart commission (1934) the province of Saskatchewan presented a formidable estimate of taxation evaded in this way.[2] Land companies, good and bad, were entrusted at various times with C.P.R. as well as other railway lands to administer, with results both good and bad for permanent settlement. The net result, however, over a range of half a century was unique for any railway on the continent and probably unique among colonizing agencies in Canada. At the hearings of the Saskatchewan Resources Commission the proud claim "We built Western Canada" was conceded on every side. "Quite right," said one counsel. "I agree with that, too," added his opponent. "Everybody must agree with that," insisted the witness, and one of the commissioners added the

[1]Mr. Frank W. Russell.
[2]Up to 1896 less than 2,000,000 of the 31,000,000 acres of railway land grants in Western Canada had been patented.

final comment, "No argument there." The C.P.R. had built a giant's causeway across the continent.

The problem of integrating and consolidating the new Dominion, nevertheless, was only half solved. In this vast enterprise many other agencies played their part. In the last analysis it was the settler who built Western Canada. The foundations of nationhood are not railways and institutions but living people. Not until the West had settled into an enduring pattern of co-ordinated provinces could the foundations of a transcontinental federation be claimed for Canadian nationhood.

Chapter Twenty-Three

"THE LAST BEST WEST"

A T the time of the transfer of Rupert's Land and the North-Western Territory to Canada in 1870 there were fewer than 15,000 inhabitants, white or mixed blood, between the Great Lakes and the Rocky Mountains. Five-sixths of the present area of Canada was still a wilderness.[1] The development of this vast region into the prairie provinces of Canada proved to be the last of a long series of agricultural "frontiers of settlement" spreading across the continent of North America like the ebb and flow of a rising tide. Many of these frontiers are now traceable only in the meagre records of the contemporary press and such impersonal evidence as survived the hurly-burly of migration. For the last of them it was fortunate that an attempt was made to recapture the elusive spirit of the frontier before it had merged with its predecessors into the routine adjustments of pioneer life.

The nine volumes of the "Canadian Frontiers of Settlement" series, projected by the late Dr. Isaiah Bowman and carried forward by the Canadian Pioneer Problems Committee under the joint editorship of Dr. W. A. Mackintosh and Dr. W. L. G. Joerg, were munificently endowed (so at least it seemed to the Canadian Committee) to observe and record the last stages of this agricultural frontier in exhaustive detail. The project was based upon five years of contemporary field-work as well as sustained research into the widest range of evidence, in all probability, ever available for such a survey.

In addition to the "Canadian Frontiers of Settlement" series no fewer than three Natural Resources Commissions, one for each province, with every access to departmental records at Ottawa and elsewhere, assembled a series of definitive investigations into almost every phase of federal administration in the prairie provinces during the sixty-year cycle of "Dominion lands." In the light of this voluminous evidence many unforeseen factors began to emerge among the "con-

[1]Cf. Fig. 21 for disposition of lands in the prairie provinces, 1911.

trols" of frontier settlement. Was the movement of population into "the last best West," as the enterprising agencies of the Department of the Interior began to boast, the result of enlightened government policy? Was it due to the impact of the free-homestead system? Was it, in terms of the plausible theory of the day, the result of "overflow" from saturated areas of contiguous settlement? Was it attainable by concerted design like the American forays into Texas and Oregon or was it dependent upon demographic "controls" much remoter and more complicated than the current *clichés* which lay upon the surface? Was there not, at the outset, a more convincing approach than the "overflow" thesis for the agricultural settlement of Western Canada?

I

The flow of population into the receding agricultural frontiers of North America has been one of the most distinctive processes of modern demography. Many of the early movements, the flow into innumerable nooks and crannies of the continent, followed the pattern of other fluids in filling available areas from the overflow of contiguous settlement. The early movements which the late Dr. Hansen sought to trace in *The Mingling of the Canadian and American Peoples* belonged largely to this category. Nova Scotia, a frontier of New England, responded in this way to the vicissitudes of that maritime economy. The rapid settlement of the Annapolis Valley in the wake of the Acadian exiles, the expansion of the Gloucester and Marblehead and Salem fishing industry to Canso and the South Shore until disorganized by the revolution, was the normal sinuous flow of population finding its own level over similar regions contiguous to New England. The early settlement of Upper Canada from New York and Pennsylvania would probably have followed a similar course. The loyalist migrations which planted a population highly selective in origin and temper in the Niagara peninsula and elsewhere in Upper Canada would probably have been anticipated by a much larger movement on purely economic grounds had there been no revolution. Such at least had been Franklin's forecast at the close of the first empire, and the migration which speedily followed in spite of the revolution —outnumbering by 1820 the loyalist population four or five to one from the contiguous states and territories of the union—would seem to confirm this thesis. The movement in turn down the Ohio into the Mississippi and Missouri prairies still followed in many respects the pattern of "overflow" from maturing frontiers into contiguous territory.

By the middle of the nineteenth century, however, it was obvious that there were other forces at work in these people-wanderings in addition to the tendency of frontier agricultural settlement to find its own level. The age of steam—the steamship on the Atlantic and the railway across the continent—lent an altogether unprecedented mobility to the process. With the land grant railways and the free-homestead system a new set of "controls," almost world-wide in their extent and prevalence, came into play. Like the ebb and flow of the tides these movements present baffling phenomena to any investigator who is concerned only with local advances in scientific agriculture, soil surveys or land policy, or other aspects of a purely local economy. It may never be possible, even by the most painstaking research, to reconstruct these early tides of migration as the agricultural frontiers ebbed and flowed across the continent. The attempt in the "Frontiers of Settlement" series[1] to diagnose at least one of these while it was actually in process has resulted in a number of conclusions with regard to Western Canada which have had the advantage of contemporary observation—a moving picture as compared with the piecemeal evidence of antiquated "stills" in the early history of frontier settlement. The story of Western Canadian settlement may be simplified by citing one or two of these conclusions at the outset.

The tidal frontiers of agricultural settlement after the appearance of the land grant railways and the free-homestead system in the United States no longer depended upon contiguous populations for their development. Vast and acquisitive enterprises were already directing the stream of migration surging towards the frontier into national channels. The prodigious vogue of Texas, confirmed by annexation and war, began a series of movements primed, in many cases, by spectacular discovery and adventure. The movement into old Oregon was directed with great resourcefulness and skill to reinforce the claims of the United States on the Pacific. The gold-rush into California was not without its influence upon the Illinois Central, the first of the land grant railways. The free-homestead system, however, was revolutionary. Though more immediately concerned, as we have seen, with the conflict between the North and the South for control of the West, it quickly transcended the issues of the Civil War and made an impact almost altogether unforeseen upon the imagination of millions in

[1]Macmillan, 9 vols. See also the exploratory volume by Isaiah Bowman, *The Pioneer Fringe* (1931). The "Frontiers of Settlement" project was intended as the first of a series of studies of vast areas of potentially important but relatively undeveloped regions in Australia, Rhodesia, Siberia, the Matto Grosso of Brazil, etc.

crowded centres of population in Europe as well as in the United States. It was "the most important step," wrote Donaldson, "in the history of the public land system. Once adopted, no person could estimate its moral, social and political effects."

Henceforth agricultural frontiers moved with seven league boots across the continent, oblivious alike of distance and direction. The settlement of the Mississippi prairies, followed by that of the Missouri prairies, quickly outran the pedestrian gait of colonial days. It was only after crossing the Rockies and the Sierras into California that the agricultural frontier returned to the spring wheat district of the Dakotas. Then it was "Canada's turn," and the factors which began to form behind the movement into Western Canada reflected as never before, perhaps, how complex was the pattern of that "golden age" in the settlement of "the last best West."

Two groups of factors are now discernible, both of them much subtler than the plausible explanations which then lay so invitingly upon the surface. The era of most rapid and permanent settlement began with the advent of the Liberal party to power in 1896, and it was easy for politics to claim the prerogatives of Providence in ordering that remarkable decade and a half of Western Canadian development. Clifford Sifton in his valedictory speech of 1905—one of the truly great speeches of the Canadian House of Commons—could review with some pride his own contribution to the era. "I shall be content," he concluded, "when the history of this country shall be written, to have the history of the last eight or nine years, as far as western administration is concerned, entered opposite my name." No abler administrator ever presided over the Department of the Interior, and his peers in that field must include two prime ministers, Sir John A. Macdonald and the Hon. Arthur Meighen. But Sifton's claim is a large order, and of the two groups of factors which are now discernible in the process one was almost world-wide in its range and complexity.

Beyond a doubt a series of local controls, largely physiographical in character, was already culminating in Western Canada—the accessibility of a new frontier endowed with resources and facilities for staple production in an expanding economy. The combination of this series of factors at the turn of the century was a circumstance of the first importance. Railway construction alone was not enough, though the completion of the main line of the C.P.R. in 1885 began a long process of bringing Western Canadian agriculture within ten miles of the railways, the accepted optimum for the economical marketing of wheat. Most of the "colonization railways" were by this time finding their way into the C.P.R. system or into the new project of the Canadian Northern under the resourceful enterprise of Mackenzie and Mann. The growing network of railways[1] will illustrate this indispensable factor for the Western Canadian frontier. The botanist and the agronomist and the frontiersman himself had also their contribution to make. Early maturing rust-resisting wheat to escape the frost, the development of dry-farming to meet the hazards of subnormal rainfall, the superb milling qualities of "number one northern" in the wheat markets of the world, all added to the sum of local factors which the shrewd entrepreneur was not slow to exploit. For a decade and a half "the last best West," as one of the most enterprising journalists of that era once observed, could be relied upon to "make the headlines" in the Canadian press.

Many of these local advantages, however, had long been expounded with great industry. Nothing devised in the twentieth century could exceed the patient resourcefulness of the C.P.R. during the grim years of the early nineties. Like the children in the marketplace they had piped and their contemporaries had not danced. Nor could federal land policy be held accountable for the lag in Western Canadian development. One of the most remarkable facts about these movements of population to the agricultural frontiers of the continent has been that cheap land or even free land has seldom been the determining factor except as it has made its impact upon population already "on the move." When "the boom was on" it was as easy to sell land as to give it away. More land in Western Canada was in fact administered by sale or for sale than as free homesteads.[2] On the other hand, when the "boom" had passed it was impossible to give the land away. There were factors here as imponderable as the swarming of bees and almost as unpredictable. At first sight the alighting of the swarm sometimes seemed due to nothing more logical than the beating of a tin pan.

It was this second series of factors which reinforced "Canada's turn" as an accessible agricultural frontier and set masses of population in America and Europe on the march towards the Canadian West. Migration was already "on the move" to the accompaniment of "good times" and a venturesome pioneering spirit already "in the air." Without these conditions, almost world-wide, in many respects, in their diversity, the most skilful advertising, the most resourceful showmanship, the shrewdest devices of official administration might have failed. With

[1] See Figs. 13 to 20.
[2] Up to 1928, 61,258,655 acres to 58,253,700. See *"Dominion Lands" Policy*, 499 ff.

them, the decade and a half at the turn of the century will stand out in Canadian demography with great distinction. For the first time in her history Canada held her own against the demographic "pull" of the United States. For the first time the Canadian-born population of the United States remained practically stationary for a whole decade. For the first time Canadian statesmen dared to hazard the prophecy that the twentieth century belonged to Canada.

II

A whole century of primitive colonization in Rupert's Land preceded this "golden age" of rapid and permanent settlement. Neither the diminutive scale of the Red River Settlement, however, nor the tragic death of Selkirk in 1820 could dwarf the ultimate importance of that strange enterprise. Seldom has the philanthropy of one man for a single decade been accountable for the survival of so vast a territory to the parent state. Had the narrow Red River corridor between Lake Winnipeg and the United States boundary followed Texas and Oregon into the American union during the forties, as every portent of demography seemed to warrant, the westward expansion of Canada could never have reached the Pacific. A vested interest of 5,000 dour and almost forgotten Scottish highlanders near the land-centre of the continent proved to be the "keystone" of its ultimate destiny. At no other point on the long transcontinental boundary would it have been possible for so small a band of pioneers, like the heroic boy in the Dutch saga, to hold back the tide by thrusting their own stolid allegiance and traditions into the hole in the dyke.

The presence there in 1846 of Colonel Crofton with his handful of infantrymen and engineers quartered at Fort Garry "under secret instructions" from the Duke of Wellington (as Colonel Crofton himself afterwards testified before the Select Committee of 1857) was a timely recognition of this basic strategy. It is now known that Lower Fort Garry was laboriously built to reinforce the security of the Upper Fort and the Settlement on the upper reaches of the Red River. Captain Warre, posing as a wandering artist whose exquisite water-colours of Red River and the Pacific coast are now "museum pieces" in the Public Archives of Canada, was a secret agent of the War Office engaged in activities far less aesthetic than sedate official circles at Fort Garry could have surmised. To the enterprising free-trader in furs Colonel Crofton's little garrison was merely another device of the old Company to reinforce its monopoly of the fur-trade and to postpone the contacts of Red River with the American outposts.

At the transfer of 1870 the population of the new "postage-stamp province" of Manitoba was scarcely more than 11,000, including those of mixed blood, both French and English. But the little village of Winnipeg, reinforced by the disbanded volunteers of the Wolseley expedition, was not long in aspiring to a metropolitan destiny. The first steam locomotive in Western Canada was floated down the Red River from the United States "with steam up and whistle blowing full-blast" to begin the northern end of railway construction to St. Paul. For nearly a decade Manitoba had been almost as isolated as the old Red River Settlement. The first wheat for export—13,000 bushels in 1877 increasing to 100,000 bushels in 1879—went out by way of Duluth. The amphibious policy of the Liberal Government for implementing the terms of union with British Columbia merely confirmed the trend towards the south. From the south came the first railway contacts with Western Canada in 1879.

With the charter of 1881 to the C.P.R. a new era, as we have seen, began for the Canadian West. A series of "booms" based on little but indiscriminate optimism was exploited by experts who rode the crest of the wave as the Hawaiian surf-rider mounts the breakers of the Pacific. Whole townsites were sold at auction in a single night. At the crest of the "boom," land near the corner of Main and Portage in Winnipeg was selling for higher prices than frontage on Madison Avenue in Chicago. The collapse of the boom in 1883 brought disillusionment and despair. Even the solid advances in agriculture through the introduction of Red Fife wheat and the technique of summer-fallowing for dry-farming could not repair the ravages of such an experience.

Group settlements nevertheless were begun in the early seventies which have since left their mark on Western Canada. Mennonites were the first to leave fearlessly the poplar swales of the river banks for the expanses of the open prairie. Their migration from Rhenish Prussia to Berdiansk on the Sea of Azov under Catherine the Great had already taught them the use of the open steppes for wheat and cattle. When Bismarck in preparation for the Franco-Prussian War renounced the suzeraignty over them which had been conceded to Prussia by Catherine the Great, the Russian government began to draft them into the army in defiance of their stubborn age-old principles of non-combatancy. After exploratory pilgrimages as far afield as South America they finally settled in Manitoba under the list of "rights" which Canada has scrupulously but all too unsympathetically observed ever since. The Icelandic settlements which left a deeper stratum of Icelandic population and culture in Western Canada than anywhere outside of Iceland passed through a more searching ordeal of adaptation. Their share not only in Canadian public life and enterprise but in the best traditions of Icelandic literature has been worthy of their Icelandic sagas. A statue to Jon Sigurdsson stands in front of the Parliament Buildings in Winnipeg, and the phenomenal Icelandic enlistments in both world wars attest the fidelity of their response. The delegation from Western Canada to Reikjavik to commemorate the thousandth anniversary of the first *Althing* in Iceland may illustrate the aptitude of that remarkable people for the parliamentary tradition in Canada. Under Letellier de St. Just, Minister of Agriculture, group settlements too from Quebec began to establish those pockets of French-Canadian life and culture in Western Canada which have never ceased their grim struggle for *survivance*. Who will say that these strands of settlement with discerning appreciation could not strengthen and enrich the fibre of Canadian character?

Meanwhile settlement was feeling its way cautiously westward to the Brandon hills, surmounting the second prairie level and retracing the receding shores of old Lake Agassiz.[1] With the completion of the C.P.R. in 1885 one at least of the prerequisites for an agricultural "frontier" began to spread its network over the prairies. Few could have known how long the other factors of permanent settlement were yet to await the propitious hour of "swarming" in Western Canada.

The decade from the completion of the main line of the C.P.R. in 1885 to the beginnings of anything like a mass movement in Western Canadian settlement exhausted every expedient of ingenious advertising and promotion. The C.P.R. cast its bread upon a sea of waters. Seed wheat was brought in free, purebred stock at $2 a head. Expert displays in Britain and on the continent spread the knowledge of "number one hard" but brought few pioneers to grow it. It was only after the tide of migration largely from the older frontiers of Missouri and Kansas and Minnesota had submerged the spring wheat areas of the Dakotas and Montana that the vast resources of the Canadian prairies came into view. Here, as the land companies came to boast, was "the last best West," and Clifford Sifton himself once referred deliberately to the Saskatchewan Valley Land Company in particular as the beginning of rapid settlement. "I make the statement advisedly,"

[1]At one time the largest body of fresh water in the world, larger than all the Great Lakes put together. Drainage at first was southward into the Mississippi, but after breaking through the ice-wall to the north into Hudson Bay, Lake Agassiz receded to Lake Winnipeg and the other lakes of the Nelson River system. Much of the road-bed of the Canadian Northern followed thriftily the old beaches of glacial Lake Agassiz. See relief map of prairie provinces, Fig. 5.

he said, "the coming in of this company was the beginning of the great success of the immigration work in the West." "I can recall no feature of our colonization policy," he added later on, "which has been attended with greater success than the efforts of this company."

III

The shareholders of the Saskatchewan Valley Land Company, many of them Canadians with experience in the western states, began by purchasing 840,000 acres from the Qu'Appelle, Long Lake, and Saskatchewan Railway and nearly 100,000 acres from the Saskatchewan and Western Railway at a very nominal price. These like all normal railway land grants were odd-numbered sections "fairly fit for settlement." The Department of the Interior joined the enterprise by selling to the company a quarter of a million acres of even-numbered sections—homestead lands—at $1 per acre on condition that twenty free-homesteaders were to be placed on the remaining free-homestead quarter-sections in each township and twelve on the lands of the Saskatchewan Valley Land Company "before they shall be entitled to the remaining even-numbered sections" purchased from the government. These ingenious details proved to be a miracle of shrewd and sound economy for the company as well as for the country, for it enabled the company to offer the prospective settler a quarter-section free as a homestead and to sell the additional acreage necessary for dry-farming at twice the price the settler would have been willing to pay had it been necessary to purchase the whole farm. It was not surprising, as one official observed complacently, that the stipulations laid down by the government were scrupulously met—the only instance on record, he reiterated, when the government's contract with a land company was scrupulously met "to the letter."

For the first time perhaps the Saskatchewan Valley Land Company was able to combine both sets of favourable factors, external as well as local, for a characteristic "swarming" upon the Western Canadian agricultural frontier. The movement from the older frontier states had long been under way to the Dakotas and Montana. The price of wheat, oats, barley, and flax was already high in world markets and there was a buyer for every bushel. A farmer who could sell his land in Missouri for $60 an acre could aspire to a fortune in Western Canada. During a state exhibition in Minnesota in September, 1902, more than 30,000 copies of the *Minneapolis Journal* with two pages of carefully prepared advertising were distributed broadcast. News of a Canadian "boom"— this time a healthy and co-ordinated movement—found its way into more than 300 American newspapers. "To show them what the country was like" the Saskatchewan Valley Land Company's excursions of pullman cars "loaded with people from the western states" carried prospective buyers and newspaper men to hotels and livery stations operated free of charge. Much of the company's acreage was sold literally "on the hoof," from the seat of the buck-board "democrat" of those days, to some of the most efficient and experienced settlers who ever came to Western Canada. It was estimated that "ninety per cent of the Americans that came in bought land" and "about half the Canadians did the same." In 1905 the Minister of the Interior reported "villages, elevators, stores, hotels, and the largest wheat field I ever saw in my life." "Canada's turn" had come and the patient enterprise of two decades was at last coming into its own.

Other land companies on a less spectacular scale took advantage of the tide and many such ventures led on to fortune. The land grants accumulated by the Canadian Northern system, now building its way feverishly across the continent under the daring management of Mackenzie and Mann, were developed after the same fashion by the Saskatchewan Valley and Manitoba Land Company. Even the C.P.R. resorted to similar administration for some of its remaining acreage to "bring the people here and locate them by view." The western "harvest excursion" of the C.P.R. became a hardy perennial of Canadian life. One of the most venturesome of the "colonization railways"—the Alberta Railway and Coal Company—had secured nearly a quarter of a million acres of its land grant in a compact block suitable for irrigation on the St. Mary's River. A Mormon migration from Utah brought vast wealth and experience to this experiment and fairly began the technique of irrigation on a large scale in Western Canadian agriculture.

Whatever the efficacy of the free-homestead system during these years of rapid settlement, it is doubtful whether government agents at remote points abroad or government land offices near the frontier itself could have duplicated the efficiency of the land companies with their own "fleets of livery rigs" directing a highly selective and experienced clientele already on the march. When it is recalled that the basis for this swarming enterprise was almost invariably the land grants originally made to the C.P.R. or to one or other of the ten "colonization railways" endowed with railway land grants, the early criticism of the Canadian railway land grant system, in its long-range results at any rate, would seem to be wide of the mark. Without it not only the whole technique of dry-farming, as we have seen, but the actual process of practical settlement might have been seriously impaired.

Certain vestigial defects of the system were still of course glaringly apparent long after the last of the railway land grants was authorized in 1894. The tardiness of the railways in selecting the acreage "earned" by railway construction and the fierce rivalry which still attended the exploration of eligible reserves came to an end only in 1908 when the Department of the Interior finally liquidated the whole system by forcing the railways to locate the remaining acreage to which they were entitled. By this time there was little choice in government policy: the system had run out of eligible land grants in odd-numbered sections "fairly fit for settlement" for the railways. Half the agricultural resources of Western Canada had gone to feed the iron horse.

The general opening of "Dominion lands," even- and odd-numbered sections alike, to homestead entry after 1908 brought a deluge of less selective migration to Western Canada. In vain the government had sought to reserve vast areas with marginal rainfall in "Palliser's triangle" for grazing and other purposes. In the queues which formed up at the land offices prospective settlers, as one observer records, "held their place in the line day and night for two or three weeks to enable them to file on certain lands," and places in the queue were frequently bought and sold for "substantial sums of money." The area of homestead entries for 1909 was larger than the whole state of Vermont; for 1910 more than twice the area of Connecticut; for 1911 larger than Delaware and New Hampshire put together; for 1912 almost as large as Maryland; for 1913 more than the whole area of Massachusetts; for 1914 more than the area of Wales.[1] For more than a decade and a half few of those abnormal vicissitudes which afterwards came to plague the development of Western Canada complicated the prospect. Two new transcontinental railways entered the field, built like the C.P.R. by private enterprise but so heavily underwritten by banks and government guarantees that public ownership afterwards became necessary to salvage governments as well as banks from bankruptcy and disaster. Abnormal rainfall, high world prices for grain, the development of Marquis and many other improved strains of early ripening and rust-resisting wheat, the prevalence of "good times" and indiscriminate optimism, all combined to suffuse the opening of what was already forecast as "Canada's century." The acreage of patented homesteads in Alberta increased from 1905 to 1930 by more than 16,450,000 acres and the population by nearly a million. In Saskatchewan the acreage

[1]See Fig. 21 for disposition of lands in the prairie provinces to 1911.

of free homesteads increased from 12,488,200 acres in 1905 to 30,729,100 in 1930, and the population from 257,763 in 1906 to 921,785 in 1931. "In thirteen and a half years," claimed the counsel for Saskatchewan before the Saskatchewan Resources Commission in 1934, "we produced seven billions of dollars." Federal counsel conceded that this was "the best contribution to Canadian prosperity that was made in those years. . . . Oh, for a return of those years."

IV

For the free-homestead era from 1908 to 1930, however, as for the railway land grant era from 1872 to 1894, there are grave revisions to be made in popular tradition. How far was it the free-homestead system which "peopled the Canadian prairies"? What was the cost in economic maladjustment, in the wastage of the human material that went into the experiment? What was the effect upon the permanent economy of the prairie provinces and upon the demography of Canada? If the railway land grant system came to an end because the government had come to the end of eligible land grants "fairly fit for settlement," is it equally true that the free-homestead system came to an end because the federal government had exhausted the range of eligible homesteads? In all three of the prairie provinces the free-homestead system was abrogated with the return of the natural resources to provincial control, and the provincial governments turned to the prosaic task of readjustment. The patient work of soil surveys and scientific land use has gone far since 1930—so far that many of the popular impressions of the early frontier now appear almost grotesquely erroneous and obsolete.

The free-homestead system in Canada, unlike that of the United States, has never been more than half a system at best in its range of application; and it has been integrated almost from the beginning with so many other categories of land for sale that it is not easy to appraise either technique except in this fortunate association. It is a remarkable fact that more land in Western Canada has been administered by sale or for sale than as free homesteads.[1] With approximately equal ingredients of each it would scarcely be accurate to regard either a "sales policy" or a "free-homestead system" as the staple of Canadian policy. The truth is that the integration of the two has been at once the chief virtue and the most distinctive characteristic of the Cana-

[1]Up to 1928 some 61,258,000 acres of "Dominion lands" had been disposed of as railway land grants, Hudson's Bay lands, school lands, pre-emption, and other categories of land for sale, while some 58,250,000 acres were under free homesteads, military homesteads, etc.

dian system. Throughout the whole range of normal agricultural settlement the free-homesteader has found contiguous land for sale to meet
the requirements of dry-farming. In 1901 not 40 per cent of Saskatchewan farms contained 200 acres. In 1926 more than 70 per cent
exceeded that size.[1] The fact that the average farm in Saskatchewan
is now 389 acres, all but 160 acres of which must have been acquired
by purchase, illustrates the growing preponderance of land sales and
the happy combination of land sales and free homesteads in the
process of permanent settlement. For the technique of dry-farming
either alone might have been disastrous. Together they have supplied
a flexibility and an adaptability that could perhaps have been acquired
in no other way.

After 1908 when the railway land grant system was liquidated and
the free homestead became the avowed staple of land policy there was
an attempt to continue the advantages of the old system in the provision for "purchased homesteads" and "pre-emptions" designed, as
the Hon. Frank Oliver stated at the time, "to keep up that stream of
desirable immigration that has added so greatly to the wealth and
prosperity of our country during the past few years." The free-homesteader could still purchase the additional acreage necessary for
dry-farming within measurable distance of his homestead. Entries for
nearly four and a half million acres in Saskatchewan and more than
five and a half million in Alberta from 1908 to 1930 attest the value
of this characteristic Canadian device; though the cancellations during
the years of war and depression and drought were in both cases
exceptionally large. On the other hand the free-homestead system
when functioning alone developed defects that were truly appalling
when measured in terms of human effort and morale. Every town and
village on the prairies was full of "homesteaders" who eked out the
minimum requirements of building and residence after homestead
entry, and turned their homesteads over to the speculator. More often
than not the doctor and the local merchant, the lawyer and the school
teacher, the barber and the hotel keeper, were themselves the worst
speculators for they were powerless to settle their quarter-sections
after the fashion of the big land companies—to bring "people here
and locate them by view."[2] The smaller land companies, too, fre-

[1]See Figs. 8 and 9, showing size of farms, 1921–26.
[2]In three small districts in Saskatchewan, according to one witness before the
Saskatchewan Resources Commission, homestead entries were made by the local
printer, three grocery clerks, the manager of a lumber yard, two school principals,
two barbers, a dentist, a drayman, two carpenters, two tailors, a plumber, a hardware merchant, two sons of a local store keeper, a harness maker, two hardware

quently exploited the system by "blanketing" adjacent homesteads by means of fictitious entries filed by power of attorney until there was a prospect of selling their own acreage to advantage. This formula must have appealed to thousands: 160 acres of free homestead *plus* 160 acres at $12 per acre provided a half-section farm at an average of $6 per acre. The settler got his land on the average at half the price charged by the land companies, and the land companies got twice as much for their land as the settler would otherwise have been willing to pay. It was one of the ironical functions of the Canadian free-homestead system that it helped to sell the rest.

Was then the traditional function of the system vindicated in practice? For Canada as for the United States the fame of the free homestead must have made a strong impact upon the imagination of that generation. The government itself frequently expounded the ingenuous benevolence of its policy: "Parliament pledged its faith to the world that a large portion of those lands should be set apart for free homesteads to all coming settlers, and another portion [school lands] . . . held in trust for the education of their children. . . . The impressive fact to the mind of the man contemplating emigration, is that . . . Government holds unfettered in its own hand the lands which it offers free." The free homestead when it functioned alone seldom justified these expectations even at its best, and at its worst it left a truly formidable legacy of frustration and maladjustment behind it. It permitted the unwary homesteader to enter marginal areas that ought never to have been broken to the plough. It has required a whole generation of patient and scientific readjustment to salvage human lives as well as land from these costly miscalculations. The ratio of cancellations to homestead entries during these exuberant years has been truly appalling. For the whole sixty-year cycle of "Dominion lands" the record is bad enough—more than 40 per cent. From 1905 to 1930 in Alberta the cancellations were nearly 46 per cent; in Saskatchewan from 1911 to 1931, about 57 per cent. Fifty-seven per cent of these homesteaders never got across no man's land to the patent registers. The record here not only of dilapidation in farm buildings and machinery but of deadly attrition in human material and morale during the best years of a settler's life and family is beyond calculation. The free homestead looked cheap but in practice it seems to have proved one of the costliest devices of frontier settle-

---

clerks, an insurance agent, two garage proprietors, an implement salesman, a druggist, and the local doctor. "I personally knew each of these people during my residence in that district."

ment. In the United States the free homestead was once defined as a wager in which the United States bet a quarter-section of land that a man could not live on it for five consecutive years. In Canada the odds were better—three years instead of five—but all too frequently the homesteader lost his wager in the silent but deadly attrition that was going on upon the frontier.

What was the effect of this decade and a half of rapid settlement in the West upon the demography of Canada? Is it true that extraneous immigration tended to supplant the native-born Canadian or to speed his departure to the United States? Here again, as in so many plausible *clichés* of the time, the evidence would seem to be to the contrary. The census of native-born Canadians in the United States shows:

    1880 — 717,000
    1890 — 980,000: a loss to Canada of 263,000
    1900 — 1,181,000: a loss of 201,000
    1910 — 1,192,000: a loss of 11,000

During the decade at the turn of the century for the first time Canada seems to have been able to stem the movement of native-born population to the United States. For the same period the census of what are now the prairie provinces indicates:

    1881 — 180,000
    1891 — 250,000: a gain of 70,000 compared with the loss of 263,000 native-born Canadians to the United States
    1901 — 420,000: a gain of 170,000 compared with the loss of 201,000 Canadians to the United States
    1911 — 1,330,000: a gain of 910,000 compared with the loss of 11,000 Canadians to the United States

While the rapid settlement of the West alone can scarcely be credited with these results for 1911, and the transit of foreign-born immigration through Canada to the United States no doubt continued, there was a growing assurance, a new sense of growth if not of maturity, in those eventful years which came to influence profoundly the sense of nationhood. With the organization of Alberta and Saskatchewan as provinces in 1905 and the extension of the boundaries of Manitoba, Ontario, and Quebec in 1912, the era of foundations was fairly over and the design of the superstructure was easily predictable. It was not by chance that some of the most venturesome of the architects for that design[1] had acquired their mastery of affairs, their unwavering sense of nationhood in the opening of the West.

V

The formation of the new provinces of Alberta and Saskatchewan in 1905, endowed with their natural resources in 1930, completed "the keystone of the arch" of sister provinces across the continent. Perhaps no phase of Canadian national development has run so nearly true to form. In biological science it is said that the early development of the individual reflects unerringly the evolution of the species. It would be possible to elaborate without fanciful embellishment a truly apt parallel between the colonial development of the territories from 1870 to full provincial status in 1905 and 1930 and the long colonial development of the Canadas from 1763 to 1867.

In both cases there was the preliminary conciliar stage: from the Proclamation of October, 1763, to the *Quebec Act* of 1774 and from the transfer of 1870 to the *North-West Territories Act* of 1875. In both cases there was a statutory conciliar stage under governor and council: from the *Quebec Act* to the normal functioning of a "royal province" in 1791, and from the *Territories Act* of 1875 to its consummation in a territorial Assembly in 1888. In both cases the ensuing contest for responsible government was as nearly inevitable as any process of government could be said to be. In the one case the long contest from 1791 to 1848, though marred by two rebellions, was resolved at last by the patient empirical tenacity of disciplined political parties during the ten years' "siege of Troy" from the Durham mission to the final concession of 1848. The winning of responsible government in the other case was a happier achievement. The outcome was of course pre-ordained by a score of precedents now evolving with practised and easy assurance all over the empire. It came in the North-West Territories in the short span of nine years from the first formal Assembly in 1888 to the Act of 1897, and it was conspicuous on the whole for goodwill and mutual understanding in a spirit of unaffected co-operation. A more fanciful parallel could perhaps be found in the two insurrections in each case which marred the experiment; but in the Territories these were fortunately over, in 1870 and 1885, before the real contest for responsible government began, though as in Canada vestigial anomalies survived to poison and impair the harmony of the result. In both the Canadas and the Territories a period of

[1]F. W. G. Haultain, A. L. and Clifford Sifton, John S. Ewart, R. B. Bennett, Frank Oliver, Arthur Meighen, J. W. Dafoe, and many others.

strenuous politics supervened between responsible government and provincial organization in the framework of confederation—in both cases marked by prodigies of skilful improvisation.

By 1905 the conventions of parliamentary government after the British model had settled convincingly into a body of political doctrine, and it will be unnecessary even in outline to review the early stages except to record the instinctiveness of the process and the growing uniformity of the result. Nowhere in Canada has there been more venturesome experimentation with new ideas in social services and legislation. Nowhere have the familiar conventions of parliamentary government been employed to serve a wider variety of governmental agencies. Nowhere, moreover, could there be a wider latitude of choice, for by the *B.N.A. Act of 1867* itself, provinces in the Canadian federation are entrusted (s. 92, subs. 1) with "the amendment from time to time, notwithstanding anything in this Act, of the Constitution of the Province, except as regards the office of Lieutenant-Governor." It is a remarkable commentary upon this phase of the long tradition we have tried to trace in these studies that neither a Social Credit Government in Alberta nor an avowedly socialist Government in Saskatchewan has departed from the time-honoured practices of the parliamentary system in implementing the most daring social programmes in Canadian politics. Nowhere in Canada meanwhile have so many plausible devices, deemed advisable at times in a republican setting, come over the border to tempt enthusiasts to similar experiments—"referendum and recall," "initiative," "single tax," and many others—only to be swallowed up, together with their exponents, in the empirical competence, upon the whole, of the parliamentary system. Conversely too the widest range of public ownership of telephones, waterpower, and for a time even grain elevators—attributed to "leftist" proclivities by casual observers south of the border—have thriven in defiance of plausible ideologies, inaugurated in many instances by Conservative governments intent upon the empirical requirements of a frontier economy.

Much of this characteristic enterprise and resourcefulness is traceable to the happier environment in which self-government grew to maturity in Western Canada. In Manitoba, it is true, the early story of "great and melancholy privation" is not pleasant to reflect upon. Precipitated into provincial status at the transfer, no community in the Commonwealth perhaps was bundled so unceremoniously into responsible government as the Manitoba of 1870: conceived in insurrection, born by caesarian scission, and eking out for forty-two years, until the Alberta and Saskatchewan terms of 1905 were made applicable to Manitoba in 1912, a menial and precarious existence in the Canadian family. Farther west, however, even the primitive stages of self-government began more auspiciously with many useful devices to soften or conciliate subordination. By the *Manitoba Act* it was provided that the lieutenant-governor of that province should function *ex officio* for the territories "by Commission under the Great Seal of Canada"; and the prosaic records of the *Minutes of the North-West Council*[1] reveal many a neat turn of fence in that friendly association. The oath of secrecy was restricted to the "Executive Functions of the said Council to the exclusion of those of a Legislative character." In its legislative capacity the Council proceeded to act with all the assurance of accredited agents for a new and thriving community. Appointed by the original *Act for the Temporary Government of Rupert's Land and the North-Western Territory when united with Canada* merely to "aid the Lieutenant-Governor in the administration of affairs" with "such powers as may be from time to time conferred upon them by Order-in-Council," they were entrusted by the Act of 1875 (s. 7) with the functions of "advice and consent" which have always foreshadowed the historic development towards self-government. The Council became from the outset in 1870 not the recipients of privilege as in the early years of the second empire but the exponents of local interests and rights as against the delinquencies of federal colonial administration. At the close of the preliminary conciliar period the Lieutenant-Governor himself was able to review the work of the Council with mutual gratification. By the *North-West Territories Act* of 1875 a separate lieutenant-governor for the territories presided over a Council of not more than five membes to be reinforced by elected members as soon as electoral districts of 1,000 square miles should be found to contain 1,000 adult inhabitants. When such elected representatives should come to number twenty-one "the members so elected shall be constituted and designated as the Legislative Assembly of the North-West Territories," and the familiar functions of elective assemblies from time immemorial in the first empire were to come into play. The hybrid Council was to become an Assembly—"the pollywog was to become a frog."

Throughout this process there is no counterpart to the fatal policy of fortifying "the connection" by special privileges and vested interests. There is no American or French revolution to palliate short-sighted policies of expediency. Self-government grew with the placid but

[1]"Not exceeding fifteen nor less than seven persons."

exuberant growth of the West. The automatic metamorphosis of the Council into an Assembly was not, it is true, a Canadian invention. It had already become a recognized device of British colonial policy, nowhere perhaps more usefully employed than in British Columbia prior to confederation. Every signpost pointed forward towards self-government, not backward as in the closing years of the first empire towards practices "dangerous and destructive of American rights."

The transition was further simplified, of course, by the fact that the territories were already integral parts of Canada with representation (after 1886) in the House of Commons and with ultimate provincial status as their manifest destiny. From the election of the first member of the Council in 1881 to the complete metamorphosis to an Assembly in the election of twenty-two members in 1888 the development was swift and eventful. There were no clergy reserves, no vested interests (fortunately abortive even for the second empire) of hereditary titles, no "family compacts." The *North-West Territories Act* of 1888 provided for an Advisory Council of four members on "matters of finance" to be chosen from the Assembly, together with *ex officio* legal advisers on matters of law; and the first act of the Advisory Council was to align itself not with the lieutenant-governor and the federal government but with the Assembly of the territories in a carefully staged contest for fully responsible government, "being with the rest of our fellow Members jealous of the rights, which were granted to us."

Within a year the Advisory Council resigned in a body (October 29, 1889) because they were "unwilling to accept responsibility without a corresponding right of control" over all "matters of finance" including not only local territorial revenues but federal subsidies from the Dominion. A new Advisory Council was promptly met by a sharp vote of want of confidence as incisive in its implications as Howe's in February, 1840. "The continuance in office of a Council not possessing the confidence of the Assembly was a gross violation of the rights and privileges of the Assembly." The parliamentary contest that ensued was regarded by the Assembly and by the press as a "fight for responsible government." Versed in the traditions of the Maritimes and of Canada, assemblymen and editors alike deployed their arguments upon as high a plane perhaps of courtesy and skill as it would be possible to find among the score and more of similar contests in British communities all over the world.

The attempt by direct action to broaden the function of the elective Advisory Council on finance to include cognate executive functions of general administration was only partially successful. For those who are still able to scale the heights of expert constitutional controversy in these anaemic and degenerate days of low altitudes, the correspondence of Sir John Thompson on the one side and F. W. G. (afterwards Sir Frederick) Haultain on the other would meet the most exacting standards of an Alpine mountaineer. Lieutenant-Governor Royal himself in his Speech from the Throne on September 16, 1893, complimented the Assembly upon their "wisdom and discretion." "Notwithstanding this controversy, no unpleasantness ever arose between me and the Assembly. . . . The Legislature to-day practically enjoys the rights and privileges of self-government." It was only in 1897, however, that provision was made (60–61 Vic., c. 28) for an Executive Council "chosen and summoned by the Lieutenant-Governor . . . to aid and advise in the Government of the Territories": the claim of the Assembly to elect an Advisory Council for general administration had come to grief upon the age-old prerogative of the crown to choose its advisers. The niceties of sound constitutional practice having been at last vindicated, the unwritten conventions of responsible government were now free to function, and within the *Territories Act* the Haultain "cabinet" was practically indistinguishable from that of a province of the Dominion itself.[1]

By the turn of the century the approach to provincial status was conceded on every hand. In 1901 (December 7) Haultain submitted to Sir Wilfrid Laurier a draft bill which became the storm centre of political controversy until "provincial autonomy" was finally conceded in 1905. In the routine of territorial government Haultain's appeal for a united front upon the threshold of unpredictable developments in Western Canada was so far successful that there was scarcely more than a nominal party of opposition in the Assembly. The imminence of provincial autonomy, however, brought the territories into the magnetic field of federal politics where divergencies of policy appeared which decided and will never cease to affect the development of Western Canada. Haultain had proposed a single province with every prospect at that time of "exceeding all others in area [404,000 square miles], in population, and in resources." It was to be endowed at once, like the other provinces of Canada except Manitoba, with the administration of its public lands, with compensation for the vast acreage already alienated "for the purposes of the Dominion." Seizing the torch well-nigh extinguished by the "finality terms" forced upon

[1]Cf. *Manitoba Act*, s. 7; *B.N.A. Act of 1867*, s. 11.

Prime Minister Norquay of Manitoba in 1885, Haultain became the Nestor of "the natural resources question" and of the time-honoured amenities of parliamentary government in the prairie provinces.[1]

Was Haultain a generation ahead of his times? With two new transcontinental railways, the Canadian Northern and the Grand Trunk Pacific, in the offing, the future of Western Canada was still undeniably obscure and unpredictable. This was still the heyday of the free-homestead system. Canada had "pledged its faith to the world" for "free homesteads to all coming settlers," with school lands to be "held in trust for the education of their children." Branch railways were still thrusting their tentacles into undeveloped territory.[2] The battle of the dinosaurs, not without uproar and turmoil, was still going on for reserves of eligible railway land grants "fairly fit for settlement." Both these historic "purposes of the Dominion" in retaining "Dominion lands" under federal administration were to persist for nearly a whole generation before the Turgeon-Crerar-Bowman Commission of 1929 could announce that "the railways have been built and the lands settled." The ugly spectre of the school question too was emerging once more to jeopardize a peaceful solution for provincial autonomy and to add, by the resignation of Clifford Sifton, to the fatal fragmentation of the Liberal party already begun by the retirement of Israel Tarte and A. G. Blair.

When the *Alberta* and *Saskatchewan Acts* appeared at last in 1905 Sir Wilfrid Laurier, in one of the most dramatic scenes of his career or of the Canadian House of Commons, surveyed the long record of law and order under "restraints and safeguards of the highest civilization." Haultain and Bulyea of the old territorial "cabinet" were seated as honoured guests for the occasion beside the Speaker's chair. The span of Canadian provinces projected by the fathers of confederation less than forty years before was now almost complete. The Dominion stood upon the threshold of a new century and perhaps of a new era. "The metal has been in the crucible," added Sir Wilfrid, "and all we have to do now is to put the stamp of Canadian nationality upon it." But the "autonomy" was not to be that projected by Haultain as the

---

[1]Haultain had been a member of the Advisory Council in 1888, chairman of the enlarged Executive Committee after 1893, and prime minister from 1897 to 1905. Though passed over for the premiership of Saskatchewan in 1905 he became Chief Justice in 1912, was knighted in 1916, lived to see the settlement of "the natural resources question" in 1930, and retired only in 1937 after fifty years of public service in Western Canada. Sir Frederick died in 1942 at the age of 84. See C. C. Lingard, *Territorial Government in Canada, passim.*

[2]See Figures 13 to 20.

territorial prime minister. There were to be two provinces instead of one. The settlement of "the natural resources question" was still to wait for a quarter of a century. For nearly a decade of this time Manitoba contented itself with a desperate crusade to acquire equality with the two new provinces by an increase in the "subsidy in lieu of lands" to equal theirs in the *Alberta* and *Saskatchewan Acts*, and by the extension of the boundary of Manitoba northward to Hudson Bay and the 60th parallel of north latitude in 1912. The prairie provinces were to become "like Cerberus three gentlemen at once," and Mrs. Malaprop herself could scarcely have devised a relationship more calculated to diffuse their political power and to complicate the interests which they have in common.

As the two new provinces moved into the orbit of federal politics it was obvious that the personnel of territorial representation at Ottawa —predominantly Liberal in party affiliation, as was perhaps to be expected—was to take right of way over the Assembly which had presided with such exemplary assiduity over the opening of the territories. F. W. G. Haultain, the central figure of a nostalgic tradition which still lingers in many quarters of Western Canada, had led an Assembly which was almost unanimous on local issues in that "golden age" of co-operation and public spirit. But the political centre of gravity was now Ottawa rather than Regina or Edmonton: the new prime minister of Saskatchewan was to be Walter Scott and the first prime minister of Alberta was A. C. Rutherford.[1] After the resignation of Clifford Sifton the domination of federal over provincial politics went on apace. Frank Oliver took over the Department of the Interior, liquidated outstanding railway land grants in 1908, and launched the Hudson Bay Railway from the proceeds of "pre-emptions" and "purchased homesteads" under the last phase of the free-homestead system. The Grand Trunk Pacific, promoted in order to "let Laurier finish his work," nearly finished many of the interests, public as well as private, which had underwritten that great project with such reckless faith in the golden age to come. The vision of a century which was to belong to Canada "trailing clouds of glory" from the infancy of western development, passed into the sombre shadows of world war and drought and depression. These too were to pass away and "fade into the light of common day"—the innumerable commonplace projects of soil surveys, strip-farming, "dug-outs" and irrigation for water conservation, "drilling" and new techniques for subnormal rainfall, and collaboration

[1]For the closing phases of the contest for provincial autonomy see Lingard, *Territorial Government in Canada*, part II.

between federal and provincial agencies in the interests of the whole nation. It has been reserved for another generation to tap the prodigious resources of oil and mineral wealth now reinforcing the fortunes of a predominantly agricultural frontier, and to recapture in the process something of the vision of "the last best West" in the early traditions of Canada.

Chapter Twenty-Four

FOUNDATIONS AND SUPERSTRUCTURE:
FUNCTIONING OF NATIONHOOD

THE spectacular approach of Canada to international recognition at the close of the First World War over by-ways "at times rough and thorny," as Sir Robert Borden once remarked, left many observers under the impression that some sudden and inscrutable impulse was at work to force a departure from Canadian traditions. Scholars of great eminence professed to find a "new British Empire" or a "third British Empire" in the making. Less scholarly observers seized upon the *Statute of Westminster* in 1931 as a sort of Declaration of Independence—a conclusion, it is safe to say, which could scarcely have survived a careful perusal of that very brief prosaic and pragmatic document. A few interpreters from abroad, still less wary, rivalled the ingenious architects found by Gulliver in the academy of Lagado who "contrived a new method of building houses, by beginning at the roof, and working downward to the foundation" after the practice of those "two prudent insects, the bee and the spider."

It is now a commonplace of Canadian history that these abrupt and sudden transitions simply did not occur. The foundations of nationhood had long since been immutably laid. By the close of the First World War the superstructure itself was so far advanced that little remained to change except the anomalies which marred or complicated the design.

Responsible government, which was the first clear attribute of nationhood to appear, was also to be the last to be completed in its widest amplitude. From first to last its inexorable expansion in range and impact was to be the most distinctive feature of Canadian nationhood. This sheltered growth was long unappreciated by Canadians themselves and unsuspected by other nations. By 1920, however, three or four axiomatic conclusions with regard to it were clearly discernible. The first had been foreseen from the outset. Responsible government,

493

though primarily concerned only with the executive—the historic little device "on the faith of the Crown" (Grey) of choosing as ministers those only who could command the confidence of the Commons—proved to be so dynamic in its implications that it came to dominate every field which its exponents chose to enter. The second conclusion, equally axiomatic, was much slower in its development but it was equally inexorable in function and effect. Beginning with local issues of immediate interest the range of responsible government expanded with growing momentum and velocity until it crossed irretraceably the boundaries of Canada in the First World War and added the sovereign functions of foreign policy, peace, and war to the scores of national attributes already encompassed in its organic growth. A third conclusion becoming obvious at the close of the war was more controversial: that the process by this time had reached a stage where certain vestigial anomalies were glaringly awkward and it was time, in General Smuts's phrase, to "tidy up the show." By 1922 these vestigial anomalies were already being tested in official controversy, all the more searching for the candour in which it was discreetly veiled. It was then found that the practice of unwritten "convention" or usage which had already functioned so satisfactorily in a score of instances to expand the range of responsible government for more than half a century was the easiest and most efficacious method of dealing with most of the anomalies that still remained. In a few instances where these anomalies were statutory in their origin—the *Colonial Laws Validity Act* of 1865, the *Merchant Shipping Act* of 1894, the *Colonial Courts of Admiralty Act* of 1890—it was necessary to resort to another British statute, the *Statute of Westminster*, 1931, for their repeal. The *Statute of Westminster* itself, however, specifically reserved the amendment of the *B.N.A. Acts* by the same statutory method. Though stipulated by Canada in 1931, this reservation too has since been partially abrogated in 1949—again necessarily by statute, 13 Geo. vi, c. 81—to the extent of permitting by federal enactment amendments to the *B.N.A. Acts* which do not involve the jurisdiction of the provinces and certain other vested rights.

Much of the controversy which attended these developments arose from the uncertainty with regard to their import. Many were still reluctant to exchange the mechanics of imperial organization for the free associations of the Commonwealth. The bitterness of this dispute at that time would be almost incredible to the present generation. It was not perhaps until the gravest crisis of the Second World War that many of these inhibitions were finally set at rest. The fact that at one time the free and autonomous nations of the Commonwealth were left standing alone in arms against the Axis was a demonstration of spontaneity rendered still more impressive by the intractable neutrality of Eire.

The controversy with regard to "status" and "autonomy" entered upon its final stage at the close of the First World War. Already the phrases come back like echoes from another world. It may now be possible to illustrate the axiomatic stages of the process outlined above without unnecessary detail, though the sequel originally planned in completion of this theme is now, alas, no longer possible.[1] Without attempting to explore or even to list the score or more of attendant controversies one general reflection may be made with regard to them. While the jurists and pundits were wrangling about "metaphysical distinctions" of procedure or protocol, the issues themselves were resolved, as a rule, by practical parliamentarians relying upon empirical adjustments undaunted by the theorists' horror of improvisation. The process itself has been unique among the nations of the modern world —a process of incubation, as we have seen, of parliamentary communities developing piecemeal into nationhood without destroying their old associations with each other and with the parent state. In more than a score of free communities in every quarter of the world the procedure has been so spontaneous that political freedom would seem to be the law of their being. No artificial design in the mechanics of government could have germinated and flourished in such a variety of environment. The result too may well be unique. Evolving freedom for themselves from within and grouping themselves into regional federations for mutual support in peaceful association to form the nations of the Commonwealth, these self-governing communities might well become an analogue of peace and freedom for other men. About this axis—their dynamic evolution towards freedom, their sovereign association towards peace—they revolve with almost the bias of natural law. The bond of the Commonwealth is a sense of common weal. "If that is not enough," exclaimed Lord Balfour, "nothing else is enough"; and "if International Law has not the sense to get over [technical irregularities] we must manage as best we can." Burke's plea for such a "contexture of this mysterious whole" on the eve of the American Revolution may still "sound wild and chimerical to the profane herd of vulgar and mechanical politicians . . . who think that nothing exists but what is gross and material. . . . But to men truly initiated and

---

[1]The functioning of Canadian nationhood in external affairs was to have been traced by the late J. W. Dafoe. See Foreward, p. xvi.

rightly taught, these ruling and master principles which in the opinion of such men as I have mentioned have no substantial existence are in truth everything and all in all."

II

Responsible government had many unforeseen consequences when applied to the British North American provinces. Many of the early reformers were more immediately concerned with the therapeutic value of responsible government for the ills of the old empire than with its hygienic value for the associations of the future. The "great principle" of Baldwin and his school enabled them, as we have seen, to by-pass the interminable "grievances" of the Mackenzie-Papineau school and to redress their own grievances. But responsible government could not stop there. Like the grain of mustard seed it contained a seminal principle of dynamic growth and power. At its planting it seemed the least of all seeds but when it was grown it waxed a great tree shooting out great branches so that in the end all the attributes of nationhood came to lodge under the shadow of it.

The most dynamic effect of responsible government, as we shall see, was this direct expansion of its range; but almost from the outset it had a profound though indirect effect upon other cognate functions of government. This was particularly true of legislation. At the Rebellion Losses Bill, for example, responsible government itself was no longer at stake. That had been irrevocably conceded when Sir John Harvey had called upon Uniacke in Nova Scotia, and when Elgin called upon La Fontaine and Baldwin in Canada, to "form a government." Elgin could have reserved or vetoed the Rebellion Losses Bill—provision was made for both reservation and veto as late as the B.N.A. *Act of 1867* (s. 55)—but it could have been reserved or vetoed in 1849 only by flouting the deliberate verdict of the legislature from both sections of the province, compromising the good "faith of the Crown" in the concession of responsible government, and throwing the governor-general, like Metcalfe, into the arms of recalcitrant opposition. A responsible government, resolute in its control of the executive, could thus on occasion dominate legislation too. A decade later this was demonstrated with almost mathematical precision by Galt's differential tariff of 1859. The Sheffield manufacturers protested against Galt's budget as an indecent reproach to free trade: "Her Majesty's Government has a right to demand that what revenue is needed shall be raised in some other way." Galt's reply, with which Newcastle is now known to have been in complete accord, proved to be unanswerable: "Her Majesty cannot be advised to disallow such Acts, unless her advisers are prepared to assume the administration of the affairs of the Colony." A responsible executive in Canada could thus enforce Canadian legislation. A formidable list of reservations nevertheless did survive confederation and it required Edward Blake's famous protest as minister of justice to remove them from the instructions to the governor-general. Section 55 of the *B.N.A. Act of 1867* has never been formally repealed but it is safe to say that the veto in federal legislation is as dead in Canada as it has been in Great Britain since the reign of Queen Anne. Its formal epitaph was written by the Imperial Conference of 1926 which brought the functions of the governor-general into alignment with those of the crown in Great Britain.

But more important than these indirect implications of responsible government for other cognate functions was the inexorable expansion of its own range to include field after field of national attributes. This has involved no change in principle. Vast changes, however, have come in the scope of its operation. From beginning to end the expanding range of responsible government has been determined by one thing and one thing only, the legitimate interest of the Canadian people. Wherever that interest has been directly involved the same stringent responsibilities have come to be exacted. In some instances this dynamic expansion was attended by bitter controversy, in others by mutual accommodation and compromise. In most cases each step had its appropriate priority in time and importance. In Prince Edward Island the most immediate concern was probably "the eternal land question." In "Canada" in the fifties it was all too apt to be the voracious appetite for "jobs": not the self-interested "log-rolling" accommodations so dear to the fiscal practices of New Brunswick, but the desire for patronage and power. Baldwin himself was ready to "throw out the anchor." The transition from this introverted doctrine began almost immediately, and it never ceased until the most extroverted attributes of nationhood were brought under control.

It is well known that Durham thought it possible to reserve four great regions of governance for imperial control: "The constitution of the form of government,—the regulation of foreign relations, and of trade with the mother country, the other British Colonies, and foreign nations,—and the disposal of public lands, are the only points on which the mother country requires a control." It is fair to add that Durham did not stipulate these reservations as indispensable.[1] Elgin with true

[1]The argument, as the context shows, was addressed to the Melbourne Whigs who at that stage were opposed to responsible government in any form. *Report*, ed. Lucas, II, 282.

Peelite sagacity foresaw that no permanent reservations were possible and that piecemeal adjustments were inevitable. Not one of Durham's reservations could remain intact, though vestigial anomalies from them long survived to challenge the ingenuity of practical statesmen.

The first to go was the imperial control of public lands—probably the most important recommendation of the *Report* in Durham's own estimation. This passed to provincial control at once as the first-fruits of responsible government, though it was not until 1854 that "clergy reserves" for Canada West and seigneurial tenures for Canada East were finally liquidated by the united province of "Canada."

The regulation of trade was a much longer and more complicated achievement with many a brisk skirmish to mark the contest at every stage. In 1849 Grey's apostolic doctrine of free trade—"the triumph of free trade not of freedom" of trade—was almost as dogmatic for the colonies as Knox's old thesis of colonial subservience "to the maritime strength and commercial interests of Great Britain." In 1849 even Hincks regarded a differential tariff for "Canada" as tantamount to independence, yet it was only a decade later, as we have seen, that Galt, with Newcastle's own connivance, on behalf of the Canadian cabinet vindicated their "responsibility in all general questions of policy . . . to the Provincial Parliament by whose confidence they administer the affairs of the country." A few months later Newcastle himself in the Colonial Office confronted the Board of Trade with a *fait accompli* by conceding freedom of intercolonial trade to the maritime provinces. With the prospective abrogation of the Reciprocity Treaty by the United States, General Michel, administrator of the government of "Canada" during Monck's absence, once sent a delegation to the West Indies and South America under the great seal of Canada, and was duly admonished by the Foreign Office for the breach of protocol.

The forays of British American ministers abroad, nevertheless, soon beat a well-trodden trail to the capitals of Europe and to Washington —Galt's negotiations with the French consul ("no official correspondence could take place"), Tupper's characteristic insouciance in forcing his way into trade negotiations with Spain and with France (1893), Sir Wilfrid Laurier's mission in Paris in 1907,[1] Fielding's negotiations of 1922, Lapointe's Halibut Treaty in 1923. In all these overtures, however, even when Canadian ministers were the negoti-

---

[1]"A treaty has been concluded with France—a treaty which applies to Canada alone, which has been negotiated by Canada alone." It was not however signed by a Canadian plenipotentiary.

ators or in Mr. Lapointe's case the sole signing plenipotentiary, the final treaty stood on the advice of the British Foreign Office. It was only after the Imperial Conferences of 1923 and 1926, as we shall see, that the technique of treaties with foreign powers was perfected—mutual consultation in matters of common interest but ratification by Canadian plenipotentiaries on the advice of Canadian ministers directly concerned. The Hyde Park agreement between Washington and Ottawa was negotiated, to the mystification of interested lobbyists on both sides of the boundary, on a still higher plane of ministerial responsibility, at a private conference between president and prime minister.

"The regulation of foreign relations" with its attendant obligations of defence, peace, and war, passed through kaleidoscopic changes during the century from Durham's *Report* to the Canadian declaration of war on September 10, 1939. The Canadian Militia Bills and Cardwell's desperate concern for defence during the process of federation have already appeared in another context.[1] Macdonald as one of the plenipotentiaries for the Treaty of Washington was appointed of course by the British Foreign Office. The subsequent ratification of the treaty by Canada despite its glaring deficiencies for Canadian interests justified Macdonald's concern for a respite from "manifest destiny" until Confederation, then "only in the gristle," could harden "into bone." The Wolseley expedition of 1870 to Red River, though commanded by a British officer, was a joint force of British regulars and Canadian militiamen. In 1885 the expedition against Riel was commanded by General Middleton but the force itself was Canadian. The same year Macdonald declined to participate in the war in the Soudan, in language (to Tupper) which could scarcely be communicated to the Colonial Office: "Our men and money would therefore be sacrificed to get Gladstone and Co. out of the hole they have plunged themselves into by their own imbecility. . . . The reciprocal aid . . . should be a matter of treaty." A decade and a half later another war in Africa found Canadian troops enlisted in South Africa. In the First World War half a million men were enlisted and during its closing months conscripted for service on the western front. The Canadian forces were finally consolidated into a Canadian Corps under Sir Arthur Currie.

The implications of this development for external relations were unmistakable. Sir Robert Borden has written with authority: "The fact that the Oversea Nations [of the Commonwealth] had put into

[1]See above, p. 345 and Stacey, *Canada and the British Army*, chaps. VI–IX.

the fighting line larger forces than any but the principal powers probably decided the issue."[1] With resolute and imperturbable goodwill Sir Robert Borden translated this record into international recognition for Canadian nationhood. To the consternation of the Foreign Office and foreign chancelleries alike, blazing a path "at times rough and thorny" in the process, the Canadian delegation forced its way to the level of high policy where empirical decisions of the first importance were effectually made. Jurists and permanent officials, obsessed with antinomies and abstractions, could prove conclusively that the appropriate thing could not possibly be done, and then responsible statesmen proceeded to do it. "In our advance along that path," Sir Robert added, "the Dominion Ministers received from the British Prime Minister and his colleagues complete sympathy and unwavering support from first to last." When the time came to project the famous Resolution ix of the Imperial War Conference stipulating "equality of nationhood"—an *ad hoc* improvisation of temporary but prodigious importance—into the peace treaty, the British Empire delegation ratified the memorandum of March 12, 1919, drafted by Borden himself, reaffirming (paragraph 2) the thesis of 1917 that "the organization of the Empire is to be based upon equality of nationhood," and stipulating the signing of the peace treaty by the plenipotentiaries of the Dominions. The indented signatures on that treaty were still anomalous, as Sir Robert Borden ruefully conceded, until the Imperial Conferences of 1923 and 1926 undertook to regularize the procedure.[2] The right of election to the Council of the League of Nations was vindicated at last by a veritable mandamus signed by Clemenceau, Woodrow Wilson, and Lloyd George (May 6, 1919). In the League of Nations, for the first time perhaps, Canadian nationhood "was recognized [to quote Sir Robert's own claim] as being in every respect equal to that of other members of the League," and the election of Canada to the Council for 1927, the diamond jubilee of Confederation, formally implemented that claim. Membership in the International Labour Organization, obstructed too by anomalies of protocol, had to be carried to the Big Four and pressed "with the most resolute insistence." "The Drafting Committee was peremptorily instructed to eliminate the objectionable clause and did so." Canada was formally elected a member of the governing body at the first International Labour Conference in Washington in 1919.

Meanwhile a legation in Washington, discussed as early as 1882,

---

[1] *Canada in the Commonwealth*, p. 96.

[2] "The British plenipotentiaries at Paris signed also for the British Dominions beyond the Seas."

was authorized (announced May 10, 1920) at the Paris Peace Conference and implemented in 1927. The technique of treaties, regularized as the result of Imperial Conferences in 1923 and 1926, led to Canadian legations or embassies in Tokyo, Paris, and a dozen points of contact for Canadian interests all over the world. It is well known that the Canadian declaration of war on Sunday, September 10, 1939 —just a week after the British declaration on September 3—was followed by the application to Canada of the *Neutrality Act* of the United States which had been applied to Great Britain during the previous week. The recognition of sovereign nationhood could scarcely go farther than this. The imponderables of the Commonwealth and a few remaining irregularities have still been known to mystify uninitiated observers, and sovereign nationhood on the part of Canada may still find it necessary at times to invoke Lord Balfour's impatient dictum in 1926: "If International Law has not the sense to get over [these difficulties] we must manage as best we can." The scope of responsible government in "foreign relations" has now expanded to the horizon of world politics.

Durham's fourth reservation—"the constitution of the form of government"—was the last to survive. Curious that British parliamentary supremacy which the thirteen colonies in 1774 and Ireland in 1782 regarded as the "intolerable" badge of subordination should have justified its survival by sheer utility above all other attributes of the second empire. Without it the constitution of Quebec, derailed by the *Quebec Act*,[1] could never have been salvaged and restored to the processes of a "royal province" in 1791. Without it the Canadian Union, which French Canada instinctively abhorred for its motives but which La Fontaine came in the end to venerate for its beneficent restoration of "his people," could never have repaired the ravages of insurrection. Without it the Canadian federation would have been impossible for that generation or perhaps for any generation with the national functions so dominant in the *B.N.A. Act of 1867*. This expedient, foreseen by Head as early as 1851, enabled the advocates of federation, as we have seen, to cut the Gordian knot of state sovereignty which dragged the United States into civil war, and to carry confederation at last with Macdonald's incomparable sense of expediency and timing.

Many of the paramount powers of the British Parliament were devolved upon the new Dominion by the *B.N.A. Act of 1871* but the process of amendment itself was still retained from the first empire for a long succession of *B.N.A. Acts* from 1871 to 1951. When the *Statute of Westminster* in 1931 repealed a whole spate of statutory

---

[1]"Revoked, annulled, and made void." 14 Geo. iii, c. 83.

anomalies and opened the way for Canadian parliamentary autonomy in other respects, the amendment of the *B.N.A. Acts* was still expressly reserved. Appeals to the Judicial Committee of the Privy Council have since been abrogated. The provinces *per se* already have full powers of constitutional amendment "except as regards the office of Lieutenant-Governor," within the range of provincial powers.[1] By the *B.N.A. Act of 1949* (13 Geo. vi, c. 81) the federal government also was empowered to amend the purely national aspects of its constitution with all the freedom and flexibility of a legislative union, reserving still however certain vested rights and strictly "federal" aspects of federal-provincial relations in the purgatorial regions of British parliamentary supremacy. It may be assumed that this supremacy, so reluctantly retained in 1931, could be given short shrift in the event of invidious federal-provincial controversy in Canada. Meanwhile Canada in common with every federal state in the modern world awaits a satisfactory method of "federal" constitutional amendment. An old chieftain of the Micmacs once bore the name of Noojecasigunodasit, which being interpreted means "tied in a hard knot." Is there any irrevocable plan of self-amendment which might not christen the Canadian federation by that ominous name? The survival of such a primordial anomaly is a curious commentary upon that fear—a curious commentary too upon the canny empirical opportunism of Canadian nationhood. "We must manage as best we can."

III

By the time of Confederation the new relationship of colony and mother country implied in this process of national incubation had already reached a stage of conscious and animated speculation. An impressive anthology could be compiled on this theme of the "new nation," "a new and vigorous nationality," the "national strength and national prestige," the resolution to "build up a nation," to "add to their national power and consideration," to attain "no unimportant position among the nations of the world." Head, as we have seen, had long contemplated "the forms and the substance of our Constitution come to maturity in this part of America under the shelter of the Crown"—"a powerful and independent State" endowed with attributes which have come to full maturity only in our own day. To Macdonald Canada was "fast ceasing to be a dependency," and nothing could illustrate

[1]*B.N.A. Act of 1867*, s. 92, ss. 1.

more effectively the true nature of this inherent growth towards nationhood than the silence of the *B.N.A. Act of 1867* with regard to this historic process in both function and method.

The value of Confederation in consolidating the trends towards nationhood was of course beyond calculation. The fact remains that the venerable instrument of 1867, by its own specific and explicit enactment, added nothing to the scope and function of self-government. Responsible government continued in the classic formula that "the Executive Government and authority of and over Canada is hereby declared to continue and be vested in the Queen." Had the preference of Macdonald and Tupper for a legislative rather than a federal union prevailed, the Act of union would simply have obliterated the interprovincial boundaries, substituted one government for three or four, and continued the expanding functions of responsible government as before without the necessity of dividing federal from provincial powers or defining the relationship between them. When federalism became necessary certain powers were funded at Ottawa and others left to function in the provinces, but the sum of self-government in both on July 1, 1867, was precisely, to start with, what it had been in the original provinces on June 30. This is stated categorically in the *B.N.A. Act of 1867* itself (ss. 12 and 65).

The effect of federation, however, in quickening the sense of nationhood and speeding its expansion is evident on every hand, and quickly repaid the consummate wisdom of the Fathers of Confederation in leaving both responsible government ("vested in the Queen") and the expansion of its range to the operation of its own ineluctable function. Within three years Canada was transformed, as we have seen, from a landless federation to a veritable empire in its own right with more than a third of the continent as its colonial appanage "for the purposes of the Dominion." Three years later its boundaries extended "from sea to sea, and from the river unto the ends of the earth." A few years later Edward Blake as minister of justice succeeded in establishing a supreme court for Canada, though his attempt to end appeals to the Judicial Committee of the Privy Council came to grief upon the threat of imperial veto. For the last time in 1875 the governor-general exercised the prerogative of pardon—to Lépine for the death of Scott—on his own "personal responsibility." At the same time a formidable list of reservations prescribed for Dominion legislation on topics ranging from divorce and treaty obligations to naval and military forces and shipping of the United Kingdom, was removed from the governor-general's instructions.

Canada [wrote Blake] is not merely a colony or a province: she is a dominion composed of an aggregate of seven large provinces federally united under an imperial charter, which expressly recites that her constitution is to be similar in principle to that of the United Kingdom. . . . She enjoys absolute powers of legislation and administration over the people and territories of the North-West, out of which she has already created one province, and is empowered to create others, with representative institutions.

A new relationship was warranted by "the vastness of her area, the numbers of her population, the character of the representative institutions and of the responsible government which as citizens of the various provinces and of Canada her people have so long enjoyed."

A few years later (August 25, 1879) an equally assertive Conservative memorandum from Macdonald, Tupper, Tilley, and Galt explored still further this new relationship. It was imperative to have "constant and confidential communications between Her Majesty's Government and Her local advisers in Canada" since imperial policy had "devolved upon Canada the administration of the whole of British North America," thus constituting her the "trustee for the Empire at large of half the continent of North America." They suggested "a resident Minister" with a "quasi-diplomatic position at the Court of St. James" capable of being "duly accredited to foreign Courts" in association with officials of the Foreign Office. Sir Michael Hicks-Beach declined (November 1, 1879) any appointment "implying a diplomatic status or position," but suggested a "Commissioner," an "officer in the home service." A Canadian Minute of Council (December 22, 1879) acquiesced under protest. It was conceded that "Canada cannot . . . maintain relations of a strictly diplomatic character . . . as respects foreign nations." Between Canada and the United Kingdom, on the other hand, the relations were different. "The Imperial Government and Parliament have so far transferred to Canada an independent control that their discussion and settlement have become subjects for mutual assent and concert, and thereby have, it is thought, assumed a quasi-diplomatic character." If a "Commissioner" there must be, let him be at least a "High Commissioner" accredited to the Colonial Office. The overtures closed (February 7, 1880) with the historic telegram: "Her Majesty's Government will recognize Sir A. T. Galt as High Commissioner under the Great Seal of Canada." The function proved almost as anomalous as the name, leaving the primitive origins of the office at last almost unrecognizable. Galt resigned after three years of frustration, but Tupper's imperturbable hardihood was equal to every occasion. Once at least, with the assistance of Lord Knutsford, he invaded the sacred precincts of the Foreign Office. In due time a

British High Commissioner to Canada helped further to sanctify an obsolete title by reciprocal offices of great value.

In the office of governor-general these evolving relations were to be seen in their simplest form. As early as 1858 Sir Edmund Head with characteristic sagacity and foresight had protested to Labouchere against the obsolete rigidity of the royal instructions: it was "most inexpedient as a general rule that the governor should be present during the discussion in council of particular measures. . . . His presence as a regular or indispensable rule would check all freedom of debate and embarrass himself as well as his advisers." Even the added prestige of the governor-general at confederation yielded, as we have seen, under Blake's resolute counsels, to the normal conventions of parliamentary government. Though "vested in the Queen," the military and naval administration, like the "executive government" itself, was not to be vested in the Queen's representative. The Dundonald incident in 1904 made it clear that "vested in the Queen" meant neither the governor-general nor the British War Office but the Canadian minister of militia. Lord Byng could command Canadian troops at Vimy Ridge in 1917 but not in 1926 as governor-general in Canada as did Dorchester and Brock and Colborne. In the *B.N.A. Act of 1867* not only the function but the appointment of the governor-general was left indeterminate—whether he was to be appointed on the advice of British ministers or of Canadian ministers as were the lieutenant-governors of the provinces. At the Imperial Conference of 1926 it was agreed that the governor-general was to hold "in all essential respects the same position in relation to the administration of public affairs in the Dominion as is held by His Majesty the King in Great Britain, and that he is not the representative or agent of His Majesty's Government in Great Britain or any Department of that Government." Appointment on the advice of Canadian ministers was a corollary of this hypothesis. Lord Bessborough's commission bore the signature: "By His Majesty's Command, R. B. Bennett" (March 20, 1931). In 1939, in a gesture of statesmanship almost beyond calculation at that time, the King and Queen of Canada discharged here the functions of their royal office in person, as truly at home in Ottawa as at Westminster. The appointment of a Canadian governor-general required nothing but the advice of Canadian ministers. This procedure has now been rounded into a cycle by Her Majesty's own title "Elizabeth II, by the Grace of God of the United Kingdom, Canada, her other realms and territories, Queen, Defender of the Faith."[1]

[1]*Royal Style and Titles Act*, 1 Eliz. II, c. 9.

Meanwhile the title of "governor" like that of "high commissioner" continues to complicate the nomenclature of the Commonwealth. Carlyle once exclaimed that of all people on earth the British were "the stupidest in speech, the wisest in action." Out of deference for Canada, which was called a "Dominion" in 1867 to avoid wounding "the sensibilities of the Yankees,"[1] the "Commonwealth of Australia" and the "Union of South Africa" were also classed as "Dominions." The original preference of the Fathers of Confederation for "Kingdom" of Canada has now come at last into its own. Would "viceroy" be more appropriate than "governor-general" for "the Chief Executive Officer . . . carrying on the Government of Canada on behalf of and in the name of the Queen, by whatever title he is designated"?[2] On the other hand no official title in America has the sanction of longer usage than "governor": it has been stereotyped by immemorial custom from the first empire, the second empire, and the Commonwealth. It survives also in forty-eight states of the American republic, stereotyped from the old colonial system by the enduring sanctions of forty-eight written constitutions. Canada has had more curious vestigial anomalies than this.

As the nineteenth century drew to a close these anomalies began to multiply. At any rate the status of Canada itself at the end of the long unbroken parliamentary tradition in America was approaching maturity under confederation. What steps were taken at the close of the First World War (as General Smuts once said) to "tidy up the show"?

IV

The appearance of Canada in national apparel at the Paris Peace Conference, in the League of Nations, in the International Labour Organization, and at the Washington Naval Conference had gone far to clothe the Dominion with the appropriate sartorial attire for the functioning of nationhood. At the same time there were still many anomalies and a few violent antinomies surviving from various stages of colonial nonage and adolescence. As the Imperial Conference of 1923 loomed upon the horizon some of these anomalies began to assume disconcerting and sinister proportions. Behind the scenes the most intensive discussion of imperial and external relations ever brought to bear at one time upon this topic began to develop upon a high plane of public spirit. Much bitterness prevailed in the press, but

[1]"The change of title from *Kingdom* to *Dominion* . . . was made at the instance of Lord Derby, then foreign minister, who feared the first name would wound the sensibilities of the Yankees." Macdonald to Lord Knutsford, July 18, 1889.

[2]*B.N.A. Act of 1867*, s. 10.

the disparagement of motives, so characteristic of public controversy, was tempered in private by much candour and mutual esteem. By 1923 certain general conclusions with regard to the substance of constitutional change were beginning to emerge with deep conviction. Perhaps the acutest controversy emerged with regard to the method.

With regard to the substance of constitutional change the conclusions of empiricists and theorists alike began to converge with convincing consensus upon certain very definite principles of policy. Much useful preliminary discussion had already taken place before the war. No more candid and honourable approach could have been made to the project of a centralized imperial federation than the *Problem of the Commonwealth* advanced by the Round Table school during the years of impending crisis from the South African union to the outbreak of the First World War in 1914. The indispensable prerequisites for a uniform foreign policy—an irreducible minimum of organic centralization, charged with the sovereign counsels of peace and war and the fiscal machinery necessary to underwrite those obligations—were canvassed with ingenuous enthusiasm in a dozen co-ordinated groups carrying forward their conclusions, favourable and otherwise, with great candour and goodwill.

Long before the outbreak of war, however, a deep and fundamental cleavage of opinion had developed in several sections of the Round Table enterprise. More than one dissentient group had reached the conviction that the Dominions had developed too far towards autonomy to surrender even the irreducible minimum stipulated by the Round Table for a uniform and centralized foreign policy. This conviction, moreover, had already been confirmed in practice by the gracious but inveterate *non possumus* of Sir Wilfrid Laurier to every tentative gesture of centralization. In 1911 this empirical belief was confirmed by the categorical statement of Asquith himself, the British prime minister, that foreign policy as administered by the Foreign Office could not be shared with the Dominions.

Athwart this exploratory enterprise the First World War broke with devastating impact and all theoretical speculation gave way to *ad hoc* improvisation. If anything was needed to demonstrate the wisdom as well as the necessity of autonomy it was to be found in the course of the war itself. No centralized authority in London could possibly have dealt with the domestic problems which emerged in South Africa, Canada, and elsewhere, or could ever have commanded the spectacular response from the Dominions forthcoming by spontaneous and voluntary co-operation in a common cause. Measured by the tasks of war the flexible associations of the Commonwealth obtained results that could never have been won by regimentation. Even the War Cabinet, an *ad hoc* improvisation of great practical value, was made up of component elements responsible to five or six different constituencies all over the world, and their ultimate responsibility to those constituencies could be relied upon to function with all the traditional stringency of responsible government for three-quarters of a century in domestic politics. The formula of 1917 in the Imperial War Conference—that "the organization of the Empire is to be based upon equality of nationhood"—was resolutely translated, as we have seen, into the memorandum of March 12, 1919, and into the Peace Treaty. The friction with permanent officials developed in the process did not always appear upon the surface. A smaller man than Sir Robert Borden "with a chip on his shoulder" might have emerged a less impressive figure in the history of these eventful years. By 1922 at any rate it was clear that many anachronisms of colonial days could no longer be ignored.

Much had already been done to explore what John S. Ewart once called these "lazy fugacities." Few had contributed more than Ewart himself to their discussion. The *Kingdom Papers* and the *Independence Papers,* published at his own expense, set a standard of public spirit which was not always recognized during the lifetime of that arch-controversialist. By 1922 a formidable list of authorities could be cited in consensus on the main thesis of Canadian nationhood.[1] Said the Hon. N. W. Rowell: "Canada not only in theory but in fact, has reached the status of a nation." Lord Milner himself, patron-saint of the Round Table school, conceded that "the United Kingdom and the Dominions are partner nations not yet indeed of equal power but for good and all of equal status." The only future for the British Empire was "an absolute out and out equal partnership of the United Kingdom and the Dominions. I say that without any kind of reservation whatsoever." In South Africa General Smuts spoke without apology of full sovereignty. Thenceforth "if a war is to affect them they will have to declare it. If peace is to be made they will have to sign it. Their independence has been achieved."

It was probably a casual revelation by Prime Minister Lloyd George in the British House of Commons on the Irish settlement of 1922 which brought the central issue of foreign policy into focus with startling clearness: "You must act through one instrument. The instru-

[1]See Sir Clifford Sifton, "Some Canadian Constitutional Problems," in *Canadian Historical Review,* March, 1922.

MAPS AND PLANS

ACKNOWLEDGEMENTS for several of these maps and plans are due to the Topographical Survey of Canada, to the Bureau of Statistics, to the National Development Bureau, and to the Department of the Interior; but especially to Principal Mackintosh, editor, and The Macmillan Company of Canada, publishers, of the *Canadian Frontiers of Settlement* (9 volumes), for permission to use material from my *"Dominion Lands" Policy* in that series. In some instances (Figs. 13 to 20) the Macmillan Company of Canada has kindly loaned the original plates for this purpose.

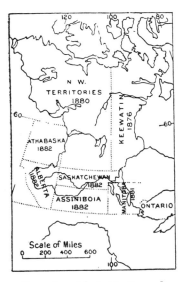

Fig. 1. Administrative divisions of "Dominion Lands," 1882.

Fig. 2. Administrative divisions of "Dominion Lands," 1898.

Fig. 3. Administrative divisions of "Dominion Lands," 1905.

Fig. 4. Administrative divisions of "Dominion Lands," 1927.

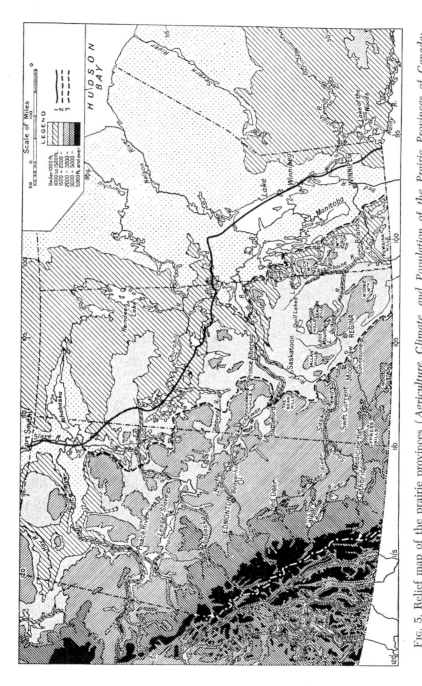

Fig. 5. Relief map of the prairie provinces (*Agriculture, Climate, and Population of the Prairie Provinces of Canada: A Statistical Atlas Showing Past Development and Present Conditions*, prepared under the direction of W. B. Hurd and T. W. Grindley, Ottawa, Dominion Bureau of Statistics, 1932).

1. Western boundary of the Precambrian Shield; 2 and 3, respectively, the boundaries between the first and second and between the second and third prairie levels.

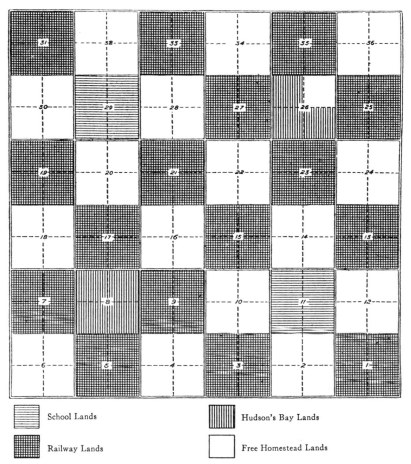

31	32	33	34	35	36
30	29	28	27	26	25
19	20	21	22	23	24
18	17	16	15	14	13
7	8	9	10	11	12
6	5	4	3	2	1

School Lands   Hudson's Bay Lands

Railway Lands   Free Homestead Lands

Fig. 6. Plan of township showing: (*a*) school lands (sections 11 and 29), (*b*) Hudson's Bay lands (sections 8 and three-quarters of 26; the whole of 26 in every fifth township), (*c*) free homestead lands (even-numbered sections, except 8 and 26), (*d*) railway lands (odd-numbered sections reserved for selection as railway land grants). Each section is bounded on three sides by road allowance (66 feet).

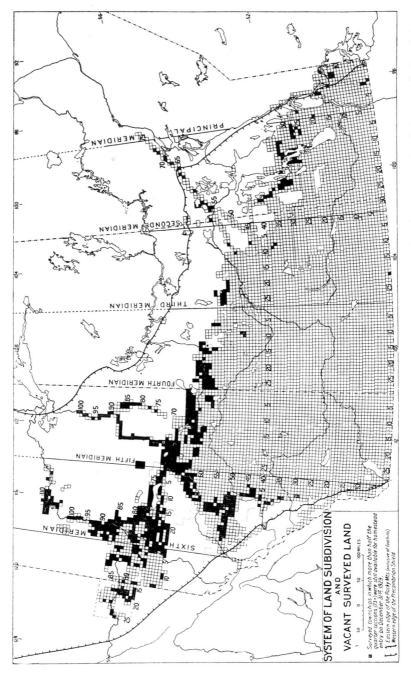

Fig. 7. System of land subdivision in the prairie provinces (data provided by the Topographical Survey of Canada). The "ranges" (horizontal series) are numbered westward from the principal meridian at Fort Garry and the "townships" (vertical series) northward from the international boundary.

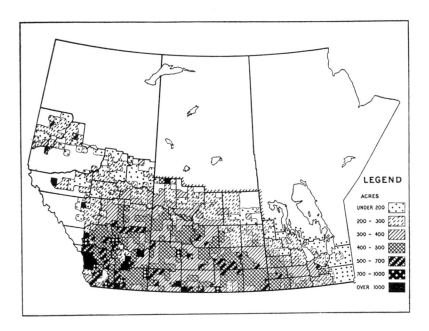

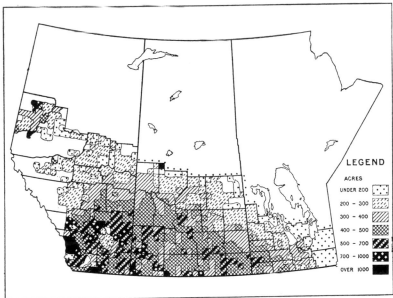

FIGS. 8, 9. Mean size of farms in 1921 (*above*) and 1926 (*below*).
Compiled from the Census of Manitoba, Saskatchewan, and Alberta, 1926.
The territorial unit is the municipality.

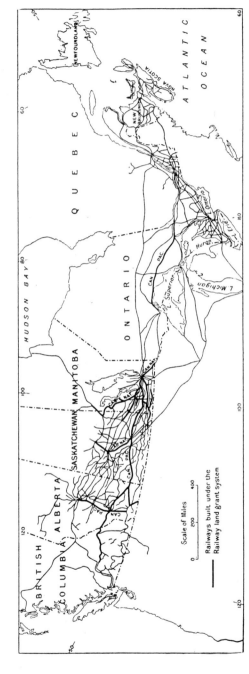

Fig. 10. Railways built under railway land grant system. From manuscript map prepared by Mr. Clifford, Department of the Interior.

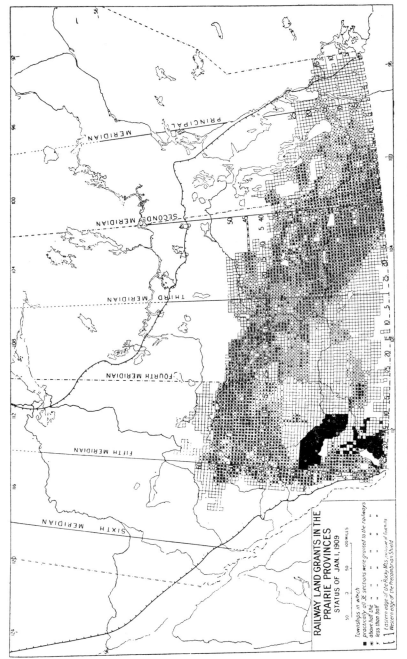

FIG. 11. Railway land grants finally "selected" by the C.P.R. and "colonization railways" in the prairie provinces. Prepared from manuscript map in the Department of the Interior as at the liquidation of the railway land grant system in 1908.

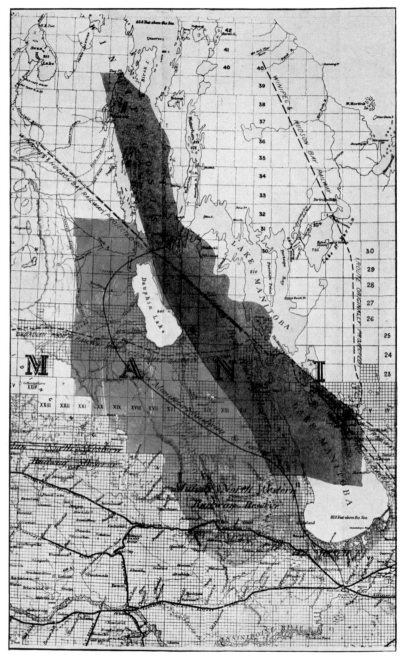

Fig. 12. Map showing railway lands reserved for "selection" by Lake Manitoba Railway and Canal Company (lightly shaded), and the Hudson Bay Railway (heavily shaded). The Manitoba and North-Western Reserve and part of the C.P.R. Reserve are also shown south of the L.M.R. & C.

From a map accompanying P.C. 1561, June 6, 1892.

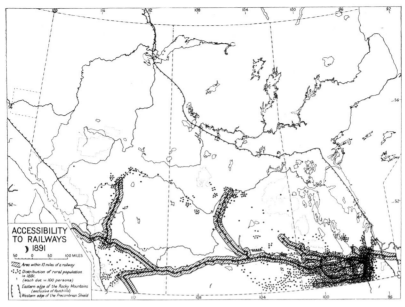

ACCESSIBILITY
TO RAILWAYS
1891

50   0   50   100 MILES

Area within 10 miles of a railway
Distribution of rural population
in 1891.
(each dot = 100 persons)
Eastern edge of the Rocky Mountains
(exclusive of foothills)
Western edge of the Precambrian Shield

FIG. 13

Figs. 13 to 20 show accessibility to railways within 10 miles, the economic range for agriculture.

Based on manuscript maps of National Development Bureau, Ottawa.

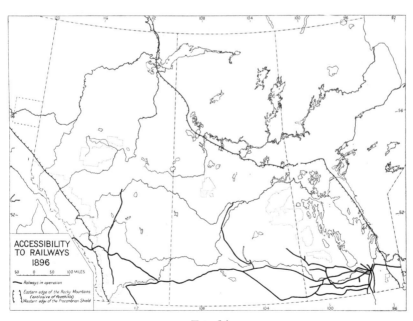

ACCESSIBILITY
TO RAILWAYS
1896

50   0   50   100 MILES

Railways in operation
Eastern edge of the Rocky Mountains
(exclusive of foothills)
Western edge of the Precambrian Shield

FIG. 14

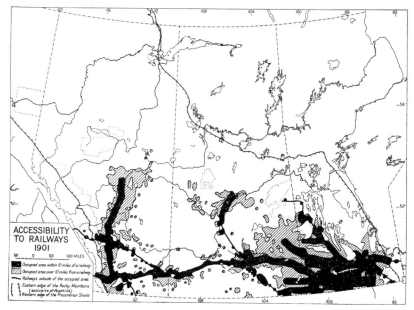

ACCESSIBILITY
TO RAILWAYS
1901

50   0   50   100 MILES

Occupied area within 10 miles of a railway
Occupied area over 10 miles from a railway
Railways outside of the occupied area
Eastern edge of the Rocky Mountains
(exclusive of foothills)
Western edge of the Precambrian Shield

FIG. 15

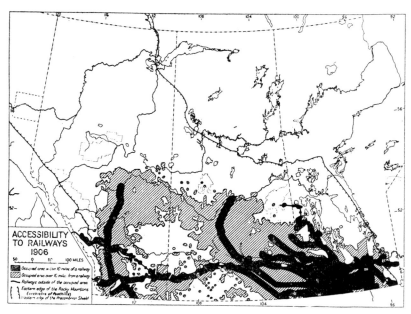

ACCESSIBILITY
TO RAILWAYS
1906

50   0   50   100 MILES

Occupied area within 10 miles of a railway
Occupied area over 10 miles from a railway
Railways outside of the occupied area
Eastern edge of the Rocky Mountains
(exclusive of foothills)
Western edge of the Precambrian Shield

FIG. 16

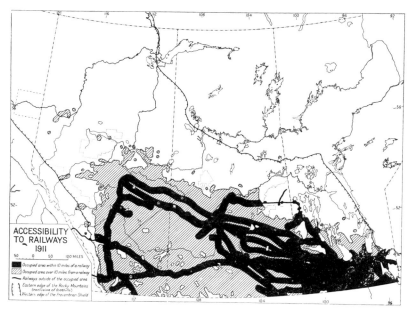

ACCESSIBILITY
TO RAILWAYS
1911

50   0   50   100 MILES

Occupied area within 10 miles of a railway
Occupied area over 10 miles from a railway
Railways outside of the occupied area
Eastern edge of the Rocky Mountains
(exclusive of foothills)
Western edge of the Precambrian Shield

FIG. 17

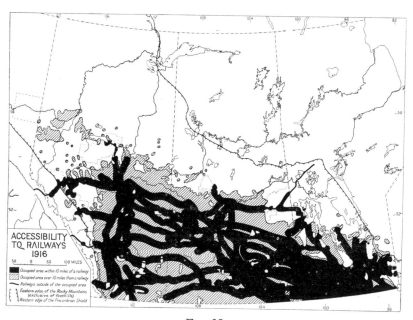

ACCESSIBILITY
TO RAILWAYS
1916

50   0   50   100 MILES

Occupied area within 10 miles of a railway
Occupied area over 10 miles from a railway
Railways outside of the occupied area.
Eastern edge of the Rocky Mountains
(exclusive of foothills)
Western edge of the Precambrian Shield

FIG. 18

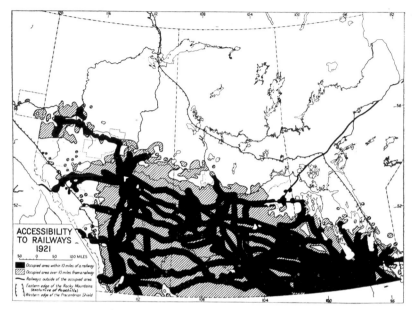

FIG. 19

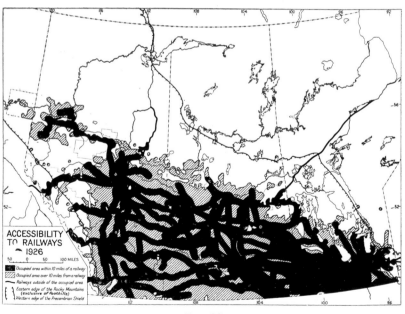

FIG. 20

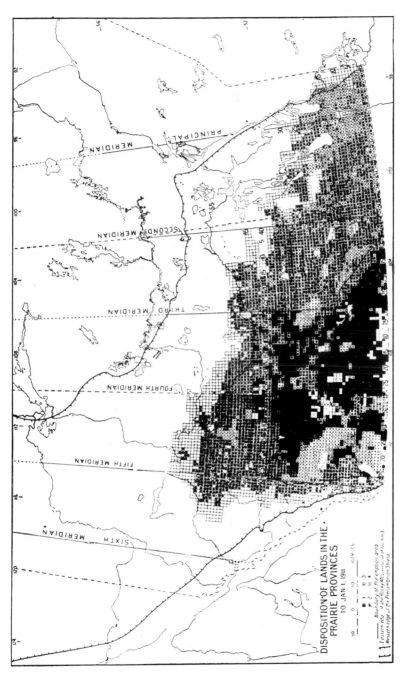

Fig. 21. Map showing by townships the disposition of "Dominion Lands" up to January 1, 1911. Solid black (see inset) shows townships in which about half or less was taken up as pre-emptions or purchased homesteads after homestead entry. Black discs show townships in which about half or more had been patented as homesteads up to January 1, 1911. Black dots show townships in which about half or more had been disposed of in categories other than homesteads. Circles in white show areas restricted to grazing leases.

ment of foreign policy of the Empire is the British Foreign Office. That has been accepted by all the Dominions as inevitable." This statement was immediately challenged. It is true that Sir Robert Borden had claimed a "voice" in the hastily improvised *de facto* War Cabinet, a voice which effectually won "equality of nationhood" at the Imperial Conference of 1917 and in the memorandum of March 12, 1919, for the impending Peace Treaty. Without that voice it is doubtful if the consolidation of the Canadian Corps under Sir Arthur Currie or the signature of the Dominions to the Peace Treaty or the national status of Canada in the Council and I.L.O. of the League of Nations could have been won. But Sir Robert Borden's "voice" had been improvised *ad hoc* in the throes of war. The formula of Lloyd George for the foreign policy of the whole Commonwealth in time of peace "through one instrument . . . the British Foreign Office" on the basis of periodical conferences of half a dozen delegations each bound at all times by a paramount responsibility to its own constituency, opened up vistas of exploitation, in Canada and South Africa particularly, too forbidding for domestic politics. By a host of advisers, official and otherwise, this thesis was impugned with impressive unanimity, confirmed by the Chanak incident and the initial *impasse* on the Halibut Treaty. In effect it was a "reversal of the policy which had been developing for fifty years" in the functioning of responsible government. The removal of such anomalies was becoming a "paramount necessity," and a veritable barrage of speculation soon began to converge upon the method.

The most venturesome project was probably that advanced by Sir Clifford Sifton. With characteristic incisiveness he urged the necessity of "clearing away restrictions and limitations that are now obsolete" and defining "Canada's constitutional relations . . . by law instead of by stump speeches." To that end he proposed a constituent convention with parliamentary sanctions to "draft an amended constitution"—"just as our statesmen in 1867 drafted the British North America Act, we now require to draft an amended constitution."[1] From this stage the discussion which ensued behind the scenes until the departure of the Canadian delegates for the Imperial Conference of 1923 and beyond to the Conference of 1926 fairly exhausted the range of feasible alternatives. It quickly emerged that the record of constituent conventions, even with parliamentary sanctions, scarcely warranted the hope of solving all the anomalies of the Canadian "constitution" at one fell swoop for all generations to come. The Quebec Resolutions of

[1]*Ibid.*, and Ottawa Canadian Club, April 8, 1922.

1864, for example, had never been formally ratified by the Maritimes nor the London Resolutions by any of the provinces. On the other hand the unwritten "conventions" which had been in process for three-quarters of a century since responsible government had already won functional nationhood *de facto* in most aspects of internal policy and could be relied upon to function willy-nilly wherever the vital interests of Canada should come to be involved. During the First World War and the Peace Conference those interests had crossed irretraceably the boundaries of Canada into international relations. The sound-barrier, so to speak, had been passed, not without "the most resolute insistence" by a series of concerted actions discerningly devised to form precedents for the future. By this method surviving anomalies could be solved one at a time, with flexible priorities, each in the order of its importance and expediency. By this method too the cumulative results could be consolidated and conserved in a constant responsiveness to public opinion which would be impossible in head-long plans for a written constitution in a hurry.

With these concerted counsels the Canadian delegation to the Imperial Conference of 1923 set itself very deliberately to demonstrate its *de facto* autonomy in foreign policy and underwrite that status in terms which could not be misunderstood. Here again "the most resolute insistence" was the order of the day; and there can be no doubt that many of those far-reaching decisions were effectually made which were to receive their formal ratification in the more spectacular Imperial Conferences of 1926 and 1930. This was true not only of the substance of constitutional status but of the method. The key in both cases was the inescapable fact that Dominion prime ministers like the British ministers themselves were responsible to their respective parliaments and could advise the crown only by virtue of that para-mount responsibility. This process "had been developing for fifty years" and nothing but frustration could result from any attempt to charge purely consultative conferences with executive powers for "a uniform policy functioning through the agency of a common instru-ment." This proved to be the most decisive and unanswerable argument of the conference. A sub-committee of the conference on the making of treaties conceded the main issue with irrefutable logic. It was "inevi-table" for Dominion ministers to advise the crown on their own affairs and for that advice nothing could absolve them from responsibility to their own parliaments. Not only the negotiation of Dominion treaties but ratification by the crown was to follow on the advice of responsible Dominion ministers acting through Dominion plenipotentiaries.

From this point forward through the classic declarations of 1926 ("in no way subordinate one to another in any aspect of their domestic or external affairs") and 1930 there was a methodical attempt to implement basic principles "appropriate to *status*" by empirical adjustments appropriate to function. Most of the anomalies were removable by the age-old method of unwritten "convention" or usage, which added new aspects of self-government to the scores already attained since 1848. The removal of certain statutory anomalies by the *Statute of Westminster* (22 Geo. v, c. 4) became necessary, as we have seen, only because a statute, the highest instrument known to the law, can be amended only by another statute. But both "convention" and statute have dealt with anomalies rather than with normal practices of government, and uninitiated observers will search in vain for anything in the nature of a new "constitution" to emerge from these fragmentary and empirical adjustments. With the removal of these vestigial anomalies the real constitution of Canada—evolved by three centuries of unbroken tradition—has been left free to function and the normal play of association free to develop without inhibitions in response to the tensions and requirements of the modern world. The mechanics of subordination have been supplanted by "broad loyalties, by the common feelings and interests—in many cases, of history—and by devotion to great world ideals of peace and freedom." "That is the bond," added Lord Balfour. "If that is not enough, nothing else is enough."

The sequel was to prove a convincing demonstration of these imponderables. Hitler predicted to Chancellor von Schuschnigg of Austria that the Dominions would not again participate in another war and that the British Commonwealth would probably disintegrate under such an impact. Five months before the Canadian declaration of war a reply was made (April, 1939) to that forecast: happily by Mr. Lapointe himself whose name had been chiefly associated with the controversial Halibut Treaty and other functional aspects of Canadian nationhood. Hitler's prediction was based on "an absolute fallacy." Neutrality in such a conflict, added Mr. Lapointe, would mean a civil war in Canada. The *Statute of Westminster* was "an agency of unity . . . unity in liberty, without which no British nation can exist. . . . We will resist all attempts to break up the Commonwealth." Six months later the Prime Minister himself, "contrary," he asserted, "to every hope and wish I have ever entertained," sponsored a Canadian declaration of war against Germany: only so could "the nations of the British Commonwealth hope to continue to enjoy the liberties which are theirs under the British Crown, and the world itself be spared a descent into a new and terrible barbarism." For more than two years Canada alone among the nations of the American hemisphere shared that conflict, and from the fall of France on June 4, 1940, to the German invasion of Yugoslavia and Greece, and finally of the U.S.S.R. on June 22, 1941, the only nations in arms left standing against the Axis were the nations of the British Commonwealth.

After the Second World War, uninhibited now by "fugacities" of "status," Canadian nationhood continued to function, a little awkwardly but instinctively, in the widest range of associations ever dictated by Canadian interests. Compared with this far-reaching maturity the sheltered growth of self-government sought by Baldwin and Howe a century ago resembles the "primordial protoplasm" of Gilbert's airy fantasy. Nevertheless that sheltered growth, that process of incubation, became one of the most distinctive features of Canadian nationhood. Though not as spectacular as revolution and bloodshed such a process has not been without its advantages. It has not, of course, been free from controversy with the parent state and with our neighbour. But the British provinces fared better than Mexico and Texas at the hands of Spain and the United States. The chief reason for this is not far to seek. The truth is that incubation at that stage was safer than independence. "The main object of our policy," Elgin wrote to Grey, "ought to be to support the hopes and courage of the Canadians until their natural advantages begin to tell." "They should stand in conscious strength," added Sir Edmund Head, "and in the full equipment of self Government as a free people bound by the ties of gratitude and affection."

That serene faith was not always realized. In comparison however with the grim memories of the past to which Eire has dedicated itself since 1922, or in comparison with the century and a half of ineradicable antipathies from the American Revolution, the manner of nationhood for the younger nations of the British Commonwealth has been harmonious and benign. In many ways this unique process has been normal and natural, and there are passages, not a few, of great magnanimity. In India and Pakistan and Ceylon the outcome is still complicated by prodigious legacies from the past. In South Africa there are insoluble problems. In the new confederacy of the Rhodesias and Nyasaland, in the Gold Coast, in the Caribbean and elsewhere, the same experiment is going forward with the goodwill and un-heralded patience of a great tradition. Such a tradition remaining unchanged in a changing world may hold a better promise than indiscriminate revolution for the peace and freedom of mankind.

V

Within four or five decades, wrote Sir John Bourinot in 1893, "Canada will probably have determined her destiny." "The history of Canada as a whole," he added, "has yet to be written." This prophecy has now been measurably fulfilled, and it may be that the added reflection too is still measurably true. More enduring history has been made than written in Canada.

The test of Canadian nationhood will be its behaviour in the unpredictable tensions of the modern world. The mere functioning of nationhood has long since lost its novelty. There can be little glamour in a sense of youth and nationhood at the present stage of perplexity in world history. During the era of the League of Nations—an introverted era of "no commitments"—it cannot be said that Canadian policy was an inspiration to still more reluctant colleagues. "The good ship 'Status', received many coats of paint but never ventured far out to sea."[1] But the maturity of recent years under the United Nations is no sporadic phenomenon. It is the product of a long and tough tradition, and every portent of Canadian history may be expected to confirm it. Many chapters of that history will continue to baffle and to challenge the unwary investigator. Over-simplification, superficial plausibilities, have always been the besetting sins of historians. History itself, the multitudinous detail of life of which it is compounded, is not always so neat. This stuff of history, not what has been written about it but history in its truly generic sense as it has been immutably made whether it has been written or not, is subject to no such discount, and the student of Canadian history in that sense is undiscerning indeed who does not perceive certain elements of character emerging from the process.

It might be a useful exercise to forget for the moment our bondage to written "histories" and to think of history as it was, and is—life in its infinite complexity, infinitely integrated but absolutely perfect in its causal sequence and comprehensiveness. This conception of history, to be sure, is apt to daunt the historian, as it ought to daunt the philosopher and the scientist, in the endless pursuit of "more and more about less and less." The multiplication of "disciplines" is the direction which the puny intellect of mankind has taken in its attempt to comprehend life by subdividing its essential unity. These are all one in the infinite play of history and everything is grist that comes to the historian's mill. The challenge of life to the historian is to try to understand a little of this infinite process—preferably before writing

[1]Vincent Massey, *On Being Canadian*, p. 76.

about it—and he must be bold indeed who does not rise from his worship at that shrine a chastened and repentant sinner.

Canadian history in that sense has been a tough and intractable business. Little of it falls into neat patterns against the background of the universe. Much of it has been a stolid and phlegmatic struggle against heavy odds. Denied the assurance of a "manifest destiny," the parliamentarian, the fur-trader, the stolid pioneer, the railway builder, the industrial entrepreneur, were almost invariably competing with superior resources. They dealt, as a rule, with forces beyond their control, in many cases the by-products of other lands. "Courage in adversity," the motto of the old Nor' Wester, remained a stark national necessity for the Canadian brigades that shot the rapids and toiled across the portages of their stormy history. Not seldom it was a blind and baffled courage. Few of the makers of Canada lived to see what they had helped to make. A few, gifted with the canny acquisitive instincts of their forbears, won a sure foothold upon fortune and ended their days in peace. For many, if the truth were told, the outlook at the end was clouded with doubt or frustration. A "goodly company" of them, whatever their achievement for posterity, never emerged from the dust and heat of conflict. Would this "goodly fellowship" now find in the gathering signs of Canadian prosperity anything to match the "courage in adversity" of their own day?

These gathering signs of Canadian prosperity have been accompanied by an increased interest in Canadian history which Canadian historians may be tempted to appropriate with unwarranted complacency. The *leit-motif* in both cases may not be altogether complimentary. One of the shrewdest of Canadian financiers has avowed the "unflattering assumption that our popularity abroad is based not so much on what we are as on what we have."[1] It may be that the more specious aspects of nationhood—two world wars, western oil, Quebec iron, the St. Lawrence seaway, the rate of exchange of the Canadian dollar, the prolific industrial expansion of recent years— have had more to do with the awakening interest in Canadian history, particularly beyond our own borders, than the long record of "courage in adversity" that went into the foundations. In any event the historian's task, like the economist's, leaves no room for complacency, for there is scarcely a major field of Canadian history where research is

[1]"Our situation is akin to that of an heiress who can never be sure that she is admired for herself and not merely for her wealth. . . . We have still to prove that we can make the most of these natural resources in building a great nation." James Muir, President of the Royal Bank of Canada.

not as imperative as in the laboratory of science or industry. If the writing of history in the United States is any criterion, this painstaking and methodical research, though not without handsome dividends in recent years, is long overdue in Canada on a scale adequate for "great history."

Beyond question great history is now being written in the United States, the culmination of an epic in the rise of the republic to world power, and the result of a range of meticulous research which has left its counterpart in Canada far behind. That much of this research was unremunerative or doomed to be appropriated, all too often without acknowledgement, by those who were content to reap where they had not strawed, can be no excuse for neglect in either country. Even when "great history" comes to be written in Canada it may not be as great as the history of greater countries, but if Canadian historians are true to their craft and go not after other gods, the growing maturity in the functioning of nationhood will not come upon them unawares.

History will continue to be made in Canada whether it is written or not. "Events stronger than advocacy, events stronger than men" will continue to challenge Canadian character. The response to that challenge will probably continue to mystify our associates and ourselves by its resourcefulness and improvisation. Few nations, young or old, can match the advantages which Canada derives from her distinctive traditions for compliance with a new world order.

The outmoded and peevish tenets of Austinian sovereignty have never been known in Canada, and the loss in the functioning of the United Nations will never be missed. Inhibitions from the old order which perplex other nations wherever they appear to curtail national sovereignty have been by-passed in Canada with scarcely a thought for the implications. In 1931 Canadian sovereignty could have been rounded out by including in the *Statute of Westminster* the amendment of the *B.N.A. Acts*. Canada chose the flexibility of constitutional amendment by the old method rather than risk the rigidities of a specious national sovereignty, and it is altogether probable that the same empirical considerations would determine Canadian policy in the United Nations if it were necessary to choose between the substance and the shadow of international security.

No nation, moreover, could have a livelier sense of the value of that security. There was a time when the safety of Canada seemed assured. In the Assembly of the League of Nations Senator Dandurand once boasted that Canada lived in a fire-proof house. But that was before the era of the hydrogen bomb and the stratosphere and the super-sonic jet plane. No city on earth would now be saved by time or distance if atomic warfare were allowed to slip the frail leash of Western civilization. Canada is now impaled between the most in-veterate antagonists of the modern world, on the cross-roads of the air by the great circles of transportation in the northern hemisphere. "Events far from Canadian borders can transform overnight our lives and our destinies."[1] The vital decisions on atomic warfare will be made elsewhere. There can be no "victory" for either side in such a struggle, and a few miles in the stratosphere by the great circles would make little difference in the impact and certainty of such a catastrophe. There are no fire-proof houses in the modern world.

But there are considerations characteristically Canadian which emerge from the long record of Canadian tradition. Randolph Churchill once reproached two of his political friends for being "men who believe in the solution of political questions." Few political prob-lems in this world are capable of definitive "solutions." More often than not, intemperate and uncompromising counsels invite solutions irremediably wrong. Rarely is it given in the infinite complexities of life to reach solutions incontestably and permanently right. Many problems are best solved by leaving them unsolved, avoiding at all costs solutions that are irremediably wrong until by patience and goodwill an acceptable compromise can be found. *Solvitur ambulando* has been an honourable device in Canadian politics. Our forbears had a word for this. *Sliddering*—call it not slithering or sliding!—is not a heroic gesture but it has been known to get around many a sharp corner and out of many a tight one. A realistic appraisal of fact is the first step towards confidence if sought, as Bagot once implored, "gradu-ally and temperately in the sober spirit of a constitutional Country." There may never be peace in our time between conflicting ideologies, but if a precious modicum of time can be found for the exercise of patience and goodwill it ought to be possible to convince both an-tagonists that an atomic war would destroy them both. Nuclear weapons are now irresistible. The banning of them in the present state of international distrust may not be feasible. Is there enough discretion in the world to avert war and survive?

Canada brings into the new world order no mean record of modera-tion and compromise and toleration, the only tradition in the Americas unbroken by revolution or civil war. Toleration has been indispensable to her own nationhood—not only toleration of opinion but that invalu-

[1]L. B. Pearson in *Canada: Nation on the March* (1953), p. 3.

able flair for what an engineer would call "tolerance" in the play of institutions and politics. To keep on keeping on, to *slidder* where we must and stand where we can, to be uncompromising only in the exercise of goodwill, are signs of national maturity. The honest international broker is seldom the most brilliant theorist but without heroics and without vainglory he may aspire to be a useful friend to world peace.

Will prosperity enervate and warp the fibre of Canadian character? The foundations of nationhood have been well and truly laid. Will the superstructure stand fast when the rains descend and the floods come and the winds blow and beat upon that house? Without sharing the profound pessimism of an Innis or a Siegfried[1] is it possible to view without concern the impact of modern "communications" of every sort upon the economic and cultural life of Canada? No other such impact is to be found in the modern world. Our friendly neighbour is a world power of the first order, with population and wealth ten times our own, with 4000 miles of a common frontier across the continent, and with command of unprecedented "communications" of language and other media across that frontier. "One or two of these conditions will be found in modern countries. But Canada alone possesses all three."[2] The incessant drum-beat of commercialized radio and television, the deluge of fresh-poured ink in books and magazines[3] and press may not reach the foundations of Canadian nationhood, but what will be the ultimate effect upon the American way of life and our own? The solution of the gravest issues in both countries is far from automatic. We have this on the best of authority, the late Hume Wrong, Canadian ambassador in Washington. "Never have the official relations between Canada and the United States been so close and friendly as they are now, but also never have they been so complicated and so difficult. More than goodwill is required to avoid future irritations, recriminations and disputes. More than ever are needed the stern virtues of sober judgment, hard work, and recognition of the general interest over local pressures and demands."[4]

In one respect at least Canada is superlatively endowed to keep the virtues of her distinctive traditions hard and true. From many of

[1]Harold A. Innis, *Changing Concepts of Time*; André Siegfried, *The Character of Peoples*.

[2]*Report of the Royal Commission on National Development in the Arts, Letters, and Sciences* (1951), p. 11.

[3]Canadian magazines have a circulation in Canada of 42,000,000, American of 86,000,000. *Id.* p. 7.

[4]*Canada: Nation on the March*, p. 197.

the worst features of undisciplined plutocracy the United States was saved during the nineteenth century by the opening of the West. From many insidious dangers of a specious but enervating prosperity Canada may be saved by the opening of the North. In both time and territory this challenge to character and resourcefulness would seem to be unpredictable. It beckons both French- and English-speaking branches of the Canadian family and the response may well be a measure of the virility, the resourcefulness, the co-operation of the Canadian people.

BIBLIOGRAPHICAL NOTE

WHEN it became obvious that the normal paraphernalia of research
—precise footnotes and an exhaustive bibliography—would increase
prohibitively the size and cost of these studies, a choice had to be
made between more feasible alternatives. The source-material, much
of it in the form of careful quotation from confidential correspondence,
might be left almost altogether unauthenticated, in barren print. The
other alternative appeared to be a fragmentary bibliographical note,
condensing into half a dozen pages material which would normally
require sixty and illustrating the original sources which had been
found especially rewarding under each "Part" of the theme. The
omission of secondary material almost altogether was one of the
penalties of this alternative.

The evaluation of this sort of evidence must of course be uncom-
fortably arbitrary. Mere bulk has little bearing upon it. Many instances
come to mind from these studies. A couple of unsigned memoranda in
the handwriting of Governor Carleton and William Knox in the Dartmouth Papers may be more convincing evidence of policy for Quebec
in the American Department during the American Revolution than so
many hundredweight of Canadian "Sundries" to the contrary. A letter
from Andrew Colvile to his sister Lady Selkirk in the Correspondence
of St. Mary's Isle reveals more conclusively than many rolls of micro-
film from the A Series of the Hudson's Bay Archives how "the Bay
beat the River" in the coalition of 1821. Thenceforth it was the
Hudson's Bay Company which held the West until the Canadian
federation was ready to take over in 1870. Baldwin's memorandum
(1836) on responsible government, though published (and forgotten)
in *The Times* and in *British Parliamentary Papers* (March 22, 1839),
is found (a well-thumbed copy) in the Durham Papers together with
correspondence which attests its influence upon the famous *Report*.
The historic alliance between Baldwin and La Fontaine, with Hincks
as its architect, is found in the La Fontaine Papers over a period of
twenty-six months in such secrecy that Sydenham surmised they had

not been "known for 24 hours" to each other. Charles Buller, the sponsor of sound party tactics for the winning of responsible government, is revealed, like a beneficent epiphany, in the Howe Papers.

Sir Edmund Head's role as the grandfather of Confederation is disclosed in the annotations of the Colonial Office and in the fragmentary Head Papers. His confidential memorandum on British American union was written privately for Earl Grey seven years before Galt's resolutions of 1858, and his project for an interprovincial conference on federation in Toronto in that year foreshadowed and antedated the Quebec Conference by six years. Watkin's letters in the Baring Papers reveal the forays of that doughty buccaneer into Canadian politics in the interests of Grand Trunk, and the purchase of a controlling interest in the Hudson's Bay Company by the International Financial Society. A single sentence from the governor-general's office ought to settle the real authorship of the *Manitoba Act* more convincingly than reams of speculation on the role of Louis Riel. The illuminating evidence of the Borden Papers, the Doherty Papers, and the Dafoe diaries is conclusive for the closing phases of Canadian nationhood. These haphazard instances could be multiplied by the score for the authentic history of Canada, and by the score too for problems which still await the research of sound scholarship.

In the circumstances the onus of appraising the most rewarding source-material for each of the four "Parts" of this theme is not an alluring task. If I have been chary of selecting so little from so much I must plead the work already done and the work still to be done in Canadian research. The accumulations in the Public Archives of Canada under Dr. Lamb's acquisitive direction go on apace and many of the provincial archivists are equally acquisitive. It remains for Canadian scholars to appropriate these treasures in the cause of Canadian history.

Part I: Survival

The correspondence in the Q Series, much of it already published in Shortt and Doughty's *Documents*, reflects a policy of great secrecy for Quebec. After the Report of the Board of Trade (1769) Carleton returned to London until 1774 where his influence is seen not only in his chart for the *Quebec Act* in the Dartmouth Papers but in negative evidences of *viva voce* consultation in the new American Department. This Department, almost exactly contemporaneous in its creation and suppression with the American Revolution, was under William Knox as permanent under-secretary, and its policy for Quebec is seen in the

Dartmouth Papers, in Knox's pamphlets, five of which were published from 1769 to 1774, and in the Knox Papers, calendared by the British Historical Commission but now in the Clements Library, University of Michigan. Knox is still unrepentant in *Extra Official State Papers* (2 vols., 1789).

The determination to deny altogether the parliamentary tradition to the "new subjects" of Quebec is seen in Carleton's memorandum ("to get rid of" it and "to restore the old Law and Constitution") and in great profusion and consistency in Knox's papers and pamphlets. Knox's conviction that "the old mode of treating our dependencies must be exploded and a new system formed" has a bearing not only upon the place of Quebec in the policy of the American Department (curiously underestimated by American scholars) but upon Knox's agreement with Carleton in the use of force ("a force can easily be raised from thence"). Dartmouth's concurrence in endowing Carleton with "the full appointments of Commander-in-Chief" in America, after a hypothetical junction with Howe from New York, is in the Q Series (11. 198), and probably marks the most fatuous reliance upon Carleton's fatal miscalculation before his disgrace and recall by Germain in 1777.

The continuation of the parliamentary tradition in Nova Scotia is seen in the A Series, the Dalhousie Papers, etc. The creation of New Brunswick for the maritime loyalists, projected by William Knox as "New Ireland" (*Extra Official State Papers*), requires careful handling. Local tradition and even the Winslow Papers are badly at fault here. The organization of Upper Canada for the overland loyalists is traceable in the Q Series, the Simcoe Papers ("the birth-certificates of Ontario"), etc. Haldimand's attempt to perpetuate the *Quebec Act* is seen in the Q Series, the Haldimand Papers, etc. The fur trade and coalition of 1821 is illuminated by the Selkirk Papers, the Selkirk Correspondence at St. Mary's Isle (since destroyed by fire), *Documents Relating to the North West Company* (ed. W. S. Wallace, Champlain Society), and the A Series in the Hudson's Bay Archives. The contemporary pamphlet material for the whole period is voluminous and valuable.

PART II: SELF-GOVERNMENT

The evidence here may be listed in an ascending scale of authenticity. The official correspondence, even the confidential files of the G Series (for Canada), C.O. 217 (for Nova Scotia), C.O. 188 (for New Brunswick), and C.O. 226 (for Prince Edward Island) are far from satisfactory for what was actually happening. Colonial Office annotations on the original despatches are frequently more revealing. Behind this façade there was the private correspondence between governors and the colonial secretaries, which could be kept out of reach in the compilation of parliamentary returns. The Bagot Papers (one of the most brilliant collections in the P.A.C.), the stolid orthodoxy of the Metcalfe Papers, the prophetic insight of the Elgin-Grey Papers, reveal convincingly how officialdom was dealing with the situation. But this was only half the story. The situation itself was the work of other men, and it is only in the revelations of the reformers, in the Howe Papers, the Baldwin Papers, the La Fontaine Papers and similar collections that the "conundrum of what, how, and why" is really answered. The newspapers, particularly the *Novascotian* and the *Chronicle* in Nova Scotia and the *Mirror*, the *Examiner*, the *Pilot*, and *Minerve* in the Canadas, are very rewarding, while the voluminous pamphlet literature is perhaps the most brilliant—and vituperative—in Canadian politics. In Part II also are many dark corners that still require illumination. The Durham Papers are of course invaluable, but Hincks's papers seem to have been destroyed after his death from smallpox in 1885. The Ryerson Papers have been admirably explored by Professor Sissons, but Clinton Murdock, Sydenham's secretary (he returned to Ottawa as Sir Clinton in 1870 to sponsor the Queen's approval of the *Manitoba Act* in accordance with the *B.N.A. Act of 1867*, s. 146) is only one of a dozen secretarial witnesses whose papers are still missing.

PART III: BRITISH NORTH AMERICAN UNION

In Part III the evidence of all sorts is so voluminous that a bibliographical note is particularly inadequate. The state papers (G Series, C.O. 188, C.O. 217, C.O. 226, etc.), while growing in importance, derive much of their value from the Colonial Office annotations upon them. The fragmentary Head Papers reveal Head's insight and "drive" for federation. His memoranda to Labouchere and Newcastle on preliminary regional unions are in the G Series but the bulk of his papers seem to have been destroyed, an irreparable loss, after his daughter's death in 1914. The Macdonald Papers (more than 500 volumes) reveal Brydges of the Grand Trunk, Galt, Tilley, Tupper, the two Grays, and many another father of confederation in new colours. Above all, they reveal Macdonald himself and his deep sense of history. (Careful copies of many of the most revealing letters are preserved for posterity in Macdonald's own immaculate handwriting.) Howe's opposition to federation, garbled in the traditions of a lost cause, is traceable in the

Howe Papers and the papers of the Anti-Confederation League. The Baring Papers, among the treasures of the P.A.C., are invaluable for Grand Trunk and Hudson's Bay Company. Galt Papers, not yet available in public repositories, were worked through by Skelton. (Many of these have since been destroyed.) A few of Brown's letters at critical junctures survive in Mackenzie's *Brown*. Later volumes of recollections (Tupper, Cartwright, etc.) like all *obiter dicta*, must be treated with great care.

The primary contemporary evidence in print is too voluminous for evaluation here. The monumental *Report* of the Select Committee of 1857 on the Hudson's Bay Company was drafted by Labouchere and based on Head's confidential memoranda. Whelan's *Union of the British Provinces* (new ed. by D. C. Harvey) comes chiefly from press reports of "banquet" speeches. It derives its chief value from the secrecy of the conferences and the dearth of contemporary news. Both for Head's "drive" of 1858 and the twin movements of 1864 (from Canada for federal union and from the Maritimes for legislative union) the press of all the provinces is almost completely at sea. After the Quebec Conference however the *Globe*, the *Leader*, the Halifax *Colonist*, and for a few weeks the *Morning Chronicle* in Nova Scotia, are more reliable. The *Confederation Debates* of 1865 are ponderous in size and comprehensiveness—more than a thousand pages, double-column, long primer type, nearly a million words of debate from 37 Canadian councillors and 76 assemblymen.

The dearth of evidence on many aspects of Confederation is largely due to the secrecy of the conferences which was also one of the main reasons for their success. Much is still shrouded in "the contingent and the unforeseen." Several large collections of papers are still resolutely inaccessible.

PART IV: EXPANSION

The background for westward expansion will be found in Part III —Head's memorandum to Labouchere in 1856, the *Report* of the Select Committee, 1857, drafted by Labouchere, the purchase of a controlling interest in the Hudson's Bay Company by the International Financial Society and Newcastle's preference for Head as Governor of the Company.

The negotiations for the transfer of Rupert's Land and the "North-Western Territory" to Canada are traceable (with many tantalizing gaps) in British blue-books and Canadian Sessional Papers. For the real origins of the *Manitoba Act* papers from the governor-general's office are very illuminating. The entry of British Columbia into confederation, to be found in Canadian Sessional Papers for 1870 and 1871, has been colourfully supplemented by provincial historians from private papers etc. though the vital decisions as a rule were made elsewhere. The "eternal land question" in Prince Edward Island is well reviewed in the report of the Howe-Gray-Ritchie Commission. The C.P.R. and other physiographical aspects of expansion are to be found in plethoric abundance in the definitive records of the three natural resources commissions. The two volumes of documents on *The Canadian North-West* (ed. E. H. Oliver) are comprehensive but uneven. There are three folio volumes on North-West autonomy in the Laurier Papers. The functioning of nationhood in the peace treaty and League of Nations at the close of the first world war is best seen in the Borden Papers (now in the P.A.C.), the Doherty Papers, and the Dafoe diaries. "Tidying up the show" in 1923 (the sequel to which was worked out in 1926 and 1931) is in Dafoe's diary for the imperial conference of that year.

The annotations on maps and plans for Part IV will indicate their sources.

INDEX

to Canada, 475; *see also* Métis; Riel
Insurrection
"Referendum and recall," 486
"Reform" party, 251 ff., *passim*; heterogeneous groups in, 252; Sandfield
Macdonald and, 252; ascendancy of,
under Blake and Mowat, 252; *see
also* Clear Grits
Regional unions: British policy for after
1857, 25–7; of "Canada" and Rupert's
Land, 25, 239 ff.; of Vancouver
Island and British Columbia, 25,
241 f.; of Maritimes, 25–6; 242 f.;
influence of Texas and Oregon on,
25, 241; chap. xii, *passim*, 226 ff.;
chap. xv, 275–96 *passim*; rip-tide
between "Canada" and Maritimes on,
275; of British Columbia implemented by Lytton, 275; of central
region and Watkin's gambit for G.T.,
275; Rouges and Clear Grits declare
for dual federation, 277 f.; dual
federation defeated in the House,
279; Lytton and mainland province
of British Columbia, 282 f.; B.C.
extended (1863), 283 f.; of B.C. and
Vancouver Island (1867), 284; of
Maritimes, *see* Maritime union
"Rep. by pop.": background of, in
"Canada," 218; its necessity conceded, 218; population trends in the
Canadas and, 245 f.; Clear Grit party
in 1857 adopts, 245; advocated by
Globe (1885), 254; development of,
256 f.; Clear Grit convention of 1859
on, 278 n.; Brown's solution for deadlock of "equal representation," 300 f.;
rising tide of, 301; exorcised for five
years by John A. and Sandfield Macdonald, 303; conceded to be inevitable by John A. Macdonald, 303;
constriction of, 309; could now be
carried by majority vote, 309 n.; key
that "wound up the clock," 315
Responsible government: influence of
American neighbourhood on, 20–4;
embryo of in N.B., 22; in N.S., 22; a
device to redress grievances, 23, 496;
Howe on, 24; influence of tendencies
towards privilege on, 87; and problems of British North American
colonies, 92; conceded first in N.S.,
100–1; decisive issue in Canada, 101;
struggle for in P.E.I., 107–9; achievement of in N.B., 111–13; theory of
an axiom in contest for self-government, 114; won by disciplined politi-

cal parties, 115, 173; gradual acceptance of, 1840–52, 115–16; leaders
of struggle for in Canada and N.S.,
118–20; and geographical factors in
N.S. and Canadas, 121; principle of
discerned in Canada and N.S., 130;
Fairbanks on, 131, 132; work of
Howe for in N.S., 134–6; opposed
by Papineau, 140–1; and Durham's
Report, 145; and Russell's despatch
of Oct. 16, 1839, 153–4; evolution
of under Sydenham, 157–8; Hinck's
arguments for, 162–3; test of in N.S.
(1840), 167–9; struggle for in U.C.,
174–5; Metcalfe on, 186–7; offered
to N.S. (1846), 191–2; achievement
of in N.S., 193–4; achievement of in
Canada, 196–8; compared by Elgin
with American system, 203; functioning of under Elgin's tutelage, 203–4;
evolution of in B.C. and union with
Canada, 444–5; in Canadas and in
N.W.T., 485; in Manitoba, 486–7;
development of in N.W.T., 487 ff.;
first clear attribute of nationhood,
493; dynamic in its implications, 494;
expansion of, 494; anomalies in, dealt
with, 494; effect of on cognate functions of government, 496; effect of
on treatment of *Rebellion Losses Bill*,
496; effect of on Galt tariff of 1859,
496–7; expanding range of, governed
by interest of the people, 497; and
provincial control of public lands,
498; broadening scope of in regulation of trade and foreign relations,
498–501; *B.N.A. Act of 1867* and,
503; conventions of and evolving
constitution, 510, 511
Revolution, American: stereotyped parliamentary tradition at colonial stage,
vi; role of Quebec in, ix–xiii, 49–55;
British defeat in, 33; tradition of
inevitability of, 98–100
Revolution, French: and Irish legislative independence, 80, 91; effect of
on Lower Canada, 92
Rhodesia, 512
Riel Insurrection, 407, 408; necessitates
creation of Province of Manitoba,
411; successful in immediate results,
411, 431; annexation not a major
issue in, 412–13; springs from problem of status of new territory in confederation, 414; American element in,
418; H.B.C. officials not involved in,
418–19; and Selkirk settlers, 419–20;